# Security and Usability

# Security and Usability

Designing Secure Systems That People Can Use

Edited by Lorrie Faith Cranor & Simson Garfinkel

# O'REILLY®

Beijing • Cambridge • Farnham • Köln • Paris • Sebastopol • Taipei • Tokyo

**Security and Usability**
*Designing Secure Systems That People Can Use*
Edited by Lorrie Faith Cranor and Simson Garfinkel

**Published** by O'Reilly Media, Inc.

1005 Gravenstein Highway North

Sebastopol, CA 95472.

**O'Reilly** books may be purchased for educational, business, or sales promotional use. Online editions are also available for most titles (*safari.oreilly.com*). For more information, contact our corporate/institutional sales department: (800) 998-9938 or *corporate@oreilly.com*.

| | |
|---|---|
| **Publishing Editor:** | Deborah Russell |
| **Production Editor:** | Mary Brady |
| **Cover Designer:** | MendeDesign |
| **Interior Designer:** | Marcia Friedman |
| **Creative Director:** | Michele Wetherbee |
| **Printing History:** | August 2005: First Edition. |

RepKover™ This book uses RepKover™, a durable and flexible lay-flat binding.

ISBN: 0-596-00827-9

[M]

# TABLE OF CONTENTS

# Preface

**T**HERE'S AN OLD JOKE THAT COMPUTERS ARE ACTUALLY EASY MACHINES TO SECURE: just turn them off, lock them in a metal-lined room, and throw away the key. What you end up with is a machine that is very secure, just not very usable.

Of course, people need to use computers, not just think about them. So while this secure computer is safe in its metal can, people who need to get their jobs done will use other computers with significantly weaker security properties. They may have their passwords recorded by keystroke loggers and sent to bad guys in Russia. They may go to web banking sites that happen to be run by illegal cartels in South America. They may use portable laptops that are targeted and stolen at trade shows. And when they are done, they may format their hard drives and throw them away—unaware that their computer's "format" command doesn't delete any data at all.

Many people believe that there is an inherent tradeoff between security and usability. A computer without passwords is usable, but not very secure. On the other hand, a computer that makes you authenticate every five minutes with your password and a fresh drop of blood might be very secure, but nobody would want to use it.

But as the world around us makes clear every day, if people are unable to use secure computers, they will use computers that are not secure. At the end of the day, computers that are theoretically secure but not usable do little to improve the security of their users, because these machines push their users away to less secure platforms.

As it turns out, the converse is also true: systems that are usable but not secure are, in the end, not very usable either. That's because these systems don't last: they get hacked, compromised, and otherwise rendered useless. In November 2002, the Honeynet Project documented that unpatched Windows 2000 computers placed on the Internet were being compromised after just five minutes.[1] And this is not a problem that is confined to Microsoft operating systems: systems running Linux and other operating systems are also compromised with alarming frequency—just not quite so fast, because there are fewer worms running loose on the Internet that can infect these systems.

## Goals of This Book

In 1975, Jerome Saltzer and Michael Schroeder[2] identified *psychological acceptability* as one of the eight key principles for building secure systems. In 1983, Donald Norman[3] noted that many user errors resulting in data loss are often the result, in part, of poor interface design. "People will make errors, so make the system insensitive to them," he wrote. Instead of simply requiring confirmation of irreversible actions—confirmations that themselves become automatic—Norman argued that systems should be designed so that their actions are both visible and undoable.

While there is much agreement among security practitioners that we need to find ways of designing secure systems that people can use, there is less agreement about how to reach this goal. In this book, we have brought together chapters that discuss case studies of usable secure system design along with the latest thinking about how to approach this problem. While we can't offer you a step-by-step foolproof approach to usable secure system design, we hope this book will inform future design efforts and give developers important insights that will lead to successful designs.

## Audience for This Book

In creating the first book to be focused entirely on the subject of usability and security, we had a difficult decision to make. Did we want an academic book, one focusing on the growing amount of research in this burgeoning field, or did we want a book for practitioners, one with a heavy emphasis on practice and many recommendations for specific actions?

---

1  The Honeynet Project, "Forensics" (Jan. 29, 2003); *http://honeynet.overt.org/index.php/Forensics.*

2  J. Saltzer and M. Schroeder, "The Protection of Information in Computer Systems," *Proceedings of the IEEE* 63:9 (1975), 1278–1308.

3  Donald A. Norman, "Design Rules Based on Analyses of Human Error," *Communications of the ACM* 26:4, 254–258.

In the end, we decided to create a book that has both academic and professional leanings, but that stresses theory and fundamental principles whenever possible. Our reasoning is simple: this is such a young field that we did not think it would be in the interest of our readers for us to spend considerable time or space documenting the "best of the worst" practices, circa 2005. Instead, we chose to present readers with information that they could use to form their own understanding of how to improve the alignment of security and usability.

That's not to say that we have shied away from practical advice: this book is filled with practical proscription on the use and evaluation of such technologies as biometrics and USB authentication tokens. We have provided step-by-step guidance to help in conducting usability studies. We have included specific recommendations for the construction of next-generation applications and operating systems that, we hope, will be both more secure and more usable.

Nevertheless, when faced with a choice, we have decided to include the results of experiments, academic references, and suggestions for future research. Our goal is to make this book useful first for researchers in the field of security and usability, then for students, and finally for professionals.

We have also taken a decidedly security-centric view in presenting this material. We view our audience as primarily security researchers and professionals who now realize the need for increased usability in their systems. We assume familiarity with security terminology, even as we pause to give step-by-step instructions on conducting user studies and the principles of user-centered design. The reason is simple: progress in the alignment of usability and security needs to come from security practitioners—the people who literally hold the keys to today's operating systems. Until they truly believe that the usability of a system is of equal importance to its theoretical security properties, we will not see significant progress in this important field. We believe this book also offers something for members of the human-computer interaction and usability communities, who we hope will be increasingly working side by side with security professionals to develop secure systems that people can use.

## Structure of This Book

This book is divided into 6 parts consisting of 34 chapters.

Part I, *Realigning Usability and Security*

In this part of the book, we state our premise: that security and usability can be synergistic. The chapters in this part argue that, with careful attention to user-centered design principles, significant progress can be made toward this goal:

- Chapter 1, *Psychological Acceptability Revisited*, by Matt Bishop, takes a new look at the question of how to align security and usability: although the need to consider usability in the design of security systems is recognized more now than it was in the past, designers still need to create systems that are easy to install, provide adequate protection mechanisms, and are unobtrusive to use. This is a solvable problem, and there is much work to do.

- Chapter 2, *Usable Security*, by M. Angela Sasse and Ivan Flechais, lays the groundwork for our volume. It argues that the actual security provided by a computer system is the product of human factors, policies, and security mechanisms. Ignore any one of them, and security suffers.

- Chapter 3, *Design for Usability*, by Bruce Tognazzini, states a truism that is ignored all too frequently: the goal of computer security professionals must be to build systems that are *actually* secure, rather than to build systems that are theoretically secure. Many security "compromises" in the interest of usability aren't compromises at all—they are frequently improvements, because the systems that are "theoretically secure" are so hard to use that people avoid or sabotage them in practice.

- Chapter 4, *Usability Design and Evaluation for Privacy and Security Solutions*, by Clare-Marie Karat, Carolyn Brodie, and John Karat, introduces tools for performing usability evaluations and shows how they can integrate into the product development life cycle. The chapter then describes how these tools were applied to two different security products at IBM.

- Chapter 5, *Designing Systems That People Will Trust*, by Andrew S. Patrick, Pamela Briggs, and Stephen Marsh, examines the issue of trust for security and privacy systems. The interface with which the end user interacts plays a central role in building or breaking that trust. It is the interface—whether it is a computer screen, a web site, a standalone kiosk, or a telephone system—that must convey all the features and limitations of the underlying service to the user. The authors show how successful trust designs can have a positive impact on both products and services.

Part II, *Authentication Mechanisms*

The chapters in this part of the book take an in-depth look at techniques for identifying and authenticating computer users to systems that are both local and remote:

- Chapter 6, *Evaluating Authentication Mechanisms*, by Karen Renaud, considers the range of authentication systems that are currently available and presents a framework for evaluating their strengths and weaknesses.

- Chapter 7, *The Memorability and Security of Passwords*, by Jeff Yan, Alan Blackwell, Ross Anderson, and Alasdair Grant, presents the results of a study of password usage among university students. The study finds that some conventional wisdom given in the choice and maintenance of passwords is correct, and other advice is "bunk."

- Chapter 8, *Designing Authentication Systems with Challenge Questions*, by Mike Just, considers the role of questions like "what is your mother's maiden name" and "who was your favorite teacher" for authenticating users. Challenge questions can be used very effectively for self-service password resetting and as an additional identifier—especially on systems that are rarely used. On the other hand, a poorly implemented challenge system can compromise security while simultaneously decreasing usability. Once again, careful design and analysis are required for favorable outcomes.

- Chapter 9, *Graphical Passwords*, by Fabian Monrose and Michael K. Reiter, considers systems that use password substitutes such as passfaces or other systems for graphical authentication. Although these systems are not popular today, their use might skyrocket in coming years as security managers struggle to find a solution to the problem of forgotten passwords. Monrose and Reiter evaluate the wisdom of such proposals.

- Chapter 10, *Usable Biometrics*, by Lynne Coventry, evaluates the applicability of biometrics for user identification and authentication. Although Coventry is interested primarily in the appropriateness of biometrics for automatic teller machines (ATMs), her findings are generally applicable.

- Chapter 11, *Identifying Users from Their Typing Patterns*, by Alen Peacock, Xian Ke, and Matt Wilkerson, evaluates keystroke dynamics as a potential biometric. This is an exciting biometric because it can be measured by practically every desktop and laptop computer on the planet; keystroke dynamics can also be measured passively by the operating system—or even covertly. Although this biometrics is relatively unused today, it has the potential to become widely adopted.

- Chapter 12, *The Usability of Security Devices*, by Ugo Piazzalunga, Paolo Salvaneschi, and Paolo Coffetti, compares the usability of smart cards, USB tokens, and multifunction USB tokens that include both memory and features for using private keys. The authors find that multifunction tokens address many of the usability problems experienced with smart cards in the past.

Part III, *Secure Systems*

The chapters in this part of the book examine how system software can deliver or destroy a secure user experience:

- Chapter 13, *Guidelines and Strategies for Secure Interaction Design*, by Ka-Ping Yee, explores specific principles and techniques that can be used for aligning security and usability in the user interfaces of desktop operating systems.

- Chapter 14, *Fighting Phishing at the User Interface*, by Robert C. Miller and Min Wu, explores systems that have been proposed for web browsers and email systems to help users resist so-called "phishing" attacks.

- Chapter 15, *Sanitization and Usability*, by Simson Garfinkel, looks at a problem that is present in practically every computer on the planet: when users instruct their computer to "delete" information, the information isn't deleted—it's simply made invisible. Garfinkel tracks the history of this problem, discusses the results of a research project that demonstrates the problem's seriousness, and then presents a concrete solution.

- Chapter 16, *Making the Impossible Easy: Usable PKI*, by Dirk Balfanz, Glenn Durfee, and D. K. Smetters, shows that many of the perceived difficulties in deploying systems based on public key infrastructure (PKI) technology can be simplified by scaling back expectations. Instead of using PKI to identify people, use it to identify computers. Instead of trying to come up with iron-clad techniques for making sure that certificates are uniquely validated, use physical locality as a proxy for trust, and give a certificate to any laptop that is present inside a secure room. Instead of trying to teach people how to use an overly complex interface, create a one-click installer that simplifies the interface under consideration. The result is that people will have a system that mostly works—a significant improvement over many of today's PKI deployments, which mostly don't work.

- Chapter 17, *Simple Desktop Security with Chameleon*, by A. Chris Long and Courtney Moskowitz, reports on an experimental system that applies the principles of compartmentalized workstations of the 1990s to 21st century desktop computing. By understanding user goals and typical roles, the authors have created a system that allows users to move from task to task, and protection level to protection level, with considerable fluidity.

- Chapter 18, *Security Administration Tools and Practices*, by Eser Kandogan and Eben M. Haber, applies ethnographic tools to the study of system administration and comes up with a surprising conclusion: despite the fact that there has been considerable work in the past 20 years on system administration tools, most administration work is painfully manual work based on the line-by-line analysis of voluminous log files. The best system administrators are programmers, cooking up quick scripts and programs to solve the problem of the minute. Is there hope? The authors think that there is. Based on their analysis of administrators' tasks, they make concrete proposals for future tool development.

Part IV, *Privacy and Anonymity Systems*

This part of the book is devoted to systems that allow people to control the release of their personal information, enabling them to use the Internet in relative anonymity if they so desire:

- Chapter 19, *Privacy Issues and Human-Computer Interaction*, by Mark S. Ackerman and Scott D. Mainwaring, provides an overview of what human-computer interaction offers to those designing and studying privacy mechanisms.

- Chapter 20, *A User-Centric Privacy Space Framework*, by Benjamin Brunk, reports on Brunk's examination of 134 privacy-enhancing tools, systems, and services. He creates a definition of what is meant by the term *privacy solution* and maps out the space of features provided by different systems. As a result of this taxonomy, it's possible to compare different solutions in terms of what the competing approaches offer.

- Chapter 21, *Five Pitfalls in the Design for Privacy*, by Scott Lederer, Jason I. Hong, Anind K. Dey, and James A. Landay, evaluates a difficult-to-use interface that the authors have created for controlling one's privacy, and draws lessons from the project's mistakes.

- Chapter 22, *Privacy Policies and Privacy Preferences*, by Lorrie Faith Cranor, discusses the World Wide Web Consortium's Platform for Privacy Preferences (P3P) system and several prototype P3P user agents designed to warn users if their privacy desires are not in line with the privacy practices of the web site that they are visiting. One of Cranor's most important discoveries is that most people have little experience articulating their privacy preferences—most people have never been asked to do so before. And because most people's privacy preferences are often complex and nuanced, people tend to make different decisions when the questions are posted in isolation versus when they are proposed in context.

- Chapter 23, *Privacy Analysis for the Casual User with Bugnosis*, by David Martin, discusses a plug-in for Microsoft's Internet Explorer that allows users to see and hear *web bugs*—those otherwise silent and invisible tracking devices that are pervasive on the Internet today. As Martin makes clear, his audience for Bugnosis was not the casual user: it was journalists. By making web bugs salient for them, Martin hoped that Bugnosis would help promote the cause of public education on this Internet surveillance system.

- Chapter 24, *Informed Consent by Design*, by Batya Friedman, Peyina Lin, and Jessica K. Miller, discusses how the underlying technologies of the Internet do and do not promote the principle of informed consent.

- Chapter 25, *Social Approaches to End-User Privacy Management*, by Jeremy Goecks and Elizabeth D. Mynatt, discusses Acumen, a browser plug-in that lets Internet users share information about how their friends, associates, and trusted opinion leaders view the privacy practices of various web sites. Instead of sharing reports or postings, Acumen does this by allowing users to learn how other users have decided to handle cookies. One of the delicious tensions in this project is the way that Acumen allows information that is inherently private to be shared in a manner that is, more or less, public.

- Chapter 26, *Anonymity Loves Company: Usability and the Network Effect*, by Roger Dingledine and Nick Mathewson, explores similar tensions in the design and deployment of anonymity technology—systems that allow users to browse the Web and communicate anonymously with one another.

Part V, *Commercializing Usability: The Vendor Perspective*

The chapters in this part of the book look at specific experiences of security and software vendors in addressing the issue of usability:

- Chapter 27, *ZoneAlarm: Creating Usable Security Products for Consumers*, by Jordy Berson, a senior product manager at Zone Labs, relates his experiences with ZoneAlarm in producing a firewall that is used by tens of millions of naïve users on a daily basis.

- Chapter 28, *Firefox and the Worry-Free Web*, by Blake Ross, a lead developer on the Firefox project, discusses the specific decisions that have been made to make a web browser that works with users to create a secure online experience—instead of tempting users into compromising their security.

- Chapter 29, *Users and Trust: A Microsoft Case Study*, by Chris Nodder, discusses similar usability and security decisions that went into the creation of Microsoft Internet Explorer—and specifically the modifications to Explorer that were made as part of the work on Windows XP Service Pack 2.

- Chapter 30, *IBM Lotus Notes/Domino: Embedding Security in Collaborative Applications*, by Mary Ellen Zurko, a longtime member of the Notes development team, discusses several specific security features in IBM Lotus Notes and Domino, a secure messaging system that has more than 100 million users, but yet whose security features are relatively hidden.

- Chapter 31, *Achieving Usable Security in Groove Virtual Office*, by George Moromisato, Paul Boyd, and Nimisha Asthagiri, shows how security properties similar to those offered by Notes/Domino can be achieved in a peer-to-peer environment where users are largely responsible for their own security.

Part VI, *The Classics*

This part of the book is our collection of classic papers on security and usability that everybody should read!

- Chapter 32, *Users Are Not the Enemy*, by Anne Adams and M. Angela Sasse, and previously published in *Communications of the ACM*, discusses the results of a user study measuring password compliance at a major corporation in the 1990s. Adams and Sasse found that even though users may be the weakest link in the chain, they don't *want* to be the weakest link in the chain. Organizations must work to give users the information and the tools necessary so that they can be part of the solution.

- Chapter 33, *Usability and Privacy: A Study of KaZaA P2P File Sharing*, by Nathaniel S. Good and Aaron Krekelberg, and previously published at the prestigious ACM CHI Conference on Human Factors in Computing Systems, discusses the results of a study in which users of the popular KaZaA file-trading program were astonished to discover just how much information the program actually makes available to others on the Internet.

- Chapter 34, *Why Johnny Can't Encrypt*, by Alma Whitten and J. D. Tygar, and previously published at the USENIX Security Conference, shows that even highly acclaimed security programs with allegedly easy-to-use interfaces can nevertheless have profound usability problems because of inherent properties in security software.

## Conventions Used in This Book

The following typographical conventions are used in this book:

*Italic*
    Used for URLs, file and directory names, emphasis, and the first occurrence of terms

`Constant width`
    Used for code examples and literals

# Safari Enabled

 When you see a Safari® Enabled icon on the cover of your favorite technology book, that means the book is available online through the O'Reilly Network Safari Bookshelf.

Safari offers a solution that's better than e-books. It's a virtual library that lets you easily search thousands of top technical books, cut and paste code samples, download chapters, and find quick answers when you need the most accurate, current information. Try it for free at *http://safari.oreilly.com*.

# How to Contact Us

Please address comments and questions concerning this book to the publisher:

O'Reilly Media, Inc.
1005 Gravenstein Highway North
Sebastopol, CA 95472
(800) 998-9938 (in the United States and Canada)
(707) 829-0515 (international/local)
(707) 829-0104 (fax)

There is a web page for this book, which lists errata and any additional information. You can access this page at:

*http://www.oreilly.com/catalog/securityusability/*

To comment or ask technical questions about this book, send email to:

*bookquestions@oreilly.com*

For more information about books, conferences, software, Resource Centers, and the O'Reilly Network, see the O'Reilly web site at:

*http://www.oreilly.com*

# Acknowledgments

In fall of 2003, we discovered that we were both thinking about editing a book on usability and security. We were in the middle of other projects at the time, but several months later we talked about it again and decided to work together on a proposal and shop it around to publishers. Our original plan was to spend about two years recruiting and editing chapters. However, when Deborah Russell at O'Reilly saw our proposal, she asked us if we could finish the book in less than a year. We agreed, and in May 2004, we began recruiting chapters.

That May we were completely engaged in the topic of usability and security. Together, we were in the process of editing a special issue of *IEEE Security & Privacy* on this topic, Lorrie was organizing a Workshop on Usable Privacy and Security Software, and Simson was finishing up a Ph.D. thesis in the area. As a result, we had a good idea of who was doing work in the domain. Most of the prospective authors we approached agreed to participate, and by September we started receiving first drafts of chapters.

We are indebted to the 62 authors who contributed the 32 chapters not written by us. Without their efforts this book would not have been possible. Unlike many edited volumes in which most chapters are slightly edited versions of conference papers, this book contains many completely original chapters that were written specifically for this book. In addition, with the exception of the classic papers in the final part of this book, the chapters that did begin as conference papers have been substantially reworked to reflect the style and emphasis of this book. We appreciate the authors' efforts to accommodate our many requests to refocus their chapters and highlight practical advice. In addition to writing and revising their own chapters, the authors also helped to review each other's chapters. As a result, every chapter in this book has benefited from the feedback of at least three reviewers.

We would like to thank the members of the CMU Usable Privacy and Security Laboratory who reviewed draft chapters, especially Rob Reeder, Cynthia Kuo, Chris Long, Jason Hong, Serge Egelman, and Matthew Geiger. We would also like to thank Robert Miller, Min Wu, and Ariel Rideout at MIT for their comments.

We are grateful to Beth Rosenberg for helping us edit several of the most difficult and demanding chapters.

Lorrie would like to thank her husband, Chuck, and her children, Shane and Maya, for all their love and support while she worked on this book. Simson would like to thank his wife, Beth, and his children, Sonia, Jared, and Draken, who barely saw their father for nearly eight months while he worked on this book, another book, and his dissertation.

We would like to thank Deborah Russell, our wonderful editor at O'Reilly, for her great editing job and for helping to keep us (mostly) on schedule. And thanks as well to the entire O'Reilly production team, including Mary Brady, the production editor; Audrey Doyle, the copyeditor; Rob Romano, the illustrator; and Nancy Crumpton, the indexer.

In addition, many of the chapters provide individual acknowledgments.

PART ONE   REALIGNING USABILITY
AND SECURITY

# CHAPTER ONE

# Psychological Acceptability Revisited

**MATT BISHOP**

IN 1987, BRIAN REID WROTE "PROGRAMMER CONVENIENCE IS THE ANTITHESIS OF SECURITY, because it is going to become intruder convenience if the programmer's account is ever compromised."[1] This belief of the fundamental conflict between strong computer security mechanisms and usable computer systems pervades much of modern computing. According to this belief, in order to be secure, a computer system must employ security mechanisms that are sophisticated and complex—and therefore difficult to use.

Today a growing number of security researchers and practitioners realize that this belief contains an inherent contradiction. The reason has to do with the unanticipated result of increasing complexity. A fundamental precept of designing security mechanisms is that, as the mechanisms grow more complex, they become harder to configure, to manage, to maintain, and indeed even to implement correctly. Errors become more probable, thereby increasing the chances that mechanisms will be configured erroneously, mismanaged, maintained improperly, or implemented incorrectly. This weakens the security of the system. So the more complex a system is, the more secure it should be—yet the less secure it is likely to be, because of the complexity designed to add security!

---

1   Brian Reid, "Reflections on Some Recent Widespread Computer Break-Ins," *Communications of the ACM* 30:2 (Feb. 1987), 105.

Finding ways to maximize both the usability of a system and the security of a system has been a longstanding problem. Saltzer and Schroeder's principle of *psychological acceptability*[2] (see the sidebar) says that a security mechanism should not make accessing a resource, or taking some other action, more difficult than it would be if the security mechanism were not present. In practice, this principle states that a security mechanism should add as little as possible to the difficulty of the human performing some action.

---

## THE PRINCIPLE OF PSYCHOLOGICAL ACCEPTABILITY

"It is essential that the human interface be designed for ease of use, so that users routinely and automatically apply the protection mechanisms correctly. Also, to the extent that the user's mental image of his protection goals matches the mechanisms he must use, mistakes will be minimized. If he must translate his image of his protection needs into a radically different specification language, he will make errors."

—Jerome Saltzer and Michael Schroeder

---

Applying this principle raises a crucial issue: difficult for whom? A programmer may find setting access control permissions on a file easy; a secretary may find the same task difficult. Applying the principle of psychological acceptability requires taking into account the abilities, knowledge, and mental models of the people who will use the system. Unfortunately, on those infrequent occasions when the principle is applied, the developers often design the mechanism to meet their own expectations and models of the system. These are invariably different from the expectations and models of the system's users, no matter whether the users are individuals at home or a team of system administrators at a large corporation.

As a result, security mechanisms are indeed cumbersome and less effective than they should be. To illustrate the problem, I focus on three examples in this chapter: passwords, patching, and configuration.

## Passwords

Passwords are a mechanism designed to authenticate a user—that is, to bind the identity of the user to an entity on the computer (such as a process). A *password* is a sequence of

---

2  Jerome Saltzer and Michael Schroeder, "The Protection of Information in Computer Systems," *Proceedings of the IEEE* 63:9 (1975), 1278–1308.

characters that confirms the user's identity.[3] If an attacker guesses the password associated with an identity, the attacker can impersonate the legitimate user with that identity.

Problems with passwords are well known; one of the earliest ARPANET RFCs[4] warned that many passwords were easy to guess. But a well-known problem is usually an unsolved problem. Reid's lament involved someone guessing a password on a poorly maintained system, and from there intruding upon a large number of systems at a major university. In the early 1990s, CERT announced that many attackers were using default administrative passwords to enter systems.[5] In the early 2000s, a CERT advisory reported a "back door" account in a database system with a known password.[6] SANS includes password selection issues as two of the current Top 20 Vulnerabilities, as well as several exploits that depend upon accounts with no passwords or with passwords set by the vendor.[7] For example, the SQLSnake/Spida Worm exploits an empty password for the default administrative account for Microsoft SQL Server.

The principle of psychological acceptability, taken literally, says that passwords should be unnecessary. But the use of passwords to protect systems adds minimal overhead for people who are using the system, provided that the passwords are easy to remember. To be effective, the passwords must also be difficult to guess. So, how can passwords be made easy to remember, yet difficult to guess?

One difficulty in solving this problem lies in balancing the ability of a human to remember a password that an attacker will find difficult to guess against the ingenuity of the attacker. The attacker has the advantage. People choose passwords that they can remember easily. Unfortunately, these are usually easy to guess. Experiments by Morris and Thompson[8] and others[9] were able to guess user passwords for between 25% and 80% of the users. The users typically picked dictionary words, names, and other common words. Amusingly, in one experiment, the analyst was able to determine who was dating whom, because many passwords were, or were derived from, the names of the users' partners.

3  Matt Bishop, *Computer Security: Art and Science* (Reading, MA: Addison Wesley Professional, 2003).

4  Bob Metcalfe, "The Stockings Were Hung by the Chimney with Care," RFC 602 (1973).

5  CERT, "Internet Intruder Warning," CERT Advisory CA-1990-02 (Mar. 19, 1990); *http://www.cert. org/advisories/CA-1990-02.html*.

6  CERT, "Interbase Server Contains Compiled-In Back Door Account," CERT Advisory CA-2001-01 (Jan. 11, 2001); *http://www.cert.org/advisories/CA-2001-01.html*.

7  SANS, "Twenty Most Critical Internet Security Vulnerabilities (Updated)—The Experts Consensus," SANS (Oct. 8, 2004); *http://www.sans.org/top20*.

8  Robert Morris and Ken Thompson, "Password Security: A Case History," *Communications of the ACM* 22:11 (Nov. 1979), 594–597.

9  Matt Bishop and Daniel Klein, "Improving System Security via Proactive Password Checking," *Computers & Security* 14:3 (Apr. 1995), 233–249.

Part of the problem is that different users have different ideas of what constitutes a password that is difficult to guess.[10] When warned not to use names as passwords, one user changed his password to "Barbara1". Foreign words are also common; one guessed password was a Mandarin phrase meaning "henpecked husband." Another was the Japanese word for "security." In the latter case, the American user was stunned when someone guessed the password quickly, because he never expected an attacker to try a Japanese word.

System administrators, system programmers, and others who have been the victims of attacks involving guessed passwords, or who run programs that guess passwords as a preventative measure, usually understand the need for passwords that are difficult to guess, and appreciate how resourceful password guessers can be. Users of home systems, who surf the Web, exchange email, write letters, print cards, and balance budgets, may or may not understand the need for good passwords, and almost always underestimate how resourceful attackers can be. The success of *war driving*, in which people attempt to piggyback onto wireless networks, attests to this. Most home wireless access points are left configured with default settings that allow anyone to use the network without a password and further allow the network to be administered with the default password. Many users simply plug in their equipment, notice that it works, and never bother to read the accompanying manual—let alone configure their equipment for secure operation. These users do not make this choice deliberately, and are generally unaware of the consequences.

Attempts to educate users meet with varied success. The most successful methods involve providing immediate feedback to the user, with an explanation of why the proposed password is poor. This must be done carefully. One organization circulated a memorandum describing how to select good passwords. The memo gave several examples. Attackers simply tried the passwords used in the examples, and found that several users had used them.

The proper selection of passwords is a classic human factors problem. Assigning passwords selected at random can be shown to maximize the expected time needed to guess a password. But passwords with randomly selected characters are difficult to remember. So, random passwords, and especially multiple random passwords, result in people either writing the passwords down on paper or forgetting them. Either outcome defeats the purpose of passwords. A proper selection method must somehow balance the need to remember a password with the need to make that password as random as possible.

Proactive password checking subjects a user-proposed password to a number of tests to determine how likely the password is to be guessed. This is a viable approach, provided that the tests are well drawn. One potential problem is that an attacker can determine from the tests which potential passwords need not be tried. The set of potential passwords must be large enough to prevent attackers from trying them all. A USENET posting[11]

---

10 See Chapter 32 of this volume, by Anne Adams and M. Angela Sasse, "Users Are Not the Enemy."

11 Frans Meulenbroeks, "Rules for the Selection of Passwords," rec.humor.funny (July 3, 1992); *http://www.netfunny.com/rhf/jokes/92q3/selpass.html*.

illustrated the necessity of this requirement. It described a (mock) set of characteristics of passwords that were difficult to guess. It then asserted that only one word met these criteria, so everyone had to use the same password!

Various attempts to balance the needs of memory and randomness mix randomly generated passwords with human-selected passwords. One common approach, used by Microsoft, Apple, and other vendors, is to supply a "wallet" or "key ring" for passwords. The user enters her passwords, and their associated target, into the key ring, and chooses a "master password" to encipher the ring. Whenever a password is needed, the user supplies the single master password, and the system deciphers the appropriate entry in the ring. This allows the user to save many passwords at the price of remembering only one. An obvious extension allows the passwords on the key ring to be generated randomly.

This approach tries to implement the principle of psychological acceptability by making passwords as invisible as possible. The user needs to remember only one password for all her different systems. But an attacker without access to the key ring must discover a different password for each system for that user. If the passwords are chosen randomly, and the set of possible passwords is large enough, guessing the chosen password is highly unlikely.

There are two important weaknesses to this approach. The first lies in the phrase "without access to the key ring." If the attacker gains that access, she needs to guess only the master password to discover all the other passwords. So, the problem of password guessing has not been eliminated; it has been reduced to the user having to select one password that is difficult to guess. The second problem springs from this need. What happens if the user forgets her master password? In most implementations of the key ring, the system cannot recover the master password (because if the system can do so, an attacker can also). Hence, the user must change all passwords on the key ring, as the originals cannot be recovered either, and select a new master password.

This demonstrates a failure to meet one aspect of the principle of psychological acceptability. If the security mechanism depends upon a human, what happens if the human fails? Logic dictates that this should never happen, and if it does, it is the human's problem. But logic must account for the frailties of human beings, and the principle of psychological acceptability speaks to human failure. How do you recover?

Another approach is to base authentication on criteria in addition to a password, such as possession of a smart card or a biometrics measurement. In principle, if a password is discovered, the attacker cannot immediately gain access to the protected system. Again, the principle of psychological acceptability comes into play; the additional requirement must be acceptable. Swiping an identification card, or entering a number displayed on a token, might be acceptable. In most cultures and computing environments, testing the DNA of the user would not be.

Other authentication techniques abound. The chapters in Part II of this book, *Authentication Mechanisms*, discuss several, including variants on passwords. The key question that one must answer in order to use the authentication techniques described in those chapters is whether the techniques balance effectiveness and usability to the satisfaction of both the users and the managers.

# Patching

Correcting problems such as default or empty passwords poses problems when the vendor distributes the correction. As an example, for many years, Microsoft's SQL Server was distributed with an empty password on its administrator account.[12] This changed when the SQLSnake/Spida Worm exploited that empty password to acquire access to servers running that database. Microsoft issued a patch to update the server and add a password.

A *patch* is an update to a program or system designed to enhance its functionality or to solve an existing problem. In the context of security, it is a mechanism used to fix a security problem by updating the system. The patch, embodied in a program or script, is placed on the system to be patched, and then executed. The execution causes the system to be updated.

Ideally, patching should never be necessary. Systems should be correct and secure when delivered. But in practice, even if such systems could be created, their deployment into various environments would mean that the systems would need to be changed to meet the needs of the specific environment in which they are used. So, patching will not go away. However, it should be minimal, and as invisible as possible. Specifically, the principle of psychological acceptability implies that patching systems should require little to no intervention by the system administrator or user.

Unfortunately, several considerations make invisible patching difficult.

The first difficulty is collecting all of the necessary patches. In a homogeneous network, only one vendor's patches need to be gathered, but a single vendor may offer a wide variety of systems. The patches for one system likely will not apply to another system. If the network has systems from many vendors, the problem of gathering and managing the patches is severe. Various tools such as Cro-Magnon[13] and management schemes using several tools[14] attempt to ameliorate this task. All require configuration and maintenance, and knowledgeable system administrators.

The second difficulty is system-specific conflicts. When vendors write and test a patch, they do so for their current distribution. But customers tailor the systems to meet their

---

12 CERT, "Microsoft SQL Server and Microsoft Data Engine (MSDE) ship with a null default password," CERT Vulnerability Note VU# 635463 (Aug. 10, 2000); *http://www.kb.cert.org/vuls/id/ 635463.*

13 Jeremy Bargin and Seth Taplin, "Cro-Magnon: A Patch Hunter-Gatherer," *Proceedings of the 13th LISA Conference* (Nov. 1999), 87–94.

14 David Ressman and John Valdés, "Use of Cfengine for Automated, Multi-Platform Software and Patch Distribution," *Proceedings of the 14th LISA Conference* (Dec. 2000), 207–218.

needs. If the tailoring conflicts with the patch, the patch may inhibit the system from functioning correctly.

Two examples will demonstrate the problem. In the first example, a site runs a version of the Unix operating system that uses a nonstandard, but secure, mail server program. When a patch for that system is released, the system administrator updates the system programs, and then reinstalls them. This entire process is automated, so the system administrator runs two commands: one to update the source code for the system, and the other to compile and reinstall all changed programs. But, whenever the system's standard mail server is one of the programs patched, the system administrator must reinstall the nonstandard mail server. Because of the architecture of the updating process, this requires a separate set of commands. This violates the principle of psychological acceptability, because maintaining the security mechanism (the nonstandard mail server) is a visible process. The system administrator must be aware of the updating process, and check that the standard mail server is not updated or reinstalled.

The second example comes from the world of finance. Many large brokerage houses run their own financial software. As the brokerage houses write this software themselves, and use it throughout the world, they must ensure that nothing interferes with these programs. If the programs cease to function, the houses will lose large sums of money because they will not be able to trade on the stock markets or carry out their other financial functions. When a vendor sends them a security patch, the brokerage houses dare not install that patch on their most important production systems because the patch may interfere with their programs. The vendor does not have copies of these programs, and so has no way to test for interference. Instead, the houses install the patch on a test system or network, and determine for themselves if there is a conflict. Again, the process of maintaining a secure system should be invisible to the system administrators, but because of the nature of the system, transparency means a possible violation of the availability aspects of the site's security policy. The conflict seems irreconcilable.

This conflict is exacerbated by automatic downloading and installation of patches. On the surface, doing so makes the patching invisible. If there are no conflicts between the patch and the current configuration, this is true. But if there are conflicts, the user may find a system that does not function as expected, with no clear reason for the failure.

This happened with a recent patch for Microsoft's Windows XP system. Service Pack 2 provided many modifications to improve both system functionality and security. Therein lay the problem. Among the enhancements was the activation of Windows Firewall, which blocks certain connections from the Internet. This meant that many servers and clients, including IIS, some FTP clients, and many games, would not function correctly. After installing the patch, users then had to reset various actions of the firewall to allow these programs to function as they did before the patch was installed.[15] The principle of psychological acceptability disallows these problems.

---

15 Microsoft Corp., "Some Programs Seem to Stop Working After You Install Windows XP Service Pack 2," Article ID 842242 (Sept. 28, 2004); *http://support.microsoft.com/default.aspx?kbid=842242*.

In the extreme, one patch may improve security, but disable necessary features. In this case, the user must decide between an effective security mechanism and a necessary functionality. Thus, the security mechanism is as obtrusive as possible, clearly violating the principle of psychological acceptability. The best example of this is another patch that Microsoft issued to fix a vulnerability in SQL Server. This patch eliminated the vulnerability exploited by the Slammer worm, but under certain conditions interfered with correct SQL Server operations.[16] A subsequent patch fixed the problem.[17]

The third difficulty with automating the patching process is understanding the trustworthiness of the source. If the patch comes from the vendor, and is digitally signed using the vendor's private key, then the contents of the patch are as trustworthy as the vendor is. But some vendors have distributed patches through less secure channels, such as USENET newsgroups or unsigned downloads. Some systems automatically check digital signatures on patches, but many others do not—and faced with the choice, many users will not bother to check, either. Unverified or unverifiable patches may contain Trojan horses or other back doors designed to allow attackers entry—an attack that was demonstrated when a repository of security-related programs was broken into, and the attackers replaced a security program designed to filter network connections with one that allowed attackers to gain administrator access to the system on which it was installed.[18] Sometimes even signatures cannot be trusted. An attacker tricked Verisign, Inc., into issuing two certificates used to authenticate installers and Active X components (but not for updating Windows) to someone claiming to be from Microsoft Corporation.[19] Although the certificates were cancelled as soon as the hoax was discovered, the attacker could have produced digitally signed fake patches during the interval of time that the newly issued certificates remained valid.

Finally, the need to tailor techniques for patching to the level of the target audience is amply demonstrated by the problems that home users face. With most vendors, home users must go to the vendors' web sites to learn about patches, or subscribe to an automated patch notification system.[20, 21] Because users rarely take such proactive actions on their own, some vendors are automating the patching mechanisms in an attempt to make

---

16 Microsoft Corp., "Elevation of Privilege in SQL Server Web Tasks (Q316333)," Microsoft Security Bulletin MS02-061 (Oct. 16, 2002); *http://www.microsoft.com/technet/security/bulletin/MS02-061.mspx.*

17 Microsoft Corp., "FIX: Handle Leak Occurs in SQL Server When Service or Application Repeatedly Connects and Disconnects with Shared Memory Network Library," Article ID 317748 (Oct. 30, 2002); *http://support.microsoft.com/default.aspx?scid=kb;en-us;317748.*

18 CERT, "Trojan Horse Version of TCP Wrappers," CERT Advisory CA-1999-01 (Jan. 21, 1999); *http://www.cert.org/advisories/CA-1999-01.html.*

19 CERT, "Unauthentic 'Microsoft Corporation' Certificates," CERT Advisory CA-2001-04 (March 22, 2001); *http://www.cert.org/advisories/CA-2001-04.html.*

20 CERT, "Continuing Threats to Home Users," CERT Advisory CA-2001-20 (July 20, 2001); *http://www.cert.org/advisories/CA-2001-20.html.*

21 CERT, "Home Network Security," CERT Tech Tips (June 22, 2001); *http://www.cert.org/tech_tips/home_networks.html.*

these mechanisms invisible to the user. As most home users reconfigure their systems very little, this effort to satisfy the principle of psychological acceptability may work well. However, the technology is really too new for us to draw any reliable conclusions.

## Configuration

Building a secure system does not assure its security: the system must also be installed and operated securely. Configuration is a key component of secure installation and operation, because it constrains what users and the system processes can do in the particular environment where the system is used. For example, a computer configured to be secure in a university research environment (in which information is accessible to everyone inside the research group) would be considered nonsecure in a military environment (in which information is accessible only to those with a demonstrated need to know). Different configurations allow a system to be used securely in different environments.

The decisions about configuration settings that a vendor faces when constructing patches are, to say the least, daunting. The vendor must balance the need to take into account the security policy of the sites to which the patch will be distributed with the need to provide a minimal level of security for those sites that cannot, or do not, reconfigure an installed patch. The principle of psychological acceptability dictates that, whatever course is followed, the installers of the patch not only should be able to alter the default configuration with a minimum of effort, but also should be able to determine whether they *need* to alter the default configuration with a minimum of effort.

An example will illustrate the dilemma. This example first arose from a system that was designed for academic research. One version was widely distributed with file permissions set by default to allow any user on the system to read, write, and execute files on the system. Once the system was installed, the file permissions could be reset to allow accesses appropriate to the site. This approach violated the principle of fail-safe defaults,[22] because the system was distributed with access control permissions set to allow all accesses. It also required all system administrators to take action to protect the system. An advantage of this is that it forced administrators to develop a security policy, even if only a highly informal one. But the price was that system administrators had to apply mechanisms after the system was installed, violating the principle of psychological acceptability. Had the system been distributed with rights set to some less open configuration, system administrators would not need to act immediately to protect the system. This would have been a less egregious violation of the principle of psychological acceptability. Fortunately, for the most part, system administrators understood enough to apply the necessary changes, and knew of the need when they received the system.

The conflict between security and ease of use arises in configurations not related to patching. Many programs allow the user to define macros, or sequences of instructions that

22 Saltzer and Schroeder, 1282.

augment or replace standard functions. For example, Microsoft Word allows the user to take special actions upon opening a file. These actions are programmed using a powerful macro language. This language allows special-purpose documents to be constructed, text to be inserted into documents, and other useful functions. But attackers have written computer viruses and worms in this language and embedded them in documents: the Melissa virus executed when an infected file was opened using Microsoft Word. Among other actions, the virus infected a commonly used template file, so any other file referencing that template would also be infected.[23] The benefit of added functionality brought with it an added security threat.

The solution was to allow the user to configure Microsoft Word to display a warning box before executing a macro. This box would ask the user if macros were to be enabled or disabled.[24] Whether this solution works depends upon the user's understanding that macros pose a threat, and the user being able to assess whether the macro is likely to be malicious given the particular file being opened. The wording and context of the warning, and the amount and quality of information it gives, is critical to help a naive user make this assessment. If macro languages must be supported, and a user can make the indicated assessment, this solution is as unobtrusive as possible and yet protects the user against macro viruses. It is an attempt to apply the principle of psychological acceptability.

## Conclusion

The lesson that we draw from the three illustrations provided in this chapter is that the solution to the problem of developing psychologically acceptable security mechanisms depends upon the context in which those mechanisms are to be used. In an environment in which only trusted users have access to a system, simple passwords are sufficient; but in a more public environment, more complex passwords or alternate authentication mechanisms become necessary. Patches designed for a known environment can modify the system with little or no user action; patches applied in an environment different from the one for which they are designed risk creating security problems. Complex configurations lead to errors, and the less computer-savvy the users are, the worse the security problems will be.

This lesson suggests an approach to improving the current state of the art. Testing mechanisms by placing them in environments in which they will be used, and analyzing the way in which those mechanisms are used, will show potential problems quickly. But this requires using human subjects to test the mechanisms. Actually testing mechanisms on the populations that are to use these mechanisms will provide useful data. Testing mechanisms on the programmers and designers of those mechanisms may give some insight into potential problems. However, this latter testing will not reveal the problems arising from

---

23  CERT, "Melissa Macro Virus," CERT Advisory CA-1999-04 (March 27, 1999); *http://www.cert.org/advisories/CA-1999-04.html.*

24  Microsoft Corp., "Word Macro Virus Alert 'Melissa Macro Virus'," Article ID 224567 (Aug. 9, 2004); *http://support.microsoft.com/default.aspx?scid=kb;en-us;224567.*

errors in installation, configuration, and operation by users unfamiliar with the mechanisms' design and implementation.

The principle of psychological acceptability is being applied more often now than it has been in the past. We have far to go, however. The primary problem with its current application is the range of users to which it must be applied. How can one create mechanisms that are easy to install, provide the protection mechanisms necessary, and are unobtrusive in use, for people ranging in skill from novice home computer users to system administrators who manage hundreds of computers from many different vendors? This remains an open question—one that may very well be insoluble.

Nevertheless, the current state of the art leaves room for considerable improvement.

## About the Author

 Matt Bishop is a professor in the Department of Computer Science at the University of California at Davis. He studies the analysis of vulnerabilities in computer systems, policy models, and formal modeling of access controls. He is active in information assurance education, is a charter member of the Colloquium on Information Systems Security Education, and has presented tutorials at many conferences. He wrote the textbooks *Computer Security: Art and Science* and *Introduction to Computer Security* (both from Addison Wesley).

*http://seclab.cs.ucdavis.edu/~bishop/*

# CHAPTER TWO

# Usable Security
## *Why Do We Need It? How Do We Get It?*

M. ANGELA SASSE AND IVAN FLECHAIS

**S**ECURITY EXPERTS FREQUENTLY REFER TO PEOPLE AS "THE WEAKEST LINK IN THE CHAIN" OF SYSTEM **SECURITY.** Famed hacker Kevin Mitnick revealed that he hardly ever cracked a password, because it "was easier to dupe people into revealing it" by employing a range of social engineering techniques. Often, such failures are attributed to users' carelessness and ignorance. However, more enlightened researchers have pointed out that current security tools are simply too complex for many users, and they have made efforts to improve user interfaces to security tools. In this chapter, we aim to broaden the current perspective, focusing on the usability of security tools (or *products*) and the *process* of designing secure systems for the real-world context (the *panorama*) in which they have to operate. Here we demonstrate how current human factors knowledge and user-centered design principles can help security designers produce security solutions that are effective in practice.

## Introduction

The need for people to protect themselves and their assets is as old as humankind. Peoples' physical safety and their possessions have always been at risk from deliberate attack or accidental damage. The increasing use of information technology means that individuals and organizations today have an ever-growing range of physical (equipment) and electronic (data) assets that are at risk. To meet the increasing demand for security, the IT industry has developed a plethora of security mechanisms that can be used to make attacks significantly more difficult or to mitigate their consequences.

A series of surveys has shown that—despite ever-increasing spending on security products—the number of businesses suffering security breaches is increasing rapidly. According to the United Kingdom's Department of Trade and Industry's Information Security Breaches Surveys,[1] 32% of UK businesses surveyed in 1998 suffered a security incident, rising to 44% in 2000 and 74% in 2002, and reaching a massive 94% in 2004. The 2004 CSI/FBI Computer Crime and Security Survey[2] reports that U.S. companies spend between $100 and $500 per employee per annum on security. But purchasing and deploying security products does not automatically lead to improved security. Many users do not bother with security mechanisms, such as virus checkers or email encryption, or do not use them correctly. Security products are often ineffective because users do not behave in the way necessary for security mechanisms to be effective. For example, users disclose their passwords, fail to encrypt confidential messages, and switch virus checkers off. Why? Because most users today:

- Have problems using security tools correctly (for an example, see the classic paper on PGP by Whitten and Tygar, reprinted in Chapter 34 of this volume)

- Do not understand the importance of data, software, and systems for their organization

- Do not believe that the assets are at risk (i.e., that they would be attacked)

- Do not understand that their behavior puts assets at risk

Whitten and Tygar have identified a "weakest link property," stating that attackers need to exploit only a single error. Frequently human frailty provides this error: humans are invariably described as the "weakest link" in the security chain. But until recently, the human factor in security has been neglected both by developers of security technology, and by those responsible for organizational security. Kevin Mitnick[3] points out that to date, attackers have paid more attention to the human element in security than security designers have, and they have managed to exploit this advantage prodigiously.

The aim of this chapter is to show how human factors knowledge and user-centered design principles can be employed to design secure systems that are workable in practice and prevent users from being the "weakest link." We view secure systems as socio-technical systems; thus, we are not just concerned with improving the usability of security mechanisms for individual users: our aim is to improve the effectiveness of security, and reduce the human and financial cost of operating it.

---

1   Department of Trade and Industry, *Information Security Breaches Survey* (2004); *http://www.security-survey.gov.uk/*.

2   Ninth Annual CSI/FBI Survey on Computer Crime and Security (2004); *http://www.gocsi.com/*.

3   Kevin D. Mitnick and William L. Simon, *The Art of Deception: Controlling the Human Element of Security* (New York: John Wiley & Sons Inc., 2003).

Security of any sociotechnical system is the result of three distinct elements: product, process, and panorama.

*Product*

What do current security policies and mechanisms require from the different stakeholders? Is the physical and mental workload that a mechanism requires from individual users acceptable? Is the behavior required from users acceptable? What is the cost of operating a specific mechanism for the organization, in both human and financial terms?

Currently, we have a relatively small set of general security mechanisms, and general policies that mandate user behavior when operating those mechanisms. Usable security requires a wider range of security policies and mechanisms, which can be configured to match the security requirements and capabilities of different users and different organizations.

*Process*

How are security decisions made? Currently, security is seen to be the responsibility of security experts. During the system development process, security is frequently treated as a nonfunctional requirement, and is not addressed until functionality has been developed. We argue that the organization's security requirements need to be determined at the beginning of the design process, and that the development of security mechanisms should be an integral part of design and development of the system, rather than being "added on." When deciding on a security mechanism, the implications for individual users (workload, behavior, workflow) need to be considered.

Usability and security are often seen as competing design goals. But in practice, security mechanisms have to be usable to be effective—mechanisms that are not employed in practice, or that are used incorrectly, provide little or no protection. To identify appropriate policies and usable mechanisms, all stakeholders have to be represented in the process of designing and reviewing secure systems.

*Panorama*

What is the context in which security is operated? Even a very usable security mechanism is likely to create extra work from the users' point of view. It is human nature to look for shortcuts and workarounds, especially when users do not understand why their behavior compromises security. User education and training have a role to play, but changing individuals' behavior requires motivation and persuasion, especially when the users' own assets are not at risk. A positive security culture, based on a shared understanding of the importance of security for the organization's business, is the key to achieving desired behavior. Effective and usable security requires effort beyond the design of user interfaces to security tools, specifically:

- *Security training in operating security mechanisms correctly*. Effective security training goes beyond instruction: it includes monitoring and feedback. Monitoring of security performance is an ongoing activity; action needs to be taken when policies are breached. For instance, mechanisms that are too difficult to operate need to be redesigned, or sanctions need to be carried out against users who refuse to comply.

- *Security education.* Users' motivation to comply is based on understanding why their behavior can put organizational assets at risk. Education needs to instill personal and collective responsibility in users, but also in security designers, administrators, and decision makers.

- *Political, ethical, legal, and economic constraints surrounding the system.* Currently, decision-making on security is largely driven by technical considerations (e.g., security mechanisms are selected according to technical performance). However, other requirements may conflict with or override technical performance.

In this chapter, we explore each of these points in more depth. As stated at the outset, our aim is to broaden the view of what is involved in building usable secure systems. At this point in time, we cannot offer a blueprint for building such systems, but we identify relevant knowledge and techniques that designers who aim to design systems that are secure in practice will find helpful.

## Product: Human Factors, Policies, and Security Mechanisms

It is unfortunate that usability and security are often seen as competing design goals in security, because only mechanisms that are used, and used correctly, can offer the protection intended by the security designer. As Bruce Tognazzini points out in Chapter 3, a secure system needs to be actually, not theoretically, secure. When users fail to comply with the behavior required by a secure system, security will not work as intended. Users fail to show the required behavior for one of the following two reasons:

- They are unable to behave as required.

- They do not want to behave in the way required.

### Impossible Demands

The current situation with computer passwords provides a good example of the first case: most users today find it impossible to comply with standard policies governing the use of computer passwords (see Chapter 7 in this volume). Remembering a single, frequently used password is a perfectly manageable task for most users. But most users today have many knowledge-based authentication items to deal with. We have multiple and frequently changed passwords in the work context, in addition to passwords and personal identification numbers (PINs) outside work, some of which are used infrequently or require regular change. The limitations of human memory make it impossible for most users to cope with the memory performance this requires.[4] As a result, users behave in ways forbidden by most security policies:

---

4   M. Angela Sasse, Sacha Brostoff, and Dirk Weirich, "Transforming the 'weakest link': a human-computer interaction approach to usable and effective security," *BT Technology Journal 2001* 19, 122–131.

- *Users write passwords down.* Externalizing items we have to remember is the most common way of dealing with memory problems. In office environments, users stick notes with passwords onto their screens, or maintain a list of current passwords on the nearest whiteboard.

  Similarly, many bank customers write their PINs on their cards. A less common remedy is to write or scratch the PIN on the ATM or its surroundings.

---

## ANECDOTAL EVIDENCE

- A reality TV show set in a police station in the UK featured a whiteboard behind a PC used to log the movement of prisoners with a prominent reminder:

  "The password is *custody*."

- The customer relations manager of a UK building society received irate phone calls after a major re-branding exercise, in which ATMs and the surrounding environments had been restyled. The customers did not object to the new corporate color scheme, but rather, to the fact that the panels and surroundings onto which they had written or scratched their PINs had been replaced, and as a result they were unable to withdraw cash.

---

- *Users share passwords with other users.* Another common way of preventing loss of data due to the vagaries of human memory is by sharing the information widely, so if you cannot remember the password, you are likely to find a colleague who can.

- *Users choose passwords that are memorable but not secure* (when the mechanism allows this). [5] Many users choose passwords or PINs that are memorable but easy to crack (names of spouses or favorite sports stars, birth dates, 1234, 8888).

The standard password mechanism is cheap to implement and—once recalled—executed quickly. But in the preceding examples, users are knowingly breaking the rules, and the examples give a feeling for the despair that the ever-growing number of passwords and PINs induces in many users. A key human factors principle is not to impose unreasonable demands on users; in fact, designers should minimize the physical and, especially, the mental workload that a system creates for the user.

Frequently used passwords—that is, passwords used on a daily basis—are not a problem for the average user in an office context. Infrequently used passwords and PINs, however,

---

5   Sacha Brostoff and Angela M. Sasse, "Ten strikes and you're out: increasing the number of login attempts can improve password usability," CHI Workshop on Human-Computer Interaction and Security Systems (Apr. 1–6, 2003, Ft. Lauderdale, FL).

can create significant problems—for instance, many people withdrawing money once a week have problems recalling a PIN. There are a number of ways in which the memory demands of passwords and PINs can be reduced:

- *Provide mechanisms that require users to recognize items rather than recall them.* Recognition is an easier memory task than recollection, and designers of graphical user interfaces (GUIs) have applied this principle for decades now. Recognition of images[6, 7] has already been used for security mechanisms; but even text-based challenge-response mechanisms (see Chapter 8) and associative passwords[8] can offer improvements over the unaided recall that current passwords require.

- *Keep the number of password changes to a minimum.* Login failures increase sharply after password changes[9, 10] because the new item competes with the old one.

- *Provide mechanisms that are forgiving.* Current password and PIN mechanisms require the item to be recalled and entered 100% correctly. Brostoff and Sasse found[11] that users do not completely forget passwords. Most of the time they confuse them with other passwords, do not recall them 100% correctly, or mistype them on entry. This means that given a larger number of attempts, most users will eventually log in successfully. They report that when the standard limitation of three attempts was removed, the number of successful logins increased from 53% to 93% within nine attempts. Not having to reset a password saves users considerable time and effort—the time, effort, and possible embarrassment involved in contacting a system administrator or help desk, and having to think of, and memorize, a new password. From the organization's point of view, a 40% reduction of resets saves considerably in system administrator or help desk time.

As mentioned previously, usability and security are often seen as competing goals. Security experts are often inclined to reject proposals for improving usability (such as the ones listed earlier) because the help given to users might help an attacker. There is a tendency to discount more usable mechanisms because they may introduce an additional vulnerability or increase risk. For example, changing passwords less frequently means that a compromised password may be used longer. However, we would argue that a usable mechanism should not be dismissed immediately because it may introduce a new vulnerability or increase an existing one. Such a sweeping dismissal ignores the importance of

6   Rachna Dhamija and Adrian Perrig, "Deja Vu: A User Study. Using Images for Authentication," *Proceedings of the 9th USENIX Security Symposium* (Aug. 2000, Denver, CO).

7   *Passfaces* (2004); *http://www.realuser.com/cgi-bin/ru.exe/_/homepages/index.htm.*

8   Moshe Zviran and William J. Haga, "Cognitive Passwords: The Key to Easy Access Control," *Computer and Security*, 9:8, 1990, 723–736.

9   Brostoff and Sasse, 2003.

10  Sasse, Brostoff, and Weirich.

11  Sacha Brostoff and Angela M. Sasse, "Are Passfaces More Usable Than Passwords? A Field Trial Investigation," People and Computers XIV—Usability or Else! *Proceedings of HCI 2000* (Sept. 5–8, 2000, Sunderland, U.K.), 405–424.

human factors and economic realities, and—as Tognazzini points out in Chapter 3—the goal of security must be to build systems that are actually secure, as opposed to theoretically secure. For example, users' inability to cope with the standard requirements attached to passwords leads to frequent reset requests. This increases the load on system administrators, and in response many organizations set up help desks. In many organizations, the mounting cost of help desks has been deemed unacceptable.[12]

To cope with the increasing frequency of forgotten passwords, many organizations have introduced password reminder systems, or encouraged users to write down passwords "in a secure manner"—for example, in a sealed envelope kept in a locked desk drawer. But such hastily arranged "fixes" to unusable security mechanisms are often anything but secure:

- *Password reminders.* These may be convenient for users and a fast and cheap fix from the organization's point of view, but they create considerable vulnerabilities that can be exploited by an attacker, and the fact that the password has been compromised may not be detected for some time. For this reason, the FIPS password guidelines[13] mandate that forgotten passwords should not be reissued, but must be reset.

- *Encouraging users to write down passwords.* This violates the cardinal principle of knowledge-based authentication: that the secret should never be externalized. The "secure manner" of writing down passwords facilitates insider attacks. And relaxing the rules may seem to help users, but also has drawbacks. Simple but strong rules ("you should never write down this password, or tell anyone what it is") are easier for users to cope with than more permissive but complex ones ("it's OK to write down your password and keep it in a sealed envelope in your desk, but it's not OK to write it on a Post-it that you keep under your mouse pad").

The risks associated with changing passwords less frequently thus need to be weighed against the risks associated with real-world fixes to user problems, such as password reminders and writing down passwords. The FIPS guidelines actually acknowledge that the load on users created by frequent password changes creates its own risks, which in many contexts outweigh those created by changing a password less frequently. Allowing users more login attempts helps only a fellow user attacking the system from the inside, but makes no difference if the main threat is a cracking attack. Frequent changing or resetting of passwords, on the other hand, tends to lead users to create weaker passwords—more than half of users' passwords use a word with a number at the end,[14] a fact that helps crackers to cut down significantly the time required for a successful cracking attack.[15]

---

12 Sasse, Brostoff, and Weirich.

13 "Announcing the Standard for Password Usage," Federal Information Processing Standards Publication 112 (May 30, 1985).

14 Sasse, Brostoff, and Weirich.

15 Jeff Yann, "A Note on Proactive Password Checking," *Proceedings of the New Security Paradigms Workshop 2001* (ACM Press, 2001).

## Awkward Behaviors

Sometimes users fail to comply with a mechanism not because the behavior required is too difficult, but because it is awkward. Many organizations mandate that users must not leave systems unattended, and should lock their screens when leaving their desks, even for brief periods. Many users working in shared offices do not comply with such policies when their colleagues are present. If a user locks the screen of his computer every time he leaves the office, even for brief periods, what will his colleagues think? They are likely to suspect that the user either has something to hide or does not trust them. Most users prefer to have trusting relationships with their colleagues. Designers can assume that users will not comply with policies and mechanisms requiring behavior that is at odds with values they hold.

Another reason why users may refuse to comply is if the behavior required conflicts with the image they want to present to the outside world. Weirich and Sasse[16] found that people who follow security policies to the letter—that is, they construct and memorize strong passwords, change their passwords regularly, and always lock their screens—are described as "paranoid" and "anal" by their peers; these are not perceptions to which most people aspire. If secure systems require users to behave in a manner that conflicts with their norms, values, or self-image, most users will not comply. Additional organizational measures are required in such situations. For example, a company can communicate that locking of one's screen is part of a set of professional behaviors (e.g., necessary to have reliable audit trails of access to confidential data), and not because of mistrust or paranoia. Labeling such behaviors clearly as "it's business, not personal" avoids misunderstandings and awkwardness among colleagues. In organizations where genuine security needs underlie such behavior, and where a positive security culture is in place, compliance can become a shared value and a source of pride.

For designers of products aimed at individual users, rather than corporations, identifying security needs and values ought to be the first step toward a usable security product. The motivation to buy, install, and use a security product is increased vastly when it is based on users' security needs and values—in Chapter 24 of this volume, Friedman, Lin, and Miller provide an introduction to value-based design and further examples.

## Beyond the User Interface

The need for usability in secure systems was first established in 1975, when Saltzer and Schroeder[17] identified the need for *psychological acceptability* in secure systems. Traditionally, the way to increase acceptability has been to make security mechanisms easier to use (by providing better user interfaces). The most widely known and cited paper on usability

---

16 Dirk Weirich and M. Angela Sasse, "Pretty Good Persuasion: A First Step Towards Effective Password Security for the Real World," *Proceedings of the New Security Paradigms Workshop 2001* (Sept. 10–13, Cloudcroft, NM); (ACM Press, 2001), 137–143.

17 Jerome H. Saltzer and Michael D. Schroeder, "The Protection of Information in Computer Systems," *Proceedings of the IEEE*, 63:9 (1975), 1278–1308.

and security, "Why Johnny Can't Encrypt" (reprinted in Chapter 34 of this volume), reports that a sample of users with a good level of technical knowledge failed to encrypt and decrypt their mail using PGP 5.0, even after receiving instruction and practice. The authors, Alma Whitten and Doug Tygar, attributed the problems they observed to a mismatch between users' perception of the task of encrypting email and the way that the PGP interface presents those tasks to users, and they proposed a redesign to make the functionality more accessible.

User-centered design of security mechanisms, however, is more than user interface design. The case of PGP presents a good example. The problem lies less with the interface to PGP and more with the underlying concept of encryption (which predates PGP). The concept of encryption is complex, and the terminology employed is fundamentally at odds with everyday language: a cryptographic key does not function like a key in the physical world, and people's understanding of "public" and "private" is different from how these terms are applied to public and private keys. This will always create problems for users who do not understand how public-key encryption works. While some security experts advocate educating all users on the workings of public-key encryption so that they can use PGP and other encryption mechanisms, we argue that it is unrealistic and unnecessary to expect users to have the same depth of understanding of how a security mechanism works. Some computing people in the 1980s argued that it would never be possible to use a computer without an in-depth knowledge of electronics and programming; arguing that all users will have to become security experts to use systems securely is similarly misguided. The conceptual design approach, pioneered by Don Norman,[18] has been used to make complex functionality available to users who don't understand the detailed workings of a system, but have a task-action model ("if I want this message to be encrypted, I have to press this button").

However, the way in which people interact with security policies and mechanisms is not limited to the point of interaction. It is a truism of usability research that a bad user interface can ruin an otherwise functional system, but a well-designed user interface will not save a system that does not provide the required functionality. Designers can expend much effort on making a security mechanism as simple as possible, and find that users still fail to use it. Using a well-designed security mechanism is still more effort than not using it at all, and users will always be tempted to cut corners, especially when they are under pressure to complete their production task (as we will discuss later in this chapter). To make an effort for security, users must believe that their assets are under threat, and that the security mechanism provides effective protection against that threat.

18 Donald A. Norman, "Some Observations on Mental Models," in D.A. Gentner and A.A. Stevens (eds.), *Mental Models* (Hillsdale, NJ: Erlbaum, 1983).

## Process: Applying Human Factors Knowledge and User-Centered Approaches to Security Design

The process of building a secure system is vital to its effectiveness. The *process* is the means by which security needs are assessed, policies are elaborated, and countermeasures are designed. As with any software development project, the right mix of participants, expertise, and methodology is vital in ensuring a system that is actually secure. To achieve this, designers of secure systems need to consider that security is not the primary goal of users and organizations. The role of security is a supporting one—to protect assets and activities that users care about or that are part of the production activity of business organizations.

### Security Is a Supporting Task

Two further concepts that are key to designing successful security applications are *goals* and *tasks*. Human behavior is essentially goal driven, so the effective and efficient execution of tasks that help users attain goals is a key principle for designing successful systems. Human factors analysts distinguish between *production tasks* (those that are required to achieve the goal or produce the desired output) and *supporting tasks* (those that enable production tasks to be carried out in the long run, or be carried out more efficiently, but are not essential to achieving the goal). Security—like safety—is a supporting task. Production tasks are the reason why a system exists, and if production tasks cannot be completed effectively and efficiently, the system will cease to exist. Users put production tasks first; organizations, sensibly enough, do the same from a higher-level perspective. This understanding leads us to a number of insights for security design:

- *Security tasks must be designed to support production tasks.* Security tasks must not make demands on users that conflict with the demands of their production tasks. The performance requirements for a security task must be derived from the performance requirements for the production task. The current reality is that security mechanisms are often chosen without consideration of the production tasks, and individual users are often left to make a choice between complying with security regulations on the one hand or getting their job done on the other—and the choice they make is predictable. When security needs require a reduction in the efficiency of a production task, the need for the extra effort has to be communicated clearly to users. Tradeoffs between production tasks and security should not be made by security experts, who naturally prioritize security over efficiency. Rather, these decisions should be made in consultation with those in charge of business processes and workflow.[19]

- *Users need to understand and accept the need for security tasks.* In an ideal world, we would have systems where security is integrated seamlessly and demands no extra effort. We could, for instance, imagine a gait recognition system that identifies users as they walk up to a door and open it to those who are authorized, remaining shut to those who are not. In reality, however, even a well-chosen and well-configured security mechanism

---

19 Sacha Brostoff and Angela M. Sasse, "Safe and Sound: A Safety-Critical Approach to Security Design," New Security Paradigms Workshop 2001.

demands extra effort—in the gait example, users may need to remember to carry a token that identifies them and to make special arrangements to take visitors into the building. To avoid users' natural inclination to shortcut security, they need to understand and accept the need for the security task, and be motivated to comply with it.

## A Process for Designing Usable Secure Systems

Zurko and Simon[20] were among the first to point out that current security mechanisms make unreasonable demands on all stakeholders: system administrators and system developers, as well as users, struggle with the increasing amount and complexity of work involved in keeping systems secure.

System administrators struggle with the increasing workload involved in securing systems at all possible levels (hardware, operating system, network, applications), keeping up with patches, registering users, and managing accounts.

Many developers feel overwhelmed by the complexity involved in securing the systems they develop. Often, security weaknesses are introduced because developers do not realize the security implications of their design decisions. Because security is seen as a nonfunctional requirement in software engineering terms, the need to secure functions is often not considered until the design is completed. Users often compound this problem by asking to see functions working as early as possible. Even when a security analysis has been done at the outset of the project, the implications for design may not be considered because they are kept in a document separate from the system specification. Today, developers are often left with the responsibility for making security decisions in new applications.

To address these issues, Flechais, Sasse, and Hailes[21] have proposed an integrated development method for secure systems that does the following:

- Brings together all stakeholders (system developers, owners, users, administrators, and security experts) to carry out a risk analysis and to consider the practical implications of proposed security mechanisms in the context of use

- Integrates security into the software engineering documentation that developers refer to throughout the development process

Appropriate and Effective Guidance for Information Security (AEGIS) is a sociotechnical software engineering methodology for creating secure systems based on asset modeling, security requirements identification, risk analysis, and context of use. The purpose is to provide system developers with simple and intuitive tools for producing a secure system

---

20 Mary E. Zurko and Richard T. Simon, "User-Centered Security," New Security Paradigms Workshop 1997.

21 Ivan Flechais, Angela M. Sasse, and Stephen Hailes, "Bringing Security Home: A Process for Developing Secure and Usable Systems," *Proceedings of the New Security Paradigms Workshop 2003.*

that takes end user needs into account and promotes security buy-in. The core processes of AEGIS are shown in Figure 2-1.

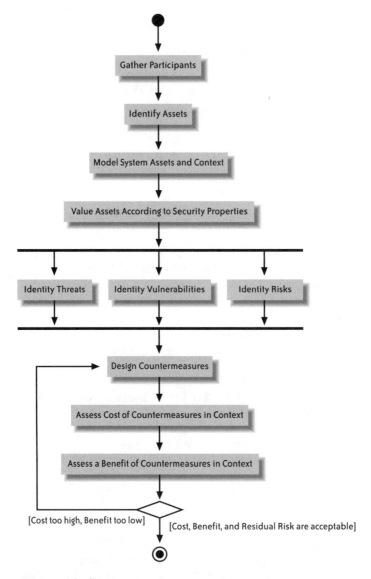

FIGURE 2-1. *AEGIS activity diagram*

The core AEGIS processes consist of:

1. *Gathering participants in the design process.* This requires identifying and ensuring the participation of key stakeholders, including users, managers, and system owners.

2. *Identifying the system's assets.* Assets represent the most fundamental valuables in a system. These include hardware or software components, physical artifacts, employees, etc.

3. *Modeling assets in the context of operation.* As seen from the HCI design technique known as *contextual design*,[22] understanding the context in which the system operates is a useful tool for designing a practical and usable system. Modeling the physical and cultural environment of the assets provides greater information about the system that can then inform the security design.

4. *Identifying security requirements on the assets.* Getting stakeholders to assign a value to the assets according to certain security properties (such as confidentiality, integrity, and availability) gives a clear insight into which aspects of the system are most important. This also provides greater clarity into which aspects of security deserve the most attention—for example, providing a high degree of availability requires a different architecture from satisfying a high confidentiality requirement. Figure 2-2 shows an example model in which assets, context, and security requirements have been recorded.

5. *Conducting a risk analysis in which vulnerabilities, threats, and risks are identified.* Together with the identification of important security requirements, this allows the identification of areas in which the system is at risk and the potential impact to the system is deemed to be high.

6. *Designing the security of the system.* This design is based on the security requirements identified by the stakeholders and the risk analysis highlighting areas where the system is unacceptably vulnerable. At this point, countermeasures are proposed and evaluated against both their cost and their effectiveness. The contextual information identified previously is important in assessing the cost of the countermeasure to the system as a whole—this includes financial, organizational, and user costs. Identifying the benefit of the countermeasure depends on an assessment of the effectiveness of that measure at preventing, detecting, or reacting to identified risks. Based on a better understanding of the impact of the countermeasure, it can then either be accepted or rejected as a part of the architecture.

By involving stakeholders in the security analysis, AEGIS provides several benefits:

• It provides increased awareness of security in the participants, allowing them to identify a number of problems and issues with security themselves, and providing a wealth of information about the needs of stakeholders. This information is elicited and recorded in the asset model, which is used throughout the security design.

• The security aspects of the system become much more accessible and personal. This can be invaluable in combating security apathy, and can be a powerful means of overcoming a lack of security motivation.

• By providing a simple model through which the security properties of the system can be discussed by stakeholders, communication during the design of security is improved—and that supports better security decision-making.

---

22 Hugh Beyer and Karen Holtzblatt, *Contextual Design* (San Francisco, Morgan Kaufmann, 1977).

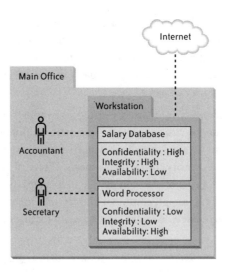

*FIGURE 2-2. Sample AEGIS asset model*

# Panorama: Understanding the Importance of the Environment

The environment surrounding the process of developing security is also extremely important to the effective operation of the product (security mechanism). During the design of the security, a number of factors not necessarily related to any security needs can influence the final product. The personal responsibility of participants for the resulting security, the enthusiasm of high-level management for security (even their presence in the design process), pressure to achieve functional features, time-to-market, personal agendas, ethical constraints, industrial involvement, and legal requirements—all influence security design in one way or another.[23]

The cultural panorama surrounding security does not stop affecting it after the design is complete, but continues even after it has been put to use. An analysis by Flechais, Riegelsberger, and Sasse[24] has identified the influences and mechanics of trust relationships in the operation of secure systems. In most current cases, existing trust relationships in an organization facilitate the breaking of security policies and practices. In fact, given the right (and currently widespread) environment, simply adhering to existing security policies can undermine social relationships within a group of peers. The authors argue that trust relationships are beneficial for organizations by promoting *social capital*[25] (i.e., trust based on shared informal norms that promote cooperation)[26] and that the organizational culture and the actual security should be designed to support both trust relationships and adherence to policy.

23 Flechais, Sasse, and Hailes.

24 Ivan Flechais, Jens Riegelsberger, and Angela M. Sasse, "Divide and Conquer: The Role of Trust and Assurance in the Design of Socio-Technical Systems," Technical Report, 2004.

25 Mitnick and Simon.

26 Brostoff and Sasse, 2001.

## The Role of Education, Training, Motivation, and Persuasion

While a well-designed security mechanism won't put off users, it also won't entice them to make the extra effort that security requires. In many home and organizational contexts, users lack the motivation to make that extra effort. User education and training can be used to explain the need for the effort that security requires, but changing users' knowledge and understanding does not automatically mean they will change their *behavior*. Dhamija and Perrig,[27] for instance, found that a sample of users with weak passwords had "received relevant training" and did know how to construct strong passwords; however, they chose not to comply with the request to construct strong passwords. The first point to make here is that there is a difference between education and training: while *education* is largely about teaching concepts and skills, *training* aims to change behavior through drill, monitoring, feedback, reinforcement, and—in the case of willful noncompliance—punishment. Because social engineering attacks often bypass technology altogether to obtain access or information, Mitnik and Simon[28] emphasize that effective security education and training should:

- Not only focus on correct usage of security mechanisms, but also address other behaviors—for example, checking that callers are who they claim to be

- Encompass all staff, not only those with immediate access to systems deemed at risk

Many organizations simply provide security instructions to users and expect these instructions to be followed. The material disseminated may even threaten punishment. However, the threat of punishment alone won't change users' behavior—rather, if users see that rules are not enforced, they will lose respect for the security in general, and the result is a declining security culture. Even though some security experts advocate rigorous punishment as a way of weeding out undesirable user behavior, this is not an easy option. Policing undesirable behavior—detection and punishment—requires considerable resources, can be detrimental to the organizational climate, and may have undesirable side effects (such as increasing staff turnover). Given that sanctions have an effect only if they are applied, and given that there may be undesirable side effects, an organization would be well advised to specify sanctions only for a small set of key behaviors that it deems to be putting key assets at risk.

Weirich and Sasse[29] identified a set of beliefs and attitudes held by many users who do not comply with security policies:

- Users do not believe they are personally at risk.

- Users do not believe they will be held accountable for not following security regulations.

27 Dhamija and Perrig.
28 Mitnick and Simon.
29 Weirich and Sasse, 2001.

- The behavior required by security mechanisms conflicts with social norms.

- The behavior required by security mechanisms conflicts with users' self-image. (The perception is that only "nerds" and "paranoid" people follow security regulations.)

There can be no doubt that security in general, and IT security in particular, currently suffers from an image problem. Education campaigns (similar to those employed in health education) can be effective only if they make users believe that something they care about is at risk. In the most recent CSI/FBI survey,[30] the overwhelming majority of respondents stated that their company needed to invest in raising security awareness. When users cannot be motivated, persuasion needs to be employed. In this chapter, we present some examples of persuasion designed to improve security behavior in the corporate context; Fogg[31] offers techniques for designing applications and interfaces that intrigue, persuade, and reward users to achieve desired user behavior in general.

## Building a Security Culture

Earlier in this chapter, we emphasized the importance of having organizations integrate security into their business processes, and argued that the best motivation for users to exhibit desired security behavior is if they care about what is being protected, and understand how their behavior can put these assets at risk. These two arguments provide the foundation for the next key point: organizations must become actively involved in security design. They need to build a security culture as much as they need to build a system of technical countermeasures. Although some organizations understand that risk analysis is the bedrock of security design, many still do not understand the role of security in their business/production processes. Too many organizations are still copying standard security policies, deploying standard security mechanisms, and leaving decisions about security largely to security experts. Security decisions are then often made in an ad hoc fashion, as a "firefighting" response to the latest threat.

Organizations need to become actively involved in making decisions about what should be protected, and how. This requires performing a risk and threat analysis, and making decisions based on what makes economic sense for the business, instead of trying to meet abstract standards set by security experts. Although many companies already use risk analysis methods, they often fail to consider the interests and needs of all stakeholders—such as users—and the economics of security are currently not well understood.

Once specific security goals appropriate to the organization have been established, role models are essential to change behavior and rebuild the security culture. This will require buy-in from the top. Currently, senior managers sometimes exhibit bad security behavior because they believe that they are too important to bother with "petty" security policies. The security experts to whom they have delegated responsibility for the organization's

---

30 Ninth Annual CSI/FBI Survey on Computer Crime and Security (2004); *http://www.gocsi.com/*.

31 B. J. Fogg, *Persuasive Technology. Using Computers to Change What We Think and Do* (San Francisco: Morgan Kaufmann, 2003).

responsibility are often unable to force senior managers—who have the power to fire them—to comply with security policies. We would argue that the ultimate responsibility for security, as for safety, always should lie with senior management. Security experts can advise, implement, and monitor, but they cannot take sole responsibility for making an organization's security work.

An additional approach worth considering is to make secure behavior a desirable trait. This can be done through social marketing or by making such behavior part of professional and ethical norms.[32] Organizations that deal with confidential customer data, for instance, must make clear to all of their staff that they have a duty to safeguard such data from unauthorized access or tampering.

## Conclusion

This chapter started with the observation that only usable security is effective security, and outlined how human factors knowledge and user-centered design techniques can be applied to increase usability. Effective security requires us to look beyond the user interface to security tools, where most of the current research and development effort is focused. Changing undesirable user behavior is a complex task, and one that cannot be achieved by education or punishment alone. An organization is a sociotechnical system, and security design needs to address both technical and human aspects. Furthermore, security needs to be integrated into the business processes of an organization to be workable in practice and economically viable.

As a first step in this direction, Brostoff and Sasse[33] have adapted Reason's model of human error (a sociotechnical model for improving safety behavior in organizational contexts) to security. Reason's model is a good starting point because safety and security share the "supporting task" problem. Two key differences are that the benefits of safety are more obvious to most users, and that safety does not have adversaries who actively seek to attack. In many Western countries, health and safety regulations have led to significant changes in organizational culture with respect to employee safety. Responsibility for safety lies with management, for they allocate resources; this chapter has made the argument that security needs to be viewed in a similar way.

32 Sasse, Brostoff, and Weirich.
33 Brostoff and Sasse, 2001.

## About the Authors

 M. Angela Sasse is the Professor of Human-Centred Technology in the Department of Computer Science at University College London. After obtaining an M.Sc. in Occupational Psychology (from the University of Sheffield) and a Ph.D. in Computer Science (from the University of Birmingham), she joined UCL in 1990 to teach and research design and evaluation of emerging technologies. Since 1997, her research has focused on user-centered approaches to security, privacy, and trust.

 Ivan Flechais is a departmental lecturer in the software engineering program at Oxford University, and his main lecturing and research interests are in the area of computer security. Prior to this, he graduated with a B.Sc. in computer science from University College London, and then stayed on at UCL with a Ph.D. researching security design and the importance of people in computer security.

# CHAPTER THREE

# Design for Usability

**BRUCE TOGNAZZINI**

**T**HE GOAL OF SECURITY IS NOT TO BUILD SYSTEMS THAT ARE THEORETICALLY SECURABLE, but to build ones that are actually secure. This requires a combination of the theoretical and the practical. It requires close examination not only of the technology, but also of the human beings that will use it.

We can easily require users to supply passwords that are theoretically unbreakable—for example, 50 characters of random ASCII data—but we must consider the capabilities and habits of real people. Everyone would immediately post their password on a little piece of paper on their monitor, then spend hours trying to enter it accurately, their errors hidden by those delightful little dots that march across our screens.

Even closing every possible loophole in the system cannot provide perfect security. Dedicated and knowledgeable spies will install software of their own, such as keyboard "sniffers" that report back every entry typed, circumventing the most elaborate precautions. The poor user ends up the victim in all this, battered by impossible memory and accuracy demands.

Fortunately, there's a solution to such misfortune. In this chapter, we'll look at ways of balancing security and usability, security and privacy, and how to achieve a comprehensive security plan that works by considering both internal *and* external factors. Finally, I will propose a way of rethinking security issues so that our solutions will offer real security, rather than just the appearance of security.

## Death by Security

Lately, automakers have been bowing to insurance companies by adding special lug nuts to each wheel, keyed to a special socket that must be used to remove the wheel. Unfortunately, some of these special lug nuts have only about 2% or 3% of the surface in contact with the tool, compared to a standard lug nut. If the wheel is overtightened at the factory, as was done with our Lexus RX-300, the custom part of the lug nut will crack right off the car when you attempt to change a spare tire on a dark road late at night, as happened to us, rendering removal of the wheel impossible.

We have installed standard lug nuts all around on both our cars now, and to heck with our auto insurance company. We want to keep our *life* insurance company happy!

Even when the auto security people aren't setting us up for a mugging, they are raising our blood pressure to dangerous heights. We had a VW Rabbit several years ago that featured a theft-proof radio, rendered useless once it was removed from the vehicle. It could only be made to function again by performing an elaborate and secret ritual, involving pressing a whole bunch of buttons in sequence while holding your right foot with your left hand and crowing to the moon.

Of course, the radio didn't really "know" it had been stolen. It only "knew" that it had lost its connection to the car battery. Therefore, the first time the battery went dead, we no longer had a radio.

VW had given us a sheet with the magical incantations, but it had warned us not to leave the sheet in the car, the equivalent to leaving passwords on a yellow sticky stuck to the side of a monitor. Ever compliant, we put the sheet in "a safe place," where it probably rests today. (I can't say for sure, since we can't remember where the safe place is.)

So we contacted our dealer, and after waiting several weeks for VW to confirm our identity through DNA analysis, we received a copy of the magic sheet. This second copy remained in plain sight in the glove box for as long as we owned the car. Strangely, no one ever stole the radio, although the buttons finally gave out from our having to repeatedly key in the special code every time we left the lights on or the car was serviced.

We are not the only users who will find ways to evade security demands that are considered unreasonably burdensome. Such circumventions are all too common among today's computer users.

## Balance Security and Usability

Balance is key to all security efforts. The same phenomenon that happens with cars happens with computers. Unless you stand over them with a loaded gun, users will disable, evade, or avoid any security system that proves to be too burdensome or bothersome. Preventing your system from becoming the victim of such "empowered" users requires a combination of engineering and education. The engineering builds security systems that are safe and usable, and the education informs users about the actual risks so that they will be motivated to use your security (or at least so that they won't disable it).

How do you find the right balance? You begin by examining and exploiting, in each new situation, the differences between the two groups.

## Exploit Differences Between Users and Bad Guys

Let's return to those "marching dots" that I mentioned in my introduction. The purpose of those dots is to protect a password from "shoulder surfing" as it is being entered. In theory, if you have a strong password that's sent over an encrypted link, shoulder surfing is the main threat that passwords face.

But the user who actually types the password is in a fundamentally different position from a potential shoulder surfer. Consider:

- The user knows what he is typing—he is only looking for errors.
- The user is close to the screen where the password is being entered—he can read text that is printed with relatively low contrast.
- The user is always present.

Now, compare that with a potential attacker:

- An eavesdropper needs to accurately reconstruct every character in the password.
- An eavesdropper is probably several feet away from the screen—if that.
- An eavesdropper might not even be present—the user might be entering the password in the privacy of his own home, for example, or on a desert island.

You can take advantage of these differences to produce an interface that promotes complex passwords, while still leaving the eavesdropper in the dark. We did that when we designed Tresor 2.2 (see the upcoming sidebar). Alternatively, you can design an interface that allows the user to choose the amount of security that he wants when entering a password. As shown in Figure 3-1, the designers of GNU Keyring followed this approach.

## Exploit Differences in Physical Location

One user may be working in an airport lounge, surrounded by people who eavesdrop from either boredom or darker motivation. Another user may be working in her private study at home, with nothing but two blank walls behind her. However, our current "one size fits all" security systems tend to ignore that difference. They arise from a single assumption: *the bad guy may be standing behind you this minute!*

## Vary Security with the Task

The task at hand is a vital component in security decision-making. Security practitioners call this *threat analysis*. Different kinds of security measures are called for protecting information that is in transit versus information that is to be stored permanently on a hard drive. Sure, both data streams might be protected with 128-bit AES encryption. But in the

# CASE STUDY: TRESOR 2.2

Tresor is a file encryption application that offers very high security. The application makes it easy to type a long "passphrase"—even for users who perpetually make typographical errors. Designed by Roland Blaser and myself, Tresor 2.2's passphrase entry design replaces "marching dots" with a new metaphor: the *rolling blackout*.

*Users in the light; eavesdropping in a blackout*

Like most web browsers, Tresor 2.2 uses those cute little dots to replace the characters in the user's password. But in Tresor 2.2, the characters are a bit slow in acting, always revealing the last few characters for a few seconds as the user types, long enough for the user to catch a typo.

But how many characters should be visible? In our first user test, we had three password characters visible and discovered that this provided enough information for an eavesdropper standing a few feet away to read the password as it was typed. The effect was startling: eavesdroppers' brains "saw" more than what was before their eyes. The security of the scheme was completely compromised.

In a follow-up test, we tried revealing just one or two characters. This foiled the eavesdropper, but users were crippled as well: they frequently didn't catch their own errors.

Our third iteration incorporated the suggestion of interaction designer, Craig Oshima: the password characters were now printed in low-contrast (light gray) characters on a white background. We still used black dots, however. This change let us return to three characters revealed. Users were able to accurately and comfortably detect errors, while the eavesdroppers failed.

*Error correction*

Error correction worked perfectly from the beginning. Pressing Delete would delete the last character and reveal one more so that three would always be visible. Yes, the eavesdropper might now pick up a fragment of a passphrase, but we decided that such revelations—happening only when the user made a mistake—were insignificant when one considered the added security that could come with a 50- or 100-character passphrase.

*Final polish*

We added a few extra safety features, including always hiding the first four characters, so eavesdroppers can't get a running start, and timing out the Delete key reveal, protecting users who wander off, and we were done.

*—continued—*

*User control*

Users are permitted to set a number of preferences, such as length of time before the "rolling blackout" hides the typed characters, with all ranges proven through user testing. Help files teach how to select secure passwords and encourage users to set preferences so that they are comfortable, making life difficult for both eavesdroppers and bad guys mounting an offline attack.

*Results*

We were able to develop a system that encouraged the use of very long passphrases. In one speed test, a user was able to type in a passphrase of approximately 50 characters 20 times in a row without a single surviving error.

*FIGURE 3-1. The GNU Keyring application allows the user to choose whether to veil the password (left) or show it (right); users in busy airports probably want to veil their passwords, and users working in the privacy and safety of their own home can have their passwords exposed, which makes it much easier to enter them using the Palm's Graffiti system*

first case, it's appropriate to use an ephemeral encryption key that is destroyed when it is no longer used; with stored documents, you might want to provide for key escrow, secret splitting, or even a secondary encryption key so that the document's contents can be recovered in the event of a problem.

Likewise, different security measures and interfaces are appropriate if your intention is to protect a laptop from a competitor or a co-worker. In the first case, you might be happy with a password that needs to be entered when the computer is powered on after it has been asleep for more than a few minutes. In the second case, you probably want a password on the screensaver—and a cable lock attaching the laptop to the table.

## Increase Your Partnership with Users

Security forces and their users are at war today, with many users in open rebellion. Security administrators need to understand that users frequently write down passwords because they cannot possibly remember all of the different codes and "secret handshakes" that are required to get through the day. Users need to learn to be discreet in their rule breaking: store the passwords on an unlabeled page of your day planner, instead of posting it on the side of your monitor.

### Trust the user

Users are not the enemy; the bad guys are. Form a partnership with your users, treat them as intellectual equals, and they will respond. Adams and Sasse found that users do a much better job of implementing and following security policies when they are given cogent explanations of both the goals of the policies and the real security threats that the organization faces.[1] Of course, you don't have to actually *believe* that users are your intellectual equals. However, if you follow such a path, you'll be amazed at how swiftly their minds will improve.

Make reasonable compromises in your design, offer users the flexibility to conform your application or service to their current conditions, and give users the information they need to make these decisions.

### Exploit the special skills of users

As one example, elderly users, while experiencing failing memory of the present, experience an actual increase in more ancient memories, such as the name of their second grade schoolmarm. Encouraging them to form passwords from such information, such as "MissMorrison2", can result in passwords they are ideally specialized to remember, while confounding all but the most aggressive attacks and guesses.

Look for similar special skills among your specific user population that you can use to their advantage.

### Remove or reduce the user's burden

We have systems that allow free and easy access; we have systems that provide high levels of security. Until recently, we haven't had many systems that do both well. For example:

---

1  Anne Adams and M. Angela Sasse, "Users are not the enemy," *Communications of the ACM* (Dec. 1999), 40–46 and reprinted as Chapter 32, this volume.

# WHY WE OVERPROTECT

For someone who has spent much of his career giving people lots of rope, I was amazed at how working on the Tresor project made me reverse roles. In less than a week, I found myself looking for new tricks, ploys, and techniques that I could use to limit the power of a user. All of these limitations, of course, were for the user's own good.

The engineer and I ended up in full role-reversal, with him as advocate for the users and me struggling to protect them, even if it killed them. I felt positively righteous about my efforts. The goal was, after all, security! It had suddenly seemed to me sacrilegious to implement anything that could even remotely help an eavesdropper, regardless of what it cost the user. I was gripped with a terrible fear that someday, some document would "get out," and it would be my fault.

When I pulled back, I stopped considering only the worst-case scenario, which for me was the user typing in passwords while standing in Grand Central Station with 12 people in trench coats hovering over her shoulder while another battery of 12 people trained high-tech cameras on her screen. I instead strove for balance between user and bad guy, and then gave the user the power to control her own use of the product.

(One might think that after slaving under the yoke of such systems for 30 years, as well as having a hand in designing more than a few of them in earlier years, I would have been a little more sympathetic toward my users. I might have been if the users weren't so stupid as to start typing in secret codes in the middle of Grand Central Station with trench-coated men floating above their shoulders!)

---

- Today, you can buy a secure USB drive that requires a fingerprint to "open" it. This works great when the fingerprint reader is cooperative, but it's maddening when it isn't. Although there is potential for biometrics-based systems to be dramatically easier to use than today's password-based systems, designers shouldn't assume that replacing a password with a fingerprint reader automatically makes a system more "usable." Much work still needs to be done to make the dream of free and easy access on the part of the authorized user a reality.

- Portable systems can be more "aware" of their environments. Are they at home, at the office, or in a restaurant or airline terminal? Knowing this, the security system can smoothly change methodologies and requirements without user intervention. (My laptop could determine that it is at home by seeing the WiFi MAC address of my home gateway, for example.) A more sophisticated approach would allow the user to choose among high, medium, and low security needs for each new environment as it is detected.

## Achieve Balanced Authentication Design

Authentication came late to the personal-computer party. Before the explosion of the Internet in the 1990s, few people needed more than a single password for their email. The personal computer was primarily a tool for developing documents that would be printed for distribution. Authentication was provided by physical access: if you could touch the keyboard, you could access the documents!

Everything changed with the arrival of the Web, and it caught the security world by surprise. Practices that had worked since the 1960s suddenly failed. Why? Because the users changed. Instead of being a few trained, dedicated employees, suddenly millions of people, with no instruction whatsoever, were faced with signing up for a dazzling array of usernames and passwords. Simultaneously, the potential for attack on protected information went up astronomically.

Unfortunately, many of the solutions that were pressed into widespread use actually prevent the user's most valiant attempts to comply.

### Remove unnecessary password restrictions

Web sites always set a low end for password selection, such as no fewer than four or six characters, a vital requirement. Some, however, go above and beyond, by setting a limit above and beyond, such as prohibiting *more* than six characters in total or requiring use of numbers only. This prevents people from using the secure passwords they've already committed to memory. My personal solution to this problem has been to create a database listing each site's username and password (currently 134 records in number). I have a shorthand for my usual password, but all others I'm forced to create are "in the clear," typed right in there for anyone with access to my machine to see. (I hesitate to reveal such a secret, lest someone break into my house some night so that they can access my free subscription to the *Podunk Shopping News*.)

Few users go to the trouble of building a database. They either avoid sites that won't accept their standard password, or register today to read the one thing they want, then immediately forget what they made up, never intending to visit again.

Many password restrictions are implemented because the passwords entered in a web site are crunched and munched and spit into some ancient application running on an IBM mainframe or something. The programmers who created the web interface felt that they had a responsibility to be faithful to the AS/400. A better solution would be to allow users to enter long or strong passwords, and then to silently drop illegal characters that can't be sent to the legacy system.

And if a password doesn't work, instead of telling the user to check his Caps Lock key, a better approach is to simply flip the case and try resubmitting. This cuts down on tech support calls without significantly impacting the security of the system as a whole.

## The Doctor and password madness

My wife, the Doctor, was working over the summer at a local hospital. This hospital is fiercely into security, requiring no fewer than four sets of passwords to navigate its system. And why not? There are confidential patient records on those systems! By golly, they ought to have eight sets of passwords, and really make things secure!

But wait! It gets worse! After being on the job for six weeks, my wife had received only two of the four sets of usernames/passwords that she needed to do her job—and she had spoken to no fewer than seven people to get them. Two weeks of further extreme effort finally produced the last two sets.

What was she doing in the meantime? Instead of spending all her time repairing people, she wasted hours camping out in another doc's offices, using his computer (and his passwords, thanks to the sticky notes) to do her work.

Meanwhile, the other doc, bumped from his office, would go and get an extra cup of coffee. The security system so carefully put in place had thus not only opened up your medical records to anyone schooled in the use of sticky notes, but also was resulting in the hospital pouring money down the drain in the form of lost productivity and company-supplied coffee.

Things get worse if my wife doesn't log in to a particular system every 90 days. This happens more than you might think, because my wife works at this particular hospital only during the summer and over the winter holidays. If she is gone for more than three months, the system will decide that her usernames and passwords are idle and will expire them.

It's almost as bad for full-time doctors. They get to keep their usernames, but have to select (and post on their computer monitors) new passwords every 90 days.

Expiring stuff is the only way this security crew has been able to prevent doctors from memorizing their passwords. You might think that memorizing passwords would be a good thing. One of the official reasons to expire passwords is to limit the amount of time an undetected attacker can use a compromised password. But this security measure is defeated easily by any attacker who can read sticky notes.

## Balance Resource Allocation

Hospitals all over the country have been panicking because of new security regulations suddenly hitting them by surprise with no more than about six years' notice. My wife called down to Emergency a couple of days after the last law struck to ask them to fax a few pages from the record of a patient they had just sent up, but they refused. Someone could steal the fax off the machine that sits right out in the hall, with easy patient access. The previous week, that was an acceptable risk. This week, it was against the law.

While the security forces had spent years staring at their computer screens, thinking up ways to require four sets of auto-expiring usernames and passwords for all the doctors, they had failed to set up the most rudimentary physical security for either computers or fax machines. The most casual field study—a walk through the hospital, informal chats with personnel on duty—would have revealed the problem years before, giving them plenty of time to move the fax machines 5 or 10 feet into a secure area.

Balance is also a critical factor in deciding where to expend resources. Cybersecurity in the absence of physical security is useless. Any new project should be launched with a thorough field study of the people who will be using the system, the places where they will use it, and the nature of the tasks they will be accomplishing. Existing efforts should go through the same kind of field review at least annually. Look specifically for aspects that are out of balance, whether they involve technology or an unsecured fax machine in the hall.

## Balance Privacy and Security

We often say "privacy and security" in the same breath, but they can often be at odds with each other.

Let us look at an example: the problem of increasing access to employees on the job. One of the earliest technologies to be deployed in this effort was a smart card that reported to a central computer, several times a minute, the current location of each and every employee so that they could always be found. It seemed only natural to make better use of this flood of data, so it was not long before bosses were receiving printouts of how much time employees were spending at the water cooler, the lunch room, and even the bathroom. In the rush to pry, the original goal of the technology was all but forgotten.

Another technology offers the same ability to maintain employees' access, while at the same time actually enhancing employees' privacy: portable telephones. Whether they be cell phones or local wireless phones, they offer the employee the ability to wander freely while still maintaining contact, and they do so without (necessarily) ratting out the employee's location.

This approach actually enhances privacy: before, should the boss ring the employee's phone in his office, she could ascertain whether he was in the office. With a portable phone, the caller has no idea where the employee is (unless sounds of a live ballgame give him away). At the same time, these phones make contact easier than with the smart cards, since the boss no longer has to slog off in pursuit.

For employers who judge their workers by how busy they look, such a scheme might well send chills down their back. For employers who, instead, judge employees by the quality of their results, such a system solves the employer's problem without shredding the last vestiges of employee privacy.

A new threat to our personal liberty is the electronic cards being used for rapid toll paying. These cards were designed to record the time the car passed through the toll station and remove the toll amount from their account. It wasn't long before they were pressed into use in tracking ongoing kidnappings, something everyone applauded (except for the Kidnapper's Union).

Recently, however, the governments in some states have started mounting card readers all along the freeways. The stated reason is that, by monitoring cars in the aggregate, they can map the flow of traffic. We've heard about aggregation before. It has a tendency to be the "introductory offer" that leads to something darker. How long will it be before the government is routinely monitoring or backtracking the movement of citizens suspected of far less violent crimes, like overdue parking tickets, or noncrimes, like being seen at a political rally?

Citizens today can buy "disposable cell phones," recycled phones that carry a certain number of prepaid minutes. They can be bought with cash and used until exhausted, all without anyone's knowledge as to who the possessor is. (Don't ask why someone would want such a phone. It's the essence of freedom that we need not declare a reason.) Prepaid toll cards could achieve the same anonymity, while achieving the same purported goal: collecting the toll.

You can do better than simply balancing privacy against security. The proper approach can actually increase both.

Privacy considerations should be separate and distinct from security. Your designs can either support or degrade privacy. You can build highly secure systems that enhance, rather than reduce privacy. For every strategy to increase security that decreases privacy, you will usually be able to devise an alternative that will not only retain it, but also enhance it.

## Build a Secure Internet

We are now engaged in the transition from isolated one-person computers to the concept of a personal network, enabling people to tap into their personal cyberspace from any point on the globe.

The most fundamental requirement of such a personal network is that individuals be able to maintain the most private of information without worry, no matter where their travels might take them. They further need to be able to monitor and control access of others both to their information and to themselves. Before that can occur, we will have to build a multiplicity of new, secure walls.

The original ARPANET, forerunner to today's Internet, was the exclusive domain of university scientists and the U.S. military. The world was neatly divided into "We" and "They." "We," the "good guys," had access to ARPANET. "They," everyone else in the world, did not. Security, in those days, consisted of keeping the "bad guys" from gaining physical access of any kind to the network.

The transition to a public Internet suddenly allowed every bad guy in the world complete access, but ARPANET's decision to have virtually no internal security was never revisited.

# DESIGN CHECKLIST

*Achieving balance:*

❏ Are you exploiting the differences between users and attackers?

    ❏ Users know what they are typing in—they are only looking for errors.

    ❏ Eavesdroppers, meanwhile, have to reconstruct every character accurately.

    ❏ Users are closer to the screen and therefore can read with lower contrast and can differentiate better between green and blue (unless they are colorblind).

❏ Are you detecting and exploiting differences in physical location?

    ❏ Home

    ❏ Office

    ❏ Airport and other public venues

❏ Are you providing a way that your software can track location changes or the user can casually indicate such changes?

❏ Are you varying security with the task?

    ❏ Temporary versus archival security

    ❏ "Here" versus "there" versus "en route"

    ❏ "Hide from co-workers" versus "Hide from competitors"

❏ Does your design exploit the special skills of your user population?

❏ Does it serve to reduce the user's burden?

*Authentication:*

❏ Are your passwords restrictive because of:

    ❏ Low upper-limits on password length

    ❏ Passwords that are system generated

    ❏ Other password rules that encourage posting the password on a yellow sticky note

❏ Is it quick and easy to obtain or replace a password?

*Methodology:*

❏ Did you begin with a comprehensive field study?

❏ Have you set up regular usability studies?

❏ Do you have systems in place to capture user feedback after release?

**Privacy:**

❏ Will your users enjoy greater privacy while using your design than they did before?

As a result, per Symantec,[2] by the close of 2004, more than 60,000 viruses, worms, etc., were crawling the Internet in search of Windows machines. An additional 60 such creatures were looking for Macs. These amateur attacks have been joined by the professional attacks of spammers, phishers, and spyware makers, rendering the character of the Internet something akin to that semi-abandoned strip mall just out of town, the one not to be visited after dark.

Today, individual application and OS developers are working frantically to secure their products, even as the "bad guys" develop more sophisticated methods of attack. This is akin to our leaving the doors to our houses wide open while expecting our flatware manufacturers to frantically develop ever-better self-protecting silverware. Patch, patch, patch is not working now, and it's never going to work. We need a fundamentally different approach.

## Ringworld

Individuals need a private network presenting a series of secure, concentric walls that surround the user and his information, with each outward wall presenting a more restrictive boundary.

Today, we have virtual private networks, or VPNs. They tend to focus on "We," with the "We" being large corporations that want their employees to continue to work at home and abroad. Everyone else in the world is the new "They." These VPNs restore the binary security model of the ARPANET era, except on a corporate rather than global level. It's a good stopgap measure, but far short of what is needed.

The computer world needs something that is at once both more personal and more general than today's VPNs, consisting of four or more separate and distinct rings. Such a system once existed in the physical world. We need only look back to the future.

### Within the Castle Keep

The "Castle Keep" of medieval times was the private realm of the castle owner and only the castle owner. This small tower in the center of the castle grounds formed the last bastion should the castle be overrun.

Each individual's VPN must be a personal Castle Keep, offering refuge from all assaults by an increasingly dangerous and aggressive cyberworld. This will be a difficult wall to construct, for the owner must be given free and easy access to his personal cyberspace from an airplane seat, a cell phone, or a hotel room in Nairobi, while at the same time, every other human being and machine on the planet, at the user's command, can be absolutely locked out. People should be able to adjust the porosity of this wall without raising the ire of those being further restricted, something that will be a good trick.

2   As reported in "Computers: Shiny Apple," *Consumer Reports* (Dec. 2004).

There's a delicacy about separating from family and friends. We usually depend on such subterfuges as telephone answering machine announcements claiming we're out when we're really watching the game. This approach should be extended into the VPN arena.

Because most of the impetus for VPNs is coming from big business, individuals have had few choices for a conveniently portable information space. A business opportunity exists for innovators to move into this space, selling to individuals the same capabilities that other companies are now offering big business.

## Within the Ramparts

The next wall surrounding the Castle Keep is the Ramparts, that outer defensive barrier (just before the crocodile-infested moat) shaping the extent of the castle grounds.

Typically, today's users will live simultaneously within two castles, their home castle and their work or school castle. Within these virtual walls of the home castle, for instance, Dad will be able to communicate freely with other members of the family residing in the castle, subject only to restrictions set by other family members' personal Castle Keeps. This will be equally true should Dad be in the living room or on safari in Nairobi. These connections will typically be more liberal than those between the family and the outside world.

Many people will elect to keep their two castles separated, dividing home/leisure from work or school. Others may encourage both to flow together, viewing their home and work lives as a continuum, rather than as two distinct activities. What will be important is to offer people the permissions and the tools to make these choices themselves, simply and fluidly.

Work on VPNs supporting the work castle (corporation) has already come to fruition, although more must be done to smooth and define the walls. Home and school lag far behind.

## The Town Wall

The area between the Ramparts and the Town Wall will represent a sharply reduced connection.

In the case of the family castle, these connections include access to trusted friends and relatives, along with businesses ranging from banks to e-commerce outlets to health care resources (all of which maintain their own private networks).

In the case of the business castle, it includes access to clients, suppliers, distributors, accounting firms, banks, etc. Much of this infrastructure for corporations, in the form of one-off efforts, has been in place for years. Wal-Mart is perhaps the best example.[3]

---

3   Sam Walton and John Huey, *Made in America* (Doubleday, 1992). If you have never read a "business book," this is the one to read. It is fun, engaging, and enlightening. (If you do read business books, you've already read this one.)

### Beyond the Town Wall

Finally, we have the connection between the greater private sphere represented by the Town Wall and the "outside world." No one lacking specific permission to enter either town or castle property must be able even to begin to breach these walls. They might send entreaties, in the form of, for example, television commercials with clickable links, but they cannot get in. No way, no how.

In addition, those begging an audience should be subject to certain rules. For example, one of my rules would be that a merchant must promise not to spam me. Tools such as the Platform for Privacy Preferences (P3P), discussed in Chapter 22, and Acumen, discussed in Chapter 25, are a start on just such a wall.

Our job in cybersecurity will not be complete until we have provided people, when in cyberspace, with greater protections than they now enjoy in physical space. This is an achievable goal, and this generation of security specialists will attain it.

### Ringworld Interface

The ideal interface is no interface at all, and most of the complexity of a multilayered security scheme could and should be hidden from the user. Those parts that are visible should enable the user to simply and flexibly change security parameters.

The top level could present the very metaphor I have, with the various elements of the medieval town, presented visually. If the user wants to add an email correspondent to his town, for example, he should be able to drag-and-drop his attached avatar onto the image of the town. (The builders of Ringworld would define these avatars.) Similarly, he could later promote that person by dragging his avatar inside the castle walls.

As users' populations grow, users could, instead, choose to see entities in text lists or iconic groupings, similar to traditional folder views. Users could fine-tune the permissions of individual entities by opening their avatars or icons, displaying a simple and compact permissions panel.

The settings of this panel and even the avatar's location in the ring would also reflect implied changes brought about, for example, by a user refusing further email from a suddenly bothersome merchant. Depending on the ramifications of the change, the user would be prompted for confirmation before making an adaptation.

Fine-tuning to the proposal will, of course, prove necessary. The goal, however, is clear: provide a multi-ring, high-security environment that supports, rather than restricts, the user, one that requires minimal setup and casual, flexible modification.

## Conclusion

The evidence of fatal flaws in today's security approach is all around us, gracing the edges of monitors across the world. We need to take the initiative. We need to look outward, to the way things "really work" once people are in the mix.

If you are a security expert, you must search for, address, test, and actively solicit feedback about every eventuality.

If you are a student who will study security, seek out professors who spend time in the field observing and studying security systems under real-world conditions. The focus of university teachings to future practitioners needs to change. The yellow sticky phenomenon has become so pandemic that it has received attention in both newspapers and business journals. Both students and professors need to do field studies of real people working in real environments.

If you are among the competent, enlightened security experts who are in the field today, you need to work to change your profession. It is in trouble. Practitioners in this field are, in my experience, uniformly bright and technically competent. They just need a new focus on users.

If you are an interaction designer who must work with a security expert whose focus ends at the edges of the computer screen, don't despair. He or she is in need of help, not criticism. Take responsibility on yourself to form a comprehensive security plan. Ensure that user, field, and quality assurance testing, along with user-feedback systems, are all in place to thoroughly and comprehensively prove out the security design.

If you are an interaction designer who gets to work with a competent security professional, thank your lucky stars. I've had the pleasure of working with more than a few, and it is a sheer joy.

## About the Author

 Bruce "Tog" Tognazzini has been part of personal computing from the beginning. He built his first electro-mechanical computer in 1959, and was employee #66 at Apple, where he spent 14 years before going on to be a Distinguished Engineer at Sun Microsystems, then Chief Designer at Healtheon/ WebMD, and finally becoming the third Principal at the Nielsen Norman Group. He publishes asktog.com, has written two books, has coauthored three others, and currently has 49 patents issued in HCI, automotive safety, and aviation.

# CHAPTER FOUR

# Usability Design and Evaluation for Privacy and Security Solutions

CLARE-MARIE KARAT, CAROLYN BRODIE, AND JOHN KARAT

**T**HIS CHAPTER SHOWS HOW YOU CAN INCORPORATE USABILITY DESIGN AND EVALUATION into the life cycle of privacy and security solutions. Here we provide you with an overview of critical-path human-computer interaction (HCI) activities that occur during the development of successful solutions and their maintenance after release. We will point you to key publications and references that you can use to gain a more in-depth understanding of HCI methods and practices in evaluating the usability of your security and privacy systems. And we will walk you through the use of these methods in a case study of a security application as well as a case study of two years of research on privacy tools for authoring and implementing privacy policies.

Of course, this chapter alone cannot make you proficient in using HCI methods. But it will guide you in understanding the value that HCI work can contribute to the success of your product.

We recommend that most projects bring an HCI expert on board early in the project's development, and that the HCI expert be a full team member. Working together, the project team should define the usability activities as a critical development path. We have seen many successful examples where the HCI lead's expertise was leveraged to train and educate the product team so that team members completed parts of the HCI project plan with consultation and collaboration from the HCI expert. We have also seen several examples of skilled computer scientists and programmers who gradually became HCI specialists, frequently with great success. One of this chapter's co-authors, Carolyn, has, in fact, followed such a career path!

## Usability in the Software and Hardware Life Cycle

Properly applied, HCI methods and techniques elicit and identify the useful information in each phase of the project life cycle. These activities can facilitate a more accurate and complete project definition during the requirements phase and an improved project design during the design phase. During the development phase, they can improve solution performance and reduce development time and costs. The benefits of HCI and usability activities continue after release, including increased user productivity and satisfaction, reduced training, support, and error recovery costs, increased sales and revenue, and reduced maintenance costs.

### Unique Aspects of HCI and Usability in the Privacy and Security Domain

Although many HCI techniques are general, there are unique aspects in the design of privacy and security systems that present challenges and opportunities.

First, a key issue to consider is that security and privacy are rarely the user's main goal. Users value and want security and privacy, of course, but they regard them as only secondary to completing primary tasks like completing an online banking transaction or ordering medications. Users would like privacy and security systems and controls to be as transparent as possible. On the other hand, users want to be in control of the situation and understand what is happening. Therein lies the rub. As a consequence, the display of information and the interaction methods related to security and privacy need to be accessible if and when desired by the user, but they shouldn't get in the way.

Second, as more of people's interactions in daily life involve the use of computing technology and sensitive information, disparate types of users must be accommodated. Security solutions in particular have historically been designed with a highly trained technical user in mind. The user community has broadened extensively as organizational business processes have come to include new types of roles and users in the security and privacy area. Many compliance and policy roles in organizations are handled by legal and business process experts who have limited technical skills. Moreover, the end user base includes virtually everyone in the population. The functionality provided by the system for people with different roles must accommodate the skill sets of each. Security and privacy are requirements for doing business as an organization and must be done well, or the organization may lose the user as a customer—or worse.

Third, the negative impact that usability problems can have is higher for security and privacy applications than for many other types of systems. Complexity is at the very heart of many security and privacy solutions; from an HCI point of view, that complexity is the enemy of success. If a system is so complex that whole groups of users (e.g., technical

# KEY REFERENCE BOOKS IN THE HCI FIELD

Please consult these books for additional information; there is a wealth of knowledge and experience contained in them.

1. Bias, R., *Cost-Justifying Usability: An Update for the Internet Age, 2nd Edition* (London: Academic Press, 2005). This book provides methods for calculating the value of HCI work and many case studies and perspectives across a variety of domains.
2. Beyer, H. and Holtzblatt, K., *Contextual Design* (New York: Morgan Kaufmann, 1997). This practitioner guide outlines a method for identification of user requirements through unobtrusive observation of users in the field and instruction on analysis of that data for the design of usable systems.
3. Diaper, D. and Stanton, N., *The Handbook of Task Analysis for Human-Computer Interaction* (Hillsdale, NJ: Erlbaum, 2003). This handbook provides instruction on how to complete task analysis in a variety of domains and information on user tasks identified in key past research.
4. Helander, M., *Handbook of Human Computer Interaction* (Amsterdam: Elsevier, 1988). This reference book provides a synthesis of HCI theory, methods, and research in many different domains and from many perspectives. It contains seminal chapters not found elsewhere.
5. Helander, M., Landauer, T., and Prabhu, P. (eds.), *Handbook of Human-Computer Interaction, 2nd Completely Revised Edition* (Amsterdam: Elsevier, 1997). This is an update of this key reference book.
6. Jacko, J. and Sears, A. (eds.), *The Human-Computer Interaction Handbook* (Hillsdale, NJ: Erlbaum, 2003). This is a key reference book with the most up-to-date synthesis of HCI theory, methods, and research and its application to a wide variety of domains.
7. Mayhew, D., *The Usability Engineering Lifecycle: A Practitioner's Handbook for User Interface Design* (San Diego: Academic Press, 1999). This is a practical guide on how to conduct HCI work as part of the development life cycle.
8. Preece, J., *Human Computer Interaction* (Wokingham, U.K.: Addison Wesley, 1994). This book provides an introduction and overview of the HCI field. This text is used in university courses.
9. Rubin, J., *Handbook of Usability Testing—How to Plan, Design, and Conduct Effective Tests* (New York: John Wiley & Sons, Inc., 1994). This is a practical guide for conducting usability tests of systems.
10. Shneiderman, B. and Plaisant, C., *Designing the User Interface* (Reading, MA: Addison Wesley, 2004). This is a key text in the field of HCI. It provides an introduction and overview of the field for university students and others interested in the topic.

---

users, business users, and end users) cannot understand it, costly errors will occur. There is a saying in the HCI field: "If the user cannot understand functionality, it doesn't exist." In the case of security and privacy, sophisticated systems that are badly designed may actually put users at more risk than if less sophisticated solutions were used. So, the increased risk of errors in this domain provides an even greater incentive to include HCI work in system research and development.

Fourth, users will need to be able to easily update security and privacy solutions to accommodate frequent changes in legislation and regulations. Different domains (e.g., health care, banking, government) frequently have unique requirements. Systems must be designed to enable easy and effective updates to them.

These are some of the challenges that provide a unique focus and strong incentive to include HCI in the system life cycle. You can probably think of more. Let's now discuss in more detail the valuable role that HCI can play.

## Usability in Requirements

It is critical that the project team be able to define the product and product goals clearly and early on. This is called the *requirements phase*.

From a usability perspective, the product definition should address who the intended users of the product are, the types of tasks for which users will use the product, and the real-world situations (the "context") in which the product will be used.

A variety of formal HCI methods are available to identify and define this information. For any specific product, the HCI expert selects the appropriate subset of methods to use, given the time, resources, risk, and business priorities involved. Some of these methods include:

*Interviews and surveys of end-user requirements*

Used to understand what top concerns and unmet needs customers, target users, and organizational stakeholders would like addressed. When you begin to work in a new domain area, it is critical that you start with end-user interviews and surveys in order to gain firsthand knowledge of the major issues and opportunities from users in their own voices. Typically these surveys involve a fairly large sample—perhaps 30 to 100 participants. Ideally, you begin with a larger survey group and follow up with in-depth interviews of a smaller group of end users and other key stakeholders (e.g., decision makers who will not necessarily use the system). Identification and refinement of the end-user profile occur as part of this work.

*Focus groups*

Used to understand and identify at a high level areas in which there are customer, target user, and other stakeholder concerns and unmet needs. Focus groups can augment surveys. An independent facilitator guides group discussions with samples of end users and probes issues in the domain area in greater depth than surveys are generally able to do. If resources are available, you might use focus groups before you conduct individual interviews.

*Field studies of end-user work context*

Used to understand and observe how current technology and business practices are being employed by users to accomplish their goals today. Find out what's working and what's not. Depending on your resources, expertise, and time available, you might conduct limited field studies to complement and validate the information gained from the preceding methods, or you might use a large sample of field studies to gain all of your information and forego the preceding steps.

*Task analysis*

Used to understand the core and infrequent tasks that users need or would like to complete to accomplish their goals. These tasks will be identified during interviews, focus groups, and field studies of end-user work context. The experts gathering the information will probe to gain the context and relative importance of the items in the set of tasks. Also, end users will provide information to help set the usability objectives of the system (see the description of deliverables later in this section).

*Benchmark studies*

Used to understand current or baseline user performance using available manual or automated processes to complete the types of core tasks that the product will address. Benchmark data can be collected during field studies of end users or in controlled laboratory studies. This is critical data that will help you to set the goals for the usability of the new system and enable you to measure the value of the improvement that the new system will deliver. Be sure to collect this data for business cases and other purposes.

*Competitive evaluations*

Used to understand the capabilities available in the marketplace at the current time and identify the strengths and weaknesses of these solutions. As with the benchmark data, this data will help you to quantify the usability objectives and the value of the solution you are going to design; you will also design a better system after you understand the strengths and weaknesses of competitive systems.

As you can see, there are many kinds of methods that you can use to collect the end-user requirements information. As a result, you must make tradeoffs in how you collect and validate the information based on the time, resources, and skilled personnel that you have available to work on a project. In a perfect world, it would probably be best to do field studies of representative samples of the different types of end users (e.g., based on age, skills, experience, roles) in a representative sample of the locations (e.g., geographic, physical conditions) and contexts (e.g., quiet indoor setting versus a mobile, public, and noisy setting) in which the system would be appropriate for use. Practically speaking, though, there are always constraints. One approach is to triangulate or cross-validate the data: ask the same questions using a variety of methods and determine whether the end users are providing you similar or different data. Thus, starting with an email survey, followed by a sample of in-depth interviews and a sample of field observation of end users, you could validate the emerging end-user requirements while keeping within time and resource constraints.

Based on the analysis of the data from the usability engineering activities during the requirements phase described earlier, the project team will have the following deliverables:

*End-user requirements definition*

The complete description of what is needed to meet the needs of the user who would like to accomplish certain tasks and goals in a specific domain.

*User profile definition*

A description of the target users of the product, including general demographic information and specific information about skills, education, and training necessary to use the product.

*Core task scenarios*

A small set of task scenarios that describe how the end users will be able to accomplish core tasks with the product to meet their goals.

*Usability objectives specification*

A quantitative goal or set of goals that needs to be met for the user to be satisfied and productive using the product.[1] An example is "95% of the users will complete the sign-on task error-free within the first three attempts at the task." The objective should surpass the results of the benchmark testing and competitive evaluations. It should also address a variety of goals: user goals for productivity and satisfaction, business goals for the streamlining of business processes, and organizational goals related to expense and risk (the cost of errors and user support). Usability objectives specification provides a means for clear communication and the development of consensus in the project team for the usability goal of the product.

These deliverables contribute to a clear and thoughtful statement about the scope of the development project, and clear objectives and measures with which to judge the success of designing and developing a usable product for the target users. HCI work in the requirements phase frequently improves communication within the development team and brings about consensus with respect to product definition in clear and quantitatively measurable terms. On numerous occasions, early HCI work on end-user requirements has surfaced large or complex issues and conflicting goals among the development team that could be resolved relatively quickly and at a cost that is much lower during the concept phase than it would be during system test or after release.[2]

Of course, conflicting goals may also exist in the customer organization. Discussions during the requirements phase can provide the opportunity to highlight and resolve these differences.

## Usability in Design and Development

During the design and development phases, the project team needs to create a clear, high-level design for the product that will be implemented during development. From an HCI perspective, the key activities during these phases are:

---

1   J. Whiteside, J. Bennett, and K. Holtzblatt, "Usability Engineering: Our Experience and Evolution," in M. Helander (ed.), *Handbook of Human Computer Interaction*, (Amsterdam: Elsevier, 1988).

2   C. Karat, "A Business Case Approach to Usability Cost-Justification for the Web," in R. Bias and D. Mayhew (eds.), *Cost-Justifying Usability* (London: Academic Press, 2005).

*Initial design development*  •

Based on the results of the HCI work during the concept phase, the HCI professional can create an initial user interface design that covers the interaction methods and flow that users will employ to complete the core task scenarios. This design will guide the development of prototypes, provide feedback to the development team, and give the project architect needed information for the system architecture.

*Ongoing data from users*

Although there is a tendency to view gathering user data as an isolated activity, design and development require information from users on an ongoing basis. HCI professionals can and should be responsible for involving target system users with the development team on an ongoing basis throughout the life cycle. Users can participate in design walkthroughs and field and laboratory evaluations of prototypes. These sessions can be a valuable tool for understanding user needs and developing a system that addresses them.

*Prototype development (low, medium, and high fidelity)*

The HCI professional can create a prototype of the user interface for the solution that illustrates how the end user would complete core task scenarios. *Low-fidelity prototypes* created early in the design and development phases might consist of static screenshots with a scenario script that walks target users through the completion of tasks. These early prototypes let the project team collect information from target users about macro-level design issues. As the design is refined, the project team can create *medium-fidelity prototypes* or *high-fidelity prototypes* that let target users have hands-on experience and provide finer-grained feedback on design issues and tradeoffs. A medium-fidelity prototype generally has certain paths through the overall design (that correspond to certain tasks) and the interaction methods (i.e., data input or access through use of voice, touch, keyboard and mouse, biometrics) working in a realistic manner, although the frontend may or may not be integrated in a real-time manner with the backend of the system. A high-fidelity prototype is a fully functional prototype of the system and may be the alpha-level version of the actual system code.

*Design walkthroughs with small groups of users*

The HCI professional can facilitate design walkthrough sessions with small groups of target users. These walkthroughs are generally conducted early in the design and development phase with low-fidelity prototypes or static screenshots. It may be very valuable to iterate on the initial design and conduct a second round of design walkthrough sessions with new samples of target users to validate the design decisions made after the first round. The target users will be able to provide data on specific aspects and capabilities of the solution, as well as the usability of the system and their satisfaction with it. Target users will also provide information essential to updating the task scenarios and user profiles.

*Heuristic evaluations and other types of inspections*

The project team may recruit HCI professionals who have expertise in the specific domain in order to have them adopt the role or roles of the target users of the system, to conduct heuristic reviews of the prototypes, and to identify issues for the project team to address. Think of these professionals as "double experts." The heuristic review consists of the experts completing the core user scenarios in the roles of the various target users and identifying usability problems that people in those roles will face with the current design of the system. The project team may also find it valuable to have these experts review competitive offerings so that the team has additional input on how their product is likely to compare to the current competition.

*Usability tests (laboratory or field) with individual users*

During development, HCI professionals can run usability evaluation sessions with one target user at a time employing medium- to high-fidelity prototypes of the solution that enable the users to have hands-on experience in using the prototyped system to complete their core task scenarios. These sessions may be conducted in a controlled usability laboratory where there is often a one-way mirror, letting members of the development team and other stakeholders observe the user interacting with the prototype firsthand. Alternatively, sessions may be conducted in the field. Although the field may have poor lighting, noise, interruptions, and a lack of privacy, it does represent the environment where the product will be deployed: testing the product in the field helps the development team to identify issues that are likely to be important later. Consider the tradeoffs between laboratory and field usability tests. If possible, it is best to use both types of tests in this phase of the project.

During these user sessions, the team should collect a variety of data including qualitative information (e.g., how hard it is to learn, their experience in using the system, and their satisfaction with it) and their quantitative performance data (e.g., time on task, completion rate, error-free rate). This data will enable the project team to determine where they stand in terms of meeting the product's usability objectives. It is best to iterate on the design and collect the usability evaluation data until the usability objectives are reached. In practice, business needs and tradeoffs are made, and the data will provide a useful basis on which to make these decisions.

Performance data can also be used to determine the severity rating of the different identified issues through use of a *Problem Severity Classification Matrix*,[3] which we describe in more detail in the first case study later in this chapter. The team can also learn whether the system as designed is good enough that the target user would like to use it, would purchase it, and how they would incorporate it into their lives. This more detailed and in-context design information from target users is very valuable and enables the project team to complete the micro-level design of the solution. From a project planning standpoint, consider that the usability tests in the design and development phases can be scheduled to dovetail with the appropriate unit, integration, and system testing.

---

3   C. Karat, R. Campbell, and T. Fiegel, "Comparison of Empirical Testing and Walkthrough Methods in User Interface Evaluation," *Human Factors in Computing Systems—CHI 92 Conference Proceedings* (New York: ACM, 1992), 397–404.

*Prototype redesign*

After a round of usability evaluation, analyze the data and present it to the project team. The whole project team can contribute to the decision-making process about which issues to tackle and how to redesign parts of the system to address them. A discussion of the problem priorities and of the different approaches to resolve those problems can be quite productive when drawing on the different skills and experience of the team members.

In the design and development phases, the main goal is to move from a fairly high-level design based on the early HCI activities in the requirements phase to a user-validated design of a highly usable system. The validated design has sufficient detail for development of the system. Usability problems in the early design are detected and resolved, and the final version of the system should meet all defined usability objectives prior to release.

Based on the analysis of the data from the usability engineering activities described earlier during the design and development phases, the project team will have the following deliverables:

*Validated and usable user interface design*

The project team can be confident that the user interface design will be successful in deployment and release based on the iterative design and evaluation with target users during the design and development phases. The validation of the design with the target users demonstrates that all significant user requirements are addressed by the system. The validation will be based on meeting the usability objectives set for the system. These will be assessed based on user performance with the system and satisfaction ratings of the system by target users during the usability evaluation of the latest iteration of the system design.

*Validated user model of the task flow*

Underlying the interface design is a model of how the target users perceive the task and their views of the flow of the task to reach the desired goal. In addition, user errors made during usability evaluation sessions are priceless to HCI practitioners in terms of highlighting differences or confusions in the design as it relates to the user model. This helps the entire project team understand and gain consensus about the design.

*Validated and updated core user task scenarios*

The user task scenarios will be refined and validated during the iterative usability evaluations in the design and development phases of the project. The project team can be very comfortable that they are addressing the critical tasks of their target users.

*Validated and updated system requirements document*

As part of the usability activities in the design and development phases, information emerges that will be used to update and validate the system requirements. This occurs through the technical discussions about the project goals, the analysis of tasks to be completed using the system, and the results of the usability evaluations.

*Validated and updated user profiles*

The usability work with target users in the design and development phases provides an up-to-date and clear definition of the target users. The project team can be comfortable that they are developing the product for the correctly defined, intended users. This information is very valuable for communication and marketing purposes.

*Objective performance data about achievement of usability objectives*

The project team will know exactly where they stand at the end of the development phase in terms of reaching the product usability objectives. As mentioned previously, in practice, tradeoffs are made in reaching these goals. The usability data provides very valuable data for these decision-making purposes.

*User interface style guide*

If the organization is going to be developing a series of products in a particular market niche for a similar set of target users, it may be valuable to capture the high-level design decisions made for the user interface for use by other teams. In this way, the initial work with users during the concept phase can be leveraged.

## Usability in Postrelease

During prerelease beta-testing and after release of the final version of the product, the product team needs to be informed of feedback from the customers who are using the product. This feedback will help the team maintain the product and can be very helpful in understanding when a new release is required. From an HCI perspective, the key activities in this phase are:

*Collection and analysis of customer data using online tools*

Tools of this kind enable remote data collection and usability evaluation. With customer consent, online tools may collect usage data through unobtrusive means and may also pop up questionnaires to collect explicit feedback from users at certain points in the use of a product. Data from these online tools can be analyzed and may highlight important issues that HCI practitioners need to follow up on with customers in individual and small group HCI work in laboratory and field settings.

*Analysis of customer support calls regarding the product*

As stated earlier, the customer support calls provide another channel for customer feedback to the product team. The HCI practitioner can work with the product team to prioritize the issues and requests. As time goes by after the release of the product, these calls may provide information that signals when a new release of the product is necessary.

*Analysis of user comments in email, list serves, or web forums about the product*

These are further channels for customer feedback about problems and for the identification of new or extended capabilities that are needed to address the customers' needs.

*Collection and analysis of survey and questionnaire data from users or through user group meetings*
The activities described earlier may be supplemented by telephone or written surveys of customers about their satisfaction with the product and any issues or requests for new functionality that they would like to communicate to the product team. Having regularly scheduled user group meetings that customers can attend is another way to collect information about problems with the current product or new customer requirements regarding usability or functionality that evolve in the changing world in which we live.

Based on the customer data from these HCI activities in prerelease and postrelease or maintenance phases, the product team will have up-to-date and accurate information about customer satisfaction and any problems or unmet needs regarding the usability and functionality of the product. The methods described in this section may be used in parallel to collect user data on issues with the system and new emerging requirements. As mentioned previously, it would be best to cross-validate user issues and new requirements through communication with users through multiple channels. If possible, periodic user group meetings (virtual or face-to-face) supplemented with user data from one or two other channels would be very valuable for the product team to have access to.

With the overview of usability in the software and hardware life cycle as context, we turn next to an examination of two case studies where HCI work was and is part of the life cycle (references to activities described earlier are shown in italics). Here we identify the variety of positive impacts that the work has provided. The first case study concerns HCI work on a security application, and the second case study describes HCI activities in a two-year privacy research project. The security case study describes a project where the HCI work on the system began when the project was well underway in the design and development phase. Although that security case study occurred some time ago, the fundamental lessons and flow of the significant HCI work on the project still remain true today. In the privacy technology case study, an example is provided of system development where HCI is incorporated as a critical component of the project beginning in the requirements phase.

## Case Study: Usability Involvement in a Security Application

*Clare-Marie Karat was the HCI lead on the development of a security application in 1989. She provides a firsthand account of the process she used to understand the user requirements and improve the usability of this product.*[4]

The project's goal was to improve the dialog of a large data entry and inquiry mainframe application used by 23,000 end users (IBM employees in branch offices across the U.S.). This large mainframe application was composed of many subapplications. The goal was to eliminate the recurring need for security authorization while performing discrete but

---

4   C. Karat, "Iterative Usability Testing of a Security Application," in *Proceedings of the Human Factors Society* (1989), 272–277.

related tasks that composed a business process. However, the project had entered the design and development phase: coding had already begun. So, before I actually joined the team, the project manager and I agreed upon the approach that I would use. I would quickly complete the HCI activities that should have been done in the requirements phase, then move ahead with the design and development phase HCI work.

Prior to the development of this security application, working with the mainframe application was like having a series of disconnected conversations for the end user. Every time a user wanted to perform a transaction, he had to re-identify, provide a password, select the appropriate application, and type a command known as a *mnemonic* that indicated the type of transaction to be performed. Further, the use of the actual mnemonics was controlled: users were only told about the mnemonics relevant to their individual job responsibilities and were instructed not to write down the mnemonics or share them with anyone.

I met with the project team to understand the *goals of the project* and define the overall *usability goal*. They were ambitious. The old security application was to be taken down on a Friday, the new application was to be installed over the weekend, and employees needed to be able to walk up and use the new security application the next Monday. The transition had to be smooth, without disrupting the end users or business. End users signed on to the target mainframe application about a dozen times a day.

After interviewing key team members, I drafted the *measurable usability objectives* for the security application and discussed them with the team during a regular status meeting. Consensus was reached that the usability objective for the security application was that "95% of the users will complete the sign-on task error-free within the first three attempts at the task." No specific usability objective was set for the time to complete the sign-on task itself; however, the team members thought users ought to be able to complete it within about 8 seconds.

### The Field Study

I went into the field (*a field study of end-user work context*) to several branch offices and observed the general workplace setting and the way the employees worked with the current system. I met with and talked to a number of the target users, collected necessary information, and was able to create the *user profile definition*. The users had an average of two years of work experience in their current jobs, and five years overall with IBM. They all had college degrees, good computer skills, and reasonable experience with the major business applications they used.

I observed their work environment and the transactions they needed to complete on the mainframe application. These users accessed the application to complete a variety of tasks and transactions related to customer relationship management, sales, and fulfillment. Employees in the branch offices were working at close quarters in open office settings with no partitions. Phones rang constantly; people carried on conversations. When sales were completed, big bells were rung to celebrate. It was a busy, exciting, fast-paced, and sometimes rather loud environment in which to work. The end users were typically attending to their terminal screens while juggling a variety of other tasks simultaneously, including communicating with other staff and customers through telephone calls and talking to people stopping by and requesting information. It was clear that the user interface to the security application needed to take these social and physical environment factors into account in the *end-user requirements* for the user interface and interaction methods for the security application.

Interviews and observation of the employees identified that the number of mnemonics that they needed to remember (for some employees, this number approached 60, with an average in the high 30s) was more than the human memory can handle. As might be expected, the users had devised their own methods of keeping track of the mnemonics they needed for their tasks. I conducted a *task analysis* to identify the key security sign-on tasks the users completed related to the various transactions they worked on each day, and then defined the set of *core user scenarios* that the security application would have to handle. These scenarios also identified a number of *end-user requirements*.

## The User Tests

Over the course of the next three months, I completed three iterations of *design and usability testing* of the security application's proposed user interface. Iterative testing provides an opportunity to test the impact of design changes made to the interface.[5] The initial test was a *field test* designed to collect data in the context of the work environment and included 5 participants. The second test was a *laboratory prototype test* involving 10 participants, and the third test was a *laboratory integration test of the live code on a test system* with 12 participants. The same set of tasks was used in all three tests. (In the examples that follow, the system and applications have been de-identified and the generic mnemonic "CMINQ" is used.)

### Test 1

For the first test, I built a *low-fidelity prototype* using the user interface design (*the initial design development*) that the project team had developed before I joined the effort. The team was very confident that it would be fine and that the users would be able to complete tasks using this design in a few seconds. The low-fidelity prototype was constructed using screenshots that I printed and covered with reusable clear laminate so that the users could write with washable pens what they would normally type into the entry fields. The reusable "paper" prototype provided a realistic approximation of the interface screens and navigation and was developed in 20% of the time that an online prototype would have required. The participants in the usability test completed a set of four sign-on tasks that covered different aspects of the changes to the sign-on process. For example, a sign-on

5    J. Gould, "How to Design a Usable System," in M. Helander (ed.), *Handbook of Human Computer Interaction* (Amsterdam: Elsevier, 1988).

task was as follows: "Please sign on to the XXX system to perform an authorized inquiry function (e.g., CMINQ) on the XXX application."

Because the usability objective concerned the users' ability to quickly learn to use the new system, all three usability tests were designed to measure learning across repetition of the same task. Therefore, the participants completed the set of four typical sign-on tasks three times (called three trials). The sets of tasks were presented in random order in each trial. The same quantitative performance and qualitative opinion measures were collected in all three usability tests. The quantitative data included participant time on task, task completion rate (regardless of the number of errors), and cumulative error-free rate across participants. The qualitative data was collected through use of a debriefing questionnaire that captured user comments on needed changes, what was confusing, and a forced-choice End User Sign-Off rating (a measure I created) about whether the product they had worked with was good enough to install without any changes.

As a way of educating the project team, I invited the lead programmer to work with me in conducting the *field test* (Test 1). We worked with one participant at a time. I introduced the participant to the purpose of the usability session, and then each participant attempted to perform the three trials of four sign-on tasks, completing a total of 12 tasks (see Figure 4-1). At the end of the third trial, the participant completed a debriefing conversation with me. During the sessions, the lead programmer sat to the side of the participants and unobtrusively completed the stopwatch timing of the participants' performances on the tasks while I ran the session and acted as the "computer" by replacing the screen on which the participants entered their text with the one they would see next on their computer screen based on their previous input. We were able to quickly move through the branch office and collect the session data, completing the *field usability test* in about 25% of the time a *laboratory test* would have required because of the time necessary to recruit and schedule participants to come to the usability lab.

I presented the results to the development team as well as the managers of associated technical and operational areas who were invited to attend the meeting. The results were shocking to those present. Only 20% of the participants (one person) could complete the sign-on task error-free. The average time on task was over 3 minutes in Trial 1, with learning improved to 48 seconds in Trial 3 (see Figures 4-2 and 4-3). Not one of the participants thought the product was good enough to install without changes. The senior managers in attendance started talking with each other about setting up a help desk for three months to handle user questions from across the country as the system was rolled out. Nobody had the funds for a help desk in their budget, though, and the conversation became heated. The team was stunned; they had been fully prepared to implement their initial user interface design as the final design for the system.

I spoke up and said that I had recommendations for how we could resolve the usability problems and eliminate the need for a help desk. During the session debriefs, the participants talked about how they were typically multitasking, described the rote manner in which they worked at the terminals, and stated that the system needed to accommodate

FIGURE 4-1. Reenactment of the field usability test of the low-fidelity prototype of the security system with a target user

their need to work in this type of atmosphere. I had analyzed all the data and identified error patterns that were the most serious for us to address using the *Problem Severity Classification Matrix (PSC)*. The PSC matrix provides a ranking of usability problems by severity and is used to determine allocation of resources for addressing user interface issues. The PSC ratings are computed on a two-dimensional scale, where one axis represents the impact of the usability problem on the user's ability to complete a task, and the other axis represents the frequency of occurrence as defined by the percentage of users who experienced the problem. Ratings range from 1 to 3, where 1 is most severe.[6] The developers were comfortable with the PSC matrix and ratings as they were used to classifying functional problems in the code in this manner.

I made four recommendations for changes to resolve the severity 1 and 2 level end-user usability issues. The redesign work included improving the clarity of information displayed on screens and its visibility, providing content in error messages that enabled users to recover gracefully from these situations, and simplifying two types of navigational complexity. Three were quickly implemented in the system code by development staff, and a new redesigned low-fidelity prototype with these design changes was tested in Test 2. The fourth recommendation could not be implemented at that time, as the team could not determine a technically feasible way to address the navigational problem.

6   C. Karat, R. Campbell, and T. Fiegel, 397–404.

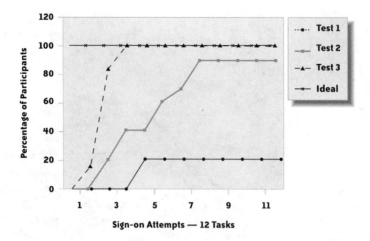

FIGURE 4-2. Cumulative percentage of participants performing tasks error-free, and ideal performance

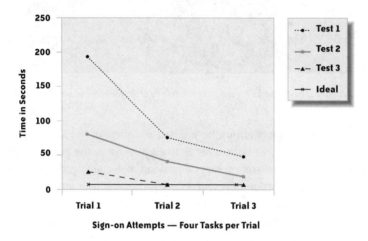

FIGURE 4-3. Median time on task in seconds for participants in the three trials, and ideal performance

## Test 2

I redesigned the low-fidelity prototype and ran Test 2 in the usability laboratory at the development site. The usability laboratory consists of a control room and a usability studio. There is a wall with a one-way mirror between the two rooms. The development team was very engaged in the usability test and took turns watching from the control room (so that the users were not disturbed) while I ran the sessions in the studio with the participants. The extra time necessary to recruit and schedule participants was offset by the significant value to the development team in their education about usability and user interface design.

The results of Test 2 were very encouraging; 90% of the participants signed on correctly after seven attempts. This was close to the 95% level specified in the usability objective, but the number of learning attempts required to achieve that level remained unacceptable. The average (median) time on task for participants in Test 2 was less than half of what it was in Test 1, and ranged from about 80 seconds in Trial 1 to about 20 seconds in Trial 3. These times were well above the project team's goal of 8 seconds.

To understand the ideal time on task that was possible with the prototype, we had an employee who had expertise in the security system and the branch office applications complete the usability test. This expert completed each task error-free and in 6 seconds. Clearly, improvement was possible.

When asked, 60% of the Test 2 participants thought the security system was good enough to install without any changes. While the team was heartened by the improvement in the usability of the security system, the low participant opinion scores in Test 2 pushed the team to find a solution to the remaining usability problem.

One severe usability problem that had been identified in Test 1 reoccurred in Test 2. This problem involved a complicated navigational flow where users navigated down two different paths depending on the mnemonic chosen at sign-on. One path was clear to the users. The second path was confusing and could not be addressed at the end of Test 1 because of technical problems. At the end of Test 2, however, the project architect, who had been thinking about the problem since the end of Test 1, created a simple and innovative solution to finesse the situation, and it was implemented. The solution involved the creation of a bridge that replaced a central navigational fork. This change both simplified and standardized the navigational flow. All users could utilize the bridge regardless of the mnemonic chosen at sign-on. The complexity in the security was transparent to users as, after authenticating with a user ID and password, they now saw only the types of transactions they were authorized to make.

**Test 3**

For Test 3, I ran the usability sessions in the lab, and the participants worked with the *live code on a test system*. In parallel, the project team was conducting the functional testing of the system. The solution implemented for the remaining major usability problem in Test 2 worked very well. In Test 3, 100% of the participants signed on error-free after the third attempt. The user performance met the *usability objective* set at the beginning of the project. User time on task ranged from 24 seconds to 7 seconds in Test 3, nearly meeting the ideal performance measure. In Test 3, 100% of the participants thought the new security system was good enough to install without any changes. The solution implemented at the end of Test 2 created one minor usability problem in Test 3, and this issue was resolved prior to the rollout of the code to the branches.

The system was rolled out to the branches on time, under budget, and with high user satisfaction. *Data analysis of support calls* regarding the product and *collection and analysis of survey data from users* documented that the system was very usable and that the users were delighted not to have to remember or keep track of all of the individual mnemonics anymore. The mnemonics for related business application tasks were now grouped under one master mnemonic. The security application simplified the sign-on process and provided the users the seamless environment across transactions that they needed to complete to provide high-quality service to IBM customers while maintaining the security of sensitive data. The architectural changes—the design and layout of the user interface, navigation, and error messages—all contributed to a simplification of the security system for the users in the branch offices.

## The Return on Investment (ROI) Analysis

The collaboration between the HCI lead and the security technical staff was essential in creating the final design. The success in designing and deploying the new security application and the resulting return on investment was achieved through the partnership between the HCI lead and the other team members on the team goal to create a usable and effective security solution. The simple cost-benefit ratio analysis provides clear data on the value of usability in the development of a security application.[7]

Postrelease costs were also significantly lower than would normally be anticipated. There were no change requests after installation, and no updates were required to the code. These achievements were unusual and they were rewarded by the organization. The product manager communicated the project results up the management chain. The entire project team was awarded bonuses for the high-quality deliverable. The division senior executive called together the team of senior product managers and reviewed the positive outcome that was the result of the inclusion of HCI work in the development project. Usability became a critical path in project planning and execution. A number of the developers became very skilled practitioners in this field. One of my colleagues from that initial experience is the manager of an HCI consulting group within the company, and we remain in regular contact.

Before I joined the project team, they had planned to implement the initial design for the system (the one evaluated in Test 1). I analyzed the cost benefit of the usability work by simply calculating the financial value of the improvement in user productivity on the security tasks for the end-user population for the first three sign-on attempts on the security system after release.[8, 9] Then the value of the increased productivity was compared to the cost of the HCI activities on the project. This resulted in a 1:2 cost-benefit ratio; for every dollar invested in usability, the organization gained two back. With the inclusion of cost savings based on further sign-on attempts, the savings related to the greatly reduced disruption of the users, and the reduced burden on the help desk staff, the ratio became 1:10.

This security application case study described a fairly small and well-defined effort: the project goals were clear, the target users were easily identified and accessible for usability design and evaluation work, and the functionality was designed and implemented using existing technology. The second case study, described in the next section, provides an overview of a project with a greater amount of complexity in the goals of the privacy tools, the

---

7   For more information on calculating the cost benefit of usability, see *ibid* and R. Bias, *Cost-Justifying Usability: An Update for the Internet Age, 2nd Edition* (London: Academic Press, 2005).

8   C. Karat, "Cost-Benefit Analysis of Usability Engineering Techniques," *Proceedings of the Human Factors Society*, 839–843.

9   C. Karat, 2005.

target users, the context of use of the privacy functionality to be designed, and the use of innovative technology that needs to integrate and work smoothly with legacy systems.

## Case Study: Usability Involvement in the Development of a Privacy Policy Management Tool

In 2002, we became involved in a research project concerned with the development of approaches for helping organizations protect the personal information (PI) that they used and stored about their customers, constituents, patients, and/or employees. Most organizations store PI in heterogeneous server system environments. In our initial review of the literature and interview research, we found that organizations do not currently have a unified way of defining or implementing privacy policies that encompass data collected and used across different server platforms.[10] This makes it difficult for the organizations to put in place proper management and control of PI that allows the data users to access and work with the PI inline with organizational privacy policies. Our task was to collect data to help us understand the problem and propose solutions that would meet the needs of organizations for privacy policy management.

This work involved a wide range of user-centered techniques (discussed earlier in the chapter). This project differs from the security application presented earlier in at least three important ways; it therefore highlights the application of different usability and evaluation techniques to the creation of a privacy application:

- The case study involves the creation and use of new software technologies rather than the addition of an incremental improvement to a system using existing technology.

- The targeted user community is broader and includes different user groups across a variety of domains and geographies.

- The solution requires integration with the organization's heterogeneous configurations, including valuable legacy applications.

To create technology to support all aspects of organizational development and use of privacy policies, we needed to understand the concerns of a large and diverse user group. The research included four steps:

1. Identify the privacy needs within organizations through email survey questionnaires.

2. Refine the needs through in-depth interviews with privacy-responsible individuals in organizations.

3. Design and validate a prototype of a technological approach to meeting organizational privacy needs through onsite scenario-based walkthroughs with target users.

4. Collect empirical data in a controlled usability laboratory test to understand the usability of privacy policy-authoring methods included in our proposed design.

---

10 A. Anton, Q. He, and D. Baumer, "The Complexity Underlying JetBlue's Privacy Policy Violations," *IEEE Security and Privacy* (Aug./Sept. 2004).

We briefly describe these activities in the following sections, and provide a reference to a more complete description of this ongoing work.

### Step One: Identifying Privacy Needs

Our initial work involved gathering data from people about their needs related to privacy-enabling technology. Interviews and surveys are generally appropriate methods for this stage of a project. We completed the initial interview research in two steps:

- An email survey of 51 participants to identify key privacy concerns and technology needs, and

- In-depth interviews with a subset of 13 participants from the original sample to understand their top privacy concerns and technology needs in the context of scenarios about the flow of PI through business processes used by their organizations

The goal of both of these activities was to create an initial draft of *the requirements definition* and the *user profile definition*. For the first step, we recruited participants from industry and government organizations who were identified as being concerned with privacy issues. These participants and their organizations represent early technology adopters concerning privacy, and we welcomed their assistance in the early identification of issues and requirements for product development. They were recruited through a variety of mechanisms including follow-ups on attendance at privacy breakout sessions at professional conferences and referrals from members of the emerging international professional privacy community.

The email survey was designed to give us an initial view of the privacy-related problems and concerns that are faced by organizations. We recognized that our target user group was made up of people with highly responsible jobs and very busy schedules, so our email survey consisted of three questions carefully chosen to help us understand their perceptions of how their organizations handled privacy issues. These were:

1. What are your top privacy concerns regarding your organization?

2. What types of privacy functionality would you like to have available to address your privacy concerns regarding your organization?

3. At this time, what action is your organization taking to address the top privacy concerns you listed above?

Participants were asked to rank-order their top three choices on questions 1 and 2 from a list of choices provided, and were also allowed to fill in and rank "Other" choices if their concern was not represented in the list. For question 3, they could choose as many options as were appropriate, or choose "Other" and explain the approaches to privacy their organizations were currently using.

From these questions, we learned that there were considerable similarities in organizations across the different geographies. We also learned that privacy protection of information held by organizations was crucial for both industry and government, although their concerns were slightly different. Both segments were concerned about misuse of PI data by internal employees, as well as by external users (hackers), the protection of PI data in legacy applications, and, for industry, the economic harm that a publicized privacy breach could have on their brand.[11] The top-ranked privacy functionality desired included:

- "One integrated solution for legacy and web data"
- "Application-specific and usable privacy policy authoring, implementation, auditing, and enforcement"
- "The ability to associate privacy policy information with individual data elements in a customer's file"
- "Privacy protection for data stored on servers from IT staff with no need to view data content"

The survey also gave us a picture of activities underway in organizations to address their needs. All of this data helped give us a picture of where to focus our efforts so that they might have the biggest impact in meeting user needs.

## Step Two: Performing In-Depth Interview Research

Our second step was to conduct in-depth interviews with target users. The goals of the interviews were to build a deeper understanding of the participants' and their organizations' views regarding privacy, their privacy concerns, and the value they perceived in the desired privacy technology they spoke of in the context of scenarios of use involving PI in their organizations. We find that having users develop and describe scenarios of use is highly effective at this stage. The majority of the interview sessions were centered on discussion of such a scenario provided by the respondent describing PI information flows in their organization.

We wanted to identify and understand examples of how PI flowed through business processes in the organization, the strengths and weaknesses of these processes involving PI, the manual and automated processes to address privacy, and the additional privacy functionality they need in the context of these scenarios. We used these to create the set of *core task scenarios* used for the rest of the project. As in Step One, we chose the participants so that they represented a range of industries, geographies, and roles. All of the interviews were completed by telephone and lasted about an hour. The team transcribed their interview notes and discussed and annotated them to create one unified view of each session. The interviews produced large amounts of qualitative data that was analyzed using contextual analysis.[12]

11 J. Karat, C. Karat, C. Brodie, and H. Feng, "Privacy in Information Technology: Designing to Enable Privacy Policy Management in Organizations," *International Journal of Human Computer Studies* (2005), 153–174.

12 H. Beyer and K. Holtzblatt, *Contextual Design* (New York: Morgan Kaufmann, 1997).

In their scenarios about the flow of PI through the organizational business processes, the interviewees shared a view that privacy protection of PI depends on the people, the business processes, and the technology to support them. As the interviewees looked to develop or acquire technology to automate the creation, enforcement, and auditing of privacy policies, they noted a number of concerns at different points in the scenario—from authoring policies to finding and deleting PI data. We noted that there are large gaps between needs and the ability of technology to meet them, particularly concerning the ability to perform privacy compliance checking.

Using the information from the interviews, we created a set of *core task scenarios* for key domains (banking/finance, health care, and government) and updated the *user profile definition* and *user requirements definition*. We reviewed these scenarios with a subset of our participants as well as a new set of target users to confirm that the scenarios correctly captured the requirements that we had identified. We used the *user requirements definitions*, *user profile definitions*, and *core task scenarios* that resulted from the survey and interview research in these two steps to guide the development of the privacy management prototype in Step Three.

## Step Three: Designing and Evaluating a Privacy Policy Prototype

Using the completed survey and interview research, the team defined and prioritized a set of requirements for privacy-enabling tools. There were many needs that customers identified, and we decided to focus our work on providing tools to assist in several aspects of privacy policy management. We call our prototype of a privacy policy management tool SPARCLE (Server Privacy ARchitecture and CapabiLity Enablement). The overall goal in designing SPARCLE was to provide organizations with tools to help them create understandable privacy policies, link their written privacy policies with the implementation of the policy across their IT configurations, and then help them to monitor the enforcement of the policy through internal audits. The project goals at this point were to determine if the privacy functionality that had been identified for inclusion in SPARCLE from Steps 1 and 2 met the users' needs, identify any new requirements, determine the effectiveness of the interaction methods for the targeted user community, and gain contextual information to inform the lower-level design of the tool.

We started with design sketches and iterated through low-fidelity to medium-fidelity prototypes, which we evaluated first with internal stakeholders and then with target customers. The first step was to sketch a set of task-based screens on paper and to discuss the flow and possible functionality associated with the task and how that should be represented in the screens. Once the team came to an agreement on these rough drawings, we proceeded to create a low-level prototype that consisted of a set of HTML screens that illustrated the steps in the user scenarios. The prototype described how two fictional privacy and compliance officers within a health care organization, Pat User and Terry Specialist, used the prototype to author and implement the privacy policies and to audit the privacy policies logs. This version of the prototype was reviewed by the team and by other HCI and security researchers internally in our organization. Based on their comments, the prototype design was updated, and it was upgraded to a medium-fidelity-level prototype by the inclusion of dynamic HTML.

The prototype has many aspects that we will not try to describe here. To illustrate one—the use of natural language parsing to author privacy policies—we briefly describe here how it became a part of our design. During the survey and interview research, many of the participants indicated that privacy policies in their organizations were created by committees made up of business process specialists, lawyers, security specialists, and information technologists. Based on the range of skills generally possessed by people with these varied roles, we hypothesized that different methods of defining privacy policies would be necessary. SPARCLE was designed to support users with a variety of skills by allowing individuals responsible for the creation of privacy policies to define the policies using natural language with a template to describe privacy rules (shown in Figure 4-4) or to use a structured format to define the elements and rule relationships that will be directly used in the machine-readable policy (shown in Figure 4-5). We designed SPAR- CLE to keep the two formats synchronized. For users who prefer authoring with natural language, SPARCLE transforms the policy into a structured form so that the author can review it, and then translates it into a machine-readable format such as XA/CML, EPAL,[13] or P3P.[14] SPARCLE translates the policies of organizational users who prefer to author rules using a structured format into both a natural language format and the machine-readable version. During the entire privacy policy authoring phase, users can switch between the natural language and structured views of the policy for viewing and editing purposes.

Once the machine-readable policy is created, SPARCLE provides a series of mapping steps to allow the user to identify where in the organization's data stores the elements of the privacy policy are stored. This series of tasks will most likely be completed by different roles in the information technology (IT) area with input from the business process experts for different lines within the organization. Finally, SPARCLE provides internal compliance or auditing officers with the ability to create reports based on logs of accesses to PI.

At the same time that our iterative design was occurring, the team worked to recrui repre- sentatives from the three selected domains of health care, banking/finance, and govern- ment who would be willing to participate in design feedback sessions to evaluate the design. Our target user group was representatives from organizations in Canada, the U.S., and Europe who are responsible for creating, implementing, and auditing the privacy pol- icies for their organizations. Note that it is a significant effort to recruit study participants, especially when the target user group is very specialized and has very limited time. We identified these individuals using a combination of methods including issuing a call for participation at a privacy session held at an industry conference, contacting and getting

13 P. Ashley, S. Hada, G. Karjoth, C. Powers, and M. Schunter, *Enterprise Privacy Architecture Language (EPAL 1.2)*, W3C Member Submission 10-Nov-2003; *http://www.w3.org/Submission/EPAL/*.

14 L. Cranor, *Web Privacy with P3P* (Sebastopol, CA: O'Reilly, 2002).

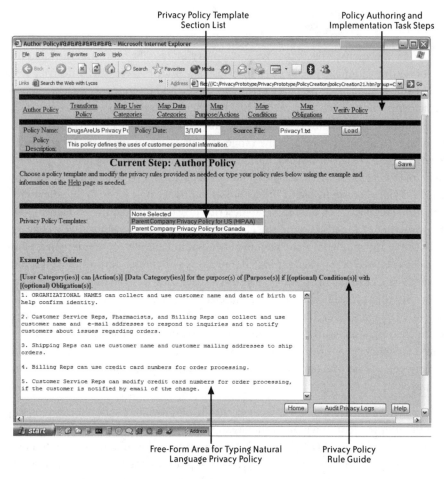

Privacy Policy Template Section List

Policy Authoring and Implementation Task Steps

Free-Form Area for Typing Natural Language Privacy Policy

Privacy Policy Rule Guide

*FIGURE 4-4. SPARCLE natural language privacy policy creation screen*

referrals from participants from the earlier studies, and employing professional and personal contacts within our department to identify potential participants.

For the review sessions, we scheduled 90-minute privacy walkthrough sessions onsite at the participants' work locations. For the first iteration of the prototype, walkthrough participants (seven participants in five sessions) rated the prototype positively (an average rating of 2.6 on a 7-point scale, with 1 indicating "highest value" and 7 indicating "no value"). During the second iteration of walkthrough sessions in which we added a capability of importing organizational or domain-specific policy templates, the participants (15 participants in 6 sessions) also rated the revised prototype very positively (an average rating of 2.5 on the same scale).

We present this summary result because it communicates the overall response to the prototype. However, the primary purpose for the sessions was to gather more qualitative responses from the participants about the value of the system to their task of managing privacy: what worked well, what was missing, and how they would like features designed.

Parsed Rule    Original Rule

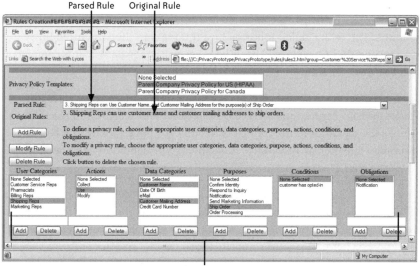

Policy Elements

*FIGURE 4-5. Expanded view of the SPARCLE structured privacy policy rule creation*

The qualitative comments were invaluable in helping us to better understand the needs of organizational users for privacy functionality and how to update the design of the prototype to better meet those needs. Based on the comments we received, we also decided to conduct an *empirical laboratory usability test* of the two authoring methods described in Step Four based on the feedback.

## Step Four: Evaluating Policy Authoring

While formal studies have become less central to usability work than they once were, they are still an important technique for investigating specific issues. We ran an *empirical usability laboratory study* to compare the two privacy policy authoring methods employed in the prototype. In order to provide a baseline comparison for the two methods (Natural Language with a Guide, and Structured Entry from Element Lists), we included a control condition that allowed users to enter privacy policies in any format that they were satisfied with (Unconstrained Natural Language). We ran this study internally in our organization employing a *user profile* describing people experienced with computers but novices in terms of creating privacy policy rules. The results will need to be validated with the target users; however, we believed that because the crux of the study was the usability of three different methods for authoring privacy rules, the use of the novice users was appropriate. It was also an extremely practical, efficient, and cost-effective strategy, as the policy experts are a rare resource, and it would be difficult or prohibitively expensive to collect this data in a laboratory setting with them.

Thirty-six employees were recruited through email to participate in the study. The participants had no previous experience in privacy policy authoring or implementation. Each participant completed one task in each of the three conditions. All participants started with a privacy rule task in the Unguided Natural Language control condition (Unguided NL). Then, half of the participants completed a similar task in the Natural Language with a Guide condition (NL with Guide), followed by a third task in the Structured Entry from Element Lists condition (Structured List). The other half of the participants completed the Structured List condition followed by the NL with Guide condition.

In each task, we instructed participants to compose a number of privacy rules for a pre-defined task scenario. Participants worked on three different scenarios in the three tasks. We developed the scenarios in the context of health care, government, and banking. Each scenario contained five or six privacy rules, including one condition and one obligation. The order of the scenarios was balanced across all participants.

We recorded the time that the participants took to complete each task and the privacy rules that participants composed. We also collected, through questionnaires, participants' perceived satisfaction with the task completion time, the quality of rules created, and the overall experience after participants completed each task. At the end of the session, participants completed a debrief questionnaire about their experiences with the three rule authoring methods. To compare the quality of the rules participants created under different conditions and scenarios, we developed a standard metric for scoring the rules.

Figure 4-6 shows the quality of the rules created using each method. We counted each element of a rule as one point. Therefore, a basic rule of four compulsory elements had a score of 4, and a scenario that consisted of five rules, including one condition and one obligation, had a total score of 22. We counted the number of correct elements that participants specified in their rules, and divided that number by the total score of the specific scenario. This provided a standardized score of the percentage of elements correctly identified that was compared across conditions.

The NL with Guide method and the Structured List method helped users create rules of significantly higher quality than did the Unguided NL method. There was no significant difference between the NL with Guide method and the Structured List method. Using the Unguided NL method, participants correctly identified about 42% of the elements in the scenarios, while the NL with Guide method and the Structured List method helped users to correctly identify 75% and 80% of the elements, respectively.

The results of the experiment confirmed that both the NL with Guide method and the Structured List method were easy to learn and use, and they enabled participants to create rules with higher quality than did the Unguided NL method. The participants' satisfaction with both the NL with Guide method and the Structured List method provided some indication that there is value in allowing users to choose between the two methods and switch between them for different parts of the task, depending on their own preferences and skills. Other feedback from the study gave us additional guidance on where to focus on our future iterations of design.

Given these results, we believe that SPARCLE is now ready to be transformed into a high-fidelity end-to-end prototype so that we can test its functionality more completely with

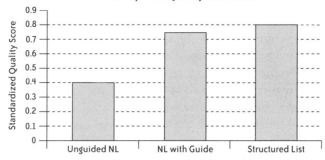

Policy Rule Quality Evaluation

FIGURE 4-6. Quality of privacy policy rules created using each method

privacy professionals. While we have used predefined scenarios with predefined policies for our evaluations so far, a prototype that has been integrated with a fully functional natural language parser and a privacy enforcement engine will enable us to conduct richer and more complete tests of functionality with the participants' organizational privacy policies before moving to product-level code.

## Conclusion

Our experiences at IBM show that HCI activities can have a positive return both for the organization creating a piece of technology and for the people who actually use it.

We encourage you to start integrating HCI activities in your development activities in the security and privacy domain. It is helpful to start with a small to medium-size project or product as a test case and learning vehicle. Bring an HCI expert on board, and leverage this person's skill and build expertise in the larger team. Hold team discussions so that you can build on what you learn in this area within your organization and in your professional associations. Communicate your successes and failures so that people within and outside your organization can benefit from your experiences.

# About the Authors

 Clare-Marie Karat is a Research Staff Member at the IBM T.J. Watson Research Center. Dr. Karat conducts HCI research in the areas of privacy, security, and personalization. She is the editor of the book *Designing Personalized User Experiences in eCommerce*, published in 2004 (Springer). She is an editorial board member of the ACM *interactions*, the British Computer Society's *Interacting with Computers*, and Elsevier's *International Journal of Human Computer Studies* journals; a reviewer for the *IEEE Security and Privacy* journal; and a technical committee member of the CHI, HFES, and INTERACT conferences, the Symposium on Usable Privacy and Security, and the User Modeling Personalization and Privacy Workshop.

*ckarat@us.ibm.com*

 Carolyn Brodie is a Research Staff Member at IBM's T.J. Watson Research Center. Dr. Brodie's current research focuses on the design and development of usable privacy and security functionality for organizations. She received her Ph.D. from the University of Illinois at Urbana-Champaign in Computer Science in 1999, where she developed a methodology for the design of military planning tools. Additional research interests include the personalization of web sites, and the use of collaboration tools to enhance information flow in organizations.

*brodiec@us.ibm.com*

 John Karat is a Research Staff Member at the IBM T.J. Watson Research Center. Dr. Karat conducts HCI research in a variety of areas including privacy, personalization, and information management. Dr. Karat is past chairman of the International Federation for Information Processing Technical Committee on HCI (IFIP TC13); North American editor for the journal *Behaviour and Information Technology*; and Editor-in-Chief of the Kluwer Academic Publishers series on HCI. He is a member of the ACM SIGCHI Executive Committee and has been actively involved in ACM CHI and DIS and in the IFIP INTERACT conferences in the HCI field.

*jkarat@us.ibm.com*

# CHAPTER FIVE

# Designing Systems That People Will Trust

ANDREW S. PATRICK, PAMELA BRIGGS, AND STEPHEN MARSH

**T**RUST IS A FUNDAMENTAL BUILDING BLOCK OF SOCIETY,[1] a means of making decisions about conferring authority or responsibility in unfamiliar or uncertain situations,[2] a method of understanding how decisions are made in context,[3] and one of the most important concepts in the security arena. Unfortunately, it also remains one of the most poorly understood concepts. A lack of trust will result in systems being ill-used at best, and not used at all at worst. A lack of understanding of trust, in both user and system, will result in the wrong decision—or no decision at all—being made in security contexts. Too much trust can be at least as dangerous as not enough, and not enough trust can be dangerous enough.

---

1   See, for example, Sissela Bok, *Lying: Moral Choice in Public and Private Life* (New York: Pantheon Books, 1978); Niklas Luhmann, *Trust and Power* (Chichester, UK: Wiley, 1979); and Barbara Misztal, *Trust in Modern Societies: The Search for the Bases of Social Order* (Cambridge, UK: Polity Press, 1996).

2   Bernard Barber, *The Logic and Limits of Trust* (New Brunswick, NJ: Rutgers University Press, 1983).

3   Stephen Marsh, "Formalizing Trust as a Computational Concept," Ph.D. Thesis, University of Stirling, Scotland, 1994; Mark R. Dibben, *Exploring Interpersonal Trust in the Entrepreneurial Venture* (Hampshire, U.K.: Business, 2000).

This chapter examines the issue of trust in security and privacy systems. These systems purportedly help users make decisions about whom to trust with access, information, or data. For example, how much, when, and for what purposes can specific information be used? They can also help make decisions for the user when the user is not available. These decisions are based on a foundation of trust.

# Introduction

Current security systems are often seen as difficult to use, or as getting in the user's way. As a result, they are often circumvented. Users should not have to delve into arcane issues of security to be able to allow access to a part of their personal information online: they don't have to in the real world, after all. In the real world, they rely on trust, an understanding of fiduciary responsibilities, and common sense. So it should be online.[4]

Fundamental questions arise when considering trust, including how to reliably represent trust in different interactions and interfaces, how to transform trust-based decisions into security decisions while maintaining the meaning of the trust-based decisions (in other words, attaining computational tractability without sacrificing meaning), how to transform in the opposite direction, and what the building blocks of trust really are in such contexts as information sharing or secure access to systems. Finally, because trust is fallible, what are its failings, how can they be addressed in this context, and what means of controlling the fallibility exist or should exist? Through investigating prior and current work in the area, this chapter arrives at recommendations for future systems and guidance for how they can be designed for use in a context of trust.

In the next section, we discuss the definitions of trust, and in the following section, we examine the context of trust, its relation to risk, and the fundamental building blocks of trust online that have arisen from e-commerce research. Later, we present formal models of trust and describe what can be learned from these models. We conclude with a set of guidelines addressing how trust can be used in security systems, and concrete suggestions for system developers.

## Definitions of Trust

Trust has not always been a subject of mainstream consideration.[5] In fact, prior to the Internet boom and bust, trust was a poor sibling to other sociological and psychological constructs. The Internet boom changed things, as people began to realize that, with trust, people will buy things, and without it, they will not.[6] As simple as this observation may

---

4   To continue this discussion, see Barber, Luhmann, and also see Helen Nissenbaum, "How Computer Systems Embody Values," *IEEE Computer* (2001), 118–120.

5   Misztal and Luhmann.

6   Cheskin Research & Studio Archetype/Sapient, "eCommerce Trust Study" (1999), *http://www.cheskin.com/think/studies/ecomtrust.html*; Cheskin Research, "Trust in the Wired Americas" (2000), *http://www.cheskin.com/p/ar.asp?mlid=7&arid=12&art=0*.

seem, it remains profound. What's more, the realization that imperfect designs can affect the trust of a user has had an equally profound effect on how people have gone about implementing user interfaces, web sites, and interactivity in general.[7] The result has been an increasing amount of well-designed, well-thought-out interfaces, and a great deal of discussion in fields such as Human-Computer Interaction (HCI) and Computer-Supported Cooperative Work (CSCW) about how to encourage, maintain, and increase trust between people and machines, and between people and other people.[8]

Unfortunately, given all of this interest in trust, a deep and abiding problem became evident: everyone knows what trust is, but no one really knows how to define it to everyone's satisfaction. Thus, we now have a great many different definitions, almost as many as there are papers on the subject, all of which bear some relation to each other, but which have subtle differences that often cannot be reconciled. Trust, it seems, is a lot of things to a lot of people.

Looking at the literature, this state of affairs is understandable because trust is multifaceted, multidimensional, and not easy to tie down in a single space.[9] The problem remains, however, that to discuss trust, one must in some way define terms. We suggest the following definition: "Trust concerns a positive expectation regarding the behavior of somebody or something in a situation that entails risk to the trusting party."[10] Problems remain with this and other definitions,[11] but it will do for our purposes.

Given the multidimensional nature of trust, we have found it useful to discuss the different *layers* of trust, because it is these layers that affect how trust works in context. We have found that trust has three basic layers: *dispositional trust*, the psychological disposition or personality trait to be trusting or not; *learned trust*, a person's general tendency to trust, or not to trust, as a result of experience; and *situational trust*, in which basic tendencies are adjusted in response to situational cues.[12] These layers work together to produce sensible

---

7  Jakob Nielsen, "Trust or Bust: Communicating Trustworthiness in Web Design," *AlertBox* (1999); *http://www.useit.com/alertbox/990307.html*.

8  See, for example, Cheskin Research, "eCommerce Trust Study" and Cheskin Research, "Trust in the Wired Americas." See also Ben Shneiderman, "Designing Trust into Online Experiences," *Communications of the ACM* 43:12 (2000), 57–59; Gary Olson and Judith Olson, "Distance Matters," *Human-Computer Interaction* 15 (2000), 139–178; Ye Diana Wang and Henry H. Emurian, "An Overview of Online Trust: Concepts, Elements, and Implications," *Computers in Human Behavior* (2005), 105–125; Cynthia L. Corritore, Beverly Kracher, and Susan Wiedenbeck, "On-Line Trust: Concepts, Evolving Themes, a Model," *International Journal of Human-Computer Studies* 58 (2003), 737–758; Jens M. Riegelsberger, M. Angela Sasse, and John D. McCarthy, "The Researcher's Dilemma: Evaluating Trust in Computer-Mediated Communication," *International Journal of Human-Computer Studies* 58 (2003), 759–781.

9  Stephen Marsh and Mark Dibben, "The Role of Trust in Information Science and Technology," in B. Cronin (ed.), *Annual Review of Information Science and Technology* 37 (2003), 465–498.

10  Marsh and Dibben (2003), 470.

11  R. C. Mayer, J. H. Davis, and F. D. Schoorman, "An Integrative Model of Organizational Trust," *Academy of Management Review* 20:3 (1995), 709–734.

12  Marsh and Dibben (2003).

trusting behavior in situations that may or may not be familiar to the truster. For example, in an unfamiliar situation, learned trust may be given less importance than dispositional trust (because no learned information is available), whereas a situation similar to others encountered in the past can allow a reliance on more learned trust. The situational trust allows cues, such as the amount of information or social expectations, to act to adjust trust levels accordingly. Clearly, the more information available, the better. Bear in mind, however, that a state of perfect information by definition removes the need to rely on trust.

Looked at in this manner, the goal of much HCI research and development is to create systems and interfaces that are as familiar as possible to the user such that the user need not make a (necessarily more limited) dispositional trusting decision, and to allow that user to make a (more solid and comfortable) learned trusting decision. The goal of security and privacy systems is to allow the user to make these decisions with as many positive situational cues as possible, or to allow the user to provide and maintain his own situational cues in situations of less than perfect information, comfort, and, ultimately, trust.

## The Nature of Trust in the Digital Sphere

The concept of trust undergoes some interesting transformations when it is brought into the digital sphere. Whereas people may be quite adept at assessing the likely behavior of other people and the risks involved in the physical, face-to-face world, they may be less skilled when making judgments in online environments. For example, people may be too trusting online, perhaps routinely downloading software or having conversations in chat rooms without realizing the true behaviors of the other parties and the risks involved. People may also have too little trust in online situations, perhaps dogmatically avoiding e-commerce or e-government transactions in the belief that such actions cannot be done securely, at the cost of missed opportunities and added convenience.[13] Online users have to develop the knowledge needed to make good trust decisions, and developers must support them by making trustable designs.

One thing that is obvious is that trust in the digital sphere is negotiated differently from trust in face-to-face situations. Take the example of eBay—one of the most successful e-commerce businesses in operation today, and one in which complete strangers routinely send each other checks in the mail (although this is becoming a less common means of payment as more sophisticated methods become available). How do eBay users develop sufficient trust in these unseen others to offset financial security concerns? One approach is eBay's reputation system that not only enhances a sense of community among eBay members but also provides a profile of user experiences. These profiles are available to all vendors and customers—something that was unheard of in the world of offline commerce. Over years, the nature and utility of such cues has changed (as we will discuss in more detail in a later section), but the principle that trust can be designed into a transaction is clearly established.

13 Batya Friedman, Peter H. Khan, Jr., and Daniel C. Howe, "Trust Online," *Communications of the ACM* 43:12 (2000), 34–40.

Another interesting example of the trust cues that can be provided to online users, and how difficult they can be to interpret, was provided in a study by Batya Friedman and her colleagues.[14] These researchers conducted detailed interviews of Internet users to explore the users' understanding of web security. They asked users to describe how they determine if a web connection is secure or not. The most frequent evidence was the appearance of the "https" protocol in the URL, and this was usually used correctly. On the other hand, the "lock" icon that appears in most browsers to indicate a secure connection was often misunderstood by the users, with many confusing the meaning of the open and closed locks. It was also common for people to use evidence about the point in the transaction (e. g., "this is the home page, so it probably is not secure"), the type of information (e.g., "they are asking for my Social Security number, so it must be secure"), and the type of web site (e.g., "it is a bank, so they must be using security"). In addition, some people just made global mistrust decisions regardless of the evidence available (e.g., "I don't think any sites are secure"). This study makes it clear that people are making trust decisions that are based on apparent misunderstanding of web security and the threats that they face.

*Phishing*, the practice of creating mirror web sites of, for example, commerce or banking sites, and then sending emails to customers asking them to "update their records urgently at the following [fake] link," is a particularly problematic exploitation of trust because it allows the fake site to obtain real account numbers, personal details, and passwords for subsequent fraudulent use on the real site. Phishing sites are often extremely sophisticated, sometimes indistinguishable from the real site. Defenses against such attacks are possible but difficult. Some developers, for example, are creating web browser plug-ins that highlight the true location of a link, rather than the normal location display that can be easily obscured.[15] Ironically, recent features in web sites that are seen as security concerns, such as using cookies to store login IDs and only asking for passwords, are an interesting defense—if I normally don't have to enter my ID, then a similar site that asks for the ID should be a clue about its authenticity. Phishing attacks are discussed in more detail in Chapter 14.

Trust (and distrust) requires at least two parties: the truster and the trustee. It requires that the truster make an informed decision. Trust is not a subconscious choice, but requires thought, information, and an active truster. The converse is not true: it is not necessary for the trustee to know that the truster is, in fact, trusting them—it may be necessary for the trustee to know that *someone* trusts them, but that's a different debate.

As discussed briefly already, it has generally been accepted that the trustee has to have some aspect of free will: that is, in this instance, the trustee can do something that the truster would find untrustworthy. In the precomputer age this was taken to mean that the

14 Batya Friedman, David Hurley, Daniel C. Howe, Edward Felten, and Helen Nissenbaum, "Users' Conceptions of Web Security: A Comparative Study," *CHI '02 Extended Abstracts on Human Factors in Computing Systems* (2002), 746–747.

15 For example, *http://www.corestreet.com/spoofstick/*.

trustee must be rational, conscious, and *real*: thus, machines could not be *trusted*, they could only be *relied upon*, a difference that is subtle, but not moot.

In an age of autonomous agents, active web sites, avatars, and increasingly complex systems, both conscious entities and complex machines can be trusted. The corresponding argument that the trustee must know when he or she acts in an untrustworthy manner is somewhat more problematic. In any case, the phenomenon of anthropomorphism, whether validly directed or not, allows us to consider technologies as "trustable" because people behave *as if* machines and technologies are trustable social entities that can in fact deceive us, and leave us feeling let down when trust is betrayed.[16]

The question remains, then, especially when active entities such as autonomous agents or interactive interfaces are in mind, as to whom or what can *trust* and whom or what can be *trusted*. In this instance, one can consider humans as trusters and trustees, and computers in similar roles. Thus, we can consider trust between humans and humans, and between humans and computers, but we can also consider trust between computers and other computers, and, finally, between computers and humans. Heretical as it may seem, there are situations where computers are trusters—sometimes even as surrogate agents for humans.

In the circumstances where the truster is a computer, there is a need for a means by which the computer can "think" about trust. Thus, a computationally tractable means of reasoning about trust is needed. It is not enough for the computer to be able to say, "I trust you, so I will share information with you." What information? How much? In which circumstance? In what context? We sometimes have a need to put some kind of value on trust; thus, "I trust you *this much*" is a much more powerful statement than "I trust you." Of course, this leads to its own questions, such as what does "*this much*" actually mean, how can we trust, and how can trust values be shared? We address these questions in subsequent sections.

Formalizations and formal models of trust do exist and more are appearing regularly.[17] With each formalization, old questions are answered, new questions arise, and we move closer to a real understanding of human trust and more capable trust-reasoning technologies. However, while formalizations exist, *computationally tractable* formalizations are much

---

16 See Byron Reeves and Clifford Nass, *The Media Equation: How People Treat Computers, Television, and New Media Like Real People and Places* (Stanford University, Palo Alto, CA: CSLI Publications, 1996); B. J. Fogg, *Persuasive Technology: Using Computers to Change What We Think and Do* (New York: Morgan Kaufman, 2002); Cristiano Castelfranchi, "Artificial Liars: Why Computers Will (Necessarily) Deceive Us and Each Other," *Ethics and Information Technology* 2:2 (2000), 113–119.

17 See below and Stephen Marsh, "Formalizing Trust as a Computational Concept"; Alfarez Abdul-Rahman and Stephen Hailes, "A Distributed Trust Model," *Proceedings of the ACM New Security Paradigms Workshop '97* (Cumbria, U.K., Sept. 19970; Cristiano Castelfranchi and R. Falcone, "Principles of Trust for MAS: Cognitive Anatomy, Social Importance, and Quantification," *Proceedings of the 3rd International Conference on Multi Agent Systems, 1998*, 72; Jonathan Carter and Ali A. Ghorbani, "Towards a Formalization of Value-Centric Trust in Agent Societies," *Journal of Web Intelligence and Agent Systems* 2:3 (2004), 167–184.

rarer. Unfortunately, it is these that are needed to better approach understanding and to better approximate trusting behaviors in computers.

## The Trust-Risk Relationship

Trust is intimately associated with risk—indeed, it is possible to argue that in the absence of risk, trust is meaningless.[18] Let's take an everyday example: I could ask a stranger to look after my seat on a train (low risk) and not feel any need to engage in an evaluation of the trustworthiness of that stranger. However, if I leave an expensive video camera or even my baby behind on the seat (high risk), a more careful trust judgment would ensue. But this example raises other issues in relation to the trust-risk relationship. In particular, it seems that the characteristics of trust are dependent upon the types of underlying risk. To pursue the example, if I would trust someone to watch my video camera, does that imply that I would trust them to look after my infant? Not necessarily, as the two trust judgments are related but somehow distinct, with the latter relying more heavily on judgments of competence and kindness and the former on judgments of honesty. So, to add to the argument made earlier, we may need to be able to phrase trust not just in terms of "I trust you this much" but also in terms of "I trust you *this much* to do *this thing*."

The same complexities occur in e-commerce. An online consumer's decision to trust an e-vendor may reflect beliefs about honesty, but is also likely to tap into decisions about competence and expertise, and it is further informed by judgments about the extent to which any information provided will remain private. Thus, a seemingly simple act of trust invokes a complex set of judgments. Once again, the risk assessment involved is crucial—there is no doubt that people are more willing to trust a site if the perceived risk is low. This was shown very clearly in a study of more than 2,500 people who said they had sought advice online.[19] Those that sought advice in relatively high-risk domains (e.g., finance) were less likely to trust and subsequently act on the advice than those who sought advice in low-risk domains (e.g., entertainment). Similar findings can be found in the well-known Cheskin/Sapient report on trust in e-commerce,[20] where, for lower-risk purchases such as books or groceries, trust was strongly associated with familiarity, whereas for high-risk purchases, such as drugs or financial services, trust remained low, even when the companies themselves were well known.

Even though some e-commerce transactions may seem to be low risk (say, involving small amounts of money), they usually involve high-risk elements such as the threat to privacy or credit card fraud. Furthermore, a typical exchange is complicated by uncertainties about whom or what is being trusted. Thus, in situations where percceived risk may be

18 Andrew Brien, "Professional Ethics and the Culture of Trust," *Journal of Business Ethics* 17 (1998), 391–409.

19 Pamela Briggs, Bryan Burford, Antonella De Angeli, and Paula Lynch, "Trust in Online Advice," *Social Science Computer Review* 20:3 (2002), 321–332.

20 Cheskin Research, "eCommerce Trust Study."

low, actual risks may be high, and the assessment of actual risk is complex. For example, when a person logs into a secure web site to do a transaction, who are they trusting and on what are they basing their trust decision? In terms of people, they are trusting the writer of the web browser, the owner of the computer system, the web host operator, the e-commerce vendor, all the network operators who handle their data, and the certificate authority that registered the web site—but each to a different extent.

## Technology Factors

Technology can alter the trust equation. When properly implemented, SSL encryption reduces the amount of trust that needs to be placed in network operators by limiting the opportunity for them to eavesdrop on TCP/IP connections, but operators must still be trusted to deliver packets to their intended destination. On the other hand, SSL does not help to protect against a keystroke logger that may be running on an Internet kiosk—a risk even when the kiosk's browser displays a secure "lock" icon in the status bar.

Customers must be prepared to place their trust not only in the people, but also in the technology that underpins an interaction. Understanding the context for trust, therefore, involves understanding issues of encryption and data security as well as understanding the development of a psychological bond. Bollier argued that it is vital to distinguish between issues of "hard trust," involving authenticity, encryption, and security in transactions, and issues of "soft trust," involving human psychology, brand loyalty, and user friendliness.[21] But as the earlier example demonstrates, hard and soft trust can easily overlap or be confused.

Riegelsberger and Sasse have broken down the risks inherent in an e-commerce transaction in two parts. First, in terms of risks that stem from the Internet, including (a) whether credit card data gets intercepted, (b) whether the data is transmitted correctly, and (c) whether the consumer uses the system correctly. Second, in terms of risks that are related to the physical absence of the online retailer, including (a) whether personal details will be kept confidential or transmitted to other parties, and (b) whether the online vendor will actually deliver the products or services.[22]

People are faced with highly complex assessments of the risks they take when engaging in e-commerce transactions. One would assume that they would be influenced by the agencies charged with communicating information about the risk[23] and also the individuals or

---

21 David Bollier, *The Future of Electronic Commerce, A Report of the Fourth Annual Aspen Institute Roundtable on Information Technology* (Aspen, CO: The Aspen Institute, 1996).

22 Jens Riegelsberger and M. Angela Sasse, "Trustbuilders and Trustbusters: The Role of Trust Cues in Interfaces to E-Commerce Applications," *Proceedings of the 1st IFIP Conference On E-Commerce, E-Business, and E-Government* (Zurich, 2001); *http://www.cs.ucl.ac.uk/staff/jriegels/trustbuilders_and_trustbusters.htm.*

23 O. Renn and D. Levine, "Credibility and Trust in Risk Communication," in R. Kasperson and P. J. Stallen (eds.), *Communicating Risk to the Public* (Dordrecht: Kluwer Academic Publishers, 1991), 175–218.

organizations charged with regulating the risk.[24] In e-commerce scenarios, the regulation of security risk is usually the responsibility of the vendor, although trust is often gained by recourse to third-party endorsers offering seals of approval. However, consumers are surprisingly willing to accept risks when other trust indicators are present. Many Internet users will be familiar with a scenario in which they are asked to input detailed personal information about themselves in order to access the facilities available on a site. Users who input this information typically do so with the assumption that (a) the company honestly communicates its privacy policy, and (b) the company is capable of honoring those privacy claims. But few users actually spend the time checking this out, or even read the policies. In practice, consumers seem to be more heavily influenced by the extent to which the facilities match their needs, whether the site has a professional look and feel, and the extent to which the exchange seems predictable or familiar.[25] Indeed, a very recent e-commerce study suggests that users are prepared to cast care to the wind and commit sensitive details to any site provided that the object of desire is compelling enough.[26] Human fallibility is often the weakest link in the security chain.

Consumers are not always as cautious as they might be, and it is possible to distinguish relatively "hasty" and "considered" processing strategies for the evaluation of trust in high- and low-risk environments. Chaiken identified two processing strategies by which an evaluation of trustworthiness may be made:

- A heuristic strategy that follows a "cognitive miser" principle—where people base decisions on only the most obvious or apparent information

- A systematic strategy that involves the detailed processing of message content[27]

Chaiken described two experiments that show that the degree of *involvement* in the issue affects the processing strategy. Those participants with low involvement adopted a heuristic approach to evaluating a message and were primarily influenced by the attractiveness, whereas those with high involvement adopted a systematic approach, presenting more arguments to support their judgment. A number of other studies in the persuasion literature support the two-process model—namely, that people use cognitively intense analytical processing when the task is an important or particularly engaging one, whereas they

---

24 W. Poortinga and N. F. Pidgeon, "Exploring the Dimensionality of Trust in Risk Regulation," *Risk Analysis* 23:5 (2003), 961–972.

25 Briggs *et al.*, "Trust in Online Advice.".

26 Kathy Dudek, Pamela Briggs, and Gitte Lindegaard, "Small Objects of Desire and Their Impact on Trust in E-Commerce" (in preparation).

27 Shelley Chaiken, "Heuristic Versus Systematic Information Processing and the Use of Source Versus Message Cues in Persuasion," *Journal of Personality and Social Psychology* 39 (1980), 752–766.

use affect or other simple heuristics to guide their decisions when they lack the motivation or capacity to think properly about the issues involved.[28]

Such studies anticipate some recent findings with regard to online credibility. Stanford *et al.* invited experts and ordinary consumers to view health and finance information sites and found that experts (those having a high involvement with a site) were highly influenced by factors such as reputation, information quality and source, and perceived motive, in contrast to ordinary consumers (those having a low involvement with the site) who were much more influenced by the attractiveness of site design.[29] The same is likely to be true of risk. In high-risk situations, or at least those situations that the user perceives as high risk, we would expect to see more evidence of careful analysis of trust indicators, as opposed to low-risk situations in which some rapid heuristic assumption of trust may be made. This high-risk/low-risk dichotomy is also played out in the trust literature where those experimental studies of initial trust where risk is imagined (would you buy from this web site?) tend to place more emphasis on the attractiveness and the professional look-and-feel of sites, whereas those (few) studies that have actually involved substantive risk have emphasized careful consideration of integrity, credibility, and competence.[30]

## Trust and Credibility

It is worth saying something here about the relationship between trust and credibility. While a number of trust models incorporate judgments of source credibility in terms of expertise and reputation factors, and therefore see credibility as a component of trust, some researchers view trust as a component of credibility. Most notable is B. J. Fogg's work on the credibility of online information. Fogg is particularly concerned with the idea of the Internet as a persuasive technology. In a series of studies, he and his colleagues at Stanford University have identified a number of factors that affect judgments of credibility. Positive factors included a real-world feel to the site, ease of use, expertise, trustworthiness, and a site tailored to the individual. Negative factors included an overly commercial

28 See, for example, G. L. Clore, N. Schwarz, and M. Conway, "Affective Causes and Consequences of Social Information Processing," in Robert. S. Wyer and Thomas. K. Srull (eds.), *Handbook of Social Cognition* (Hillsdale, NJ: Erlbaum, 1994), 323–417; D. J. McCallister, "Affect-Based and Cognition-Based Trust as Foundations for Interpersonal Co-Operation in Organisations," *Academy of Management Journal* 38 (1995), 24–59; R. E. Petty and D. T. Wegener, "The Elaboration Likelihood Model: Current Status and Controversies," in S. Chaiken and Y. Trope (eds.), *Dual-Process Theories in Social Psychology* (New York: Guilford Press, 1999), 41–72; D. Albarracin and G. T. Kumkale, "Affect as Information in Persuasion: A Model of Affect Identification and Discounting," *Journal of Personality and Social Psychology* 84:3 (2003), 453–469.

29 Julianne Stanford, Ellen R. Tauber, B. J. Fogg, and Leslie Marable, "Experts vs. Online Consumers: A Comparative Credibility Study of Health and Finance Web Sites," Consumer Web Watch [Accessed November 19, 2002]; *http://www.consumerwebwatch.org/news/report3_credibilityresearch/slicedbread abstract.htm*.

30 B. Chong, Z. Yang, and M. Wong, "Asymmetrical Impact of Trustworthiness Attributes on Trust, Perceived Value and Purchase Intention: A Conceptual Framework for Cross-Cultural Study on Consumer Perception of Online Auction," *Proceedings of ICEC 2003* (2003).

orientation and amateurism.[31] Fogg has interpreted this research in terms of a theory capable of explaining how web-credibility judgments are made. His prominence-interpretation theory posits two processes in the formation of a credibility judgment: *prominence* (the extent to which something is noticed) and *interpretation* (a considered judgment about the element under consideration).

Fogg argues that five factors affect prominence, and three factors affect interpretation,[32] as follows:

Prominence:

1. The involvement of the user in terms of his motivation and ability to scrutinize web content

2. The topic of the web site

3. The nature of the user's task

4. The user's experience

5. Individual differences—for example, in learning style or literacy level

Interpretation:

1. The assumptions in a user's mind (derived from examples, cultural influences, or past experiences)

2. The skills and knowledge a user brings to bear

3. The context for the user (in terms of environment, expectations, etc.)

There are interesting areas of overlap with the two-process model discussed earlier. Heuristic judgments clearly reflect the more "prominent" aspects of an interaction, and analytic judgments reflect the interpretative processes outlined earlier. Perhaps the important issue for trust research is that the predictions made by prominence-interpretation theory (in terms of patterns of user involvement, skills, and experience) are consistent with those derived from the two-process theory, and the guidelines that result are also in accord.

## The Time-Course of Trust

The research on trust reviewed in earlier sections suggests a need for more explicit consideration of the ways in which trust develops over time. It is certainly worth distinguishing

---

31 B. J. Fogg *et al.*, "What Makes a Web Site Credible? A Report on a Large Quantitative Study," *Proceedings of ACM CHI 2001 Conference on Human Factors in Computing Systems* (2001), 61–68.

32 B. J. Fogg, "Prominence-Interpretation Theory: Explaining How People Assess Credibility Online," *Proceedings of ACM CHI 2003 Conference on Human Factors in Computing Systems* (2003), 722–723.

between the kinds of trust that support transient interactions and those that support longer-term relationships.[33] A number of authors[34] have suggested that three phases are important: a phase of initial trust, followed by a more protracted exchange, which then may or may not lead to a longer-term trusting relationship. If one considers trust in this developmental context, some of the findings in the literature make more sense. In particular, consideration of a developmental context helps to reconcile the tension between those models of trust suggesting that trust is a concept grounded in careful judgment of vendor expertise and experience, process predictability, degree of personalization, and communication integrity,[35] and those models suggesting that trust decisions depend much more heavily on the attractiveness and professional feel of a site.[36]

The importance of visual appeal in the early stages of interaction with a web site is not unexpected given that in face-to-face interaction, we often make judgments on the basis of the attractiveness of an individual, giving rise to the well-known *halo effect*.[37] Other influences on first impressions in face-to-face conversation include the small talk that strangers engage in. Some trust designers have tried to capture this in the design of relational agents that promote early trust. Thus, Bickmore and Cassell describe the use of small talk to build "like-mindedness" between interlocuters in the early stages of an interaction.[38] Although there is less documented research concerning trust in such interactions, the issue of how to make an agent trustworthy is likely to be important for future security systems.[39]

33 For example, D. Meyerson, K. E. Weick, and R. M. Kramer, "Swift Trust and Temporary Groups," in R. M. Kramer and T. R. Tyler (eds.), *Trust in Organizations: Frontiers of Theory and Research* (Thousand Oaks, CA: Sage Publications, 1996), 166–195.

34 Elizabeth Sillence, Pam Briggs, Lesley Fishwick, and Peter Harris, "Trust and Mistrust of Online Health Sites," *Proceedings of the 2004 Conference on Human Factors in Computing Systems* (2004), 663–670; Florian Egger, "From Interactions to Transactions: Designing the Trust Experience for Business-to-Consumer Electronic Commerce," Ph.D. Thesis, Eindhoven University of Technology, The Netherlands, 2003; *http://www.ecommuse.com/research/publications/thesis.htm*.

35 For example, A. Bhattacherjee, "Individual Trust in Online Firms: Scale Development and Initial Trust," *Journal of Management Information Systems* 19:1 (2002), 213–243; J. Lee, J. Kim, and J.Y. Moon, "What Makes Internet Users Visit Cyber Stores Again? Key Design Factors for Customer Loyalty," *Proceedings of CHI '2000* (2000), 305–312; D. H. McKnight, V. Choudhury, and C. Kacmar, "Developing and Validating Trust Measures for E-Commerce: An Integrative Typology," *Information Systems Research* 13:3 (2002), 334–359.

36 U. Steinbruck, H. Schaumburg, S. Duda, and T. Kreuger, "A Picture Says More Than a Thousand Words—Photographs as Trust Builders in E-Commerce Websites," *Proceedings of Conference on Human Factors in Computing Systems CHI 2002 (Extended Abstracts)* (2002), 748–749.

37 See, for example, N. R. Bardack and F. T. McAndrew, "The Influence of Physical Attractiveness and Manner of Dress on Success in a Simulated Personnel Decision," *Journal of Social Psychology* 125 (1985), 777–778; K. Dion, E. Bersheid, and E. Walster, "What is Beautiful is Good," *Journal of Personality and Social Psychology* 24 (1972), 285–290.

38 T. Bickmore and J. Cassell, "Relational Agents: A Model and Implementation of Building User Trust," *Proceedings of Conference on Human Factors in Computing Systems CHI 2001* (2001), 396–403.

39 Andrew S. Patrick, "Building Trustworthy Software Agents," *IEEE Internet Computing* 6:6 (2002), 46–53.

Another advantage of considering the developmental nature of trust is that it facilitates consideration of those factors that help to build trust and those that destroy it. A very early study of trust in automated systems demonstrated the intuitive finding that trust is slow to build up but can be destroyed very quickly.[40] This asymmetry is one of the reasons that researchers have suggested that the underlying processes involved in making or breaking trust are likely to be different. Thus, for example, McKnight *et al.*[41] describe two models, one for trust and one for distrust, and argue that disposition to trust and institution-based trust affects low/medium-risk perceptions, while disposition to distrust and institution-based distrust affects medium/high-risk perceptions. The authors found that in contexts where people were merely exploring a site, the disposition to trust was most salient. Once they had made up their minds to engage in a higher-risk interaction with the site, the disposition to distrust became more important. McKnight *et al.* also found that promoting some initial exploration of the site was easy initially (because of the readiness to trust) and that this initial exploration could then be used subsequently to overcome the inclination to distrust when the user went on to engage in risky behavior. Interestingly, McKnight also observed a kind of halo effect such that a professional and well-designed site was associated with a disposition to trust.

These findings are consistent with the heuristic-systematic models described earlier if we consider that people are initially disinclined to look for hard evidence of trust (in the form of systematic assessment of expertise and careful investigation of privacy and security policies), but are instead happy to engage with sites on the basis that they are attractive and easy to use.

## Models of Trust

Researchers have developed a variety of models of trust components, antecedents, and/or consequences.[42] The advantage of models is that they may make fuzzy concepts clearer by defining terms and concepts. They can also provide structure where none existed before. More practically, developing a model may lead to specific metrics of interest that can be measured in research studies using questionnaires or other instruments. Models of trust can also lead to specific development advice. Some researchers working in the trust area, such as Egger, have used their models to develop criteria or checklists that practitioners can use to evaluate and improve a web site or similar service. In this section, we review

40 J. Lee and N. Moray, "Trust, Control Strategies and Allocation of Function in Human-Machine Systems," *Ergonomics* 35:10 (1992), 1243–1270.

41 D. Harrison McKnight and Norman L. Chervany, "Trust and Distrust Definitions: One Bite at a Time," in R. Falcone, M. Singh, and Y.-H. Tan (eds.), *Trust in Cyber-societies, LNAI 2246* (Springer, 2001) 27–54.

42 For a review, see Sonja Grabner-Krauter and Ewald A. Kaluscha, "Empirical Research in On-Line Trust: A Review and Critical Assessment," *International Journal of Human-Computer Studies,* 58 (2003), 783–812.

some of the models of trust, pointing out the similarities and differences, and we conclude with some specific lessons that the models can provide for developers.

## Early Work on Modeling Trust

Some of the earliest work on modeling trust focused on different components of the concept. Mayer *et al.*[43] proposed that trust is based on a set of beliefs about trustworthiness, and that the most important beliefs concerned ability, integrity, and benevolence:

- Ability is the capacity for a trustee to be able to fulfill a promise made in a trusting relationship.

- Integrity relates to the promises made by the trustee—does he promise more than he can deliver?

- Benevolence refers to acting in another's best interest.

Gefen[44] operationalized this model of trust components by developing a questionnaire that addressed the three concepts of ability, integrity, and benevolence. Students who used the Amazon.com web site were asked questions related to Amazon's ability (e.g., "Amazon.com knows about books"), integrity (e.g., "I expect that Amazon.com will keep promises they make"), and benevolence (e.g., "I expect that Amazon.com has good intentions toward me"). Analysis of the results showed that these concepts are reliable, statistically independent, and valid for predicting past shopping behavior and future intentions.

## Bhattacherjee's Model of Trust

Bhattacherjee took a different approach and focused on the antecedents and consequences of trust for e-commerce situations.[45] That model consists of three components and, like many others, Bhattacherjee uses a flow diagram to illustrate the proposed relationship between the components, illustrated in Figure 5-1. The component of *familiarity* is defined as knowledge of the trustee based on prior interactions or experiences. Trust is assumed to be made up of beliefs in ability, benevolence, and integrity, based again on the pioneering work of Mayer *et al.* In this model, familiarity can lead to trust, which in turn can lead to a *willingness to transact*. In addition, familiarity can lead to a willingness to transact directly, even without feelings of trust. Such a situation might occur if a customer continues to transact with a vendor out of habit or convenience, even though there may be a lack of trust. Like Gefen, Bhattacherjee developed questionnaire items to operationalize each of the components in the model, and then demonstrated in an empirical study that the concepts were related in the expected statistical manner.

43 R. C. Mayer, J. H. Davis, and F. D. Schoorman, "An Integrative Model of Organizational Trust," *Academy of Management Review* 20:3 (1995), 709–734.

44 D. Gefen, "Reflections on the Dimensions of Trust and Trustworthiness Among Online Consumers," *The DATA BASE for Advances in Information Systems* 33:3 (2002), 38–53.

45 A. Bhattacherjee, "Individual Trust in Online Firms: Seale Development and Initial Trust."

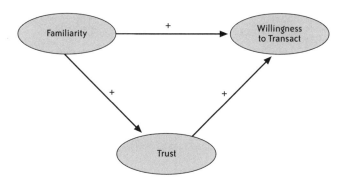

*FIGURE 5-1. Bhattacherjee's model of trust*

## Lee, Kim, and Moon's Model of Trust

A similar model of trust for e-commerce was developed by Lee, Kim, and Moon.[46] The model, illustrated in Figure 5-2, also describes antecedents to trust, this time focusing on three concepts: *comprehensive information, shared values*, and *communication*. In a way, these antecedents are describing the things that might be learned in the familiarity component proposed by Bhattacherjee, so the two models are similar in that respect. What makes the Lee *et al.* model unique is the addition of a *transaction cost* component that is seen as being in opposition to trust. In this model, trust and cost are combined, in opposite directions, when customers make their decisions about e-commerce behaviors (in this case, customer loyalty). Lee, Kim, and Moon describe three antecedents to transaction cost: *uncertainty*, the *number of competitors*, and *specificity* (the nature of the store or transaction).

This model is important because it describes both trust and cost as being independent, opposing factors. According to the model, customers will choose to continue a relationship with a vendor if factors leading to trust are strong and factors leading to transaction costs are weak. We have recently adapted the model to replace transaction costs with the more general concept of perceived risk, and found it to be useful for explaining trust in a different domain.[47]

## Corritore's Model of Trust

Corritore *et al.* also included trust and risk in their model (see Figure 5-3), although they proposed that increased perceptions of risk lead to decreased trust, instead of having trust and risk be independent factors.[48] This model also includes perceptions of *credibility* as a concept related to risk, and as we have seen, assessments of credibility are seen to be related to perceptions of honesty, expertise, predictability, and reputation. Corritore *et al.* also include *ease of use* in their model, and this is meant to measure how easy it is for a truster to achieve his goals (e.g., find the desired goods or complete the transaction). They propose that ease of

46 Lee, Kim, and Moon.

47 Patrick.

48 Corritore *et al.*

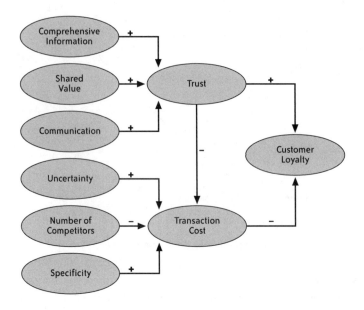

FIGURE 5-2. Lee, Kim, and Moon's model of trust

use affects both credibility and perceptions of risk. Finally, this model also includes *external factors* that might affect a trust judgment. Such external factors include the environment or context of the transaction, the characteristics of the truster (e.g., a risk-seeking or risk-averse personality), the characteristics of the trustee (e.g., web site design), and the overall risk related to the transaction (e.g., the amount of money involved).

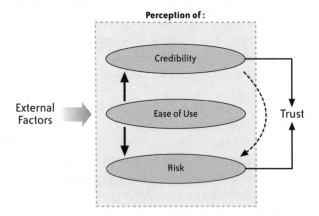

FIGURE 5-3. Corritore et al.'s model of trust

## Egger's Model of Trust

In another model of trust in e-commerce situations, Egger also proposed an important role for external factors.[49] In Egger's MoTEC model (see Figure 5-4), *pre-interactional filters* are included to describe those factors in place before any transaction takes place. Included in this concept are factors such as the truster's disposition to trust, prior knowledge or experience, information and attitudes transferred from others (friends, the media, etc.), the reputation of the industry and company involved, and trust in information technologies and the Internet in general.

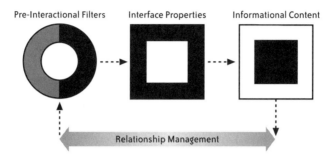

FIGURE 5-4. *Egger's MoTEC model of trust*

Two other important concepts in Egger's model are special roles for *interface properties* and *informational content*. Egger argues that interface properties, such as the visual appearance caused by graphic and visual designs, are important for creating first impressions that affect trust. Egger describes how trusters new to a situation or transaction make rapid assessments based on superficial cues about the usability, navigation, and reliability of an e-commerce application or web site. Later, the trusters may pay attention to the informational content in a slower, secondary phase of trust judgments. Here, trusters assess competence and risk as they learn more about the transaction. Finally, MoTEC includes a *relationship management* component to explain the trust that may build up over time. Here, trusters assess the responsiveness and helpfulness of a vendor, and how well transactions are completed over time, including fulfillment and after-sales support. In this way, Egger proposes a three-stage model of trust:

1. Rapid, superficial trust based on interface properties
2. Slower, reasoned trust based on an analysis of information content
3. Relationship trust based on a history of transactions

## McKnight's Model of Trust

Taking into account the different models of trust described so far, each one proposing both common and distinct features or components, it is not surprising that there have been some attempts to build larger, more comprehensive models of trust. For example,

49 Egger.

McKnight and his colleagues[50] have developed a relatively complex model that includes many of the components proposed before (see Figure 5-5). This model outlines antecedent factors to trust in an e-commerce situation. Included are the factors of *disposition to trust* and trust in technology and the Internet (*institution-based trust*), as we have seen before. The model also includes the various attributes of a trustee, such as competence, integrity, and benevolence, which can contribute to *trusting beliefs*. One unique feature of the McKnight model is the distinction between *trusting intentions* and *trusting behaviors*. This is an important distinction because, although the theory of planned behavior[51] states that actions follow intentions, research shows that this is not always the case. It is one thing to state that you intend to do something (trust a vendor), but it may be quite another to actually do it. Very little trust research has actually measured true trusting behaviors, such as having trusters spend their own money in e-commerce transactions.

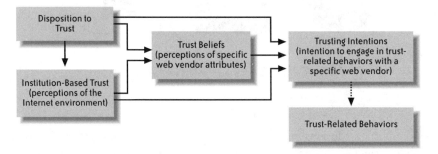

*FIGURE 5-5. McKnight et al.'s proposed web-trust model*

McKnight and his colleagues have also made their concepts concrete by operationalizing them. Specific question topics for each concept are shown in Table 5-1, and questionnaires have been developed to ask trusters about each of these areas. As others have done, McKnight *et al.* have tested these questionnaires and shown that the concepts hold the statistic relationships that were predicted.

50 McKnight *et al.*, "Developing and Validating Trust Measures for E-Commerce: An Integrative Typology"; D. H. McKnight and N. L. Chervany, "What Trust Means in E-Commerce Customer Relationships: An Interdisciplinary Conceptual Typology."

51 I. Ajzen, "The Theory of Planned Behavior," *Organizational Behavior and Human Decision Processes* 50 (1991), 179–211.

TABLE 5-1. McKnight et al.'s operationalization of trust concepts

| | Dispositional | Structural | Interpersonal | | |
| --- | --- | --- | --- | --- | --- |
| | | | Perceptual | Intentional | Behavioral |
| Conceptual Level | Disposition to Trust | Institution-Based Trust | Trusting Beliefs | Trusting Intentions | Trust-Related Behavior |
| Operational Level | • Faith in humanity<br>• Trusting stance | • Structural assurance<br>• Situational normality | • Competence<br>• Benevolence<br>• Integrity<br>• Predictability | • Willingness to depend<br>• Subjective probability of depending | • Cooperation<br>• Information sharing<br>• Informal agreements<br>• Decreasing controls<br>• Accepting influence<br>• Granting autonomy<br>• Transacting business |

## Riegelsberger's Model of Trust

Another attempt at a comprehensive model has recently been described by Riegelsberger *et al.*[52] This model is somewhat different in that it focuses on the incentives for trustworthy behavior rather than on opinions and beliefs about trust or perceptions of trustworthiness. This model (see Figure 5-6) describes the trust situation for both the truster and the trustee. Both the truster and the trustee can choose to interact by performing *trusting actions* (truster) and *fulfilling promises* (trustee), or they can *withdraw* or *not fulfill*. Riegelsberger *et al.* describe what factors play a role in the decisions to take trusting actions and fulfill promises.

The first step in the model is for the actors to communicate by sending *signals* about a desire to interact. Often the situation is complex because the actors are *separated in space* (e.g., e-commerce buyers and sellers) and the actions are *separated in time* (e.g., delivery delays for e-commerce goods). Thus, signals can be important for showing trust-warranting properties. Signals are a method to demonstrate important intrinsic properties, such as benevolence, and they allow the actors to infer motivations and abilities.

Riegelsberger *et al.* also include contextual factors in their model (see Figure 5-7), including temporal, social, and institutional properties. Social properties include things like reputation, while the institutional context is meant to convey things like the assurance given by job roles (e.g., bank tellers), regulations, and threats of punishment. This is similar to the *situation normality* concept included in the McKnight model. Riegelsberger *et al.* also describe different stages of trust that develop over time, and they discuss early, medium, and mature forms of trust. These concepts are not included in their model diagrams, however.

52 Jens Riegelsberger, M. Angela Sasse, and John D. McCarthy, "The Mechanics of Trust: A Framework for Research and Design," *International Journal of Human Computer Studies* 62:3 (2005), 381–422.

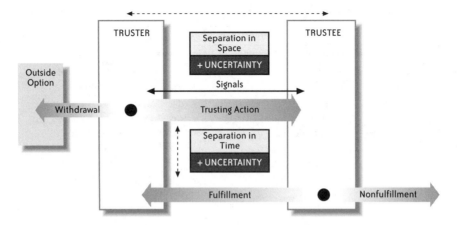

FIGURE 5-6. Riegelsberger et al.'s proposed trust situation

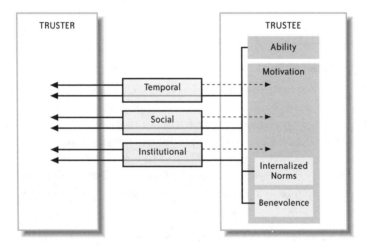

FIGURE 5-7. Riegelsberger et al.'s proposed trust-warranting properties

## Looking at the Models

What are we to make of all these models? Although they may all seem quite different, there are some common themes among them. More importantly, the research on the models can lead to specific advice to developers who want to build a trusted service:

- Developers may learn that trust concepts can be operationalized into specific attributes or questions that can be examined in research and designs.

- One of the key findings is that trust seems to be related to beliefs about another's ability, integrity, and benevolence.

- Trust and risk are related concepts, and factors that reduce risk perceptions (e.g., reducing uncertainty) may be beneficial for increasing trust or decreasing the need for trust.

- Ease-of-use characteristics, such as the ease of finding information and completing transactions, may affect trust.

- External factors or context that may seem to be unrelated to the situation may affect trust, such as the characteristics of the truster and the type of risk involved in the transaction.

- Trust probably develops in stages. In the first stage, superficial interface properties, such as colors and designs, may have a large effect on initial trust decisions. Later, users may make trust decisions based on more reasoned analysis of information. Eventually, long-term trust decisions are based on direct experience and personal service.

---

## TRUST DESIGN GUIDELINES

The trust models presented here have been developed with a view to making it easier for designers to identify those elements capable of promoting trust and those capable of destroying it. We have developed a composite set of trust guidelines, extracted from the literature. The order of the various guidelines suggests the point at which they are influential in interaction. Thus, the lower-numbered factors are likely to influence snap judgments made within seconds of visiting a site, and the higher-numbered factors are likely to come into play in the longer term.

1. Ensure good ease of use.
2. Use attractive design.
3. Create a professional image—avoid spelling mistakes and other simple errors.
4. Don't mix advertising and content—avoid sales pitches and banner advertisements.
5. Convey a "real-world" look and feel—for example, with the use of high-quality photographs of real places and people.
6. Maximize the consistency, familiarity, or predictability of an interaction both in terms of process and visually.
7. Include seals of approval such as TRUSTe.
8. Provide explanations, justifying the advice or information given.
9. Include independent peer evaluation such as references from past and current users and independent message boards.
10. Provide clearly stated security and privacy statements, and also rights to compensation and returns.
11. Include alternative views, including good links to independent sites within the same business area.
12. Include background information such as indicators of expertise and patterns of past performance.
13. Clearly assign responsibilities (to the vendor and the customer).
14. Ensure that communication remains open and responsive, and offer order tracking or an alternative means of getting in touch.
15. Offer a personalized service that takes account of each client's needs and preferences and reflects its social identity.

---

## Trust Designs

There are some examples available of successful designs that have promoted trust in online users. For example, gambling over the Internet using an off-shore, unregulated casino is an act that requires a great deal of trust. Such sites require that the gambler trust the casino operator to provide fair odds and to handle money securely and properly. Shelat and Egger examined factors that online gamblers use when deciding to trust Internet gambling sites.[53] Conducted within the framework of the MoTEC model, the study revealed that:

- Informational content was the most important factor. People were most trusting when they could easily find information about the casino, its staff, and its policies.

- The second most important factor was relationship management, and trust-building attributes were an ability to contact the casino and rapid, high-quality responses and payments.

- The third most important factor was interface properties, which included usability and the ease of finding information.

- Pre-interactional factors were the least important, with a positive attitude toward gambling being the most important determinant of trust in this category.

As noted earlier, one of the greatest success stories in terms of designing trust into a system is eBay. A number of trust design factors have been identified by Boyd,[54] including those listed next.

- The use of a simple reputation system in which buyers and sellers give feedback about each other regarding issues such as promptness of payment.

- The use of bulletin boards to reinforce the sense of community and to police undesired behavior.

- A clear status system that relates not only to feedback but also to longevity with the vendor. This is reinforced with the use of icons such as the prestigious "shooting star"— an icon posted next to the usernames of people with a feedback rating of more than 10,000.

Reputation systems are in operation in many sites, but Boyd notes that such design elements are cleverly worked into the community elements of eBay to reinforce the sense that its members genuinely help to build the company and are part of an "in group" of people engaged in an exciting venture.

---

53 B. Shelat and Florian Egger, "What Makes People Trust Online Gambling Sites?" *Proceedings of the Conference on Human Factors in Computing Systems, 2002 Extended Abstracts* (2002), 852–853.

54 J. Boyd, "In Community We Trust: Online Security Communication at eBay," *Journal of Computer-Mediated Communication* 7:3 (2002); *http://www.ascusc.org/jcmc/vol7/issue3/boyd.html*.

Another example of a trusted design is the study that investigated the factors that lead to trust in online health advice.[55] This study examined the design factors that led a group of menopausal women to place their trust in sites that offered advice regarding hormone replacement therapy (HRT). The researchers found that most of the women preferred sites that were run by reputable organizations or had a medical or expert feel about them. They trusted the information on such web sites, especially when the credentials of the site and its authors were made explicit. Sites that indicated that the advice originated from a similar individual were also well received. Most participants showed some distrust of the advice and information on web sites sponsored by pharmaceutical companies or those explicitly selling products. One of the most trusted sites was "Project Aware"—a "web site by women for women." This site is split into menopause stage–specific areas, covers a wide variety of relevant topics, and provides links to original research materials. The language is clear and simple, and the layout is easy on the eye. Most importantly, however, the site establishes clear social identity signals, similar to those described for eBay, that tell readers that they are members of a community and part of the in group.

One point worth making about successful trust designs, however, is that they are only as trustworthy as the people who use them, and trusted people can fail to be trustworthy, particularly when interacting with supposedly secure systems.[56] Trust design features do not in themselves guarantee a trustworthy system, and no amount of design work can compensate for a careless or malicious user. The phishing examples described at the beginning of this chapter provide food for thought—these attacks capitalize on our willingness to trust messages adorned with familiar and seemingly secure logos. Orgill *et al.* describe such "social engineering" attacks and argue that ultimately user education will provide the best defense.[57] Certainly, few users seem to fully evaluate the trustworthiness of different systems, even though they are influenced by the design factors described earlier.

## Future Research Directions

We began this chapter with a discussion of some of the reasons why considerations of trust will be important for future privacy and security systems. Let us end the chapter with some explicit considerations of the trust issues raised by future technologies. We know that researchers and developers are increasingly excited about the concept of *Ambient Intelligence* (AmI). This term, first coined by the Advisory Group to the European Community's Information Society Technology Programme (ISTAG), refers to the convergence of ubiquitous computing, ubiquitous communication, and interfaces that are both socially aware and capable of adapting to the needs and preferences of the user. It evokes a near future in

---

55 Sillence *et al.*

56 Gregory L. Orgill, Gordon W. Romney, Michael G. Bailey, and Paul M. Orgill, "The Urgency for Effective User Privacy-Education to Counter Social Engineering Attacks on Secure Computer Systems," *Proceedings of the 5th Conference on Information Technology Education* (2004), 177–181.

57 *Ibid.*

which humans will be surrounded by "always-on," unobtrusive, interconnected intelligent objects, few of which will bear any resemblance to the computing devices of today.

One of the particular challenges of AmI, which distinguishes it from many other developments, is that the user will be involved in huge numbers of moment-to-moment exchanges of personal data without explicitly sanctioning each transaction. Today we already carry around devices (mobile phones, personal digital assistants) that exchange personal information with other devices, but we initiate most exchanges ourselves. In the future, devices embedded in the environment, and potentially in the body, will use software agents to communicate seamlessly about any number of different things: our present state of health, our preferences for what to eat, our schedule, our credentials, our destination, our need for a taxi to get us there in 10 minutes. Agent technologies will be required to manage the flow of information, and a great deal of exciting technical work is ongoing in this field. But many privacy and security concerns remain unanswered. How might we instruct these agents about when, where, and to whom certain intensely personal details can be released?

We are involved in several new research projects that address these issues, and some things have become clear:

- User engagement in such technologies is crucial if we are to ensure a future devoid of suspicion and paranoia, but most users don't understand the complex technologies at issue here, and so new research methods inviting proper participation are required.

- It is not enough to simply ask people about trust, privacy, or security in the abstract, because what people say and what they do are two different things.

- Our future will be one in which many decisions are taken on our behalf by trusted third parties, so a great deal more information is required about the prerequisites for trust in regulatory bodies and agents. As we've already noted, a great deal of information is available concerning building and breaking trust in e-commerce, yet only very sparse literature is available on the ways in which people come to trust third parties in a mediated exchange. The time is right for a proper agenda for trust research with specific respect to security and privacy systems, as opposed to only e-commerce. A related issue concerns the transfer of trust from one agent to another, and recommender systems provide some interesting insights into this issue, particularly concerning the kinds of networks that support the transfer of trust from one individual to another.

- We need to know a great deal more about what happens following loss of trust. From what we know already, it seems that loss of trust can be quite catastrophic in a one-to-one relationship, but how does it percolate throughout a network of agents, each with its own set of trust indices? Such questions will be crucial for the development of privacy and security systems that people can genuinely trust.

# About the Authors

 Andrew S. Patrick is a Senior Scientist at the National Research Council of Canada and an Adjunct Research Professor at Carleton University. He is currently conducting research on the human factors of security systems, trust decisions in privacy and e-commerce contexts, and advanced collaboration environments. Dr. Patrick holds a Ph.D. in Cognitive Psychology from the University of Western Ontario.

*http://www.andrewpatrick.ca/*

 Professor Pamela Briggs currently holds a Chair in Applied Cognitive Psychology and the position of Acting Dean in the School of Psychology and Sport Sciences at the University of Northumbria, Newcastle upon Tyne, U.K. She also is Director of the PACT Lab—a new research laboratory for the investigation of Psychological Aspects of Communication Technologies. She has worked as a consultant for multinational organizations, and her most recent work on trust and privacy issues in computer-mediated communication is funded by the Economic and Social Research Council's E-Society initiative.

 Steve Marsh is a Research Officer at the National Research Council's Institute for Information Technology (NRC-IIT), and is based in Moncton and Fredericton, New Brunswick. He is the Research Lead for IIT's Privacy, Security and Trust initiative. His research interests include trust, HCI, socially adept technologies, artificial life, multi-agent systems, social computers, complex adaptive systems, critical infrastructure interdependencies, and advanced collaborative environments.

*http://www.stephenmarsh.ca/*

PART TWO   AUTHENTICATION
MECHANISMS

# CHAPTER SIX

# Evaluating Authentication Mechanisms

**KAREN RENAUD**

**T**HE END USER PLAYS A VITAL ROLE IN ACHIEVING SYSTEM SECURITY. If a security system is designed to accommodate the average user's needs and limitations, it is more likely that the system will succeed. Bear in mind that computer users are primarily goal directed and engaged in carrying out some task—and that maintaining security is usually not an integral part of that task. Hence, security systems are sometimes seen as an intrusion to be dealt with as quickly as possible so that users can continue with their primary task. Jonathan Grudin[1] found that humans would subvert any technology that did not directly benefit them in a group-based technological environment. This finding appears to apply to authentication mechanisms too: people often work around these mechanisms, which are put there explicitly to protect them, because they do not fully understand the benefits that will accrue from observation of security guidelines. Of course, security mechanisms *do* benefit end users, but they sometimes have a limited understanding of the whole security arena and do not have an insight into the benefits of taking the time to behave securely.

---

1  J. Grudin, "Social Evaluation of User Interfaces. Who Does the Work and Who Gets the Benefit?" in H-J Bullinger and B. Shackel (eds.), *Proceedings of INTERACT 1987 IFIP Conference on Human Computer Interaction* (Elsevier,1987), 805–811.

Password-based authentication is currently the most common authentication mechanism, but passwords are notoriously weak, mostly because of human information-processing limitations. People have too many passwords and PINs to remember, so they resort invariably to choosing easily remembered weak passwords, writing down the strong passwords, or using the same password with multiple accounts. All of these strategies weaken the password authentication mechanism.

Biometrics is another common authentication mechanism. Besides being usually more expensive than passwords, biometrics is also somewhat unreliable because human beings are, by their very nature, variable. For example, fingerprint readers can misread if given dirty or damaged fingers; they can also be confused by users who don't place their fingers correctly on the reader. Some biometrics can also be readily compromised; for example, people can also unknowingly leave enough skin oil residue on the reader to enable an attacker to duplicate their fingerprints.

This chapter provides an overview of the different authentication mechanisms and proposes a technique for comparing these mechanisms to support developers in making an informed choice for their systems.

## Authentication

Security systems are designed to let authorized people in (the *permission* problem), and to keep unauthorized people out (the *prevention* problem[2]). This involves three distinct steps: identification, authentication, and authorization.

- *Identification*. The identification step asks a person to identify himself—usually by means of a token or an identification string such as an email address or account number.

- *Authentication*. Once the identification token has been tendered, the person will have to provide evidence of his identity—the authentication step.

- *Authorization*. Authorization allows an authenticated person to take a set of actions once permission has been granted.

People authenticate themselves by what they *know (memometrics[3])*, by what they *recognize (cognometrics)*, by what they *hold*, or by what they *are (biometrics)* (see Figure 6-1). In the case of the first three, the system and the person share a secret[4] (the authentication key). At enrollment, the user and the system agree on what the secret is; at authentication time, the system determines whether the person being authenticated has possession of the pre-agreed secret. If the user proves knowledge of the secret, the system will authenticate her. In the case of biometrics, the system records a digital representation of some aspect of a person's physiology or behavior at enrollment, and this is confirmed at authentication time.

---

2   B. Schneier, "Sensible Authentication," *ACM Queue* 1 (2004), 74–78.

3   Nomenclature introduced by *http://www.realuser.com/technology/*.

4   R. E. Smith, *Authentication: From Passwords to Public Keys* (Reading, MA: Addison Wesley, 2002).

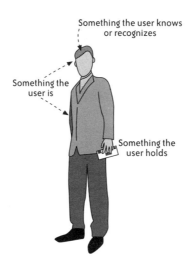

Something the user knows
or recognizes

Something the
user is

Something the
user holds

*FIGURE 6-1. Authentication types*

Many authentication scenarios can be strengthened through the use of *public key cryptography*. For example, a user can have a *smart card* that contains a *public key* and a matching *private key*. Instead of a password, the user's public key can be placed on file at the remote computer system. To authenticate the user, the remote computer sends the user a random *challenge*. The user signs the challenge with his private key and sends the result back to the remote server, which verifies the signature with the public key that is on file. In this way, the remote system can verify that the user has possession of the private key without ever having to receive it. Instead of having the public key on file at the remote system, the smart card can submit both the signed challenge and a *public key certificate* that has been signed by a third party. In this case, the use of public key technology is called *PKI* (*public key infrastructure*).

One way to think about authentication systems based on public key cryptography is that the user must authenticate himself to a local system (the smart card) through the use of a password, a biometrics, or mere possession. The card then authenticates itself to a remote system using public key cryptography. Because the remote system believes that the smart card is reliable, the remote system trusts the card's assertion that the subject has been properly authenticated. This is an example of *transitive trust*.

Figure 6-2 depicts the entities involved in the authentication process. At each stage of the process it is possible for an attacker to gain access to the authentication key. Cryptographic techniques can be used effectively to protect transmission of the key over the network, key handling at the server, and key storage in the file store. The real areas of vulnerability are the input mechanism and the user. In the case of knowledge-based authentication, the user has to keep a secret, something people are mostly not very good at doing. A secret can be told, discovered, or stolen if the user records it physically. Users may tell someone their secret either because they have been tricked or forced into doing so, or because they don't understand the possible consequences of sharing it. Even if the user does not reveal her key prior to authenticating, it is still possible for it to be discovered, either because the user can be observed during the key entry process (if she has chosen a secret that is easy to guess) or because the key may be duplicated by an attacker interfering with the input mechanism.

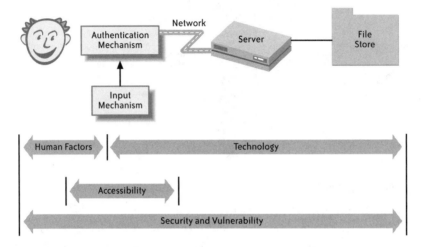

FIGURE 6-2. Entities involved in the authentication process

Clearly security cannot be solved in a purely technical way because the user forms an integral part of the system. The following subsections discuss the areas pertinent to a user-centered approach to authentication: accessibility barriers, human factors, security, and context and environment.

### Accessibility Barriers

Particular authentication mechanisms can disenfranchise users based on disabilities or limitations they may have. Examples of accessibility barriers are:

- *Physical.* Some authentication mechanisms rely on the ability to use a mouse, which can severely affect users with a variety of physical disabilities.

- *Cognitive.* Examples of the kinds of disabilities to be considered are dyslexia, dyspraxia, or reduced memory skills. Dyslexia affects a user's ability to work with text, and dyspraxia affects the user's ability to remember and execute sequences of actions in the right order. Users with reduced memory skills may find it difficult to correctly recall a knowledge-based authentication key.

- *Sensory.* For example, authentication mechanisms that rely on visual acuity are a problem not only for blind users but also for aging users.

- *Technical.* For example, authentication mechanisms that require large amounts of data to be exchanged may be inconvenient for users accessing a system via modem. Likewise, those that require users to recognize graphical images may be inaccessible to users accessing a system via a small mobile device.

## Human Factors

Because many authentication mechanisms require cognitive activity, it is important to consider human information-processing characteristics and memory limitations that will directly determine the success of any knowledge-based mechanism.

Figure 6-3 demonstrates how humans process the information they receive from their senses, which is interpreted in terms of previous experience. The information passes from the sensory short-term storage to primary memory if the person is paying attention. The information in primary memory will be transferred to long-term memory only by further processing and encoding. This processing usually entails the organization of the new information in terms of previously encoded information, or the categorization or other encoding of the new material. The quality of the encoding is vitally important because it has a direct effect on the ease with which a user remembers the item later. To remember the item the user has to have some "hooks" that he can use to extract the item again—encoding links the new item to these hooks, which are usually called *cues*.

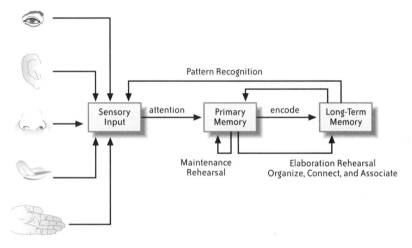

*FIGURE 6-3. Memory and information processing*

A nonmeaningful item can be learned effectively if the person puts some effort into learning it, but it will frequently decay within 30 days.[5] Sometimes, however, an item can be made meaningful by linking it to a previously learned item, which has established hooks. An example of a meaningful item in authentication is the use of a well-established knowledge item, such as a family birthday, as a PIN. Another way of linking is the definition of a *process* that allows *deduction* of the item. An example of a deduction-based item is a user who has a scheme by which he uses the name of the first item he purchases from any e-commerce site as the password. For example, the first book he purchased from Amazon

---

5  H. Ebbinghaus, *Memory: A Contribution to Experimental Psychology* (New York: Dover Publications, 1964). Translated by H. A. Ruger and C. E. Bussenius. Originally published 1885.

was *Jane Eyre,* so when he needs to log into Amazon in the future, he remembers that, and types JaneEyre as the password.

There are three ways that a person can remember an item:

- *Uncued recall.* With no assistance, it is up to the user to extract the item from memory, which is why a meaningful or deducible item with established hooks or processes makes things much easier.

- *Cued recall.* The person is given a cue and uses it to extract the item from memory. Cues, such as re-establishment of context, can support recall,[6] making it easier to remember the stored item.

- *Recognition.* The person is shown the item and then has to confirm whether this is the previously encoded item. This is the best possible cued-recall situation,[7] but recognition must be used with caution in authentication because one has to factor in the effects of guessing.

A stored item can be forgotten as a result of decay or fading, interference from other similar items in memory,[8] or simply because it gets lost—perhaps because it was not encoded in the person's memory with sufficient hooks to enable extraction when required. The first category of remembering makes forgetting much more likely. Computer users, only too aware of this, react by making authentication keys meaningful to ease remembering, which unfortunately increases predictability and compromises security. Predictability is exacerbated by the provision of cues so that in providing a cued recall or recognition-based authentication mechanism, one has to walk a fine line between helping the legitimate user to remember and giving an attacker enough cues to guess the key.

## Security

The authentication mechanism must be commensurate with the access being provided. Thus, access to a safety-critical system requires a much stronger authenticator than non-critical access to a shared resource. The authentication mechanism will therefore either make or break the security system and should be chosen with due forethought to support the kind of security required by the data being protected or the access being provided.

## Context and Environment

One also has to consider the effects of the environment. For example, some organizations have security policies that require regular renewal of knowledge-based authentication keys so that users have to repeatedly memorize new keys. This is often done to limit the

---

6  E. Tulving and S. Osler, "Effectiveness of Retrieval Cues in Memory for Words," *Journal of Experimental Psychology* 77 (1968), 593–601.

7  M. Eagle and E. Leiter, "Recall and Recognition in Intentional and Incidental Learning," *Journal of Experimental Psychology* 68 (1964), 58–63.

8  K. A. Ericsson and W. Kintsch, "Long-Term Working Memory," *Psychological Review* 102 (1995), 211–245.

damage that can be done by an impersonator if a key should be leaked, but the side effects of this policy are often far worse than the original problem—users react to forced changes by choosing predictable keys or by using the same key with a different suffix, to make it easier for them to remember the frequently changing key.

Another important factor is how often the user will use a system where he is authenticated by a knowledge-based key. If the system is used infrequently, it is even more important for the key to be memorable to counteract the inevitable decay problems of memory. One also has to take users' security motivation into account. Organizations can attempt to enforce good security practices, which should raise security awareness, but sometimes this can be counterproductive because users may simply become more inventive at getting around the system. Furthermore, overly restrictive policies can prevent users from averting disasters in unusual situations.[9]

Biometrics authentication mechanisms should be used with caution in an uncontrolled environment because of the potential for abuse of the mechanism, by attackers either masquerading or forcing legitimate users to authenticate to gain illegal access to the system.

## Authentication Mechanisms

This section discusses authentication mechanisms grouped according to whether they are based on what users *are*, what users *know*, what users *recognize*, or what users *hold*.

### What the User Is—Biometrics

Biometrics mechanisms (Figure 6-4) fall into two distinct categories:

- *Behavioral biometrics.* These can be based on mouse usage patterns, keystroke latencies or dynamics, or signature dynamics.

- *Physiological characteristics.* These can be based on fingerprints, voice, iris or retina, vein pattern, face, hand, or finger geometry, or even ear shape.

Biometrics, while appearing infallible, can actually suffer from some potentially insuperable flaws, depending on the actual biometrics. In the first place, they are easy to forge in an uncontrolled environment. For example, facial recognition systems can be fooled by a photograph of the individual held up to the camera—and in some cases, even by a drawing.

They also present problems in terms of convenience because the user's biometrics has to be captured securely at enrollment and at each authentication attempt, potentially a time-consuming process that requires a controlled environment to ensure that people are not being forced to authenticate themselves for someone else's benefit.

Biometrics are covered in more detail in Chapter 10.

---

9  D. Povey, "Optimistic Security: A New Access Control Paradigm," *Proceedings of the 1999 Workshop on New Security Paradigms* (ACM Press, 2000), 40–45.

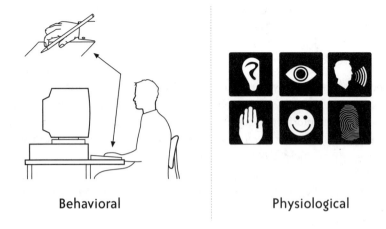

Behavioral                    Physiological

*FIGURE 6-4. Biometrics*

## What the User Knows—Memometrics

There are two types of passwords:

- *Random.* The random approach uses a random sequence of characters and digits (which may be generated randomly or selected by each user), and is called a *password* (if it is a word), a PIN (if it is composed only of digits), or a *passphrase* (if it consists of more than one word).

- *Cultural.* The cultural approach relies on the memory of a concept or a phrase, and is sometimes also called a *cognitive* or a *semantic* password.

### Random passwords (uncued recall)

Currently, the most pervasive and popular authentication mechanism is the random password. Passwords have the potential to be very secure, but this potential is seldom realized in the real world, especially in an uncontrolled environment such as the Web. There is evidence that users remember passwords better if they choose them,[10] and even though the system-assigned password will probably be stronger, most systems allow users either to choose their own passwords or to change a system-assigned password. The reason is that users frequently will resort to writing down random passwords that are difficult to remember.

Unfortunately, many end users do not choose strong passwords.[11] This is primarily a result of their being overloaded with too many passwords and PINs to remember. They choose easily guessed passwords and reuse those passwords out of self-defense; it is the only way

---

10 M. Zviran and W. J. Haga, "Cognitive Passwords: The Key to Easy Access Control," *Computers and Security* 9 (1990), 723–736.

11 A. McCue, "Is Your Cat a Target for Password-Stealing Hackers?" *Silicon.com* (Aug. 11, 2004); *http:// software.silicon.com/security/0,39024655,39123066,00.htm.*

to cope in a world that places increasing burdens on users without any consideration given to the cumulative effects of similar demands being placed upon them by other security systems. (For further discussion of password memorability, see Chapter 7.)

An example of the use of a passphrase is demonstrated by Spector and Ginzberg.[12] Their approach compensates for differences in syntax to determine whether users remember the semantics of the passphrase at authentication, even if the user has forgotten the actual words used at enrollment. This is a good alternative to passwords because it addresses both the memorability and the predictability issues, but it does require special software and is potentially more time consuming at authentication than simple passwords.

### Cultural passwords (cued recall)

Cultural passwords rely on a deductive process to produce the required password. This contrasts with random passwords, where any word or phrase will do; it is up to the user to make it meaningful in some way. Cultural passwords will typically present the user with a challenge question and obtain, in response, an answer, which requires some thought (see Figure 6-5). The theory is that the user will have fewer problems recalling these passwords because the cultural password requires recall of an established fact or opinion. However, it is not a secret in the strict sense of the word—opinions will have been shared, as will facts about the user's life. The design of these systems is nontrivial, as can be seen from the discussion in Chapter 8.

*FIGURE 6-5. Example of recognition-based graphical password (VIP)*

12 Y. Spector and J. Ginzberg, "Pass-Sentence—A New Approach to Computer Code," *Computers and Security* 13 (1994), 145–160.

Examples of this approach can be seen in the work of Zviran and Haga, who tested cognitive passwords in terms of memorability and predictability and found that they performed better than random passwords. Smith[13] proposes the use of word association during authentication, and Haskett[14] proposes the use of pass-algorithms where users respond to challenge questions based on the current algorithm, which is communicated to valid users only.

## What the User Recognizes—Cognometrics

The idea of graphical authentication relies on the knowledge that visual memory is extremely powerful. Classic cognitive scientific studies have shown that humans have a vast, almost limitless memory for pictures,[15] and visual memory does not seem to be significantly affected by the general decline of cognitive capabilities associated with aging.[16]

Graphical codes are becoming increasingly popular in personal technology. Two main approaches can be identified, involving different types of skills:

- *Recognition-based systems.*These require the user to select target pictures among a set of distractors. This approach relies on pure visual memory, and exploits the ability to recognize previously seen visual objects among others.

- *Position-based systems.* These require the user to identify target objects within an individual picture, or to draw a previously drawn object on a grid. This approach relies on both the visual and the spatial aspects of the visuo-spatial memory, and on precise movements.

### Recognition-based systems

Example recognition-based systems are Passfaces,[17] Déjà Vu,[18] and the Visual Identification Protocol (VIP).[19] They all follow the same paradigm—identify target images among distractors—but use very different visual stimuli. Passfaces uses faces, Déjà Vu uses abstract art, and VIP uses simple representative images. The user clicks on a sequence of

13 S. Smith, "Authenticating Users by Word Association," *Proceedings of the Human Factors Society—31st Annual Meeting* (1987), 135–138.

14 J. A. Haskett, "Pass-Algorithms: A User Validation Scheme Based on Knowledge of Secret Algorithms," *Communications of the ACM* 27 (1984), 777–781.

15 A. Madigan, "Picture Memory," in J. C. Yuille (ed.), *Imagery, Memory and Cognition: Essays in Honour of Allan Paivio* (Erlbaum, 1983).

16 D. C. Park, "Aging and Memory: Mechanisms Underlying Age Differences in Performance," *Proceedings of the 1997 World Congress of Gerontology* (1997).

17 S. Brostoff and A. Sasse, "Are Passfaces More Usable Than Passwords? A Field Trial Investigation," in *People and Computers XIV—Usability or Else! Proceedings of HCI 2000*, S. McDonald (ed.), (Springer, 2000), 405–424

18 R. Dhamija and A. Perrig, "Déjà Vu: A User Study Using Images for Authentication," *Proceedings of USENIX 'Security Symposium* (2000).

19 A. De Angeli, M. Coutts, L. Coventry, and G. I. Johnson, "VIP: A Visual Approach to User Authentication," *Proceedings of the Working Conference on Advanced Visual Interfaces* (AVI, 2002), 316–323.

images in much the same way as she would click on a sequence of numbers on a PIN pad, as shown in Figure 6-6.

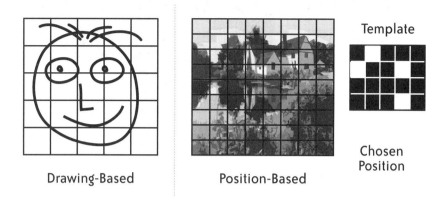

*FIGURE 6-6. Example of cultural passwords*

Initial results for many of these systems are encouraging, but evaluations suggest that design issues for this kind of authentication mechanism are not yet fully understood. Graphical passwords are discussed further in Chapter 9.

### Position-based systems

The original approach to graphical authentication relied on different types of position-based systems. In 1996, Blonder patented a graphical password that required the user to touch predetermined areas of an image in a fixed sequence for authentication.[20] Further work in this area, illustrated in Figure 6-7, can be seen in Draw-a-Secret by Jermyn *et al.*[21], which requires the user to reproduce a previously drawn picture, and Jiminy,[22] which requires the user to position a colored template onto an image with a grid superimposed over it in order to reveal a PIN or password.

### What the User Holds

Authentication can be based on something the customer holds. Such an object is typically called a *token*.

A good example of a token is the SecureID manufactured by RSA Security.[23] The token contains a lock and a secret key. The two are combined by a cryptographic function to produce a numeric code that is displayed on the token's LCD display. To authenticate herself,

20 G. E. Blonder, "Graphical Password," U.S. Patent 5559961, 1996.

21 I. Jermyn, A. Mayer, F. Monrose, M. K. Reuter, and A. D. Rubin, "The Design and Analysis of Graphical Passwords," *Proceedings of the 9th USENIX Security Symposium* (2000).

22 K. V. Renaud and A. De Angeli, "My password Is Here! Investigating Authentication Schemes Based on Visuo-Spatial Memory," *Interacting with Computers* (2005). To appear.

23 *http://www.rsasecurity.com.*

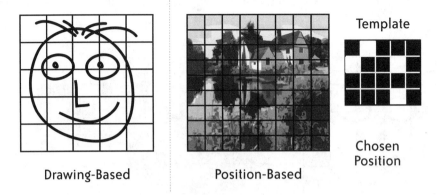

Template

Chosen
Position

Drawing-Based          Position-Based

*FIGURE 6-7. Examples of drawing-based and position-based graphical passwords*

a SecureID user types the displayed number at a prompt. The authenticating server also knows the time of day and the secret stored in the user's token. The server performs the same cryptographic function. If the computed value matches the value that the user entered, the user is assumed to be in possession of the token.

Another good example is the Universal Serial Bus (USB) authentication token, which contains a smart card chip and a smart card reader. These devices typically contain a private key, a public key, and a certificate issued by a certification authority. The remote system issues a challenge to the token to verify that the user in fact has control of the matching private key. Next, the system consults a database to verify that the name on the certificate corresponds to an identity that is authorized to have access. The usability of these devices is discussed in Chapter 12.

Tokens can be provided by either hardware or software devices. The hardware token has a lifetime battery and displays a security code on an LCD display. The software token runs on the user's personal machine, with the user's key being stored securely on the desktop computer rather than on the hardware token.

Although such hardware devices offer security benefits over regular passwords, they do have some disadvantages. The devices have an associated cost, which may make them less viable than other mechanisms. The user also has to remember to carry the hardware token. If users have many relationships that require the use of hardware tokens, transporting all of these tokens may prove somewhat onerous. Furthermore, users need some way of remembering which token to use for different systems. Software tokens alleviate these problems by storing keys on the user's own computer, but this binds the user to that machine when accessing a particular system: software tokens are also less secure than hardware tokens, because the user's computer may be compromised.

Finally, some token-based systems may require that the user remember a PIN, which has all the problems related to uncued recall discussed in the previous section.

## Two-Factor Authentication

The chances of an erroneous positive authentication can be reduced by requiring that users perform multiple authentications with different systems in order to gain access. The most common strategy is known as *two-factor authentication* because it combines two systems. This allows each system to make up for the other's weakness.

For example, token-based authentication systems are commonly combined with passwords. This protects the user against compromise by a lost token (because the attacker will not know the password) and compromise by a stolen password (because the attacker will not have the token). Two-factor authentication also complicates usability, because the user must now remember both her password *and* the token.

While two-factor authentication works well against many kinds of security compromises, these systems can also be circumvented by a sufficiently motivated attacker. Against some kinds of attacks, two-factor authentication provides little increased security at all. For example, ATM machines use two-factor authentication: they require that a bank depositor both *have* an ATM card and *know* a password in order to withdraw money. But these two factors do not offer increased protection to a depositor who has been kidnapped and is forced at gunpoint to both hand over the ATM card and reveal the password.

## Quality Criteria

Authentication mechanisms often have deficiencies in one or more areas. To support meaningful comparison of authentication mechanisms, we propose a set of evaluation criteria that can be used to assign relative deficiency values to each authentication mechanism. Once these values have been assigned, the characteristics of the environment within which the authentication mechanism will be used are identified and used to group the criteria into four different groups—*critical, vital, significant*, and *incidental*—indicating their relative importance to the developer. The assigned deficiency values in each group can then be used to support an informed decision as to which authentication mechanism to use in a particular situation.

Three fundamental authentication mechanism deficiency categories can be isolated from the previous discussion: *accessibility, memorability,* and *security*. A *cost* category will also be included, because a cost-benefit analysis is part of any decision process. Each of these categories has several dimensions, which are discussed in the following sections. In our discussion, we describe how these criteria can be applied generally to several types of authentication mechanisms. The deficiency values for specific instances of each of these mechanisms may be somewhat different. However, after reading this section, you should be able to use these criteria to evaluate any authentication mechanism yourself.

### Accessibility

Figure 6-8 depicts the various aspects of this dimension, which reflects how easy it is for users to use a particular authentication mechanism. The aspects are described in the list that follows.

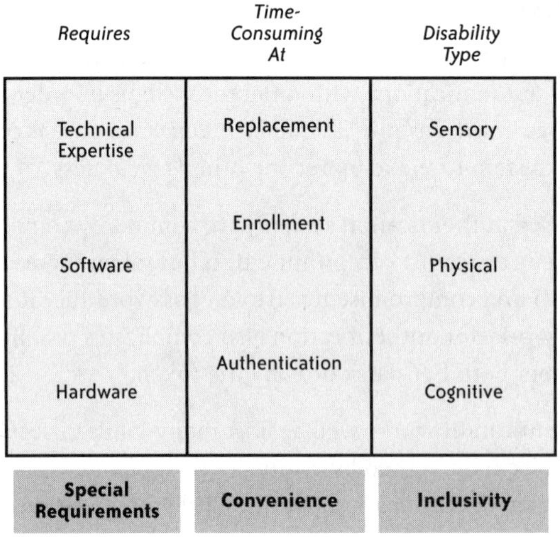

| Requires | Time-Consuming At | Disability Type |
|---|---|---|
| Technical Expertise | Replacement | Sensory |
| Software | Enrollment | Physical |
| Hardware | Authentication | Cognitive |
| **Special Requirements** | **Convenience** | **Inclusivity** |

FIGURE 6-8. Accessibility

*Special hardware and software requirements*

This aspect refers to the minimum hardware, software, or technical expertise required to support the authentication mechanism. If only one of these is required at the user's machine, only a minor deficit can be applied; if two are required, it is obviously more serious; and if all are required, it can be considered to be a major deficit.

Many authentication systems can have special requirements. Most obvious are biometrics such as fingerprint- or iris-based identification, which naturally requires a fingerprint or iris scanner. On the other hand, biometrics systems such as voice recognition or identification by keystroke dynamics can often be performed using standard PC hardware. And biometrics or smart card readers may be built into the terminal used by the target population—for example, there are mobile phones with integrated fingerprint or smart card readers—and thus the special requirements may not pose any problems at all.

Even a token-based authentication system that displays a code may require that the server be equipped with special software or hardware to verify the tokens. Smart cards further require that the user have access to a smart card reader, and USB tokens require that the user have a computer that has an available USB connector.

Special requirements must always be carefully considered for authentication mechanisms that are likely to be accessed from small, handheld devices.

*Convenience*

There are three aspects of convenience to be considered: enrollment time, authentication time, and key replacement time. Authentication time is the most relevant (it will mount up), so a large deficiency can be applied if this is time consuming. A smaller deficit can be applied if the mechanism is time consuming only at either enrollment or replacement. A large deficit results if all stages are time consuming.

Only random passwords are fast and convenient both at enrollment and at authentication, with replacement being potentially time consuming depending on how it is handled. Graphical passwords, both recognition-based and position-based, are considerably more time consuming at all stages, but less so than cultural passwords where users have to answer a succession of questions. The most time consuming are biometrics, where the user has to potentially spend a substantial amount of time enrolling and being authenticated (depending on the biometrics mechanism and the level of control applied).

*Inclusivity*

This aspect addresses the issue of the exclusion of users. Three kinds of disability are considered here—cognitive, physical, and sensory—and the deficit should be assigned based on whether users in the disability categories are excluded. The deficit gets larger as more categories of disabled users are excluded. If users in all categories are excluded, that constitutes a maximal deficit.

Cultural passwords do not exclude users with any type of disability—assuming that an accommodation has already been made so that the user can enter a response—whereas random passwords affect users with cognitive disabilities, such as users with memory difficulties.

Recognition-based graphical authentication systems affect the same disabilities, but also exclude people affected with cognitive disabilities such as dyspraxia.

Biometrics possibly affects users with physical disabilities, such as amputees in the case of fingerprint devices. Physiological changes, such as those that occur in retinas during pregnancy, may affect users' use of retinal screening devices. Position-based devices may exclude users with both sensory and physical disabilities—or even people who are simply too short or too tall, depending on how the biometrics system is mounted.

In general, this deficit depends on the actual type of authentication strategy being used and should be tailored accordingly.

## Memorability

Figure 6-9 depicts the various aspects of this dimension, which reflects the importance of the memorability of authentication mechanisms. Most authentication mechanisms are knowledge-based, so this dimension is especially important.

Biometrics mechanisms have minimal deficits with respect to any of the memorability criteria because the only burden they place on the user is that the user must remember how to use the biometrics device. Other mechanisms are essentially knowledge-based so that they impact on the users' memory load to a lesser or greater extent. The memorability aspects are:

*Retrieval strategy*

Users find it easier to recognize than to recall. Hence, a system that requires only recognition or a system that does not require the user to remember at all has no deficit. A mechanism that relies on recall has a maximal deficit in terms of retrieval, and a mechanism that provides cues has a smaller deficit.

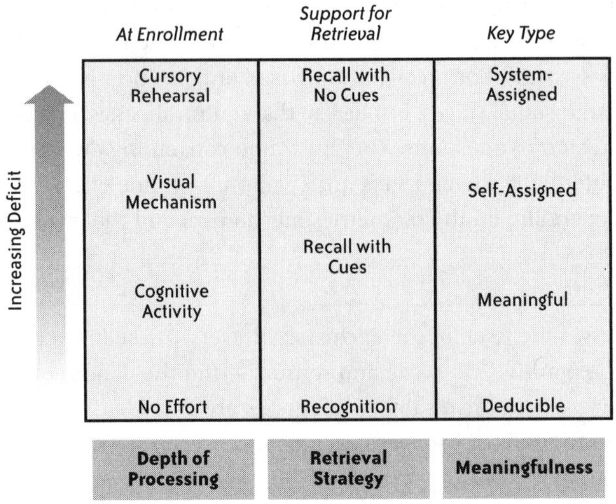

| At Enrollment | Support for Retrieval | Key Type |
|---|---|---|
| Cursory Rehearsal | Recall with No Cues | System-Assigned |
| Visual Mechanism | | Self-Assigned |
| Cognitive Activity | Recall with Cues | Meaningful |
| No Effort | Recognition | Deducible |
| **Depth of Processing** | **Retrieval Strategy** | **Meaningfulness** |

↑ Increasing Deficit

FIGURE 6-9. Memorability

The retrieval strategy used by recognition- and position-based graphical passwords is recognition, so there is no deficit in the retrieval strategy criterion. Cultural passwords provide a cued recall situation that is better than the uncued recall required by random passwords, which is assigned a maximal deficit.

*Meaningfulness*

Humans remember things best if they are deducible and very well if they are meaningful. Hence, if the authenticator is self-assigned and deducible by means of a special scheme, no deficit is assigned. If it is self-assigned and meaningful to the user, there is only a small deficit. If it is self-assigned but not necessarily meaningful or deducible, the deficit is significantly larger. If it is assigned arbitrarily by the system, it has a maximal deficit in terms of meaningfulness.

Cultural passwords are very meaningful, so they have no deficit for meaningfulness. Random passwords are usually meaningful to the user, and a position chosen in a position-based graphical password is also usually meaningful. Graphical passwords, if assigned by the system, may not be meaningful at all. If a recognition-based graphical password is chosen by the user, it will have the same deficit as a position-based graphical password, if the images are chosen by the system. If the images are provided by the user, they become very meaningful and no deficit is assigned here.

*Depth of processing*

Humans remember things better if, at the encoding stage, there is some cognitive activity associated with the process.[24] The cognitive activity involved in the encoding of an authenticator based on something the user knows will determine how well the user can retrieve the authenticator later. An authentication system that does not require effort to

---

24 V. H. Gregg, *Introduction to Human Memory* (London: Routledge & Kegan Paul, 1988).

remember (such as biometrics) has no deficit. The deficit increases as less and less cognitive activity is involved at enrollment time. A maximal deficit can be assigned if only cursory and shallow cognitive activity, such as rehearsal, is involved at enrollment.

Cultural passwords link the "password" to things the user already knows so that at enrollment, there is a substantial processing of information. Position-based passwords require users to choose a particular position, which also requires some cognitive activity. Graphical passwords, using images, allow dual encoding of the "password," which will encode better than a simple random password (which generally requires very little cognitive activity at enrollment).

## Security

Figure 6-10 depicts the various aspects of the security dimension, which are related and interdependent but do need to be considered separately because of their different characteristics.

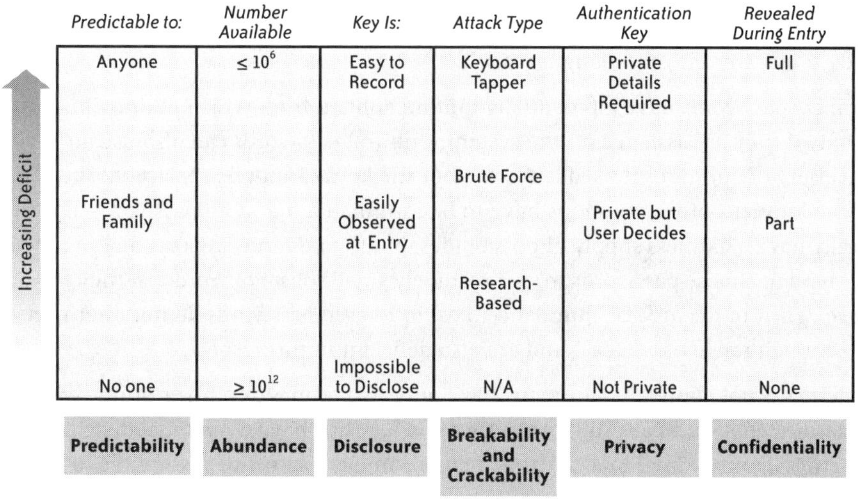

| | Predictable to: | Number Available | Key Is: | Attack Type | Authentication Key | Revealed During Entry |
|---|---|---|---|---|---|---|
| (Increasing Deficit ↑) | Anyone | $\leq 10^6$ | Easy to Record | Keyboard Tapper | Private Details Required | Full |
| | | | | Brute Force | | |
| | Friends and Family | | Easily Observed at Entry | | Private but User Decides | Part |
| | | | | Research-Based | | |
| | No one | $\geq 10^{12}$ | Impossible to Disclose | N/A | Not Private | None |
| | **Predictability** | **Abundance** | **Disclosure** | **Breakability and Crackability** | **Privacy** | **Confidentiality** |

FIGURE 6-10. Security

Note that the predictability of a key is affected by the abundance of the key for knowledge-based keys, but not for biometrics keys, which are neither abundant nor predictable. Abundance also affects breakability for knowledge-based keys, but once again not for biometrics keys. They are described in the following list.

*Predictability*

Predictability of an authentication key is a big issue: the plethora of password choice recommendations on the Web is a bleak testimony to the tendency of people to choose weak authentication keys. There is no deficit if the authentication key is completely unpredictable, as is the case for a public encryption key. A varying deficit can be assigned depending on how many people find the key predictable.

Random and position-based graphical passwords are very predictable and can be assigned a maximal deficit value. Biometrics are unpredictable, and so are system-assigned recognition-based graphical passwords. If a graphical password is chosen by the user, it becomes as predictable as random passwords. Cultural passwords are assigned a deficit halfway between maximum and minimum because although they can tap into a user's childhood memories, which hold facts generally known to few others, they can be uncovered by means of a research-based attack.

### Abundance

The user should be able to either choose from, or be assigned, one of a wide number of possible authenticators. Abundance has two aspects—one is the number of keys that are available for usage if the key needs to be replaced, and the other is the number commonly used in practice. So, for example, there is potentially an extremely large number of passwords if one includes all possible combinations of letters, both upper- and lower-case, and digits and special characters. In practice, however, people use very few of the available passwords because they usually restrict themselves to recognized words, reducing the number of passwords in practice to a number close to $10^6$ (for English words, and fewer for other languages).

Graphical passwords have a potentially infinite domain from which to draw images—but only if they are assigned by the system. Cultural passwords can also use an unlimited variety of questions if used correctly, but the keys cannot be replaced if they become known—other questions have to be formulated. Random passwords also theoretically have a limitless supply of possibilities, but the literature reports that in practice, users tend to choose passwords from a relatively small subset of words, so they too have a large deficit in the area of abundance. Position-based passwords do not offer users a large enough range of choice[25] and are also deficient in this respect.

Biometrics is not abundant—humans have only two retinas, ten fingerprints, two hand geometries, etc.—so as a result, biometrics mechanisms have a maximal deficit. If the biometrics device is used in a controlled environment that is not susceptible to replay attacks, abundance will not be an issue because it is unlikely that the biometrics will ever have to be replaced, but in an uncontrolled environment, this lack of abundance may be serious.

### Disclosure

An authenticator should not be disclosed to another user; otherwise, authentication fails. Hence, the mechanism is clearly deficient if a user can easily record his authenticator, and if it can be purposely disclosed, observed by, or stolen by another person. There is no deficit if is impossible for the user to do this, and a varying deficit can be applied between these extremes to denote the ease with which disclosure can occur.

Cultural passwords and both types of graphical passwords can be observed at key entry time, so there is a deficit in this area, but it is not the maximal deficit, which is assigned

25 *Ibid.*

to random passwords based on the literature reporting widespread recording of passwords in insecure locations.

Biometrics need to be disclosed in order to be verified, so they have a maximal deficit in this respect.

Private keys do not need to be disclosed in order to be used, so they have no disclosure deficit. Token-based systems that do not use public key technology are typically based on a shared secret that does not need to be disclosed for the user to be authenticated, but the shared secret does need to reside on the system verifying the token. Thus, they are subject to disclosure.

*Confidentiality*

Authentication requires the user and the system to exchange a pre-agreed key. If the user has to supply the full key at authentication, it is possible for a transmission sniffer to observe the key, or for some other person to observe it and reuse it. If there is another way for the user to demonstrate knowledge of the key without revealing it, that makes the authentication mechanism less vulnerable. Hence, an authenticator that relies on the full authentication key being revealed is assigned a maximal deficiency value. If the user doesn't have to reveal the key at all, or if the revealed key cannot be reused, there is no deficit. Values in between can be assigned depending on how much of the key has to be revealed.

Random passwords generally reveal the entire key at authentication, which assigns a maximal deficit to confidentiality. Cultural passwords may capture the answers to many questions at enrollment time, and then only use a few at authentication time, so that the deficit is not as large. If a password mechanism can be tailored to only ask for particular letters or digits, the confidentiality deficiency decreases. Authentication systems that involve responding to a random challenge with a response that is signed with a private key may not have any confidentiality deficit.

*Privacy*

An authenticator may record many details about the user to support authentication or key replacement, which, if not stored securely, could compromise other systems for which the person is required to use the same details, because a key reused is a key weakened.[26] It can also violate the person's privacy.[27] If an authenticator requires the user to reveal personal details, a maximal deficiency value is assigned. No deficiency is assigned if no personal details are required. An approach that allows users to decide which personal details to reveal will earn a deficiency value depending on the type and number of details that have to be revealed.

---

26 B. Ives, K. R. Walsh, and H. Shneider, "The Domino Effect of Password Reuse," *Communications of the ACM* 47 (2004), 75–78.

27 H. Berghel, "Identity Theft, Social Security Numbers and the Web," *Communications of the ACM* 43 (2000), 17–21.

Assigned random and graphical passwords generally do not reveal any personal details, so they have no deficit in the privacy area. This changes if users are permitted to specify their own "random" passwords or provide their own images for graphical-based authentication. User-specified passwords may also compromise the security of other systems, if the same password is used in multiple locations. Cultural passwords and biometrics both reveal very personal details, so they have a maximal deficit.

Because of a century-long association with law enforcement, many users feel that fingerprints represent private or confidential information. As a result, these users may feel that the use of biometrics systems based on fingerprints constitutes an inherent privacy violation. Although users do not seem to have similar associations with iris biometrics at this time, such associations could emerge in the future.

*Breakability and crackability*

The values will be assigned depending on the time an attacker would have to spend to attack the authenticator. The higher the price an attacker must pay in terms of time and effort, the less vulnerable an authentication mechanism is. A research-based attack is inevitably time consuming for anyone other than close friends and family. Thus, if the authentication mechanism is vulnerable to a research-based attack, a relatively small deficiency value can be assigned. If the authentication key is vulnerable to dictionary or brute force attacks, which are more common, a larger deficit can be assigned. If the authenticator is vulnerable to a key logger,[28] a maximal deficit can be assigned. Many users do not have virus software or firewalls running on their home computers, and this cracking mechanism is particularly cheap from an attacker's point of view.

Cultural passwords are vulnerable to research-based attacks, which are very time consuming, so they have a small deficit for breakability and crackability.

Biometrics can be subject to replay[29] and reverse engineering[30] attacks, depending on how the biometrics is implemented. The entropy or information content of the biometrics also needs to be considered: some biometrics, such as handprint geometry, do not have enough "randomness" that they can successfully distinguish between all members of a nation-size population. Other biometrics, such as iris recognition, have so much entropy and variance that it is unlikely that two people will ever be found who have matching biometrics values.

28 A key logger is a program that can be surreptitiously loaded onto your computer to record all of your key presses on the keyboard. In this way, many passwords can be obtained and reported back to the attacker.

29 A replay attack records the authentication key as the user provides it or as it is transmitted; then, when an attacker wants to get into the site, he simply provides the system with the previously recorded key.

30 Reverse engineering is a technique that obtains the stored description of a person's biometrics, such as his voiceprint or fingerprint description. The attacker uses software to derive a description of the voice or fingerprint that can be entered into the biometrics device as an authentication key.

Recognition-based and password-based graphical passwords are both subject to brute force attacks, and random passwords are subject to dictionary attacks, so they have the maximal deficit because such attacks can be largely automated.

## Cost

No set of criteria can be complete without considering cost, in terms of both time and money. Cost has various dimensions:

- Software

- Hardware

- Enrollment

- Authentication

- Key replacement

- Securing key details

- Maintenance, such as backup and expiration/retraction of keys

Random passwords appear to be a relatively cheap option, until you consider the salaries paid to help-desk teams to replace forgotten passwords in an online banking environment and the risk that these individuals might fall prey to a social engineering attack. It may be worth spending a bit more on software and having a time-consuming enrollment to reduce the replacement and maintenance costs of the system by automating the key replacement stage. In order to apply a deficit to cost, all the different cost factors should be considered and a cumulative cost assessment performed to come up with a deficit value.

Biometrics has the greatest costs because you need extra hardware *and* software, and you have to assist users being enrolled and authenticated. Graphical passwords need special software, but enrollment, authentication, and replacement can be automated. Random passwords need no special hardware or software and have almost no cost at enrollment and authentication, but secure replacement can involve humans and can be expensive. Cultural passwords are time consuming at enrollment, but this helps make replacement a rare event, and even if it is required, it can be easily automated.

# Environmental Considerations

This section explains how to determine a ranking of the criteria introduced in the previous section. To help the system developer make a decision, it is necessary to rank the criteria so that deficiencies in the more important criteria will tend to carry more weight. We will use the characteristics of the environment to classify criteria as *critical, vital, significant,* or *incidental.* All criteria will be initially assigned to the *significant* category, and moved into the other categories based on an environmental analysis.

There may be certain situations where a large deficiency of a particular aspect or dimension can completely disqualify the authentication mechanism for use in a particular environment. For example, the developer may decide that the system controls access to such critical data that only a completely nonpredictable mechanism will suffice. These criteria are termed *critical*. Mechanisms with unacceptable deficiencies in these criteria can be withdrawn from consideration if requirements are stringent.

Environmental factors are identified in terms of the category in which they fall, provided in the following subsections. The list of environmental factors given here does not attempt to be exhaustive but, rather, is intended merely to give an example of the kinds of environmental factors that can affect the relative importance of the different criteria.

### Accessibility

*Control of environment*

> For example, a web environment is completely uncontrolled, whereas an ATM is an example of a moderately controlled environment because the network used to communicate with the server is not public, and it is a relatively easy matter to control extra hardware and software that is required by the mechanism.

> This factor determines how important all the criteria in the accessibility category will be in the calculation of the final quality measure because accessibility barriers can be partially alleviated in a controlled environment. If the environment is uncontrolled, these criteria become vital, and if the environment is controlled, these criteria remain significant.

*Range of users*

> For example, if the users are a small group of technically competent individuals who can be accommodated on a one-on-one basis if they are unable to use the authentication system, *inclusivity* may be merely incidental. If, on the other hand, we need to ensure that members of the general public must be able to use the authentication system without additional accommodation, *inclusivity* becomes vital.

### Memorability

*Frequency of use*

> Usage can be categorized as low (less often than once a month), medium (once a week), or high (daily) because more frequently used items are remembered more easily.[31] This factor determines how important all criteria in the *memorability* category will be. Thus, high usage makes memorability criteria incidental; medium usage makes them significant; and infrequent usage makes them vital.

*Forced renewal*

> This refers to the organizational rules, which require users to change authentication keys regularly. This factor determines how important all criteria in the *memorability* category will be. A forced renewal policy will make the memorability criteria vital, whereas no forced renewal policy will make these criteria only significant.

---

31 M. Kinsbourne and J. George, "The Mechanisms of the Word-Frequency Effect on Recognition Memory," *Journal of Verbal Learning and Verbal Behaviour* 13 (1974), 63–69.

## Security

*Access*

> This refers to the information being protected or the kind of access being granted. If the access being provided is noncritical, the security deficiency becomes less important; but if the data being protected or the access being provided is potentially damaging, the security deficiency becomes more important.
>
> If it will not be damaging to the user if another user gains access, *predictability* and *abundance* become incidental; if wrongful access can affect only the user himself, *predictability* and *abundance* become significant; and if wrongful access can affect more than one user, *predictability* and *abundance* become vital.
>
> If a particular user has authorized access to many users' details, *breakability and crackability* become vital because illegal access in this person's name could be very damaging.

*Trust*

> This refers to how much the user trusts the person or organization requesting authentication. If there is trust between them, as there is between an employer and an employee, or between a patient and a doctor, *privacy* and *confidentiality* become incidental. If, however, the user does not have any firsthand knowledge of the organization or the host of an e-commerce web site, these criteria become significant. If the user is being asked to authenticate for a system hosted by another country, such as a web site, which means that it is more difficult for the user to be protected by her own country's legislation, these criteria become vital.

*Security motivation*

> This refers to the degree to which the environment can put measures in place to require the user to act in a secure and responsible way. If some sanction can be applied to a user who behaves irresponsibly, the *disclosure* criteria is only significant; if no sanction can be applied, it becomes vital.

*Auditing*

> A system that actively audits in real time can be less vulnerable to attacks. Such auditing procedures can activate some other security measure if something suspicious is detected. If no auditing is done, the *breakability and crackability* criteria become vital; if auditing is carried out, it becomes merely significant.

## Cost

If there are financial constraints on the person commissioning the system, *cost* is significant; otherwise, it becomes incidental. If the authentication system is protecting finances, *cost* becomes vital.

# Choosing a Mechanism

To evaluate an authentication mechanism, it is useful to divide the selection criteria into four categories:

*Critical*
> Used to disqualify mechanisms with an unacceptably large deficit.

*Vital*
> Used to come up with a cumulative deficit for authentication mechanisms across these criteria, to identify candidates for use in the system.

*Significant*
> Used to confirm the decision made by using the vital criteria only. If a chosen mechanism happens to have a maximal deficiency in a significant criterion, we should consider other options based on the vital criteria.

*Incidental*
> These criteria are not important and usually would not be weighed as part of the decision-making process.

Clearly, different applications will put different criteria into different categories.

## An Online Banking Example

Consider the case of a bank that wants to authenticate its customers for an online banking portal. Three approaches have been proposed:

*Password approach*
> The bank has each customer choose a password in the branch office when an account is created.

*TAN approach*
> The bank prints on the customer's monthly statement a set of Transaction Authorization Numbers (TANs). These TANs can each be used a single time to gain access to the bank's web site. Essentially, the TANs are a set of one-time passwords that may each be used once to log into the bank's web site.

*Token approach*
> Customers who desire online access may purchase a security token with a changing PIN. The customer must type both his password and the PIN into his computer each time he wants to access the web site.

The bank can use the evaluation strategy presented in this chapter to decide between these three authentication strategies.

### The critical criterion: accessibility

First, it is useful to see if any of the alternatives have such deficits that they must be disqualified. Because the bank does business with the public, it has both moral and potential legal requirements for inclusivity. Because the bank wants to make its online portal accessible to all of its customers, it needs to consider any special requirements.

Of the three proposed approaches, only the *token approach* has a significant inclusivity deficit: tokens with LCD screens cannot be used by people who are blind. This problem can be overcome through the use of USB tokens. The bank may want to substitute USB tokens for LCD tokens, or it may want to give customers the choice of using *either* token.

Both the *TAN approach* and the *token approach* have special requirements: the TAN approach requires that the user have a copy of his bank statement in order to engage in online banking, and the token approach requires that the user have his token. Although either might represent a significant deficit for an entertainment service that was designed to be used throughout the day, this deficit might be acceptable for an online banking portal that users might want to use only in the evening when they are at home.

### The vital criterion: security

Vital to the bank's selection of an authentication mechanism will be the security that the mechanism provides. Of the three alternatives, the *password approach* offers the lowest amount of security. Because passwords must be disclosed in order to be used, they can be inadvertently shared with an attacker—for example, the password can be entered at the wrong web site. Passwords that are chosen by the user may be further compromised by being used at multiple web sites. Passwords are also susceptible to being broken through brute force or password-guessing attack. Thus, the bank will need to have software that detects such an attack and behaves accordingly.

The *TAN approach* has a different security deficit: because the TANs are printed on the customer's statement, any individual who is able to intercept the customer's paper mail will be given complete access to the customer's bank account. For this reason, the bank may wish to supplement the TANs with a password chosen by the user. This would be an example of two-factor authentication.

### The significant criteria: memorability and cost

Memorability is a significant criterion to the bank because a high deficit will increase customer support costs. The *password approach* has a low memorability deficit because consumers have the ability to pick their own passwords. A scheme that requires users to change their passwords on a regular basis will increase this deficit. Such a scheme might be warranted, however, if there is a chance that a percentage of users will have their passwords compromised on a regular basis.

Neither the *TAN approach* nor the *token approach* has low memorability deficits: the user must both remember how to use the scheme and carry the TAN booklet or the token. Otherwise, however, there is no information that must be remembered. The token approach does place an additional cost on customers, who must purchase the token.

### The incidental criterion: nothing

Because of the bank's scale of operation, in this example there are no incidental criteria. On the other hand, if the bank were a small private bank that offered service only to high-net-worth individuals, the cost of the authentication strategy might not be a factor.

## Conclusion

Random passwords are currently the most popular user authentication mechanism, but passwords are inherently weak, and it is becoming necessary for system developers to consider other authentication mechanisms. Using the techniques explained in this chapter, an objective and informed choice can be made based on the mechanism, the environment within which it will be used, and customer preferences.

## About the Author

 Karen Renaud is a Senior Lecturer in the Department of Computing Science at the University of Glasgow in Scotland. She previously lectured at the University of South Africa. She does research in a variety of areas including usability of security systems, distributed systems, Internet technology, design patterns, and issues related to recovery from interruptions. She is also actively involved in developing and testing alternative web authentication mechanisms.

# CHAPTER SEVEN

# The Memorability and Security of Passwords

**JEFF YAN, ALAN BLACKWELL, ROSS ANDERSON, AND ALASDAIR GRANT**

**M**ANY THINGS ARE "WELL KNOWN" ABOUT PASSWORDS, such as the fact that people can't remember strong passwords and that the passwords they can remember are easy to guess. However, little research on the subject would pass muster by the standards of applied psychology.[1]

In the study presented here, we confirmed some widely held folk beliefs about passwords. However, we also observed a number of surprising phenomena that run counter to the established wisdom. Our study shows that the methods of applied psychology can bring new insights and solid results for security research and development.

## Introduction

Many of the deficiencies of password authentication systems arise from the limitations of human memory. If humans were not required to remember the password, a maximally secure textual password would be one with maximum entropy: it would consist of a string

---

1   Based on "Password Memorability and Security: Empirical Results," by J. Yan, A. Blackwell, R. Anderson, and A. Grant, *IEEE Security & Privacy*,2:5 (2004),  25–31. © 2004 IEEE.

as long as the system allows, made up of characters selected from all those allowed by the system, and in a manner that provides no redundancy—that is, a totally random selection.

Each of these requirements is contrary to a well-known property of human memory:

- Human memory for sequences of items is temporally limited,[2] with a short-term capacity of around seven (plus or minus two items).[3]

- When humans remember a sequence of items, those items cannot be drawn from an arbitrary and unfamiliar range, but must be familiar "chunks," such as words or familiar symbols.[4]

- Human memory thrives on redundancy—we are far better at remembering information that can be encoded in multiple ways.[5]

Password authentication, therefore, appears to involve a tradeoff. Some passwords are very easy to remember (e.g., single words in the user's native language) but also very easy to guess with dictionary searches. In contrast, some passwords are very secure against guessing but are difficult to remember. In the latter case, the security of a superior password may be compromised as a result of human limitations, because the user may keep an insecure written record of it or resort to insecure backup authentication procedures after forgetting it.[6]

In 1999, we started an empirical study investigating this tradeoff in the context of an actual population of password users. Research in cognitive psychology has defined many limits of human performance in laboratory settings where experimental subjects are required to memorize random and pseudorandom sequences of symbols. However, it is very difficult to generalize from such research to password users, who can select the string themselves, are able to rehearse it while memorizing, and need to recall it at regular intervals over a long period of time.

We show that this user context allows the exploitation of mnemonic strategies for password memorization. Many successful mnemonic techniques can be used to achieve

---

2   G. J. Johnson, "A Distinctiveness Model of Serial Learning," *Psychological Review* 98:2 (1991), 204–217.

3   G. A. Miller, "The Magical Number Seven, Plus or Minus Two: Limits on Our Capacity for Processing Information," *Psychological Review* 63 (1956), 81–87.

4   *Ibid.*

5   A. Paivio, "The Empirical Case for Dual Coding," in J.C. Yuille (ed.), in *Imagery, Memory and Cognition: Essays in Honor of Allan Paivio* (Hillsdale, NJ: Erlbaum, 1983), 307–322.

6   This doesn't mean we accept the common doctrine that writing down passwords is always wrong. For machines not in publicly accessible areas, it may be good sense to have a long, random-boot password written down in an envelope taped to the machine, as one can then have a strict policy that passwords are never, under any circumstances, to be disclosed over the phone. However, the prevention of "social engineering" attacks is beyond the scope of this chapter.

impressive performance when memorizing apparently random sequences. Password alternatives such as *passfaces* exploit superior human memory for faces, for example.[7] However, instead of changing the password authentication procedure, we investigate changing the advice that is given to the user when selecting a password.

## Existing Advice on Password Selection

Adams and Sasse[8] note that users are not enemies of security, but collaborators who need appropriate information to help maintain system security. They observe that users, when not told how to choose good passwords, make up rules for password generation, resulting in insecure passwords. They therefore recommend that organizations "provide instruction and training on how to construct usable and secure passwords."

Later research by Sasse, Brostoff, and Weirich, based on a survey of system users, found that 90% of them had difficulty with standard password mechanisms and that they welcomed advice on password generation.[9] The authors conclude that, "instructions for constructing and memorizing a strong password...should be available when a password needs to be chosen or changed."

Many large organizations do give specific advice to new users about how to select a "good password." A good password, in terms of the preceding discussion, should aim to be reasonably long, use a reasonably large character set, but still be easy to remember. There are some subtleties about whether the attacker is going to try many passwords over a network or whether she has obtained a copy of the password file and is cracking it offline, but we propose to ignore these for the purposes of the present study.

We made an informal survey of advice given to new users at large sites by searching on the Web for the terms "choose," "good," and "password." Many sites did not recognize the importance of memorability, merely emphasizing resistance to brute force search. Some typical pieces of advice were:

> "[A good] password should consist of mixed characters or special characters, and should not consist of words found in the dictionary. It should not be written down in an easily accessible place and especially not next to login. It may be either all in capital or all in small type letters."
> "Use the output from a random password generator. Select a random string that can be pronounced and is easy to remember. For example, the random string 'adazac' can be pronounced a-da-zac, and you can remember it by thinking of it as 'A-to-Z'. Add uppercase letters to create your own emphasis—e.g., aDAzac.2."
> "Good passwords appear to be random characters. The wider the variety of characters, the better. Mixing letters with numbers is better than letters alone. Mixing special characters with number and letters is better still."

---

7   H. Davies, "Physiognomic Access Control," *Information Security Monitor* 10:3 (Feb. 1995, 5–8.

8   A. Adams and M. A. Sasse, "Users Are Not The Enemy," *Communications of the ACM* 42:12 (Dec. 1999), 40–46.

9   M. A. Sasse, S. Brostoff, and D. Weirich, "Transforming the 'Weakest Link': A Human-Computer Interaction Approach to Usable and Effective Security," *BT Technical Journal* 19:3 (July 2001), 122–131.

One recommendation that seems increasingly popular is the "passphrase" approach to password generation. A typical description of this is as follows:

> A good technique for choosing a password is to use the first letters of a phrase. However, don't pick a well-known phrase like "An apple a day keeps the doctor away" (Aaadktda). Instead, pick something like "My dog's first name is Rex" (MdfniR) or "My sister Peg is 24 years old" (MsPi24yo)."

Of course this informal survey does not include sites where no advice at all is given on password selection. We believe that many sites simply tell new users the minimum requirement for a valid password (length and character set), and give no further advice regarding security or memorability. Others, in our experience, enforce rules such as:

> Passwords must be at least eight characters long and must contain at least two non-letter characters. They must also be changed at least once a month.

The usual response of users to such rules appears to be to devise a personal password generation system of which a simple example is "Juliet03" for March, "Juliet04" for April, and so on. In our own study described in this chapter, we did not include advice of this kind, so we are unable to offer additional empirical evidence. Nevertheless, we believe that this policy is clearly weak. Other attempts to compel user behavior have backfired. For example, Patterson reports that when users were compelled to change their passwords and were prevented from using the previous few choices, they changed passwords rapidly to exhaust the history list and then returned to their favorite password. A response, of forbidding password changes until after 15 days, meant that users couldn't change possible compromised passwords without help from the system administrator.[10] Once again, this proves Adams and Sasse's finding that users will circumvent restrictions that they find tedious.

So, the design of the advice given to users, and of the system-level enforcement that may complement this, is an important problem. It involves subtle questions of applied psychology to which the answers are not obvious.

The existing literature on password selection and memorability is surprisingly sparse. Grampp and Morris's classic paper on Unix security reports that after software became available, forcing passwords to be at least six characters long and have at least one non-letter, they made a file of the 20 most common female names, each followed by a single digit. Of these 200 passwords, at least one was in use on each of several dozen machines they examined.[11] Klein records collecting 13,797 password file entries from Unix systems and attacking them by exhaustive search; about one-quarter of them were cracked.[12] Password

---

10  B. Patterson, letter to *Communications of the ACM* 43:4 (Apr. 2000), 11–12.

11  F. T. Grampp and R. H. Morris, "UNIX Operating System Security," *AT&T Bell Laboratories Technical Journal* 63:8 (Oct. 1984), 1649–1672.

12  Daniel V. Klein, "Foiling the Cracker: A Survey of, and Improvements to, Password Security" (revised paper), *Proceedings of the USENIX Security Workshop* (1990).

management guidelines from the U.S. Department of Defense[13] recommended the use of machine-generated random passwords.

Zviran and Haga[14] conducted an experiment in which they asked 106 students to choose passwords, writing them on a questionnaire. The questionnaires also assigned a random password to each student, and they were asked to remember both. Three months later, they found the following results:

|  | Self-selected | Random |
|---|---|---|
| Successful recall | 35% | 23% |
| Wrote it down | 14% | 66% |

However, the students were not actually using the password during the intervening three months. So, although this provides a quantitative point of reference for the difficulty of random passwords, it does not closely model a real operational environment.

As previously noted, Adams and Sasse[15], and Sasse, Brostoff, and Weirich[16] report the results of studies in which system users were surveyed and asked to report their experiences with password usage. They discussed memorability issues and concluded that users should be instructed to construct secure and memorable passwords. However, they did not, as commented by Abrahams,[17] put much effort into identifying "specific, positive advice" on how to "compose passwords that are both easy to remember and difficult to crack."

## Experimental Study

To investigate the tradeoff between security and memorability in a real-world context, we conducted an experiment involving 400 first-year students at the University of Cambridge. The experiment compared the effects of giving three alternative forms of advice about password selection, and measured the effect that this advice had on the security and memorability of passwords.

The experimental subjects were students who had arrived to start a degree in our School of Natural Sciences, which includes physics, chemistry, geology, and materials science. All Natural Sciences students are provided with an account on a central computing facility, using a user ID and a randomly generated initial password. They also have access to a number of other facilities. At the time they receive these account details, students are generally advised to select their own password. Some students receive this advice informally from a computer officer in their department or hall of residence. Many students attend an

13 Department of Defense, "Password Management Guideline," CSC-STD-002-85 (1985).

14 M. Zviran and W. J. Haga, "A Comparison of Password Techniques for Multilevel Authentication Mechanisms," *Computer Journal* 36:3 (1993), 227–237.

15 Adams and Sasse.

16 Sasse, Brostoff, and Weirich.

17 P. Abrahams, letter to *Communications of the ACM* 43:4 (April 2000), 11.

introductory lecture to learn about the central facilities, followed by a tutorial session under the supervision of demonstrators.

## Method

In October 1999, students attending the introductory lecture were told that they would be subjects (with their consent) in an experiment on password selection. At the tutorial session, they were then asked for consent and were randomly assigned to one of three experimental groups. Each student was given a sheet of advice depending on the group to which they had been assigned. The three different types of advice were:

- *Control group.* Students in this group were given the same advice as in previous years, which was simply that "Your password should be at least seven characters long and contain at least one non-letter."

- *Random password group.* Students in this group were given a sheet of paper with the letters A–Z and the numbers 1–9 printed repeatedly on it. They were told to select a random password by closing their eyes and picking eight characters at random. They were advised to keep a written record of the password, but to destroy it once the password was memorized. This is very similar to the advice given by banks when issuing PIN numbers, which are issued in written form, but with the user advised to destroy the written slip as soon as it has been memorized.

- *Passphrase group.* Students in this group were told to choose a password based on a mnemonic phrase.

The text of the instructions given to the three groups is reproduced in Figures 7-1, 7-2, and 7-3, respectively.[18]

Our hypothesis was that the random password group would have stronger passwords than the passphrase group, but would find them harder to remember and/or easier to forget, while the passphrase group would stand in the same relation to the control group.

One month after the tutorial sessions, we took a snapshot of all password files, and conducted four types of attack on the passwords:

- *Dictionary attack.* Simply use different dictionary files to crack passwords. This attack was attempted against all passwords.

- *Permutation of words and numbers.* For each word from a dictionary file, permute with 0, 1, 2, and 3 digit(s) to construct possible password candidates. Also, make common number substitutions, such a 1 for I, 5 for S, etc. This attack was attempted against all passwords.

- *User information attack.* Exploit user information collected from password files (e.g., user ID, user full name, initial substring of name) to crack passwords. This attack was attempted against all passwords.

---

18 Lent and Easter are the names of the second and third academic terms in Cambridge, respectively. We started this experiment in the first term.

This sheet offers some advice on how to choose a good computer password. We are giving you this sheet as part of the password security experiment that was described in your introductory lecture. Different people are receiving different advice (but all advice should result in passwords at least as secure as you would choose if not participating in the experiment). Please do not discuss the experiment, this advice, or your choice of password with your friends.

Please log on using the initial password you have been issued, and choose a new password not known to anybody else. The "Windows NT Tutor" tells you how to do this on pages 1.6–1.7.

Your password should be at least seven characters long and contain at least one non-letter.

If you have already changed your initial password to one of your choice, and your new password meets this standard, then you do not need to change it again. However, we strongly recommend that you change your password from time to time—at least once a term. As the experiment will run for the duration of this academic year, please keep this sheet and use this advice again when you choose your new passwords for Lent and Easter.

FIGURE 7-1. Control group instruction sheet; participants were asked to choose a seven-character password with at least one non-letter

This sheet offers some advice on how to choose a good computer password. We are giving you this sheet as part of the password security experiment that was described in your introductory lecture. Different people are receiving different advice (but all advice should result in passwords at least as secure as you would choose if not participating in the experiment). Please do not discuss the experiment, this advice, or your choice of password with your friends.

A secure password is one that is very difficult to guess. Words that appear in a dictionary, or the names of people or places, are easy to guess. The most difficult passwords to guess are random sequences of letters. To help you choose a random sequence of letters for your password, we have printed a grid of random letters overleaf. Choose your password by closing your eyes and pointing at a random place on the grid. Choose eight characters this way and write them down on a scrap of paper.

Now log on using the initial password you have been issued, change your password to the new random password which you have chosen. The "Windows NT Tutor" tells you how to do this on pages 1.6–1.7.

You may find your password difficult to remember at first. Make sure that the scrap of paper on which you have written it is in a secure place, such as the back of your wallet or purse.

You should find that once you have entered it a dozen times or so, you will be able to remember it. Once you are sure you can remember it, destroy the scrap of paper where you wrote it down.

Finally, we strongly recommend that you change your password from time to time—at least once a term. As the experiment will run for the duration of this academic year, please keep this sheet and use this advice again when you choose your new passwords for Lent and Easter.

FIGURE 7-2. Random password group instruction sheet; group members chose their passwords by closing their eyes and pointing randomly to a grid of numbers and letters

This sheet offers some advice on how to choose a good computer password. We are giving you this sheet as part of the password security experiment that was described in your introductory lecture. Different people are receiving different advice (but all advice should result in passwords at least as secure as you would choose if not participating in the experiment). Please do not discuss the experiment, this advice, or your choice of password with your friends.

To construct a good password, create a simple sentence of 8 words and choose letters from the words to make up a password. You might take the initial or final letters; you should put some letters in uppercase to make the password harder to guess; and at least one number and/or special character should be inserted as well. Use this method to generate a password of 7 or 8 characters.

An example of such a composition might be using the phrase "It's 12 noon I am hungry" to create the password "I's12&Iah" which is hard for anyone else to guess but easy for you to remember. By all means use a foreign language if you know one: the password "AwKdk.Md" from the phrase "Anata wa Kyuuketsuki desu ka ... Miyu desu" would be an example. You could even mix words from several languages. However, do not just use a word or a name from a foreign language. Try being creative!

Now log on using the initial password you have been issued, and change your password to the new password which you have chosen. The "Windows NT Tutor" tells you how to do this on pages 1.6–1.7. Do not write your new password down.

Finally, we strongly recommend that you change your password from time to time–at least once a term. As the experiment will run for the duration of this academic year, please keep this sheet and use this advice again when you choose your new passwords for Lent and Easter.

*FIGURE 7-3. Passphrase group instruction sheet; group members were asked to choose passwords based on mnemonic phrases*

- *Brute force attack.* Try all possible combinations of keys. We performed this attack on any passwords that were only six characters long (the password system used in our study allows us to know the length of a password without cracking it).

We collected information on the distribution of password lengths and on the number of cracked passwords in each group. We monitored the number of times that users requested that their passwords be reset by the system administrators, on the assumption that passwords that were difficult to remember may be forgotten. In such a case, the user would either have to ask for his password to be reset, or stop using the central facilities in favor of those provided elsewhere. We also surveyed all experimental subjects by email four months after the tutorial session, asking whether they'd had any difficulty remembering their password. This survey asked the following questions:

- How hard did you find it to memorize your password, on a scale from 1 (trivial) to 5 (impossible)?

- For how long did you have to carry around a written copy of the password to refer to? Please estimate the length of time in weeks.

We also tested the validity of our experimental sample by making the same attacks on the accounts of 100 first-year students who had not attended the introductory lecture or received any experimental instructions.

# Results

Of the 300 students we asked, 288 consented to participate in the experiment. They were allocated randomly to experimental groups as follows:

Control group               95
Random password group       96
Passphrase group            97

The selected passwords were, on average, between seven and eight characters long (7.6, 8.0, 7.9, respectively) with no significant difference between the three groups. All experimental groups chose slightly longer passwords than did the comparison sample of 100 students who had not attended the introductory lecture. Mean length of password in that group was 7.3, with analysis of variance (ANOVA) statistically significant at F=8.3, p<.001.

The most successful cracking method was the permuted dictionary attack. Cracking based on user information was not successful in any case, probably because of the very limited amount of user information available in these password files (they do not include first names or forenames, for example). All six-character passwords were cracked successfully using a brute force attack. Table 7-1 summarizes these results (treating brute force attacks separately).

TABLE 7-1. Results of password crack, by test group

| Group | Passwords cracked using first three attacks | | Passwords cracked using brute force attacks |
|---|---|---|---|
| | Number | Percent of total | |
| Control group | 30 | 32 | 3 |
| Random password group | 8 | 8 | 3 |
| Passphrase group | 6 | 6 | 3 |
| Comparison sample | 33 | 33 | 2 |

Modern computers are sufficiently fast that all six-character passwords are susceptible to brute force attack. The experimental password selection advice had no effect on this. In each experimental condition, a small number of users ignored the advice regarding password length and chose an insecure password. This also occurred among the comparison sample.

Of the passwords that were longer than six characters, far more of these were cracked successfully in the control group than in either the random character group or the passphrase group (significant at $\chi^2$=24.8, p<.001). The proportion of passwords cracked in the control group was lower than in the comparison sample. In addition, 13% of the comparison sample (13 out of 100 students) used six-character passwords versus 5% in the control group (5 out of 95 students). Among those cracked, 13 passwords in the comparison sample were verbatim dictionary words versus 3 in the control group.

For those passwords that were cracked successfully in the random-character and passphrase groups, all the cracked passwords were dictionary words, or permutations of dictionary words and numbers, that were not compliant with the advice given to the student. These results, together with the number of six-character passwords, provide a reasonable estimate of the level of user noncompliance with password selection advice.

By examining all cracked passwords, we also observed that nobody used special characters (i.e., neither letters nor numbers) except in the passphrase group, whose instructions had given examples of passwords containing punctuation. So, a strong lead in the direction of passwords containing a mix of alpha, numeric, and special characters seems to be advisable.

Very few users asked the system administrator to reset their passwords. Within a period of three months after the tutorial session, only six users (2%) had requested administrator resets. The proportion of these in each experimental group is shown in Table 7-2. The difference between the three groups is not significant ($\chi^2=0.97$, p=0.61). As far as we are aware, all reset requests resulted from the user having forgotten his password, although it is possible that other users who forgot their passwords simply stopped using the system—this possibility is considered in the discussion of survey results, since any such users would then not have responded to the final survey.

TABLE 7-2. Number of requests for password reset

| Group | Number of requests |
|---|---|
| Control group | 2 |
| Random password group | 1 |
| Passphrase group | 3 |

A total of 242 students replied to the email survey, of which 13 responses indicated that the students had not used their accounts, or had dropped out of the course. Of the valid responses, there was a clear difference between the groups, as Table 7-3 shows.

TABLE 7-3. Responses to the email memorability survey

| Group | Responses | Difficulty level (1-5) | Weeks |
|---|---|---|---|
| Control group | 80 | 1.52 | 0.7 |
| Random password group | 71 | 3.15 | 4.8 |
| Passphrase group | 78 | 1.67 | 0.6 |

Users assigned to the random password group reported that they found their passwords more difficult to remember than did those in the control group (significant at t=8.25, p<.001), and that they carried a written copy of their passwords for far longer than those in the control group (significant at t=6.41, p<.001). This confirms the results of Zviran and Haga in an operational setting. There was no significant difference in reported difficulty between the passphrase group and the control group.

The differences in response rates were not significant, so we do not believe that our results were skewed significantly by students in the random password group finding our advice so difficult that they gave up using the computer facilities.

It is worth noting that 22 members of the random character group were still carrying the written copy of the password at the time of the survey, compared with 3 members of the control group and 2 members of the passphrase group. We cannot compare the effect of our experimental treatment on users' decisions to write down the password, because only the random group was advised to write down the password. Neither of the other groups was specifically asked to write down the password, although some clearly chose to do so.

More interesting is that the random group was specifically advised to destroy the note as soon as they had memorized it. Other groups were not advised to destroy written records, so we might expect (if the initial instructions caused any bias in these results) that more members of the control group and the passphrase group would keep their written records instead of destroying them. However, despite the specific instruction to destroy the written record, 22 members of the random group had not done so, presumably (given the reported difficulty of memorizing) because they had been unable to memorize the password. This indicates the degree of threat that can result from the use of system-generated passwords that must be written down and then destroyed. Worryingly, this is very similar to the advice given by banks when they issue written advice for PIN numbers for card security. We speculate that a similar survey of bank card users might find many of them still carrying the PIN advice slip issued by their bank.

## Discussion

Our study confirms a number of widely held folk beliefs about passwords, and debunks some others:

- *Users have difficulty remembering random passwords.* This belief is confirmed, both in users' subjective reports and in their actions—the latter in a manner that has worrying parallels to common practice in the issue of bank PIN numbers.

- *Passwords based on mnemonic phrases are harder for an attacker to guess than naively selected passwords are.* This belief is confirmed.

> **NOTE**
> Theoretically, random passwords should provide the maximum security. This result highlights the importance of studying systems as they are used in practice.

- *Random passwords are better than those based on mnemonic phrases.* However, each type appeared to be just as strong as the other. So this belief is debunked.

- *Passwords based on mnemonic phrases are harder to remember than naively selected passwords are.* However, each appeared to be reasonably easy to remember, with only about 2%–3% of users forgetting passwords. So this belief is debunked.

- *By educating users to use random passwords or mnemonic passwords, we can gain a significant improvement in security.* However, both random passwords and mnemonic passwords suffered from a noncompliance rate of about 10% (including both too-short passwords and passwords not chosen according to the instructions). While this is better than the

35% or so of users who choose bad passwords with only cursory instruction, it is not really a huge improvement. The attacker may have to work three times harder, but in the absence of password policy enforcement mechanisms, there seems no way to make the attacker work a thousand times harder. In fact, our experimental group may be about the most compliant a system administrator can expect to get. So this belief appears to be debunked.

**NOTE**

There was a significant noncompliance rate for all groups, regardless of password policy. This suggests the following:

- It counters the established wisdom that educating users to construct stronger passwords will result in a significant security gain.
- In applications where one user can be harmed by another user's negligence, compliance monitoring and enforcement may be just as important as education.

Previous work suggests that the noncompliance rate could be even higher when users are required to remember multiple passwords, which usually increases the user's cognitive overhead and decreases memorability.[19] However, the issue of multiple passwords is beyond the scope of our experimental study.

Our empirical study on password security and memorability is merely a first step toward a better understanding of the applied psychology aspects of computer security. Many questions remain to be answered, and we plan to continue our experiments with future cohorts of students.

In the meantime, our tentative recommendations for system administrators are as follows:

- *Users should be instructed to choose mnemonic-based passwords*. These are just as memorable as naively selected passwords, while being just as hard to guess as randomly chosen ones. So, they give the best of both other options.

- *Size matters*. With systems like Unix, which limit effective password lengths to eight characters, users should be told to choose passwords of exactly eight characters. With systems such as Netware, which allows 14 characters but is not case sensitive, one might encourage users to choose passwords of 10 or more characters in length; perhaps this will further encourage the use of mnemonics. (This is a topic for our future work, as is enforcement generally.)

- *Entropy per character also matters*. Users should be told to choose passwords that contain numbers and special characters as well as letters. If such a lead isn't given, then most of them will choose passwords from a very small subset of the total password space.

- *Compliance is the most critical issue*. In systems where users can put only themselves at risk, it may be prudent to leave them to their own devices. In that case, it must be expected that about 10% will choose weak passwords despite the instruction given. In

19 Adams and Sasse.

# PASSWORD SECURITY

*Facts and Recommendations*

- Users have difficulty remembering random passwords.

- Instruct users to choose mnemonic-based passwords, as these are as memorable as naively selected passwords while being as hard to guess as randomly chosen ones.

- In applications where one user can be harmed by another user's negligence, screen users' password choices and reject weak ones.

- When devising your advice to users and writing your password-screening code, pay attention to password length but also to entropy per character.

*Lessons Learned*

- Theoretical analysis does *not* guarantee the security of systems. It is often necessary to study systems as they are used in practice.

- What engineers expect to work and what users actually make to work are two different things. Rigorous experimental testing of interface usability is one of the necessary ingredients for robust secure systems.

---

systems where one user's negligence can impact other users as well (for example, in systems where an intruder who gets a single user account can rapidly become root—that is, illicitly get a system administrator's privileges—using well-known and widely available techniques), consideration should be given to enforcing password quality by system mechanisms.

- *Central assignment may matter*. If there is a benefit to be had from the use of centrally assigned random passwords, it appears to come from the fact of central assignment (which enforces compliance) rather than randomness (which can be achieved just with mnemonic phrases).

An interesting and important challenge is to find compliance enforcement mechanisms that work well with mnemonic password choice. We expect that proactive password checkers,[20] which verify that a password is not part of a known weak subset of the password space, may be an effective tool. But as our empirical study has shown, what engineers expect to work and what users actually make to work are two different things. In our view, rigorous experimental testing of interface usability is one of the necessary ingredients for robust secure systems.

---

20 J. Yan, "A Note on Proactive Password Checking," *Proceedings of the 2001 ACM New Security Paradigms Workshop* (New Mexico, Sept. 2001), ACM Press.

Moreover, because the subject samples used in our experiment (all young undergraduates) were likely to be biased by age, gender, and race, it would be very interesting to look into how widespread the behaviors characteristic of our experimental groups might be in a broader environment.

## Acknowledgments

We thank Sacha Brostoff, Lorrie Cranor, Simson L. Garfinkel, and anonymous reviewers whose comments helped us improve this chapter.

## About the Authors

Jeff Yan is a lecturer in the School of Computing Science, Unversity of Newcastle, in England. He is interested in most aspects of information security, both theoretical and practical. His recent research is largely about systems security, applied crypto, and human aspects of security. He has a Ph.D. in Computer Science from Cambridge University.

*jyan@cantab.net*

Alan Blackwell is a lecturer in the Cambridge University Computer Laboratory, with qualifications in professional engineering and experimental psychology. His research interests include design practice and human-computer interaction. He is a Fellow of Darwin College, Cambridge.

*Alan.Blackwell@cl.cam.ac.uk*

Ross Anderson leads the security group at the Computer Laboratory, Cambridge University, where he is a professor of security engineering. He was one of the founders of the study of information security economics. A Fellow of the IEEE, he was also one of the pioneers of peer-to-peer systems, of API attacks on cryptographic processors, and of the study of hardware tamper resistance. He was one of the inventors of Serpent, a finalist in the competition to find an Advanced Encryption Standard. He wrote the standard textbook *Security Engineering—A Guide to Building Dependable Distributed Systems*. Contact him at *Ross.Anderson@cl.cam.ac.uk*.

*http://www.cl.cam.ac.uk/~rja14/*

Alasdair Grant is a technical lead on code generation in the compilation tools group at a leading CPU vendor. His research interests include program correctness, static analysis, and binary translation. He has an M.A. in Math and Computer Science from Cambridge University and is a member of the ACM and SIGPLAN.

*algrant@acm.org*

# CHAPTER EIGHT

# Designing Authentication Systems with Challenge Questions

MIKE JUST

**W**HAT IS YOUR MOTHER'S MAIDEN NAME?" "What is your date of birth?" Such questions are often used to authenticate an individual. The answers often represent information well known to the individual, but (one hopes) not so widely known so as to be available to a potential impersonator. These *challenge questions* require an individual to recall and present previously registered answers when authenticating.

In this chapter, I review the design and evaluation of authentication systems that use challenge questions and answers to identify or authenticate individuals. I pay particular attention to ensuring that the design satisfies the security, usability, and privacy requirements of the authentication system.

While systems today use challenge questions for recovering forgotten passwords, they can be used more broadly for other forms of authentication, such as routine user login. This chapter focuses on password recovery but considers other applications as appropriate.

## Challenge Questions as a Form of Authentication

Most people are familiar with passwords as a form of authentication. Passwords or Personal Identification Numbers (PINs) are two examples of using "something you know" in order to authenticate. Biometrics, such as a fingerprint or voice recognition, represent "something you are," and a physical token, such as a bank card, represents "something you have." These three "something" categories are the common means of classifying authentication techniques. Challenge questions (and their corresponding answers), like passwords, are a form of "something you know" because they represent information that is known to an individual.

When I refer to challenge questions in this chapter, I am referring to questions and answers that are deposited or registered by an individual. For the purposes of subsequent authentication, the questions are posed to the individual who is required to repeat the original answer as his response.

An alternative form of "challenge questions" does not require the explicit deposit of information by an individual. Rather, the individual responds to questions posed by the account manager. In the case of a financial institution, for example, the individual might be asked to provide the monetary amount of his most recent transaction. I refer to such information as *shared secrets*, as they represent information shared *a priori* with the account manager.

## Using Challenge Questions for Credential Recovery

Security credentials such as passwords and physical security tokens are issued in a variety of situations. Sometimes an initial identification step takes place in which an individual must show a passport or other identification papers. In other cases—for example, when establishing an account to read a free online newspaper—individuals identify themselves, and no efforts are made to verify a claimed identity. If an individual should forget a password or lose a security token, he might be able to recover his lost credential by re-identifying himself to the credential issuer. However, this is often inconvenient and generally requires a physical rather than an online interaction. In cases where an individual initially identified himself without providing any identification papers, re-identification may not be possible without the use of a shared secret or challenge questions.

Differing somewhat from passwords that are often memorized by an individual in support of future, routine authentication, challenge questions are most often based upon information already known to the user. While password construction might similarly rely upon information known to an individual, password rules (e.g., requirements to include both alphabetic and numeric characters) typically necessitate some additional memorization. Thus, challenge questions are particularly well-suited for credential recovery, as they do not require individuals to memorize additional information that subsequently could be forgotten.

## Using Challenge Questions for Routine Authentication

While offering some advantage for the purpose of credential recovery, challenge questions can also be used for the day-to-day authentication of an individual. However, challenge questions may be inconvenient for day-to-day authentication for a number of reasons:

- *A challenge question system may require an additional step to obtain the challenge questions.* Unlike a system whereby the individual submits his username and password in one step, when questions are specific to the individual, the username must be provided first and the appropriate questions retrieved and presented to the individual for his response. Such delay may be intolerable to individuals.

- *A challenge question system may choose not to obscure display of the answers.* To prevent "shoulder-surfing" attacks, credentials such as passwords are often obscured (e.g., each password character is replaced with a "*" when displayed on the screen). Because challenge questions may prompt answers that include varying capitalization and punctuation, challenge question systems often allow users to enter responses unobscured.

- *A challenge question system may use more than one question-answer pair.* In this case, the use of multiple questions will most certainly require more time for authentication, at least when compared to password authentication.

- *A challenge question system may make use of an "out-of-band" authentication step.* This might require, for example, sending mail to the individual's address of record (e.g., his home address). Such a step may introduce unacceptable delay for routine authentication.

In addition, because the answers to challenge questions are not constructed in the same way as passwords (e.g., with no requirements for including punctuation, capitalization, etc.), the answers may be "dictionary searchable." By using challenge questions for routine authentication, a system may give an attacker more opportunity to validate his answer guesses. A recovery process can be controlled more easily; because recovery attempts are less frequent, each such attempt can result in a notice to the individual account owner. A poorly designed challenge question system can dramatically weaken the security of an otherwise strong password system.

## Criteria for Building and Evaluating a Challenge Question System

We begin our introduction to the design of challenge question systems by introducing criteria that are helpful in both their design and evaluation. These criteria relate to the privacy, security, and usability of the challenge question system.

### Privacy Criteria

In environments that use personal information, it should be common practice to follow recognized privacy principles to protect answers to challenge questions.[1] For the use of challenge questions and answers to authenticate users, one principle in particular seems relevant: *collection limitation*. This criterion serves to limit the collection of personal user

---

1   "Guidelines on the Protection of Privacy and Transborder Flows of Personal Data," Organization for Economic Co-operation and Development (OECD),  1980.

information to what is necessary for the purpose of authenticating an individual. Adherence to this principle helps to ensure that only information necessary to support a suitable level of security and usability is maintained.

Designers should give particular caution to using questions that ask for personal information, such as "What is your mother's maiden name?", because the answer, while possibly obscured (hashed), will be stored at the account server. Preference should be given to asking nonpersonal questions, provided that they offer sufficient security and usability.

In addition, answers to challenge questions should be used only for the purpose of recovering user access to one's account—conforming to a *use limitation* principle. If challenge questions are to be used for other purposes, individuals should be notified and their consent obtained. Furthermore, care should be taken when asking for answers that users may find sensitive. Therefore, best practice involves offering as much choice as possible (while maintaining a suitable security level) to individuals for question selection, allowing individual control over the answers that are provided.

## Security Criteria

The security of a challenge question system is related directly to the confidentiality of the challenge question answers. Other properties such as integrity and availability are also important to the security of the overall system, but are not the focus of our framework. The following security criteria apply primarily to the content of individual questions and answers:

*Guessing difficulty*

Answers should be difficult to guess and have an answer space with a fairly uniform distribution. Questions that can be guessed successfully in a small number of attempts (for example, "What is your eye color?") do not make good challenge questions.

*Observation difficulty*

The answers to challenge questions should be difficult for an attacker to retrieve or observe easily. In particular, the answers should not be available from public sources. Questions that individuals are often asked to answer, such as "What is your mother's maiden name?", do not pose much observation difficulty. Unlike guessing difficulty, a determination of a question's observation difficulty is more subjective, as the difficulty of determining the answer is dependent upon a number of factors (e.g., the availability of the answer). In addition, observation difficulty will differ for individuals that have different relationships with the user—for example, family, friends, acquaintances, colleagues, or strangers.

For an authentication system that consists of multiple questions, additional criteria should be considered, including the total guessing and observation difficulty for the entire set of questions. In addition, answers should be unrelated so that both their availability and entropy can be maintained independently when multiple questions are used. One way to support answer independence is to use independent questions (questions that would encourage the submission of independent answers).

## Usability Criteria

The usability of a challenge question system is concerned with providing a user-friendly experience at the stages of both answer registration and subsequent answer presentation. The following usability criteria should be used when evaluating a challenge question system:

*Applicability*

> The applicability criterion attempts to characterize the size of the target population for which a question might be applicable. For example, a question about pets would not apply to those individuals who have never owned a pet. Attempts should be made to support highly applicable questions, although not at the expense of other criteria. A sufficiently large quantity of possible questions can be used to ensure enough coverage across the population of individuals.

*Memorability*

> An answer is memorable as long as the user is able to recall the answer. This generally implies that the answer would be personally significant. Information that is used frequently will be more memorable, indicating that answers reflecting the habits, activities, or practices of users provide suitable answers. For an answer with high recall, only the likelihood of recalling an answer rather than the likelihood of knowing some answer is considered for the memorability criterion. For example, although many people may not know their high-school locker combination, those who do know the combination are likely to be able to continue to recall the answer. However, such a question would be applicable (as discussed for the applicability criterion) to only a smaller set of individuals that would know of an answer.

*Repeatability*

> There are at least two aspects of answer repeatability to consider. First, answers should have few syntactic representations. For example, a question involving an address might be answered with "St." or "Street," and the word contractions (e.g., "St." versus "Street") may cause a discrepancy. Second, answers should have a semantic value that remains the same over time. For example, questions about favorites may be susceptible to the answer changing over time. For this reason, questions asking for "favorites" should be avoided in favor of "first time" or perhaps "memorable" qualifiers.

Additional usability issues include the number of questions and answers stored and the number of answers required to authenticate. These issues are discussed further in the next section.

## Types of Questions and Answers

In this section, we present a candidate classification of questions and answers. For both questions and answers, three different types are described: fixed, open, and controlled. Depending on the system needs, various combinations of questions and answers can be used.

## Question Types

The two types of questions that are likely to be most familiar are fixed questions and open questions. A *fixed question* provides a list of preset questions to a user, where the user's choice of question can be taken only "as is" from this list. At the other extreme is an *open question*, where a user has complete choice and control over the question; guidance as to the question construction may be provided to the user, but the user enters the question in free-form text.

A *controlled question* lies between the extremes of a fixed question and an open question; it is a question whose content is partially fixed, although modifiable by the user. Two potential variations of a controlled question follow:

- The fixed question might allow for additional text to be added, forming a modification of the original question. The modified question would be presented subsequently to the individual for authentication. For example, consider the following question that supports customized addition of a name by an individual to the original question. In this case, the individual would choose an appropriate *Name* along with his answer to the question, and at subsequent authentication, the question would be asked along with the individual-provided name.

  ```
  What is Name's middle name?
  ```

- The fixed question might support a combination with an optional user-provided hint, where the hint would be presented to the individual for authentication. For example, to the following original fixed question the user might provide the following hint: "Dog." The question and the hint would be provided to the user at authentication time. For the user, this hint might indicate a special date associated with his pet dog, such as its date of purchase. In this case, during answer registration, the individual is asked to provide a hint, and during answer presentation, the hint is provided for the user as an aid to recalling his answer.

  ```
  Answer Registration
  What is a memorable date for you? Date
  Hint: Hint

  Answer Presentation
  What is a memorable date for you? Date
  Hint: Dog
  ```

## Answer Types

A similar distinction applies for fixed answers, controlled answers, and open answers. A *fixed answer* set involves user selection of an answer from a preset list of answers. At the other extreme, an *open answer* involves a user manually entering his response. Guidance may be provided as part of answer registration, but the answer is entered in free-form by the user.

A subtle variation is a *controlled answer,* where the answer space is neither fixed nor open. Some ways in which this might be achieved are:

- Providing a fixed set of answers where the answer space is large enough so that most potential answers are allowed. For example, in case an individual answers with a geographic location, the answer may be entered using drop-down menus listing all possible cities, states/provinces, and countries for some region.

- The individual is able to enter an answer, but the format of the answer is controlled—answers that do not conform are rejected. For example, an individual might be asked to provide a memorable numeric value so that alphabetic and punctuation characters would not be permitted for inclusion in the answer text.

# Designing a Challenge Question Authentication System

Previous sections presented options for question and answer types and criteria upon which to evaluate a challenge question system design. This section discusses the design of a complete authentication system.

## Determining the Number of Questions to Use

Usability tends toward requiring fewer questions and answers. This lessens the recall requirements for an individual, and also introduces fewer repeatability mistakes. For reasons of security, however, it is often necessary that more than one question-answer pair be registered by a user. This is to ensure a sufficient difficulty for either guessing or observing the answer. To ensure a sufficient level of protection against guessing, the entropy for the answers should provide a level of security similar to that for routine authentication (that may be performed with a password). In situations in which no complementary security measures are used (see the later section, "Complementary Security Techniques"), the entropy for the answers should be at least that for the routine authentication. In terms of *guessability* considerations, the strength of a challenge question system can be measured explicitly against password-based authentication. For example, an 8-character password constructed from the set of 52 upper- and lowercase characters, 10 numbers, and 32 punctuation characters, has approximately $2^{52}$ possible passwords. An 8-character answer to a question that uses only lowercase characters has only $2^{38}$ possibilities.

Unfortunately, this number is misleading. Answers to questions cannot be expected to conform to the same, strict rules as for passwords; otherwise, the answers effectively become passwords. Instead, we would expect many answers to be dictionary words. This can be a problem, as most dictionaries have only between $2^{16}$ and $2^{20}$ words, while studies show that many adults have vocabularies between $2^{15}$ and $2^{17}$ words. Thus, even with these extremely optimistic values, at least two questions would need to be asked to ensure security similar to that provided by an 8-character password. In addition, as discussed earlier under "Security Criteria," *observability* is important, but unfortunately is less quantifiable.

When more than one question is asked, both the interface and the administrative storage for the answers should ensure that multiple answer attempts are all validated before an indication of success or failure is given. Through the interface, for example, if two questions are asked, an indication of success or failure should be given only when both questions have been answered. If not, an attacker can guess answers to one question at a time, even though the entropy level of only one question might not provide a sufficient level of security. Similarly, as with the storage of passwords, answers should be obscured (hashed), but additionally, when multiple answers are used, they should be obscured in such a way that if the obscured answers are compromised, an attacker would have to guess all answers before determining the success of his guess. This can be achieved, for example, by inputting all answers to a single hash rather than by separately hashing each answer.

Variations exist where the number of questions presented at recovery is less than the number of questions registered. There are at least two models:

- The user registers $n$ questions, but is presented only $t \leq n$ questions upon recovery. All $t$ questions must be answered properly in order for the recovery process to continue.

- The user registers $n$ questions, and is presented $t \leq n$ questions upon recovery. Differing from the previous model, only $r < t$ questions must be answered in order for the recovery process to continue.

The first model is an attempt to offer a level of security equivalent to that of $n$ questions, but to provide a usability benefit at the time of recovery, with fewer questions to the user. However, the usability benefits appear only to reduce the time required for recovery and do not affect the arguably more important concerns of memorability and repeatability (the user still has to remember the answers for $n$ questions, as it is not known what questions will be posed at recovery). Yet there is some benefit for users who register $n$ questions, but after a period of time happen to forget the answers to some of these questions. The purpose of the second option is to tolerate mistakes upon answer presentation. However, it seems that an additional question is being used to tolerate such mistakes whereas a more usable system might attempt to reduce the number of questions used.

For a set of candidate questions, some form of *question grouping* might be beneficial. For example, supposing that three questions are to be registered, it may be advantageous to require that one fixed and two controlled questions be selected, and for these questions, that a combination of fact-based and opinion-based questions be used. Alternatively, questions might be classified based on their topic so that users might have to select one question that required them to enter a "date" response, while the second might require a numeric response and the third, an alphabetic response. Finally, if one can classify users' questions based on their security strength, the system could offer multiple classes where a user must select one question from each class as part of registration.

### Determining the Types of Questions and Answers to Use

The types of questions and answers used contribute to both the security and the usability of the challenge question authentication system.

### Determining the appropriate question type

With fixed questions, individuals are not required to conceive of their own questions at registration, perhaps offering an advantage to some. An open question has potential for improved memorability and improved applicability for individuals who are better able to recognize information that is more memorable to them, and to construct an appropriate question from this information. However, asking for a completely open question might require too much novelty. A controlled question seems to support a reasonable compromise whereby only part of the question development is delegated to the individual. For example, a question may be as simple as "Enter a number that is memorable for you" (giving some content control and guidance for the individual), and the individual can provide the hint, "Grade 8 locker," thereby providing some equivalence to an open question. However, controlled questions also share the weaknesses of open questions, as the question or hint entered can be insecure by providing too much guidance for the answer to an attacker. Notice, however, that the repeatability and the memorability of the hint are not a concern because the hint is shown to the user upon answer presentation.

With a fixed question, individuals are prevented from a potentially insecure question selection (e.g., "What color are my eyes?") whose answer space is exhausted easily, thereby providing a security advantage to an attacker. With an open question, individuals might select a question that is potentially insecure, although capable individuals are able to select more secure questions—for example, individuals are able to customize questions directly related and meaningful to their childhood. In addition, with open questions, individuals can form associative word pairs (e.g., the word "cat" might associate with the word "my pet," or possibly with "shedding").

When developing questions for a challenge question system, further distinctions can be made. One such distinction is that of *fact-based* versus *opinion-based* questions.[2] Fact-based questions relate to factual statements regarding an individual. Such questions might be expected to have less varying answers over time, and can be constructed as such (e.g., by asking for the first place the individual lived rather than his most recent residence). Care must be taken, though, as the answers to such questions (involving factual information about a user) might be more readily available to an attacker. Opinion-based questions relate to beliefs an individual has, and thus may be more susceptible to change over time. However, they should be less pervasive than the answers to fact-based questions, as opinions might be less frequently presented and recorded as part of the individual's day-to-day activities.

### Determining the appropriate answer type

Individuals can be prevented from selecting insecure answers if the system requires choosing an answer from a set of fixed answers. Such systems must be designed to disallow answers that would be very common and thus easily guessed by an attacker. However, memorability and repeatability may be hampered if there is no unique answer to satisfy an individual's preference (either the individual's first choice is not available, or more than

---

2   W. Haga and M. Zviran, "Question-and-Answer Passwords: An Empirical Evaluation," *Information Systems* 16:3 (1991), 335–343.

one satisfactory choice is available). With open answers, larger variation in the answer space is provided, although for certain questions, a user would be able to select highly probable answers. Memorability may be better than with fixed answers, although repeatability can be problematic if the registered answer is ambiguous (e.g., "St." versus "Street"). Controlled answers offer an alternative whereby a large answer space can be used, but control over the possible values improves repeatability. There do not seem to be any significant security advantages offered by using a controlled answer instead of by supporting a large answer space.

An interesting option is supported with answers whereby the answer registered and the answer presented need not be of the same type. Two such options are:

- *Fixed answer at registration; open answer at authentication.* When registering his question and answer, the individual is provided a fixed answer set corresponding to the question. However, at subsequent authentication, an open answer is designed, allowing the individual to enter his response, rather than choosing from a list. Still, as noted earlier, fixed answers at registration are problematic.

- *Open answer at registration; fixed answer at authentication.* When registering his question and answer, the individual provides a free-form response. However, at subsequent authentication, a fixed list of answers is provided, one of which is the correct answer originally chosen by the individual. This option offers improved repeatability and can be an advantage to individuals with poor memories.

Expanding upon the open-fixed option, a likely implementation might involve the storage of a set of "fake answers" along with the user's given answer upon registration. At answer presentation, the user's answer would consistently be presented along with the same set of fake answers. There are numerous issues to consider regarding the secure implementation of such a system. In particular:

- The "fake answer" set must not be repeated across users; otherwise, an attacker could easily determine the fake answer sets (and thus eliminate and recover the user's submitted answer) by attempting to recover two or more users.

- The fake answer set must be consistent from one recovery attempt to the next; otherwise, an attacker could identify the user's answer as the only consistent answer across a number of recovery attempts.

- The fake answer set must be changed should the user choose to modify his submitted answer; otherwise, an attacker (aware of a potential answer update) could determine the user's answer from the variance in the answer sets from before and after the update.

Care must be taken in the selection of the fake answer sets for each user so that the user's submitted answer is sufficiently concealed by the fake answers. For example, suppose that the user is asked the question "What is your favorite fruit?" but answers with the word "mushroom." In this case, if only fruits were provided as part of the fake answer set, the user's submitted answer would be easily distinguishable. Optionally, "incorrect" fake answers might be provided in order to anticipate any user variance and serve to confuse would-be attackers. Finally, two security problems present themselves with this scenario:

- The size of the fake answer set should be large enough to resist exhaustive guessing attacks against the individual user.

- The user's submitted answer must not be hashed, as it must be presented to the user as part of answer presentation. Thus, while great care must be taken for this solution, it does offer an interesting variation.

## Complementary Security Techniques

In addition to the construction, evaluation, and grouping of questions, additional techniques can be used for authenticating individuals, some of which are more suited to a recovery system than to general user authentication. Most notably, mailing to an address of record is a useful tool. For example, if the address of record is an email address, then as part of the recovery process an appropriate message can be emailed giving instructions. Some recovery systems will even choose to rely only upon a mailing, and not include any additional authentication (e.g., with a challenge question). While it is certainly possible for an attacker to intercept unprotected email (if an individual needs to recover, he likely won't have key material to support a protected email message), the decision to use an additional factor is a risk management decision. When combined with a challenge question recovery system, an additional factor is used, and an email might be sent immediately after the user has answered the challenge questions successfully. By using an address of record, additional security is provided, as other security precautions are typically in place to control access to that address.[3] Adding another communication step does impact usability; however, the extent to which this is true depends primarily upon the amount of time required for this step to be completed. For some accounts, such latency may not be tolerable.

In addition, there are additional security measures that can greatly improve the usability of a challenge question system by reducing the security rigor that is applied to each question and possibly reducing the number of questions. These include:

- A system lockout feature whereby access to the recovery functionality would be reduced or removed after a number of failed attempts.

- A "graduated lockout" feature that would reduce access over time, perhaps locking out recovery for a fixed period of time after some number of failed recovery attempts, and fully blocking the recovery after some number of temporary lockouts.

Of course, the denial-of-service implications of using such features must be considered carefully. Reverse Turing Tests (e.g., CAPTCHA[4]) help reduce the likelihood of success for

---

3   S. Garfinkel, "Email-Based Identification and Authentication: An Alternative to PKI?", *IEEE Security and Privacy* (Nov./Dec. 2003).

4   The CAPTCHA Project; *http://www.captcha.net/*.

# CANADA'S GOL SOLUTION

A candidate challenge question system, based upon the framework in this chapter, was recently designed in support of Canada's Government OnLine solution.[a] Input to some of the design decisions came from a focus group consisting of 17 individuals from the general population that had Internet experience. Compared to a previous five-question system that was perceived negatively, participants of the current group appreciated the following three-question system:

- *Question 1.* Consists of 15 fixed questions, where the focus group input was used to determine several of these questions. The corresponding answer is open, both at registration and recovery. Some of the fixed questions proposed for this fixed list include: "What was my first pet's name?" "Where did I first meet my significant other?" and "What was the last name of my childhood best friend?"

- *Question 2.* Consists of a controlled question, "Please choose a person who is memorable to you," and an open hint. Originally, a fixed hint was used, but participants were not comfortable with the choices it offered, as they had difficulty mapping their desired hint to a single selection of a fixed hint.

- *Question 3.* Consists of a controlled question, "Please choose a date that is memorable to you," and an open hint. The corresponding answer is controlled at both registration and recovery, consisting of drop-down selections for each of year, month, and day.

Free-form answers are normalized, removing whitespace, some punctuation, and capitalization. A confirmation page is displayed to confirm the user's answers. Some additional lessons learned from the focus group include the following:

- Although questions related to "first-time" events are good for repeatability, they can be more difficult for older users to recall.

- Regarding questions with calendar date answers, participants indicated an inability to recall more than a half-dozen dates. However, even in this situation, such a question offers strength against a random attack, while being more susceptible to a targeted attack. Thus, additional questions and/or complementary security techniques should also be used.

- Although participants indicated a preference for open questions, the candidate list of questions they provided did confirm the designers' assumptions that an insufficient level of security would be attained for open questions.

---

[a] Mike Just, "An Overview of Public Key Certificate Support for Canada's Government On-Line (GoL) Initiative," *Proceedings of the 2nd Annual PKI Research Workshop* (April 2003).

automated attacks.[5] Client puzzles[6] offer a variation for limiting the effectiveness of denial-of-service attacks, whereby the client is required to perform additional computations before his request can be processed.

## Some Examples of Current Practice

Challenge questions are used at a variety of web sites, often in combination with additional protections such as mailing to an address of record (typically an email address). For example, web email sites such as Yahoo! and Hotmail, and e-commerce sites such as Amazon, eBay, Chapters, and FutureShop, each use challenge questions in support of account recovery. In addition, online banking services similarly support a challenge question system.

From a privacy point of view, personal information is sometimes used as part of identification during recovery for some of these systems. Several banking sites use personal information (shared secrets) as part of account recovery. This is perhaps not too surprising, as the personal information used was related directly to information already retained by the banks. However, some of the web email sites, for example, do collect additional personal information (such as a date of birth) with the apparent, sole purpose of recovery.

From a security point of view, of those solutions in which a user registers a recovery question, only one such question is registered. In most cases, the use of personal information, or mailing to an address of record, is used to provide additional security. In cases where recovery questions are used, users are asked to choose from a list of questions (an option described earlier as a "fixed question").

### About the Author

 Mike Just is a policy and business strategist with the Canadian Federal Government. He is also an adjunct professor at Carleton University. His interest is in ensuring the delivery of secure yet usable online solutions for government. Prior work includes federal government IT security policy development, and work as an information security specialist at Entrust. He holds a Ph.D. in computer science from Carleton University and is active in the computer-security community.

*http://www.scs.carleton.ca/~just/*

5   G. Mori and J. Malik, "Up to the Challenge: Computer Scientists Crack a Set of AI-Based Puzzles," *SIAM News* (Nov. 2002).

6   J. Brainard and A. Jules, "Client Puzzles: A Cryptographic Defense Against Connection Depletion," *Proceedings of the Network and Distributed System Security (NDSS) Symposium* (Feb. 1999).

# CHAPTER NINE

# Graphical Passwords

**FABIAN MONROSE AND MICHAEL K. REITER**

**A**GRAPHICAL PASSWORD IS A SECRET THAT A HUMAN USER INPUTS TO A COMPUTER WITH THE AID OF the computer's graphical input (e.g., mouse, stylus, or touch screen) and output devices. In this chapter, we review the arguments supporting graphical passwords as being potentially superior to text passwords, present several graphical password designs, and discuss some analyses of graphical password memorability and security.

## Introduction

The ubiquity of graphical user interfaces and input devices, such as the mouse, stylus, and touch screen, that permit other than typed input, has enabled the emergence of graphical passwords. Graphical passwords are particularly useful for systems that do not have keyboards. In addition, they offer the possibility of addressing known weaknesses in text passwords. History has shown that the distribution of text passwords chosen by human users has entropy far lower than possible,[1, 2, 3, 4] and this has remained a significant weakness of user authentication for over 30 years. Given the fact that pictures are generally more easily remembered than words,[5, 6] it is conceivable that humans would select and remember graphical passwords that are stronger than the text passwords they typically select.

The goal of this chapter is to review some proposed graphical password schemes and the analyses that have been performed to evaluate their security and/or usability. Where appropriate, we explain these schemes in the context of results from the psychological literature. In surveying this information, we also hope to elucidate those topics in graphical passwords that are candidates for future research.

Today, text passwords have many uses, but these uses can be grouped into two types:

- *Authentication.* The first and most common is as a method of user *authentication*—that is, to confirm the claimed identity of a human user. The output of this process is one bit: "1" means that the user is as claimed, "0" indicates that he is not.

- *Key generation.* The second is as a method of *key generation* by the human user, for the purpose of using the resulting key in a cryptographic algorithm. A common example of this type is file or disk encryption using a password: the user inputs her password, and this password is used to encrypt or decrypt certain stored contents of the device. Unlike authentication, key generation requires an output of many more bits (e.g., 80), and each bit should be unpredictable to an adversary who does not know the password.

In both cases, the output should be repeatable by a user who knows the password.

In order to stand in for text passwords, graphical passwords supporting both types of use are needed. While arguably the two types of use can be supported via a common mechanism—the only difference being whether the entered password is compared against a stored template (as in the authentication case) or output directly—most proposed graphical password systems have a password space that could be searched exhaustively by an automated program in a short time. Because this is exactly the attack that user-based key generation is intended to address, such schemes may not be useful for key generation;

1   R. Morris and K. Thompson, "Password Security: A Case History," *Communications of the* ACM 22:11 (Nov. 1979), 594–597.

2   D. Feldmeier and P. Karn, "UNIX Password Security—Ten Years Later," *Advances in Cryptology—CRYPTO '89* (Lecture Notes in Computer Science 435), 1990.

3   D. Klein, "Foiling the Cracker: A Survey of, and Improvements to, Password Security," *Proceedings of the 2nd USENIX Security Workshop* (Aug. 1990), 5–14.

4   T. Wu, "A Real-World Analysis of Kerberos Password Security," *Proceedings of the 1999 ISOC Symposium on Network and Distributed System Security* (Feb. 1999).

5   D. L. Nelson, U. S. Reed, and J. R. Walling, "Picture Superiority Effect," *Journal of Experimental Psychology: Human Learning and Memory* 3 (1977), 485–497.

6   S. Madigan, "Picture Memory," *Imagery, Memory, and Cognition* (Hillsdale, NJ: Erlbaum, 1983), 65–86.

nevertheless, they may still be useful for user authentication. We thus find it useful to separate the two notions.

As with text passwords, most graphical password schemes can be configured to permit the user to choose the password, or to have the password generated by the system and given to the user. In the latter case, the security of the graphical password is presumably high, whereas the usability might suffer. In the former case, usability might be better, but as we will show, the security of the graphical passwords might be weakened.

## A Picture Is Worth a Thousand Words

One of the most compelling reasons for exploring the use of a graphical password scheme stems from the fact that humans seem to possess a remarkable ability for recalling pictures, whether they are line drawings or real objects. The so-called *picture effect*—the effect of pictorial and object representations on a variety of measures of learning and memory—has been studied for decades.[7, 8, 9, 10, 11, 12] For the most part, cognitive scientists and psychologists have shown that there is a substantial improvement of performance in recall and recognition with pictorial representations of to-be-remembered material over verbal representations.

The picture effect has itself been the focus of numerous debates related to perception, and the most prevalent theory in its support is known as the *dual-code theory*, which postulates that language and knowledge of worlds are represented in functionally distinct verbal and nonverbal memory systems. Examples of dual process theory can be found in experiences that we have all had at some time or another: we meet someone, know them to be familiar, but do not know who they are; we recognize a melody, but fail to remember its name or when or where we heard it before; we read a line of a poem, know it, but do not know where we have read it before, much less the title or author of the poem. In all these cases, we experience a sense of familiarity, but we have, at least at first, no access to any contextual information.[13, 14]

7   M. W. Calkins, "Short Studies in Memory and Association from the Wellesley College Laboratory," *Psychological Review*, 5 (1898), 451–462.

8   R. N. Shepard, "Recognition Memory for Words, Sentences, and Pictures," *Journal of Verbal Learnings and Verbal Behavior* 6 (1967), 156–163.

9   A. Paivio, T. B. Rogers, and P. C. Smythe, "Why Are Pictures Easier to Recall Than Words?" *Psychonomic Science* 11 (1968),137–138.

10  L. Standing, "Learning 10,000 Pictures," *Quarterly Journal of Experimental Psychology* 25 (1973), 207–222.

11  G. H. Bower, M. B. Karlin, and A. Dueck, "Comprehension and Memory for Pictures," *Memory and Cognition* 2 (1975), 216–220.

12  S. Smith, "Authenticating Users by Word Association," *Proceedings of the 31st Annual Meeting of the Human Factors Society* (1987), 135–138.

13  G. Mandler, "Your Face Looks Familiar but I Can't Remember Your Name: A Review of Dual Process Theory," *Relating Theory and Data* (1991), 207–225.

14  Paivio, Rogers, and Smythe.

Whatever the underlying reason, our ability to recall images may lend itself naturally to building robust human authentication and key generation technologies. In fact, much of the work that we see today on graphical passwords is motivated in part by the scientific literature in psychology and perception. Although we do not provide a complete survey of proposed schemes here, the following subsections present a set of representative examples in the three main areas: image recognition, tapping or drawing, and image interpretation.

## Image Recognition

The most widely explored paradigm for graphical passwords is that of image recognition—that is, the user enters her "password" by recognizing the images that comprise it from among many more images. These images might be those of persons, everyday objects, or abstract images such as those in Figure 9-1, showing illustrative examples of "random art" which has been proposed for use in graphical password schemes based on image recognition.[15] A typical presentation of the interface would be to place a panel of several images in front of the user, from which the user would select one or more that she recognizes as being part of her password. After this, other panels may be placed in front of the user, for selection of additional images. In some cases, multiple images from a single panel can be selected, and in some schemes, the password includes the order in which the images are selected.

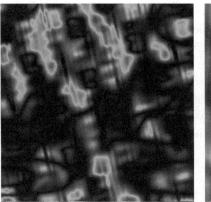 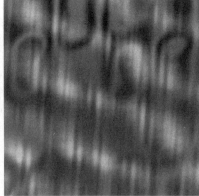

FIGURE 9-1. *Illustrative examples of "random art," which has been proposed for use in graphical password schemes based on image recognition*

Generally, a scheme based on image recognition requires that the images within each panel be the same each time the panel is presented. Because the password images must always be present, doing otherwise would permit an attacker who is interacting with the system to determine those images in the password as those that appear repeatedly in the panel. In addition, it is commonplace for these schemes to present the (same) panel

---

15 Some examples of "random art" used in graphical password schemes can be found at *http://www.random-art.org/*.

images permuted in a random fashion each time so that the user chooses images based on the image itself, as opposed to the position the image occupies in the panel.

Because of the limited size of the password space in image recognition schemes, these systems are generally not suitable for key generation; an automated search would easily exhaust the space of possible passwords. Thus, they are generally used only for authentication, and then only when there is an online reference monitor that can stop an automated search. This is commonplace with short text passwords (e.g., PINs) as well, where an account might "lock out" after five incorrect password guesses, for example. Whether such a graphical password scheme is sufficiently secure depends on a number of factors. Later in this chapter, we give an example of two graphical password schemes that allow users to select their passwords, and show that the type of images can have a significant effect on security.

## Tapping or Drawing

Other techniques that have been explored regarding the design of graphical password schemes include displaying a reference image and asking the user to utilize a mouse or stylus to draw or click in reference to the object. In these schemes, the object is placed to provide the user a reference point for placing her drawing or clicks so that her input will be repeatable. For example, Blonder proposes a scheme in which a figure (e.g., a face) is displayed to the user, and the user is asked to click in various "tap regions" (e.g., the left ear), possibly in a particular order.[16] The sequence of tap regions constitutes the password. Jermyn *et al.* propose an approach, called "Draw-a-Secret" or DAS, in which they utilize merely a grid as the reference object.[17] Then, the user is asked to draw free-form on the grid, as shown in Figure 9-2. The sequence of line crossings on the grid constitutes the password in this scheme.

Jermyn *et al.* performed an analysis that suggests that the space of passwords in the DAS scheme, as well as the entropy of "memorable" such passwords, will be sufficiently large to enable the use of DAS for key generation. Such a claim can only be evaluated with substantial user studies, which to our knowledge have not yet been performed. However, recent analysis suggests that the scheme may not be as secure in this sense as initially thought (see the later discussion).

## Image Interpretation

Recently, Stubblefield and Simon have proposed a graphical password scheme based on the notion of image interpretation.[18] In this scheme, a series of *n* inkblots are generated

---

16 G. E. Blonder, "Graphical password," U.S. Patent 5559961, Lucent Technologies, Inc. (Murray Hill, NJ), Aug. 30, 1995.

17 I. Jermyn, A. Mayer, F. Monrose, M. Reiter, and A. Rubin. "The Design and Analysis of Graphical Passwords," *Proceedings of the 8th USENIX Security Symposium* (Aug. 1999).

18 A. Stubblefield and D. Simon, "Inkblot Authentication," Microsoft Technical Report MSR-TR-2004-85 (Aug. 2004).

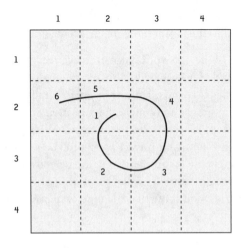

*FIGURE 9-2. An example password in DAS; in DAS, a password is the sequence of line crossings made by the user's drawing*

and displayed one at a time. For each image, the user forms a word association and enters it via the keyboard. For example, for the inkblot in Figure 9-3, she might enter "batman." After each word association is entered, the next inkblot in the series is displayed, and the final password is derived from the words—for example, concatenating the first and last letters of each word. This scheme presumes that words prompted by inkblot-like images are easier to recall than passwords recalled without such prompting, and moreover, that there is significant entropy in the word associations ascribed by users, even for the same set of inkblots. In fact, the authors believe that this entropy is sufficiently high that this scheme might be useful for key generation, not only for authentication. Again, such claims can only be adequately evaluated with sufficiently large user trials, but unfortunately, no such studies on this scheme have been conducted to date.

*FIGURE 9-3. An example inkblot; the password is derived from word associations made for each inkblot in a series of images*

# Picture Perfect?

In this section, we summarize several analyses that have been performed to evaluate the security and usability of graphical passwords. While the old adage that a picture is worth a thousand words might indeed be true, it's not entirely clear that user-chosen graphical passwords of the type suggested to date offer additional security over text passwords. An alternative may be to utilize only system-chosen passwords, although we might expect that this would sacrifice some degree of memorability; we do not explore this avenue here, as we are unaware of empirical results to evaluate this conjecture in general.

## Security

As with usability analyses, which we examine later in this chapter, the most compelling security analyses for graphical password schemes permitting user password selection are those performed on the basis of extensive user experiments. After all, the security weaknesses of text passwords were revealed only by their use in practice. That said, to date there are few such user studies, and so graphical password design efforts have appealed to surrogate analyses in an effort to reason about the security of particular proposals.

### Key generation

The graphical password scheme that has been the topic of most such analyses is the Draw-a-Secret (DAS) scheme.[19] In the paper that originally proposed this scheme, Jermyn *et al.* reason about the size of the memorable password space, giving a counting argument that the number of memorable DAS passwords (i.e., those having a simple algorithm to generate them) quickly outpaces the number of text passwords that are commonly chosen, as measured by the size of dictionaries commonly applied to break them. As discussed previously in this chapter, the password space is particularly important when considering the use of this scheme to generate cryptographic keys.

Recently, however, Thorpe and van Oorschot have postulated that the memorable DAS passwords are those that exhibit mirror symmetry. If true, they show that the security of DAS against dictionary attacks may be far less than originally hypothesized.[20] They argue that a similar weakness results if users select DAS passwords that are simple by various pattern complexity measures[21]—for example, selecting only a small number of strokes.[22] If the DAS passwords selected by users in practice are consistent with the hypotheses of Thorpe and van Oorschot, then these works may point to ways to strengthen DAS passwords, perhaps by implementing restrictions on DAS passwords similar to those levied on text passwords today.

---

19 Jermyn *et al.*

20 J. Thorpe and P. C. van Oorschot, "Graphical Dictionaries and the Memorable Space of Graphical Passwords," *Proceedings of the 13th USENIX Security Symposium* (Aug. 2004).

21 F. Attneave, "Complexity of Patterns," *American Journal of Psychology* 68 (1955), 209–222.

22 J. Thorpe and P. C. van Oorschot, "Towards Secure Design Choices for Implementing Graphical Passwords," *Proceedings of the 20th Annual Computer Security Applications Conference* (Dec. 2004).

## Authentication

To our knowledge, the only significant user study on the security of graphical passwords for authentication was performed by Davis and the present authors.[23] In that work, we studied the security of two schemes based on image recognition, denoted "Face" and "Story," which are described shortly. This study focused specifically on the impact of user selection of passwords in these schemes, and the security of the passwords that resulted. We recount some of the notable results from this study, and the methodologies used to reach them, as an illustration of some of the challenges that graphical passwords can face. In particular, this study demonstrated that graphical password schemes can be far *weaker* than textual passwords when users are permitted to choose their passwords.

In the Face scheme, the password is a collection of $k$ faces, each selected from a distinct set of $n > 1$ faces; for our evaluation we used $k = 4$ and $n = 9$. So, while choosing her password, the user is shown four successive $3 \times 3$ grids containing randomly chosen images (see Figure 9-4(a), for example), and for each, she selects one image from that grid as an element of her password. Images are unique and do not appear more than once for a given user. During the authentication phase, the same sets of images are shown to the user, but with the images permuted randomly.

In the Story scheme, a password is a sequence of $k$ unique images selected by the user to make a "story," from a single set of $n > k$ images, each derived from a distinct category of image types. The images are drawn from categories that depict everyday objects, food, automobiles, animals, children, sports, scenic locations, and male and female models. A sample set of images for the story scheme is shown in Figure 9-4(b).

We chose to study the Face scheme, in particular, because of a depth of psychological literature that revealed factors that could potentially be sources of bias in password selection. For example, the scientific literature abounds with studies that show that people tend to agree about attractiveness even across cultures,[24] and psychologists have argued for decades that the old adage that "beauty is in the eye of the beholder" may be largely false. A natural question is whether general perceptions of beauty (e.g., facial symmetry, youthfulness, averageness)[25, 26] might influence graphical password choices. Similarly, the "race effect" refers to the innate ability of people to better recognize faces from their own race

23 D. Davis, F. Monrose, and M. K. Reiter, "On User Choice in Graphical Password Schemes," *Proceedings of the 13th USENIX Security Symposium* (Aug. 2004), 151–164.

24 J. Langlois, L. Kalakanis, A. Rubenstein, A. Larson, M. Hallam, and M. Smoot, "Maxims and Myths of Beauty: A Meta-Analytic and Theoretical Review," *Psychological Bulletin* 126 (2000), 390–423.

25 T. Alley and M. Cunningham, "Averaged Faces Are Attractive, But Very Attractive Faces Are Not Average," *Psychological Science* 2 (1991), 123–125.

26 A. Feingold, "Good-Looking People Are Not What We Think," *Psychological Bulletin* 111 (1992), 304–341.

than faces of people from other races.[27, 28, 29] Again, this raises the question as to whether race might influence a user's choice for graphical passwords in the Face scheme.

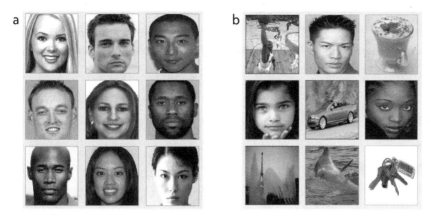

FIGURE 9-4. (a, left) In the Face scheme, a user's password is a sequence of k faces, each chosen from a distinct set of n > 1 faces; (b, right) in the Story scheme, a user's password is a sequence of k unique images selected from one set of n images to depict a "story"; in the above examples, n = 9, and images are placed randomly in a 3 × 3 grid

To study both the Story scheme and the Face scheme, we collected user data during the fall semester (roughly the four-month period of late August through early December) of 2003, of graphical password usage by three computer engineering and computer science classes at two universities. Each student used one of the graphical password schemes for access to content including his grades, homework, homework solutions, course reading materials, etc., via standard Java-enabled web browsers.

For the purposes of the experiment, facial images were classified into nonoverlapping categories, namely:

| | |
|---|---|
| Typical Asian males | Asian male models |
| Typical Asian females | Asian female models |
| Typical black males | Black male models |
| Typical black females | Black female models |
| Typical white males | White male models |
| Typical white females | White female models |

27  D. Levin, "Race as a Visual Feature: Using Visual Search and Perceptual Discrimination Tasks to Understand Face Categories and the Cross Race Recognition Deficit," *Quarterly Journal of Experimental Psychology: General* 129 (4), 559–574.

28  T. Luce, "Blacks, Whites and Yellows: They All Look Alike to Me," *Psychology Today* 8 (1974), 105–108.

29  P. Walker and W. Tanaka, "An Encoding Advantage for Own-Race Versus Other-Race Faces," *Perception* 23 (2003), 1117–1125.

To simplify the analysis, we made the assumption that images in a category are equivalent—that is, the specific images in a category that are available do not significantly influence a user's choice in picking a specific category.

If we simply consider the set of images chosen by men and women using the Face scheme (see Figure 9-5), some differences are apparent immediately: for one, different populations exhibit strong differences in their password choices.

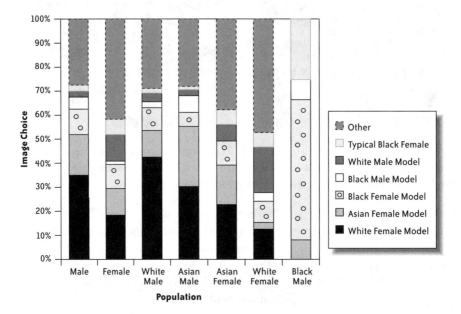

FIGURE 9-5. *Category selection based on gender and race for the Face scheme; the graph shows the distribution of choices from sets of images consisting of typical Asian males, typical Asian females, typical black males, typical black females, typical white males, typical white females, Asian male models, Asian female models, black male models, black female models, white male models, and white female models*

Insight into what different groups tend to choose as their passwords in the Face scheme is shown in Tables 9-1 and 9-2, which characterize selections by gender and race, respectively. As can be seen in Table 9-1, both males and females chose females in Face significantly more often than males, and when males chose females, they almost always chose models (roughly 80% of the time).

Moreover, perceptual differences were also observed when we examined image selection across racial categories. In that case, the "race effect" described earlier seemingly influenced the selection of passwords. As depicted in Table 9-2, Asian females and white females chose from within their races roughly 50% of the time; white males chose whites over 60% of the time.

*TABLE 9-1. Gender and attractiveness selection in Face; the results show that "beauty" appeared to play a significant role in the choices of images selected by both genders, albeit more so for males*

| Population | Female model | Male model | Typical female | Typical male |
|---|---|---|---|---|
| Female | 40.0% | 20.0% | 28.8% | 11.3% |
| Male | 63.2% | 10.0% | 12.7% | 14.0% |

*TABLE 9-2. Evidence of the "race effect" can be seen in the selection of images for the Face scheme; this effect is quite startling in the case of black males, although the reader is cautioned that there were only three black males in the study, and so any conclusion along those lines requires greater validation*

| Population | Asian | Black | White |
|---|---|---|---|
| Asian female | 52.1% | 16.7% | 31.3% |
| Asian male | 34.4% | 21.9% | 43.8% |
| Black male | 8.3% | 91.7% | 0.0% |
| White female | 18.8% | 31.3% | 50.0% |
| White male | 17.6% | 20.4% | 62.0% |

The categories of images chosen by each gender and race in the Story scheme are shown in Figure 9-6. The most significant deviations between males and females is that females chose animals twice as often as males did, and males chose women twice as often as females did. Less pronounced differences are that males tended to select nature and sports images somewhat more than females did, and females tended to select food images more often.

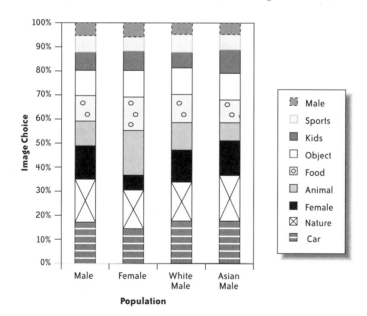

*FIGURE 9-6. Category selection based on gender and race for the Story scheme; the graph shows the distribution of choices from sets of images representing the nine categories: animals, cars, women, food, children, men, objects, nature, and sports*

## USERS' COMMENTS ON THEIR PASSWORD CHOICES

- "In order to remember all the pictures for my login (after forgetting my "password" four times in a row), I needed to pick pictures I could *easily* remember—kind of the same pitfalls when picking a lettered password. So, I chose all pictures of beautiful women."

- "I started by deciding to choose faces of people in my own race ... specifically, people that looked at least a little like me. The hope was that knowing this general piece of information about all of the images in my password would make the individual faces easier to remember."

- "I simply picked the best-looking girl on each page."

Given these differences across populations in both the Face scheme and the Story scheme, we set out to measure the ability of an attacker to guess the password of a user in each scheme. We summarize our findings in the following discussions. In our analysis, we let $p$ denote a password selected in either the Face scheme or the Story scheme. Then, $\Pr[p]$ for any $p$ denotes the probability that the scheme yields the password $p$, where the probability is taken over both user choice and random choices in the scheme.

Given accurate values for $\Pr[p]$ for each $p$, a measure that indicates the ability of an attacker to guess passwords, is the *guessing entropy* of passwords.[30] Informally, guessing entropy measures the expected number of guesses an attacker with perfect knowledge of the probability distribution on passwords would need in order to guess a password chosen from that distribution. Guessing entropy supposes that the attacker examines his guesses in an optimal order to minimize his expected number of guesses. So, if we enumerate passwords $p_1$, $p_2$, ... in nonincreasing order of $\Pr[p_i]$, then the guessing entropy is simply:

$$\sum_{i>0} i \cdot \Pr[p_i]$$

Because guessing entropy intuitively corresponds closely to the attacker's task in which we are interested (guessing a password), we will mainly consider measures motivated by the guessing entropy.

30 J. L. Massey, "Guessing and Entropy," *Proceedings of the 1994 IEEE International Symposium on Information Theory* (1994).

The direct use of the preceding formula to compute guessing entropy is problematic for two reasons:

- Pr[$p$] for each $p$ can be estimated only from the data observed in our experiments. In our experience, the use of these probabilities was sensitive to various parameter settings in our methodology.

- An attacker guessing passwords will be offered additional information when performing a guess, such as the set of available categories from which the next image can be chosen. For example, in Face, each image choice is taken from nine images that represent nine categories of images, chosen uniformly at random from the twelve categories. This additional information constrains the set of possible passwords, and the attacker would have this information when performing a guess in many scenarios.

To account for the first of these issues, we use the probabilities only to determine an enumeration $\Pi = (p_1, p_2, \dots)$ of passwords in nonincreasing order of probability.[31] This enumeration is far less sensitive to parameter variations than are the numeric probabilities, and leads to a more robust use. We use this sequence to conduct tests with our data set in which we randomly select a small set of "test" passwords from our dataset (20% of the data set), and use the remainder of the data to compute the enumeration $\Pi$.

We then guess passwords in order of $\Pi$ until each test password is guessed. To account for the second issue identified earlier—namely, the set of available categories during password selection—we first filter from $\Pi$ the passwords that would have been invalid given the available categories when the test password was chosen, and obviously do not guess them. By repeating this test with nonoverlapping test sets of passwords, we obtain a number of guesses per test password.

Tables 9-3 and 9-4 present results for the Face scheme and the Story scheme, respectively. Populations with less than 10 passwords are excluded from these tables. The results in these tables should be considered in light of the number of available passwords. In particular, the Face scheme (in the configuration we tested) has $9^4 = 6,561$ possible passwords (for fixed sets of available images), for a maximum guessing entropy of 3,281. However, our results show that for Face, if the user is known to be a male, then the worst 10% of passwords can be guessed easily on the first or second attempt. This observation is sufficiently surprising as to warrant restatement: an attacker can succeed in merely *two guesses* for 10% of male users. Similarly, if the user is Asian and his gender is known, then the worst 10% of passwords can be guessed within the first six tries.

31 Davis, Monrose, and Reiter.

*TABLE 9-3. Per-password guesses required to find test paswords in the Face scheme; the results show that while the chosen configurations yield 6,561 possible passwords, an attacker requires only two guesses to find the passwords of 10% of male users*

| Population | Average number of guesses | Median number of guesses | Guesses to find weakest 25% | Guesses to find weakest 10% |
|---|---|---|---|---|
| Overall | 1374 | 469 | 13 | 2 |
| Male | 1234 | 218 | 8 | 2 |
| Female | 2051 | 1454 | 255 | 12 |
| Asian male | 1084 | 257 | 21 | 5.5 |
| Asian female | 973 | 445 | 19 | 5.2 |
| White male | 1260 | 81 | 8 | 1.6 |

The Story-based scheme offers far fewer possible passwords, namely $9 \times 8 \times 7 \times 6 = 3,024$, yielding a maximum possible guessing entropy of 1,523. Nevertheless, Table 9-4 shows that it is more secure, in that the biases observed in the Face scheme do not tend to be as prominent in the Story scheme.

*TABLE 9-4. Guessing entropy for the Story scheme; the results show that if the attacker knows the target user is an Asian male, then an outline dictionary attack would succeed in 20 guesses for 10% of these users*

| Population | Average number of guesses | Median number of guesses | Guesses to find weakest 25% | Guesses to find weakest 10% |
|---|---|---|---|---|
| Overall | 790 | 428 | 112 | 35 |
| Male | 826 | 404 | 87 | 53 |
| Female | 989 | 723 | 125 | 98 |
| White male | 844 | 394 | 146 | 76 |
| Asian male | 877 | 589 | 155 | 20 |

It is also interesting to note that for both schemes the average number of guesses to find a test password is always higher than the median number, implying that there are several good passwords chosen that significantly increase the average number of guesses an attacker would need to perform, but that do not affect the median. The most dramatic example of this is for white males where the average is 1260 versus a median of 81 using the Face scheme, and the average is 844 versus a median of 394 for the Story scheme. This seems to imply that with better user education, the passwords selected by users of these schemes might be hardened against online attacks. We hope that larger-scale studies will better evaluate that claim.

## Usability

To date, a handful of studies have analyzed, albeit on small populations, the recall rate of authentication systems based on image recognition. For the most part, these studies have shown that memorability is indeed far better for these types of graphical passwords than for their textual counterparts. For instance, Brostoff and Sasse report the results of a three-month trial investigation with 34 students that shows that fewer login errors were made when using Passfaces™ (a commercial scheme based on image recognition) compared to textual passwords, even given significant periods of inactivity between logins.[32] Similarly, other recent studies have confirmed the memorability of other schemes based on image recognition.[33, 34, 35]

For our study, we also evaluated the effect of user choice on the memorability of the chosen passwords. Figure 9-7 shows the percentage of successful logins versus the time since that user's last login attempt. A trend that emerges is that while memorability of both schemes is strong, Story passwords appear to be somewhat harder to remember than Face passwords. One potential reason for users' relative difficulty in remembering their Story passwords is that apparently few of them actually chose stories, despite our suggestion to do so. This contributed very significantly to incorrect password entries resulting from misordering their selections. For example, of the 236 incorrect password entries in Story, over 75% of them consisted of the correct images selected in an incorrect order.

---

## IMPACT OF ORDERING ON MEMORABILITY

- "I had no problem remembering the four pictures, but I could not remember the original order."

- "No story, though having one may have helped me to remember the order of the pictures better."

- "... but on the third try I found a sequence that I could remember: fish-woman-girl-corn. I would screw up the fish and corn order 50% of the time, but I knew they were the pictures."

---

As such, it seems advisable in constructing graphical password schemes to avoid having users remember an ordering of images. For example, we expect that a selection of $k$ images, each from a distinct set of $n$ images (as in the Face scheme, although with image categories not necessarily of only persons), will generally be more memorable than an ordered selection of $k$ images from one set. If a scheme does rely on users remembering an ordering, then the importance of the story should be reiterated to users, because if the

32 S. Brostoff and M. A. Sasse, "Are Passfaces™ More Usable Than Passwords? A Field Trial Investigation," *Proceedings of Human Computer Interaction* (2000), 405–424.

33 R. Dhamija and A. Perrig, "Déjà Vu: A User Study Using Images for Authentication," *Proceedings of the 9thUSENIX Security Symposium* (Aug. 2000).

34 Stubblefield and Simon.

35 M. Zviran and W. J. Haga, "A Comparison of Password Techniques for Multilevel Authentication Mechanisms," *The Computer Journal* 36:3 (1993), 227–237.

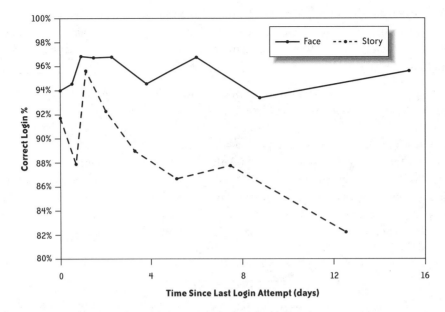

*FIGURE 9-7.* Memorability versus time since last login attempt; each data point represents the average of 90 login attempts; of the 236 incorrect password entries in Story, over 75% of them consisted of the correct images selected in an incorrect order

sequence of images has some semantic meaning, it is more likely that the password will be memorable (assuming, of course, that the sequences are not too long[36]).

## Discussion

These results demonstrate that graphical password schemes can suffer from drawbacks similar to those of textual password schemes; most notably, they exhibit similar biases in human tendencies to select memorable passwords. Moreover, forthcoming evaluations of which we are aware may further elucidate the depth of this problem. For example, Sasse is exploring the susceptibility of graphical passwords to the *spouse-test*, where spouses play the role of informed impostors.[37] Early evidence suggests that graphical password schemes of the type we consider here may indeed be vulnerable to such "adversaries." One alternative to strengthen graphical passwords is to prohibit user selection of passwords, so that each user's password is system-generated. However, it is widely considered that such measures have failed in the case of textual passwords as a result of usability concerns, and more research is needed in the context of particular graphical password schemes to ascertain whether this is a reasonable measure.

36 G. A. Miller, "The Magical Number Seven, Plus or Minus Two: Some Limits on Our Capacity for Processing Information," *Psychological Review* 63 (1956), 81–97.

37 M. A. Sasse, personal communications, *Dimacs Workshop on Usable Privacy and Security* (July 2004).

The range of memorability studies undertaken thus far have all been limited in a number of respects. For one, the effects of image confusion has yet to be evaluated, and it is unclear whether the impressive recall rates observed thus far (albeit in small user trials) will be adversely affected as we become more exposed to graphical authentication systems. To illustrate the risk of image confusion, let's imagine that graphical password schemes became widespread. Furthermore, suppose for argument's sake, that the Story scheme becomes the de facto scheme of choice. It remains entirely plausible that as a user becomes exposed to more instances of the scheme (say, for example, for accessing web-based email, online banking services, news subscriptions, etc.) the user will confuse stories used to access each of these services, particularly if the image categories selected by the user for one of her stories appear as distractors during the authentication stage for a different service. To date, no evaluation of graphical password schemes of which we are aware has taken this effect into consideration—for example, by forcing users to create new graphical passwords every so often. In that regard, we believe that exploring the impact of this effect on long-term recall rates remains an area of research that warrants further investigation.

## Let's Face It

Given the psychological evidence supporting the assertion that humans can better remember pictures than they can text, graphical passwords are an attractive approach to better user authentication and key generation. There is already empirical evidence that this approach can yield user authentication schemes offering better memorability. The analysis we surveyed here suggests that it is possible to design a graphical authentication scheme permitting user-chosen passwords (e.g., the Story scheme) that should provide adequate user authentication, provided that only a limited number of incorrect guesses are permitted before the account is "locked." However, the study also shows that the design of such a scheme requires care; in particular, the Face scheme fails significantly when users select their own passwords.

An issue that is much less clear at this point is the extent to which repeatable key generation can be achieved satisfactorily using graphical passwords. To our knowledge, only two classes of schemes have been proposed for this purpose, and neither has been evaluated empirically.[38, 39] We consider this to be an area warranting significant future research in both design and evaluation.

Our collective understanding of graphical passwords is still in its infancy, and for this reason, we caution users from adopting them (even for user authentication) without careful consideration of alternatives. We do believe that some designs will prove to be more usable than text passwords and adequately secure for user authentication, in terms of the measures that we have discussed here. However, they may fall prey to other attacks that

38 Jermyn *et al.*
39 Stubblefield and Simon.

we have not considered here; for example, passwords based on image recognition, tapping, or drawing may be more easily observed by an onlooker while a user is entering the password. In contrast, text passwords in which the characters are not echoed (or, more typically, echoed with nondescript characters such as asterisks) provide few on-screen cues as to what the password is. So, considering whether to adopt a graphical password scheme requires attention to a range of system factors, as well.

## About the Authors

Fabian Monrose is an assistant professor of Computer Science at Johns Hopkins University. Previously, he was a member of the Secure Systems Group at Bell Labs. His interests include computer and network security, with particular interest in biometrics and techniques for strong user authentication.

Michael K. Reiter is a professor of Electrical & Computer Engineering and Computer Science at Carnegie Mellon University. He joined AT&T Bell Labs in 1993 and became a founding member of AT&T Labs—Research when NCR and Lucent Technologies (including Bell Labs) split from AT&T in 1996. He returned to Bell Labs in 1998 as director of secure systems research, and then joined Carnegie Mellon in 2001.

# CHAPTER TEN

# Usable Biometrics

**LYNNE COVENTRY**

**B**IOMETRICS OFFER A TECHNOLOGICAL SOLUTION TO THE AUTHENTICATION OF INDIVIDUALS. Biometrics confirm that the actual person, rather than merely his or her token or identifier, is present. Thus, biometrics may reduce the effort of a person's trying to identify himself and in doing so potentially reduce the chances of authentication fraud.

The term *biometrics* is derived from the Greek *bio* (life) and *metric* (measure). Biometrics, as a means of identification, can be traced back to both ancient Egypt[1] and China. Pioneering work on modern biometrics technologies dates back to the late 1960s, when researchers began looking at voice patterns, fingerprints, and hand geometry as a means for establishing unique individual identity. By the mid-1980s, the biometrics industry was established and the first systems went live in controlled environments. In recent years, with the heightened security concerns gripping much of the world and the rising amount of fraud in the commercial sector, biometrics technologies have received a great deal of attention. However, the application of biometrics spans all industries.

To date, the growth of biometrics technologies has been driven by a mainly system-centered approach, dealing with the problems of unique digital identifier extraction,

---

1   B. Miller, "Vital Signs of Identification," *IEEE Spectrum* (Feb. 1999), 422–430.

template handling, and recognition algorithms. With very few exceptions,[2, 3, 4] the usability community has not been involved in the design or evaluation of biometrics, and the traditionally quoted biometrics performance measures are no guarantee of real-world performance. The success of the biometrics approach is strongly influenced by user factors including the size and range of the user population. To facilitate successful biometrics implementations, more research is required into these user factors.

After a brief introduction to biometrics and their uses, this chapter investigates the user factors that will ultimately impact the successful implementation of biometrics security. We primarily focus these ideas within the context of self-service applications such as Automated Teller Machines (ATMs), to highlight the technical and user factors to consider when implementing a biometrics solution. Some technical issues of biometrics are outside the scope of this chapter; these include the handling of templates and images, integration issues, and standards.[5, 6, 7, 8]

## Introduction

*Biometrics* is the comparison of live anatomical, physiological, or behavior characteristics to the stored template of a person. *Physiological* biometrics include those based on finger-prints, hand and/or finger geometry, and the patterns of retinas, veins, irises, and faces. *Behavioral* biometrics techniques include those based on voice, signature, and typing behavior.

Table 10-1 provides a brief description of the most well-developed biometrics technologies.

2   L. Coventry and G. Johnson, "More Than Meets the Eye! Usability and Iris Verification at the ATM Interface," in S. Brewster *et al.* (eds.), *Proceedings of the IFIP TC 13 International Conference on Human Computer Interaction*, (Edinburgh, 1999).

3   F. Deane, K. Barrelle, R. Henderson, and D. Mahar, "Perceived Acceptability of Biometric Security Systems," *Computers and Security* 14 (1995), 225–231.

4   F. P. Deane, R. D. Henderson, D. P. Mahar, and A. J. Saliba, "Theoretical Examination of the Effects of Anxiety and Electronic Performance Monitoring on Biometric Security Systems," *Interacting with Computers* 7 (1995), 395–411.

5   F. L. Podio *et al.*, "A Biometric Application Programming Interface Industry Standard—Benefits for the Users and the Enterprise," *Proceedings of CTST 2000*; *http://www.ctst.com*.

6   Biometric Application Programming Interface (BioAPI) Specification, Version 1.0, March 1.

7   ANSI X9.84, *Biometric Information Management and Security* (2000); *http://www.x9.org*.

8   F. L. Podio *et al.*, "NISTIR 6529 Common Biometric Exchange File Format" (cited Jan. 3, 2001); *http://www.nist.gov/cbeff*.

TABLE 10-1. Common types of biometrics

| Biometrics | Description |
|---|---|
| Fingerprint | Patterns found on the fingertip, including the location and direction of ridge endings and bifurcations |
| Palm print | A larger-scale version of the fingerprint biometrics |
| Vein pattern | Vein and capillary patterns on the back of the hand |
| Hand geometry | Shape of the hand including height and width of bones and joints in the hands and fingers |
| Finger geometry | 3D features of index and middle finger of leading hand |
| Retina | Layer of blood vessels in the back of the eye |
| Iris | Inherent radial pattern and visible characteristics (e.g., freckles, rings, furrows, corona) of the iris |
| Facial | Facial characteristics such as position and shape of nose and position of cheekbones, eye sockets, and mouth (but not hairline area, which is prone to change) |
| Voice | Voice characteristics (frequency, duration, cadence) |
| Signature | Time, stroke speed, spacing, letter formation, stylus pressure, etc. |
| Typing dynamics | Typing habits including speed and patterns for particular words |

Other biometrics systems have been proposed but not brought to market. These include the recognition of a person's earlobe, ear shape, smell, gait, and pressure with which keys are pressed. Recently, recognition of laughter, bones in the finger, facial thermograms, inner ear bones, and lip shape have also been discussed. However, many of these techniques are still in the realms of fantasy. Moreover, no biometrics system has yet been developed that appears to be well suited for all applications.

Current biometrics research is being driven primarily by the military. The Defense Advanced Research Projects Agency (DARPA), for example, sponsors much of the research in the United States, with "Human ID at a distance" being one of their ongoing projects.[9]

## Biometrics Types

Before continuing, I must distinguish between two specific types of biometrics applications:

- *Biometrics for identification*. Those that require identifying an individual from the set of all possible users (by matching an acquired biometrics image to all possible templates)

- *Biometrics for verification*. Those that require verifying a particular identity (by matching an acquired biometrics image against a specific template)

Biometrics used for identification must ensure the uniqueness of each member of the target population. As the size of the population grows, so grows the probability that more than one user will fall within the match criteria. Fingerprints, retinal scanning, and iris

---

9  The Defense Advanced Research Projects Agency (DARPA), "Human ID at a Distance";
   *http://infowar.net/tia/www.darpa.mil/iao/HID.htm.*

scanning are the only biometrics techniques that can accurately identify a person from a large database. Facial systems are often used to create a manageable subset of possible identities, but they then must be scrutinized by a human observer. Thus, facial systems may not be suitable for real-time identification.[10]

Even when an individual can be uniquely identified using a biometrics system, the processing time required makes biometrics identification unsuitable for many uses. In applications such as border control and ATMs, the potential user base is in the millions and the processing time needed to identify someone from a biometrics measurement would be prohibitive. However, biometrics may be used for verification purposes.

For biometrics verification, an *identifier* is provided to allow the system to determine which identity is being claimed, and therefore which template to utilize in the verification process. Traditionally within the banking industry, the *token* is the conventional bank card used to activate the self-service terminal or ATM. Within other systems, tokens may include a national identification card, driver's license, or passport—all of which have either been tested with, or are being considered for, being embedded with some form of biometrics identifier. However, any sufficiently individual token—for example, a radio frequency tag—could be used. Alternatively, the user could simply key in a unique identifier such as a personal account number or a Social Security number. The system then needs to check the biometrics information (template) associated with the claimed identity against the biometrics information that is currently being provided for verification.

## Issues of Biometrics Specificity

Biometrics technologies are difficult to compare against one another. A variety of technologies can be used to verify a single biometrics characteristic. Further, each characteristic and technology brings with it a unique set of both technical and user issues, and significant differences exist between the software algorithms used to compare two samples.

Biometrics technologies have a wide range of accuracy, reliability, and usability. Thus, despite the difficulty in comparing biometrics, they will always have some comparable accuracy versus usability balance that can be compared with other technologies. The biometrics that are easiest to use are those that can be captured passively (e.g., some facial recognition systems). However, some systems that are more difficult to use (e.g., those requiring a user to align a particular body part with a sensor) currently produce more accurate results.

## The Fingerprint Example

The fingerprint biometrics illustrates the range of issues each biometrics technology must address, the range of technologies available, the impact of the user, and his attitudes on the system's performance.

10 "Tomorrow's Markets," *Biometric Technology Today* (May 2004), 7–9.

There are several commercially available methods of capturing the initial fingerprint image: optical, capacitive, ultrasonic, thermal, and pressure. Fingerprint systems require the user to place his finger flat on the sensor, or to move his finger across the sensor. Both methods require that the finger remain flat during this process. This may seem simple but has not proved natural or intuitive to untrained users who point down, or roll their fingers either side to side or bottom to top.[11]

According to *Biometrics Report*,[12] fingerprint quality is affected by race, gender, occupation, and age: caucasians have better defined prints than other races; women have finer prints than men; manual workers can have worn or damaged prints; children have softer skin and thus less well-defined prints than adults; older adults lose moisture and skin elasticity. Optical systems themselves are affected by dirt, cold fingers, and finger damage, and are otherwise prone to fraud.[13] Capacitive systems are not susceptible to dirt or fraud but have more placement issues, require a specific pressure to be applied, and are affected by cold fingers and age-related issues.

For a fingerprint sensor to be considered successful, it must be able to respond to "outlying" cases (those unable to effectively present their biometrics to the system). Independent test data[14] has shown the ultrasonic to be more effective than either the optical or the capacitive sensors, as it is of higher resolution and can deal with dry fingers. However, the vibration experienced by users may feel strange. Many companies produce software algorithms[15] for fingerprint recognition that work on any image.

User concerns about fingerprint sensors include hygiene, association with crime (although this is diminishing), fear of attacks aimed at removing fingers, and fraud from severed or artificial fingers or from images of the print. Some vendors offer life-testing sensors as an option, although "no fingerprint system—currently on the market—is 100% foolproof."[16]

## Where Are Biometrics Used?

Each biometrics technique has its own unique set of advantages and disadvantages. Cost, size, and method of use often dictate applicability to any given situation. For example, a telephone-based system could use only voice as a biometrics.

11 L. Coventry, A. De Angeli, and G. Johnson, "Biometric Verification at a Self-Service Interface," *Proceedings of the British Ergonomic Society Conference* (Edinburgh, April 2003).

12 *Biometrics Report 2000–2005*; *http://www.biometricgroup.com*.

13 L. Thalheim, J. Krissler, and P. M. Ziegler, "Bodycheck: Biometric Access Protection Devices and Their Programs Put to the Test," *C'T*, 11 (May 22, 2002); *http://www.heise.de/ct/english/02/11/114/*.

14 The National Biometric Test Centre, San Jose State University, San Jose, CA; *http://www.engr.sjsu.edu/biometrics/*.

15 D. Maio *et al.*, "Fingerprint Verification Competition 2000," *Proceedings of the 15th International Conference on Pattern Recognition* (Barcelona, Sept. 2000); *http://www.csr.unibo.it/research/biolab*.

16 *Biometric Technology Today* 9:6 (Oct. 2001), 9.

Early biometrics were cumbersome to use and very expensive, and therefore were used only in very high-security applications. However, as the technology has improved, the number of applications has increased. This section introduces some other areas of application, including physical access control, border control, surveillance, people tracking, and online transaction security.

## Physical Access Control

Physical access control is the largest and most commercialized application of biometrics systems, in part because a relatively small user base exists for each system, and in part because these devices could be sold and deployed as standalone systems, allowing for incremental deployments. Physical access security ranges from access to secure locations such as prisons or military facilities, to secure work areas such as bank vaults, to general workplaces, and now to countries via border controls. Nowadays, we are also seeing biometrics used in conjunction with clocks for time cards, to confirm "season passes" at attractions, for access to schools or subsidized meals at school cafeterias, and as an alternative to keys for a car, house, hotel room, or locker.[17] The most commonly used biometrics in this area are hand geometry and fingerprint. Biometrics researchers are also looking at identification alternatives including iris, retina, and hand vein.

## Immigration and Border Control

A specific set of problems arises when dealing with border control between countries. Here, the user base can be extraordinarily large, and systems in different countries must interoperate. As of this writing, iris, fingerprint, and facial biometrics are being incorporated in passports. In some cases, this means that people must adopt a particular pose when providing a passport photograph. For instance, Canadian, British, and U.S. citizens are no longer permitted to smile in their passport photos, to prepare for facial biometrics that capture only "neutral" expressions.[18]

More and more surveillance is being deployed worldwide that attempts to use biometrics technology to identify people at a distance. Much of this technology is being implemented covertly, raising issues of privacy and civil liberties in many countries. Another application of "distance biometrics" is face recognition to track photographs or videos of specific people. These systems can be used either at special screening stations or with covert imagery shot in banks, casinos, and shopping malls, and at borders. While not completely reliable, this technology reduces human search efforts; for example, recorded images can be compared automatically with faces of known terrorists, and a human screener can be alerted when there is a close match. Perhaps in the future, more identification accuracy could be achieved with iris recognition.

---

17 "Biometric Tech Puts ID at Your Fingertips," (Aug. 11, 2004); *http://www.cnn.com/2004/TECH/ptech/08/11/biometrics.ap/index.html.*

18 M. Lockie, "Commentary," *Biometric Technology Today* (Sept. 2004), 12.

## Law and Order

Some countries are investigating issuing ID cards or drivers' licenses with embedded biometrics. Biometrics is currently being used to prevent welfare fraud by checking for multiple identities and to ensure that the real recipient collects the correct benefits. Biometrics are also being deployed in other social services settings. In South Africa, for example, a project in the Western Cape region is registering and tracking street children to ensure that they are not placed in adult prison and are identified correctly.[19]

## Transaction Security

Biometrics is being used to secure many different transactions, including those taking place at a single server or over a network, the Internet, or telephones, as well as being used in voting systems and at ATMs.[20] However, remote biometrics authentication is neither trivial nor foolproof. The assumption that anyone who can provide my fingerprint can also complete any transaction in my name is risky. This requires a trusted biometrics sensor, one that is sufficiently tamper-resistant and provides trustworthy liveness detection. Remote, unsupervised authentication provides greater opportunity for fraud.

# Biometrics and Public Technology: The ATM Example

As different application areas place different requirements on biometrics technology, we must consider the appropriateness of different technologies for a specific application. This section explores the applicability of the different biometrics technologies for use within an ATM or other self-service environment.

For a number of reasons (to be enumerated in the following sections), I assume here that *verification* rather than *identification* will be utilized at an ATM.

## ATM Fingerprint Verification

Integration of fingerprint sensors into an ATM for verification is feasible, especially if contact silicon (capacitance or thermal swipe) devices are used (see Figure 10-1). Optical sensors and static capacitance systems are not viable for ATMs because of dirt and latent prints that accumulate with use. Swipe devices, on the other hand, at least have the potential for self-cleaning with use. Unfortunately, the physical positioning of the sensor may be difficult for all users (left-handed/right-handed aside) to get their fingers flat on the reader. Smart cards equipped with fingerprint sensors—where the fingerprint is used to allow use of a private key—could remove many of the technical problems of deploying biometrics in the self-service environment.

19 *Biometric Technology Today* (Sept. 2004), 3.

20 M. Alpert, "Security at Your Fingertips," *Scientific American* (May 24, 2004).

FIGURE 10-1. Fingerprint reader

## ATM Face Verification

Another possibility for ATMs is the integration of facial biometrics systems (see Figure 10-2). In many cases, a security camera is already present; this camera could be used for both video recording and biometrics verification.

Because face verification could be a universal biometrics—everybody has a face—most research on this technology to date has focused on the potential negatives. Several complicating factors have been identified:

- The system's field of view must cover a wide range of heights, from the tallest standing user to a user in a wheelchair.

- Today's technology requires that users find and look at the camera at the right time, facing straight on and with a neutral expression.

- Lighting must be uniform and consistent—with good front lighting and little back lighting—posing a significant problem in many locations.

- Some systems can be tricked into accepting photographs or even drawings of faces.

- It is possible that people could attempt to defraud the system through decapitation of a legitimate user. The use of masks is another avenue for potential fraud.

- Likewise, an attacker could coerce a legitimate user to look at a camera to complete an authentication under duress.

- There are unknown accuracy rates, with a high chance of false negatives.

On the positive side, face recognition presents no hygiene-related health concerns and no current association with criminology. This biometrics technique can also be used without the user's cooperation or even his knowledge, as a backup or addition to any other biometrics deployed, potentially raising privacy concerns.

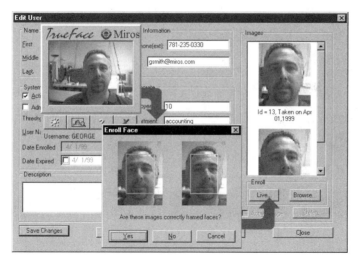

FIGURE 10-2. Face recognition

## ATM Iris Verification

Iris verification is the most reliable biometrics, but currently it is still very expensive for systems that do not require the user to put her eye in close proximity to the camera (see Figure 10-3). (Such positioning could cause problems in an ATM environment for the same reason that it is problematic for face recognition.) Iris verification has already been piloted in ATMs.

On the positive side:

- The method is noncontact and noninvasive.

- It can be located anywhere.

- The physical attribute it uses is relatively stable and it is a proven system in the ATM field.

On the negative side:

- The risk of fraud by the use of force is possible.

- Criminals who are not familiar with how the technology works could attempt fraud through mutilation of the user. Although this would not work, as a responsive eye is required, the mere thought of such a crime is exceedingly distasteful and could impact adoption or use.

- The technology requires more user cooperation than face recognition would.

If performance accuracy were the only criterion for adoption, this system would be more popular. However, the difficulty of positioning the eye remains a problem. Advances in both algorithms and robotics to direct the camera to the eye instead of requiring the user to position the camera or eye manually will surely make this technology more successful.

FIGURE 10-3. Iris scanner

## ATM Retina Verification

Many reasons exist for not using retina verification and existing retina systems in ATMs. These include:

- The technique is invasive.

- The technique requires training and patience to use.

- Although the system requires no physical contact, users must still place their eyes very close to it, making sensor location difficult to accommodate all users.

- Users must look into the output from a laser.

- Questions exist as to the stability of the measured feature (body temperature and fatigue, for example, have been quoted as possible causes of variance within the pattern).

Retina verification systems may evolve, and theoretically their performance is attractive, but at present they have too many negative aspects to deploy in any capacity.

## ATM Hand Verification

The finger geometry system has some potential, but at present the integration of a hand sensor into an ATM would be difficult for a number of reasons:

- The size of the larger systems can be prohibitive (9 cm (W) x 15 cm (H) x 14 cm (D)).

- As with all optical devices, dirt can pose a problem in self-service environments.

- Positioning of the sensor may be difficult for all users (left-handed/right-handed aside) to get their hands flat on the plate or their fingers in place.

- Fraud through the use of severed hands may or may not work. Forcing someone to present his or her hand is also a possibility.

- Vandalism or accidental damage of the units could be a problem.

## ATM Speaker Verification

Speaker verification uses the user's voice as an authenticator. There are many advantages to this technique at an ATM:

- It involves simple integration of the necessary voice-recognition sensors.

- The sensor need not be at the ATM at all. For example, a mobile phone could be used.

- The system is more resistant against coercion, because it is more difficult to force someone to speak than to physically move that person to the location of the sensor.

- In the event of coercion, the stress of forced speech could alter the voice sufficiently that the user would no longer authenticate.

However, there are some negatives:

- Background noise—for example, aircraft flying overhead or the noise of rainstorms—can cause serious difficulties. (Handsets would ease this problem but would create others.)

- Enrollment is time consuming (unless mobile phones are part of the system).

- Template size may create problems not associated with other biometrics techniques.

- Recording of the human voice may create a simple fraud potential, although some companies claim recorder detection.

## ATM Signature Verification

With a signature verification system, the computer verifies a physical signature that the user writes with either pen-and-ink or a special pen on an electronic pad (see Figure 10-4). This system is very attractive for use with financial transactions because of the long historical and present-day association between signature and financial authorization. What's more, an image of the signature can be preserved for later human scrutiny.

Signature verification systems can be integrated directly into an ATM, although the location of small tablets and pens can pose a usability problem for some users.

Although this technology is intriguing, it has not yet proven to be reliable.

## ATM Typing Verification

It is unlikely that everyone would have sufficient typing skills or practice to be comfortable with the typing verification technique, even if a standard alphanumeric keyboard were available on all ATMs. Such a keyboard would require space and careful placement so that its use could mimic that of a desktop-based keyboard. If full keyboards were to become the norm on many self-service devices, one could see the attraction of this relatively unknown biometrics technique, but otherwise, the technique is infeasible.

*FIGURE 10-4. Signature verification*

## Evaluating Biometrics

Testing biometrics is complicated and requires objective comparisons.[21] That's because biometrics authentication is not a simple yes/no process. It involves complicated statistical analysis of the incoming live signal from the biometrics device. Performance metrics should indicate how well a system performs, but it is difficult to get reliable data on particular systems, and in general, more independent testing is required.

To this end, a standard for biometrics testing should be created. A number of private and public testing laboratories have been set up to promote such a standard. These organizations include the U.S. National Biometric Test Center[22] at San Jose State University, the Biometric Consortium,[23] and programs at the International Computer Security Association,[24] the U.S. National Institutes of Standards and Technology[25] (NIST), and the UK National Physical Laboratory.[26] The International Biometric Group[27] is a private initiative offering independent testing that purports to include a usability perspective.

21 P. J. Phillips, A. Martin, C. L. Wilson, and M. Przybocki, "An Introduction to Evaluating Biometric Systems," *Computer* (Feb. 2000), 56–62.

22 *http://www.engr.sjsu.edu/biometrics/*.

23 *http://www.biometrics.org/*.

24 *http://www.icsa.net/*.

25 *http://www.nist.gov/*.

26 A. J. Mansfield and J. L. Wayman, "Best Practices in Testing and Reporting Performance of Biometric Devices," *NPL Report CMSC* 14:2 (Aug. 2002).

27 International Biometrics Group. Comparative biometric testing; *http://www.ibgweb.com/reports/public/comparative_biometric_testing.html*.

## Performance Metrics

The performance of a biometrics system must be high if users are to trust and accept it. A system's theoretical performance is often quoted by vendors and looks impressive, but it does not necessarily reflect the system's real-world performance. Furthermore, the methods used to measure performance can greatly affect the results. A system that performs well in the laboratory with trained, cooperative users will generate a completely different set of values with inexperienced or less cooperative users in a real-world environment.

Performance is typically measured in terms of two measures:

- *False accept rates (FAR)*. The likelihood that the wrong person will be able to access the system

- *False reject rates (FRR)*. The likelihood that a legitimate person will be denied access

The problem is the interconnection between these two measures: as FAR improves, FRR worsens, and vice versa. In fact, reported values for FAR and FRR are usually based on theoretical calculations performed with clean, high-quality data, instead of on actual observations and real-world performance. Reported values should indicate how the numbers were calculated and the basis for including and excluding users, images, and other data from the calculations.

Both the methods by which these figures are gathered and the human subjects used in their gathering seriously impact subsequent performance. The realized performance may not be as good as the predicted performance. Performance estimates are often far more impressive than actual performance.[28] Systems tested in laboratory conditions with a small homogeneous set of "good," trained, young, cooperative users may generate completely different results than testing in a live environment with inexperienced and less-cooperative users. Many systems do not live up to expectations because they prove unable to cope with the enormous variations among large populations, or fail to take into account people's needs and behaviors.[29]

NIST's 2003 Fingerprint Vendor Technology Evaluation[30] test found that poor-quality fingerprints reduced matching accuracy. The relevance of tests is therefore limited if the distribution of fingerprint quality is not known in the test sets. A variety of user factors affect fingerprint quality, however, and only some of them can be controlled by operational procedures. The poorer the quality, the higher the false rejects. This study also found that the false reject rate increased as subject age increased, particularly when the subjects were over the age of 50.

Two other metrics, described next, must be considered in biometrics usability.

28 Mansfield and Wayman.

29 S. G. Davies, "How Biometric Technology Will Fuse Flesh and Machine," *Information Technology and People* 7:4 (1994).

30 *http://fpvte.nist.gov/*.

- *Failure to enroll (FTE).* The FTE rate is very important, as it identifies people who can never use the system.

- *Failure to acquire (FTA).* The FTA rate depends on the number of users that fail to generate an appropriate image when using the device. The FTA is often affected by difficult systems, or systems that require a high level of user cooperation.

FTE and FTA necessitate manual or alternative processing of that user. These figures will vary with the user base, the application area, and the biometrics system. The fallback strategy for these people must be acceptable, usable, and secure. It is essential to ensure that they do not result in a security loophole.

## Incorporating User Factors into Testing

Biometrics researchers have determined that real-life users are the biggest variable in system performance. Thus, performance measures must be qualified with an understanding of that system's user base. Ashbourn[31] provides an index of user characteristics that can impact predicted biometrics system performance; we reprint this index in Table 10-2.

*TABLE 10-2. Ashbourn's index of user characteristics that can impact predicted biometrics system performance*

| User characteristic | Description |
| --- | --- |
| Acceptance of biometrics concept | If the user is hostile toward the idea of using the biometrics in a given application, his behavior may not be optimal. This will influence behavior if the user is forced to use the biometrics, or the user may completely opt out of the application if given a choice. |
| Knowledge of technology and computers in general | If the user is technology literate and comfortable using and exploring new technology, he will be better able to optimize his behavior with the system. |
| Familiarity with biometrics characteristic | If the user if familiar with the characteristic and how it should be used to optimize security, he will be more able to use the system appropriately. For example, with a fingerprint system, the core should be within the image captured. If the user knows the location of the core, he will incorporate a better finger position. |
| Experience with the specific device being used (and other devices) | Each device has its own way of working and its own user requirements. Users who have used that particular device extensively may feel particularly positive or negative toward it. If a user has been habituated to a certain device, he may use a new device inappropriately. |
| Environment of use | User stress when using a device can have an influence on the ability to acquire and the quality of an image. Public or private milieus, the presence of a queue, time pressure, and environmental conditions affect overall performance, as will assistance from either a human or an effective interface design. |
| Transaction criticality | The transaction's degree of criticality will affect user stress levels and, potentially, user performance. |

31 J. Ashbourn, "Biometrics," *Advanced Identity Verification* (London: Springer Verlag, 2000).

Considerations of *age*, *long-term stability*, *gender*, and *ethnicity* also need to be taken into account when a biometrics system is evaluated. All claims should be qualified with the user categories on which the biometrics has actually been tested.

Fully understanding the user's role in the performance and acceptance of biometrics requires the utilization of a number of research methods through different stages of development of new biometrics technologies. (The most extensive research has been carried out on iris and fingerprint verification.[32, 33]) These methods include focus groups to identify consumers' understanding, misconceptions, and barriers to acceptance of biometrics techniques—although conclusions drawn from focus groups may or may not correlate with actual user behavior. Specific studies help to understand how well a technology works with the general, untrained public, and to assess whether it can be adapted to a self-service environment.

Developers must work with an iterative design and evaluation process to create a successful biometrics application. Field trials are imperative to fully test the performance and acceptance of any self-service application, as experience with the actual technology can change people's attitudes in either a positive or a negative direction.

## Size of User Base

Within some application areas, including the financial self-service environment, the potential size of the user base can be extraordinarily large. Even small financial institutions can have millions of customers, and with cross-institution relationships, we must consider the possibility that any biometrics system might ultimately have to be applicable to the entire banking population of the planet and all the variations within it! This drives a number of factors associated with biometrics, such as the use of verification (as opposed to recognition), template storage, accessibility, the handling of "outliers," enrollment, and user acceptance.

## Designing a Biometrics Solution to Maximize the User Experience

Developers must take into account a number of design considerations for a biometrics solution, if it is to fully accommodate a wide range of potential users in a socially acceptable manner. Consideration must be given to the design of the enrollment process, the biometrics capture device itself, the device's user interface, and the user acceptance issues for the particular application.

## Enrollment

Any person wishing to use a system with biometrics security first must be enrolled. The person's biometrics template must be sampled and stored along with his identification. The difficulty of this task scales with the size of the population to be identified.

---

32 DARPA, "Human ID at a Distance."
33 Thalheim, Krissler, and Ziegler.

Enrollment is similar to verification in that the user provides a series of biometrics measurements for the same biometrics artifact. These biometrics measurements are then processed, producing a template that is representative of the biometrics artifact. But while enrollment sounds simple, it is extremely problematic. Enrollment is often the first time a user might have seen a particular biometrics device, which can be confusing and disconcerting.

The effectiveness of biometrics depends on the quality of the enrollment image; thus, a good enrollment template is key to efficient and accurate verification. It is unfortunately difficult to obtain a high-quality image in an unattended self-service environment. ATM owners cannot afford customer dissatisfaction through false rejection, nor can they allow the ATM to become a target for fraud through false acceptance.

An attended enrollment is thus a critical part of a successful solution, as it maintains the integrity of the information stored, provides an opportunity for education and training, and dispels misconceptions. Such enrollment should include:

*Education about the biometrics itself*
> For example, with fingerprint biometrics, users must understand the importance of the fingerprint core and where it is located on their finger.

*Training to enable the consistent use of the technology*
> For example, users must be told how to use the technology and its limits. This might focus around, for example, accurate placement of the biometrics within the required range.

*Explanation of interface support*
> Users need some understanding of how the software interface will support them if they have not placed their biometrics accurately.

*Use of a trainer*
> A "trainer" should lead the user through the interaction, and the user should be provided with feedback about how to correct his placement.

*Supervised "playtime"*
> Time is needed for the user to explore how to use the system (e.g., the pressure required, positioning the biometrics). This should continue until the user can provide consistent images.

Readers who first learned graphical user interfaces two decades ago might remember a similar situation: extensive training was required at the start, but it soon became superfluous. If biometrics becomes ubiquitous, the population will become habituated to the technology and will no longer need this level of early support. Until then, it is unlikely that unassisted enrollment will be effective.

## Biometrics Capture

A biometrics device requires that the user actively participate in, or at least collaborate with, the biometrics system in order for the system to obtain a biometrics measurement. A user might have to provide a fingerprint image—for example, by placing his finger on a specified device, swiping his finger across a fingerprint reader, or collaborating with a camera-based system in order for it to obtain a good picture of his face or of his iris.

Biometrics vendors assume that their systems are intuitive and easy to use—perhaps because of their familiarity with their own technology—but usability evaluations are proving this not to be the case. Users find that they must interact with this new technology correctly and consistently. This may be a physical challenge for anyone until they become habituated to the technology, but may be especially problematic for elderly or disabled users. Therefore, the nature and timing of the feedback to the user are essential to capture consistent and high-quality images.

Many factors affect the quality of the data and the appropriateness. For example, a user must apply correct pressure when providing a fingerprint to a capacitive sensor. However, exact pressure varies between individuals depending on their skin. Meanwhile, users must also accurately place their fingerprint core on the device. Overall, the user's interaction with the biometrics device and the feedback provided by the system are crucial for success.

In general, approaches based on external cues (e.g., an indentation where the finger should be placed or a red line against which to position the base of the fingernail) are too general and can create problems resulting from the discrepancies between varied human finger sizes and shape. This is particularly problematic if the user does not understand what goal he is trying to achieve.

It is essential for user comprehension to provide an image of the biometrics on the screen. This image should also have a marker showing where the user's core is located relative to the ideal location of the fingerprint's core. The image also can be used to give users feedback about the amount of pressure they need to apply; for example, a very black image indicates too much pressure. Greater user feedback reduces the number of poor enrollments, and thus the subsequent percentage of false rejects. Further, the resulting images will be more consistent and of higher image quality.

## Outliers and Fallback Strategies

There is currently no biometrics that can be used by everyone in the world, and so the system must consider how it will handle cases where it is not possible to use the biometrics system. As a result, "outliers" and those temporarily excluded from a specific biometrics system must be accommodated without causing either discrimination or weakened system security.

*Exception handling* offers an easy bypass to this issue if biometrics authentication is part of a security process.

### Exception handling of outliers

Extreme examples of "unenrollable" users are those people who do not have the required characteristic—for example, no eyes or no fingers. Conversely, someone with a very manual job may have such poor fingerprint definition that some fingerprint systems will be unable to capture enough of the fingerprint for verification. Still others may find it physically impossible to present the required characteristics (e.g., as a result of arthritis or loose eyelids). It may be possible to deal with such cases through individually based quality acceptance levels—with the attendant security implications. Alternatively, an entirely different authentication system could be used.

### Exception handling of temporary exclusions

Injury, illness, or current environmental conditions (e.g., tremors, glaucoma, traumas, or injuries such as a cut finger or a broken hand) may prevent an enrolled user, on one or more occasions, from presenting his biometrics at the required quality level for obtaining access. While ATMs might fall back on PINs, it is quite possible that a user who has become habituated to biometrics would have forgotten his PIN altogether. Fear of lack of access might even encourage the user to write down his PIN number and carry it with him so that he has it available for the few occasions on which he goes to a machine without the appropriate biometrics system. This, of course, is a terrific security risk all its own—and paradoxically defeats the security provided by the biometrics in the first place.

### Exception handling of aging

Because the body changes over time, the statistical algorithms that match the live image with the template must be sufficiently flexible to continually match the two as the body ages. Some systems perform minor updating of the template over time with each successful authentication, and other systems require periodic re-enrollment.

### User Acceptance

Users' fundamental attitude toward a technology will affect their behavior with that technology. For consumers to adopt biometrics (assuming that they are given any choice), they must find the technology:

- Socially acceptable
- Appropriate for a given environment
- Filling a perceived need
- Fundamentally understandable
- Usable
- Not destructive to personal privacy

Further, user acceptance of biometrics varies with the biometrics being used and the application to which it is being applied. Therefore, it is essential to understand user acceptance of specific rather than general situations. Negative factors affecting user acceptance include the newness of the technology, fear of being unable to use the technology, and privacy concerns.

## Promoting user acceptance

There is a general lack of public understanding of how biometrics works. This understanding gap is often expressed in terms of suspicion, distrust, or blind acceptance. However, the base level of consumer acceptance has increased over the last few years: a December 2002 study[34] showed that 78% of the American public would find biometrics verification at ATMs acceptable.

A few years ago, there was little perceived need for the addition of biometrics. However, the press coverage around "shoulder surfing" and card skimming has raised worries about PIN security. Meanwhile, terrorist threats have raised even bigger security concerns in general, and biometrics is often thought to be a more secure solution to both issues. It seems that fear of these threats is driving up public acceptance without a corresponding understanding of or experience with the technology: in a recent survey of 1,067 silicon.com readers, 75% believed that biometrics is more secure than traditional security methods.[35]

On the other hand, many consumers have difficulty believing that some "futuristic" technologies can work well. They think they stand a real chance of being rejected and not getting access, or that the technology may seem intimidating. People do not like rejection; it is embarrassing, particularly if it happens in public. Subsequent attempts to use the biometrics may be affected by the higher level of emotions created by the previous rejection. If a consumer already has a negative attitude toward the technology, any negative interaction will only serve to confirm his negativity.

Usability studies have shown that experience with an actual biometrics device can improve acceptance,[36, 37] but a system that exhibits poor usability can equally drive acceptance down. Thus, effective user enrollment, training, and lead-through when using the system are key to maintaining usability and thus, user acceptance.

Some users have expressed concerns about the hygiene of touch-based fingerprint devices, and the health risks of more advanced technologies such as iris or retina recognition. Some even fear that criminals will kill them in order to steal their eyes or fingers. This view is perpetuated by films such as *Mission Impossible* and *Minority Report*.

## Privacy

Privacy is a thorny issue that can generate poor user acceptance of biometrics. Any kind of biometrics technology implemented on a national scale raises all sorts of privacy and data protection issues. While there have been cases where user caution has been justified,[38] it

34 A. Westin, "Biometrics in the Main Stream: What Does the U.S. Public Think," *Privacy and American Business Newsletter* 9:8 (Dec. 2002).

35 T. Hallett, "Give Me Some Skin: Biometrics Get Thumbs Up," Silicon.com (Jan. 6, 2004).

36 Davies.

37 DARPA, "Human ID at a Distance."

38 C. Piller, J. Meyer, and T. Gorman, "Criminal Faces in the Crowd Still Elude Hidden ID Cameras," *Los Angeles Times* Section 1 (Feb. 2, 2001), 1.

is unclear if such fears are unwarranted. There are a number of ethical concerns[39] that biometrics advocates claim are unwarranted in general. Currently the technology is not as good as some people believe, and those technology limitations mean that privacy is maintained, at least for now. It is currently not possible to identify an individual from a large population; information is kept local because there are no interoperability standards; data capture requires cooperation and so cannot be covert; and template algorithms are built securely as the vendors want to maintain their confidentiality. But these weaknesses are slowly being eroded, as the technology is refined. In some cases, facial biometrics can be used without the person's knowledge, although this has privacy law implications as seen at Super Bowl XXXV in the U.S. in 2000.[40]

Another aspect of biometrics privacy issues involves cultural or religious concerns. Some people believe that the control and use of any part of the human body is a violation of a basic moral tenet of their civilization, or of their own religious beliefs. Other people worry that giving a biometrics may reveal extremely personal information—for example, whether an individual has a genetic disorder or HIV.

Also important is a general concern about the potential misuse of personal data, which would potentially violate both privacy and civil liberties. These views vary between countries and cultures and are reviewed extensively in Woodward (1997).[41] Simon Davies, executive director of Privacy International, believes that "We are on the verge of creating a biometrics system in which privacy and anonymity will vanish forever."[42] Some of us believe that protecting privacy in a "database nation" is the most pressing threat to liberty, particularly if there is a compulsory database encompassing everyone (e.g., national IDs with biometrics identifiers will mean constant surveillance).

It is not the biometrics concept itself that is seen as a threat to individual rights and privacy, but rather, the potential danger that an unspecified third party would be able to access the data and use it for applications for which the owner had not given permission. This can be controlled by applying preventative measures including encryption and by not storing an actual image.

## Conclusion

The assumption that biometrics is inherently a usable form of security is flawed. For the system to be secure, input must be controlled and the system must provide appropriate education, training, and lead-through to support the user in providing the required input.

39  A. Allerman, "Ethical Issues in Biometric Identification," *Ethics and Information Technology* 5 (2003), 139–150.

40  J. D. Woodward Jr., "Superbowl Surveillance: Facing Up to Biometrics," *Rand Arroyo Centre* (2001), 7.

41  J. D. Woodward, "Biometrics: Privacy's Foe or Privacy's Friend?" *Proceedings of the IEEE*, 85:9 (1997), 1480–1492.

42  W. Grossman, "Ever Feel You're Being Watched?" *The Independent* (May 14, 2003).

On the surface, there appear to be many valid reasons to adopt biometrics—for example, to replace PINs at the ATM. From a high-level perspective, biometrics appears to be a viable alternative to other forms of security. Field trials and surveys have shown that both system performance and consumer acceptance of biometrics is both promising and improving.[43, 44, 45, 46]. Public exposure to biometrics is increasing; and the cost of biometrics devices is coming down. And yet, there has been no large-scale deployment of consumer biometrics in the ATM environment.

This may be because many issues still exist with respect to adopting biometrics at ATMs. Many of these problems relate to the environment of use and the diversity of the user base—problems that are typically ignored by biometrics advocates.

Although biometrics technologies are still improving, inherent performance limitations remain and are extremely difficult to work around, except perhaps by combining multiple technologies or by providing for a bypass. In our work, we have found that certain participants simply cannot use certain systems, and we have been unable to identify the reasons for the failure. This situation would be unacceptable at an ATM if it prevented people from accessing their money.

In addition, the environment—both meteorological and social—is not always conducive to easy biometrics use. Rapidly changing illumination levels, and hot, cold, wet, and dry weather conditions, can all affect usage. Imagine that you are trying to use an ATM on a cold, wet night, with a queue of people waiting behind you. You repeatedly try to give your biometrics but are rejected. This makes you anxious and on each failure you are less likely to be accepted as you get more anxious, feel more rushed, and are more distracted by the surrounding activity.

Our ability to predict consumer acceptance of new technologies and services requires that we acknowledge some of the inherent limitations of focus groups and surveys. Research clearly demonstrates that there is no substitute for "hands-on" user experience with functional, contextually apropos prototypes, to ensure that predicted behavior will be converted into real behavior. The earlier we engage consumers with prototypes of the intended system, the better. However, more research is required to enable the design of usable biometrics to ensure that the experience with the system is satisfactory.

Every biometrics device has its own set of usability issues, and more work is required to ensure that more users can correctly access the system, and that the system itself is more accessible. Further, biometrics technologies do not resolve the usability/security tradeoff, and must establish fault tolerance limits. Narrowly setting these limits maximizes security

43 DARPA, "Human ID at a Distance."

44 Thalheim, Krissler, and Ziegler.

45 *Ibid.*

46 Tomorrow's Markets.

but decreases usability. Further research is required to understand the relationship between security and issues such as false rejects and failure to acquire.

Progress in the definition and resolution of usability in any proposed system will require a pluralist approach in methodology. Qualitative techniques are useful in identifying potential barriers to biometrics usage, and sophisticated technology is required to determine user positions and envelopes.

Biometrics usability, while essential to the success of biometrics implementations, is not the only factor that will affect user acceptance. The social issues surrounding biometrics are complex. While currently there may be a stigma attached to keeping records that include aspects of unique biological identifiers, this is not necessarily justified. If biometrics systems are properly regulated and not used for intrusive record-keeping of an individual's life, consumer groups should not be worried. However, it will be many years before biometrics is incorporated into the current authentication environment.

There is a common perception within the biometrics industry that some consumers will never adopt biometrics technologies, decrying them as intrusive. Other experts believe that consumers will resist adopting biometrics technologies only if these technologies prove to be susceptible to failure, time consuming, or otherwise inconvenient.

For this technology to be of real value to consumers, industry consensus must be reached before biometrics devices become ubiquitous. Biometrics devices will become more accurate and reliable as technology evolves, and more affordable as development costs are recouped and production techniques progress. In a financial service environment, it will be some time before biometrics technologies can be implemented on a large scale. Standards are required that allow greater interoperability between biometrics systems; and biometrics system accuracy depends on how many identifiable data points the system is able to map. A system that combines different sources of biometrics data is invariably more accurate and more reliable. Such a system will also be more expensive and more difficult to tune.

Today, it appears that biometrics is interesting and even appropriate for certain niche market applications, but it will be some time before biometrics is implemented *en masse*. There are many issues to resolve before it will be ready for applications with large, diverse, and untrained user populations.

Certain biometrics vendors (iris and fingerprint) are currently striving to achieve the goal of identifying individuals quickly, accurately, and reliably among a sample size of millions. But it appears that this objective is a long way from becoming commercially viable.

## About the Author

 Lynne Coventry holds a B.Sc. in Computing Science and Psychology, an M.Sc. in Software Engineering, and a Ph.D. in Human Computer Interaction. She joined NCR in 1995 and is part of a multidisciplinary advanced research group. She is responsible for the HCI research for future self-service technologies. Her work includes the design and evaluation of alternative authentication concepts such as biometrics and graphical authentication techniques.

# CHAPTER ELEVEN

# Identifying Users from Their Typing Patterns

**ALEN PEACOCK, XIAN KE, AND MATT WILKERSON**

**A**S DEFICIENCIES OF TRADITIONAL PASSWORD-BASED ACCESS SYSTEMS BECOME MORE ACUTE, researchers have turned their focus to *keystroke biometrics*, an approach that seeks to identify individuals by their typing characteristics. Since 1980, a number of techniques have been proposed for accurately harnessing a user's unique typing pattern for system authentication and other novel uses. But do these systems deliver on their promise to increase system security and simultaneously ease the burden of logging into systems and remembering passwords? And do databases of users' keystroke profiles present additional privacy concerns?

## Typing Pattern Biometrics

Many current computer systems ask users to enter a username and password pair before granting access. This method of authentication relies on the password's secrecy and, in some cases, the username's secrecy. If secrecy is not compromised, the system asserts that these tokens uniquely identify a valid user.

The problems associated with maintaining the secrecy of passwords are well understood.[1] Passwords that consist of common words, common phrases, or terms associated with a

1    M. Kotadia, "Gates Predicts Death of the Password," CNET News.com (Feb. 2004); *http://msn-cnet. com/2100-1029_3-5164733.html.*

particular user are generally considered to be weak because of the relative ease with which such passwords can be guessed by a third party or found through dictionary attacks. But because users find obscure passwords hard to remember, usability suffers. Not only must users choose obscure passwords, but they also must choose new ones often: many systems require that users periodically choose new passwords as part of security policies designed to deal with account compromises that are undetected. Add to this difficulty the fact that users are frequently encouraged to choose different unique passwords for each system that they access so that one exposed password does not jeopardize all systems. In practice, many individuals find the burden of remembering many unique, obscure, constantly changing passwords too heavy to carry, so they instead shed the weight of complying fully with these policies and recommendations by choosing weak passwords or reusing the same password over and over again.[2] Even if users do follow the best-recommended practices, passwords are still easily transferable from one party to another, whether transferred inadvertently or not; users sometimes write passwords down on paper, store them in accessible text files, accidentally expose them by entering them in the username field, and so on.

Over the past quarter-century, researchers have developed authentication systems based on the uniqueness of a user's typing pattern. The hope is that these systems will improve the security of traditional password systems while increasing, or at least not decreasing, usability. These systems work by measuring typing characteristics that are believed to be unique to the physiology and behavior of an individual, and thus are hard for impostors to imitate. The exact characteristics that are measured to form these biometrics vary, but almost universally they rely on timings between the press and release of various key combinations.

In the remainder of this chapter, we will outline several applications of this technology, compare results from existing research, discuss the impact of patents, and explore possible attacks on systems built to take advantage of typing patterns.

## Applications

The first suggested use of keystroke characteristics for identification appeared by 1975,[3] but observations about the uniqueness of an individual's typing characteristics stretch as far back as the end of the 19th century when telegraph operators observed that they could often identify one another by listening to the rhythm of each individual's Morse code keying pattern.[4] For a more complete introduction to research leading up to the invention of

---

2   A. Adams and M. A. Sasse, "Users Are Not the Enemy," *Communications of the ACM* 42 (Dec. 1999), 40–46. See also this volume, Chapter 32.

3   R. Spillane, "Keyboard Apparatus for Personal Identification," *IBM Technical Disclosure Bulletin* 17: 3346 (1975).

4   W. L. Bryan and N. Harter, *Studies in Physiology and Psychology of the Telegraphic Language* 6 (New York: New York Times Co., 1973), 35–44.

keystroke biometrics, see Leggett *et al.*[5] In this section, we highlight some of the most pertinent and interesting ways in which keystroke patterns can be applied.

---

## EXAMPLE USAGE: IDENTIFYING A USER

Virtually all strategies for identifying an individual from his typing patterns entail collecting timing information on individual keystroke events. As the user types, a background process collects timestamps that indicate when the user presses and releases each key.

The most common method used by researchers utilizes *keystroke digraphs*—the timings of two successive keyboard events. Figure 11-1 illustrates the various timing metrics that can be extracted from a digraph. Researchers have also examined techniques using three or more successive keystroke sequences, and have proposed measuring keystroke force and other features.

Generally, identification requires two stages:

- Enrollment, in which a number of keystroke traces are collected to form a profile
- Classification, in which the user provides a typing sample for comparison to the profiles in order to identify the user

Enrollment methods include requiring the user to type long texts, collecting traces transparently as the user works normally, and collecting traces only for a static set of words (such as the login typing pattern).

Classification methods range from statistical comparison to machine learning and pattern recognition techniques. Much of the body of research in keystroke biometrics focuses on creating and evaluating classifiers.

By far the most commonly researched usage scenario, *keystroke-enhanced login*, collects enrollment data from users while they sign into a system (either transparently, during a transition period, or in a session that collects a number of login samples in one or more sittings). Once enrolled, the system continues to collect keystroke timing information from each user during sign-in, using the initial profile to either accept or reject the user. If either the keystroke classifier rejects the user or the password value does not match the expected value, the user is rejected. The process is completely transparent to the user under such a scheme, as long as the keystroke biometrics classifier achieves accurate classification.

---

5   J. Leggett, G. Williams, M. Usnick, and M. Longnecker, "Dynamic Identity Verification Via Keystroke Characteristics," *International Journal of Man-Machine Studies* 35:6 (1991), 859–870.

## Authentication

Harnessing a user's typing patterns for authentication is highly attractive because it can be layered transparently onto existing systems. Applications involving financial transactions are excellent candidates for utilizing keystroke pattern authentication systems. Gartner Group estimates that online retailers in the U.S. lost $1.64 billion to fraudulent sales in 2002 and rejected another $1.82 billion in legitimate sales that looked suspicious.[6] Not only are these applications among the most likely to be targeted by attackers, but also consumers' tolerance for inconvenient security solutions is tempered by laws and regulations that frequently place the burden of financial loss on retailers. Because users would not perceive the difference between a traditional username/password login and one that had been modified to use keystroke biometrics, financial applications could add this type of authentication with little fear of user rejection.

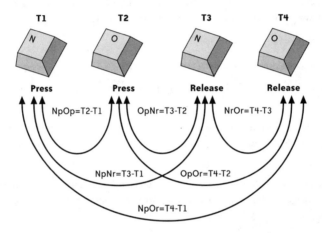

FIGURE 11-1. Digraph latencies for the typed sequence "no"; the most commonly used metric of a digraph is the time between the pressing of the first key and the pressing of the second key, but there are a total of six such metrics, as illustrated

Another likely candidate for this type of authentication is digital rights management. Here, the interests of consumers and content providers are not entirely aligned. Content providers desire to discourage individuals from sharing accounts, but without alienating legitimate users through additional complexity. Keystroke biometrics-based access controls to digital media accounts could largely eliminate account sharing without imposing additional hurdles to legitimate user access.

A compelling space for implementing password-based typing pattern authentication is the World Wide Web, where it is infeasible to outfit client machines with traditional biometrics devices. While other multifactor solutions exist,[7] they come with significantly higher

---

6   R. Richmond, "Fed Up with Fraud," *The Wall Street Journal Classroom Edition* (April 2003); *http://www.wsjclassroomedition.com/archive/03apr/BIGB_retailer.htm*.

7   For example, see RSA SecureID at *http://www.rsasecurity.com/products/securid/*.

infrastructure and usability costs. A web-based authentication solution incorporating keystroke biometrics replaces a standard form-based login with one that is capable of collecting keystrokes. The feasibility of implementing a Java applet to perform this function has been demonstrated by several research studies,[8, 9, 10] and source code is available.[11] Besides being supported by all recent browsers and operating systems, an applet can keep keystroke timing information private by sending it through an encrypted SSL connection to the server, which performs the processing. Any server responses can then be redirected back to the browser just as if a normal form-based login had occurred.

The first, and currently the only, commercial product suite that offers the ability to enhance authentications with keystroke patterns is BioPassword, distributed by BioNet Systems, LLC (*http://www.biopassword.com/*). The company's flagship product targets the standard Windows login, and has been deployed by several dozen customers. A related software development kit (SDK) allows developers to integrate the technology into their own Windows applications. A web authentication product, as well as multiplatform implementations of the BioNet SDK, are expected soon.

An interesting issue that has yet to be addressed by existing research is the degree to which keystroke dynamics–based authentication solutions scale as the number of users increases. The largest research study conducted to date collected samples from fewer than 200 users. The largest installation of BioPassword has fewer than 3,000 users. The user base of most consumer web applications is undoubtedly orders of magnitude larger.

Policy decisions abound in authentication, and they directly impact a system's usability and effectiveness. A primary concern is what to do when the check on the password text succeeds, but the check on the typing pattern fails. Should the user be rejected outright, or should some additional authentication step be performed? A successful supplemental check, such as requiring the user to answer a secret question, could lead to relaxing or adapting the thresholds on matched keystroke patterns, attempting to collect keystroke data once again, or simply allowing access and alerting administrators to watch the account closely. Frequent additional checks carry additional usability costs, so it is important that systems be built with high levels of accuracy to begin with.

8   S. Cho, C. Han, D. Han, and H. Kim, "Web-Based Keystroke Dynamics Identity Verification Using Neural Network," *IEEE Journal of Organizational Computing and Electronic Commerce* 10 (Dec. 2000), 295–307.

9   M. Tapiador and J. A. Sigüenza, "Fuzzy Keystroke Biometrics on Web Security," tech. rep., Escuela Técnica Superior de Informática, Universidad Autonoma de Madrid, Cantoblanco, Madrid, Spain, (March 2000).

10  A. Peacock, "Learning User Keystroke Latency Patterns" (April 2000); *http://pel.cs.byu.edu/~alen/personal/CourseWork/cs572/KeystrokePaper/*.

11  X. Ke, R. Manuel, M. Wilkerson, and L. Jin, "Keystroke Dynamics: A Software-Based Biometric" (2004); *http://web.mit.edu/xke/Public/kd/*.

## Identification and Monitoring

Closely related to the problem of authentication is the identification of a user from a set of potential candidates. One can imagine a scenario where physical access to a system is restricted to a set of users, and the system is able to decipher which one of those users is at the keyboard solely by observing typing patterns.

An identification scheme can also monitor when one user takes over for another on a given machine. The idea of detecting changes in identity through continuous monitoring of freely typed text has been touched upon in existing research, but tested empirically only with a very limited sample size.[12] The benefit of monitoring is in its ability to prevent an intruder from taking over a previously authenticated session. A user who forgets to lock down his machine before leaving it could, for example, rely upon the automatic lockdown by the monitoring system when it detects someone with a significantly different typing pattern.

Keystroke monitoring can also allow a system to detect uncharacteristic typing patterns of valid users caused by drowsiness, distraction, stress, or other factors.[13] In a task where alertness matters, for example, such an application could automate or augment monitoring tasks currently performed by human supervisors.

The allure of biometrics systems for use in monitoring and surveillance has become increasingly popular among law enforcement and security-sensitive private businesses in recent years. Public sentiment is becoming more sympathetic to these uses after a worldwide increase in terrorist activities, making it likely that even keystroke dynamics have been or will be deployed in the name of safety.

A number of privacy issues arise for any system designed to constantly monitor users. We discuss these in greater detail in the later "Privacy and Security Issues" section. Of course, usability questions abound here as well; too many alerts because of the typing inconsistencies of a single individual would be a significant hindrance to productivity.

## Password Hardening

A hardened password based on typing patterns can be used to create long-term, cryptographically stronger secrets for login and encryption. Monrose, Reiter, and Wetzel have defined a scheme for creating and storing such a hardened password that requires the user not only to know the correct password, but also to type it with the correct timings (within some threshold).[14] Their solution thwarts attempts to decipher the password using the

---

12 D. Song, P. Venable, and A. Perrig, "User Recognition by Keystroke Latency Pattern Analysis" (April 1997); *http://citeseer.nj.nec.com/song97user.html.*

13 F. Monrose and A. D. Rubin, "Keystroke Dynamics As a Biometric for Authentication," *Future Generations Computing Systems* 16:4 (2000), 351–359.

14 F. Monrose, M. K. Reiter, and S. Wetzel, "Password Hardening Based on Keystroke Dynamics," *Proceedings of the 6th ACM Conference on Computer and Communications Security* (ACM Press, 1999), 73–82.

server's stored content by a multiplicative factor and also prevents an attacker from gaining access to the system with knowledge of the password text alone.

### Beyond Keyboards

The concept behind keystroke typing patterns is not limited to the traditional keyboard. Any interface where keys need to be pressed can benefit from similar techniques. Application domains include authenticating personal identification numbers (PINs) at automatic teller machines and phone numbers entered through cellular devices. Early studies indicate that there is potential for authenticating users from input on a numerical keypad, although levels of accuracy are, as one might expect, worse than with a keyboard.[15, 16] Advances in identification of users through keypads and other button-dependent devices may lead to greater accuracy in typing pattern identification systems; the variety of keyboard types, shapes, and sizes surely affects user classification accuracy.

## Overview of Previous Research

The first studies on the effectiveness of keystroke characteristics as personal identifiers occurred in 1977[17] and 1980[18] (for a fuller treatment of work prior to 1990, see Joyce and Gupta[19]). Over the years, many different classifiers have been evaluated in an effort to improve recognition capabilities of keystroke biometrics, ranging from statistical analysis to neural networks. It is beyond the scope of this chapter to delve into the details of each approach. In general, each classifier measures the similarity between an input keystroke timing pattern and a reference model of the legitimate user's typing pattern. The model is built from training samples previously provided by each user and maintains varying characteristics depending on the classifier. The time required to generate each model also varies according to the classifier, with neural networks generally taking significantly longer than other approaches.

Table 11-1 compares the various experimental designs and techniques that have been analyzed in key published research. We include as much information as we have available

15 T. Ord and S. M. Furnell, "User Authentication for Keypad-Based Devices Using Keystroke Analysis," *Proceedings of the Second International Network Conference (INC 2000)*, (Plymouth, UK), IEE (July 2000), 263–272.

16 N. L. Clarke, S. M. Furnell, P. L. Reynolds, and P. Rodwell, "Advanced Subscriber Authentication Approaches for Third Generation Mobile Systems," *Third International Conference on 3G Mobile Communication Technologies*, 489 (May 2002), 319–323.

17 G. Forsen, M. Nelson, and R. Staron, "Personal Attributes Authentication Techniques," Rome Air Development Center Report RADC-TR-77-1033, Air Force Base Griffis (New York, 1977).

18 R. Gaines, W. Lisowski, S. Press, and N. Shapiro, "Authentication by Keystroke Timing: Some Preliminary Results," Technical Report Rand report R-256-NSF, Rand Corporation (1980).

19 R. Joyce and G. Gupta, "Identity Authentication Based on Keystroke Latencies," *Communications of the ACM* 33:2 (1990), 168–176.

from the relevant papers, though often experimental details are omitted from the primary source.[20]

*TABLE 11-1. Comparison of published research, 1980–2004*

| Authors/<br>Year | Input Data | Design | Features | Preprocessing | Classifiers | Notes |
|---|---|---|---|---|---|---|
| Gaines, Lisowski, Press, and Shapiro[a]; 1980 | Three 300–400 character passages | Seven professional secretaries typed two samples each with a delay of four months between samples | Interkey delays | Used only the 87 digraphs that had at least 10 or more replications per sample and per user; eliminated outliers; took logarithm of values | Two-sample t-test on whether the means of each value were the same assuming that variances were the same | Identified five core digraphs that discriminated perfectly: in, io, no, on, and ul |
| Umphress and Williams[b]; 1985 | Fixed 1,400-character reference input, 300-character test input | 17 programmers typed samples with a delay of at least one month; errors allowed | Interkey delays | Single low-pass temporal filter to remove outliers | Closeness between test value and corresponding reference value, measured according to a standard deviation threshold and a passing ratio | |
| Leggett and Williams[c]; 1988 | Two samples of fixed 537-character input | 36 individuals typed samples with a delay of at least one month; errors allowed | Interkey delays; mean of delays | Various; resulted in 12 different subsets of feature vectors to analyze | Closeness measure as in Umphress and Williams | Found that means of delays do not further discriminate between users; using all lowercase digraphs yielded best results |

20 Feature vectors representing keystroke characteristics are derived from key press times, key release times, and information on which keys are being pressed. Times are usually measured in milliseconds, although the granularity can vary according to the experiment setup, and is not generally reported. *Duration*, or *hold time*, represents the time between the press of a key and the release of the same key. *Digraph latency* is the delay between the release of one key and the press of the next key. In early literature, the term *interkey delay* is also used; that term may refer to either the digraph latency or the time from the press of one key to the press of the next key. We will refer to the latter feature as *key press delay* to avoid confusion. Timing information between three consecutive keystrokes, known as *trigraphs*, has also been analyzed. Unless otherwise indicated, samples involving input errors or the use of the backspace key are not analyzed. In addition, most experiments have subjects type on a single machine and keyboard, with the notable exception being the web-based experiments that rely on Java applets to collect keystrokes.

*TABLE 11-1.* Comparison of published research, 1980–2004 (continued)

| Authors/ Year | Input Data | Design | Features | Preprocessing | Classifiers | Notes |
|---|---|---|---|---|---|---|
| Joyce and Gupta[d]; 1990 | Username, password, first name, last name | 33 users typed all samples in a single session | Key press delays | None | Minimum distance from reference model, with verification threshold according to each user's typing variance | Found that more experienced users were more difficult for imposters to replicate |
| Bleha, Slavinski, and Hussein[e]; 1990 | Username and fixed 32-character phrase | 32 users typed samples over a period of weeks | Digraph latencies | Combined two samples into one; dimension reduction to reduce size of feature vector | Normalized minimum distance; normalized Bayesian | Applied different fixed thresholds for authentication |
| Leggett and Williams et al.[f]; 1991 | Same as 1988 | Same as 1988 | Interkey delays | N/A | N/A | Introduced dynamic characterization of users by their typing patterns |
| Bleha, Knopp, and Obaidat[g]; 1992 | Fixed 32-character phrase | Users typed the sample at least once per day for five weeks | Digraph latencies | None | Linear perception | |
| Brown and Rogers[h]; 1993 | First and last name | 25 users typed on a single keyboard | Digraph latencies | Removed outliers | Minimum distance; back-propagation neural network; partially connected back-propagation neural network | Found that partially connected back-propagation network performed the best |
| Obaidat[i]; 1995 | Username and password | 15 users typed on a single keyboard over 8 weeks | Durations; digraph latencies | None | Various pattern recognition (k-means, cosine measure, minimum distance, Bayesian, potential function); various neural networks (BP, SOM, ART-2, RBFN, LVQ, RNN, SOP, HSOP) | Potential function and Bayesian performed the best, while cosine measure performed the worst; using only durations was more successful than using only latencies |
| Lin[j]; 1997 | Password | 90 valid users and 61 invalid users logged into system | Durations; key press delays | Derived invalid vectors by extending valid vector with random numbers and multiplying by a factor | Three-layer back-propagation neural network | |

*TABLE 11-1. Comparison of published research, 1980–2004 (continued)*

| Authors/ Year | Input Data | Design | Features | Preprocessing | Classifiers | Notes |
|---|---|---|---|---|---|---|
| de Ru and Eloff[k]; 1997 | Password | 30 users typed on single keyboard; used assembler code to produce time intervals in clock cycles | Interkey delays; category indicating typing difficulty of password | Related precise delays to four time interval categories (a value can belong to more than one category through probabilistic assignment) | Fuzzy logic with four categories and five rules | Found typing difficult to be less discriminating than timing interval |
| Song, Venable, and Perrig[l]; 1997 | Continuous monitoring of keystrokes | Several hours of keystroke data gathered for each user; coarse timing granularity of 10 ms due to X server implementation | Digraph, trigraph, and wordgraph key events for each incoming keystroke | Measured closeness of incoming key events to the respective digraph, trigraph, and wordgraph models for that user | Final probabilistic prediction based on a weighted sum of the incoming keystroke's closeness measurement and the previous keystroke's closeness measurement | Empirical observations on a single user showed promise, but lack of quantitative results |
| Robinson et. al.[m]; 1998 | Username | 140 students routinely logged into campus network; replaced standard login module with one that collected keystrokes | Digraph latencies | Randomly selected 10 usernames for training and 10 usernames for testing; discarded 24% of samples due to typing errors | Minimum distance; nonlinear measure similar to Umphress and Williams; inductive learning based on nonparametric density estimation | Found that inductive learning classifier using both duration and latencies performed the best; using duration time alone was better than latencies |
| Monrose, Reiter, and Wetzel[n]; 1999 | Fixed eight-character password | 20 users logged into server at least five times over six months; Java applet recorded keystrokes | Durations; digraph latencies | Selected distinguishing features based on mean and standard deviation, and thresholds | Binary classification (slow and fast) for each distinguishing feature | Attempted to demonstrate how passwords can be more securely stored on servers, and did not seek to minimize FAR |
| Monrose and Rubin[o]; 2000 | N/A | 63 users typed on local Sun workstations at their convenience over 11 months | N/A | Selected most significant features | Minimum distance; weighted and nonweighted probability; Bayesian | Bayesian classifier performed the best |
| Peacock[p]; 2000 | Username, password, fixed nine-character word | 11 users typed samples from own machines in one session; Java applet recorded keystrokes | Durations; digraph latencies | None | K-nearest neighbor | |

*TABLE 11-1. Comparison of published research, 1980–2004 (continued)*

| Authors/ Year | Input Data | Design | Features | Preprocessing | Classifiers | Notes |
|---|---|---|---|---|---|---|
| Cho, Han, Han, and Kim[q]; 2000 | Seven-character password | 25 users typed samples over several days | Durations; digraph latencies | Removed two users; 6%–50% of training data discarded for every user | Minimum distance; autoassociative neural network | Neural network performed the best |
| Haider, Abbas, and Zaidi[r]; 2000 | Seven-character password | Users typed samples into DOS-based application | Interkey delays | None | Fuzzy logic with five categories; three-layer neural network; statistical confidence interval; combinations thereof | A combination of approaches performed the best |
| Changshui and Yanhua[s]; 2000 | Fixed 1,100-character text | 24 users typed sample 18 times | Durations; key press delays | Removed outliers | Autoregressive model with coefficients by the Yule-Walker and Burg methods | Low accuracy relative to previous results |
| Wong et al.[t]; 2001 | User-selected password | 10 users typed on 2 dedicated machines; 100 unauthorized attempts | Interkey delay | Removed outliers | Single-layer perceptron network; minimum distance | Tradeoff between FRR and FAR for the two classifiers used, with the neural network having a high FAR |
| Bergadano, Gunetti, and Picardi[u]; 2002 | Fixed 683-character text | 44 users typed sample over one month, with no two samples from a user collected on the same day; errors allowed | Trigraph durations | None | Disorder between arrays of sorted trigraph durations | The method was also tested on digraphs, 4-graphs, and 6-graphs, but trigraphs performed the best |
| Clarke et al.[v]; 2002 | Four-digit number, fixed phone number, varying phone numbers | 16 users typed on mobile handset | N/A | N/A | Back-propagation neural network | |
| Kacholia and Pandit[w]; 2003 | Username and password | 20 users typed on a single machine | N/A | N/A | Clustering to produce reference models; threshold deviation for classification | |

TABLE 11-1. *Comparison of published research, 1980–2004 (continued)*

| Authors/ Year | Input Data | Design | Features | Preprocessing | Classifiers | Notes |
|---|---|---|---|---|---|---|
| Yu and Cho[x]; 2003 | Seven-character password | 25 users typed samples over several days (data from same experiment as Cho, 2000) | Durations; digraph latencies | Various, with the best results after performing feature selection based on a genetic algorithm—SVM-based wrapper | Support Vector Machine (SVM) novelty detector models | SVM approach is about 1,000 times more efficient than multilayer perceptrons but has the same degree of accuracy; large training sample needed to attain most accurate results |

[a] Gaines *et al.*

[b] D. Umphress and G. Williams, "Identity Verification Through Keyboard Characteristics," *International Journal of Man-Machine Studies* 23: 3 (1985), 263–273.

[c] J. Leggett and G. Williams, "Verifying Identity Via Keystroke Characteristics," *International Journal of Man-Machine Studies* 28: 1 (1988), 67–76.

[d] Joyce and Gupta.

[e] S. Bleha, C. Slivinsky, and B. Hussein, "Computer-Access Security Systems Using Keystroke Dynamics," *IEEE Transactions on Pattern Analysis and Machine Intelligence* 12:12 (1990), 1217-1222.

[f] Leggett and Williams.

[g] S. A. Bleha, J. Knopp, and M. S. Obaidat, "Performance of the Perceptron Algorithm for the Classification of Computer Users," *Proceedings of the 1992 ACM/SIGAPP Symposium on Applied Computing* (ACM Press, 1992), 863–866.

[h] M. Brown and S. J. Rogers, "User identification Via Keystroke Characteristics of Typed Names Using Neural Networks," *International Journal of Man-Machine Studies* 39:6 (1993), 999–1014.

[i] M. S. Obaidat, "A Verification Methodology for Computer Systems Users," Proceedings of the 1995 ACM Symposium on Applied Computing (ACM Press, 1995), 258–262.

[j] D.-T. Lin, "Computer-Access Authentication with Neural Network Based Keystroke Identity Verification," *IEEE International Conference on Neural Networks* 1 (June 1997), 174–178.

[k] W. de Ru and J. Eloff, "Enhanced Password Authentication Through Fuzzy Logic," *IEEE Expert* 12 (Nov./Dec. 1997), 38–45.

[l] Song, Venable, and Perrig.

[m] J. A. Robinson, V. W. Liang, J. A. M. Chambers, and C. L. MacKenzie, "Computer User Verification Using Login String Keystroke Dynamics," *IEEE Transactions on Systems, Man, and Cybernetics, Part A* 28 (March 1998), 236–241.

[n] Monrose, Reiter, and Wetzel.

[o] Monrose and Rubin.

[p] Peacock.

[q] Cho, Han, Han, and Kim.

[r] S. Haider, A. Abbas, and A. K. Zaidi, "A Multi-Technique Approach for User Identification Through Keystroke Dynamics," *IEEE International Conference on Systems, Man, and Cybernetics* 2 (Oct. 2000), 1336–1341.

[s] Z. Changshui and S. Yanhua, "AR Model for Keystroker Verification," *IEEE International Conference on Systems, Man, and Cybernetics* 4 (Oct. 2000), 2887–2890.

[t] F. W. M. H. Wong, A. S. M. Supian, A. Ismail, L. W. Kin, and O. C. Soon, "Enhanced User Authentication Through Typing Biometrics with Artificial Neural Networks and K-Nearest Neighbor Algorithm," *Conference Record of the Thirty-Fifth Asilomar Conference on Signals, Systems and Computers* 2, (Nov. 2001), 911–915.

[u] F. Bergadano, D. Gunetti, and C. Picardi, "User Authentication Through Keystroke Dynamics," *ACM Transacations on Information and System Security*, 5:4 (2002), 367–397.

[v] Clarke *et al.*

[w] V. Kacholia and S. Pandit, "Biometric Authentication Using Random Distributions (BioART)," *Proceedings of the 15th Canadian IT Security Symposium (CITSS)*, Government of Canada (May 2003).

[x] E. Yu and S. Cho, "GA-SVM Wrapper Approach for Feature Subset Selection in Keystroke Dynamics Identity Verification," *Proceedings of the IEEE International Joint Conference on Neural Networks* 3 (July 2003), 2253–2257.

# Evaluating Previous Research

The majority of academic papers published on keystroke biometrics systems since 1980 have presented independent studies, each collecting its own samples from unique sets of individuals. These samples were collected through diverse methods, varying widely in the mechanics of user input, the granularity of measured data, the amount of input required to train the system and authenticate users, the number of test subjects employed, and the diversity of the typing experience of these subjects. Such nonuniformity alone makes comparison among different studies difficult; add to this difficulty the diversity of keystroke pattern classification approaches and the application of these technologies to different domains, and the task becomes more complex.

In this section, we will compare results from the field with commonly used metrics for measuring accuracy, and propose new metrics for measuring the usability of keystroke systems. Unfortunately, much of the literature in this area lacks sufficient reported data to measure all of the preceding features. We therefore restrict results reported in the following sections to the subset of reports reviewed in the earlier section titled "Overview of Previous Research" that do provide the necessary numbers. Notably missing in all these comparisons is the only commercial offering, for which published numbers are scant (although public documents at the BioNet web site[21] do claim that performance is on par with some of the earliest published results).

## Classifier Accuracy

Three metrics are commonly used to describe biometrics classifier performance with regard to accuracy:

- *FRR.* False Rejection Rate—the percentage of valid (genuine) user attempts identified as imposters

- *FAR.* False Acceptance Rate—the percentage of imposter access attempts identified as valid users[22]

- *ERR.* Equal Error Rate—the crossover point at which FRR = FAR, given some independent variable(s) that can be adjusted to produce curves for FRR and FAR

Although ERR is a desirable metric in terms of its ability to condense FAR and FRR into one value, the amount of data needed to turn FAR and FRR into curves (usually through the introduction of an independent variable) is usually prohibitive. Few researchers report

---

21 Net Nanny Software International, Inc., "Biopassword Keystroke Dynamics," Technical Report, 2000–2001.

22 In much of the literature regarding keystroke patterns, the terms *Imposter Pass Rate (IPR)* and *False Alarm Rate (FAR)* are used interchangeably with FAR and FRR as defined here, respectively. The existence of two terms whose meanings are opposite but which are both denoted by *FAR* can cause some confusion. We have adopted the FAR/FRR terminology throughout this article.

ERR in their published results. For this reason, we present an alternative approach to combining FAR and FRR: averaging the two values. We will call this value:

- *AFR.* Average False Rate—the average of FAR and FRR. Empirically, AFR closely approximates ERR for those few papers that did report ERR.

In 2000 and 2002, the U.K.'s Biometrics Working Group produced guidelines for "Best Practices in Testing and Reporting Performance of Biometric Devices."[23] Going forward, we hope that researchers in the field of keystroke typing patterns will consider these guidelines when reporting results. The main corpus of results we review herein, however, did not have the advantage of access to these standards, and therefore did not present data that we could use to produce such useful evaluation criteria as Receiving Operator Characteristic (ROC) or Detection Error Trade-off (DET) curves.[24] In this light, AFR can be viewed as a useful stopgap for comparing overall classifier accuracy.

Figure 11-2 graphs the performance of each of the highlighted systems in terms of AFR, FRR, and FAR. Although we make no claim about the validity of a system designed to favor either FAR/FRR over the other (such as password hardening[25]), we feel that in the absence of reported ERR, AFR is a good descriptor of the overall accuracy of a given classifier in terms of discriminating between users.

This figure demonstrates that the very best reported results are able to achieve an AFR of less than 1%, and roughly one-third are capable of AFR near 2%—values generally considered to be acceptable for this type of system. The worst performers have average AFR values between 8% and 27%, and are not likely to provide sufficient accuracy for common usage.

### Usability

Two other commonly used metrics in the realm of biometrics are:

- *FTR.* Failure to Enroll Rate—the percentage of users who lack enough quality in their input samples to enroll in the system

- *FTA.* Failure to Acquire Rate—the percentage of users for whom the system lacks sufficient power to classify, once enrolled

These metrics are proposed primarily as a way to measure classifier accuracy, and not as a means of measuring system usability,[26] although they can provide some limited insight into system usability. We found that FTR and FTA are seldom reported; this may stem

---

23 A. J. Mansfield and J. L. Wayman, "Best Practices in Testing and Reporting Performance of Biometric Devices," Technical Report Version 2.0, U.K. Government Biometrics Working Group (Aug. 2002).

24 These curves plot pairs of error rates measured at different algorithm parameters.

25 Monrose, Reiter, and Wetzel.

26 The authors of "Best Practices in Testing and Reporting Performance of Biometric Devices" go so far as to explicitly exclude human factors from consideration when defining FTR and FTA.

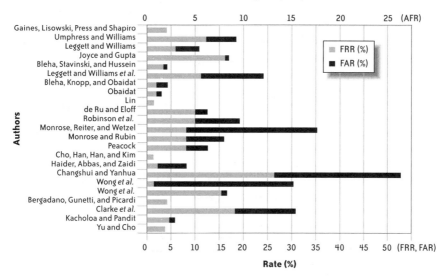

**Accuracy: FRR, FAR, and AFR**

FIGURE 11-2. *False Rejection Rate, False Acceptance Rate, and Average False Rate for each of several approaches; Average False Rate is the average of FRR and FAR, and is shown by the top axis; systems with lower FRR, FAR, and AFR are more accurate in discriminating between users, and are thus capable of being more secure*

from the fact that most studies do not use thresholds for rejecting users during enrollment, which in turn may stem from the relatively small groups of users studied in most reports (see "Confidence in Reported Results" later in this chapter).

False Rejection Rate (FRR) also partially addresses usability, as it is a measure of how often a user may have to reauthenticate after being misidentified by the system. But none of these metrics addresses usability directly. We therefore propose two new metrics that do quantify usability explicitly:

- *CUE.* Cost to a User to Enroll—the number of keystrokes a user needs to submit to the system before enrolling as a valid user

- *CUA.* Cost to a User to Authenticate—the number of keystrokes a user needs to submit to the system each time he needs to authenticate

CUE and CUA arise from the need to measure usability in terms of how much work an individual must perform when accessing a system successfully, rewarding classifiers that perform well with less input from the user. Unlike FTR/FTA, these metrics ignore the extra work required of users as a result of classifier failures, instead focusing on the usability costs associated with *successful* enrollment and access. If FTR/FTA data was available from the studies cited in this survey, we could combine these with CUE/CUA data to give a more complete picture of overall system usability.

Figure 11-3 plots CUE and CUA for each of several approaches.[27] The graphs show a wide range of requirements both for enrollment (from 24 required keystrokes to nearly 3,500) and for authentication. Authentication costs in this figure fall into three categories: those that require on the order of 10 keystrokes (these are almost universally the systems that monitor only password patterns), those that require tens of keystrokes, and those that require several hundred keystrokes. Note that if we were to eliminate those systems that required more than 1,000 keystrokes to enroll and/or more than 100 keystrokes to authenticate, we would eliminate a few of the better performers from "Classifier Accuracy," but would retain a large number of systems that perform accurately *and* have low usability costs.

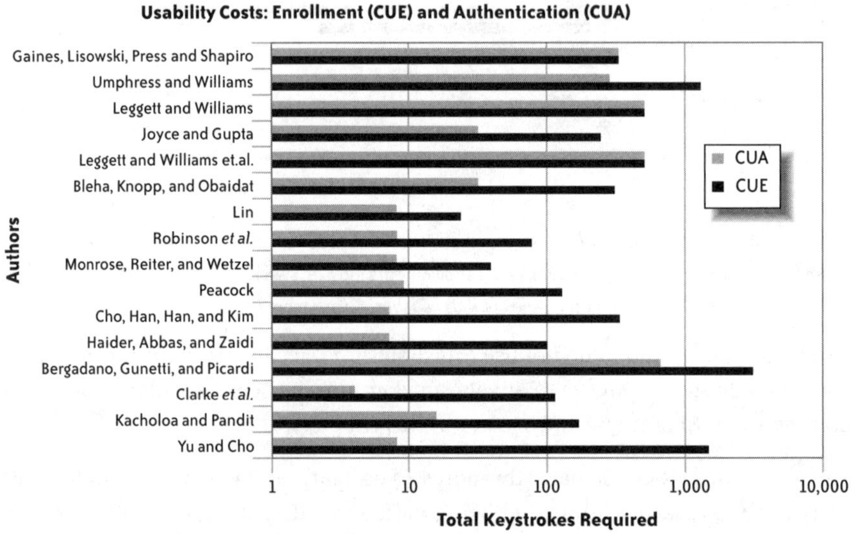

FIGURE 11-3. *The cost to a user (in keystrokes) to enroll and to authenticate for a given approach; systems that can enroll and authenticate with fewer keystrokes are easier to use*

## Confidence in Reported Results

There is wide variance in the amount of data researchers collect to perform their studies and to demonstrate the effectiveness of their systems. Is a system that is able to determine the identities of 5 users with 100% accuracy better than a system that is able to determine the identities of 300 users with 99% accuracy? To measure the amount of confidence we can place in reported results, we compare the various studies according to:

- *Sample size.* The number of test subjects taking part in the study
- *Valid access attempts.* The number of valid authentications attempted
- *Imposter access attempts.* The number of imposter authentications attempted

27 Many of the password-based approaches failed to publish average password length. The data presented in this article assumes a password length of eight characters in that case.

The results shown in Figure 11-4 are not very encouraging; only two of the published studies used more than 50 test subjects, with the majority using fewer than 25. The lack of extensive test data demonstrates an important deficiency: keystroke biometrics will almost certainly be used for groups of users larger than 25, yet only two of the approaches compared in the figure demonstrated competence on samples large enough to validate their results on large systems. Large sample sets are particularly important for web-based systems, the largest of which may scale to millions of users. To be fair, harnessing a significant number of human test subjects is a difficult task. Perhaps these numbers indicate the need for a central repository of input data for keystroke biometrics analysis. Such a repository would also serve as a source for common benchmarking to compare various approaches. Alternatively, researchers could independently make their own data available upon publication.

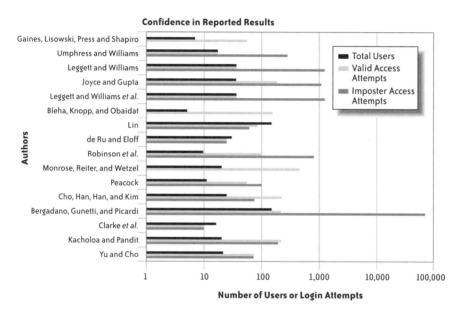

*FIGURE 11-4. The involvement of more users and more valid/imposter logins lends credence to reported results, but even the largest studies in the keystroke patterns field to date fall short of proving competence on large systems*

Figure 11-4 also shows the number of valid and imposter accesses attempted on each system. Valid attempts fall roughly into three categories: those with fewer than 100 attempts, those with close to 200 attempts, and one[28] with close to 500 attempts. Imposter attempts have four divisions: a few with no imposter attempts, many with 100 or 1,000 imposter attempts, and one[29] with over 70,000 imposter attempts. Larger numbers provide more convincing proof of workable, secure systems. It is also worth pointing out that a small handful of the best combined performers from the earlier sections, "Classifier Accuracy"

28 *Ibid.*
29 Bergedano *et al.*

and "Usability," such as Lin,[30] maintain reasonable—if not stellar—performance in relation to the current body of work.

---

## TIPS FOR PRODUCING USEFUL AND COMPARABLE RESULTS IN KEYSTROKE BIOMETRICS STUDIES

In our review of user studies involving keystroke biometrics, we noticed that a clear explanation of experimental procedures greatly enhanced the clarity and comparability of presented results. The following list of attributes culled from successful experiments is intended as a checklist for future researchers:

- Include, as a minimum:
  - Total number of subjects involved.
  - Input sample length as number of keystrokes, averaged where applicable. The sample length may be different for enrollment and for access (if so, include both lengths).
  - Number of samples required for a user to enroll.
  - Number of valid users (and valid access attempts).
  - Number of imposter users (and imposter access attempts).

- Describe the testing methodology. What system did the users interact with? What were they told about the experiment? How often did they access the system? Under what circumstances did they access the system? How long did the experiment last?

- If possible, make the raw collected data available. This allows other researchers to independently verify your results, as well as to try the same datasets with new classifiers in order to perform direct comparisons.

We didn't encounter any researchers who omitted their final results. However, there are several things to keep in mind when reporting future findings:

- For each result, make it clear what supporting experimental setup was used, including the facts from the above list.

- If you report CUE and CUA (which we heartily encourage), avoid the temptation to omit reporting the number of valid and imposter users, and the input sample length.

- Consider using Receiving Operator Characteristic (ROC) or Detection Error Trade-off (DET) curves. [a]

---

[a] Mansfield and Wayman.

30 Lin.

# Privacy and Security Issues

If keystroke dynamics gain widespread acceptance, privacy and security issues must be evaluated carefully. Of concern are databases that maintain the keystroke timing patterns of users. With this information, attackers can subvert authentication systems that rely on keystroke biometrics.

If an attacker is able to obtain a particular user's keystroke timing profile, he may be able to guess which keys the user is typing simply by analyzing the timing of keystrokes. Such an attack may succeed against encrypted keystrokes as they are sent over a network, without ever needing to decrypt the data. For example, if it is known that the user spends 800 milliseconds typing the digraph **io** but usually spends around 1,400 milliseconds typing **yr**, an attacker can narrow the search space of plausible keystrokes, with the hope of finding an interpretation of the timings that results in a plausible original text. In 2001, researchers proved that this attack could work when they deciphered encrypted passwords sent through version 2 of the SSH protocol (used for remote access to computer terminals). Their technique allowed them to find the password an average of 50 times faster than brute force methods by utilizing a weakness in the protocol that allowed an attacker to determine precise timings for each keystroke and a database of user keystroke profiles.[31] Even when user-specific keystroke profiles are not available, generic keystroke profiles created from any representative population subset have been found to weaken security. In addition, the attacker may be able to employ this tactic with very low-tech means—for example, by using a tape recorder to listen to the click-clack of a user typing at a keyboard.

Systems that monitor typing patterns (see the earlier section, "Identification and Monitoring") must also guard against privacy breaches. If the monitoring process produces records, these records must be protected by both a policy regarding their use and a mechanism to prevent unauthorized access to the records. But such safeguards do not protect against covert monitoring and tracking of individuals, wherein a third party might secretly collect a keystroke profile from an unsuspecting user to monitor the user's activities in the future, or to subvert keystroke authentication systems by posing as the legitimate user with the collected biometrics. A governmental agency, for instance, could collect keystroke traces of targeted individuals from computer terminals in public libraries or at other official public kiosks. This data could be used to monitor and track an individual as he moves from one public system to the next. A private entity could do likewise from a private but publicly accessible system, such as an online registration application. Once an entity has a copy of a user's keystroke biometric, its ability to perform identity theft against other keystroke biometrics-enabled systems is greatly enhanced.

---

31 D. X. Song, D. Wagner, and X. Tian, "Timing Analysis of Keystrokes and Timing Attacks on SSH," *Tenth USENIX Security Symposium* (2001); *http://www.usenix.org/events/sec01/song.html*.

## INTELLECTUAL PROPERTY AND THE CURRENT MARKET LANDSCAPE

The biometrics security market is expected to grow from $1 million in 2004 to $4.6 billion in 2008. So why have keystroke biometrics not become a booming part of this trend? Either current implementations do not meet performance and usability standards, or other factors, such as broad patent claims, have hindered commercial development of this technology.

For a technology that has made little progress outside the ivory tower, the field of keystroke patterns has a substantial body of patents covering every possible interpretation and incarnation as a product. At worst, these patents negatively impact academic research to improve viability of the biometrics. In 2001, one of the authors of this chapter was asked by one of the holders of these patents to cease and desist from making keystroke collection and classification tools available on the Internet. Undoubtedly, other researchers have encountered similar obstacles.

The first patent that actually defined typing patterns as a method was John D. Garcia's 1986 patent.[a] It describes a general method for verifying whether someone is part of a predetermined group using a similarity measure based on timing vectors. It also describes a "personal identification apparatus," covering possible input devices such as a typewriter keyboard, numerical keypad, or piano keyboard. Garcia describes both a method and an apparatus so that the interpretation of the invention is broad.

The 1989 James R. Young and Robert W. Hammon patent[b] forms the basis for claims protecting BioNet Systems' BioPassword.[c] This patent specifically targets computer keyboards, uses templates to classify users, and includes keystroke pressure measurement as a novel feature addition.

In 1996, the U.S. Patent Office granted Marcus E. Brown and Samuel J. Rogers a patent[d] that describes a number of improvements based on specific classifiers such as neural networks and Euclidean distance measures, and presents a method for purifying training data by discarding outlying input.

The most recent patent to be accepted in the area of typing patterns is the 2002 Zilberman patent.[e] Zilberman's improvements include a keyboard device that dispenses physical tokens as a unique key to access the system, a data matrix for storing timing characteristics, and an embedded microcontroller for authentication.

*—continued—*

Whether seen as a device, an apparatus, a process, or a method, keystroke dynamics has clearly been well thought out by inventors positioning themselves for the crossing of this technology into the steadily growing information security market. The success of any commercial offering will either herald the acceptance of typing pattern authentication into the marketplace or signal the need for more research and better implementations.

[a] J. D. Garcia, "Personal identification apparatus," U.S. Patent 4,621,334 (1986).
[b] J. R. Young and R. W. Hammon, "Method and apparatus for verifying an individual's identity," U.S. Patent 4,805,222 (1989).
[c] BioNet Systems, LLC, "Biopassword—Questions and Answers," Technical Report, 2002; *http://www.biopassword.com/home/FAQs/BP_General_FAQs_112502.pdf*.
[d] M. E. Brown and S. J. Rogers, "Method and apparatus for verification of a computer user's identification, based on keystroke characteristics." U.S. Patent, Washington, D.C., 1996. Patent Number 5,557,686.
[e] A. G. Zilberman, "Security method and apparatus employing authentication by keystroke dynamics." U.S. Patent, Washington, D.C., 2002. Patent Number 6,442,692.

## Conclusion

Although keystroke biometrics systems have been pursued actively by academics and inventors for over a quarter of a century, the field is still maturing. Lack of a shared set of standards with regard to data collection, benchmarking, and measurement has prevented, to some degree, growth that comes through collaboration and independent confirmation of techniques. Patents encumber many of the most basic of strategies. Until privacy concerns regarding the building of databases of keystroke biometrics data are resolved, wide adoption of this technology may meet opposition from civil libertarians and privacy advocates.

Still, the field of keystroke biometrics holds great promise for creating systems that are both more secure and more usable than their predecessors. Because keystroke biometrics can be collected without the need for special hardware, and because software to perform identification and authentication has shown great potential in this regard, keystroke biometrics may be poised to become a standard method of proving one's identity both online and offline. Keystroke biometrics maintains an advantage over most other biometrics authentication schemes: user acceptance.[32] As users are already accustomed to authenticating themselves through the entry of username and password, the majority of proposed keystroke biometrics methods are completely transparent to users.

32 Gaines *et al.*

Continuing research and commercial activities in the field, and the popularity of the keyboard as the primary input device for applications, ensure that the technology will not fade into history. As the keystroke biometrics field matures, observers should watch for several trends that will indicate when the technology is ready for more widespread adoption:

- Greater depth in performance measurement, with the average study involving at least thousands of users

- The creation of datasets that can be shared between studies, enabling researchers to focus on perfecting their classification methods instead of burdening them with the task of building usable sample data

- Introduction of schemes that ensure the privacy of collected biometrics data

- Expiration or relaxation of existing intellectual property claims, with resultant competition that this will foster

Whether the use of keystroke biometrics ultimately become a ubiquitous part of the security landscape will be determined not only by how much we trust these systems to uniquely identify individuals and provide a comfortable authentication process, but also by how much we trust systems that collect the immutable piece of ourselves known as a biometrics.

## About the Authors

Alen Peacock currently works as a software developer for Novell, Inc. and as a research consultant at the Massachusetts Institute of Technology's Lincoln Laboratory, researching topics in airborne mobile networking. His current research interests include application of cognitive processes to ad hoc network topology formation, and the design of resilient, decentralized data storage. He has an M.S. in computer science from Brigham Young University.

*alenpeacock@gmail.com*

Xian Ke is a program manager with Microsoft's Security Business Unit. Her research interests include practical computer security applications and information systems. She has an M.E. in computer science from the Massachusetts Institute of Technology.

*xke@mit.edu*

Matt Wilkerson is a graduate of the Massachusetts Institute of Technology, with degrees in Computer Science and Management Science. While at MIT, his research interests included information security, computer graphics, and streaming video applications. He currently works as an investment banking analyst in the Media and Communications Group at Morgan Stanley.

*mwilker@mit.edu*

# CHAPTER TWELVE

# The Usability of Security Devices

**UGO PIAZZALUNGA, PAOLO SALVANESCHI, AND PAOLO COFFETTI**

**A**N INCREASING NUMBER OF HARDWARE DEVICES ARE BECOMING AVAILABLE TO HELP USERS ACHIEVE A higher level of security in authentication systems. However, little research has been performed on the usability of these devices. This chapter takes a first step toward understanding the usability issues associated with security devices. After briefly reviewing security devices, we define an experimental approach suitable for their usability evaluation. We apply this approach to evaluating cryptographic smart card devices, and we report and comment on the results, including the impact of usability on security. We conclude by presenting general recommendations to minimize usability problems while deploying security devices.

## Introduction

A variety of hardware devices are employed to increase computer security. This chapter focuses on those portable devices designed to increase the security of authentication systems. Smart cards and "one-time password" tokens are perhaps the best-known examples of security devices; they fit easily in pockets or on keychains, embed an integrated circuit, and are used to log into networks or web sites securely.

Vendors of security devices strive for a design that is both secure and usable. But are they successful? In this chapter, we will attempt to address this question by suggesting an experimental approach to evaluating security devices as a whole, then applying that approach to a particular subclass of security devices: smart cards and USB tokens.

Previous work on the usability of identification and authentication mechanisms, particularly in the area of password usability, emphasizes the importance of a systemic approach to usability.[1, 2] We believe the same holds true for security devices. We cannot speak about the usability of these devices without taking into account their social contexts, physical characteristics, and software, as well as typical users and applications. This systemic view of usability is essential to defining a comprehensive set of usability attributes.

Defining these attributes represents the first step of our proposed approach to assessing usability. The second step is the objective measurement of these attributes, as many usability claims are not supported by any research or experimental evidence.

The primary purpose of our approach is for evaluation. However, experimental studies are valuable not only for evaluation and comparison purposes, but also as a source of suggestions for better system design. Indeed, this process may provide larger insights into system design beyond the hardware security device itself. For example, a security device may be used in conjunction with email software. A proper design of both could help avoid or limit usability problems. Similarly, an experimental study of usability may help the designer identify the weak components or interactions between components, and may thus inform a redesign process.

## Overview of Security Devices

Security devices provide the "something I have" factor for authentication systems.[3] Passwords, an example of the "something I know" factor, lend themselves to a plethora of security attacks. Security devices can offer an alternative or, even better, a complement to the knowledge factor to increase security.

Take, for example, the process of withdrawing cash from an ATM. You need to insert your card (the "something you have") and enter its corresponding PIN ("something you know"). Similarly, a security device lets you securely withdraw precious electronic resources, like logging into your laptop or accessing your company's private networks, from anywhere.

There are a number of ways to categorize security devices. As you do with your ATM card, you need to carry your security device with you to access electronic resources. But, depending on the type of device, you may or may not need to physically insert it into your

---

1   A. Adams and M. A. Sasse, "Users Are Not the Enemy," *Communications of the ACM* 42:12 (1999). See also Chapter 32, this volume.

2   M. A. Sasse, S. Brostoff, and D. Weirich, "Transforming the 'Weakest Link': A Human-Computer Interaction Approach to Usable and Effective Security," *BT Technology Journal* 19:3 (1999), 122–131.

3   See Chapter 6, this volume.

computer or a separate reader device. One way to distinguish among different security devices is according to whether they need to be physically *plugged in*, as follows:

*Smart cards*

Smart cards[4] are among the smallest computers we currently handle in our daily life. Smart cards are essentially plastic credit cards that include an integrated circuit (IC) whose current computational power is similar to the desktop PCs of the 1980s.[5] However, smart cards must be plugged into a reader. Other kinds of security devices do not require a special reader. Universal Serial Bus (USB) tokens, for example, use the USB port built into most computers.

*One-time password (OTP) tokens*

OTP tokens[6] fall into the category of security devices that do not have to be plugged in. Similar in shape to a small pocket calculator, OTP tokens display authentication data that users type in manually. The authentication data changes each time a user authenticates (or, in some cases, after a designated small time interval regardless of whether an authentication has taken place)—hence the name "one-time password" token. The fact that OTP tokens do not require a hardware reader means that they can be used with more kinds of computers than USB tokens can—for example, an airport Internet kiosk may not expose its USB ports to travellers. On the other hand, the fact that the user must physically type the value displayed on the OTP token can be an annoyance, make OTP tokens slower to use, and introduce the opportunity for transcription errors.

Devices that must be plugged in can be further subcategorized: can they be plugged into an existing port on a typical laptop or desktop computer, or do they require a special reader?

*Passive storage* versus *active storage* is an additional way to categorize security devices. Let's go back to our ATM card example: our "secret" authentication information is stored passively on the magnetic strip. On the other hand, OTP tokens and cryptographic smart cards embed a small computer that actively performs the computations needed for authentication.

We can further subcategorize "active" security devices by considering their external cryptographic functionalities. OTP tokens, for example, provide no *cryptographic functionality* externally. Cryptographic smart cards, on the other hand, provide wider cryptographic services like random number generation and public key cryptography. Cryptographic smart cards can enable users to securely access systems based on public key cryptography. Desktop machine logon, Virtual Private Network (VPN) access, wireless client authentication, and email protection are just a few examples where smart cards enhance security.

---

4   K. M. Shelfer and J. D. Procaccino, "Smart Card Evolution," *Communications of the ACM* 45:7 (2002), 83–88.

5   U. Flohr, *The Smartcard Invasion* (Byte, 1998).

6   R. E. Smith, *Authentication: From Passwords to Public Keys* (Reading, MA: Addison Wesley, 2002).

Indeed, examples like these are a current driving force for deployment of cryptographic devices such as smart cards.[7]

Table 12-1 summarizes the classifications introduced so far and plots them against particular security devices.

*TABLE 12-1. A schematic classification of security devices*

| Type of security device | OTP tokens | Smart cards | USB tokens |
|---|---|---|---|
| Plug-in | No | Yes | Yes |
| Reader required | No | Yes | No |
| Active device | Yes | Yes | Yes |

With these general classifications in mind, we'll now describe four form factors of security devices (including biometrics devices, which do not appear in the table). Note, however, that we do not intend this to be a comprehensive list.

## OTP Tokens

- *Description:* similar in shape to small pocket calculators, OTP tokens show on a small display the authentication code that the user must enter to authenticate. The code needs to change each time it is used—hence the name "one-time password" token.

- *Classify as*: no plug-in; no reader required; active device.

- *Pros*: no special hardware required.

- *Cons*: user must type the authentication code each time; can be used only for authentication; server and token may get out-of-sync.

- *Product examples*: RSA Security SecurID, Secure Computing SafeWorld.

- *Additional comments*: different form factors are available; for example, cellular phones can be used to compute and display the authentication data. "Sound" smart cards represent another example: they compute the authentication data, encode it as a sound sequence, and play it. This eliminates the need for the user to type the code, but introduces additional complexity in the client software.

## Smart Cards

- *Description*: smart cards add an integrated circuit (IC) to the familiar plastic credit cards. The IC has a computational power similar to the desktop PCs of the 1980s.

- *Classify as*: plug-in; reader required; either passive storage *or* active device (depending on the integrated IC).

- *Pros*: form factor familiar to millions of people; low cost (but excluding the reader costs).

- *Cons*: require a reader; users can fail to insert the smart card properly in the reader.

---

7   E. Messmer, "Microsoft Sold on Smart Cards," *Network World* [cited 03/22/2004]; *http://www. nwfusion.com/news/2004/0322mssecurity.html.*

- *Product examples*: Axalto CryptoFlex, Oberthur ID-One, Gemplus GemXpresso.
- *Additional comments*: different form factors are available (see the description of USB tokens next).

## USB Tokens

- *Description*: USB tokens include both a smart card IC and a smart card reader in a single object.
- *Classify as*: plug-in; either passive storage *or* active device (depending on the integrated IC).
- *Pros*: no reader required; easy to plug in.
- *Cons*: existing tokens have a limited area for printing (hardly suitable as an ID document).
- *Product examples*: Aladdin eToken, Eutron CryptoIdentity.
- *Additional comments*: variants of these devices may include additional functionality, such as general-purpose mass storage, RFID for physical access, or fingerprint sensors; see also "Biometrics Devices," next.

## Biometrics Devices

- *Description*: security devices or their associated readers can also embed biometrics sensors, in most cases fingerprint sensors. Examples include biometrics smart card readers and USB tokens.
- *Classify as*: not applicable (depends on the actual security device).
- *Pros*: replace PIN with fingerprint verification.
- *Cons*: fingerprint security is still debated; potential privacy concerns.
- *Product examples*: G&D StarSign® BioToken 3.0, Omnikey Cardman fingerprint 7120 smart card reader, Sony Puppy.

One last comment regarding this list: plug-in devices, unlike OTP tokens, are connected to the potentially hostile host machine. Malicious programs, for example, can compromise the PIN or trick the device into performing an operation different from the one intended by the user—for example, signing a modified transaction.[8] Placing both a PIN pad and a small display on a security device or reader can prevent these types of attacks; on the other hand, it makes such devices considerably more expensive. For financial applications where costs may not be a concern, FINREAD-compliant smart card readers[9] offer this maximum level of security. However, their small-size display can raise nontrivial usability issues. For example, how would you use it to review a page-long email that you need to sign?

8   N. Ferguson and B. Schneier, *Practical Cryptography* (New York: John Wiley & Sons, Inc.,2003).

9   *http://www.finread.com*.

# Usability Testing of Security Devices

Security devices, like other security technologies, are deployed in a physical and social context to allow users to complete their tasks. Thus, it is essential to perform usability studies on the system as a whole—in other words, taking into consideration the specific contexts, users, and tasks users must perform.[10] In the testing described in this chapter, we have tried to capture many of the important usability attributes that will be applicable generally. Do keep in mind, however, that while we are striving for general attributes, you should review your own actual environment to identify additional attributes that might affect your usability, or drop one or more of those we have identified.

## Setting Up the Test

Our attributes definition draws on prior research[11, 12] and the ISO 9126 standard.[13] The ISO 9126 software quality model defines six independent software quality characteristics, each of which is broken down into a set of subcharacteristics. However, usability studies of security devices deal not only with software but also with systems. Therefore, while the ISO standard is an important reference point, we have had to extend and adapt it to accommodate our specific aspects of interest.

The usability attributes we adopted are an extension of the following three ISO 9126 usability subcharacteristics:

- *Learnability.* How difficult/easy is it for users to learn how to use the security devices?

- *Operability.* How difficult is it for users and their organizations to carry out the assigned tasks properly while using the security devices?

- *Attractiveness.* To what extent are the security devices attractive to users?

Operability is a very broad attribute. Therefore, we have broken it down into the following subattributes:[14, 15]

- *Mobility.* Organizations' procedures and structures are increasingly encompassing remote and mobile employees. Are applications that require security devices easily operable from different computers?

---

10 Sasse, Brostoff, and Weirich.

11 B. Pinkas and T. Sander, "Securing Passwords Against Dictionary Attacks," *Proceedings of the 9th ACM Conference on Computer and Communications Security* (ACM Press, 2002), 161–170.

12 A. Whitten and J. D. Tygar, "Why Johnny Can't Encrypt: A Usability Case Study of PGP 5.0", *Proceedings of the 8th USENIX Security Symposium* (Aug. 1999). See also Chapter 34, this volume.

13 ISO, *International Standard ISO/IEC 9126. Information technology—Software product evaluation—Quality characteristics and guidelines for their use*, International Organization for Standardization, International Electrotechnical Commission, Geneva (1991).

14 Pinkas and Sander.

15 Whitten and Tygar.

- *Installability.* In order to operate security devices properly, users must be able to install them. Can users do so without too much difficulty?

- *User friendliness.* Can users operate the devices easily? Are the devices prone to user error?

- *Low operating costs.* Do the security devices require customer support calls? Is too much user time spent merely trying to interact with the devices?

- *Security interaction.* Do the security devices provide enhanced security without creating the potential for dangerous error? More specifically, what influence, if any, does the devices' usability have on security? Do usability problems lead to security failures?

One controversial topic is how security devices that require a reader should be evaluated using this framework. A company that is promoting these devices might want an evaluation to consider only the device itself, and assume that the readers are ubiquitous. We take an opposing view: given today's computer hardware—that is, the system's physical context—these issues will be raised unless the reader is already in place. This situation can create both usability and security issues if the user is forced to carry around extra hardware and software in order to operate the device.

Here, we must make some additional comments about the adaptation of the ISO model of software quality to the specific type of systems in our study. The first comment concerns the hierarchical relationship between the attributes. In our approach, each subattribute of operability has the same relevance level of learnability and attractiveness; the subattributes are simply classified under the common name of *operability*. The second comment is related to the security interaction; somewhat arbitrarily, we have placed it under the head *operability*. In fact, the ISO standard does not model this type of attribute, because the attribute does not describe a property in a hierarchy, but an interaction between properties (usability and security).

Our experimental approach is driven by the usability attributes defined in this section. In other words, each attribute will be evaluated through a set of metrics detailed in the experiments.

## Related Work

Little research has been published on the usability of security devices. One recent study performed by Wu *et al.* compares the usability of mobile-phone-based authentication interfaces.[16] Herzberg,[17] and Mallat *et al.*[18] describe financial services that can be enabled through mobile phones, but their focus on usability is minimal. Fulcher discusses the

---

16 M. Wu, S. Garfinkel, and R. Miller, "Secure Web Authentication with Mobile Phones" [cited 11/2004]; *http://www.mit.edu/~minwu/*.

17 A. Herzberg, "Payments and Banking with Mobile Personal Devices," *Communications of the ACM* 46:5 (May 2003).

18 N. Mallat, M. Rossi, and V. K. Tuunainen, "Mobile Banking Services," *Communications of the ACM* 47:5 (May 2004).

deployment of a cryptographic USB token in an "eHealth" project, but neither analyzes its usability nor discusses usability tradeoffs of other security devices that might be used in the same context.[19] The usability characteristics of other types of authentication mechanisms are discussed in Part II of this book.

A recent study by Scholtz and Consolvo[20] proposes a framework for conducting a usability study of ubiquitous computing applications. The goals of their framework—that is, to allow researchers to learn from each other's results and to create effective evaluation techniques and design guidelines—could apply equally to the evaluation of security devices. The approach we propose in this chapter may be considered a first step in defining a more complete framework similar to the one proposed by these researchers.

## Usability Testing Methodology

The following steps summarize the methodology we adopted in our usability testing:

1. *Purpose and scope definition.* We define the aims of the test (e.g., comparing the usability of two types of devices) and set the test's limits.

2. *Context and roles definition.* We define the context for the experimental scenario, including the simulated environment, user roles, tasks they need to achieve, and so on. Each role must be specified clearly, including the possible actions of a supervisor.

3. *User selection.* We define the selection criteria of users based on the selected context and aims of the test. We must select a user sample wide enough to assure statistical significance.

4. *Task definition.* We define the set of tasks to be executed by each user (sequence of steps, input data, output data).

5. *Measurement apparatus design.* We choose a set of metrics and specify their relationships with the usability attributes. For each metric, we define name, description, scale, and procedure to collect the raw data and compute the measurement.

6. *Execution and data collection.* We execute the test and collect the data.

7. *Processing for statistical significance.* We process the data to ensure its statistical significance.

8. *Computation of the quality attributes scores.* We compare the quality profile of each device. In the ISO 9126 quality model, product usability is linked to a set of attributes, and each attribute is evaluated through a set of metrics. Note that this procedure has to consider various types of measures, including both quantitative and qualitative ones.

19 J. Fulcher, "The Use of Smart Devices in eHealth," *Proceedings of the 1st International Symposium on Information and Communication Technologies*, Trinity College Dublin (2003), 27–32.

20 J. Scholtz, S. Consolvo, "Towards a Discipline for Evaluating Ubiquitous Computing Application," National Institute of Standards and Technology and Intel Research [cited 01/2004]; *http://www. intel-research.net/Publications/Seattle/022520041200_232.pdf.*

9. *Results interpretation and explanation.* We interpret our set of results and suggest possible causal explanations that will be useful for generating design recommendations.

# A Usability Study of Cryptographic Smart Cards

This section describes the aim, scope, context, user selection, task definition, measurement apparatus, processing, and results of our usability study.

## Aim and Scope

The aim of this usability study was to compare alternative form factors of cryptographic smart cards—that is, comparing traditional smart cards with USB tokens.

Smart cards are often praised for their usability:[21] they are mobile, can be used in multiple applications, and carry lower administrative costs than systems based on multiple usernames/passwords. On the other hand, smart cards are also criticized for their low market acceptance.[22, 23] Garfinkel states that "few people use this [smart card] added security option because smart cards and readers are not widely deployed."[24] However, alternative form factors to the familiar plastic smart card are emerging, and proponents of these technologies claim that they overcome the limitations of smart cards.[25]

## Context and Roles Definition

The scenario set up for this study compares three form factors: the traditional plastic smart card with a USB smart card reader, and two types of USB tokens (see Figure 12-1). We label these two types of USB tokens *base* and *advanced*; the advanced type is identical to the base one, but has an additional feature, as described shortly.

The base type of USB token integrates, in one single object, both the smart card reader and the cryptographic smart card IC. The IC embedded in the tokens used in the usability test is the same one embedded in the smart cards. The advanced USB token adds mass storage to the base type; when connected to the host system, this token will make available as separate resources both the smart card (and its reader) and a removable hard drive for general-purpose storage. The tokens used in our study contain 64 MB of storage and embed the same smart card IC found in the smart card and base token.

The "advanced" USB tokens' additional mass storage resource motivated our decision to include these tokens in our testing. We were interested in discovering whether usability

21 RSA Security, "The Cryptographic Smart Card: A Portable, Integrated Security Platform" [cited 2001]; *http://www.rsasecurity.com/products/securid/whitepapers/smart/CSC_WP_0301.pdf.*

22 *http://www.finread.com.*

23 S. Garfinkel, "Email-Based Identification and Authentication: An Alternative to PKI?", *IEEE Security & Privacy* 1:6 (2003), 20–26.

24 *Ibid.*

25 C. Kolodgy, "Identity Management in a Virtual World," IDC White Paper (June 2003).

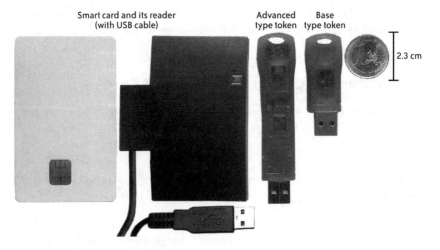

Smart card and its reader (with USB cable)     Advanced type token     Base type token

2.3 cm

*FIGURE 12-1. The three form factors deployed in the usability test*

could be enhanced by deploying, in a single hardware device, not only cryptographic material but also software and data on how to use the software (e.g., installation software). On the other hand, smart card IC and mass storage components are isolated; therefore, this additional functionality does not introduce security vulnerabilities to the smart card IC. (Figure 12-2 shows a schematic diagram of both types of tokens.)

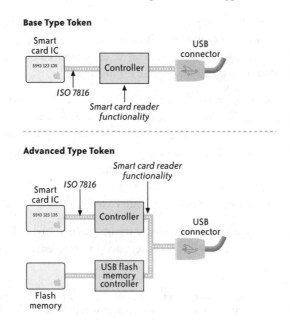

**Base Type Token**

Smart card IC          USB connector

5543 123 135          Controller

ISO 7816

Smart card reader functionality

**Advanced Type Token**

Smart card reader functionality

Smart card IC     ISO 7816          USB connector

5543 123 135          Controller

USB flash memory controller

Flash memory

*FIGURE 12-2. Schematic diagram of base and advanced USB tokens*

Except for low-level drivers, all three form factors share the same middleware (e.g., Microsoft CAPI). The software used in the study was Microsoft Outlook Express running on the Windows XP and Windows 2000 operating systems. These were chosen so that users would see no difference at the software level while using any of the three devices.

Furthermore, given the standard interfaces between the application-level software and the devices provided by the middleware, the specific devices used in these experiments could just as well be replaced by any other cryptographic smart card or cryptographic USB token (so long as this replacement provided the same standards-compliant middleware). The outcome of this usability evaluation applies, therefore, to any specific instance of these kinds of devices.

The social context, or "setup," for the user tests draws inspiration from the work of Whitten and Tygar.[26] Each participant was told to imagine that they were responsible for the preparation and launch of an advertising campaign to promote a new product. Tasks for this job position included frequent travel between the different company sites, and most of the material to be delivered for the campaign had to be sent to colleagues through emails. Given the high competition in the market targeted by the new product, a strong level of security protection was demanded on all email communications. To this end, we prepared a cryptographic device with the user's personal digital certificates. The imaginary company provided a technical support team to assist the user, should any trouble arise with the device. However, the subject's manager advised the subject to minimize calls to the support team, as it had limited staff.

This scenario motivates users to actively "protect some secret they consider worth protecting."[27] and includes the use of security while carrying out certain tasks, as opposed to instructing participants "to perform a security task directly."[28] Indeed, security itself is not a user function. The user wants to send a protected email, not use an encryption algorithm. This means that security tools and devices should be integrated seamlessly into the applications.

The test's active participants were the user and the supervisor (experimenter). The supervisor had the following roles:

- Drove the briefing phase, giving the user all the required inputs
- Collected the measures during the test
- Acted as the customer support service during the test execution
- Drove the debriefing phase to collect the final questionnaire

## User Selection

We selected 10 participants for the user test. All were in their second or third year of undergraduate studies at an engineering college. While all were skilled in the use of email

26 Whitten and Tygar.
27 *Ibid.*
28 *Ibid.*

and computers, none had any previous experience with securing email or cryptographic devices.

## Task Definition

The user test consisted of the following three phases:

*Briefing phase*

Before the execution of the user test, the supervisor introduced each participant to the test scenario, described the task to be executed, and explained the role of the supervisor. The supervisor gave the user a brief document describing the context of the study and the tasks to be completed. A set of manuals on the installation and use of the devices was made available for reference, together with the hardware needed for the first form factor to be tested.

*Execution phase*

During this phase, the participant had to move across three company sites where her work was required. Three workstations in three different university labs simulated this setup. At each site, the user had to execute the following tasks:

- Install drivers and software for the device.

- Send an encrypted and signed email to a colleague through the standard Outlook encryption and signing procedure, which required the user to provide the password to authorize the signature operations on the device. The email's text and recipient were contained in the documents handed out prior to the experiment, and the email client was configured beforehand to include the recipient's digital certificate.

After the user completed the first set of tasks, the supervisor gave the user the hardware for the second form factor and the user repeated the tasks for the three sites. The same process was executed for the third form factor.

One of our concerns was that the sequence of presentation of each device might affect the results of the test, in the event that the user's experience with the first device influenced her opinion of the other two. Thus, sequences of presentation were rotated for every user.

During the execution phase, the supervisor measured the values of the defined metrics (e.g., the time for sending an email or the number of errors during the installation) using a standard sheet to write the results and, if needed, additional comments.

If users failed to complete a task correctly, they had to re-execute it. The supervisor surveyed the operations and requested the task repetition as needed.

*Debriefing phase*

At the end of the test, the user was given a debriefing questionnaire.

## Measurement Apparatus

Figure 12-3 lists the metrics we defined for this experiment and compares their relationships with the usability attributes. For example, the number of requests to customer service and the time for sending email contribute to the "low cost to operate" attribute value.

| Metrics | Learnability | Attractiveness | Installability | User friendliness | Low cost to operate | Security interaction | Mobility |
|---|---|---|---|---|---|---|---|
| Number of references to the manual | ■ | | | | | | |
| Number of requests to customer service | | | | | ■ | | |
| Time for installation | | | ■ | | | | |
| Number of errors during installation | | | ■ | | | | |
| Number of hesitations during installation | | | ■ | | | | |
| Time for sending email | | | | ■ | | | |
| Number of errors in sending email | | | | ■ | | | |
| Number of hesitations in sending email | | | | ■ | | | |
| Number of security errors | | | | | | ■ | |
| Number of mobility errors | | | | | | | ■ |
| Evaluation of mobility (questionnaire) | | ■ | | | | | ■ |
| Evaluation of usability (questionnaire) | | ■ | | | | | |
| Discretional use (questionnaire) | | ■ | | | | | |

*Attributes*

FIGURE 12-3. Metrics and their relationships to usability attributes

The following provides clarification of some of the metrics:

*Security errors*

For purposes of this study, we classified the following user errors as "security errors":

• Failure to encrypt an email.

• Failure to sign an email.

• Failure to bring the cryptographic device in the new location. The device is left on the desk or plugged into the workstation; this situation may allow attackers to get access to the user's private key.

*Hesitations*

We defined *hesitations* as conditions in which the user had doubts on how to proceed further; these do not necessarily imply an error. Although hesitations are less important than errors from a usability perspective, they offer an additional metric for user friendliness.

*Mobility errors*

We defined *mobility errors* as those that involved moving from site to site. For example, the user might fail to bring along the CD-ROM containing the installation software, or forget the smart card, reader, or token.

*Overall metrics*

The last three metrics shown in the table are based on answers given in the debriefing questionnaire: participants were asked to score from 1 (poor) to 5 (excellent) the overall usability and mobility of the device. The supervisor also asked the user what form factor she would prefer to purchase, assuming that the user addressed security in a similar but real scenario.

## Processing for Statistical Significance

After all users completed the experiment, the collected data was processed to assure its statistical significance. Where applicable, the measured results were processed to compute the mean value and the standard deviation. Given a set of three mean values (and the associated standard deviations) coming from a metric applied to the three devices, we computed the *t-test* to each couple of values. This procedure tested the statistical significance of the differences. Using a student's *t* distribution and assuming two populations with different standard deviations and 10 samples for each population (10 participants for each device), we computed the samples' reference variance, the degrees of freedom, and the *t* value. Then we used a *t* distribution table (mapping the value of *t* and the degrees of freedom to the probability) to find the significance level of the difference between the two mean values. We applied this procedure to each applicable metric. Figures 12-4, 12-5, 12-6, 12-7, and 12-9 show some examples of these measured values, their standard deviations, and the related probability levels.

## Computation of the Quality Attributes Scores

Next, we processed the data to compute the quality attributes scores. The computation had to take as input the whole set of values coming from a number of metrics. Some metrics provided quantitative values (e.g., the mean time required for a user to send an email); others were based on qualitative evaluations (e.g., the subjective perceptions relative to ease of mobility). We computed the end data through the use of *interpretation functions*, which map the measurement values (e.g., the mean time is 3 minutes) onto merit values (e.g., the mean time is high), and integrated a number of merit values into a unique score.

The computation is composed of the following two steps:

- A mapping function translates the value of each metric into a qualitative space: "Very High, High, Medium, Low." For example, the range of values measuring the number of errors is divided into four intervals of equal amplitude, each pointing to a qualitative value.

- The score of each attribute is derived from the contribution of a set of qualitative values. Each set of values is integrated into a unique attribute score through a decision table. The table maps a set of "Very High, High, Medium, Low" values into a quality score from 1 (poor) to 7 (excellent). For example, a two-entry decision table maps the pair of values "Very High, Very High" into the score 7 and the values "Very High, High" into the score 6.

Note that this procedure is somewhat arbitrary. Nevertheless, it does provide a global quality profile that may be used to present the results and discuss them together with specific, more relevant quantitative measures.

## Results and Interpretation

Figure 12-4 shows the mean time the subjects needed to perform each one of the three email protection tasks. We noticed that using the smart cards took about twice as long as using the tokens; the existence of more than one hardware piece and the user's need to connect them properly were the main reasons for this result.

This difference is certainly exacerbated by the nomadic nature of the user test; in a real-life situation, a user would probably be configuring the smart card at a familiar workstation, thus decreasing task time. Nevertheless, considering that this result is the average of the three executions, and also considering that we could anticipate difficulties, and therefore a longer execution time, on the first trial, it is surprising that the measured time spent on the second and third smart card trials is still significantly higher than for the USB tokens. In fact, the slowdown in smart card task completion is the result of many repeated user errors inserting the smart card in the reader.

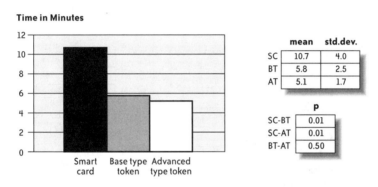

*FIGURE 12-4. Mean time required for a user to send three protected emails*

In Figure 12-4 (and Figures 12-5, 12-6, 12-7, and 12-9), *std.dev.* is the standard deviation of the collected data (10 users); *mean* is the mean of the collected data; *p* is the significance level of the difference between the mean values for two devices; *SC, BT,* and *AT* denote, respectively, the smart card, the base type token, and the advanced type token.

Figure 12-5 depicts the mean number of user requests to "customer service" in order to complete all tasks. Out of a total of nine requests, seven occurred while subjects were using the smart card. Most queries to "customer service" resulted from confusion users had regarding the hardware pieces they had to handle: the smart card and the reader. For example, it was not obvious when to insert the smart card into the reader, or how the reader, smart card, and computer had to be interconnected.

Figure 12-6 shows the mean number of errors that occurred while sending three protected emails.

Figure 12-7 shows the mean number of mobility errors that occurred while completing the tasks on the three sites.

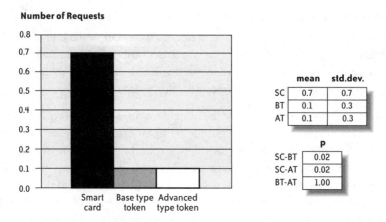

*FIGURE 12-5. Mean number of requests to "customer service" to complete all tasks*

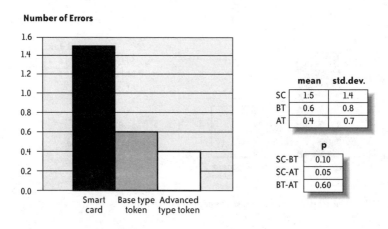

*FIGURE 12-6. Mean number of errors that occurred while sending three protected emails*

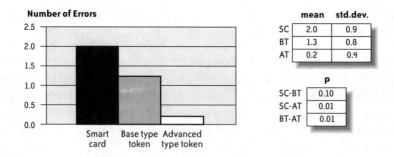

*FIGURE 12-7. Mean number of mobility errors that occurred while completing the tasks on the three sites*

The overall impact of these errors on the test scenario can be estimated by considering the entire number of single tasks involved. For example, the test case for sending protected emails required the user to send at least three emails for each device. More than three emails per user were actually sent because users failed to send the first as expected. Considering the average total of 3.5 email tasks per user and per device, the frequency of errors is 43% for smart cards, 20% for the base tokens, and 9% for the advanced tokens. Similarly, the mobility task involved in moving among workstations averaged about 4.17 times among the three devices. The percentage of error is, in this case, 42.6% for smart cards, 27.7% for the base tokens, and 4.3% for the advanced tokens.

In retrospect, we could have anticipated this difference of errors for the mobility task as a consequence of the difference in the number of pieces users had to carry. However, the large difference for the email protection task is somewhat unexpected. To analyze this result further, Figure 12-8 reports the types and frequencies of errors that occurred while subjects were using the smart card.

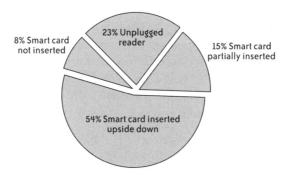

FIGURE 12-8. Type and frequency of errors while using the smart card for protecting emails

In fact, 69% of these errors occurred because users inserted the smart card in the reader incorrectly—either upside down or incompletely. Users queried customer service about half of these times, and in the other half were able to correct the error independently.

Figure 12-9 shows the mean number of security errors that occurred while completing the tasks on the three sites. The result is the reverse of common-sense expectations: indeed, one could expect that because the software and smart card IC are identical for all three devices, little or no substantial difference should be found. However, the numbers reveal a different situation: of a total of 35 security errors, 21 occurred while using smart cards, 9 while using the base tokens, and only 5 while using the advanced tokens. Users executed a total of 230 email and mobility tasks—these 35 security errors represent 15% of this total number.

Most of the errors were the result of users connecting the devices improperly, or failing to bring along the hardware when moving to a different location. Only five errors were the result of the user's failure to explicitly request signature and encryption, either because the user forgot or because the email software client failed to make the user aware of it. This result indicates further that the number of hardware components users must deal with increases complexity and decreases security.

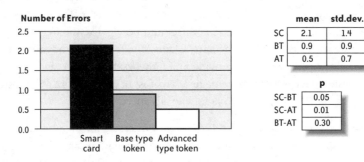

Number of Errors

| | mean | std.dev. |
|---|---|---|
| SC | 2.1 | 1.4 |
| BT | 0.9 | 0.9 |
| AT | 0.5 | 0.7 |

| | p |
|---|---|
| SC-BT | 0.05 |
| SC-AT | 0.01 |
| BT-AT | 0.30 |

*F I G U R E 12-9. Mean number of security errors while completing all tasks*

The advanced token appears to be the least error-prone of the devices, for obvious reasons. Because it is a single hardware piece and is thus self-sufficient for carrying out every task, users were less likely to forget it. Test participants also praised the advanced token's mass storage functionality; perhaps participants cared more about this object because it had a greater value to them. The few errors that occurred with the advanced token appeared to be linked to installation; because the token is bundled with its own installation software, users plugged it in as soon as they reached a new location—thus, they had already plugged it in for the email protection task.

It is worth further investigation to determine whether the advanced token does indeed provide better usability in contexts where, for example, installation can be carried over from a network, or when installation is not needed at all. On the other hand, contexts in which the software using the cryptographic device (a) cannot be assumed to be available in the host machine and (b) can be executed from the filesystem on the device itself (without the need for a specific installation step) are likely to exhibit better usability for the advanced token.

The last component of the experiment was a debriefing questionnaire, which included some questions about how well the users comprehended the suggested context, and other questions about the users' perceptions of the devices' attributes. The three main questions were:

- "How do you evaluate the mobility attribute (ease of transport) for the three devices? Please assign a score between 1 (poor) and 5 (excellent)."

- "How do you evaluate the overall usability? Please assign a score between 1 (poor) and 5 (excellent)."

- "Given a similar context, which device would you prefer to buy?"

Figure 12-10 shows the outcome of the questionnaires. The advanced token scored very well, obtaining excellent scores for mobility and usability (a, left). The base token obtained good scores, particularly for usability. The smart card had low scores for mobility and medium for usability. In the last question, 70% of users chose the advanced token as their preferred device, while 30% chose the base token (b, right). No user chose smart cards.

## (a) Mean score values of the users' evaluation of mobility and usability

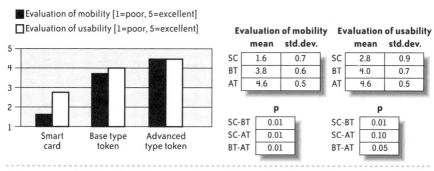

■ Evaluation of mobility [1=poor, 5=excellent]
□ Evaluation of usability [1=poor, 5=excellent]

| Evaluation of mobility | | | Evaluation of usability | | |
|---|---|---|---|---|---|
| | mean | std.dev. | | mean | std.dev. |
| SC | 1.6 | 0.7 | SC | 2.8 | 0.9 |
| BT | 3.8 | 0.6 | BT | 4.0 | 0.7 |
| AT | 4.6 | 0.5 | AT | 4.6 | 0.5 |

| | p | | | p |
|---|---|---|---|---|
| SC-BT | 0.01 | | SC-BT | 0.01 |
| SC-AT | 0.01 | | SC-AT | 0.10 |
| BT-AT | 0.01 | | BT-AT | 0.05 |

## (b) User purchase preference

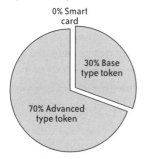

0% Smart card

30% Base type token

70% Advanced type token

*FIGURE 12-10. Results of the debriefing questionnaire*

Figure 12-11 provides a graphical summary of the usability attributes scores. While the procedure used to compute them is arbitrary (see the section "Computation of the Quality Attributes Scores" earlier in this chapter), they nonetheless give a global view of the usability evaluation.

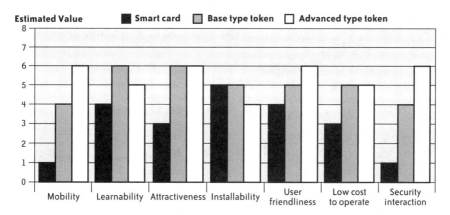

*FIGURE 12-11. Comparison of the usability attributes of the three form factors; attribute scores are between 1 (poor) and 7 (excellent)*

## Some Initial Conclusions

The smart card form factor is familiar to millions of people, and the USB token is not. The experimental results reported here, however, indicate that familiarity does not translate into good usability and security, at least when the smart card is used actively for security purposes on present-day computers. Indeed, current smart card deployment often seems to ignore a simple but hardly surprising usability issue: correct card insertion.

For example, the graphics printed on an Amex Blue or Target smart card do not provide users with a clear visual clue about which side and edge need to be inserted into the reader. Further, many smart card readers do not offer users clear visual feedback when the smart card is positioned properly. The introduction of visual clues printed on the smart card, as well as good visual feedback from card readers, would likely limit the usability problems related to proper smart card insertion.

USB tokens' better usability is rooted in their relatively small number of components, as well as the usability of the USB connector (there is only one way to plug in a USB device). In addition, the advanced tokens' better results are linked to a side effect of a software usability issue in the email client: the token was already plugged in because of its use in installation. In other words, it bypassed the failure of the software to remind users to insert the device for signing emails.

Let's not forget, however, that the usability of these form factors is a systemic property, and is affected by the software using each device. Email client software, for example, should check and give warnings to users regarding the usage of cryptographic devices; it should also check and give specific feedback that the device is plugged in and, therefore, that the certificate and the associated private key are available for email signature.

Reminding users to unplug a security device when they finish a session (e.g., at logoff or closure of the email software client) could also help users to remember to carry along their cryptographic credentials. Smart card login and automatic logoff might reinforce the metaphor of the cryptographic device as a door key, thus helping to limit this usability issue. Further addressing this issue might also increase security, as security can be in danger if users forget their cryptographic devices.

# Recommendations and Open Research Questions

What lessons have we learned about the usability of cryptographic smart cards? How many of these lessons can be generalized? We believe the following recommendations hold for any security device:

*The system as a whole matters*

Good behaviors, as well as dangerous ones, arise from the interaction of social, human, and technical components. Every evaluation or design activity must take into account the system as a whole.

*Devices that require a reader affect mobility*

Ease of mobility affects security. If the user must carry around a reader, we must ensure that the reader, host, and security device all connect without potential for gross error. Further, we must devise countermeasures to limit these potential errors.

*Add value to the security device[29]*

If the devices have multiple values to users, users will care about them more—for example, they won't forget them. Mass storage or RFID technology for building access are examples of how to increase value.

*Simple is secure*

Users prefer simple devices to those that are more complex or those that have more parts. Users will also make fewer security errors with them.

*Tune and adapt the software*

Doing so helps to avoid or limit usability and security issues.

*Conduct experimental usability studies, even small ones*

Such studies might catch use-time simple issues that could cause global usability and security problems.

This chapter has reported our efforts in attempting to cover the lack of studies on the usability of security devices. The following is a short list of actions that we believe deserve further research efforts:

- Evaluate the effects on usability and security of the interaction between software applications and security devices. Doing so may lead to identifying integrated criteria for system design.

- Provide general abstractions, guidelines, checklists, etc., to educate software developers in implementing software that minimizes usability issues with security devices.

- Provide quantitative usability evaluations for a wider spectrum of security devices.

- Investigate which complementary technologies enhance usability while maintaining comparable or increased levels of security. For example, are USB tokens with fingerprint sensors both more usable and at least as secure as normal USB tokens? Can we keep integrating additional technologies without impairing usability?

## Conclusion

In the description and analysis of our usability study, we have provided an approach for evaluating the usability of security devices. This approach both introduces general usability attributes and calls for their experimental evaluation. We have applied our systemic approach to measure the usability of alternative form factors of a subclass of security devices, cryptographic smart cards. The study results clearly show that different form factors do have different levels of usability. In the (plausible) scenario where mobility is

29 Ferguson and Schneier.

demanded and no smart card reader infrastructure is in place, smart cards scored lower on many usability attributes—costs, mobility, etc.—and security, as compared to the USB tokens evaluated.

## Acknowledgments

We would like to thank Lorrie Cranor, Chris Long, and Karen Renaud for the many constructive comments and suggestions provided on a draft of this chapter.

## About the Authors

Ugo Piazzalunga is technical director at Eutron Infosecurity Srl. He joined Eutron in November 2000 after four years at IBM Global Services and three years in research labs in European and U.S. universities. His current research interests include software security and the design of secure, usable USB devices.

*ugo.piazzalunga@eutron.it*

Paolo Salvaneschi is associate professor of software engineering at the University of Bergamo, Faculty of Engineering. He joined the University after spending 20 years as a software architect and head of software development groups in industry and research labs. His interests include quality evaluation of software products, software design methods, and AI-based data interpretation.

*pasalvan@tin.it*

Paolo Coffetti is a graduate student in computer science at the University of Bergamo, Faculty of Engineering. His thesis studied the usability of smart cards and USB tokens.

*coffetti@katamail.com*

PART THREE **SECURE SYSTEMS**

# CHAPTER THIRTEEN

# Guidelines and Strategies for Secure Interaction Design

**KA-PING YEE**

**A**LTHOUGH A RELIABLE, USABLE AUTHENTICATION METHOD IS ESSENTIAL, it is far from the only human interface concern. After a user signs in to a system, the system has to carry out the user's wishes correctly in order to be considered secure. The question of secure interaction design, addressed in this and the other chapters in this part of the book, is:

> How can we design a computer system to protect the interests of its legitimate user?

To give you a sense of how important it is to look beyond authentication, consider some of today's most serious security problems. Viruses are a leading contender, with email viruses making up a large part. Spyware is growing into a nightmare for home users and IT staff. Identity theft is becoming widespread, perpetrated in part through "phishing" scams in which forged email messages entice people to give away private information. None of these problems is caused by defeating a login mechanism. They would be better described as failures of computers to behave as their users expect.

This chapter suggests some guidelines for designing and evaluating usable secure software and proposes two strategies for getting security and usability to work in harmony: *security by designation* and *user-assigned identifiers*. I'll begin by providing a little background for our discussion, then present the guidelines and strategies, and finally look at real design problems to show how these strategies can be applied in practice.

# Introduction

This section introduces the topic of secure interaction design, touching briefly on mental models, the apparent conflict between security and usability, and the overall issues underlying interaction design.

## Mental Models

For software to protect its user's interests, its behavior should be consistent with the user's expectations. Therefore, designing for security requires an understanding of the *mental model*—the user's idea of how the system works. Attempting to make security decisions completely independent of the user is ultimately futile: if security really were independent, the user would lack the means to predict and understand the consequences of her actions. On the other hand, users should not be expected to speak the language of security experts or think in terms of the security mechanisms to get their work done safely. Thus, usable secure systems should enforce security decisions based on the user's actions while allowing those actions to be expressed in familiar ways.

A common error in security thinking is to classify an entity as "trusted" or "untrusted" without carefully defining *who* is doing the trusting and exactly *what* they trust the entity to do. To ignore these questions is to ignore the mental model. For example, suppose that a user downloads a file-deletion program. The program has been carefully tested to ensure that it reliably erases files, leaving no trace. Is the program secure or not? If the program is advertised as a game and it deletes the user's files, that would be a security violation. However, if the user intends to erase files containing sensitive information, the program's *failure* to delete them would be a security violation. The only difference is in the expectations. A digital signature asserting who created the program[1] provides no help. The correctness of a program provides no assurance that it is secure, and the presence of a digital signature provides no assurance that it is either correct *or* secure.

## Sources of Conflict

At the heart of the apparent conflict between security and usability is the idea that security makes operations harder, yet usability makes operations easier. Although this is usually true, it's imprecise. Security isn't about making *all* operations difficult; it's about restricting access to operations with undesirable effects. Usability isn't about making *all* operations easy, either; it's about improving access to operations with desirable effects. Tension between the two arises to the extent that a system is unable to determine whether a particular result is desirable. Security and usability come into harmony when a system correctly interprets the user's desires.

---

[1]   Today's code-signing schemes are designed to provide reliable verification that a program came from a particular source. They don't warrant what programs are supposed to do. They usually don't even specify the author of a program, merely the entity whose key was used to sign it.

Presenting security to users as a secondary task also promotes conflict. Some designs assume that users can be assigned extra homework: users are expected to install patches, run virus scanners, set up firewalls, and/or check certificates in order to keep their computers secure. But most people don't buy computers and take them home so that they can curl up for a nice evening of firewall configuration. They have better things to do with their computers, like keeping in touch with their friends, writing documents, playing music, or organizing their lives. Users are unlikely to perform extra security tasks and may even circumvent security measures to make their main task more comfortable.

As Diana Smetters and Rebecca Grinter have suggested,[2] security goals should be closely integrated with the workflow of the main task to yield *implicit security*. Extracting information about security expectations from the user's normal interactions with the interface enables us to minimize or eliminate the need for secondary security tasks.

## Iterative Design

Security and usability are qualities that apply to a whole system, not features that can be tacked on to a finished product. It's regrettably common to hear people speak of "adding security features," even though they would find the idea of adding a "correctness feature" absurd. Trying to add security after the fact is rarely effective and often harms usability as well. Likewise, although usability is also often described in terms of particular features (such as icons, animations, themes, or widgets), *interaction design* is much deeper than visual appearance. The effectiveness of a design is affected by whether work flows smoothly, whether the symbols and concepts make sense to the user, and whether the design fits the user's mental model of actions and their consequences.

Instead of adding security or usability as an afterthought, it's better to design software in iterations consisting of three basic phases: analysis of needs, then design, then testing. After a round of testing, it's time to analyze the results to find out what needs to be improved, then apply these discoveries to the next round of design, and so on. With each cycle, prototypes become more elaborate and polished as they approach product quality. This advice is nothing new; software engineers and usability engineers have advocated iterative design for many years. However, iterative design is particularly essential for secure software, because security and usability design choices affect each other in ways that are difficult to predict and are best understood through real tests.

Every piece of software ultimately has a human user, even if that user is sometimes a system administrator or a programmer. Therefore, attention to usability concerns is always necessary to achieve true security. The next time someone tells you that a product is secure, you might want to ask, "How much user testing was done?"

---

2   Diana Smetters and Rebecca Grinter, "Moving from the Design of Usable Secure Technologies to the Design of Useful Secure Applications," *Proceedings of the 2002 Workshop on New Security Paradigms* (New York: ACM Press, 2002).

## Permission and Authority

Much of the following discussion concerns the management of authorities. By an *authority*, I mean the power to make something happen, in contrast to *permission*, which refers to access as represented by settings in a security mechanism.[3]

For example, suppose that Alice's computer records and enforces the rule that only Alice can read the files in her home directory. Alice then installs a program that serves up her files on the Web. If she gives Bob the URL to her web server, she is granting Bob the authority to read her files even though Bob has no such permission in Alice's system. From the system's perspective, restricted permissions are still being enforced, because Alice's files are accessible only to Alice's programs. It's important to keep in mind the difference between permission and authority because so many real-world security issues involve the transfer of authority independent of permissions.

# Design Guidelines

Having established this background, we are now ready to look at the main challenge of secure interaction design: minimizing the likelihood of undesired events while accomplishing the user's intended tasks correctly and as easily as possible. Let's dissect that general aim into more specific guidelines for software behavior.

Minimizing the risk of undesired events is a matter of controlling *authorization*. Limiting the authority of other parties to access valuable resources protects those resources from harm. The authorization aspect of the problem can be broken down into five guidelines:

1. Match the most comfortable way to do tasks with the least granting of authority.

2. Grant authority to others in accordance with user actions indicating consent.

3. Offer the user ways to reduce others' authority to access the user's resources.

4. Maintain accurate awareness of others' authority as relevant to user decisions.

5. Maintain accurate awareness of the user's own authority to access resources.

Accomplishing the user's intended tasks correctly depends on good *communication* between the user and the system. The user should be able to convey his or her desires to the system accurately and naturally. I'll discuss the following additional guidelines concerning the communication aspect of the problem:

6. Protect the user's channels to agents that manipulate authority on the user's behalf.

7. Enable the user to express safe security policies in terms that fit the user's task.

8. Draw distinctions among objects and actions along boundaries relevant to the task.

---

3   These definitions of permission and authority are due to Mark S. Miller and Jonathan Shapiro. See Mark S. Miller and Jonathan S. Shapiro, "Paradigm Regained: Abstraction Mechanisms for Access Control," in Vijay A. Saraswat (ed.), *Proceedings of the 8th Asian Computing Science Conference, Lecture Notes in Computer Science* 2896, (Heidelberg: Springer-Verlag, 2003); *http://erights.org/talks/asian03/*.

**9.** Present objects and actions using distinguishable, truthful appearances.

**10.** Indicate clearly the consequences of decisions that the user is expected to make.

These guidelines are built on straightforward logic and are gleaned from the experiences of security software designers. They are not experimentally proven, although the reasoning and examples given here should convince you that violating these guidelines is likely to lead to trouble. I'll present each guideline along with some questions to consider when trying to evaluate and improve designs. Strategies to help designs follow some of these guidelines are provided in the second half of this chapter.

## Authorization

### 1. Match the most comfortable way to do tasks with the least granting of authority.

*What are the typical user tasks?*

*What is the user's path of least resistance for each one?*

*What authorities are given to software components and other users when the user follows this path?*

*How can the safest ways of accomplishing a task be made more comfortable, or the most comfortable ways made safer?*

In 1975, Jerome Saltzer and Michael Schroeder wrote a landmark paper on computer security[4] proposing eight design principles; their *principle of least privilege* demands that we grant processes the minimum privilege necessary to perform their tasks. This guideline combines that principle with an acknowledgment of the reality of human preferences: when people are trying to get work done, they tend to choose methods that require less effort, are more familiar, or appear more obvious. Instead of fighting this impulse, use it to promote security. Associate greater risk with greater effort, less conventional operations, or less visible operations so that the user's natural tendency leads to safe operation.

A natural consequence of this guideline is to default to a lack of access and to require actions to grant additional access, instead of granting access and requiring actions to shut it off. (Saltzer and Schroeder called this *fail-safe defaults*.) Although computer users are often advised to change network parameters or turn off unnecessary services, the easiest and most obvious course of action is not to reconfigure anything. Wendy Mackay has identified many barriers to user customization: customization takes time, it can be hard to figure out, and users don't want to risk breaking their software.[5]

Consider Microsoft Internet Explorer's handling of remote software installation in the context of this guideline. Just before Internet Explorer runs downloaded software, it looks

---

4   Jerome Salzter and Michael Schroeder, "The Protection of Information in Computer Systems," *Proceedings of the 4th Symposium on Operating System Principles* (ACM Press, 1973); *http://web.mit.edu/ Saltzer/www/publications/protection/*.

5   Wendy Mackay, "Users and Customizable Software: A Co-Adaptive Phenomenon," (Ph.D. Thesis, Massachusetts Institute of Technology, 1990); *http://www-ihm.lri.fr/~mackay/pdffiles/MIT.thesis.A4.pdf*.

for a publisher's digital signature on the software and displays a confirmation window like the one shown in Figure 13-1. In previous versions of this prompt, the default choice was "Yes". As this guideline would suggest, the default is now "No", the safer choice. However, the prompt offers an option to "Always trust content" from the current source, but no option to *never* trust content from this source. Users who choose the safer path are assured a continuing series of bothersome prompts.

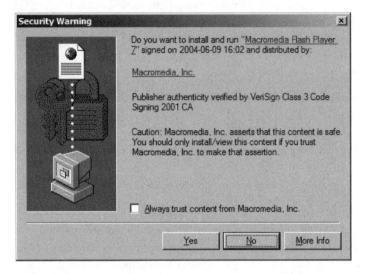

*FIGURE 13-1. Internet Explorer 6.0 displays a software certificate*

Regardless of the default settings, the choice being offered is poor: the user must either give the downloaded program complete access to all the user's resources, or not use the program at all. The prompt asks the user to be sure he or she trusts the distributor before proceeding. But if the user's task requires using the program, the most comfortable path is to click "Yes" without thinking. It will always be easier to just choose "Yes" than to choose "Yes" after researching the program and its origins. Designs that rely on users to assess the soundness of software are unrealistic. The principle of least privilege suggests that a mechanism for running programs with less authority would be better.

**2. Grant authority to others in accordance with user actions indicating consent.**

*When does the system authorize software components or other users to access the user's resources? What user actions trigger these transfers of authority?*

*Does the user consider these actions to indicate consent to such access?*

The user's mental model of the system includes a set of expectations about *who* can do *what*. To prevent unpleasant surprises, we should ensure that other parties don't gain access that exceeds the user's expectations. When a program or another user is granted access to the user's resources, that granting should be related to some user action. If another party gains access without user action, the user lacks any opportunity to update his or her mental model to include knowledge of the other party's access.

The authorizing action doesn't have to be a security setting or a response to a prompt about security; ideally, it shouldn't feel like a security task at all. It should just be some action that the user associates with the granting of that power. For example, if we ask users whether they expect that double-clicking on a Microsoft Word document would give Word access to its contents, and the vast majority say yes, the double-click alone is sufficient to authorize Word to access the document.

In other situations, a user action can be present but not understood to grant the power it grants. This is the case when a user double-clicks on an email attachment and gets attacked by a nasty virus. The double-click is expected to open the attachment for viewing, not to launch an unknown program with wide-ranging access to the computer.

### 3. Offer the user ways to reduce others' authority to access the user's resources.

*What types of access does the user grant to software components and other users?*
*Which of these types of access can be revoked?*
*How can the interface help the user to find and revoke such access?*

After granting authorities, the user needs to be able to take them back in order to retain control of the computer. Without the ability to revoke access, the user cannot simplify system behavior and cannot recover from mistakes in granting access.

Closing windows is an example of a simple act of revocation that users understand well. When users close a document window, they expect the application to make no further changes to the document. This reduces the number of variables they have to worry about and lets them get on with other tasks.

Lack of revocability is a big problem when users are trying to uninstall software. The process of installing an application or a device driver usually provides no indication of what resources are given to the new software, what global settings are modified, or how to restore the system to a stable state if the installation fails. Configuration changes can leave the system in a state where other software or hardware no longer works properly. Microsoft Windows doesn't manage software installation or removal; it leaves these tasks up to applications, which often provide incomplete removal tools or no removal tools at all. Spyware exploits this problem: most spyware is designed to be difficult to track down and remove. An operating system with good support for revocability would maintain accurate records of installed software, allow the user to select unwanted programs, and cleanly remove them.

### 4. Maintain accurate awareness of others' authority as relevant to user decisions.

*What kinds of authority can software components and other users hold?*
*Which kinds of authority impact user decisions with security consequences?*
*How can the interface provide timely access to information about such authorities?*

To use any software safely, the user must be able to evaluate whether particular actions are safe, which requires accurate knowledge of the possible consequences. The consequences are bounded by the access that has been granted to other parties. Because human memory is limited and fallible, expecting users to remember the complete history of authorizations is unrealistic. The user needs a way to refresh his or her mental model by reviewing which programs or other users have access to do which things.

Special attention must be paid to powers that continuously require universal trust, such as intercepting user input or manipulating the internal workings of running programs. For example, Microsoft Windows provides facilities enabling programs to record keystrokes and simulate mouse clicks in arbitrary windows. To grant such powers to another entity is to trust that entity completely with all of one's access to a system, so activation of these authorities should be accompanied by continuous notification.

Spyware exploits both a lack of consent to authorization and a lack of awareness of authority. Spyware is often included as part of other software that the user voluntarily downloads and wants to use. Even while the other software isn't being used, the spyware remains running in the background, invisibly compromising the user's privacy.

### 5. Maintain accurate awareness of the user's own authority to access resources.

*What kinds of authority can the user hold?*
*How is the user informed of currently held authority?*
*How does the user come to know about acquisition of new authority?*
*What decisions might the user make based on his or her expectations of authority?*

Users are also part of their own mental models. Their decisions can depend on their understanding of their own access. When users overestimate their authority, they may become vulnerable to unexpected risks or make commitments they cannot fulfill.

PayPal provides a good example of this problem in practice. When money is sent, PayPal sends the recipient an email message announcing "You've got cash!" Checking the account at the PayPal site will show the transaction marked "completed," as in Figure 13-2. If the sender of the money is buying an item from the recipient, the recipient would probably feel safe at this point delivering the item.

FIGURE 13-2. PayPal sends email notifying a recipient of "cash" and displays the details of a "completed" transaction

Unfortunately, PayPal's announcement generates false expectations. Telling the recipient that they've "got cash" suggests that the funds are concrete and under the recipient's control. Prior experience with banks may lead the recipient to expect that transactions clear after a certain period of time, just as checks deposited at most banks clear after a day or two. But although PayPal accounts look and act like bank accounts in many ways, PayPal's policy on payments[6] does not commit to any time limit by which payments become permanent; PayPal can still reverse the payment at any time. By giving the recipient a false impression of access, PayPal exposes the recipient to unnecessary risk.

## Communication

### 6. Protect the user's channels to agents that manipulate authority on the user's behalf.

*What agents manipulate authority on the user's behalf?*
*How can the user be sure that he or she is communicating with the intended agent?*
*How might the agent be impersonated?*
*How might the user's communication with the agent be intercepted or corrupted?*

When someone uses a computer to interact in a particular world, there is a piece of software that serves as the user's agent in the world. For example, a web browser is the agent for interacting with the World Wide Web; a desktop GUI or command-line shell is the agent for interacting with the computer's operating system. If communication with that agent can be spoofed or corrupted, the user is vulnerable to an attack. In standard terminology, the user needs a *trusted path* for communicating with the agent.

The classic way to exploit this issue is to present a fake password prompt. If a web browser doesn't enforce a distinction between its own password prompts and prompt windows that web pages can generate, a malicious web site could use an imitation prompt to capture the user's password.

Techniques for preventing impersonation include designating reserved hotkeys, reserving areas of the display, and demonstrating privileged abilities. Microsoft Windows reserves the Ctrl-Alt-Delete key combination for triggering operating system security functions: no application program can intercept this key combination, so when users press it to log in, they can be sure that the password dialog comes from the operating system. Many web browsers reserve an area of their status bar for displaying an icon to indicate a secure connection. Trusted Solaris reserves a "trusted stripe" at the bottom of the screen for indicating when the user is interacting with the operating system.

Eileen Ye and Sean Smith have proposed adding flashing colored borders[7] to distinguish window areas controlled by the browser from those controlled by the remote site. The

---

6   PayPal, "Payments (Sending, Receiving, and Withdrawing) Policy" (Nov. 21, 2004); *http://www. paypal.com/cgi-bin/webscr?cmd=p/gen/ua/policy_payments-outside*.

7   Zishuang (Eileen) Ye and Sean Smith, "Trusted Paths for Browsers," *Proceedings of the 11th USENIX Security Symposium* (USENIX, 2002); *http://www.usenix.org/events/sec02/ye.html*.

borders constantly flash in a synchronized but unpredictable pattern, which makes them hard to imitate, but would probably annoy users. For password prompts, the Safari web browser offers a more elegant solution: the prompt drops out of the titlebar of the browser window and remains attached (see Figure 13-3) in ways that would be difficult for a web page script to imitate. Attaching the prompt to the window also prevents password prompts for different windows from being confused with each other.

FIGURE 13-3. *Password prompts in Safari fall out of the titlebar like a flexible sheet of paper and remain attached to the associated window*

### 7. Enable the user to express safe security policies in terms that fit the user's task.

*What are some examples of security policies that users might want enforced for typical tasks?*
*How can the user express these policies?*
*How can the expression of policy be brought closer to the task, ideally disappearing into the task itself?*

If security policies are expressed using unfamiliar language or concepts unrelated to the task at hand, users will find it difficult to set a policy that corresponds to their intentions. When the security model doesn't fit, users may expose themselves to unnecessary risk just to get their tasks done.

For instance, one fairly common task is to share a file with a group of collaborators. Unix file permissions don't fit this task well. In a standard Unix filesystem, each file is assigned to one owner and one group. The owner can choose any currently defined group, but cannot define new groups. Granting access to a set of other users is possible only if a group is already defined to contain those users. This limitation encourages users to make their files globally accessible, because that's easier than asking the system administrator to define a new group.

## 8. Draw distinctions among objects and actions along boundaries relevant to the task.

*At what level of detail does the interface allow objects and actions to be separately manipulated?*

*During a typical task, what distinctions between affected objects and unaffected objects does the user care about?*

*What distinctions between desired actions and undesired actions does the user care about?*

Computer software systems consist of a very large number of interacting parts. To help people handle this complexity, user interfaces aggregate objects into manageable chunks: for example, bytes are organized into files, and files into folders. User interfaces also aggregate actions: downloading a web page requires many steps in the implementation, but for the user it's a single click. Interface design requires decisions about which distinctions to expose and hide. Exposing pointless distinctions generates work and confusion for the user; hiding meaningful distinctions forces users to take unnecessary risks.

On a Mac, for example, an application is shown as a single icon even though, at the system level, that icon represents a set of folders containing all the application's files. The user can install or remove the application by manipulating just that one icon. The user doesn't have to deal with the individual files, or risk separating the files by mistake. This design decision simplifies the user's experience by hiding distinctions that don't matter at the user level.

On the other hand, the security controls for web page scripts in Mozilla neglect to make important distinctions. Mozilla provides a way for signed scripts to gain special privileges,[8] but the only option for file access is a setting that grants access to all files. When the user is asked whether to grant that permission, there is no way to control which files the script is allowed to access. The lack of a boundary here forces the user to gamble the entire disk just to access one file.

## 9. Present objects and actions using distinguishable, truthful appearances.

*How does the user identify and distinguish different objects and different actions?*

*In what ways can the means of identification be controlled by other parties?*

*What aspects of an object's appearance are under system control?*

*How can those aspects be chosen to best prevent deception?*

In order to use a computer safely, the user needs to be able to identify the intended objects and actions when issuing commands to the computer. If two objects look indistinguishably similar, the user risks choosing the wrong one. If an object comes to have a misleading name or appearance, the user risks placing trust in the wrong object. The same is true for actions that have some representation in the user interface.

Identification problems can be caused by names or appearances that are hard to distinguish even if they aren't exactly the same. For example, in some typefaces, the lowercase

---

8 Jesse Ruderman, "Signed Scripts in Mozilla"; *http://www.mozilla.org/projects/security/components/ signed-scripts.html.*

"L" looks the same as the digit "1" or the uppercase "I", making some names virtually indistinguishable; later in this chapter, we'll look at a phishing attack that exploits just this ambiguity. Unicode adds another layer of complexity to the problem, because different character sequences can be displayed identically: an unaccented character followed by a combining accent appears exactly the same as a single accented character.

No interface can prevent other parties from lying. However, unlike objects in the real world, objects in computer user interfaces do not have primary control over their own appearances. The software designer has the freedom to choose any appearance for objects in the user interface. Objects can "lie" in their appearances only to the extent that the user interface relies upon them to present themselves. The designer must choose carefully what parts of the name or appearance are controlled by the system or controlled by the object, and uphold expectations about consistent parts of the appearance.

For instance, Microsoft Windows promotes the convention that each file's type is indicated by its extension (the part of the filename after the last period) and that an icon associated with the file type visually represents each file. The file type determines how the file will be opened when the icon is double-clicked. Unfortunately, the Windows Explorer defaults to a mode in which file extensions are hidden; in addition, executable programs (the most dangerous file type of all) are allowed to choose any icon to represent themselves. Thus, if a program has the filename *document.txt.exe* and uses the icon for a text file, the user sees a text file icon labeled *document.txt*. Many viruses have exploited this design flaw to disguise themselves as harmless files. By setting up expectations surrounding file types and also providing mechanisms to violate these expectations, Windows grants viruses the power to lie.

### 10. Indicate clearly the consequences of decisions that the user is expected to make.

*What user decisions have security implications?*
*When such decisions are being made, how are the choices and their consequences presented?*
*Does the user understand the consequences of each choice?*

When the user manipulates authorities, we should make sure that the results reflect what the user intended. Even if the software can correctly enforce a security policy, the policy being enforced might not be what was intended if the interface presents misleading, ambiguous, or incomplete information. The information needed to make a good decision should be available before the action is taken.

Figure 13-4 shows an example of a poorly presented decision. Prompts like this one are displayed by the Netscape browser when a web page script requests special privileges. (Scripts on web pages normally run with restricted access for safety reasons, although Netscape has a feature allowing them to obtain additional access with user consent.) The prompt asks the user to grant a privilege, but it doesn't describe the privilege to be granted, the length of time it will remain in effect, or how it can be revoked. The term "UniversalXPConnect" is almost certainly unrelated to the user's task. The checkbox labeled "Remember this decision" is also vague, because it doesn't indicate how the decision would be generalized—does it apply in the future to all scripts, all scripts from the same source, or repeated uses of the same script?

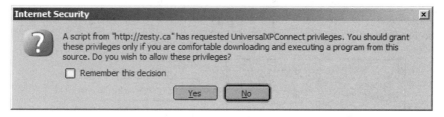

*FIGURE 13-4. A script requests enhanced privileges in Netscape 7.2*

An interface can also be misleading or ambiguous in nonverbal ways. Many graphical interfaces use common widgets and metaphors, conditioning users to expect certain unspoken conventions. For example, a list of round radio buttons indicates that only one of the options can be selected, whereas a list of square checkboxes suggests that any number of options can be selected. Visual interfaces also rely heavily on association between elements, such as the placement of a label next to a checkbox or the grouping of items in a list. Breaking these conventions causes confusion.

## Design Strategies

Two strategies—security by designation and user-assigned identifiers—can be used to implement some of the aforementioned guidelines in a broad range of situations. After describing them, I'll propose ways to solve some everyday security problems using these strategies.

### Security by Admonition and Security by Designation

Users often want to make use of things they do not completely trust. For example, it's reasonable for people to want to run programs or visit web pages without having to understand and audit their source code. Instead of trusting the unknown entity, users trust an agent (such as a secure operating system or a secure web browser) to protect their interests by placing constraints on the unknown entity. The agent's challenge is to determine the correct constraints.

Consider two contrasting styles of establishing these security constraints that I'll call *security by admonition* and *security by designation*. Security by admonition consists of providing notifications to which the user attends in order to maintain security. With security by designation, the user simultaneously designates an action and conveys the authority to perform the action.

The case of an operating system constraining a potentially dangerous program provides an example to illustrate these concepts. I'll use Venn diagrams to depict the space of the program's possible actions. In each run of the program, its actions form a path through this space, represented by a sequence of black dots. Arrows represent user actions that trigger these program actions. The rectangle delimits the actions that the system allows; it is a simple shape to signify the rigidity of a typical policy specification. The shaded region is the set of actions acceptable to the user; its shape is irregular to signify that the user's desires are probably complex and imprecisely specified. Figure 13-5 displays these notational conventions.

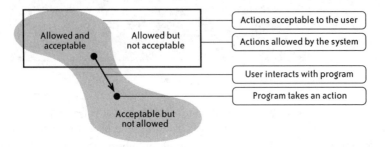

FIGURE 13-5. *This Venn diagram of the space of program actions shows the notational conventions to be used in the next two figures*

### Security by admonition

Figure 13-6 shows a system that enforces a static, preestablished security policy. Because the policy is only finitely detailed, it can only roughly approximate the user's desires. Because the policy is static, it must accommodate a wide range of situations other than this particular run of the program. Thus, the solid box in Figure 13-6 includes large areas outside the shaded region. On Mac OS, Unix, and Microsoft Windows systems, programs usually run with the user's full authority, creating a vast discrepancy between the sets of allowed and acceptable actions. For example, even though I may start a program intending to edit only one file, the system allows it to modify or delete any of my files, send email in my name, upload my files to the Internet, and so on.

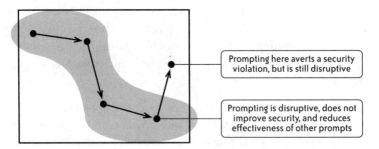

FIGURE 13-6. *With security by admonition, the system has to guess when to warn the user of potential dangers*

To prevent the program from taking undesirable actions, the admonition approach would be to show a warning so that the user has an opportunity to intervene before the undesirable action happens. Commercial products like ZoneAlarm (see Chapter 27) do just this, stepping in with a prompt when programs access the network. Unfortunately, the computer can't read the user's mind, so it has to guess when to warn and when to proceed. Warning too little places the user at risk; warning too much annoys the user. The larger the discrepancy between acceptable and allowed actions, the more severely we are forced to compromise between security and usability.

### Security by designation

Figure 13-7 acknowledges that user expectations change over time and that the security policy should change to match. In this approach, the program starts out with minimal authority (solid box). As before, the user can interact with the program's user interface (solid arrow) to have the program carry out actions using its initial authority. When the user wants to take an action requiring new authority, the user interacts with the system's user interface (dotted arrows) to express both the command and the extension of authority (dotted box) at the same time. Combining the authorization with the designation of intent in a single user action maintains a close, dynamic match between the allowed set and the acceptable set of actions. Users don't have to establish a detailed security policy beforehand and don't have to express their intentions twice.

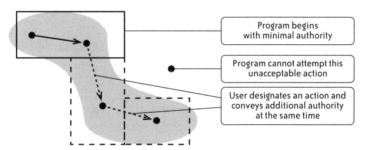

*FIGURE 13-7.* With security by designation, the user simultaneously designates an action and conveys the authority to take that action

### Advantages of designation

Software commonly employs a mix of these two approaches. Launching a program is a case of security by designation: users don't have to select a program and then separately grant memory to the newly created process; a single action accomplishes both. Sending an email attachment is another example of designation: users don't have to select a file to attach and then separately assign read permissions to the recipient of the message; dropping the attachment into the message designates the attachment, the recipient, and the intended authorization in a single act. When a web browser asks for confirmation before submitting a form, or when Microsoft Word asks whether to enable macros upon opening a document, these are cases of security by admonition.

When security by designation is possible, it is convenient and straightforward because it achieves the ideal of integrating security decisions with the user's primary task. On the other hand, security by admonition demands the user's attention to a secondary source of information. With designation, the authorization is part of a user-initiated action, so the user has the necessary context to know the reason for the authorization. With admonition, the request for authority is initiated outside the user, so the user may not have the context needed to decide whether to approve it.

### Implementing security by designation

To implement the designation strategy, we have to find an act of designation with which to associate the authorization. When we are tempted to ask the user whether a particular action is acceptable, we instead determine how the user originally specified that action. The action may have been conveyed through several software components, so we must follow it back to the originating user interaction. Then we move that user interaction into a software layer that the user trusts to handle the relevant authority and convey the authority together with the designation of the action. The example in the later "Securing file access" section will demonstrate how this is done.

### Implementing security by admonition

It may be necessary to fall back on admonition when security by designation isn't feasible—for example, if the original designating interaction is inaccessible or untrustworthy. It is usually better to inform users without interrupting their workflow. Forcing users to answer a prompt is a terrible way to present a notification: it teaches users that security issues obstruct their work and trains them to dismiss prompts carelessly instead of making meaningful decisions.

Seek designs that are noticeable by their proximity and relevance to the matter at hand, not by their aggressiveness. For example, the Firefox web browser notifies the user when an unknown site tries to install software by adding a transient bar to the browser window; the bar does not prevent the user from viewing the page as a prompt box would. Notifications concerning a particular operation can be displayed just for the duration of the operation. Later in this chapter, Figure 13-15 shows a note about passwords appearing next to a password field while the field is active; the note disappears when the user moves to another field. Displaying tips near the mouse cursor or changing the mouse cursor are also ways to provide clear yet noninterrupting feedback.

### User-Assigned Identifiers

Practically every user interaction depends on the correct designation of an object or action. The names by which a user refers to objects and actions come from many different sources: some are assigned by the user, some are assigned by other users, some are allocated by global or local organizations, and some are assigned by programs.

Giving objects the power to choose their own names places the user at a significant disadvantage. Unless another naming mechanism is provided, the user is forced to work with identifiers controlled by outside parties—potentially, to communicate with his or her most trusted software agents using terms defined by an adversary. Each name that enters the user's sphere is a potential avenue of attack if it can be made misleading or confusing.

A good way to avoid the danger of identification problems is to let users assign and use their own local identifiers for objects and actions. Computers are harder to confuse than humans; they can take care of the translation between users' familiar names and the names used by machines or other people.

You already use user-assigned identifiers all the time. For example, each file on your desktop has a name that you can assign. The true, unique identifier for each file is a number that tells the system how to locate the file on the disk. But you never have to deal with that number; you assign a filename, and the operating system takes care of translating between the name and the number. Imagine how difficult it would be to identify files if the desktop displayed only disk addresses instead of filenames, or how inconvenient it would be if files all chose names for themselves that you couldn't change.

Another means of user-controlled identification is the assignment of positions to icons. Preserving the positions of the icons on the desktop helps you find them later. Some systems also let you assign colors to icons. These mechanisms give you more control over how you identify objects, improving your ability to designate them accurately.

## Applying the Strategies to Everyday Security Problems

Let's look at a few examples to see how security by designation and user-assigned identifiers help us address security problems in practice.

### Email viruses

Self-propagating email attachments have caused widespread havoc in the last few years. Some exploit software bugs in the operating system or mail program, but bugs are not the whole story. Many email viruses, such as MyDoom, Netsky, and Sobig, rely on humans to activate them by opening executable attachments, and would continue to spread even with bug-free software.

On Microsoft Windows and Mac OS systems, double-clicking serves two very different purposes: opening documents and launching applications. Whereas documents are usually inert, starting an application grants it complete access to the user's account. Thus, a user can double-click an attachment, intending only to read it, and instead hand over control of the computer to an email virus.

The missing specification of intent here is the choice between *viewing* and *executing*. The user is not given a way to make this choice, so the computer guesses, with potentially dangerous consequences. A bad solution would be to patch over this guess with a prompt asking the user "Do you really want to run this application?" every time an application icon is double-clicked. To find a better solution, we need to consider how users specify the intent to run a new application.

What do users already do when they install applications? On a Mac, most applications are installed by dropping a single icon into the Applications folder. So, suppose that double-clicking files in the Applications folder launches them, and double-clicking files elsewhere only passively views them. Suppose also that the Applications folder can only contain files that the user has placed there. The resulting system would respect a distinction between viewing and executing established by the convention users already know. Programs would run only if installed by the user. The main propagation method of email attachment viruses would be eliminated with virtually no loss of usability, because Mac users normally run their applications from the Applications folder. As for Windows, dropping a single icon is simpler to do and understand than running a multistep application installer, so switching to a drag-and-drop style of installation would simultaneously improve *both* security and usability for Windows users.

### Other viruses and spyware

Although distinguishing viewing from execution would be better than what we have now, it provides a defense only when opening email attachments. Any program the user installs voluntarily, including downloaded programs that might contain viruses or spyware, would still run with the user's full access rights, exposing the user to tremendous risk.

The lack of fine-grained access controls on application programs is an architectural failure of Windows, Mac OS, and Unix systems. Such fine-grained control would enable a true solution to the virus and spyware problems. Let's consider how to control two major kinds of access exploited by viruses: file access and email access.

### Securing file access

How do users specify the intent to read or write a particular file? In current graphical user interfaces, files are mainly designated in two ways: by pointing at file icons and by selecting filenames in dialog boxes. With Mac OS and Windows, both of these functions are implemented in the operating system. However, selecting a file passes the file's name to an application, not the file itself. The application then asks the operating system to open the file by name, receiving an object called a *filehandle* that represents the file. Applications on Windows, Mac OS, and Unix systems assume the user's identity when accessing the disk, so they can ask the system to open any of the user's files.

Here's an analogy to illustrate the concept of filehandles. Suppose that I have a telephone and I'd like to call my mother to wish her a happy birthday, but unfortunately I am a terrible singer. On the other hand, you have no telephone, but you have a wonderful voice and kindly offer to sing "Happy Birthday." I have two options: I could let you use my telephone, give you my mother's phone number, and ask you to call her (Figure 13-8a). But that would let you dial any number and call anyone with my phone, just as an application can "dial up" any file by its name. Instead, I could call my mother on the phone and then hand you only the receiver (Figure 13-8b). That way, I'd be sure that you were speaking only to her, and I wouldn't have to reveal her phone number to you. I could even disconnect you if necessary. Handing you a telephone receiver that's connected to another party is like giving a filehandle to an application.

FIGURE 13-8. (a, left) Handing over the entire telephone conveys the authority to dial any number; (b, right) handing over only the receiver is more consistent with the principle of least authority

To perform security by designation, we would stop providing applications with all the user's authority to access the disk; applications would start with access only to their own program files and a limited scratch space. Instead of returning a filename, the file dialog would open the selected file and return a filehandle to it (Figure 13-9). Similarly, dropping a file on an application would send the application a filehandle rather than a filename. The user experience of opening files would be exactly the same, yet security would be improved significantly because programs would get access only to user-selected files. Viruses and spyware wouldn't be able to install themselves or modify files without the user's specific consent.

Some special programs, such as search tools and disk repair utilities, do require access to the entire disk. For these programs, the user could convey access to the entire disk by installing them in a "Disk Tools" subfolder of the Applications folder. This would require a bit more effort than dropping everything in the Applications folder, but it isn't an alien concept: on Windows systems, for example, disk utilities are already kept in an "Administrative Tools" subfolder of the Start Menu.

### Securing email access

How do users specify the intent to send email to a particular person? They usually choose recipients by selecting names from an address book or by typing in email addresses. To control access to email capabilities, we might add a *mailhandle* abstraction to the operating system, which represents the ability to send mail to a particular address just as a filehandle

**A) Excess authority**

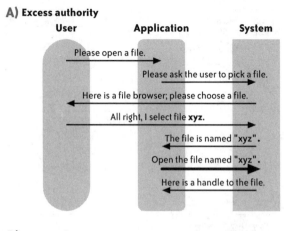

**B) Least authority**

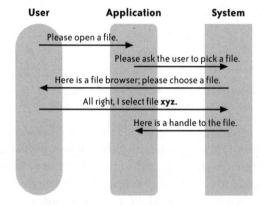

*FIGURE 13-9. (a, top) In today's Mac OS and Microsoft Windows systems, file dialogs return a filename; applications use their unlimited user file access (bold arrow) to open the selected file; (b, bottom) returning a filehandle is simpler and more secure while requiring no visible changes to the user interface; applications' access to user files is restricted to only files that the user designates, thereby protecting the user from malicious programs such as viruses and spyware*

represents the ability to read or write a particular file. Then, selecting names from a standard system-wide address book would return mailhandles to the application, just as a secure file selection dialog would return filehandles. Using mailhandles would allow us to stop providing general network access to all programs, rendering viruses unable to email themselves to new victims.

### Cookie management

Cookies are small data records that web sites ask browsers to retain and present in order to identify users when they return to the same site. They enable web sites to perform automatic login and personalization. However, they also raise privacy concerns about the tracking of user behavior and raise security risks by providing an avenue for circumventing logins. Users need some control over when and where cookies are sent.

Many browsers address this issue by prompting users to accept or reject each received cookie. But cookies are so ubiquitous that this causes users to be constantly pestered with irritating prompt boxes. To reduce workload, some browsers provide an option to accept or reject all cookies from the current site, as in Figure 13-10. After one has chosen a site-wide policy, it can be tricky to find and reverse the decision. Yet the decision to *accept* cookies is immaterial, as the real security risks lie in *sending* cookies. Moreover, the term "cookie" refers to an implementation mechanism and has no relevance to user tasks; if cookies appear at all in the interface, their appearance should relate to the function they serve.

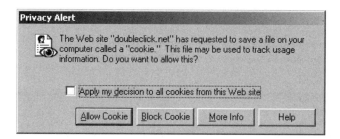

*FIGURE 13-10. Internet Explorer 6.0 prompts the user to accept a cookie*

The missing specification of intent here is whether the user, upon returning to a web site, wants to continue with the same settings and context from the last session. To find a better solution, consider how users specify that they want to return to web sites they've seen before.

The existing user interface mechanism for this purpose is the bookmark list: users designate the site they want by selecting a bookmark. Therefore, suppose that each bookmark has its own associated "cookie jar." One jar at a time would be the active cookie jar, from which cookies are sent and where received cookies are stored. When the user creates a bookmark, the cookies for the current session are placed in the new bookmark's cookie jar,[9] and it becomes the active cookie jar. When the user selects a bookmark, its cookie jar becomes active. This is a change from today's typical browsers, but the usage is easily explained: "Bookmark a site if you want to continue later where you left off."

Bookmarks containing cookies would be displayed with a mark to show that they are personalized. In the example in Figure 13-11, personalized bookmarks are marked with a small heart symbol. A bookmark icon in the location bar would indicate whether there are bookmarks for the current site, and it would also be marked to show whether the current view is personalized. Clicking on the icon would show a menu of bookmarks for the site as in Figure 13-12, enabling users to switch to a personalized session if they want.

9  Some cookies are temporary, marked to expire automatically at the end of a session. Others are persistent, marked to be saved for future sessions. In the design proposed here, only persistent cookies issued by the bookmarked site would be stored in the cookie jar with a bookmark. Cookies issued by third parties would be ignored.

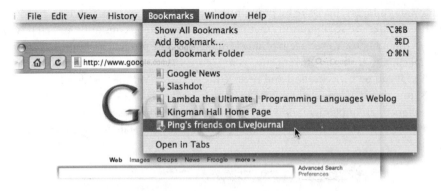

*FIGURE 13-11.* In the proposed design, bookmarks that the user has created for personalized sessions are marked with a small heart in the bookmark list; selecting such a bookmark restores the session

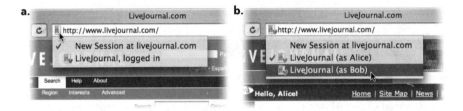

*FIGURE 13-12.* (a, left) A bookmark icon next to the URL indicates that the user has bookmarks for the current site; the user can select a bookmark to switch to a personalized session; (b, right) an advanced user has created and named bookmarks for two different logins; the bookmark icon next to the URL is marked with a small heart to show that the current session is personalized, and the drop-down menu allows the user to switch to a different personalized session

This solution would eliminate the need for prompts or lists of cookie-enabled and cookie-disabled sites to manage. In fact, there would be no need to mention "cookies" in the user interface at all; one would simply describe some sessions as personalized. Login cookies would no longer be left lingering on public-access machines. Users' privacy would be better protected. Sites would no longer mysteriously change their appearance depending on hidden state. And users would gain additional functionality: advanced users could manage multiple logins or multiple suspended transactions simply by creating bookmarks. Security and usability would both be simultaneously improved.

Notice that security by designation has helped us to arrive at a design that follows several of the guidelines identified earlier: by requiring a user action to save cookies instead of a user action to reject cookies, we match the safer option with the path of least effort. By activating cookies based on the selection of a bookmark, we associate the sending of cookies with an authorizing act. By identifying which session is active, we help the user maintain awareness of the authority the user wields. And instead of having to express policy decisions in the unfamiliar language of cookies, the user expresses these decisions by creating and using bookmarks, which serve a useful and familiar task.

## Phishing attacks

Forged email messages and web sites designed to steal passwords are a common method of stealing private information. SMTP, the dominant Internet mail protocol, places no restrictions on the "From:" field of an email message, so messages can be easily forged to appear to come from anyone. In a typical so-called *phishing attack*, a user receives an email message that appears to be from a bank, asking the user to click on a link and verify account information. The link appears to point to the bank's web site, but actually takes the user to an identity thief's web site, made to look just like the bank's official site. If an unsuspecting user enters personal information there, the identity thief captures it.

Here, the missing specification of intent is the intended recipient of the form submission. In one scam, for example, an imitation of PayPal was hosted at *paypai.com*. This problem is tricky because the system has no way of knowing whether the user intended to go to *paypal.com* and was misdirected to *paypai.com*, or whether the user really wanted to go to *paypai.com*. The intention resides only in the user's mind.

The designation at the heart of this security problem is the link address. Yet the specification of that address does not come from the user; the user merely clicks in the email message. Our problem would be solved if we could secure the email channel and determine the source of the message. But until we can convince most users to switch to secure email, there is no trustworthy designation on which to hang a security decision.

In this case, practical constraints make security by designation infeasible. The user is required to identify a web site by observation rather than by designation. The site has total control over its appearance; even the URL is mostly chosen by the site itself.

To protect the user, we have to provide some helpful information. Traditional admonition-style thinking would suggest warning the user when submitting forms to a suspicious-looking site. Such a prompt might look something like Figure 13-13.

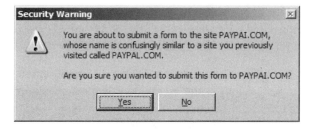

*FIGURE 13-13. Prompting is a traditional method of phishing protection*

Indeed, this is exactly the approach taken by many antiphishing tools. Perhaps the most sophisticated is a commercial program called Web Caller-ID, which employs "hundreds of routines that examine the elements of a web site" to decide whether a site is fraudulent.[10]

10 WholeSecurity, "Web Caller-ID Core Technology"; *http://wholesecurity.com/products/wcid_core_technology.html*.

This type of solution is unreliable because it makes guesses based on assumptions about good and bad sites. The creators of Web Caller-ID claim that their routines can detect 98% of spoof sites—an impressive figure. But because there are more than 1,400 different phishing attacks per month (and this number is rising),[11] and each one could target thousands of users, the missed 2% can still do considerable damage. Moreover, any scheme based on heuristics generates spurious warnings. A false-positive rate of even 1% could be enough to train users to ignore warning messages.

A better solution is to give the user control over the name used to identify the site. The petname toolbar[12] provides a text field, as shown in Figure 13-14, where the user can enter a *petname* for the current site (a nickname for the site specific to just this user). The user would assign a name to a site when registering for an account at the site.

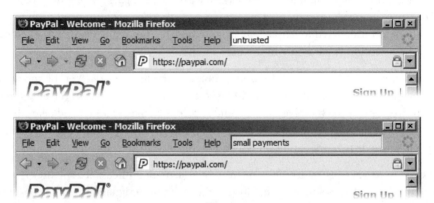

FIGURE 13-14. *The petname toolbar, shown in untrusted (top) and trusted (bottom) states, supports user-assigned site names*

The user-assigned name appears in the text field whenever the user returns to the same site. If the user hasn't assigned a name, the field shows that the site is unknown. As long as the user is aware of the petname, it doesn't matter what domain name a scammer uses. The act of assigning the name is initiated by the user, at the time the user chooses to enter a trust relationship with the site, in a context that the user understands.

This way of browsing would be completely safe against misidentification, without any heuristics or false positives, as long as the user notices the petname in the toolbar. Checking the toolbar is a change from current practice, so an admonition that brings the petname closer to the user's natural workflow might be needed to help users migrate. Figure 13-15 shows a message that might appear as the user enters a password on a site he or she hasn't named. The admonition is a temporary message, not a prompt window, so it informs the user without interrupting. Interrupting the user with a prompt would defeat

11 Anti-Phishing Working Group, "Phishing Attack Trends Report, June 2004"; *http://antiphishing.org/APWG_Phishing_Attack_Report-Jun2004.pdf.*

12 Waterken Inc., "Petname Toolbar"; *http://www.waterken.com/user/PetnameTool/.*

our purpose: it would encourage users to assign petnames to sites in response to the prompt, instead of assigning names on their own initiative.

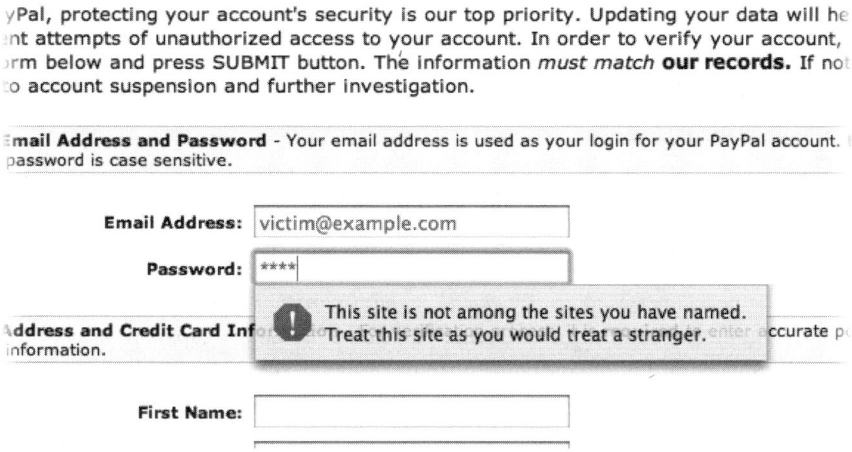

*FIGURE 13-15. An admonition appears while the user is entering a password into a scam site*

This petname scheme contrasts with today's centralized public key infrastructure (PKI) of digital certificates issued by certification authorities. PKI was intended to prevent just the type of misidentification that is exploited in phishing attacks, yet phishing is rampant. Some might say the problem is that users don't check certificates. But users rightly feel no compulsion to rely on a naming system with which they have no involvement and no trust relationship. (I'll bet you don't know who issued the certificate for the last secure web site you visited.) Carl Ellison has identified many problems with centralized PKI.[13, 14] Chapter 16 describes how key management can be made vastly simpler and more useful by using local namespaces instead of centralized authorities. Enabling users to assign personally meaningful names frees users from external sources of confusion, political battles, or dependence on unfamiliar third parties. See the Pet Name Markup Language[15] for further elaboration of the petname concept.

13  Carl Ellison and Bruce Schneier, "Ten Risks of PKI: What You're Not Being Told About Public Key Infrastructure," *Computer Security Journal* 16 (Winter 2000); *http://www.schneier.com/paper-pki.pdf*.

14  Carl Ellison, "Improvements on Conventional PKI Wisdom," *Proceedings of the 1st Annual PKI Research Workshop* (NIST, 2002); *http://www.cs.dartmouth.edu/~pki02/Ellison/*.

15  Mark Miller, "Lambda for Humans: The Pet Name Markup Language"; *http://erights.org/elib/capability/pnml.html*.

**Real implementations**

CapDesk[16] and Polaris[17] are two research projects that apply the design ideas and strategies described in this chapter:

- *CapDesk.* A desktop shell that lets users safely run downloaded software in a familiar graphical environment. The CapDesk system and applications are written in the secure programming language, E.[18]

- *Polaris.* A safe environment for running existing Microsoft Windows applications. With Polaris, one can use programs normally, enable macros, and open email attachments without experiencing ill effects from viruses or spyware.

Both of these projects are based on the *object-capability paradigm*,[19] in which combining designation with authority is a central design principle. The object-capability model has a long history of development in computer systems research, particularly secure operating systems[20, 21] and secure programming languages.[22] It is no coincidence that object-capability design yields benefits at the user level as well as the system level: the object-capability model has its roots in object-oriented programming, which was a breakthrough at both levels.

# Conclusion

This chapter has offered advice at two levels: the guidelines describe qualities that usable secure software should have, and the strategies describe ways to design software with those qualities. Although these strategies address only some of the guidelines and are far from a complete solution, they have been effective in many situations. As we saw in our discussion of how phishing exploits email's weaknesses, integrating with insecure installed systems yields some of the toughest design problems and can prevent the direct application of these strategies. Even in such cases, the guidelines and strategies can help highlight vulnerable areas of a system and improve the design of countermeasures.

16 David Wagner and Dean Tribble, "A Security Analysis of the Combex DarpaBrowser Architecture"; *http://combex.com/papers/darpa-review/index.html*.

17 Marc Stiegler, Alan Karp, Ka-Ping Yee, and Mark S. Miller, "Polaris: Virus Safe Computing for Windows," HP Labs Technical Report HPL-2004-221; *http://www.hpl.hp.com/techreports/2004/HPL-2004-221.html*.

18 Mark Miller, "E: Open Source Distributed Capabilities"; *http://erights.org/*.

19 Miller and Shapiro.

20 Norman Hardy, "The KeyKOS Architecture," *Operating Systems Review* 19 (October 1985), 8–25; *http://www.cis.upenn.edu/~KeyKOS/OSRpaper.html*.

21 Jonathan Shapiro, "EROS: A Fast Capability System," *Proceedings of the 17th ACM Symposium on Operating Systems Principles* (New York: ACM Press, 1999); *http://www.eros-os.org/papers/sosp99-eros-preprint.ps*.

22 Miller, "E: Open Source Distributed Capabilities."

The theme of user initiation links the two strategies presented here. With security by designation, the user proactively designates an action instead of reacting to a notification that appears out of context. With user-assigned identifiers, the user proactively assigns names instead of reacting to names that are controlled by another party. Security based on actions initiated by the user more accurately captures the user's intentions than security based on the user's response to external stimuli. When the user initiates, security works for the user instead of the user working for security.

## Acknowledgments

The 10 guidelines in this chapter are based on an earlier set of principles[23] developed in collaboration with Miriam Walker through a series of discussions with Norm Hardy, Mark S. Miller, Chip Morningstar, Kragen Sitaker, Marc Stiegler, and Dean Tribble. Thanks to Morgan Ames, Tyler Close, Lorrie Cranor, Paul Eykamp, Simson Garfinkel, Jeremy Goecks, Alan Karp, Linley Erin Hall, Marti Hearst, Siren Torsvik Henriksen, Rebecca Middleton, Mark S. Miller, Diana Smetters, and Marc Stiegler for their many helpful suggestions, and to David T. Wallace for his advice on illustrations.

## About the Author

Ka-Ping Yee is a Ph.D. student at the University of California, Berkeley. His research interests include interaction design, capability-based security, information visualization, and computer-supported argumentation.

*http://zesty.ca/*

23  Ka-Ping Yee, "User Interaction Design for Secure Systems," in Robert Deng, Sihan Qing, Feng Bao, and Jianying Zhou (eds.), *Proceedings of the 4th International Conference on Information and Communications Security, Lecture Notes in Computer Science 2513*, (Heidelberg: Springer-Verlag, 2002); *http://zesty.ca/sid/*.

# CHAPTER FOURTEEN

# Fighting Phishing at the User Interface

ROBERT C. MILLER AND MIN WU

**A**S PEOPLE INCREASINGLY RELY ON THE INTERNET FOR BUSINESS, PERSONAL FINANCE, AND INVESTMENT, Internet fraud becomes a greater and greater threat. Internet fraud takes many forms, from phony items offered for sale on eBay, to scurrilous rumors that manipulate stock prices, to scams that promise great riches if you will help a foreign financial transaction through your own bank account.

One interesting and fast-growing species of Internet fraud is *phishing*. Phishing attacks use email messages and web sites designed to look as if they come from a known and legitimate organization, in order to deceive users into disclosing personal, financial, or computer account information. The attacker can then use this information for criminal purposes, such as identity theft, larceny, or fraud. Users are tricked into disclosing their information either by providing it through a web form or by downloading and installing hostile software.

A phishing attack succeeds when a user is tricked into forming an inaccurate mental model of an online interaction and thus takes actions that have effects contrary to the user's intentions. Because inferring a user's intentions can be difficult, building an automated system to protect users from phishing attacks is a challenging problem.

# Introduction

Phishing attacks are rapidly increasing in frequency; many are good enough to fool users. According to the Anti-Phishing Working Group (APWG),[1] reports of phishing attacks increased by 180% in April 2004 alone, and by 4,000% in the six months prior to April. A recent study done by the antispam firm MailFrontier Inc. found that phishing emails fooled users 28% of the time.[2] Estimates of losses resulting from phishing approached $37 million in 2002.[3]

## Anatomy of a Phishing Attack

The Anti-Phishing Working Group collects and archives examples of phishing attacks, a valuable service because the web site used in an attack exists only for a short time. One example on APWG is an attack against eBay customers, first reported on March 9, 2004.[4]

The attack begins when the potential victim receives an email (Figure 14-1), purporting to be from eBay, that claims that the user's account information is invalid and must be corrected. The email contains an embedded hyperlink that appears to point to a page on eBay's web site. This web page asks for the user's credit card number, contact information, Social Security number, and eBay username and password (Figure 14-2).

Beneath the surface, however, neither the email message nor the web page is what it appears to be. Figure 14-3 breaks the deception down schematically. The phishing email resembles a legitimate email from eBay. Its *source* (listed in the "From:" header) appears to be *S-Harbor@eBay.com*, which refers to the legitimate domain name for eBay Inc. The link embedded in the message also appears to go to eBay.com, even using an encrypted channel ("https:"). Based on these *presentation* cues and the content of the message, the user forms a *mental model* of the message: eBay is requesting updated information. The user then performs an *action*, clicking on the embedded hyperlink, which is presumed to go to eBay. But the user's action is translated into a completely different *system operation*—namely, retrieving a web page from IP address 210.93.131.250, a server from a communication company registered in Seoul, South Korea. This company has no relationship with eBay Inc.

The phishing web site follows a similar pattern of deception. The page looks like a legitimate eBay web page. It contains an eBay logo, and its content and layout match the format of pages from the actual eBay web site. Based on this presentation, the user forms a

---

1   Anti-Phishing Working Group, "Phishing Attack Trends Report, April 2004"; *http://antiphishing.org/APWG_Phishing_Attack_Report-Apr2004.pdf*.

2   Bob Sullivan, "Consumers Still Falling for Phish," MSNBC (July 28, 2004); *http://www.msnbc.msn.com/id/5519990/*.

3   Neil Chou, Robert Ledesma, Yuka Teraguchi, and John C. Mitchell, "Client-Side Defense Against Web-Based Identity Theft," *11th Annual Network and Distributed System Security Symposium* (2004); *http://theory.stanford.edu/people/jcm/papers/spoofguard-ndss.pdf*.

4   Anti-Phishing Working Group, "eBay—NOTICE eBay Obligatory Verifying—Invalid User Information" (March 9, 2004); *http://www.antiphishing.org/phishing_archive/eBay_03-09-04.htm*.

*FIGURE 14-1. Screenshot of a phishing email (source: Anti-Phishing Working Group)*

mental model that the browser is showing the eBay web site and that the requested infor-mation must be provided in order to keep the user's eBay account active. The user then performs an action, typing in personal and financial data and clicking the Submit button, with the intention of sending this information to eBay. This action is translated by the web browser into a system operation, encoding the entered data into an HTTP request sent to 210.93.131.250, which is not a legitimate eBay server.

## Phishing as a Semantic Attack

Bruce Schneier has observed that methods for attacking computer networks can be cate-gorized in waves of increasing sophistication and abstraction. According to Schneier, the first wave of attacks was *physical* in nature, targeting the computers, the network devices, and the wires between them, in order to disrupt the flow of information. The second wave consisted of *syntactic* attacks, which target vulnerabilities in network protocols, encryption algorithms, or software implementations. Syntactic attacks have been a primary concern

eBay Registration - Microsoft Internet Explorer

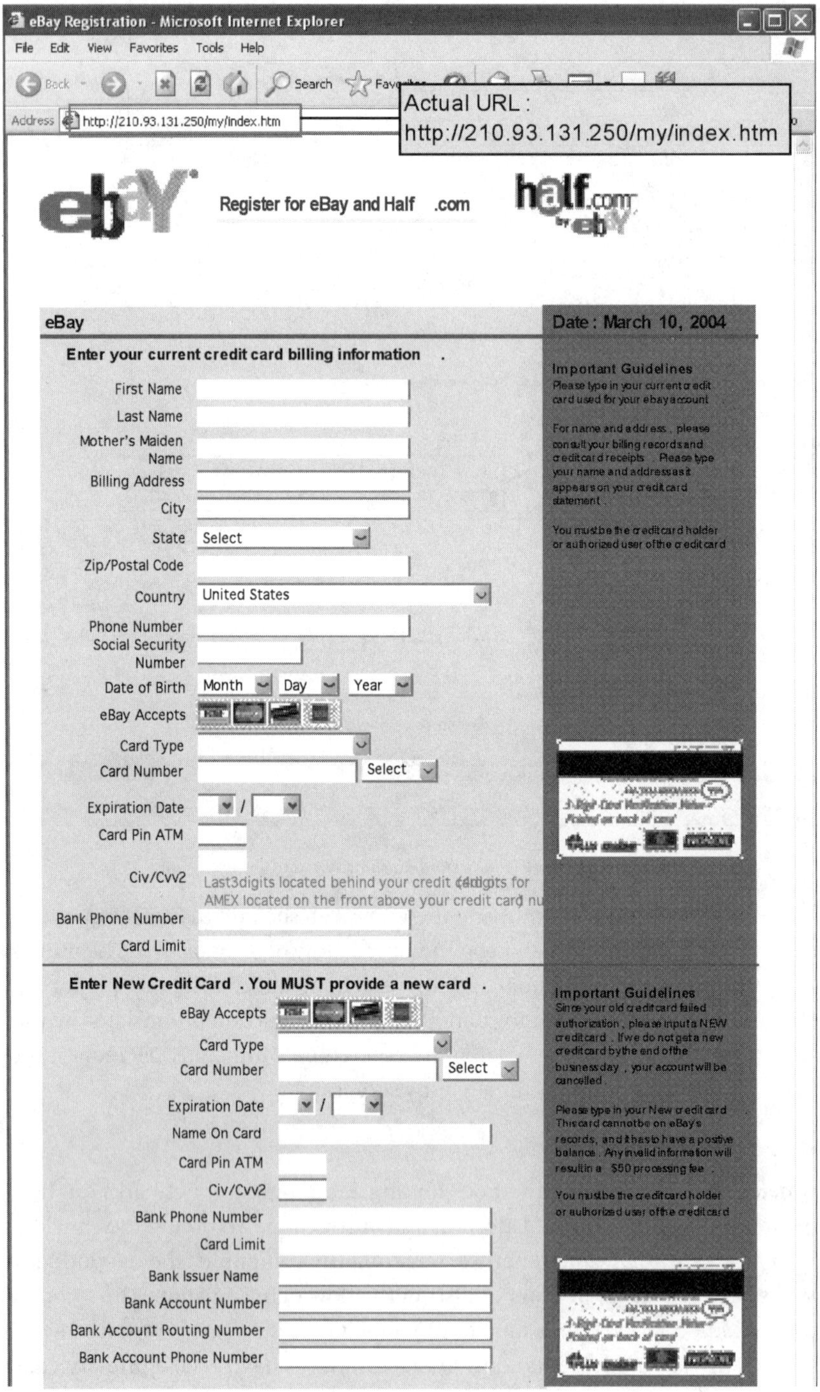

File   Edit   View   Favorites   Tools   Help

Back     Search   Favorites

Address   http://210.93.131.250/my/index.htm

Actual URL :
http://210.93.131.250/my/index.htm

eBay          Register for eBay and Half   .com        half.com

| eBay | Date : March 10, 2004 |

**Enter your current credit card billing information .**

First Name

Last Name

Mother's Maiden Name

Billing Address

City

State          Select

Zip/Postal Code

Country        United States

Phone Number

Social Security Number

Date of Birth   Month      Day      Year

eBay Accepts

Card Type

Card Number          Select

Expiration Date      /

Card Pin ATM

Civ/Cvv2      Last3digits located behind your credit cardigits for AMEX located on the front above your credit card nu

Bank Phone Number

Card Limit

**Important Guidelines**
Please type in your current credit card used for your ebay account

For name and address , please consult your billing records and credit card receipts . Please type your name and address as it appears on your credit card statement .

You must be the credit card holder or authorized user of the credit card

3-Digit Card Verification Value Printed on back of card

**Enter New Credit Card . You MUST provide a new card .**

eBay Accepts

Card Type

Card Number          Select

Expiration Date      /

Name On Card

Card Pin ATM

Civ/Cvv2

Bank Phone Number

Card Limit

Bank Issuer Name

Bank Account Number

Bank Account Routing Number

Bank Account Phone Number

**Important Guidelines**
Since your old credit card failed authorization , please input a NEW credit card . If we do not get a new credit card by the end of the business day , your account will be cancelled.

Please type in your New credit card . This card cannot be on eBay's records , and it has to have a positive balance . Any invalid information will result in a  $50 processing fee

You must be the credit card holder or authorized user of the credit card

3-Digit Card Verification Value Printed on back of card

FIGURE 14-2. Screenshot of a phishing web page pointed to by the phishing email (source: Anti-Phishing Working Group)

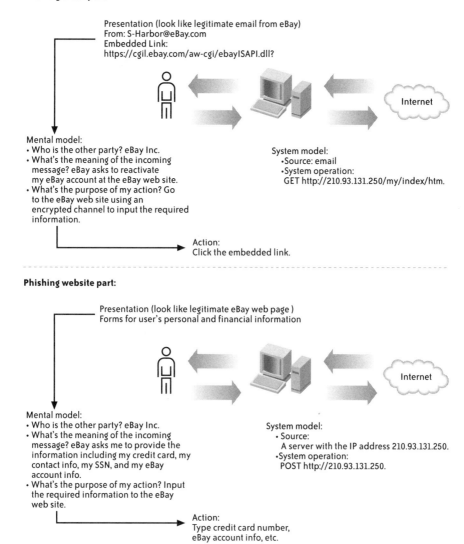

**Phishing email part:**

Presentation (look like legitimate email from eBay)
From: S-Harbor@eBay.com
Embedded Link:
https://cgil.ebay.com/aw-cgi/ebayISAPI.dll?

Internet

Mental model:
• Who is the other party? eBay Inc.
• What's the meaning of the incoming
  message? eBay asks to reactivate
  my eBay account at the eBay web site.
• What's the purpose of my action? Go
  to the eBay web site using an
  encrypted channel to input the required
  information.

System model:
•Source: email
•System operation:
  GET http://210.93.131.250/my/index/htm.

Action:
Click the embedded link.

**Phishing website part:**

Presentation (look like legitimate eBay web page )
Forms for user's personal and financial information

Internet

Mental model:
• Who is the other party? eBay Inc.
• What's the meaning of the incoming
  message? eBay asks me to provide the
  information including my credit card, my
  contact info, my SSN, and my eBay
  account info.
• What's the purpose of my action? Input
  the required information to the eBay
  web site.

System model:
• Source:
  A server with the IP address 210.93.131.250.
•System operation:
  POST http://210.93.131.250.

Action:
Type credit card number,
eBay account info, etc.

*FIGURE 14-3. Anatomy of a phishing attack*

of security research for the last decade. The third wave is *semantic*: "attacks that target the way we, as humans, assign meaning to content."[5]

Phishing is a semantic attack. Successful phishing depends on a discrepancy between the way a user perceives a communication, like an email message or a web page, and the actual effect of the communication. Figure 14-4 shows the structure of a typical Internet

5 Bruce Schneier, "Semantic Attacks: The Third Wave of Network Attacks," *Crypto-Gram Newsletter* (Oct. 15, 2000); *http://www.schneier.com/crypto-gram-0010.html#1.*

communication, dividing it into two parts. The *system model* is concerned with how computers exchange bits—protocols, representations, and software. When human users play a role in the communication, however, understanding and protecting the system model is not enough, because the real message communicated depends not on the bits exchanged but on the semantic meanings that are derived from the bits. This semantic layer is the user's *mental model*. The effectiveness of phishing indicates that human users do not always assign the proper semantic meaning to their online interactions.

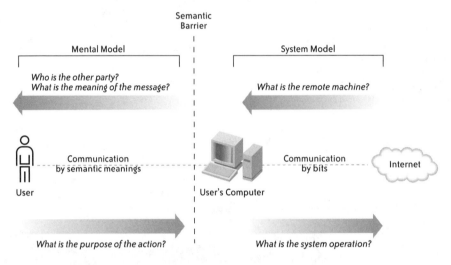

*FIGURE 14-4. Human-Internet communication*

When a user faces a phishing attack, the user's mental model about the interaction disagrees with the system model. For example, the user's intention may be "go to eBay," but the actual implementation of the hyperlink may be "go to a server in South Korea." It is this discrepancy that enables the attack, and it is this discrepancy that makes phishing attacks very hard to defend against. Users derive their mental models of the interaction from the presentation of the interaction—the way it appears on the screen. The implementation details of web pages and email messages are hidden, and are generally inaccessible to most users. Thus, the user is in no position to compare his mental model with the system model, and it would take extra effort to do so. On the other hand, email clients and web browsers follow the coded instructions provided to them in the message, but are unable to check the user's intentions. Without awareness of *both* models, neither the user nor the computer is able to detect the discrepancy introduced by phishing.

One extreme solution to the phishing problem would simply discard the presentation part of an Internet communication—the part that produces the user's mental model—because it can't be trusted. Instead, a new presentation would be generated directly from the implementation. If the user's computer is trustworthy, then, the presentation seen by the user would be guaranteed to be related to the actual implementation. Unfortunately, the cost of this idea in both usability and functionality would be enormous. Most online messages are legitimate, after all, with the presentation correctly reflecting the implementation. Phishing messages are rare (but pernicious) exceptions. So this solution would improperly sacrifice the freedom of legitimate senders to present and brand themselves in order to block a small number of wrongdoers.

So we must accept the fact that users will see messages with mismatched presentation and implementation. Attempts to fight phishing computationally, which are discussed in this chapter, try to enable the computer to bridge the gap between the user's mental model and the true system model. But the human user must be the final decision-maker about whether a message is phishing. The reason is that phishing targets how users assign semantic meaning to their online interactions, and this assignment process is outside the system's control.

## Attack Techniques

Phishing attacks use a variety of techniques to make the presentation of an email message or web page deceptively different from its implementation. In this section, we catalog a few of the techniques that have been seen in the wild:

*Copying images and page designs*

A phishing attack often copies a legitimate page nearly verbatim, including its style, layout, and embedded images. The eBay attack shown in Figure 14-2 is an example of this approach. Because logos and page style are the most prominent indicators of a site's identity—the "face" of a web site—unsuspecting users are likely to fall for this very simple deception.

*Similar domain names*

Another way that users authenticate web sites is by examining the URL displayed in the address bar. To deceive this indicator, the attacker may register a domain name that bears a superficial similarity to the imitated site's domain. Sometimes a variation in capitalization or use of special characters is effective. Because most browsers display the URL in a sans-serif font, *paypaI.com* has been used to spoof *paypal.com*, and *barcIays.com* to spoof *barclays.com*. More commonly, however, the fake domain name simply embeds some part of the real domain: *ebay-members-security.com* to spoof *ebay.com*, and *users-paypal.com* to spoof *paypal*. Most users lack the tools and knowledge to investigate whether the fake domain name is really owned by the company being spoofed.

*URL hiding*

Another way to spoof the URL took advantage of a little-used feature in URL syntax. A username and password could be included *before* the domain name, using the syntax *http://username:password@domain/*. Attackers could put a reasonable-looking domain name in the username field, and obscure the real domain amid noise or scroll it past the end of the address bar (e.g., *http://earthlink.net%6C%6C...%6C@211.112.228.2*). Recent updates to web browsers have closed this loophole, either by removing the username and password from the URL before displaying it in the address bar or (in the case of Internet Explorer) by simply forbidding the username/password URL syntax entirely.

*IP addresses*

The simplest expedient to obscuring a server's identity is to display it as an IP address, such as *http://210.93.131.250*. This technique is surprisingly effective. Because many legitimate URLs are already filled with opaque and incomprehensible numbers, only a user knowledgeable enough to parse a URL, and alert enough to actually do so, is likely to be suspicious.

*Deceptive hyperlinks*

The text of a hyperlink is completely independent from the URL to which it actually points. Attackers exploit this built-in distinction between presentation and implementation by displaying one URL in the link text, while using a completely different URL underneath. Even a knowledgeable user, having seen an explicit URL in the message, may not think to check its true URL. The standard means for checking the destination of a hyperlink—hovering over it and examining the URL in the status bar—may also be spoofed, using JavaScript or URL hiding techniques.

*Obscuring cues*

Instead of tweaking URLs, a sophisticated attack may spoof identification cues like the address bar or the status bar by replacing them entirely. One recent attack used Java-Script to create a small, undecorated window on top of Internet Explorer's address bar, displaying a completely innocent URL.[6]

*Pop-up windows*

A recent attack against Citibank customers[7] has taken page copying a step further, by displaying the true Citibank web site in the browser but popping up an undecorated window on top to request the user's personal information.

*Social engineering*

Phishing attacks also use nontechnical approaches to persuade users to fall for the attack. One tactic is urgency so that the user will feel rushed to comply and be less likely to take time to check the message's authenticity. Another tactic is a threat of dire consequences if the user fails to comply, such as terminating service or closing accounts. A few attacks promise big rewards instead ("You've won a great prize!"), but threatening attacks are far more common. It may be human nature that users would be more suspicious of getting something for nothing.

Phishing attacks to date have several other noteworthy properties:

*Short duration*

Most phishing web sites exist for a very short period of time, on the order of days or even hours.

6   Anti-Phishing Working Group, "US Bank—Maintenance Upgrade" (July 6, 2004); *http://www.antiphishing.org/phishing_archive/07-06-04_US_Bank_(usBank.com_Maintenance_upgrade).html.*

7   Anti-Phishing Working Group, "Citibank—Your Citibank Account!" (July 13, 2004); *http://www.antiphishing.org/phishing_archive/07-13-04_Citibank_(your_Citibank_account!).html.*

*Sloppy language*

Many phishing messages have misspellings, grammar errors, or confusing wording.

## Defenses

As we showed earlier in the example of the eBay attack, we can separate an online interaction into four steps (Figure 14-5):

- *Message retrieval.* An email message or web page arrives at the user's personal computer from the Internet.

- *Presentation.* The message is displayed in the user interface, the user perceives it, and the user forms a mental model.

- *Action.* Guided by the mental model, the user performs an action in the user interface, such as clicking a link or filling in a form.

- *System operation.* The user's action is translated into system operations, such as connecting to a web server and submitting data.

In this section, we survey existing defenses against phishing attacks, classifying them according to which of these four steps they address.

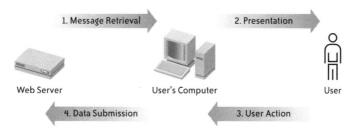

*FIGURE 14-5. Four steps of human-Internet interaction*

### Message Retrieval

In an ideal world, the best defense against phishing would simply block all phishing communications from being shown to the user, by filtering them at message retrieval time. The essential requirement for this solution is that the computer alone must be able to accurately differentiate phishing messages from legitimate ones. Defenses that filter at message retrieval depend on message properties that are easily understood by a computer.

### Identity of the sender

One of these properties is the identity of the sender. *Black listing* is widely used to block potentially dangerous or unwelcome messages, such as spam. If the sender's IP address is found in a black list, the incoming message can be categorized as spam or even simply rejected without informing the user. A black list may be managed by an individual user, the approach taken by Internet Explorer's Content Advisor (Figure 14-6). Alternatively, it may be managed by an organization or by collaboration among many users. For phishing, the EarthLink Toolbar alerts the user about web pages that are found on a black list of known fraudulent sites.[8]

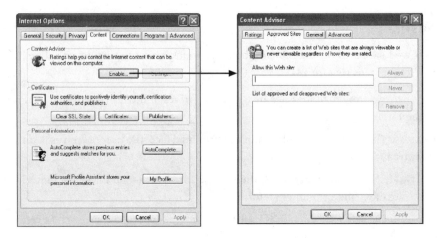

*FIGURE 14-6. Internet Explorer's Content Advisor*

Black listing is unlikely to be an effective defense on today's Internet, because it is so easy to generate new identities such as new email addresses and new domain names. Even new IP addresses are cheap and easy to obtain. The black list must be updated constantly to warn users about dangerous messages from newly created sources. Because phishing sites exist for only a short time, the black list must be updated within hours or minutes in order to be effective at blocking the attack.

The converse of black listing is *white listing*, allowing users to see messages only from a list of acceptable sources. For example, Secure Browser controls where users may browse on the Internet using a list of permitted URLs.[9] White listing avoids the new-identity problem because newly created sources are initially marked as unacceptable. But defining the white list is a serious problem. Because it is impossible to predict where a user might need to browse, a predefined, fixed white list invariably blocks users from accessing legitimate web sites. On the other hand, a dynamic white list that needs the user's involvement puts a burden on users because, for every site they want to visit, they must first decide whether to put it in the white list. This also creates vulnerability: if a phishing site can convince users to submit sensitive data to it, it may also be able to convince them to put it into a white list.

**Textual content of the message**

Another property amenable to message filtering is the textual content of the message. This kind of content analysis is used widely in antispam and antivirus solutions. Dangerous messages are detected by searching for well-known patterns, such as spam keywords and virus

---

8   EarthLink Toolbar: Featuring ScamBlocker; *http://www.earthlink.net/earthlinktoolbar/download/*.

9   Tropical Software Secure Browser; *http://www.tropsoft.com/secbrowser/*.

code signatures. In order to beat content analysis, an attacker can tweak the content to bypass the well-known filtering rules. For example, encryption and compression are added to existing viruses in order to bypass antivirus scans.[10] Random characters are inserted into spam emails to enable them to bypass spam filters. One sophisticated phishing attack used images to display text messages so that they would defeat content analysis.[11]

Spam filtering is one defense that applies at message retrieval time. Because nearly all phishing attacks are currently launched by spam, getting spam under control may reduce the risk of phishing attacks significantly. Unfortunately, the techniques used by many spam filters, which scan for keywords in the message content to distinguish spam from legitimate mail, are insufficient for classifying phishing attacks, because phishing messages are designed expressly to mimic legitimate mail from organizations with which the user already has a relationship. Even if spam filters manage to reduce the spam problem substantially, we can anticipate that phishing will move to other transmission vectors, such as anonymous comments on discussion web sites, or narrowly targeted email attacks rather than broadcast spam.

## Presentation

When a message is presented to the user, in either an email client or a web browser, the user interface can provide visual cues to help the user decide whether the message is legitimate.

Current web browsers reflect information about the source and integrity of a web page through a set of visual cues. For example, the address bar at the top of the window displays the URL of the retrieved web page. A lock icon, typically found in the status bar, indicates whether the page was retrieved through an encrypted, authenticated connection. These cues are currently the most widely deployed and most user-accessible defenses against phishing, and security advisories about phishing warn users to pay close attention to them at all times.[12, 13, 14]

Unfortunately, these visual cues are vulnerable for several reasons. First, the cues are displayed in the peripheral area of the browser, separately from the page content. Because the content is central and almost always is the user's focus of attention, a peripheral cue must fight to draw the user's attention. Second, these cues can be attacked directly by phishing. As we mentioned earlier, URL hiding and domain name similarity are evidence that the address bar is susceptible to deception. JavaScript and Java applets have also been

10  F-SECURE, "F-Secure Virus Descriptions: Bagle.N"; *http://www.f-secure.com/v-descs/bagle_n.shtml.*

11  Anti-Phishing Working Group, "MBNA—MBNA Informs You!" (Feb. 24, 2004); *http://www.antiphishing.org/phishing_archive/MBNA_2-24-04.htm.*

12  eBay Inc., "Email and Websites Impersonating eBay"; *http://pages.ebay.com/ help/confidence/isgw-account-theft-spoof.html.*

13  Federal Bureau of Investigation, Department of Justice, "FBI Says Web 'Spoofing' Scams Are a Growing Problem" (2003); *http://www.fbi.gov/pressrel/pressrel03/spoofing072103.htm.*

14  PayPal Inc., "Security Tips"; *http://www.paypal.com/cgi-bin/webscr?cmd=p/gen/fraud-prevention-outside.*

used to hide or fake other security cues, including the address bar, status bar, authentication dialog boxes, SSL lock icon, and SSL certificate information.[15, 16, 17]

---

## PEOPLE MAY IGNORE SECURITY CUES

A general problem with the presentation of security cues is that users may disregard them, or attribute their presence to causes other than malicious attack. We observed this effect recently while developing a new authentication mechanism for logging in to web sites through an untrusted, public Internet terminal. Instead of requesting a secret password through the untrusted terminal (where it may be recorded by a key logger), authentication is performed on the user's cell phone using SMS messages and WAP browsing. To defend this approach against spoofing, however, it was necessary to associate a unique *session name* with the login attempt.

The user's only task was to confirm that the session name displayed in the untrusted web browser was the same as the session name displayed on the cell phone. In a user study of 20 users, however, the error rate for this confirmation was 30%. In other words, out of 20 times that we simulated an attack in which the session name on the phone differed from the session name on the terminal, users erroneously confirmed the session 6 times—giving the attacker access to their account.

Some users erred simply because they had stopped paying attention to the session names. Others made telling comments:

- "There must be a bug because the session name displayed in the computer does not match the one in the mobile phone."
- "The network connection must be really slow because the session name has not been displayed yet."

We subsequently changed the user interface design so that instead of simply approving the session name (Yes or No), the user is obliged to choose the session name from a short list of choices. Not surprisingly, the error rate dropped to zero, because the new design forces users to attend to the security cue and prevents them from rationalizing away discrepancies.

---

15 J. D. Tygar and Alma Whitten, "WWW Electronic Commerce and Java Trojan Horses" *Proceedings of the Second USENIX Workshop on Electronic Commerce* (1996).

16 Edward W. Felten, Dirk Balfanz, Drew Dean, and Dan S. Wallach, "Web Spoofing: An Internet Con Game," *20th National Information Systems Security Conference* (1996).

17 Zishuang Ye, Yougu Yuan, and Sean Smith, *Web Spoofing Revisited: SSL and Beyond*, Technical Report TR2002-417, Dartmouth College (2002).

eBay's Account Guard (Figure 14-7) puts a site identity indicator into a dedicated toolbar.[18] Account Guard separates the Internet into three categories, described next.

- Web sites truly belonging to eBay or PayPal, indicated by a green icon
- Known spoofs of eBay or PayPal, indicated by a red icon
- All other sites, indicated by a neutral gray icon

One problem with this approach is its lack of scalability. Of course, phishing attacks are not limited to eBay and PayPal. As of October 2004, the Anti-Phishing Working Group has collected attacks targeted at customers of 39 different organizations. It is impossible to cram all the possible toolbars, each representing a single organization, into a single browser. A better approach would be a single toolbar, created and managed by a single authority such as VeriSign or TRUSTe, to which organizations could subscribe if they have been, or fear becoming, victims of phishing attacks. VeriSign might do this right away by rolling out a toolbar that automatically certifies all members of its VeriSign Secured Seal program.[19]

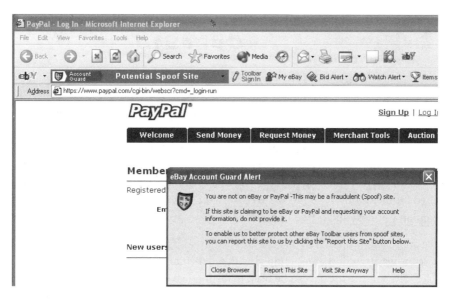

*FIGURE 14-7. eBay Account Guard toolbar*

SpoofStick (Figure 14-8) is a browser extension that helps users parse the URL and detect URL spoofing by displaying only the most relevant domain information on a dedicated toolbar. For example, when the current URL is *http://signin.ebay.com@10.19.32.4*, Spoof-Stick displays "You're on 10.19.32.4". When the current URL is *http://www.citibank.com.*

18 eBay toolbar; *http://pages.ebay.com/ebay_toolbar/.*

19 VeriSign Secured Seal Program; *http://www.verisign.com/products-services/security-services/secured-seal/ index.html.*

*intl-en.us*, SpoofStick displays "You're on intl-en.us". Because it uses a large, colorful font, this toolbar is presumably easier for users to notice. But SpoofStick cannot solve the similar-domain-name problem: is *ebay-members-security.com* a domain owned by eBay, or is *mypaypal.com* a legitimate domain for PayPal? If the user's answer to either of these questions is yes, then the user will be tricked even with SpoofStick installed. Moreover, it is unknown whether seeing an IP address instead of a domain name raises sufficient suspicion in users' minds, because some legitimate sites also use bare IP addresses (e.g., Google caches).

*FIGURE 14-8. SpoofStick toolbar*

In order to address the problem of faked cues, Ye and Smith have proposed *synchronized random dynamic boundaries*.[20] With this approach, all legitimate browser windows change their border colors together at random intervals. Because a spoofed window generated by a remote site has no access to the random value generated on the local machine, its border does not change synchronously with the legitimate window borders. This approach was considered for inclusion in the Mozilla web browser, but was dropped out of concern that users wouldn't understand it (see Chapter 28).

A related approach, proposed by Tygar and Whitten,[21] is *personalized display*, in which legitimate browser windows are stamped with a personal logo, such as a picture of the user's face. The same principle can be used to distinguish legitimate web pages from phishing attacks. For example, Amazon and Yahoo! greet registered users by name. Anti-phishing advisories suggest that an impersonal email greeting should be treated as a warning sign for a potential spoofed email.[22] PassMark goes even further, by displaying a user-configured image as part of the web site's login page, so that the user can authenticate the web site at the same time that the web site authenticates the user.[23]

---

20 Zishuang Ye and Sean Smith, "Trusted Paths for Browsers," *ACM Transactions in Information Systems Security* 8:2 (May 2005), 153–186..

21 Tygar and Whitten.

22 eBay, Inc., "Tutorial: Spoof (fake) Emails"; *http://pages.ebay.com/education/spooftutorial/*.

23 PassMark Security; *http://www.passmarksecurity.com/twoWay.jsp*.

Personalization is much harder to spoof, but requires more configuration by the user. Configuration could be avoided if the web site automatically chose a random image for the user, but a system-chosen image may not be memorable. Another question about personalization is whether the lack of personalization in a phishing attack would raise sufficient warning flags in a user's mind. The *absence* of a positive cue like personalization may not trigger caution in the same way that the *presence* of a negative cue, like a red light in a toolbar, does.

## Action

Phishing depends on a user not only being deceived but also *acting* in response to persuasion. As a result, security advisories try to discourage users from performing potentially dangerous actions. For example, most current phishing attacks use email messages as the initial bait, in order to trick the recipient into clicking through a link provided in the email, which points to a phishing server. Security tips suggest that the user should ignore links provided by email, and instead open a new browser and manually type the URL of the legitimate site.

This advice is unlikely to be followed. Considering the low frequency of phishing attacks relative to legitimate messages, this suggestion sacrifices the efficiency of hyperlinks in legitimate emails in order to prevent users from clicking misleading links in very few phishing emails.

## System Operation

In the final step of a successful phishing attack, the user's action is translated into a system operation. This is the last chance we have to prevent the attack. Unfortunately, because phishing does not exploit system bugs, the system operations involved in a phishing attack are perfectly valid. For example, it is ordinary to post information to a remote server. Warnings based solely on system operations will inevitably generate a high rate of false positive errors—that is, warning users about innocent actions (Figure 14-9). These false-positives eventually cause users to disable the warnings or simply to become habituated to "swatting" the warning away.

*FIGURE 14-9. Warning based on system operations*

A more interesting approach involves modifying the system operation according to its destination. *Web password hashing* applies this idea to defend against phishing attacks that steal web site passwords.[24] The browser automatically hashes the password typed by the user with the domain name to which it is being sent, in order to generate a unique password for each site—and hence sending useless garbage to a phishing site. Web password hashing assumes that users will type their passwords only into a password HTML element. But this element can be spoofed, and a sophisticated attack may be able to trick users into disclosing their passwords through other channels.

## Case Study: SpoofGuard

The most comprehensive solution thus far for stopping phishing at the user interface is SpoofGuard, a browser plug-in for Internet Explorer.[25] SpoofGuard addresses three of the four steps where phishing might be prevented.

At message retrieval time, SpoofGuard calculates a total *spoof score* for an incoming web page. The calculation is based on common characteristics of known phishing attacks, including:

- Potentially misleading patterns in URLs, such as use of @
- Similarity of the domain name to popular or previously visited domains, as measured by edit distance
- Embedded images that are similar to images from frequently spoofed domains, as measured by image hashing
- Whether links in the page contain misleading URLs
- Whether the page includes password fields but fails to use SSL, as most phishing sites eschew SSL

At presentation time, SpoofGuard translates this spoof score into a traffic light (red, yellow, or green) displayed in a dedicated toolbar. Further, when the score is above a threshold, SpoofGuard pops up a modal warning box that demands the user's consent before it proceeds with displaying the page.

For the action step, SpoofGuard does nothing to modify the user's online behavior. The user is free to click on any links or buttons in the page, regardless of their spoof score.

SpoofGuard becomes involved again in the system operation step, however, by evaluating posted data before it is submitted to a remote server. The evaluation tries to detect whether sensitive data is being sent, by maintaining a database of passwords (stored as hashes) and comparing each element sent against the database. If a user's eBay password is sent to a site that isn't in *ebay.com*, then the spoof score for the interaction is increased. This evaluation is also linked with the detection of embedded images so that if the page also contained an eBay logo, the spoof score is increased still more. If the evaluation of the

---

24 Dan Boneh, John Mitchell, and Blake Ross, "Web Password Hashing," Stanford University; *http://crypto.stanford.edu/PwdHash/*.

25 Chou *et al.*

system operation causes the spoof score to exceed a certain threshold, then the post is blocked and the user is warned.

The evaluation of posted data depends on some assumptions that may not be valid for sophisticated attacks. For example, data must be posted from an HTML form; an attacker might defeat this by using Flash form submission. Further, a password must be submitted as a single piece of clear text to be detected, but JavaScript could easily hash it.

In general, however, SpoofGuard is an impressive step toward fighting phishing attacks at the client side.

## Looking Ahead

Phishing attacks are likely to grow more sophisticated in the days ahead, and our defenses against them must continue to improve. Phishing succeeds because of a gap between the user's mental model and the true implementation, so promising technical solutions should try to bridge this gap, either by finding ways to visualize for the user details of implementation that would otherwise be invisible, or by finding ways to see the message from the user's point of view.

If technical solutions fail, we might ask whether there are legal or policy solutions. As a species of wire fraud, phishing is, of course, already illegal; no new legislation is required to prosecute an attacker. So, legal and policy solutions may have to restrict legitimate access instead, in order to make phishing attacks easier to detect or attackers easier to track down. One policy measure, already being undertaken by some companies, is to stop using email for critical communications with customers. AOL, one of the earliest targets of phishing attacks in the Internet era, has a unique message system for "Official AOL Mail" that cannot be spoofed by outsiders or other AOL members. More recently, eBay has responded to the spate of phishing attacks against it by setting up a private webmail system, "My Messages," for sending unspoofable messages to its users.

The success of phishing suggests that users authenticate web sites mainly by visual inspection: looking at logos, page layout, and domain names. The web browser can improve this situation by digging up additional information about a site and making it available for direct visual inspection. How many times have I been to this site? How many other people have been to this site? How long has this site existed on the Web? How many other sites link to it, according to a search engine like Google? Reputation is much harder to spoof than mere visual appearance. Authentication by visual inspection would be easier and more dependable if these additional visual cues were not all buried in the periphery of the web browser, but were integrated into the content of the page, in the user's locus of attention.

Another potential opportunity arises in the action step of an online interaction. A phishing attack is harmless unless the user actually *does* something with it. If earlier analysis suggests that the risk of phishing is high, then the system can suggest alternative safe paths ("Use this bookmark to go to the real eBay.com"), or ask the user to choose which site they really want to receive the information ("eBay.com in California, or 210.93.131.250 in South Korea?").

The ideal defense against phishing might be an intelligent security assistant that can perceive and understand a message in the same way the user does so that it can directly compare the user's probable mental model against the real implementation and detect discrepancies. This ideal is likely to be a long way off. In the meantime, phishing will remain a problem that must be tackled by both a user and a computer, with an effective user interface in between.

## About the Authors

 Robert Miller is an assistant professor in MIT's Department of Electrical Engineering and Computer Science and a member of the MIT Computer Science and Artificial Intelligence Laboratory. He received his Ph.D. in computer science from Carnegie Mellon University in 2002. His research concerns intelligent user interfaces, end-user programming, and applications of usability to security, including authentication, secure email, and network visualization.

 Min Wu is a Ph.D. candidate in electrical engineering and computer science at MIT. He received his M.S. in electrical engineering and computer science at MIT in 2001. He is interested in different techniques to deal with Internet fraud.

# CHAPTER FIFTEEN

# Sanitization and Usability

**SIMSON GARFINKEL**

**D**ELETION POSES A FUNDAMENTAL QUANDARY TO SECURE USABILITY. On the one hand, users would like to be able to undo their mistakes—to undelete files after they have been deleted accidentally. On the other hand, users would like to know that sensitive data is actually removed from a disk when they delete it—removed so that it cannot be recovered by an adversary.

Anybody who has a paper shredder lives with this quandary. If you get one of those preapproved credit card offers in the mail and you don't need it, you can always just throw it into a recycling bin. If you change your mind and decide that the 0% introductory rate might help you finance a new laptop, you can always pull the offer out of the bin and fill it out. Of course, these preapproved offers can also be used by crooks in the commission of identity theft: if you are *really* sure that you don't want to take out that new credit card, you're better off shredding the offer and perhaps even the envelope in which it came. The best paper shredders make it easy for you to inspect the chad to make sure that the information is no longer intelligible. Some companies that care about their data security let their employees throw whatever documents they wish into recycling, but the paper is then shredded before it is given to a waste hauler.

Today's computers use the metaphors of folders, files, recyclers, and paper shredders frequently to describe how information is stored and erased, but few actually work the way that these metaphors imply. In fact, they work in a way that is perverse and truly anti-user: when a file is deleted—perhaps by putting it in the Windows Recycle Bin and then emptying the recycler—normal users can no longer recover the contents of their files, but specialists armed with special *forensic tools* frequently can. Simply put, the DELETE key lies.

Nobody set out to make delete a deceitful act, it just sort of happened. And it's something that can be undone. If computers were programmed to simply overwrite data when that data was "deleted," a process commonly called *sanitization*, this problem would not exist. But changing the behavior of a function that's nearly 40 years old can be hard work.

This chapter addresses the question of sanitization and usability. My argument, based on an analysis of operating systems and the results of a data forensics investigation, is that the time has come to redesign the way that operating systems implement DELETE.

## Introduction

Visibility is a powerful tool for aligning security and usability. All too often, hidden properties, functionality, or data storage that is part of a complex system can make it very difficult for a user to operate a system in a secure manner. Although it is possible, with significant effort, to teach users about hidden aspects of a system, an attractive alternative is to remove the opportunities for a system's visible state to be inconsistent with its internal state.

Many of the specific security and privacy problems facing users of the World Wide Web today are a direct result of the mismatch between what is visible to the user and what is actually happening inside the computer. Much of the initial furor over *web cookies* in the popular press that accompanied the introduction of Netscape's 2.0 browser centered upon the fact that cookies were a hidden tracking device that was not generally visible to web site visitors. The same resentment was played out several years later when web sites and email marketers started tracking page views with *web bugs*. (For more discussion of web cookies and web bugs, see Chapters 24 and 23, respectively.)

Web browsers contain much personal information that is hidden from the average user, including browser caches, history lists, and databases used for form completion. In many cases, information left behind by the browser has revealed information that the computer user would have preferred to remain hidden. Novice Internet users are rarely aware of the fact that their browser records such information. But even advanced users can easily forget to clear their browser's history, empty the browser's cache, and explicitly delete the "form filling" database after using a borrowed browser.

This chapter looks at another way that private information may be compromised by modern computer systems: the improper sanitization of disk space when the files on the disk are "deleted." Although the need to sanitize magnetic media properly has been recognized for more than 30 years, as of this writing, operating system developers have still refused to make proper sanitization a standard part of any computer system that is widely available today. In the first section of this chapter, I present the results of a study that demonstrates the need for clean deletion in mass-market operating systems such as Windows, Mac OS, and Linux. In the second section, I explore sanitization standards and academic studies, and discuss support for sanitization in today's operating systems. In the final section, I present a plan for incorporating sanitization into today's mass-market systems.

## The Remembrance of Data Passed Study

In August 1998, I was chief technology officer of a computer security start-up. One of my jobs involved setting up a test bed of modem-equipped computers that would answer incoming phone calls and respond with a variety of different prompts. Instead of purchasing new computers for this somewhat mundane task, I bought 10 used machines at $20 each from a small-town computer store. Most of the computers had been sitting on a shelf for more than a year, and the store's owner didn't even know if they worked. My plan was to mix and match the components until I had five or six operational systems.

When I got the computers back to my house and started to inventory the parts, I discovered that the computer store had neglected to sanitize the hard drives prior to selling me the machines. Intrigued, I inventoried the drives and discovered the following:

- One of the larger machines, a '486-class system with a 40-gigabyte hard drive, had been the Novell file server for a small law firm. The computer had considerable client material on it, including contracts, wills, and billing records.

- A second computer had been used by an organization that delivered mental health services to community residents under contract to a state agency. The computer included a FileMaker Pro database that had the names, addresses, and diagnoses of several dozen individuals living in the community.

- A third machine had belonged to a writer who worked for a national magazine and also wrote novels. This machine contained many unpublished works, works-in-progress, and correspondence.

- A fourth machine had letters sent between a woman and her daughter in college. This computer also had a copy of Quicken, which the woman apparently used to manage her finances.

All of this information was visible once the computers were turned on; no special disk recovery software was needed at all. I called the store's owner. Once he got over his shock and embarrassment, he asked me to wipe the systems as a favor. Apparently, he had meant to sanitize the machines before he sold them, but he had forgotten to do so.

## Other Anecdotal Information

My experience with data left on disks that were subsequently sold on the secondary market is hardly unique. In recent years, there have been numerous reports of such cases, including:

- In April 1997, a woman in Pahrump, Nevada, purchased a used IBM PC and discovered records from 2,000 patients who had prescriptions filled at a Smitty's Supermarkets pharmacy in Tempe, Arizona.[1]

- In August 2001, more than 100 computers from the consulting firm Viant containing confidential client data were sold at auction by Dovebid following the closure of Viant's San Francisco office.[2]

- In spring 2002, the Pennsylvania State Department of Labor and Industry sold computers containing "thousands of files of information about state employees."[3]

- In August 2002, a Purdue student purchased a used Macintosh computer at the equipment exchange and discovered that the computer contained a FileMaker database with names and demographic information of 100 applicants to the Entomology Department.

- Also in August 2002, the United States Veterans Administration Medical Center in Indianapolis retired 139 computers. Some of these systems were donated to schools, others were sold on the open market, and at least three ended up in a thrift shop where they were purchased by a journalist. Examination of the computer hard drives revealed sensitive medical information, including the names of veterans with AIDS and mental health problems. Also found were 44 credit card numbers used by the Indianapolis facility.[4]

- In June 2004, the UK computer security firm Pointsec purchased 100 hard disks on eBay as part of a project on the "life cycle of a lost laptop." Although all of the hard drives had "supposedly" been "wiped clean" or "reformatted," the company was able to recover data from approximately 70 of the drives. The company also purchased laptops at auction that had been lost at airport terminals in England, Germany, Sweden, and the U.S. and verified that police did not sanitize the laptops prior to selling them. Reportedly, the laptop recovered from Sweden "contained sensitive information from a large food manufacturer. The data recovered included four Microsoft Access databases containing company and customer-related information and 15 Microsoft PowerPoint presentations containing highly sensitive company information."[5]

1   John Markoff, "Patient Files Turn Up in Used Computer," The *New York Times* (April 4, 1997).

2   Jay Lyman, "Troubled Dot-Coms May Expose Confidential Data," *NewsFactor Network* (Aug. 8, 2001); *http://www.newsfactor.com/perl/story/12612.html*.

3   Matt Villanano, "Hard-Drive Magic: Making Data Disappear Forever," The *New York Times* (May 2, 2002).

4   Judi Hasson, "VA Toughens Security After PC Disposal Blunders," *Federal Computer Week* (Aug. 26, 2002).

5   John Leyden, "Oops! Firm Accidentally eBays Customer Database," *The Register* (June 7, 2004); *http://www.theregister.co.uk/2004/06/07/hdd_wipe_shortcomings/*.

While these cases are certainly notable, they represent a tiny fraction of the number of hard disks that are being repurposed, recycled, or otherwise resold on the secondary market.

According to the market research firm Dataquest,[6] nearly 150 million disk drives will be retired in 2002—up from 130 million in 2001. Dataquest estimates that 7 disk drives will be retired for every 10 drives that ship in the year 2002; this is up from a 3-for-10 rate of retirement in 1997. Thus, more and more drives are being retired every year!

But the term *retired* is something of a misnomer. As the experience at the VA Hospital demonstrates, many disk drives that are "retired" by one organization can appear elsewhere. Indeed, mainstream businesses are increasingly turning to used equipment in an effort to cut costs—the editors at *CIO Magazine* even ran a cover story giving their readers advice on finding the best deals.[7]

These anecdotal reports are interesting both because of their similarity to each other and because of their relative scarcity. Clearly, confidential information has been disclosed through computers sold on the secondary market more than a few times. Why, then, have there been so few reports of unintended disclosure?

In the initial publication detailing this study,[8] Shelat and I proposed three possible hypotheses to answer this question:

- Disclosure of so-called "data passed" information, while it occurs from time to time, is nevertheless exceedingly rare.
- Confidential information might be disclosed so often on retired systems that such events are simply not newsworthy.
- While used equipment is awash with confidential information, nobody is looking for it—or at least, few people who are looking for this data are publicizing the fact.

This chapter argues that the third hypothesis is correct. Based on a combination of the information found on the drives and interviews conducted with some of the original data owners, it seems that most confidential information on these "retired" drives is erased but not overwritten. As a result, I believe that many repurposed drives contain significant amounts of personal or confidential information, but few of the drives' current users are aware of this fact.

6   John Monroe, "Personal Communication," Gartner Dataquestion (Sept. 23, 2002).

7   Scott Berinato, "Good Stuff Cheap: A New Hardware Market Is Developing to Give CTOs What They Want Most: Good Stuff Cheap. This Is Its Story," *CIO* (Oct. 15, 2002).

8   Simson Garfinkel and Abhi Shelat, "Remembrance of Data Passed," *IEEE Security and Privacy* (Jan.2002).

## Study Methodology

Between January 1999 and January 2003, I purchased 235 used hard drives on the secondary market in an effort to determine what information they contained and what, if any, means were taken to clean the drives before they were discarded. Initially the drives were purchased at used computer stores such as WeirdStuff in Sunnyvale, California, and PC Recycle in Belleview, Washington. The majority of drives were purchased as the result of winning bids on the eBay online auction web site. Most purchases consisted of between 3 and 5 drives; in no case were more than 20 drives at a time from the same vendor.

Modern hard disks store information in individually addressable *blocks*, with each block being 512 bytes in length. A 50-gigabyte disk thus has approximately 10 million blocks.

On receipt, each drive was cataloged and entered into a database. Each drive was then attached to a computer running the FreeBSD operating system and the contents were copied off, block for block, using the command:

```
dd if=/dev/ad2 of=NNN.img conv=noerror,sync
```

where /dev/ad2 is the raw device of the disk, noerror instructs that the dd command should continue copying data even if an error is encountered, and sync specifies that error-containing blocks should be written to the output stream as all zeros.

A *filesystem* is the piece of a computer's operating system that controls the allocation of disk blocks to individual files. Popular filesystems are FAT32 (used by Windows 3.1, Windows 95, and Windows 98), NTFS (used by Windows NT, 2000, and XP), FFS (used by BSD Unix), and ext2fs (used by Linux). The following discussion is for the FAT32 filesystem, but it applies to all modern filesystems with only minor changes.

Once the images were created, they were mounted with FreeBSD's "memory disk" driver. I then attempted to read the data in the image using FreeBSD's native filesystem implementations for the FAT, NTFS, Novell, and Unix filesystems.

Of the 235 disks, 59 were dead on arrival, and the remaining 176 had data that could be read, for a total of 125 gigabytes of image files. Of these drives, 11 disks contained no data at all—that is, every block on these disks had been overwritten with ASCII NUL bytes. Another 22 disks appeared to have been overwritten completely and then formatted using the Windows FORMAT command. On these 22 disks, more than 99% of the blocks were blank. For the majority of the remaining disks, it appeared that little if anything had been done to remove the data of their previous owners.

Further examination appeared to contradict this conclusion. The remaining disks contained relatively large amounts of recoverable data. Nevertheless, a relatively small percentage of this data seemed to actually reside in files. There were only 168,459 files on the

176 readable drives, accounting for just 38,296,903[9] of the 190,681,765 non-zero disk blocks. Examining the files by file type, I found just 783 Microsoft Word files, 184 Microsoft Excel files, 30 Microsoft PowerPoint files, and just 11 Outlook PST files—numbers that seemed suspiciously low given that these were *used* disk drives.

Typical of the disks recovered was Disk #70, an IBM DALA 3540 that was purchased for $5 on eBay from a Massachusetts retail store. The disk contained 541 megabytes of data in 1,057,392 disk blocks (each disk block holds 512 bytes). Only 6% of the disk blocks were filled with ASCII NUL bytes; the rest contained data. Yet when the disk was mounted, just three files were observed—two of which were marked as "hidden" by the operating system:

```
IO.SYS         (hidden)
MSDOS.SYS      (hidden)
COMMAND.COM
```

Where was the rest of the data?

## FORMAT Doesn't Format

Broadly speaking, modern disk drives have the ability to store two kinds of information. The majority of information stored by the device is *directly addressable user data*—these are the actual blocks that are written by the computer's operating system onto the drive's media in response to WRITE commands, and read back into the computer in response to READ commands. The second kind of information stored on the disk drive is *hidden data* that is used for the proper operation of the disk drive itself. This information includes the disk's firmware and spare blocks that the drive will use when blocks containing directly addressable user data begin to fail.

When a manufacturer delivers a drive to the computer maker or end user, all blocks that will be used to hold directly addressable user data are filled with the ASCII NUL character—that is, the blocks are zeroed. (The hidden blocks generally are not zeroed, but they cannot be accessed by the computer's operating system; for most practical purposes, these blocks do not exist.)

When a disk is formatted with the FAT filesystem, the Windows FORMAT command scans the entire disk, reading every block to make sure that the block is functioning. The FORMAT command then writes down *boot blocks*, the disk's root directory, and finally a *file allocation table* that is used to distinguish blocks that are in use by the filesystem from those that are not. This process typically takes between 10 and 20 minutes, owing to the time required to read every block on the drive.

---

9   This figure takes into account the fact that a 1-byte file takes an entire block, and a 1,025-byte file takes three blocks.

Once the root directory is written out, any information that was previously on the disk is rendered inaccessible. The data is still on the disk, but it cannot be retrieved using Windows because the files and directories of the disk cannot be reached by starting at the disk's now empty root directory. Thus, the Windows FORMAT command doesn't really erase the contents of the disk: it actually reads the entire disk and writes a new root. (Overwriting the FAT *does* make it more difficult to reassemble files that have been fragmented—that is, written partially in one location and partially in one or more others. This tends to make it harder, although not impossible, to recover large files.)

The failure of the FORMAT command to zero or otherwise initialize a hard drive has an interesting history. The first version of DOS, MS-DOS 1.0, worked only with floppy disks. At the time, floppies were sold without any track or sector information on their magnetic surface and they needed to be "formatted" before they could be used. In the process of formatting the disk, any bad blocks were detected and noted in the disk's FAT so that they would not be used accidentally. If a floppy disk containing data was formatted, the information that it contained would necessarily be overwritten. This process took a few minutes. Thus, the initial meaning of "format" to PC users in 1981 was "a process that initializes a piece of magnetic media, making it usable, and destroying any data that the media might contain in the process."

With the introduction of DOS 2.0, the first version of DOS that directly supported hard-disk drives, FORMAT of hard disks was made nondestructive. Because hard drives were sold already initialized, it was only necessary for the FORMAT command to literally write a format of data structures into the disk's logical blocks so that the disk could be used with the operating system. But the FORMAT command continued to scan the entire disk for bad blocks—a process that might take between 10 and 30 minutes.

Thus, the FORMAT command *gave the impression* that it was overwriting the entire disk because it took a long time and because the resulting disk appeared to contain no data. But, in fact, no such overwriting took place. Not only does the FORMAT command turn visible data into invisible data, but it furthermore does so in a manner that is *misleading*. Equally misleading is the warning that the command displays:

```
A:\>format c:

WARNING, ALL DATA ON NON-REMOVABLE DISK
DRIVE C: WILL BE LOST!
proceed with Format (Y/N)?y

Formatting 1,007.96M
100 percent completed.
Writing out file allocation table
Complete.
Calculating free space (this may take several minutes)...
Complete.
```

```
Volume label (11 characters, ENTER for none)?
1,054,851,072 bytes total disk space
1,054,851,072 bytes available on disk

      4,096 bytes in each allocation unit.
    257,531 allocation units available on disk.

Volume Serial Number is 4026-1EFC

A:\>
```

The DOS 2.0 FORMAT command *could* have overwritten the entire disk, but this would have doubled the amount of time that the command required to prepare a new hard drive because every block would have needed to be both *written and then read*. The program's creators appear to have made a tradeoff here between usability and security—increasing one while decreasing the other. Unfortunately, it was an invisible, undocumented tradeoff.

Microsoft could have done things differently. For example, the program's creators could have put in a command-line switch that would have forced the program to first overwrite each block with NULs before it was read back. Then, the program could have been modified so that it would display one of two different messages. The "ALL DATA … WILL BE LOST" message could have been used when the disk was actually overwritten, and a different message could have been used for the less severe option.

One reason that Microsoft's engineers may not have gone in this direction is that the hard drives that were sold in the 1980s generally came with their own separately packaged "disk utilities." Invariably, one of the "utilities" was a program that performed a so-called "low-level format" on the physical disk. The details of what a "low-level format" actually did varied from manufacturer to manufacturer and from drive to drive, but it generally was viewed as destroying all of the user-addressable information that the disk might contain. Mueller's 1991 book, *Que's Guide to Data Recovery*, noted that the key difference between a *low-level format* and a *high-level format* was that "you can recover data—unformat—from a high-level format."[10] Nevertheless, such knowledge did not diffuse into the general computer-user population.

It is incredibly misleading for an operating system to give the impression that all of the information has been removed from a disk when, in fact, the information has merely been made inaccessible to users who have not obtained special data recovery tools. Such a situation is an invitation for mishap: given a freshly formatted hard disk, there is no way for a user to audit the disk and determine if it is, in fact, clean, or if it has a treasure-trove of hidden, confidential information.

10 Scott Mueller with Alan C. Elliott, *Que's Guide to Data Recovery* (Que Corporation, 1991), 99.

Modern versions of the Windows FORMAT command also have the ability to "quick format" a disk, which omits the media scan step. In this case, the entire disk can be formatted in just a few seconds. When Microsoft created the "quick format" option, the company could have gone back and changed the behavior of FORMAT when the "quick" option wasn't selected. Ideally, a non-quick format would actually overwrite the data on the disk. This would have aligned once again the internal workings of the commands with the effects that are visible to the user. Unfortunately, Microsoft left the behavior of the command as it was.

## DELETE Doesn't Delete

Just as today's FORMAT command doesn't actually format disks, it turns out that commands for erasing individual files do not actually perform that function, either. Instead of overwriting the actual data, commands like DELETE and ERASE simply remove the entry in the file's containing directory and return the file's blocks to the free list. What happens after the file is deleted depends upon many factors, including the amount of free space on the disk and the system's pattern of usage.

Once again, the usability problem is that the operating system gives the user the *appearance* that the data has been removed from the computer when, in fact, the data has merely been made *inaccessible by ordinary means*. The usability problem for end users is compounded by the fact that there is no mention of this behavior in the Microsoft documentation. For example, the Windows built-in help for the DELETE command simply states that DEL "deletes one or more files."

As before, this systematic deception on the part of DELETE and ERASE wasn't exactly secret—a 1987 advertisement for the Mace Utilities appearing in *The New York Times* noted that the $59.95 program could "Unformat, Undelete, Diagnose & Remedy" and much more.[11] But mention that files could be undeleted did not appear in a feature article until 1990, and then only in Peter Lewis's "Executive Computer" column on the 11th page of the Business section of *The Times*.[12]

## A Taxonomy of Sanitized Recovered Data

Now we have an explanation for what happened to the data on Disk #70: the disk was formatted with the Windows FORMAT command before it was resold. Indeed, running the Unix strings(1) command over the disk's image file reveals many interesting things about the disk's previous owner, including the fact that the disk had a copy of IBM AntiVirus

---

11 Display Ad 57—No Title, *The New York Times* (Feb. 8, 1987), 57. An April 26, 1983 advertisement for the Norton Utilities fails to mention if the Norton's programs can undelete or unformat.

12 H. Peter Lewis, " 'Little Black Boxes' That Can Save a Hard Drive," *The New York Times* (April 29, 1990), F11.

Trial Edition installed (Example 15-1) and that the disk was used in some kind of medical application (Example 15-2). Additional investigation revealed that this disk had been used in a computer that belonged to a mail-order pharmacy.

*EXAMPLE 15-1. The contents of block #854420 from Disk #70*

```
Displaying block 854420
Notes to Users of IBM AntiVirus version 3.0 build 307..=======
=====================================....This file conta
ins important notes for all users of IBM AntiVirus,..including a
 summary of highlights in this release and last-minute..changes
to the printed documentation.  It is divided into these..section
s:....   Introduction..   Highlights of release 300..   Highligh
ts of release 301..   Highlights of release 302..   Highlights o
f build 304..   Highlights of build 306..   Highlights of build
```

*EXAMPLE 15-2. The contents of blocks 315782 and 315783 from Disk #70*

```
Displaying block 315782
*.......&@......u@.ALLERGY ALERT.......@.DPC5.......&@..... u@.D
RUG TO DRUG INTERACTION.......@.DPC4.......&@.....0u@.THERAPEUTI
C DUPLICATION.......@.DPC,.......&@.....@u@.HIGH DOSE ALERT.....
..@.DPC-.......&@.....Pu@.TOO EARLY REFILL.......@.DPC/........@
.....`u@.EXCESSIVE DURATION.......@.CMB=.......&@.....pu@ INFERR
ED DRUG DISEASE PRECAUTION.......@.DPC(.......&@......u@.DRUG GE
NDER.......@.DPCO.......&@......u@.DRUG AGE PRECAUTION.......@.D
PC+.......&@......u@.LOW DOSE ALERT.......@.DPC........*@.......
Displaying block 315783
 09/30/1981  03:00   DUPLICAT.ION
@.SUSPENDED LICENSE.......@.RTPO........@.......@.DIABETIC STRIP
S - C.......@.CMBO........@.......@.DIABETIC STRIPS - B.......@.
CMB7.......$@.......@.GENERIC PROD. SUBST-REFILL.......@.DAW>...
....$@.......@!GENERIC PROD. SUBST-NEW & REFILLS.......@.DAW;...
....&@......v@.BENEFICIARY NOT ELIGIBLE PRIME.......@.DPC2......
.O@.......@.MNFR. SPECIFIED ON RX.......@.NIS........&@..... v@.
DUPLICATION CLAIM.......@.DPC-.......&@.....Ov@.REQUIRES RECIEPT
.......@.DPC/.......&@.....@v@.DRUG NOT AVAILABLE.......@.DPC-..
```

In order to facilitate the discussion of sanitization tools and practices, Shelat and I created a *sanitization taxonomy* (see Table 15-1). Using this taxonomy to discuss Disk #70, we can say that the disk contained one Level 0 file (*COMMAND.COM*) and two Level 1 files (*IO.SYS* and *MSDOS.SYS*—both files that were "hidden") and approximately 508 MB of Level 3 data.

*TABLE 15-1. A sanitization taxonomy*

| Level | Type of data | Description |
|---|---|---|
| 0 | Regular files | Information contained within the filesystem. Includes filenames, file attributes, and file contents. By definition, there has been no attempt to sanitize the information that is contained within Level 0 files. Level 0 also includes information that is written to the disk as part of any sanitization attempt. For example, if a copy of Windows 95 is installed on a hard drive in an attempt to sanitize the drive, then the files contained within the *C:\WINDOWS* directory would be considered Level 0 files. No special tools are required to retrieve Level 0 data. |
| 1 | Temporary files | Temporary files, including print spooler files, browser cache files, files for "helper" applications, and files in "recycle bins." Most users either expect that these files will be deleted automatically in time or are not even aware that these files exist. |
| | | Note that Level 1 files are a subset of Level 0 files. Experience has shown that it is useful to distinguish this subset, because many naive users will overlook Level 1 files when they are browsing a computer's hard drive to see if it contains sensitive information. No special tools are required to retrieve Level 1 data, although special training is required so that the operator knows where to look. |
| 2 | Deleted files | When a file is deleted from a filesystem, most operating systems do not overwrite the blocks on the hard disk on which the file is written. Instead, they simply remove the reference to the file from the containing directory. The file's blocks are then placed on the free list. These files can be recovered using traditional "undelete" tools such as Norton Utilities. |
| 3 | Retained data blocks | Data that can be recovered from a disk but that does not obviously belong to a named file. Level 3 data includes information in slack space, swap space for virtual memory, and Level 2 data that has been partially overwritten so that an entire file cannot be recovered. |
| | | One common source of Level 3 data is disks that have been formatted with the Windows FORMAT command or the Unix newfs command. Even though these commands give the impression that they overwrite the entire hard drive, in fact they do not, and the vast majority of the information on a formatted disk can be recovered with Level 3 tools. |
| | | Level 3 data can be recovered using advanced data recovery tools that can "unformat'" a disk drive, and using special-purpose forensics tools. |
| 4 | Vendor-hidden data | This level consists of data blocks on the drive that can be accessed using only vendor-specific commands. This level includes the drive's controlling program, blocks used for bad-block management, and the Host Protected Area (HPA) of modern hard drives. |
| 5 | Overwritten data | Many individuals maintain that information can be recovered from a hard drive even after it is overwritten. Level 5 is reserved for such information. |

The combination of the taxonomy and the statistical analysis of the operational disks provides a simple answer to the questions posed earlier in this chapter. Although the disks that were purchased contained large amounts of personal information, most of this information consisted of Level 2 and Level 3 files: a casual examination of the disks showed disks that were either formatted or had the user files deleted, leaving only the program files. Most potential recipients of disks sold on the secondary market, lacking tools for accessing Level 2 and Level 3 information, probably never encounter the confidential information on disks that they purchase.

## DELETE DOESN'T DELETE BACKUPS, EITHER

There is another kind of data that the DELETE command doesn't delete: information stored on backup tapes. This point was made in a very public manner during the 1987 Congressional Iran-Contra hearings. Prior to the hearings, investigators had been able to reconstruct the Reagan Administration's illegal "arms-for-hostages" scheme by accessing stored email messages from the National Security Council's PROFS (Professional Office System) backup tapes. (The original messages had long since been deleted by staff members trying to cover their tracks.) As Lt. Colonel Oliver North stated during his congressional testimony, "We all sincerely believed that when we sent a PROFS message to another party and punched the button 'Delete' that it was gone forever. Wow, were we wrong."[a]

One way to deal with the problem of deleting information on backup tapes is to encrypt every file on the backup with a different key: when it is necessary to sanitize a file, the key can also be deleted. Of course, this contradicts the express purpose of backups: to enable information that is deleted accidentally to be recovered. Certainly, the key can be deleted after a waiting period of minutes or hours, but in some cases, organizations may simply not want to give individuals the ability to delete files from backups—this is a way to protect the organization against possibly hostile employees.

---

[a] National Public Radio news broadcasts (1992).

This answer was confirmed, in part, by a series of interviews conducted between December 2003 and October 2004 with the previous owners of 16 of the drives. In some cases (Drives #7, #11, #73, #74, #75, #77, #94, and #134), the organization had a procedure in place for sanitizing the drives, but that procedure was not sufficient to do the job. In other cases (Drives #21 and #44), there was no formal procedure in place. Many owners that were not sophisticated had trusted their reseller to perform the sanitization process—a trust that was betrayed (Drives #54, #193, and #205). In the remaining cases of drives that were traced back to their owners, no determination could be made (Drives #6 and #128).

## Related Work: Sanitization Standards, Software, and Practices

Confidential information that is stored on a computer system can be protected by numerous mechanisms, including operating system mechanisms, physical isolation of the computer system itself, and even the use of cryptography. The first two of these techniques fail when media is physically discarded: discarded media is, by definition, no longer contained within a protected perimeter. And once a disk or tape drive is removed from the computer on which it was created and is taken elsewhere, other operating systems are free to honor or ignore meta information such as file protection attributes. Only cryptographic measures survive when a disk is discarded. Yet experience has shown that many kinds of confidential information are not stored with encryption. Interestingly, the risk that confidential information could be released inadvertently on discarded media has been recognized since the 1960s.[13]

## DoD 5220.22-M

In the 1970s, each of the armed services adopted their own standards for sanitizing discarded media. These were combined into the unified Department of Defense standard 5220.22-M.[14] According to the standard, nonremovable rigid disks may be "cleared" simply by "overwrit[ing] all addressable locations with a single character," which is generally taken to mean writing an ASCII NUL onto all user-addressable locations. Sanitizing requires that the media be degaussed with a Type I or Type II degausser, that a three-pass sanitization process be implemented, or that the disk be physically destroyed—"disintegrate, incinerate, pulverize, shred, or melt."

DoD's three-pass procedure has been the subject of some debate. According to the standard, the procedure is: "Overwrite all locations with a character, its complement, then a random character and verify. THIS METHOD IS NOT APPROVED FOR SANITIZING MEDIA THAT CONTAINS TOP SECRET INFORMATION." [Emphasis in original.] This is normally implemented with the following algorithm:

1. Seed a cryptographically secure random number generator with a random seed R1.
2. Write the output of the generator to the entire disk.
3. Reseed the random number generator with the same seed R1.
4. Write the complement[15] of the generator's output to the entire disk.
5. Seed the generator with a new random seed R2.
6. Write the generator's output to the entire disk.
7. Reseed the random number generator with the seed R2.
8. Read the contents of the entire disk, verifying that the contents of each block match the output of the random number generator.

This process is designed to guard against a hard-disk drive that claims to be accepting write commands but that does not actually write data onto the disk.

There has been much debate as to why the standard's authors have taken such great pains to specify that this standard is not approved for sanitizing media that contains "top secret"

---

13 National Computer Security Center, *A Guide to Understanding Data Remanence in Automated Information Systems* (1991), NCSC-TG-025; *http://www.secinf.net/rainbow_series/NCSCTG025_Green_book_.html*.

14 U.S. Department of Defense, "Cleaning and Sanitization Matrix" (1995), DOS 5220-22-M; *http://www.dss.mil/isec/nispom_0195.htm*.

15 That is, for each output byte *d*, write the byte 255-*d*.

information. The implication is that organizations such as the National Security Agency have capabilities for recovering information that has been overwritten using this procedure. An alternative explanation is that the NSA does not possess this capability, and that the NSA doesn't want the targets of its collection efforts to employ 5220-22-M to sanitize *their media*!

Peter Gutmann explored the issue of recovering overwritten information in his 1996 USENIX paper, "Secure Deletion of Data from Magnetic and Solid-State Memory." Gutmann notes that it should be possible to recover information that has been overwritten once or twice—or possibly even more times—depending on the particular recording technology in question. For example, when a 1 is written over a 0, the resulting magnetic field sensed by the read head is going to be different from when a 1 is written over a 1. Gutmann then presents a variety of patterns for overwriting data that are designed to interact with various recording schemes used by different generations of disk drives. In total, 35 different patterns are presented, covering several generations of disk-drive technology.

Surprisingly, a few developers of sanitization tools have adopted all 35 patterns, writing one after the other. Gutmann sneered at this misreading of his paper, and added this postscript to the online version:

> "In the time since this paper was published, some people have treated the 35-pass overwrite technique described in it more as a kind of voodoo incantation to banish evil spirits than the result of a technical analysis of drive encoding techniques. As a result, they advocate applying the voodoo to PRML and EPRML drives even though it will have no more effect than a simple scrubbing with random data. In fact, performing the full 35-pass overwrite is pointless for any drive since it targets a blend of scenarios involving all types of (normally used) encoding technology, which covers everything back to 30+-year-old MFM methods (if you don't understand that statement, reread the paper). If you're using a drive which uses encoding technology X, you only need to perform the passes specific to X, and you never need to perform all 35 passes. For any modern PRML/EPRML drive, a few passes of random scrubbing is the best you can do. As the paper says, 'A good scrubbing with random data will do about as well as can be expected.' This was true in 1996, and is still true now."

It is readily apparent that overwriting provides sufficient sanitization for the vast majority of computer users. Yet overwriting has not been built into operating systems until very recently, and even current operating systems do not implement it in a uniform or even consistent manner. This creates profound usability problems: not only does the computer user need to understand that the deleted files aren't actually deleted, but also the user must obtain and use specially written software to properly sanitize his media if he wishes to discard it without risk.

The remainder of this section discusses a variety of techniques that have been developed to allow end users to overwrite data—either selectively or across an entire drive.

# CRYPTOGRAPHIC APPROACHES

Cryptography provides one of the simplest and possibly the best way to handle the problem of data passed. If information is simply encrypted when it is written to a disk and decrypted when it is read back from the disk, then a disk can be sanitized simply by throwing away the cryptographic key in question.

One of the simplest ways to encrypt data on a disk is to use a cryptographic filesystem. Such filesystems can operate on a file-by-file basis, as is the case with Matt Blaze's Cryptographic File System[a] and Microsoft's Encrypted File System, or they can operate on individual blocks, as is the case with PGP:Disk.

Another approach is to use an active hardware device that sits between the computer and the hard disk. Such devices have been made by a variety of manufacturers for both tape drives and disk drives.

The cryptographic approach has also been applied to the problem of email sanitization. The system, developed in the 1990s by a company that was coyly known as Disappearing Ink, turned ordinary HTML email into JavaScript-enabled email that contained a small decryption engine and a block of encrypted data. Each message would have a certain date, $D$, after which it could not be read. When the engine was run by the receiving mail client, the engine would download the decryption key for day $D$ from the Internet and, if the key was still available, decrypt the message. Disappearing Ink promised that on day $D+1$, it would delete the key for day $D$. The Disappearing Ink system couldn't protect against printouts or malicious pastings of the message text into an ordinary word processor, but it did provide a system whereby cooperating email partners could assure that all copies of messages in their control (including copies on backup tapes) would be deleted after a certain date.

All of the schemes discussed in this section rely on the ability to delete a key properly. Deleting keys may be difficult in practice, a problem discussed by both Crescenzo et al.[b] and Gutmann.[c]

---

[a] Matt Blaze, "A Cryptographic File System for Unix," *1st ACM Conference on Communications and Computing Security* (Nov. 1993), 9–16.

[b] Giovanni Di Crescenzo, Niels Fergurson, Russell Impagliazzo, and Markus Jakobsson, "How to Forget a Secret," *16th International Symposium on Theoretical Aspects of Computer Science (STACS '99)* (Springer Verlag, 1999), 500-509; *http://www.macfergus.com/niels/pubs/forget.html*.

[c] Peter Gutmann, "Secure Deletion of Data from Magnetic and Solid-State Memory," *Sixth USENIX Security Symposium Proceedings* (1996); *http://www.cs.auckland.ac.nz/~pgut001/pubs/secure_del.html*.

## Add-On Software

Although sanitization has not been built into operating systems until recently, third-party and add-on programs to perform some kind of overwriting have been available for personal computers for more than two decades. Programs have emerged to target all manner of data on a hard drive:

*Existing files (Level 0 and Level 1 data)*

Programs such as Norton Disk Doctor, PGP, and the Linux `shred` command have the ability to delete specific files securely. These features typically are implemented by opening the disk file through the operating system, seeking to the beginning of the file, and repeatedly issuing the `write( )` system call.

*Free blocks (Level 2 and Level 3 data)*

A program can sanitize the contents of blocks on the free list using two approaches. The easiest technique is for the program to open a file for writing and write to the file until the file fills the entire disk. The operating system necessarily allocates most or all of the disk's available free space to the new file. A problem with this approach is that the computer necessarily spends some time with no free disk space available; this can impact normal operations. A second problem is that it does not overwrite files that are small enough to be stored in the Windows MFT or in the Unix inode. Nevertheless, Microsoft's *CIPHER.EXE*, distributed with the Windows operating system, uses this technique to sanitize blocks on the free list.

A second technique is to have a program that understands the computer's filesystem open the raw disk device, interrogate the list of free blocks, and systematically overwrite the contents of each block on the free list. The advantage of this technique is that it does not compromise the computer's "free space," but this technique requires much closer integration with the computer's operating system. This approach should not be employed on a disk that is actually in use by the filesystem.

*Slack space (Level 3 data)*

Although disk drives typically write data in 512-byte blocks, many operating systems allocate storage in clusters that consist of two, four, eight, or more blocks. If a file consists of only a few bytes, it is not uncommon for an operating system to write only the first block of the cluster and leave the rest with their previous contents: this is both a performance optimization, because it takes less time to write one block than four, and a memory optimization, because the data written to the disk needs to come from somewhere. The unused blocks at the end of the cluster are frequently referred to as *slack space*. They can contain the contents of older files that have long since been deleted.

*The entire disk (Level 1, 2, and 3)*

A number of programs simply overwrite the contents of the entire disk. These programs typically are run from bootable floppy disks or CD-ROMs and are typified by DBAN (Dirk's Boot and Nuke).

Add-on programs are not without their risks: a poorly written program that reads and writes directly to the disk without going through the operating system risks corrupting the entire volume. Programs that go through the operating system run the risk that there may be a mismatch between the primitives that the operating system offers to programs and the way those abstractions are implemented on the actual disk surface. For example, a user who types `pgp -w` *filename* to erase the contents of *filename* on a journaling filesystem may be surprised to learn that data that "overwrites" may actually be written to another location of the disk. That's because journaling systems write modifications to an expanding journal, instead of modifying data that is stored in place, to protect the filesystem against inadvertent corruption that might occur if the computer fails during a disk write.

Another risk of add-on programs is that they may not actually perform the way that they claim to. Although users would certainly notice and complain about a program that was advertised to sanitize slack space but that actually overwrote Level 0 files, a program that overwrote only the first few bytes of a file being "wiped" would not be so easy to detect. Indeed, for several years, the Linux *wipe* command did just that.

But the biggest risk of relying on add-on programs, quite simply, is that users do not know that they exist. Driving this point home, a proactive white paper written by Guidance Software, evaluating the Windows *CIPHER.EXE* program, concludes:

> **Results**: All unallocated space was filled with random values (which greatly affected file compression in the evidence file); however, the cipher tool affected only the unallocated clusters and a very small portion of the MFT [Master File Table]; 10–15 records were overwritten in the MFT, and the majority of the records marked for deletion went untouched). The utility does not affect other items of evidentiary interest on the typical NTFS partition, such as: file slack, registry files, the pagefile, and file shortcuts.
>
> In terms of its anticipated end-user adoption, the cipher feature is a burdensome command-line utility that is difficult to find and operate. Notably, the cipher function is available on the Professional version, but not included in the Home version of XP and Windows 2000. Despite some speculation, the function is not set by default or even selected for repeated execution on an ongoing basis. The cipher must be executed from a command line each time the user wants to employ it. There is very little documentation supporting this feature, which is largely intended for programmers and system administrators for use in limited circumstances.[16]

Once again, usability is compromised because of an underlying failure in the operating system: not only does the user need to know that he must obtain a special sanitization program, but he also needs to be sure that the program works as advertised. Unlike a word processor or a spreadsheet, it is remarkably difficult for a user to test a sanitization program to determine if it is functioning properly.

## Operating System Modifications

An alternative to third-party sanitization tools is to have sanitization technology embedded directly into the computer's applications and operating system. Arguably this is where they belong, on the grounds of both usability and correctness. Certainly usability is enhanced when the operating system provides for proper sanitization of media that potentially has confidential information. Correctness is also furthered, because an implementation of sanitization within the operating system should take into account any implementation peculiarities (such as journaling filesystems) that might be hidden to the application program but that are relevant to the sanitization process.

---

16 Kimberly Stone and Richard Keightley, "Can Computer Investigations Survive Windows XP?", (Guidance Software, 2003); *http://www.guidancesoftware.com/corporate/whitepapers/downloads/XPwhitepaper.pdf.*

For example, version 0.4 of the Linux ext2fs filesystem introduced the concept of the per-file s attribute. Set with the chattr command, any file with the s attribute set was overwritten with ASCII NULs when the file was unlinked. Remy Card's implementation was quite simple—only four places in the ext2fs source code needed to be modified to handle the secure deletion attribution.[17]

Card's implementation was certainly open to criticism: blocks were overwritten only once, not three times or more. And because the write was only scheduled, there was a chance that a block queued for being overwritten might not actually get overwritten at all —the system might crash, or the blocks might be reallocated to another file and the confidential information might end up in the slack space at the end of a file. In any event, the code for "secure deletion" was removed from ext2fs in the Linux 2.2 kernel, apparently for performance reasons.

It's interesting to note that even though the Linux 2.2 kernel dropped the actual secure deletion, the s attribute can still be set by the chattr command. Doing so, however, no longer does anything! Adding to the confusion is the fact that the chattr command's documentation still discusses the s, c (automatic compression), and u (allow undeletion) attributes, but notes at the bottom:

```
BUGS AND LIMITATIONS
        As  of Linux 2.2, the 'c', 's',  and 'u' attribute are not
        honored by the kernel filesystem code.   These attributes
        will be implemented in a future ext2 fs version.
```

Here, then, is another example of the disconnect between usability and security caused by poor programming and visibility, rather than an inherent disconnect between the two. Does the phrase "not honored by the kernel filesystem code" mean that secure deletion happens somewhere else, or that it doesn't happen at all? The only way for an expert user to know is to inspect both the source code and a running system. The only way for a novice user to know is to ask an expert.

Others have reimplemented secure deletion for Linux, but these modifications have not been incorporated into the mainstream Linux kernel. Bauer and Priyantha[18] describe a modification to the Linux operating system to support secure deletion using the very same attribute bits developed by Card. Instead of implementing secure deletion directly in the unlink( ) system call, the implementation uses a scheduled kernel process. Unfortunately, this code was not integrated into the mainstream Linux kernel, and it can no longer be integrated because the Linux kernel has continued to evolve.

Following the publication of the "Remembrance of Data Passed" paper, Apple Computer added a Secure Empty Trash function to the Finder component of its Mac OS. According

17 Remy Card, "Announce 0.4" (Oct. 7, 1996); *http://www.ibiblio.org/pub/historic-linux/ftp-archives/tsx-11.mit.edu/Oct-07-1996/packages/ext2fs/old/announce.0.4*.

18 Steven Bauer and Nissanka B. Priyantha, "Secure Data Deletion for Linux File Systems," *Proceedings of the 10th USENIX Security Symposium* (2001), 153–164.

to interviews conducted with Apple's security group on January 12, 2003, the security group had long wanted to put a secure delete-file function in the operating system's interface: such efforts had been deemed by Apple's management to be not a priority until the "Remembrance" paper was published.

Like the Windows Recycle Bin, the Macintosh Trash is actually a special directory that is managed by the graphical file manager (which Apple calls the Finger). Dragging a file to the Trash moves the file to this special directory. Emptying the Trash causes all of the files in the directory to be unlinked with the `unlink( )` system call. Choosing the Secure Empty Trash feature, added by Apple in Mac OS 10.3, causes the contents of the files to be overwritten before they are unlinked.

The Mac OS 10.3 interface is subtle in the way that it informs the user of the difference between Empty Trash and Secure Empty Trash. Choosing either option from the Finder menu causes an alert panel asking for confirmation to appear. The wording on the Empty Trash panel states:

> Are you sure you want to remove the items in the Trash permanently?
>
> You cannot undo this action.

In contrast, the wording on the Secure Empty Trash panel states:

> Are you sure you want to remove the items in the Trash permanently using Secure Empty Trash?
>
> If you choose Secure Empty Trash, you cannot recover the files.

What is the difference between an operation that cannot be undone and one that cannot be recovered from? The answer is found in the Finder's Help system when one types in Secure Empty Trash.

> Even after emptying the trash, deleted files may still be recovered using special data-recovery software. To delete files so that they cannot be recovered, choose Finder → Secure Empty Trash. Files deleted in this way are overwritten completely by meaningless data. This may take some time, depending on the size of the file. You may want to use Secure Empty Trash if you sell or give away your computer.

Although this author finds it personally rewarding that a paper published in January 2003 would result in a significant modification to an operating system used by tens of millions of people in less than a year's time, there is much to critique in Apple's initial implementation of Secure Empty Trash from a usability perspective:

- Because Secure Empty Trash is such a slow procedure, it seems that it would be advantageous to be able to specify files to be erased securely on a file-by-file basis. However, there is no way to make such distinctions.

- Likewise, there is no way to securely erase a specific file but leave the other files in the Trash untouched. This poses an inconvenience to users who habitually keep hundreds or thousands of files in their Trash directories and who wish to securely delete a single file from time to time. (There is a rather straightforward, albeit annoying, workaround for this problem: simply move all of the files that are in the Trash into a second, temporary directory, leaving behind the files to be sanitized. Choose Secure Empty Trash. Finally, move the files from the temporary directory back into the Trash.)

- If the user inadvertently chooses Empty Trash… rather than Secure Empty Trash, there is no way to go back and securely overwrite the disk blocks once the files have been unlinked from the Trash directory.

- Implementing Secure Empty Trash in the Finder, rather than in the operating system's kernel, means that there is no way to securely delete files that are deleted by programs other than the Finder (e.g., using rm or Emacs). Likewise, the contents of temporary files that are created and then deleted will not be sanitized.

- There is no way to remove from a disk the information that was contained in files that have been "overwritten" using the Save As… feature of many document-based applications. That's because Save As is implemented by a four-step process that involves saving the requested file to a temporary file, renaming the file to be overwritten to a temporary name, renaming the new file to the final destination filename, and finally *unlinking* the file being "overwritten." In this way, no data is lost if the computer fails during the procedure. Unfortunately, the interface promises that the new file will "overwrite" the original file, as demonstrated in Figure 15-1.

*FIGURE 15-1. This pop-up window is displayed when an existing file is specified using the Save As? command; Mac OS 10.3 promises that the new file will "overwrite [the] current contents" of the file being replaced; in fact, Mac OS does not overwrite the file: it saves the new file to a temporary location, renames the original file to a temporary filename, renames the new file to the original filename, and then uses the unlink() system call to delete the original file*

- Finally, by the time you are thinking of selling or giving away your computer, it's too late! The files have already been unlinked and can no longer be "securely emptied!"

Apple's implementation of Secure Empty Trash has the look of a quick hack—it adds functionality without properly integrating that functionality into the user experience. Indeed, the very user interface is inconsistent: the menu item Empty Trash… appears with a trailing ellipsis, indicating that choosing the command will bring up another window, while the menu item Secure Empty Trash appears without an ellipsis. Meanwhile, the context-sensitive menu on the Trash Can icon was not modified between Mac OS 10.2 and Mac OS 10.3 to reflect the new functionality: a user who *only* empties the trash by using the context-sensitive menu might miss the new functionality in the operating system. Both of these user interface errors are shown in Figure 15-2.

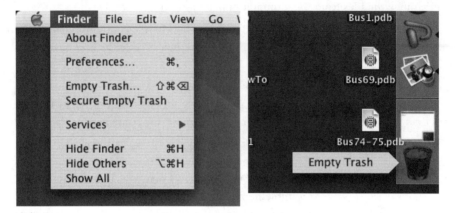

FIGURE 15-2. Modifications to the Mac OS 10.3 user interface to support the Secure Empty Trash command were inconsistent and applied haphazardly

While Apple should be commended for making an attempt to address the issue of file-by-file sanitization, the company has not lived up to its reputation of interface thoughtfulness, consistency, and user experience. Apple needs to rethink its implementation of file sanitization and come up with a new interface that both is easier to use and promotes improved security. Thoughts on such an interface are presented in the next section.

## Moving Forward: A Plan for Clean Computing

Although the need for proper sanitization of magnetic recording media has long been recognized as a serious issue for computer security practitioners, the problem has traditionally been addressed through the use of add-on software or physical destruction of the media itself. Only recently has the question of sanitization been addressed by computer operating system vendors themselves, and in the cases that we have considered, both Microsoft and Apple have addressed it poorly.

Some researchers have told me that operating system developers did not deploy sanitizing file deletion in the 1970s and 1980s so that accidentally deleted files could be recovered using special tools. I have looked and have found no evidence to support this claim. Indeed, had recoverability of accidentally deleted data been a goal, companies like Microsoft and Apple would have distributed such tools themselves—either as part of their operating system offerings or as aftermarket additions. (DOS 5.0 included an UNFORMAT command-line utility that could, in some cases, recover a volume that had been formatted inadvertently. But this looks like an after-the-fact attempt to make use of a DOS 2.0 idiosyncrasy, rather than an intentional design attribute that was put into DOS 2.0 and realized only when DOS 5.0 finally shipped.)

Instead, it seems that the lack of a sanitizing delete-file is a historical accident. The first multiuser computer systems did not need a sanitizing delete because of the ways in which they were operated. The developers of the Compatible Time Sharing System (CTSS) at MIT in the 1960s did not consider the problem of sanitizing disk blocks after deleting files because the computer system frequently ran with disks that were full or nearly full: blocks that were freed were quickly overwritten with new data.[19] The CTSS disk drives were rented from IBM and, thus, were never offered on the secondary market. Indeed, the real data security problem was not that data on a disk returned for service might be sent accidentally to another IBM customer—the real problem was trying to keep data on the disks that were having head crashes every few days! In any event, while there was a general belief that CTSS should prevent one user from crashing a program being run by another user, overall the system did not have strong internal disclosure controls: the developers did not believe that CTSS was secure enough to store sensitive information.

Internal security between users was a design goal of the Multics operating system. But Multics did not have files as we know them today. Instead, it had named memory segments that could be created, placed in a hierarchical filesystem, and extended as needed. When a process created a new segment, the disk blocks for that segment were cleared (that is, overwritten with NULs) *when the segment was allocated*. Thus, there was no need to overwrite the blocks when the segment was erased. Clearing on allocation doesn't solve the data remanence problem, but that problem applies to both deleted and undeleted information. If a Multics disk was decommissioned, the system's operators would have understood the importance of erasing all of the information from the device.

Unix was developed in a research environment in which security was not a priority: when Unix first transitioned into the commercial world, it ran on large systems that were run by trained system operators who, presumably, were aware of the sanitization issue. Although Unix provided no tools for sanitizing disks, the dd command did an excellent job, as previously noted.

In the world of PC operating systems, an overwriting delete would have caused significant performance degradation (similar to Mac OS 10.3's Secure File Delete) on any operating system that did not have asynchronous access to the filesystem and disk device. Windows did not have such capabilities until 32-bit clean disk drivers were available under Windows 95 and NT. Apple did not have such capabilities until it migrated to Mac OS X.

Today, matters have changed. Unlike the systems of the 1960s and 1970s, most of today's desktop computers spend most of their time idle. Likewise, many—perhaps most—of today's desktop computers are not managed by professional IT staffs that are aware of the sanitization problem. What is needed, then, is some straightforward way to add a sanitizing delete-file function.

19 Jerome Saltzer, "Re: sanitizing delete file," personal communication (Dec. 2004).

Although a simple approach would be to resurrect Bauer and Priyantha's Linux implementation, I believe that this is only half of the story. Although it's good for overwriting to happen asynchronously with other activities, bringing truth to the phrase "rm is forever" is not a particularly user-friendly way to move forward. Many usability experts have noted that humans make frequent mistakes; simply adding a warning box saying something to the effect that "rm deletes all of your files" not a particularly strong barrier to improper use.

An alternative construct would be to remove the Empty Trash and Secure Empty Trash commands in the Macintosh user interface and replace them with a new command: Shred Trash. Executing this command would perform much the same function as the Secure Empty Trash, except that the overwriting would be performed asynchronously. There are two advantages to this approach:

- The term *Shredder* is superior to Secure Empty Trash because most people know what a paper shredder does; most people do not know what it means to securely empty trash. Thus, less initial user education would be required.

- Because the shredding would be performed asynchronously, there would be no perceived penalty for using the feature.

The second change required is to allow the user to create rules that specify conditions under which the contents of the Trash directory are shredded automatically. Typical rules might include:

- Shred any file that has been in the Trash more than 30 days.

- Shred all files in the Trash when the user clicks the "Shred all files now" button.

- Shred all files in the trash at 7:00 a.m. every day.

- If a file is selected and the user chooses the Shred command from the File menu:
  - — If the file is not in the Trash directory, move the file to the Trash directory and schedule for it to be shredded in 5 minutes.
  - — If the file is in the Trash directory, shred it immediately.

These rules give users a chance to change their minds (as recommended by Cooper[20]), but nevertheless provide for the possibility of immediate shredding, should such an action be necessary. Figure 15-3 shows a hypothetical user interface to implement this rule set.

The third change required is to change the semantics of the POSIX unlink( ) system call, so that calling unlink( ) on a file has the effect of moving that file to the user's Trash, instead of actually releasing the blocks. Such a move, while drastic, would overcome the problems

---

20 Alan Cooper, *The Inmates are Running The Asylum: Why High-Tech Products Drive Us Crazy and How to Restore the Sanity* (Sams Publishing: 1999).

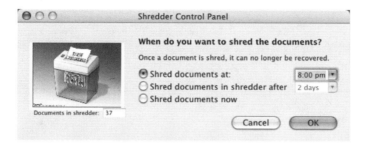

*FIGURE 15-3. Hypothetical design of a Shredder rules interface (Icon by Danziger, used with permission.)*

that arise when a file is deleted by an application other than the Finder. This approach would also handle the problem discussed earlier with the Save As command.

A naïve implementation of this third recommendation would degrade system performance dramatically. This is because many small files are constantly being created and deleted on a typical computer system. But temporary files still need to be sanitized. Moving them to a shredder—perhaps with a tag that marks them for "immediate" shredding—assures that this will happen. The files can then be shredded in the background when the computer is not otherwise in use. For servers and computers that are *constantly* in use, the computer's filesystem can simply use disk blocks in the shredder and marked for shredding as a convenient source of new blocks when they are needed for writing out new files. This would effectively sanitize the blocks in the same manner as blocks were sanitized on CTSS back in the 1960s.

## Acknowledgments

The credit card numbers in the forensics study were found using a program written by Abhi Shelat. David Clark and Ron Rivest provided much support, suggestions, and guidance on the original forensics study, as did Brian Carrier, Peter Gutmann, Rich Mahn, Eric Thompson, and Wietse Venema. Matthew Geiger and Lorrie Cranor provided useful comments on an earlier draft of this chapter.

## About the Author

Simson Garfinkel has been working in the field of computer security since 1986. He recently completed his dissertation on patterns and principles for aligning usability and security at MIT and is now a postdoctoral fellow at Harvard University's Center for Research on Computation and Society.

*http://www.simson.net/*

# CHAPTER SIXTEEN

# Making the Impossible Easy: Usable PKI

DIRK BALFANZ, GLENN DURFEE, AND D. K. SMETTERS

THE WIDESPREAD PERCEPTION THAT USABILITY AND SECURITY ARE AT ODDS WITH ONE ANOTHER OFTEN leads systems designers to shun powerful security technologies. A quintessential example is provided by public key infrastructure (PKI) technology: despite the high degree of security PKI technology can provide, designers frequently avoid this technology because of its notoriously complex deployment and the incomprehensibility of such an infrastructure to end users.

This chapter explains how by designing usability in from the start, one can make PKI-based systems easy to deploy and use. The resulting systems, however, are not large, general-purpose infrastructures, but PKIs that are small, dedicated, easy to set up, and application specific. We refer to these as *instant PKIs* (iPKIs). Several case studies illustrate interaction paradigms for building such usable, secure iPKIs.

## Public Key Infrastructures

Before the invention of public key cryptography, methods for secure digital communications were all but unavailable to mainstream computer users. The reason for this was the difficult problem of *key distribution*: for Alice to send a secure message to Bob, they first would have to agree on a shared secret (e.g., a key or password). The only way to do this would be for Alice (or Bob, or a third party) to generate such a key and then deliver that key to Bob (or Alice, or both). While in transit, the key not only had to be kept secret but also had to be protected from tampering.

Once Alice and Bob shared a secret key, Alice could do two things: first, she could *encrypt* messages with the shared key and be sure that only Bob would be able to read those messages. Second, if Bob used a *message authentication code*, Alice could be convinced that those messages indeed came from Bob and nobody else. Because Alice and Bob both used the same key, and because this key was used for both encryption and decryption, this kind of cryptography is usually called *symmetric key cryptography*.

Public key cryptography makes the key distribution problem much easier. Bob generates a *key pair* consisting of a *private key* and a *public key*. Now, all Alice needs to do is obtain a copy of Bob's public key. As the name suggests, a public key does not need to be kept secret. For example, people could publish their public keys in a central database. Alice would then simply connect to that database and request Bob's public key to be able to communicate with Bob securely. Again, this allows two different things: first, by encrypting messages with Bob's public key, which can only be decrypted using Bob's private key, Alice can ensure that only Bob can read them. Second, by using Bob's public key to verify a *digital signature* on a message, Alice can be convinced that the message indeed came from Bob—such a signature can only be created using Bob's private key.

How does Alice know that the public key she requests from the central database is indeed Bob's (and hasn't been tampered with while in transit to Alice)? *Certification authorities* (CAs) solve this problem, and also get around scalability issues with the central database. A certification authority digitally signs a statement consisting of Bob's public key together with an assertion that this key belongs to someone named "Bob." This signed statement is called a *certificate*. We assume that everybody knows the certification authority's public key. (In practice, these public keys today are part of operating system distributions such as Microsoft's Windows or Apple's Mac OS.) Using the certification authority's public key, Alice can now verify Bob's certificate, no matter where she obtained it. If the name on the certificate is indeed Bob's, and the certification authority's signature indeed verifies, Alice can be sure that she is now in possession of an authentic copy of Bob's public key.

Certification authorities can also issue certificates for *intermediate certification authorities*, which in turn issue digital certificates either to further intermediate CAs, or to *end entities* such as Bob. A hierarchical arrangement of certification authorities and end entities to allow certification of public keys is called a *public key infrastructure* (PKI).

Public key infrastructures have a number of advantages:

- Participants in the PKI can generate their keys independently of the parties with whom they want to communicate: new keys do not need to be generated and shared for every private communication desired.

- Public keys do not need to be kept secret. This vastly simplifies the key distribution problem.

- To ensure authenticity of public keys as they are passed around among members of the PKI, a certification authority issues public key certificates that include both a member's public key and some identifying attributes such as the member's name. Every member is assumed to trust the certification authority and know the CA's public key.

- Once the certificates are issued, any two members of a PKI can establish a secure connection without anybody else's help. They use *public key protocols* to ensure the integrity and secrecy of messages.

These are just the most important advantages of public key infrastructures, as compared to shared key systems. There are many more details and subtleties to PKIs that cannot be covered in this short introduction. What is important to remember is that these are not simply theoretical ideas. The concepts of public key cryptography and public key infrastructures have been implemented, and many implementations follow established standards. For example, we can use *X.509*[1] certificates to exchange public keys, and can use public key protocols such as *Secure Sockets Layer*[2] (SSL) or *Transport Layer Security*[3] (TLS) to secure communication between web browsers and web servers.

## Problems with Public Key Infrastructures

PKI technology was originally designed to be deployed globally. The idea was to have a single certificate infrastructure in which all users and devices would participate. Despite all the advantages of such a system, this has proven impractical: the amount of coordination and trust required to establish a global infrastructure is enormous, and no one has been able to do it in the 25 years since a global PKI was originally proposed.

Apart from such political problems, usability—or, rather, a lack of usability—is the main reason for the failure of public key infrastructures. Usability issues hamper PKI deployment even at much smaller scales, such as within a single company or within a supply chain. Here is a list of usability problems that people are confronted with when trying to use a PKI:

- Users don't have an intuitive understanding of public key cryptography. A study conducted by Whitten *et al.* shows that users have trouble understanding the difference between public and private keys, as well as the role that certificates play.[4] There is no intuitive model that explains the security properties of a PKI. (In contrast, in the physical world, we understand that, say, those who have the key to our house can open the front door.)

---

1  R. Housley, W. Ford, W. Polk, and D. Solo, "Internet X.509 Public Key Infrastructure Certificate and CRL Profile," IETF—Network Working Group, The Internet Society, RFC 2459 (Jan. 1999).

2  Alan O. Freier, Philip Karlton, and Paul C. Kocher, "The SSL Protocol Version 3.0," IETF—Transport Layer Security Working Group, The Internet Society (Nov. 1996).

3  T. Dierks and C. Allen, "The TLS Protocol Version 1.0," IETF—Network Working Group, The Internet Society, RFC 2246 (Jan. 1999).

4  Alma Whitten and J. D. Tygar, "Why Johnny Can't Encrypt: A Usability Evaluation of PGP 5.0," *Proceedings of the 8th USENIX Security Symposium* (1999), 169–184. See also Chapter 34, this volume.

- Users don't understand the connection between the PKI and the application goal they are trying to achieve. For example, the application goal might be to send a confidential email message. It is not clear to the average user what this has to do with certification authorities, key pairs, etc. Lamentably, the standard practice of reusing certificates across applications ensures that users will be exposed to gory PKI details: they must configure their applications to use certificates, understand when to request and how to install certificates, and so on.

- Not only do users not understand why they need certificates in the first place, but tasks such as requesting and installing certificates are often too cumbersome[5, 6] (see the sidebar, "Case Study: Traditional PKI Deployment for an Enterprise Wireless Network").

- As mentioned earlier, certificates often attest that a certain public key belongs to a certain name (usually referred to as *identity certificates*), as names are considered easier for users to work with. However, in large PKIs , this changes the problem of finding the correct certificate for someone into a naming problem (e.g., knowing the "John Smith" in marketing from the one in accounting). It also means that for a CA to issue a certificate to the "right" person, it must have the ability to tell that the recipient is indeed the rightful owner of a particular name, not just a particular key pair.

As a result, organizations simply don't even bother issuing certificates to end users, limiting the use of certificates to servers that have been painstakingly configured by trained administrators.

## Making PKI Usable

Can PKI technology be made usable? The following examples argue strongly that with new approaches to design, it is possible to build "instant" public key infrastructures that are both easy to use and, through the use of public key cryptography, highly secure.

### Case Study: "Network-in-a-Box"

Wireless local area networks are becoming increasingly popular in homes and small offices. Unfortunately, such networks have been subject to a number of high-profile security problems, leaving users' machines vulnerable to attackers—not only those on their block, but also those accessing their network from quite a distance using high-gain antennas. Such networks can be secured, using new standards. However, the more secure the network, the more difficult it usually is to set up and configure (see the following sidebar for an example).

---

5   P. Doyle and S. Hanna, "Analysis of June 2003 Survey on Obstacles to PKI Deployment and Usage" (2003); *www.oasis-open.org/committees/pki/pkiobstaclesjune2003surveyreport.pdf*.

6   P. Gutmann, "Plug-and-Play PKI: A PKI Your Mother Can Use," *Proc. 12th USENIX Security Symposium* (2003), 45–58.

# CASE STUDY: TRADITIONAL PKI DEPLOYMENT FOR AN ENTERPRISE WIRELESS NETWORK

When we set up a wireless local area network (WLAN) at the Palo Alto Research Center (PARC), we opted for a PKI-based solution. This promised better security and better ease of use than a password-based system. The idea was to give each of about 200 users an X.509 certificate and to use the 802.1x wireless standard's *Extensible Authentication Protocol* in TLS mode (802.1x EAP-TLS[a, b]) to authenticate to the wireless network.[c] Users requested and retrieved their certificates via a fairly automated, standard web-based interface, and configured their devices via the GUI-based 802.1x configuration software supplied with Microsoft Windows XP. To help users enroll, our administrators produced an elaborate set of instructions.

We studied eight subjects' experiences enrolling in the wireless PKI. Our subjects were sophisticated computer users, typically holding Ph.D.s in computer science. Despite using the GUI-based interface for enrollment and configuration of their machines, the process involved a total of 38 distinct steps. Each of these presented an opportunity for end users to make frustrating mistakes. The average time that it took them to request and retrieve their certificate and then configure their system was 140 minutes.[d]

Almost all of the subjects printed the instructions, and even those determined to understand what they were doing soon began following the instructions mechanically. In the end, many test subjects described enrollment as the most difficult computer task that PARC had ever asked them to do. All subjects had little idea of precisely what they had done to their computers. Several commented that if something were to go wrong, they could not perform even basic troubleshooting. For several subjects, this was the first time that they had ever experienced the inability to administer their own machines. Ironically, while PKI technology may have secured their machines for wireless use, it simultaneously reduced these end users' ability to configure and maintain their own machines.

---

[a] B. Aboba and D. Simon, "PPP EAP TLS Authentication Protocol (EAP-TLS)," IETF RFC 2716 (Oct. 1999); *http://www.ietf.org/rfc/rfc2716.txt.*

[b] ANSI/IEEE Std. 802.1x, Port-Based Network Access Control, IEEE (2001).

[c] D. Balfanz, G. Durfee, R. Grinter, and D. Smetters, "In Search of Usable Security—Five Lessons from the Field," *IEEE Security & Privacy* 2:5 (Sept./Oct. 2004).

[d] Dirk Balfanz, Glenn Durfee, R.E. Grinter, D.K. Smetters, and Paul Stewart, "Network-in-a-Box: How to Set up a Secure Wireless Network in under a Minute," *Proceedings of the 13th USENIX Security Symposium* (2004), 207–221.

A recent study investigates how to build a wireless network that is extremely easy to set up and that, at the same time, provides the strongest grade of wireless security currently available. The authors of the study call their system a "Network-in-a-Box" (NiaB).[7]

---

7   Balfanz *et al.*, "Network-in-a-Box."

This high level of security is provided by the 802.1x protocol,[8] which authenticates each wireless client before it can access the network, and then provides them with encryption keys that change rapidly and automatically to protect their data. Networks that use 802.1x ask clients to authenticate themselves using a choice of mechanisms. The most secure of these is a protocol called EAP-TLS,[9] which asks clients and the wireless infrastructure to mutually authenticate each other using digital certificates via the standard TLS[10] key exchange protocol. Deploying such a network means setting up a certification authority and an authentication infrastructure, and issuing certificates to each new client. As the example in the earlier sidebar shows, this is extremely difficult in an enterprise staffed by professional administrators. It is normally inconceivable for an average home user.

What was needed was a small-scale PKI (an instant PKI), one that covered a single wireless network and its clients, and one that could be configured and set up automatically. Users also needed a secure way to indicate which clients should be able to join that network, and a way to automatically have those clients obtain a certificate and be set up to use it.

The NiaB access point (NiaB AP), shown in Figure 16-1, is the solution to these problems. It provides a complete 802.1x-secured wireless network.[11] Clients who want to enroll in that network run a small enrollment application. In addition to being an access point, the NiaB AP has the authentication services necessary to support 802.1x, a certification authority to issue certificates to wireless clients, and an enrollment component (described later) to add new clients to its network securely. When the NiaB AP is switched on for the first time, it configures itself automatically. The access point component chooses a wireless network name and channel. The CA component generates a root key pair and root certificate. The NiaB AP is configured to automatically use an upstream Internet connection if one is available, and to act as a gateway for its clients—it provides all of the services necessary for its wireless clients to safely access the Internet, such as a DHCP server, a firewall, etc. Even if the NiaB AP does not have an external connection to the Internet, it still provides a useful wireless network to its clients, allowing a group of users to easily configure a secure local wireless network.

FIGURE 16-1. Network-in-a-Box makes it easy to enroll in a secure wireless network

8   ANSI/IEEE Std. 802.1x.

9   B. Aboba and D. Simon, "PPP EAP TLS Authentication Protocol (EAP-TLS)," IETF RFC 2716 (Oct. 1999); *http://www.ietf.org/rfc/rfc2716.txt*.

10  T. Dierks and C. Allen, "The TLS Protocol Version 1.0," IETF RFC 2246 (Jan. 1999); *http://www. ietf.org/rfc/rfc2246.txt*.

11  Balfanz *et al.*, "Network-in-a-Box".

The process to easily and securely add new clients to this network is called *gesture-directed automatic configuration*: a user wishing to add his laptop to the NiaB network runs a small enrollment application, which tells him to "point out" the NiaB AP whose network he wishes to join. In the NiaB implementation, he points out the AP using the infrared (IR) port on his laptop (although other mechanisms could be used[12]). For a second or two, the devices exchange a small amount of information over infrared. Then, the user is prompted to separate the devices to continue the automatic configuration of the laptop. After a few more seconds, the user is informed that his laptop is ready to use. These simple steps provide a previously unconfigured laptop with everything needed to get a "network dial tone."

This gesture-based approach to configuration is simple and intuitive for the user and, at the same time, highly secure. When the user's laptop and the NiaB AP communicate over infrared, they are actually exchanging digital fingerprint information with each other that will allow them to securely recognize each other's public keys, and the AP tells the client the name of the wireless network it should join. The infrared channel is an example of a *location-limited channel*.[13] Location-limited channels are channels that can be used to bootstrap secure communications between devices.

The client enrollment software on the laptop then makes a secure connection over the wireless network to the NiaB AP, authenticating each other by proving they have the private keys corresponding to the public key fingerprints they exchanged over IR. This takes the user's clear intention to have his laptop talk to that *particular* NiaB AP, and turns it directly into a secure connection over which the laptop can be configured. Over that secure connection, the enrollment software on the laptop requests a certificate from the NiaB AP's CA, and then retrieves the new certificate and installs it on the laptop. The enrollment software then configures the laptop to use the new certificate to access the NiaB network securely in the future. From then on, standard software in the laptop will automatically access and authenticate to the NiaB network whenever it is in range, without further intervention from the user.

By setting up and joining a NiaB network, the user is managing an "instant" public key infrastructure—a small, dedicated PKI—without even realizing it. Instead of burdening the user with complicated certificate management semantics, this iPKI provides a simple and intuitive security model: a device can participate in the wireless network if and only if, during enrollment, it can be brought into close enough physical proximity of the access point to exchange information over infrared. For example, if a NiaB AP were to be deployed in a home, someone wishing to gain access to its wireless network would have to be able to physically enter that home. (Especially concerned users might even lock their

12 Dirk Balfanz, D.K. Smetters, Paul Stewart, and H. Chi Wong, "Talking to Strangers: Authentication in ad hoc Wireless Networks," *Proceedings of the 2002 Network and Distributed Systems Security Symposium* (NDSS'02), Internet Society (2002), 23–35.

13 *Ibid.*

NiaB AP in a closet.) This is a simple, intuitive trust model that is quite effective for many situations.

The gesture-based interface for enrolling in a NiaB network is designed to be as simple and intuitive as possible. Most importantly, it asks the user to perform only an action that he would have to perform anyway—to indicate *which* network he would like to join. User studies confirm that this approach is very easy to use—it took a population of 12 users on average only 2 steps and 51 seconds to set up a laptop to use a secure NiaB network, and they rated the system's ease of use very highly.[14] The interface also follows Yee's guideline:

> Grant authority to others in accordance with user actions indicating consent.[15]

The user action indicating consent is the physical pointing out of the laptop to the access point. The authority granted is the network access given to the laptop. Without this explicit user action, no authority is granted to the laptop.

The authors of the study arrived at this easy-to-use design through an iterative process. Their interdisciplinary team (consisting both of security experts and ethnographers) first designed a prototype that they then tested with users for usability flaws. The test users indeed pointed out issues with the prototype that were addressed in the final design. The timing and satisfaction results cited earlier refer to that final design.

## Case Study: Casca

Casca is an application that shows how small, dedicated iPKIs can be used to secure workgroup applications.[16] In Casca, users create shared virtual spaces for collaborating with other users. Each space is represented by an (initially empty) canvas on the user's screen. Users can invite others to join a space, and such members can then add objects to that space (e.g., files, cameras, or speakers) by dragging objects' representations (i.e., icons) onto the space's canvas (see Figure 16-2). For example, if Alice invites Bob to join her space, and then drags her screen component onto the space's canvas, Bob (along with any other member of that space) will have access to Alice's screen. (Bob will see an icon representing Alice's screen on his canvas, and will be able to display documents on Alice's screen by simply dragging those documents onto the icon.)

The shared spaces provide a natural basis for security: only users that are members of a space can access the objects in that space. By making sharing a top-level primitive of the application, the design makes it easy for users to understand what they are sharing and with whom. Moreover, users don't have to do anything extra in order to specify who

---

14 Balfanz *et al.*, "Network-in-a-Box."

15 See Chapter 13, this volume.

16 W.K. Edwards, M. Newman, T.F. Smith, J. Sedivy, D. Balfanz, D.K. Smetters, H.C. Wong, and S. Izadi, "Using Speakeasy for ad hoc Peer-to-Peer Collaboration," *Proceedings of the ACM 2002 Conference on Computer Supported Cooperative Work* (CSCW 2002), (ACM Press, 2002), 256–265.

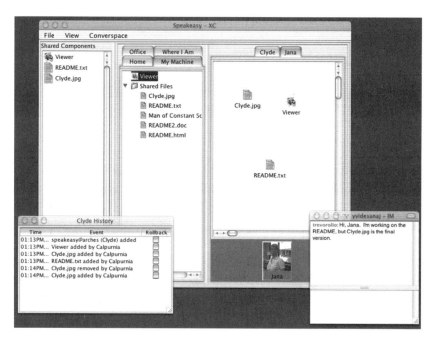

*FIGURE 16-2. A screenshot of the Casca application*

should have access to (and who should be barred from access to) shared resources: assembling a workgroup to participate in a shared virtual space automatically sets up a security mechanism that enforces access control along workgroup boundaries.

It turns out that instant public key infrastructures are an ideal tool to implement the security requirements for Casca in an easy-to-use manner. Whenever a user creates a new blank canvas (thus creating a shared space that only he is a member of), a new root certificate is created for that shared space. The creator of a shared space essentially becomes the certification authority for that space (of course, the user is unaware of this). Inviting others to join the space means issuing them a new certificate signed by the space's root public key. The new member's public key is authenticated using location-limited channels (see the previous case study). Two members of a space authenticate each other by proving that their respective certificates stem from the same root. Again, all this happens under the covers—users do not see the setup or use of certificates.

The user experience is similar to the previous case study. In order to invite a new member, *some* sort of action is necessary on behalf of the group owner. In Casca, this happens to be a gesture that aligns the infrared ports of the group owner's computer and the new member's computer. As a result of the gesture, the group owner sees a new member alongside the group's canvas. The new member sees the group's canvas and immediately has access to all objects made available through the shared space. In addition, this also serves as an example of Yee's guideline:

> Enable the user to express safe security policies in terms that fit the user's task.[17]

In Casca, users assemble groups of colleagues with whom they wish to collaborate. This is a very task-centric activity (Casca is a *collaboration* tool). At the same time, this group of colleagues also represents a security policy in that it specifies that these and only these collaborators have access to the group's converspace.

## Case Study: Usable Access Control for the World Wide Web

Instant PKIs do not always have to use location-limited channels to enroll new clients. Balfanz describes a system where web servers themselves take on the role of certification authorities, issuing certificates for potential clients of the web sites they're serving.[18] The system is designed for small-time web publishers such as hobby photographers or keepers of online diaries who want to restrict access to their online content to a select group of people. After they create new content, Balfanz suggests that a natural part of the "workflow" for these small-time web publishers is to inform their clients of the new content by announcing to them (and only to them) the creation of the new content. This intention of access control (which is expressed, say, by sending an email announcement to a select group of people) is enforced by a small, dedicated iPKI: when a recipient of such an announcement visits the web site for the first time, he automatically receives a certificate issued by the site (as opposed to some general-purpose certification authority). This certificate is then used to authenticate to the site, during both the first and subsequent visits.

Why does the site issue a certificate to any (!) client that connects, only to turn around and test for the possession of such certificates as proof of access? The idea is that the legitimate recipient of the announcement email will visit the site before any attacker, thus obtaining the certificate. The web site honors only the first certificate request from each user; subsequent requests are rejected. If, for some reason, an attacker manages to visit a web site before the legitimate recipient of the certificate does, that legitimate user will encounter an error message asking him to contact the web site's publisher. Upon such contact, the publisher can easily revoke the existing certificate (assuming that it was issued to an illegitimate user), and instead issue a new certificate to the legitimate user.

This threat model is similar to the widely used tool *ssh*, where there is a small chance of a man-in-the-middle attack on the first connection to a remote host. If and when such a first connection is successful, subsequent connections are secured by the full strength of the underlying protocol (in this case, SSL or TLS with client authentication).

---

17  Yee.

18  D. Balfanz, "Usable Access Control for the World Wide Web," *Proceedings of the Annual Computer Security Applications Conference*, IEEE Computer Society (2003), 406–415.

The result is a system that, while protected with an iPKI, is to the users almost indistinguishable from a system that does not employ any security mechanisms at all—that is, the additional security does not place an additional burden on the user. As in an insecure system, web publishers publish information through a web server and announce this fact in an email message to a select group of people. And as in an insecure system, recipients of the announcement click on a link in that message and have immediate access to the published content. The only difference in the implemented system is that during their first visit, clients encounter a few "setup" screens they have to walk through. The users (both publishers and clients) never notice that they are managing, and partaking in, a public key infrastructure. What's more, this is actually an example of Yee's guideline:

> Match the most comfortable way to do tasks with the least granting of authority.[19]

Because the secure version is (almost) indistinguishable from the insecure system, it represents a mechanism that users are already very comfortable with. At the same time, however, authority is granted to no one but the individuals addressed in the announcement.

## Instant PKIs

The examples in the previous sections show that, with careful design, public key technology can be made not only useful but also *usable*. A set of five principles for secure and usable system design can be drawn from these and other examples.[20] Together they suggest a general new approach to usable PKI design:

*You can't retrofit usable security*
Just as security cannot be "bolted on" to an existing system late in its design, existing unusable systems cannot be fixed simply by adding a better GUI. Systems must be designed to be both secure and usable from the ground up.

*Tools aren't solutions*
Components like SSL/TLS, public key cryptography, and digital certificates are important resources in building secure systems. However, by themselves, they are not solutions to a user's problem—they must be applied effectively in a well-designed application context.

*Keep your customers satisfied*
The only way to tell if a system is usable is to ask users—usability testing is key to being sure that a system's design is successful.

*Think locally, act locally*
Make technology easier to deploy and use by tailoring it to the application at hand, and by avoiding external deployment dependencies.

---

19 Yee.
20 Balfanz *et al.*, "In Search of Usable Security."

*Mind the upper layers*

Users are trying to accomplish goals expressed in the context of the application at hand. Don't ask them to make security decisions or take actions outside that context—use the context to automate necessary security steps.

While the first three of these are important general principles for the design of any usable, secure system, the last two lead to very specific indications of how we should design a usable PKI. *Think locally, act locally* suggests that we should avoid designs that require establishing large, coordinated trust hierarchies, or certificates that are predesigned to fit every possible future application. This not only simplifies deployment by reducing the need for interorganization coordination, but also allows greater opportunity for autoconfiguration.

*Mind the upper layers* suggests that users should be allowed to focus on the task at hand, and that systems should take contextual information about what is needed to accomplish that task into account in order to figure out what security-related actions need to be performed. Users should not be asked to think about certificates directly—either how to obtain one or whether to trust a particular CA. An increasing amount of research and experience finds that users are very confused by such requests.[21, 22, 23, 24] Instead, certificate management should be integrated into the task at hand. For instance, in the Network-in-a-Box system described earlier, users were asked to indicate by a gesture what wireless network they wanted to join. The fact that joining that network required them to obtain a certificate was not something they had to find out explicitly.

This approach to simplified PKI deployment can be generalized and reused for a wide variety of applications. When used in combination with intuitive approaches to initial user authentication like the gesture-directed approaches described earlier, the combined system is secure, easy to use, and easy to deploy. As we've mentioned, the term *instant PKI* (iPKI) is used throughout this chapter to describe such systems.

## What Makes a PKI Instant?

An iPKI is a lightweight PKI centered around a standalone CA—one that doesn't participate in a larger CA hierarchy. Certificates issued by that CA are usually used for a single, specific application. The goal of an iPKI is to make it so simple and easy to issue certificates and configure them for use (while not sacrificing security) as to make it easier to issue a new certificate than reuse an old one. These small, special-purpose PKIs turn out to be considerably easier to configure and set up than a reusable PKI—most often, PKI setup can be completely automated. And because the certificates issued are closely linked to an

---

21 *Ibid.*

22 Doyle and Hanna.

23 Gutmann.

24 Whitten and Tygar.

## CASE STUDY: USABLE PKI DEPLOYMENT FOR AN ENTERPRISE WIRELESS NETWORK

With the principles for instant public key infrastructures in mind, we redesigned the procedure for joining the wireless network at PARC described in the earlier sidebar. We reused many of the design choices from the NiaB system to greatly simplify the user experience.

A user wishing to join a laptop to the wireless network walks to a room that houses an *enrollment station*. The user installs and launches a client application that instructs her to align the laptop's infrared port with that of the enrollment station; she is then told that a certificate request has been received, and she can leave the room. After administrator approval, the user receives an email asking her to rerun the client application, which automatically retrieves the certificate and installs it for use with the wireless network.

This system provides an intuitive trust model. Our enrollment station is locked in a room, so someone who has physical access to the room can request a certificate, while someone who doesn't have physical access cannot. At PARC, users need to present their badges to a system administrator to enter the enrollment room.

Usability studies demonstrate that this approach is simpler and more intuitive for end users than setting up security using traditional methods. It takes users an average of 1 minute and 39 seconds, and a total of four steps, to add a new device to the wireless network. The system also gets much higher marks than the traditional system in user satisfaction and confidence. Even our system administrators, who by this time had become quite familiar with the traditional system, prefer the new system to the point where they exclusively use it to enroll end users' computers.

---

application context, it's much easier to make enrollment and certificate use comprehensible and easy for the end user, who prefers not to have to think about certificates at all.

A number of elements are common to iPKIs:

*Application-specific, lightweight CA*
An iPKI is used for a particular narrow application context (e.g., to identify all the devices that can access a particular wireless LAN, or all the devices that are allowed to use a shared repository of resources). Instead of reusing existing certificates, in an iPKI it's often easier to get a new one for a different application or different trust condition.

*Automated PKI and CA setup*
To make it possible to deploy many lightweight iPKIs, it must be as simple as possible to set each one up—ideally requiring no user intervention at all.

*Simple, intuitive enrollment mechanism*

To make it feasible for users to obtain multiple certificates, it must be simple for them to get each one. More importantly, each certificate and enrollment action should be embedded in a task the user knows he wants to perform (e.g., enrolling in a particular wireless LAN or inviting someone to participate in a shared repository of resources). The user should be asked to do nothing more than would be necessary to indicate what he wants to do, such as pointing out the AP serving the WLAN he wants to join via IR, instead of being asked to do separate, security-specific steps.

*A simple, intuitive trust model*

It should be simple and clear to the user who will and will not be able to join the iPKI. More importantly, that access model should be expressible in application terms. In the NiaB example described earlier, only people who can get physical access to the NiaB AP (close enough to exchange IR) can get onto its wireless network.

*Secure bootstrapping*

Making the enrollment mechanism intuitive doesn't mean that it should also then be insecure—giving out certificates without enforcing a well-thought-out trust model for who should get them, and effectively enforcing that model. In the examples presented in this chapter, authentication over location-limited channels provided a strong cryptographic binding between the user's intention (e.g., demonstrating a desire to join a WLAN and physical access to the AP and pointing out who he wants to join his shared space), and the system trust model. This form of ad hoc authentication acts to bootstrap trust in the resulting PKI.

*Certificates as capabilities*

Although an iPKI may issue standard X.509 identity certificates, these certificates are rarely used for their ability to provide identity information. Instead, they usually play the role of simple, easy-to-verify capabilities—"anyone owning a valid certificate issued by this iPKI is allowed to do X," where X might be participating on a particular network, accessing a particular set of files, etc. (Ownership here is defined in the sense of proving possession of the private key corresponding to the public key in a certificate signed by the iPKI's CA.) This simplifies the design and implementation of applications that will use the PKI.

*No need for direct user interactions with certificates*

One of the corollaries of automated enrollment is that users don't have to directly manipulate certificates or even know they are in use. This improves the user experience dramatically.

The "instant PKI" approach is not all-or-nothing—it's simply a collection of design choices that make it easier to deploy small, usable PKIs. Subsets of these design choices can be combined with traditional PKI techniques to generate all sorts of *hybrid* solutions, which are more usable than traditional PKI enrollment, while still keeping centralized management features that may be necessary in certain organizations or situations. The sidebar, "Case Study: Usable PKI Deployment for an Enterprise Wireless Network," shows an example of such a hybrid.

We close this chapter by remarking that many of the concepts discussed here are applicable above and beyond CA-based infrastructures that use public key certificates. An instant public key infrastructure is really only one example of an *Instant Trust Infrastructure* (ITI). Instant Trust Infrastructures may differ in the security mechanisms they employ: certificates, shared secret keys, more complicated forms of cryptographic credentials, etc. What they have in common is that they are just the right size, are application specific, and provide an easy bootstrap mechanism and an intuitive security model. Armed with those properties, Instant Trust Infrastructures in general, and iPKIs in particular, show us how to make the impossible easy and combine usability and security in one system.

## About the Authors

 Dirk Balfanz joined the Palo Alto Research Center (formerly Xerox PARC) in 2001 after receiving his Ph.D. from Princeton University for work on distributed systems security. Dirk is interested in end-to-end security, which means the correct interplay of human factors, systems security, and cryptography in distributed systems such as the Internet. Most recently he has focused on usability issues for securing computer networks. For recent publications, see his web site:

*http://www.parc.com/balfanz*

 Glenn Durfee is a member of the computer and network security research group at the Palo Alto Research Center. His interests range from mathematical cryptography to the development, implementation, and deployment of next-generation security systems. Currently he has been especially interested in security for wireless and mobile devices. Glenn received his Ph.D. in Computer Science from Stanford University in 2002, and has since worked at the Palo Alto Research Center. More information and a list of publications can be found at his web site:

*http://www.parc.com/csl/members/gdurfee*

 D. K. Smetters has been a member of the security research group in the Computer Science Laboratory at the Palo Alto Research Center since 1999. Her current research focuses primarily on the usability of security and security for wireless networks and mobile devices, and around problems of key distribution and key management. She obtained her Ph.D. in 1995 from MIT. Additional biographical details and a list of publications can be found at her web site:

*http://www.parc.com/smetters*

# CHAPTER SEVENTEEN

# Simple Desktop Security
# with Chameleon

A. CHRIS LONG AND COURTNEY MOSKOWITZ

**C**HAMELEON IS A DESKTOP INTERFACE AIMED AT HOME COMPUTER USERS THAT IS DESIGNED TO REDUCE the damage caused by malicious software, or malware—for example, viruses, worms, and Trojan horses. Malware is especially a problem for home computer users, in part because on most home computers all software runs with full access to all parts of the system. For example, an email attachment or a file downloaded from the Web has freedom to do anything to any part of the computer.

## Introduction

The Chameleon design philosophy is to put the user, and thus the user interface, first. Frequently, security practitioners design detailed security models and mechanisms, then implement them in software or hardware, then design interfaces to expose the security features to users, or to application programmers who then expose them to users. In contrast, our project began with a very high-level idea of the security model of the system, and then moved straight to the user interface design. Details of the security model and decisions about the implementation are driven by the primary focus of making the interface easy to understand and convenient to use.

In the physical world, we have reasonable security in spite of a lack of fine-grained security mechanisms. For example, we routinely allow only partly-trusted people into homes, such as friends for socializing and repairmen to fix our utilities. We often monitor them only loosely, because that is all that is required to ensure that the plumber is not looking through our CDs instead of fixing the pipes. This level of supervision is easy because CDs and pipes are typically not near one another. In general, the varied locations of different types of objects and activities in the home provide a convenient, albeit coarse, security mechanism.

In information space, no analogous mechanism exists. On typical home computers, all programs run by the user have access to all data, and in some circumstances implement security policies the users do not intend.[1] Users do not necessarily store files for different purposes in separate places. Even when they do, current security mechanisms do not automatically take advantage of this, and it is too much to expect users to set good permissions on every file or directory (e.g., using permission bits under Unix[2] or access control lists under modern versions of Microsoft Windows[3] and other operating systems). However, just as people coarsely sort their possessions in the physical world into separate rooms, they may be willing to coarsely sort their files and applications. This sorting may enable the system to protect data from malware more effectively than it does at present.

In Chameleon, users coarsely sort their files and applications by assigning each file to one specific category, called a *role*,[4] and installing applications into one or more roles.[5] Files are put into one role or another based on how secure the file should be or on the types of activities you do with the file.

The idea of a role-based system is not new. The Chameleon security model borrows ideas from previous security research, especially compartmented mode workstations,[6] sandboxing,[7] and role-based access control.[8] It is also similar to the WindowBox project.[9]

---

1   Nathaniel S. Good and Aaron Krekelberg, "Usability and Privacy: A Study of Kazaa P2P File-Sharing," *Proc. CHI 2003, CHI Letters* 5:1 (April 2003), 137–144. See also Chapter 33, this volume.

2   Fred T. Grampp and Robert H. Morris, "UNIX operating system security," *AT&T Bell Laboratories Technical Journal* 63:8 (Oct. 1984), 1649–1672.

3   Karanjit S. Siyan, *Windows NT Server4: Professional Reference*, 2nd Edition (Indianapolis: New Riders Publishing, 1997).

4   For readers familiar with role-based access control (RBAC), note that roles in Chameleon are similar, but not identical to roles in RBAC.

5   A program is stored as files, so for a program to be runnable from multiple roles, it must be installed using Chameleon tools that set up this behavior. Regular files are visible only to a single role.

6   Jeffrey L. Berger, Jeffrey Picciotto, John P. L. Woodward, and Paul T. Cummings, "Compartmented Mode Workstation: Prototype Highlights," *IEEE Transactions on Software Engineering* 16:6 (1990), 608–618.

7   Vassilis Prevelakis and Diomidis Spinellis, "Sandboxing applications," *Proceedings of the FREENIX Track: 2001 USENIX Annual Technical Conference* (Boston, June 2001), 199–126.

8   David Ferraiolo and Richard Kuhn, "Role-Based Access Controls," *15th NIST-NCSC National Computer Security Conference* (1992), 554–563.

9   Dirk Balfanz and Daniel R. Simon, "WindowBox: A Simple Security Model for the Connected Desktop," *Proceedings of the 4th USENIX Windows Systems Symposium* (Aug. 2000), 37–48.

Chameleon is novel because of its focus on making a role-based system easy to use. To make our interface intelligible and convenient, we keep it extremely simple. Although this entails some sacrifices in flexibility, a simple system that is actually used provides more security than an elaborate one that is not. Another key part of our security philosophy is to give users control over trust decisions. This control does allow users to make insecure decisions, but we believe that users will not adopt a system if it is too restrictive, especially on their home computer.

Based on our research so far, we think that the following set of roles strikes a good balance between security and usability:

- *Vault.* A safe place to put valuables you want to keep safe. Only trusted programs are given access to the Vault.

- *Communications.* The role for working with email and the Web. Because email and the Web are the most common ways computers get infected with malware, important files are not stored in this role.

- *Default.* This role is for files that are not particularly sensitive and for programs that are fairly trustworthy. It is the typical workspace for most files.

- *Testing.* The role for installing and trying out new, and potentially untrustworthy, programs. No important data is kept here.

- *System.* The role for files that the system itself requires. Only trusted programs from trusted sources are installed here.

One way for malware to spread and to cause damage is by making applications change files that they would ordinarily never need to change. Chameleon mitigates this problem by keeping each application confined to its own role. An application cannot read or write files that don't belong to its role (and, in fact, the application doesn't even know they exist). For example, the email application might be restricted to run only in the Communications role, so if a virus is received in an email message, it cannot affect files in other roles, such as important financial files stored in the Vault. Although an application can be installed to be available in all roles, installing it in only some roles provides an extra layer of security because it prevents the application from being started accidentally in the "wrong" role. If an application is available in multiple roles, it can be running in more than one of them simultaneously. However, each instance of the application is separate from the others and is confined to its role.

Some security exploits rely on one program to start another application and tell it to do something dangerous. For example, if an email message contains a malicious attachment, the email application launches the attachment application, and that is what causes the damage. In Chameleon, damage from chaining applications together like this is contained because an application can start applications only in its own role, unless specifically given permission by the user. So, for example, an email client running in the Communications role could not automatically start a work processor in the Vault role.

Because of its simplicity, Chameleon's security model does not allow users to express as wide a variety of security policies as traditional systems do. However, Chameleon's ease and convenience mean that it will be used (effectively) more often, and so in practice it will have greater security than traditional systems.

The following sections briefly describe Chameleon's security design for file organization, program communication within the system and outside, and advanced role features. Implementation details are covered in later sections.

### File Organization in Chameleon

The additional security Chameleon provides comes largely from protecting files, so an important design decision for Chameleon was how to organize files. The two important issues are ease of use and security.

The most obvious course is to let people continue organizing files however they wish, in whatever directories they wish. Although this seems like the most user-friendly approach, it means that to make roles useful, the user would have to set the role for every file individually. Even though choosing one role from a handful is a lot less work than typical file control mechanisms—for example, Windows lets you set multiple rights (e.g., read, write, create) separately for each user on the system—it is still much more complicated and cumbersome than we wanted Chameleon to be.

Instead, in Chameleon, files are organized by role, based on their security level. For example, the Testing role is for files that are not trusted, and the Vault role is for highly trusted files. Fortunately, most users are already familiar with grouping files together using directories. For these reasons, Chameleon uses directories to group together those files belonging to the same role.

More specifically, there is a home, or top-level, directory for each role, and all files for each role are stored under that directory. Users can organize files within a role by creating directories in the home directory, and subdirectories under those, and so on. The restriction Chameleon has is that all files in the same directory belong to the same role.

This organization has the advantage that it is simple to understand, and we believe that it will be easy for most people to use. There may be people who are used to putting all their files in one directory, and they will have to do some sorting to separate files into different roles to get the advantages of Chameleon's security. However, our testing so far supports our belief that this is not too onerous. If future testing reveals that many people want a more flexible model—for example, to allow a file to belong to more than one role simultaneously—such features could be added to Chameleon.

### Interrole Communication and Network Access

Roles affect what files a program can access and what access it has to other programs on the same computer. Programs running in the same role have the same access to each other as programs run by the same user have to each other in existing systems. Programs running in different roles have essentially the same access as programs run by different users—that is, a program in one role may be able to communicate using network protocols or other interprocess protocols (e.g., shared memory) with a program in another role, but it cannot look into the private memory space of the other program nor kill the other program.

Because different roles in Chameleon contain information of differing sensitivity and can run programs of varying trustworthiness, Chameleon limits communication with external computer systems, based on role:

- *Vault.* Because the Vault stores the most sensitive documents, it has highly restricted network access. Programs in the Vault can send, but not receive, email, and can connect to web sites, but only sites on the "white list" of trusted sites. If a program in the Vault attempts to connect to a site not on the white list, Chameleon will ask the user for approval before allowing the connection. The user can also add new sites to the white list. The Vault cannot receive incoming network connections (e.g., it cannot run servers).

- *Communications.* Only email, web, and instant messaging connections are allowed into and out of this role.

- *Default.* This role has no network restrictions.

- *Testing.* Programs in this role are not trusted, so they are not allowed any network access without user permission.

- *System.* This role implements network restrictions so is not itself restricted. However, networking programs should not be installed here because a security breach in this role could be very damaging.

## Advanced Role Features

A benefit of the role paradigm in Chameleon is its flexibility. Chameleon allows users to have more roles if they want greater compartmentalization of their files. Chameleon lets users "clone" one of the built-in roles to create a new role with the same security level (e.g., network access). Although the new role has the same type of security as its parent, it is a separate role, so, for example, neither role has access to the other's files. These new roles can also be deleted when no longer needed. For example, important work documents and important personal documents could be kept separate from each other using two separate Vault-level roles. Or a new Testing role could be created to temporarily try out a particular program, and could then be deleted.

An application that was written for Chameleon could take greater advantage of roles. For example, email attachments are a common source of malware. To help protect a user from potentially malicious attachments, a role-aware email client could create a new role on-demand when a user opens an attachment. After the attachment is closed, the email client would then destroy the role.

The main benefit of Chameleon is in helping users protect their own files from programs they themselves run. However, many users have files that are shared with other people, for example, on corporate fileservers. To make other users' files available, Chameleon uses an interface similar to the "Map network drive" dialog in Microsoft Windows. In addition to the existing authentication needed to authorize access to the files, the user also specifies the role in which the files should appear. Note that when the files are mapped and appear to be in a certain role, it does not change the files, for two reasons: the owner of the files may have a different set of roles, and the system the files are stored on may not be running Chameleon and thus not have roles at all.

To share files, the user has to specify what files to share, with whom to share them, and what type of access to give (e.g., read, write). In keeping with the rest of the Chameleon security model, the unit of sharing is the role—that is, entire roles are shared or not shared. To limit what is shared, users can create new roles. Each role keeps a list of which users it is shared with. Many sharing mechanisms allow sharing with groups of users, but Chameleon does not have groups because, for home users, this would only add complexity and rarely, if ever, be needed. In keeping with Chameleon's philosophy of simplicity, files are shared on an all-or-nothing basis. That is, if a file is shared with another user, that user may perform any operation on it: read, write, delete, and so on.

Only two roles in Chameleon are suitable for sharing files: Default and Testing. Because the Vault and System roles contain the sensitive documents, they cannot be shared, nor can foreign files be mapped to them. The Communications role is specifically for communications applications, so it also cannot be shared nor mapped into.

## Chameleon User Interface

This section describes the current version of the Chameleon interface and highlights issues we considered in its design that are specific to security interfaces.

Security as a secondary (or tertiary, or lower-priority) task means not only that the security operations must be easy to use, but also that they cannot interfere too much with the primary task or tasks. We designed the Chameleon interface to be easy to use itself, and also to not intrude on the ordinary activities that people want to perform.

To make Chameleon easy to understand and use, we used popular interfaces such as Microsoft Windows and the Macintosh as a starting point. Chameleon uses separate, overlapping windows to display applications and to browse and manage files. The Chameleon design attempts to add or modify this interface style only as much as necessary to support roles. The role features are designed to be simple, so they are easy to understand and convenient to use. Chameleon has evolved over time through two low-fidelity (paper) prototypes and one software prototype, based on lessons learned in user studies. These old versions of the interface are shown in Figures 17-1 and 17-2.

The current implementation is under development; a schematic of how its screen will be laid out is shown in Figure 17-3.

# WHY LOW-FIDELITY PROTOTYPING?

In developing Chameleon, we used a technique called *low-fidelity prototyping* (or *low-fi prototyping* for short). In general, prototyping is invaluable in many design activities, and user interface design is no exception. Prototyping allows designers to gather feedback early, consider many alternatives, and keep design centered on the user.

Low-fi prototyping usually involves tools like paper-and-pen media that are unstructured and easy to work with. In contrast, typical high-fidelity prototyping uses animation or software tools such as Macromedia Flash or Director, or Visual Basic.

Low-fi prototyping has several advantages over high-fi prototyping. Because it is created with simple, natural media, it is faster and easier to create the prototypes.[a] Even the most advanced software tools for building animations or graphical user interfaces require much more time than paper, pen, scissors, and tape to create simple interfaces.

Low-fi prototyping can also be used much earlier in the design process. Earlier evaluation and feedback about designs is valuable because it allows designers to compare design ideas before a lot of time and energy have been invested.

An advantage of low-fi prototyping that may be surprising is its ability to elicit *better* early-stage feedback about the interface than high-fi prototypes. When presented with high-fi prototypes, people get the impression that the design is finished and their comments tend to focus on details, such as font sizes or alignment of widgets. In the early stages of design, though, what is really valuable is high-level comments about the interface, such as whether it's on the right track at all. Low-fi prototypes look much less finished, so people are more willing to be critical, which is exactly what designers need.

---

[a] Marc Rettig, "Prototyping for tiny fingers," *Communications of the ACM*, 37:4 (April 1994), 21–27.

If you design user interfaces or web sites, low-fi prototyping can be a very useful tool. If you'd like to learn more, consult the books devoted to low-fi prototyping.[10]

Users need to be aware of what role each program and file belong to. Otherwise, a user might put an untrustworthy application, such as a game downloaded from an untrusted web site, in the same role as valuable data, such as personal financial records. To make roles visible, all windows and icons in Chameleon have a colored border that shows what role they belong to. Windows also have the role name in their titlebar. As an extra cue indicating what role the user is currently working with, all windows that do not belong to

---

10 Carolyn Snyder, *Paper Prototyping: The Fast and Easy Way to Design and Refine User Interfaces* (Morgan Kaufman, 2003).

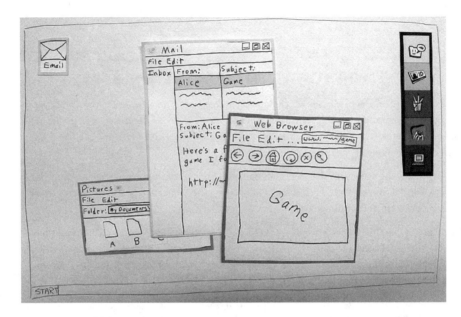

FIGURE 17-1. Low-fidelity prototype

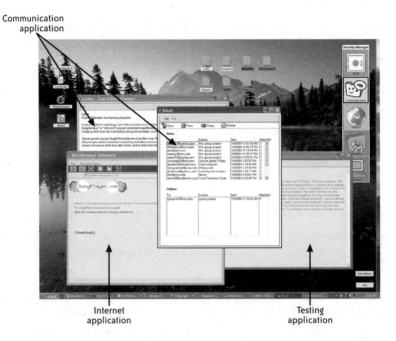

FIGURE 17-2. Visual Basic prototype

the currently active role are dimmed slightly. We plan to study whether this level of notification will give users a sufficient level of role awareness.

Chameleon desktop schematic

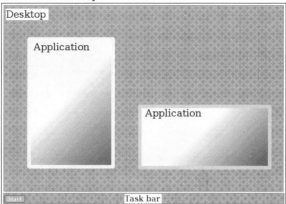

*FIGURE 17-3.* *Schematic of the Chameleon X Windows implementation; cross-hatched regions are controlled by trusted software; gradient areas are controlled by end-user applications; application borders indicate their role*

Of course, in addition to being aware of roles, users also need to interact with roles. Specifically, Chameleon supports these role-based actions:

- Copying and moving files across roles
- Specifying the role in which to start an application
- Specifying the role(s) in which to install an application

Based on user testing, the current design provides the following methods for these actions.

Because the role to which a file belongs is tied to what directory it is in, the user can copy and move files across roles, just like copying and moving files within a role, simply by dragging and dropping the file from a folder that belongs to one role to a folder that belongs to another. A file can also be copied or cut to the clipboard in one role, and pasted into another.

Sometimes, a user may want to access a file that belongs to role A from an application that belongs to role B. For example, the email application running in the Communications role might want to attach a file from the Vault role. The user could copy the file to the Communications role, but this would be cumbersome. An easier way is to use a file dialog box that has been enhanced to know about roles, as shown in Figure 17-4.

An important issue with the design of security interactions in Chameleon is how easy they *should* be. Security in Chameleon comes from role separation. So if, for example, moving or copying files across roles is too easy, people might do it too readily, without considering the security implications. Although this is a risk, Chameleon errs on the side of convenience because experience with other security technologies shows that people are very willing to work around mechanisms they deem too inconvenient. Even if users move or copy some files across roles in a way that exposes them, that is better than abandoning Chameleon altogether and losing its benefits for all their other files, too.

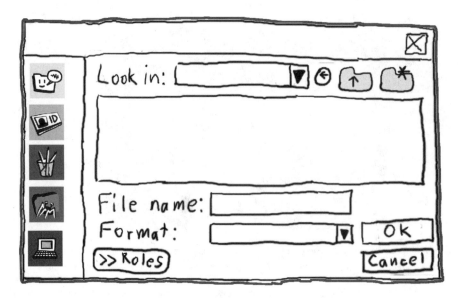

*FIGURE 17-4. Role-aware file dialog box from low-fidelity prototype; the role palette on the left side chooses the role to browse; the "Roles" button hides and shows the role palette*

The decision to require all files in the same directory to belong to the same role seemed simple, straightforward, and easy to understand and use. Then we considered the desktop, where it is likely that people will want to put files and applications from different roles side by side. Showing all files from all roles at the same time could make for a messy desktop. But showing only files that belong to the currently active role could be confusing, and would require users to remember what role a file belonged to.

Applications, too, can be installed in multiple roles—for example, a simple text editor might be useful in many roles. As with files, we considered a verbose and a concise option for displaying desktop icons for an application installed in multiple roles. The verbose option is to show a separate icon for each role in which the application could run. The concise option is to show only a single icon but to change the color of its border depending on the role of the active window. If the application is available in the active role, we would color its icon border to match; otherwise, we would color it gray to indicate that it is not available in that role.

Our user studies so far indicate that people have strong preferences about which display style to use for icons—strong, but different, preferences, unfortunately. There is a slight preference for separate icons for files and applications, so that is the default. Given that nearly half of people prefer the other, it should be easy to change.

The next section describes the interface development process, and issues that we discovered from user testing and analysis.

## SURFACE SIMPLICITY, HIDDEN COMPLEXITY

In Chameleon, applications are limited to accessing only files in their role. However, this sometimes conflicts with user desires, for example, to attach to an email message a file from a different role. Chameleon solves this problem by enhancing the traditional file dialog box (see Figure 17-4). This decision illustrates how simple decisions in the interface may entail adding complexity "under the hood."

The reason this simple interface complicates the underlying system is that allowing applications access to files belonging to other roles—even to browse the directories and see what files are there—violates the security model that is crucial to the security Chameleon provides. The problem is how to allow users to do the simple, obvious, intuitive thing of opening a file in another role without introducing a security vulnerability by violating the security model.

For interface consistency and ease of programming, most applications use the file dialog that the system provides, and run the same code from the same shared library. However, this dialog box is created and controlled by the application, with the rights and permissions of whatever application made it. In Chameleon, if the dialog box has the same rights as the application, it can't access other roles' files.

The solution Chameleon uses is to change who owns the file dialog box. The Chameleon file dialog box is not controlled by the application, but by the system, and so has the ability to look at other files and directories. What this dialog box passes back to the application is a name that provides access only to the file specified by the user in the dialog. This access is OK because it is specified explicitly by the user.

# Chameleon Interface Development

User interfaces, like many other complex artifacts, are virtually impossible to create perfectly the first time. For this reason, a key element of good user interface design is iteration through the design, implementation, and evaluation phases. The Chameleon interface is currently on its third major version, after a paper prototype and a Visual Basic prototype. The paper prototype was evaluated with two different user studies, and the Visual Basic prototype with one study.

Chameleon presents a new paradigm of application and file organization—roles—so the primary goal with our evaluations has been to determine, at a high level, whether Chameleon is easy enough to understand and convenient enough to operate that people would use it and, if not, how to improve the interface to make it usable. Toward that end, our experiments focus on the subjective impressions of participants, gathered by observing how they use the system and from questionnaires participants filled out after using the system.

This section describes our goals for each iteration of the interface, how we evaluated each one, and what we learned. (An in-depth discussion of the user studies with the paper prototypes is given in our technical report.[11])

## Study 1: Paper Prototype (Security in Context)

We began the design of the Chameleon interface with sketches and storyboards on paper. The goal at this early stage was to determine what elements the interface needed for the user to interact with the security features of Chameleon, such as copying or moving files across roles. The sketches and storyboards served as vehicles for brainstorming how people might use Chameleon and how its security features might interact with nonsecurity tasks.

In the next stage, we wanted to find out how people would react to the basic role idea of Chameleon, how easy the security features were to use, and how much impact they had on the realistic tasks. We also wanted to learn user preferences about two issues specific to the Chameleon interface: explicit versus implicit role switching and how to display desktop file icons.

Explicit versus implicit role switching is an interesting issue because it is a tradeoff between security and usability. Explicit role switching means that if an application running in role A is active, and the user wants to use an application running in role B, role B must first be explicitly activated. With implicit role switching, the user can simply click on the application running in role B and automatically change role. Explicit role switching may have a security advantage because it is much less likely that users would accidentally change roles than with implicit switching. On the other hand, implicit role switching is much more convenient.

We recruited 10 people from around our campus to use the paper prototype while we observed them and listened to their comments about what they found confusing, easy, difficult, helpful, etc. Participants also filled out a web-based questionnaire about their experiences using the prototype.

Overall, participants were positive about the Chameleon interface, both verbally during and after the experiment and in the post-experiment questionnaire. For example, one section in the questionnaire asked participants to rate the security features of Chameleon with opposing word pairs on a scale of 1 to 9, as shown in Table 17-1.

11 A. Chris Long, Courtney Moskowitz, and Greg Ganger, "A Prototype User Interface for Coarse-Grained Desktop Access Control," Technical Report CMU-CS-03-200, Carnegie Mellon University, Pittsburgh (Nov. 2003).

*TABLE 17-1. Reactions to security features in the paper prototype user studies, on a scale of 1 to 9 (1 being the most negative, 9 being the most positive)*

| Word pair | | Median rating | |
|---|---|---|---|
| Intrusive | Helpful | Study 1 | Study 2 |
| Annoying | Pleasant | 6.0 | 8.0 |
| Hostile | Friendly | 5.5 | 6.0 |
| Cumbersome | Convenient | 7.5 | 7.5 |
| Confusing | Clear | 6.0 | 6.0 |
| Difficult | Easy | 6.5 | 7.0 |
| | | Overall average 7.5 | Overall average 7.0 |

Seven of the ten participants made positive comments, such as "I definitely would like it," and "[It is] easy to operate," and two expressed interest in finding out when the software would be ready. However, four made negative comments, such as "annoying for the lazy user who doesn't want to deal with the 'roles' each time they use the computer." The main concerns involved the convenience of transferring files across roles and of switching roles. Participants varied in their opinion of the likelihood of other people using Chameleon. Some participants thought that it was very similar to current interfaces and would be learned easily, while others thought it would not be easy for a computer novice or that only people who had been affected by malware would use it.

Several participants commented that they would be very motivated to use our system because they had been affected by viruses or were concerned about being affected.

Most participants did not think that the roles we used in the study were ideal. Of those who specified why, all said that they wanted fewer roles. One wanted only two roles: one for "files I absolutely knew were safe" and the other for "files that were suspect."

Our observations of participants using the system and their comments about it confirmed our belief that a role-based desktop was workable. However, it also highlighted the importance of making the low-level interface mechanisms, such as menus, convenient. To determine the best mechanisms to use for role-related operations, we conducted a second user study.

## Study 2: Paper Prototype (Security Mechanisms)

During the first user study, we had observed that people were sensitive to how convenient the security operations were to perform. For the second study, we wanted to determine how people would prefer to perform key role-related operations. We gave each study participant a set of tasks with multiple methods that could be used to complete each task. We asked them to try each method and rank them. An abridged description of the tasks and methods is shown in the following list (note that participants were given more detailed instructions than are shown here). An * indicates the methods most preferred by participants.

1. Open a URL in an email message (which is in the Communications role) in the Unsafe role.[12]

   a. Copy to clipboard with context menu and use activation option in Security Manager menu (see Figure 17-5 and Figure 17-6).

   b.*Use context menu in application and select Activate in/Unsafe.

2. Move the *Test.doc* file from the Communications to the Personal role.

   a. *Drag-and-drop to the Security Manager and use a directory dialog box (see Figure 17-4).

   b.Copy to clipboard, transfer clipboard to new role with the Security Manager (see Figure 17-5 and Figure 17-6), and paste.

   c. Use context menu in application, select Copy to/Personal, and use a directory dialog box.

   d.Change to new role, open My Documents, and drag-and-drop file from old role to new role's My Documents.

3. Save an open text file that is being edited into the Communications role.

   a. *Use menu item File/Save to/Communications and use Save As dialog.

   b.Use menu item File/Save as to save the file, then move it to the Communications role.

   c. Use menu item File/Save as and open Roles to save directly to Communications role (see Figure 17-4).

4. You are in the Communications role. You want to open the *to do* file that is in the Personal role.

   a. Files for all roles are shown, with role-appropriate colored borders. Double-click the *to do* file.

   b.Files for all roles are shown, with role-appropriate colored borders, but icons for nonactive roles are dimmed. Double-click the *to do* file.

   c. *Only files for active role are shown. Change to Personal role, then double-click the *to do* file.

5. Some applications are installed in more than one role. You are in the Communications role and want to open the web browser in the Personal role.

   a. *There is one web browser icon onscreen, with a border in the active role color. Change to the Personal role; the web browser icon border changes to match. Double-click to start the browser.

   b.Several icons for the web browser are visible, each with a border of a different role's color. Double-click the Personal one to open it.

---

12 The paper prototype had slightly different roles than we introduced in this chapter.

6. You want to send a file to a friend. The file is in the Personal role, but the email to which you want to reply is in the Communications role.

   a. Move the file to the Communications role. Use the Attach button in the email client and the Open dialog box that appears.

   b. Click the Attach button. Open Roles to load directly from the Personal role.

   c. *Move the file to the Communications role. Drag-and-drop the file into the email message.

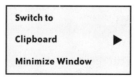

FIGURE 17-5. *Context menu for the Security Manager*

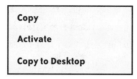

FIGURE 17-6. *Context submenu for the Security Manager, from the "Clipboard option"*

For tasks with two or three methods, we balanced the method ordering across participants. This was not possible for task 4 because it has four methods, so we chose unique orders for the participants to be as different as possible.

Upon completion of each task, the participants were asked to rank the methods by preference. As in the first study, participants filled out a web-based questionnaire at the end. Participants took 45–70 minutes to complete the experiment.

Participants in this study also generally liked the security features in Chameleon. The biggest concern participants expressed was that some operations have several steps. One participant was not worried about getting a virus and thought the roles were extra, unnecessary work. However, the other five participants were positive about the interface and said they would use it. One said, "I wish some of [your] designs...would be common practice among big leading software companies."

In this study, participants ranked the interface methods for performing each task. We used these rankings to assign points to each method and summed them to determine the most preferred method for completing each task. Participants had strong preferences related to tasks 1 and 5, and fairly strong preferences related to task 6. However, preferences were less clear for tasks 2, 3, and 4.

Some methods shared common interface mechanisms of clipboard use, context menus, drag-and-drop, and role-aware file dialog boxes. Overall, the strongest preference was against using the clipboard. The most common comment about specific mechanisms was that they liked drag-and-drop, although in the rankings this method is similar to other popular methods.

## Study 3: Visual Basic Prototype

As mentioned earlier, a concern we had with the Chameleon interface was how aware of roles users would be. Our ideas for making roles visible included graying out windows owned by inactive roles and animation; both methods are difficult to implement with paper prototypes. Also, it would be hard to learn about user awareness from a paper prototype because it is so visually different from the final software. For these reasons, we decided to move to a software prototype for this iteration.

Based on what we learned from the studies with the paper prototype, we built a software mock-up in Visual Basic (see Figure 17-2). It was used to explore different interface alternatives, did not have any real security, and did not run real applications. It included several mock-up applications, based loosely on Microsoft Windows applications.

In addition to observing how participants used the interface in general, we introduced a trick into the interface at a few points in order to test how aware of roles participants were. Specifically, at a few points during the study, participants saw a window that appeared to be in one role, but was actually in another (see Figure 17-7). The goal of this deception was to attempt to get participants to take actions that would be a security risk in a real system, such as entering a password into an untrusted application.

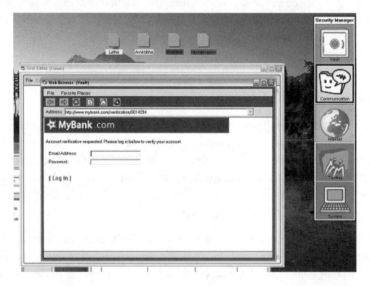

*FIGURE 17-7. A malicious application appears to be a text editor and tries to trick the user by drawing a fake window inside itself that looks as if it is in a different role*

As with the previous studies, participants were generally quite positive about using Chameleon. What was surprising was that very few of them noticed our trick (illustrated in

Figure 17-7). We are not sure why this occurred, but we believe that our participants may not have done enough security-related operations, or that our feedback about the active role was not overt enough. More work on how to provide role awareness is needed. Ideas for feedback include:

- Playing a brief sound when the active role changes, with a different sound for each role
- A soft ambient sound playing continuously, with a different sound for each role
- Continuously animating the icon in the Security Manager for the active role
- Animating the border of each window to show what role it belongs to
- When a window becomes active (e.g., the user clicks in it to give it focus), emphasizing its role by temporarily showing lines from the corners of the window to the appropriate role icon in the Security Manager

## Chameleon Implementation

The current implementation of Chameleon is being written in C and C++ for X Windows on Linux (kernel 2.4.x). It will support existing applications and allow new role-aware applications to be developed.

The X Windows implementation does not put support for the Chameleon security model directly into X Windows or the operating system, but instead layers the Chameleon model on top, using existing security features. A schematic of the desktop for the X Windows implementation is shown in Figure 17-3. Because they deal with multirole windows and objects, the desktop and the taskbar are managed by trusted programs. Applications, however, need not be trusted.

The following section describes how this implementation enforces role separation in three places: the windowing system, the filesystem, and the network.

### Window System Partitioning

In the Chameleon security model, applications are not allowed to see what is in windows in other roles, or to send input events (e.g., mouse clicks, key presses) to windows in other roles. However, in X Windows, once an application connects to the server, it is allowed to inspect the contents of, and send input to, all windows. To enforce role separation, Chameleon uses a separate X server for each role (see Figure 17-8).

Applications connect to an X server as usual, but it is actually a virtual X server (Xvfb, from the standard X Windows distribution) that writes its output to a buffer in memory instead of to a display, and does not connect to a mouse or keyboard. Chameleon uses a new program, *cproxy*, to monitor each role-specific X server for output. *cproxy* takes the output and copies it to the X server with which the user interacts. *cproxy* also takes the input from the user (via the desktop X server) and sends it to the appropriate X server, depending on which window has input focus. For example, if a window from the Vault role has focus, input will be sent to the X server for the Vault role, which will forward it to

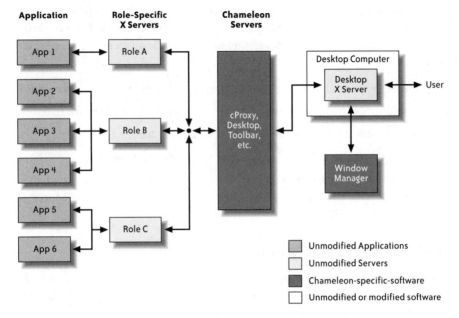

Application | Role-Specific X Servers | Chameleon Servers

App 1 ↔ Role A

App 2 ← Role B ↔

App 3 ← Role B

App 4 ←

cProxy, Desktop, Toolbar, etc.

Desktop Computer
Desktop X Server ↔ User

Window Manager

App 5 ← Role C

App 6 ←

Unmodified Applications
Unmodified Servers
Chameleon-specific-software
Unmodified or modified software

FIGURE 17-8. Architecture of Chameleon in X Windows implementation

the appropriate application. If a window moves or resizes on a role-specific X server or on the desktop X server, *cproxy* mirrors this change on the corresponding display to keep them synchronized. Interactions with the desktop and the taskbar do not need to be forwarded, because they are connected directly to the desktop X server.

In addition to *cproxy*, Chameleon contains these custom software components:

- *cselman*. Manages selections and the clipboard across the X servers and makes it appear to applications that the system has a shared clipboard.[13] When an application requests pasting the selection from another role, *cselman* asks the user for permission before allowing access.

- *cxdnd*. Manages the X drag-and-drop protocol so that it works across X servers.

- *Desktop*. Manages the icons the user sees on the desktop (e.g., My Computer, the trash can).

- *Toolbar*. Provides a menu for easy access to launch programs. It also shows an icon for each running program so that it can be (de)iconified, closed, etc., easily.

- *Role managers*. There is a role manager for each role, which provides a central point for operating on all applications in a role at once, for example, to iconify or kill them.

---

13 Actually, X Windows has multiple "selections," of which the clipboard is one (along with PRIMARY and SECONDARY). *cselman* makes each one shared as a single selection.

Each role manager needs access only to its own role, so it is run as that role. However, the other Chameleon components interact with programs and servers from multiple roles, so they must be trusted. For example, the Desktop and Toolbar may launch applications in any role.

All nonapplication software components are started by Chameleon. The trusted Chameleon components are told where the desktop and role X servers are when they start, and are notified if role X servers are created or destroyed later.

This architecture has several advantages. The primary advantage is that it provides good separation of roles. When a program is launched by Chameleon (e.g., by the Toolbar), the only X server to which it is given access is the one for its role, so it cannot affect other roles or the desktop X server—in fact, it doesn't even know they exist. And because it has no access to the other X servers, it cannot give greater access to any program it launches. Even if a role-specific X server crashed, other roles would not be affected. This architecture also allows X applications that are unaware of Chameleon and roles to run normally, without modification. At the same time, it allows applications that are role aware to run side by side. It is also considerably less work than building role awareness into the X server, primarily because the X server manages many different resources internally (e.g., windows, properties, fonts, colormaps, keyboard maps), and access to all of them would have to be controlled based on role.[14] And it has the deployment advantage that each user can run the same X server on his desktop that he normally uses.

This architecture has the disadvantage that it consumes more resources than an architecture where there is one X server that is role-aware. However, because X Windows is designed for distributed operation, it would be easy to spread the CPU and memory requirements across multiple computers.

### Filesystem Security

This prototype prevents applications in one role from accessing files belonging to another role by using a separate user account for each role, and setting the operating system's built-in file permissions appropriately. Chameleon provides a graphical interface to the filesystem that makes all files for the same user appear to belong to different roles rather than to different user accounts.

The advantage of this scheme is that it does not require a new security infrastructure based on roles, but instead takes advantage of existing file security mechanisms. However, it has the disadvantage that what the user sees is different from what is going in the filesystem, and this difference is visible to applications. In particular, programs that are not Chameleon-aware will likely expose the different user accounts.

14 For a discussion of building security into the X server, see Doug Kilpatrick, Wayne Salamon, and Chris Vance, "Securing the X Window System with SELinux," NAI Labs (March 2003); *http://www.nsa.gov/selinux/x11-abs.html.*

It was a compromise to make the implementation of this prototype simple. In the future, we may use other security systems that can support the Chameleon model more directly (e.g., SELinux[15]).

## Network Security and Interprocess Communication

This prototype does not implement network access control based on role, as a result of the lack of support in the underlying operating system (Linux). Extensions such as SELinux include the mechanisms needed to include this feature in Chameleon, and may be used in the future.

Controls on interprocess communication are managed by the operating system. Because separate roles run as separate users, programs cannot kill programs in other roles or access them except with mechanisms that work across users, such as with sockets. The environment for Chameleon, home use, is not a high-security one, so Chameleon does not attempt to control covert channels. The Chameleon architecture allows each role to be run on a separate physical or virtual machine, which would make it more difficult for programs running in different roles to find one another and communicate.

## Software Architecture for Usability and Security

Although in the Chameleon project we are focused primarily on designing paradigms and interfaces for usable security, we are also interested in how to architect the software to make it easier to implement in a way that is both usable and secure. One issue in particular concerns in which part of the software system the security should go. In high-level terms, there are three places it might go: the operating system, the application, or a toolkit or library sitting between them. Each of these has advantages and disadvantages:

*Operating system*
> Traditionally, security is implemented in the operating system. This has the advantage that a single implementation is available to all applications, which makes it easier to ensure that the security is implemented correctly.
>
> However, the operating system provides only low-level primitives, and it is up to the application writer to present these in a way that makes sense to the user. To look at it another way, the operating system has no context for operations. For example, if the operating system receives the command to reformat a disk, it does not know if that is a secure operation. It could be a legitimate user preparing for a reinstall, or it could be malware.

*Applications*
> Security today is often found in applications, such as email clients that include encryption functionality or secure web browsers. From a usability perspective, applications have an enormous advantage over operating systems, because the application knows the higher-level goal the user is trying to accomplish. So the application can, at least in theory, put the security operations in the context of the user's normal workflow so that they are easy to understand and convenient to use.

---

15 National Security Agency, "SELinux"; *http://www.nsa.gov/selinux/*.

Unfortunately, it is undesirable to implement security features separately in every application, because doing so introduces more opportunities for bugs that introduce security vulnerabilities, and for inconsistent user interfaces.

*Toolkit*

We believe that application authors need help bridging the gap between the security features users desire and the security primitives operating systems provide. A toolkit that provides features such as the role-aware file dialog box in Chameleon (see Figure 17-4) may be able to combine the advantages of operating systems and applications. A toolkit has a higher-level context for what the user is trying to accomplish than does the operating system. Also, a platform may require security features to be included in only one (or a small number of) toolkits, which reduces the number of implementations greatly, compared to the application level.

The disadvantage of the toolkit level is that we do not currently know what the most useful abstractions are for developers of usable, secure applications. Toolkits will still depend on the operating system for enforcing security policies, and they will not automatically make applications usable, but they can be helpful in combining usability and security. We believe that Chameleon will be a useful platform for exploring this issue.

## Conclusion

Users need awareness of their computer security environment—but just the right level of awareness. An interface that gives the user too much information about security, or gives the information at the wrong time, or in the wrong way, will be confusing or annoying, or both, and the user will turn it off. On the other hand, if awareness information is too subtle, the user will be oblivious when the situation is dangerous. Like Goldilocks' porridge, the level of awareness has to be "just right."

As discussed in other chapters,[16] too many controls can overwhelm users and prevent them from effectively setting their preferences. However, controls that are too simple may also fail if they do not allow users enough flexibility to express their security needs—for example, the High, Medium, and Low security settings in Internet Explorer are too simplistic for some users. As with awareness, the complexity of controls has to be just right.

Most application developers are not experts in security and usability. Tools such as widget libraries and graphical user interface builders are available for helping them with usability, and libraries exist for fundamental security primitives such as encryption. However, the field of usable security is too new for us to know yet what abstractions application developers need. Development of applications that incorporate usable security will help us understand what they need.

Chameleon provides a simple means to partition data and applications from each other to reduce the harm suffered by typical desktop computer users from malware. User studies

16 In particular, see Lorrie Cranor, Chapter 22, this volume.

with prototypes of Chameleon indicate that many users desire more protection and like the Chameleon model. We believe that it will continue to be a fruitful framework for exploring issues in usable security.

## Acknowledgments

Thanks to the participants in the user studies, and to Lorrie Cranor, Dirk Balfanz, Alen Peacock, and Karen Renaud for their valuable comments. This work was funded in part by Carnegie Mellon CyLab.

## About the Authors

A. Chris Long is a Postdoctoral Research Fellow in the Electrical and Computer Engineering Department at Carnegie Mellon University. He is working with Greg Ganger on human-computer interaction and security, in particular on improving security for typical desktop computers. He is also interested in other areas where HCI and security intersect. In the past, he has done research on a variety of interface types, including digital video editing, pen-based interaction, and virtual reality.

*http://www.cs.cmu.edu/~chrisl*

Courtney Moskowitz recently completed her master's degree in Human-Computer Interaction at Carnegie Mellon University, where she worked with A. Chris Long. As an undergraduate at Cornell University, she studied psychology and human development. She is currently interested in the convergence of design and technology. She enjoys creating more usable products and is glad to have had the opportunity to work on this project.

# CHAPTER EIGHTEEN

# Security Administration Tools and Practices

### ESER KANDOGAN AND EBEN M. HABER

T ODAY, HUNDREDS OF MILLIONS OF USERS DEPEND ON RELIABLE ACCESS TO COMPUTING AND INFORMA-
tion services for business, educational, and personal activities. The growth of the Internet
puts a world of information and services at our fingertips, yet also opens computers to
attack from anywhere around the globe. The same networks that permit a tourist to read
email from an airport in Singapore also permit a student in Romania to release a computer
virus that disables computers and the businesses that depend on them. In addition, as the
complexity of computer systems increases, new vulnerabilities are discovered each day.
There is a worldwide community of people, usually referred to as hackers or crackers, who
work to discover and exploit such vulnerabilities to attack and gain control of systems,
sharing their techniques through various underground channels. Computers across the
Internet have been subject to worms, denial-of-service attacks, password-sniffing, and
other malicious activity, leading to significant inconvenience and loss of productivity for
legitimate users. On the other side, vendors and computer system administrators race to
discover vulnerabilities and to create, release, and apply patches before those vulnerabilities are exploited. On the front lines of this battle are *security administrators*, the people
responsible for continually monitoring both their own systems and the ever-evolving
security landscape in order to detect new attacks and prevent known attacks. Their work
is crucial because, simply put, we cannot afford critical data and systems to get into the
hands of hackers.

In this chapter, we provide an overview of the tools and work practices of security administration based on our ethnographic field studies at various computing centers. We profile two representative security administrators and detail five case studies to illustrate security work and the challenges faced by security administrators. Based on these findings, we outline some of the opportunities that lie ahead to improve security administration tools.

## Introduction

Security administration takes place in an ever-changing landscape of new systems, new vulnerabilities, and new tools. As threats to computer security evolve, so too do the practices and tools of security administration. On one level, computers are being used in larger numbers and broader applications, forcing security administrators to deal with increasingly large volumes of information and placing correspondingly more demands on their tools. Many existing tools place much of the cognitive load for analysis onto the user, an unacceptable situation given the trends of ever more computers and network traffic to monitor. Administrators would clearly benefit from advances in analytics, automation, and visualization tools. On another level, computer systems are increasingly connected, providing access for an ever-wider variety of client systems including laptops, cell phones, PDAs, etc. The diversity of computing devices complicates security management and planning significantly. Increasingly complex software architectures create more opportunities for vulnerabilities to arise. With more components integrated and interacting in various ways in these architectures, there is a growing potential for unanticipated vulnerabilities. Sometimes, security breaches take advantage of multiple vulnerabilities in systems, making patterns of attack hard to predict. As a result, security administrators need to know how various devices and systems work and interact to analyze developing situations. In short, all of these changes to the information technology landscape make the job of the security administrator increasingly difficult.

So, how do security administrators secure our computing systems, defend them against attacks, limit damage proactively, and recover from attacks rapidly? In this chapter, we describe results from our ongoing field studies of system administration at various computing centers across the U.S. In these studies, we examined the work practices, tools, organization, and environments of security, database, web, storage, and operating system administrators. So far, we have conducted 10 such field studies, where we observed approximately 25 administrators over a total 40 days.[1, 2] We collected about 250 hours of video, which we analyzed to varying degrees of detail. In these studies, our approach has

---

1   R. Barrett, E. Kandogan, P. P. Maglio, E. Haber, L. Takayama, and M. Prabaker, "Field Studies of Computer System Administrators: Analysis of System Management Tools and Practices," *Proceedings of the ACM Conference on Computer Supported Cooperative Work (CSCW '04)* (Chicago, Nov. 6–10, 2004); (ACM Press, 2004), 388–395.

2   P. P. Maglio, E. Kandogan, and E. Haber, "Distributed Cognition and Joint Activity in Collaborative Problem Solving," *Proceedings of the Twenty-fifth Annual Conference of the Cognitive Science Society (COGSCI '03)* (Boston, July 31–Aug. 2, 2003), 758–763.

been ethnography, which involved entering the system administrators' environments and observing their practices, tools, and interactions for extended periods of time. Our analysis is based on Grounded Theory,[3, 4] in which we do not use ethnography to validate a previously formulated hypothesis, but instead draw all our conclusions from what we observed.

## ETHNOGRAPHY

Ethnography, defined literally as writing about people, is a technique commonly used in anthropology where one immerses one's self in a culture for extended periods of time to better understand the people and their practices. Ethnography traditionally has been practiced for understanding foreign cultures, but more recently it has been applied and has been highly effective in understanding the work practices of computer users in context, informing the design of computer systems to better suit their needs.[a, b, c]

Ethnography is almost always used to generate qualitative rather than quantitative data. Ethnographic techniques include observation, often as a full participant in daily activities, direct interviews, and collection of artifacts. Observers take notes and frequently record events using cameras, video, and audiotape. An ethnographer typically engages with a small number of subjects to study their daily lives in depth to get an understanding of the particular circumstances that drive behavior as opposed to drawing statistically significant conclusions about the whole culture. Ethnographic accounts aim to provide a rich description of events with as much detail as possible, not only expressing what happened but also interpreting the meaning and significance of events.

[a] E. Hutchins, *Cognition in the Wild* (Cambridge, MA: MIT Press, 1995).
[b] P. Luff, J. Hindmarsh, and C. Heath, *Workplace Studies: Recovering Work Practice and Information System Design* (Cambridge, MA: Cambridge University Press, 1999).
[c] J. E. Orr, *Talking About Machines: An Ethnography of a Modern Job* (Ithaca, NY: Cornell University Press, 1996).

In this chapter we focus only on our findings in the area of security administration. We start with an overview of the attacks that security administrators work to prevent, and the tools that they use toward this end. We then give an overview of the current practices of security administration by profiling two representative security administrators, and detail five case studies to illustrate security work and the challenges faced by security administrators. We also discuss how current tools support or fail security administrators' practices.

3   Barney G. Glaser and Anselm L. Strauss, *The Discovery of Grounded Theory: Strategies for Qualitative Research* (Chicago: Aldine, 1967).

4   Barney G. Glaser, *Basics of Grounded Theory Analysis: Emergence vs. Forcing* (Mill Valley, CA: Sociology Press, 1992).

Lastly, based on these findings, we outline some of the opportunities that lie ahead to improve security administration tools.

## Attacks, Detection, and Prevention

The security administrators we observed face two broad categories of attack: autonomous software such as worms and viruses that spread from machine to machine, and human-directed intrusions in which an attacker tries to compromise machines manually or by using semi-automated tools. While most virus attacks appear to have the goal of disrupting computer operations, most human-directed attacks aim to gain control of machines. These privileges are then used to attack other machines, steal data or computational resources, and occasionally destroy data. Some attackers appear to do little damage, instead concentrating on obtaining access to as many systems as possible to gain recognition from their peers. When discovered and blocked by security administrators, however, attackers sometimes strike back and try to damage the administrators' data and machines.

We saw security administrators using a variety of tools for detecting and preventing attacks. These tools include:

*Global intrusion detection tools*
These monitor network traffic to analyze and report suspicious patterns—for example, Bro.[5]

*Scanning tools*
These probe machines remotely for known vulnerabilities in their installed software—for example, Nessus.[6]

*File/host integrity tools*
These run locally to check for compromised states; such tools include:

- Virus detection and repair tools—for example, Symantec AntiVirus.[7]

- Change management tools that track and compare system configuration information, including file organization, and that alert administrators when unauthorized changes occur—for example, Tripwire.[8]

- Rootkit hunters (a *rootkit* is a prepackaged set of programs and/or files used to exploit a vulnerability and gain control of a machine), etc.

*Communication tools*
These are used to coordinate work and share information between administrators, such as email, phone, instant messaging, and chat rooms.

5   Bro Intrusion Detection System; *http://bro-ids.org*.
6   Nessus Open Source Vulnerability Scanner Project; *http://www.nessus.org*.
7   Symantec AntiVirus; *http://www.symantec.com*.
8   Tripwire Change Auditing Solutions; *http://www.tripwire.com*.

*Samples of code*

Such code exploits vulnerabilities and runs in a secure setting (e.g., VMWare) to better understand attacks.

*Honeypots*

These are tools that emulate information system resources to attract attacks and capture attack data—for example, Sebek.[9]

*Public information sources*

These contain data about vulnerabilities and attacks, including mailing lists and web sites such as FIRST (Forum of Incident Response and Security Teams[10]), bugtraq,[11] unisog,[12] CERT (Computer Emergency Readiness Team[13, 14]), and SANS (SysAdmin, Audit, Network, Security[15]).

Administrators spend considerable time on prevention, researching new vulnerabilities and finding vulnerable machines. When faced with an automated attack, work becomes much more hectic as compromised machines are detected and isolated from the network to prevent the attack from spreading. Human-directed attacks are sometimes stopped in the same way, but occasionally security personnel will allow an attacker to continue in a controlled manner in order to trace the attack back to its source. In the next section, we describe security administrators and their work in more detail based on our studies.

## Security Administrators

Over the last two years, we have conducted a number of ethnographic field studies looking at database management, web hosting, operating system administration, and security administration. We observed activities ranging from database backup and recovery to configuration of geographic load balancers, from patch management to computer security forensics. Most system administrator activities are either directly related to security or have security implications.

In this section, we profile two typical security administrators, Joe and Aaron. In the following section, we describe five security administration case studies from our observations. Finally, based upon our observations and interviews, we discuss the unique aspects of security administration work, and how well this work is supported by available tools.

9   Sebek Open Source Honeypot; *http://www.honeynet.org/tools/sebek.*

10  Forum of Incident Response and Security Teams (FIRST); *http://www.first.org.*

11  SecurityFocus.com, bugtraq; *http://www.securityfocus.com/archive/1.*

12  University Security Operations Group, unisog; *http://www.dshield.org/mailman/listinfo/unisog.*

13  Computer Emergency Readiness Team (CERT); *http://www.cert.org.*

14  J. H. Allen, *The CERT Guide to System and Network Security Practices* (Reading, MA: Addison Wesley, 2001).

15  The SysAdmin, Audit, Network, Security (SANS) Institute; *http://www.sans.org.*

## Profile of a Security Manager—Joe

Joe is a senior security engineer at a computing center in a large public university. He has been in this position for over four years. Previously, he worked as a system administrator at the same center and in various software development positions at different companies. The computing facilities at the center provide services for about 300 employees and external collaborators throughout the U.S. Joe manages a team of three other security administrators. Together their responsibilities include setting up, configuring, and monitoring intrusion detection systems and responding to alerts reported. They work to proactively protect systems, detect attacks, and perform forensic analysis on compromised systems. As a manager, he is also responsible for defining policies and dealing with policy issues, and interacting with other concerned groups within the university as well as at other institutions. His motto is "Know Thy Network." Joe proudly claims that he learned most of the necessary skills primarily on the job. As shown in Figure 18-1, Joe's office has a bookcase full of various kinds of puzzles and games, and he considers this hobby as a nice metaphor for his day job.

FIGURE 18-1. Puzzles in Joe's office

Joe typically starts the day at 9:00 a.m. One of the first things he does is to start clients to read email and a MOO (An Object Oriented MUD—Multiple User Dialog). MOO is essentially a persistent messaging system composed of a set of virtual rooms representing dedicated spaces for admins to communicate on pre-agreed topics. Joe likes the MOO system, as it provides him a way to catch up on things quickly in the morning using its history function that shows past messages. Joe frequently checks both the MOO and email throughout the day. While the MOO allows him to feel the pulse of administration activity at the university, email provides updates from automated monitoring tools as well as security news from the outside world. Joe also participates in regular meetings and phone conferences with his counterparts at other organizations to share information concerning recent and emerging threats. When he hears about new vulnerabilities through these channels, Joe often researches them further using a variety of web sites, some created by the security community, others by hackers.

Joe and others recently finished a five-month project to revamp the center's security policies. Because they work at a center within a larger university, they need to abide by the university's policies, yet they also need more restrictive policies in areas such as file sharing, wireless networks, connecting personal computers to the university network, external collaborator use, and so on. One of the biggest problems is to make the policies usable by making the policy document short enough so that all employees can read, remember, and follow it. Joe thinks a lot of education still needs to be done, as policy issues still do come up frequently. Users often read the policy document only once, when required to at the beginning of their employment, so continuing education and discussion are needed.

Joe typically leaves work around 5:00 p.m., but he quickly logs back in again from home so that he can be in touch with his colleagues. At 9:00 p.m., email reports from the center's change management and analysis tool are sent, and he usually likes to look at these before going to bed so that he can sleep with some peace of mind. Joe has been officially on call 24/7 for the last eight years, although he has received few off-hour calls in the last few years. He really enjoys the challenges of his work, but at times it can be a little too demanding on his personal life.

### Profile of a Security Engineer—Aaron

Aaron is a security engineer who reports to Joe. He graduated with a master's degree in Computer Science last year, and has been working in this position ever since. He shares an office with Tom, another security administrator, and their office is full of computers and displays, as shown in Figure 18-2.

Aaron's schedule is similar to Joe's, but offset an hour or two later. The security group members deliberately stagger their hours to ensure better coverage at both ends of the workday. In fact, one of their team members works remotely from several time zones away, further increasing coverage. The rhythm of Aaron's day is centered on email, which he checks frequently (5 to 10 times per hour), looking for email notifications of security alerts. Through experience, he knows that certain alerts may be ignored on-sight, and others cause him to perform an immediate investigation such as looking through monitoring logs, checking network ports, searching for vulnerability/exploit data on the Web, and consulting with his co-workers via the MOO and face-to-face. He also checks the MOO regularly, but less frequently than email; he uses the MOO primarily for getting advice from more experienced admins.

When Aaron is not investigating a particular alert, he has assigned projects, such as scanning all the machines on the network for a newly discovered vulnerability. Any free time is occupied reading security mailing lists, though Aaron receives more mail from these lists than he has time to read. When he hears about new vulnerabilities through alerts or mailing lists, he usually performs web searches to learn more, and he occasionally downloads

FIGURE 18-2. *Aaron's workspace*

sample code for the attack to better understand how it works and which machines are vulnerable. Aaron has fewer meetings than Joe, and during meetings he always continues to monitor the network and research new potential attacks from his laptop. At the end of the day, Aaron heads home and, like his manager, connects in again after dinner to continue his tasks through the evening.

Aaron is the most junior member of the security team, but his educational background is strong. He spends much of his time educating himself to improve his knowledge of security. He is very motivated and really enjoys his work, and he seems to like the role of being a "good guy" helping fend off the "bad guys."

## Security Administration: Cases from the Field

In this section, we describe the specifics of a number of actual security cases encountered by the security administrators profiled in this chapter. These cases fall into two categories: security checkup and attack analysis.

### Security Checkup

One of the primary responsibilities of security administrators is to check the health of the systems in their charge. System "checkup" activities are performed routinely to ensure that systems are secure with the latest fixes, that only permitted applications are running with the proper approved releases, and that the system is generally free of viruses and worms. While intrusion detection systems are constantly on alert, notifying the security administrators of any emerging suspicious patterns, administrators also proactively scan their systems through various remote security tools to reduce the risk of an attack by eliminating any known vulnerabilities. This, however, is a very intensive task with high cognitive demands on the admin.

While scanning tools produce a comprehensive list of possible vulnerabilities, it is up to the administrator to examine this list, assess the risks involved, judge whether these risks are applicable in their situation, and take the appropriate actions. To illustrate the complexity of the "checkup" tasks we'll take a look, in the following subsections, at cases where we observed Aaron handling a virus incident, dealing with alerts sent by an intrusion detection system, and going through a report generated by one such security scanner tool.

### Case 1: MyDoom

Having learned through various security news groups and web sites of the emergence of a new variant of the MyDoom virus, Aaron did a network scan of systems in his subnet. Much to his dismay, he discovered that one of the systems had suspicious and increasing network traffic activity involving port 1034 (used by MyDoom for network communications). Immediately acting upon these findings, he notified the system's owner of the situation and had the system taken off the network. Now, he wanted to examine the situation closely, assess the damage, verify whether this system had actually been involved in a virus attack, and get the system cleaned before bringing it back online.

First, he wanted to understand whether other systems were affected by this incident. To do that he needed to analyze logs from the network monitoring tools. Network monitoring systems generate several gigabytes of data per day, making it impossible for a human to read and understand the logs directly. Instead, Aaron created an ad hoc command-line analysis tool using a series of commands to get the list of all IP addresses associated with port 1034 activity, as shown here:

```
./bin/ra -xcz args.out -port 1034 | awk `{print $7}' - | awk -F.
   `{print $1, $2, $3, $5}' | sort -u
```

He then copied the list into a file called *mydoom.o* to process it further by associating each IP address with its hostname using the following commands:

```
for a in `cat mydoom.o'; do echo $a; host $a | awk `{print $5}' -; done
```

These results suggested that four other systems were potentially infected by the virus. So Aaron decided to collect more information on the MyDoom virus to understand how the virus works. A Google search on the subject quickly got him the information he needed and confirmed his suspicions that 1034 is the MyDoom port. Based on the information he found, he explained to us that this particular version of the virus was also causing problems on some search engines because it queried them for valid email addresses within a particular domain (and thus kept them extremely busy). Talking to his office mate, he added that this made the virus very easy to spot, as it leaves a clear signature in the web logs, which could be scanned to search for matches to the URL templates used by the virus in querying search engines. He then told Joe about the new machines involved in the attack so that they too would be taken off the network.

Within hours, users began to note that their systems had been disconnected, and one of them sent him an email about the situation. He spoke to that user on the telephone and gave instructions on how to clean up the machine so that it could be put back on the network.

### Case 2: Intrusion alert—false alarm

Throughout the day, security administrators receive email alerts from intrusion detection systems. Typically, these alerts take the highest priority in their work schedule, because such alerts might indicate an ongoing attack. While detection is for the most part automated, classification of events as normal behavior or an attack requires human judgment. On normal days, most of the alerts are either false alarms or harmless, but it is up to the administrator to make the call. This requires an intimate knowledge of the environment—that is, system workload patterns, network packet traffic, application use, hardware and software architectures, and so on. This case study examines the use of human judgment by Aaron. During our observations, we observed Aaron stop a reporting task he was working on after receiving one such alert, shown here:

```
Following alerts in tcpred.  These seem to be coming from the known compromised
systems.  Please take time to investigate.
External IP (Once compromised IP's)
123.123.10.10 #once.compromised.host.edu
> Jul 27 15:10:14 123.123.10.10 0.1kb > 210.210.10.10/http 711kb 9,9m %12345
```

The alert specified that network traffic was detected involving the IP address of a once-compromised system. While the system had been repaired, extra attention is given to such systems in case the fix was insufficient and the machine is still compromised. Specifically, the HTTP log indicated that a file of 711 KB in size was transferred from the formerly compromised machine to another internal machine. Noting that the alert was referring to the HTTP log with the ID 12345, Aaron did a search on the HTTP log for this particular ID using:

```
grep %12345 http.log
```

which returned:

```
109090.04476 %12345 start 123.213.10.10 > 210.210.10.10
%12345 GET download/perftool-tar.gz
```

The HTTP log provided more information for Aaron to investigate. Specifically, it revealed what file was downloaded (*perftool-tar.gz*). This gave him sufficient leads to pursue it further. He first found the hostname of the machine using the host command and used this information to query the owner of this particular machine (using the center's online administrative tools). He then did a Google search for this particular user and found a number of documents related to parallel programming on his web page. At this point, he was reasonably sure this could be a legitimate file; he commented:

> If this is a person doing parallel programming, it should be all right.

Just to make sure, he pointed his web browser to the web server on this particular machine to find out what it was being used for. Realizing that the machine was used as a web server for a research group doing performance analysis of parallel programming systems, he commented:

> I think this guy basically wrote this thing. It should be legitimate.

Relieved, he further commented that this case was fairly straightforward because they knew what application was downloaded and who downloaded it. However, he added:

> But then there are times when somebody would download a tar file, source code, or something. Then we need to see if it is an exploit or something.

### Case 3: Real-time network monitoring

Most sites perform continuous network monitoring to watch for traffic that could indicate an attack. This monitoring can be surprisingly thorough, as demonstrated in this case. While we observed a meeting discussing hacker tools, the security administrators started discussing a package called *ettercap*. Being unfamiliar with this tool, one of the observers began searching the Web for information about *ettercap* from his laptop over the wireless network. A few minutes later, Aaron informed us that Fred, a security administrator working remotely, had detected this traffic and asked about it on the MOO:

```
Fred: any idea who was looking for ettercap?  dhcp logs say <observer's machine name>
is a netbios name.  nothing in email logs (like pop from that IP address).
Fred: seemed more like research.
Fred: smtp port is open on that host, but it doesn't respond as smtp.  That could be a
hacker defender port.
Aaron: we were showing how <hacker> downloaded ettercap.  One of the visitors started
searching for it.
Fred: ah, ok.  thanks.
```

In the space of only a few minutes, the security administrator had detected web searches for the dangerous *ettercap* package, identified the name of the machine in question, checked the logs for other activity by that machine, and probed the ports on the machine. Fred could see that it was probably someone doing research, but checked the MOO to verify that it was legitimate.

### Case 4: Security scan

Security administrators routinely probe their systems using various remote security scanner tools to identify potential vulnerabilities. When the security admins discover potential problems, they work with other administrators such as network administrators and operation system administrators to patch systems, turn off unused services, etc., to eliminate these risks. Typically these scans produce reports that are quite detailed, giving the administrators information on the potential vulnerability, an assessment of the risk factors, possible solutions, and further references to the issue for examination, as shown in Figure 18-3.

| Vulnerability | ssh (22/tcp) | You are running a version of OpenSSH older than OpenSSH 3.2.1<br><br>A buffer overflow exists in the daemon if AFS is enabled on your system, or if the options KerberosTgtPassing or AFSTokenPassing are enabled. Even in this scenario, the vulnerability may be avoided by enabling UsePrivilegeSeparation.<br><br>Versions prior to 2.9.9 are vulnerable to a remote root exploit. Versions prior to 3.2.1 are vulnerable to a local root exploit. Solution : Upgrade to the latest version of OpenSSH Risk factor : High CVE : CAN-2002-0575 BID : 4560 ID : 10954 |
|---|---|---|

*FIGURE 18-3. Output from a scan report*

During our observations, Aaron spent quite a bit of time going through one such report. Essentially what he did was to look at the list of potential vulnerabilities to understand the risks of each one and how they work, to test the exploits on safe, isolated systems, and, when a serious problem was found, to notify the responsible admins to patch the system in question.

One of the vulnerabilities reported had to do with NIPrint (a print service) that could allow an attacker to remotely overflow an internal buffer and thereby allow arbitrary code to execute. Unfortunately, at the time, this high-risk vulnerability had no solution, and the admin was referred to the vendor site for the latest information. Aaron tried the vendor web site to see if there were new fixes for this problem, but no new information was available. Then he did a Google search on "NIPrint exploits" and quickly found sites that not only had more information, but also provided source code for the exploit. Aaron examined the code in depth and decided that he should try it out. So, he copied the source code, compiled it, and ran it on the system in question. The exploit, however, returned an error code, indicating that print services were not available to the host. This led him to check to see if the port was open through a utility that determines what hosts are available on the network, what services (application name and version) these hosts are offering, what operating systems (and versions) they are running, and so on. Based on the information, he concluded that:

> This is also a false positive. You see NIPrint has a vulnerability on Windows machines. From the utility I just ran, I see that the port is open but it is a BSD machine, which tells me that it is not vulnerable. Most probably that is why it has not been compromised so far.

A number of other vulnerabilities were suggested by the report as potential risks. Aaron went through most of them, collecting information through the references provided by the report, seeking further information on various search engines and security web sites, and occasionally testing the exploits himself. In a number of other cases, he found applications and services (such as FTP and web servers) running old versions with significant vulnerabilities, prohibited software (such as peer-to-peer file-sharing services and game servers), and open vulnerable services (such as SMTP) left unused. He typically collected all this information and reported it to the responsible admins, requesting that they fix them as soon as possible. At the end of the day, he told us that of the 15 machines he had scanned so far, only one machine was appropriately secure and had a clean report.

## Attack Analysis

While attacks are not uncommon, the level of sophistication in these attacks varies widely. Most incidents are fairly easy to handle, as attackers leave some kind of footprints in the compromised systems that lead to their identification. When confronted, attackers typically stop their malicious activities. Only rarely are hackers so persistent in their attacks that they cause damage (financial or otherwise), and seldom do they manage to avoid identification for a long time. In such cases, security administrators typically contact the appropriate authorities to attempt prosecution of the perpetrators. In the following section, we look at one such case in detail.

### Case 5: Persistent hackers

During the four months before our visit, Joe had been defending against an ongoing attack on his university and several other universities. This incident was consuming close to 100% of his time and was not yet resolved at the time of our observation. According to Joe, these attackers (or perhaps even just a single person) had been persistently breaking into research centers and universities. Whenever an attack was discovered and the vulnerability patched, the attackers would find another way in. As a result, Joe had been in regular contact with 10 or so senior security admins at various institutions through phone meetings and email to share information and coordinate the response.

Attacks of this scale require not only good coordination among the involved parties, but also sophisticated information organization, processing, and interaction skills and tools. Joe was particularly skilled in using various information processing commands to analyze the voluminous log files containing hints of the attackers' activities. He was also following good information management strategies, as he and his colleagues organized information on exploits, incidents, people (including hackers), sites, etc., in various file directory structures. Naturally, coordinating information of this scale requires sophisticated information interaction tools, which was evident in Joe's environment, a virtual windowing system of nine or more virtual desktops spread across two large physical screens.

One of the invaluable pieces of information Joe and his colleagues collect in such incidents is attacker session logs. Sometimes, vulnerabilities in the attack tools permit security administrators to capture a detailed log of the attacker's activity. Examination of these sessions reveals a wealth of information about the tools and techniques attackers use, as well as information such as source hostnames, that could potentially lead to the identification of the hackers.

Joe and his colleagues had worked closely to focus on figuring out the access path of the compromised machines and the various techniques that hackers use in their attacks. Joe was particularly meticulous in these efforts, and kept a master file of attacker actions; there, he would copy interesting segments of the sessions, comment them with findings, and jot down references to other information. The closer the security administrators got to the originating machine, the closer they were to identifying the hackers and potentially prosecuting them. However, this case had been particularly challenging, as the attackers frequently changed their access path. In addition, not all of the compromised sites were helpful. There were various reasons for this lack of cooperation. This was the case particularly for large ISPs, which do not have the time to deal with such cases. Sometimes, sites would provide one of these session logs, which provide the admins new leads. Other times, sites would not deal with the attack beyond simply shutting down compromised machines. This, however, delayed tracking activities, as the admins would then need to wait for the attackers to come in through some other compromised machine.

In one session log that they had just received, Joe was able to find some of the toolsets that attackers were using. A directory listing in the log revealed the name of one of the tools (e.g., *abcd.tgz*), and Joe did a web search on the tool. In this case, he was not particularly lucky, however, as the only information he could find was another admin's report of a similar situation. The other admin did find that the tool was an exploit for a Domain Name Service (DNS) server vulnerability.

On occasion, Joe has been able to find the full source code of an exploit on underground attacker sites, including all the source files, README files, and Makefiles, as he did for one of the other exploits used in this ongoing incident. That exploit, he found out, allowed a user to stealthily access a root shell on the machine via HTTP requests. Thus, all attack traffic was on port 80, which made it difficult to spot because all web traffic uses the same port. This added further complication to an already complicated case involving multiple exploits. In this particular situation, three different vulnerabilities were exploited, including a web server backdoor, a Secure Sockets Layer (SSL) buffer overflow, and a DNS exploit.

At another point of the session log, Joe was able to find an unzipped listing of the tool files and, much to his surprise, a view of one of the source code files for the vulnerability. Apparently, during the session, the hacker, for some reason, opened an editor to view one of the exploit files. Joe explained later that this happens when hackers actually copy and paste exploit source code as opposed to downloading it from a web site to prevent leaving any traces in web server logs. In any case, this was a break, so Joe quickly copied the source code onto his machine. First he spent quite a bit of time to understand what the exploit was doing. Later, he compiled it and ran it on another system. Normally when security admins try out downloaded exploits and rootkits, they do so in a quarantine environment. In any case, this particular executable did not yield much new information, but Joe stated that a lot of their work is for educational purposes to understand what the attackers are trying to do.

At one point, one of Joe's colleagues, Tom, told him that in another part of the session, he saw a process listing, and a particular process caught his eye (`ssh abc@111.111.10.10`). This was a secure connection to a particular site, and if that site's administrators were cooperative, the logs could give Joe more information. Tom also saw a DNS session where the hacker changed his server from one site to another site. In the process of doing so, Tom was able to capture the username and password used by the attacker, probably for a compromised account at this particular site. This, they decided, was another lead, but they would need to think further about how they could best use it. They could potentially prepare traps for the hacker through mirroring of the IP packets, but they considered that this could be tricky, as the attacker might notice it. They also joked about changing his password.

This had been another long day. The security administrators had found some new leads, particularly information on new tools that the hackers added to their portfolio. Unfortunately, this was not good news: it simply meant that the attackers were getting better and better, and Joe and his colleagues just wanted to put a stop to their efforts. Joe's organization had not been the prime target of attacks for some time, but he felt obligated to work on the project. The various administrators were getting closer to where the hackers were, so Joe took it upon himself to track the attackers and help out those other sites that were being compromised.

## The Need for Security Administration Tools

Security administrators have a variety of tools at their disposal. In the cases we examined, we saw the use of intrusion detection systems based on network monitoring, remote and local scanning tools, public information sources, data analysis tools, etc. While these semi-automated tools help the administrators significantly overall, it is clear that security as a whole would be very difficult to automate fully—much of the analysis requires intelligence and judgment to determine whether a certain system behavior is the result of legitimate activity. For example, in case 2, Aaron investigated the research activities of the machine owner in question to determine whether a particular file download was reasonable. In case 5, Joe needed to download and examine source code, read online reports of similar problems, and coordinate activities across multiple institutions. Simply put, there isn't much room for brute force automation. Yet obviously tools can help administrators do their jobs more effectively. Advanced analytical and visualization techniques could help admins manage large amounts of information. In our observations, we saw little or no use of data-mining technologies to analyze patterns of activity. Automatic classification could help the administrator to focus on questionable activities rather than the obvious false alarms. We also saw little or no use of visualization techniques put into practical use.

Real-time and post-incident visualization of activities could improve the ability of security administrators to develop situational awareness.[16, 17]

The case studies also show that an important aspect of security administration work is the integration of data from various parts of the system to construct and understand the real story. This work may involve relating data up and down and across various components in the system. However, this can be particularly challenging, for several reasons:

- There is simply too much to look at.

- In addition to the vast quantities of data in log files, there is no single standard data format describing the various events produced from all the monitoring and scanning tools.

- In distributed systems, out-of-sync system clocks make it difficult to correlate events with timestamps.

In summary, the various security tools are not well integrated. When one tool would produce a certain piece of information, we observed admins using manual tools to derive other information—for example, looking up machine names by network address and vice versa, or looking up machine owner names using online directories. With little integration, the security administrators typically take charge of integrating and correlating data using various ad hoc tools and commands to process, combine, and make sense of the data. When processing information, security admins frequently create scratch documents to hold data as a stage for further processing, as part of a report for a colleague, or for future reference. While the security administrators we observed were fairly proficient in the tools they used, many opportunities remain for further improvement, particularly in the area of workspace/activity management—specifically in activity reuse in information processing. In our observations, we clearly observed many patterns of activity where administrators examined logs to correlate events, yet each new incident required them to perform similar information processing. Instead of skipping back and forth repeatedly between different tools and manually integrating information using command-line tools and temporary files, security admins could benefit from integration that automatically (or manually via a user-defined data flow) processed the information, encapsulating activities and best practices in an executable form.

Time is a crucial factor for security administrators. Their work style is event driven: typically security admins stop their routine tasks whenever they receive an intrusion alert. Time is also an enemy, as security admins are very well aware of the fact that, given enough time, many systems are compromisable. Thus, security administrators need to be more current in their field than do other system operators. New vulnerabilities and attacks are discovered daily. At high-profile computing centers, attacks can come very quickly

16 C. Brodley, P. Chan, R. Lippman, and B. Yurcik, ACM Workshop on Visualization and Data Mining for Computer Security (Washington, D.C., Oct. 29, 2004).

17 J. R. Goodall, W. G. Lutters, and A. Komlodi, "I Know My Network: Expertise in Intrusion Detection," *Proceedings of the ACM Conference on Computer-Supported Cooperative Work (CSCW '04)*, (Chicago, Nov. 6–10, 2004); (ACM Press, 2004), 342–345.

after vulnerabilities are discovered. Proactive work pays off later on. Security admins must constantly watch for new vulnerabilities and proactively scan their systems for possible exploits. Security administrators also need to understand how various systems, architectures, and tools work, which components connect to each other and over which port, and which files are created and where, to distinguish legitimate activity from subtle attacks. Here again, tools are not very effective, particularly because each environment is different—thus, Joe's motto: "Know Thy Network!" Experience takes years to build, and brute force tools, while useful, fall short of meeting administrators' needs.

Security administration requires collaboration between people at many levels. Co-workers frequently check with each other face-to-face or via chat rooms to verify the validity of activities. Across organizations, they share their experiences, problems, scripts, and tools, and they collaborate to track down the most serious attacks. The "we are all in this together" mentality is widespread and most appreciated. Better tools for facilitating this collaboration may also be needed. Currently such communication is done through phone, email, scratch notes containing contact information, etc. Clearly, security administrators are in search of better means to collaborate and are exploring interesting approaches such as the use of MOOs. MOOs are a particularly interesting approach, as messages could be produced and consumed by programs such as bots. While we have not yet seen much exploration of this possibility, there are interesting opportunities where human and software information processing agents can collaboratively and cooperatively manage security. Bots can form the first line of defense, handling the obvious cases and notifying security administrators in questionable and critical cases.

## VISUALIZATION FOR SECURITY

Security work is likely to remain highly human intensive, yet the work is becoming increasingly challenging. High-volume, multidimensional, heterogeneous, and distributed data streams need to be analyzed both in real time and historically. In security practice, visualization tools are currently underutilized. Visualization for security is challenging, as current techniques try to match the needs of security administrators to gain situational awareness, correlate and classify security events, and improve their effectiveness by reducing noise in the data. Visualization coupled with data mining is likely to help security administrators make sense of network flow dynamics, vulnerabilities, intrusion detection alarms, virus propagation, logs, and attacks.

One approach is to provide multiple coordinated visualizations, as in the NVisionIP[a] interface shown in Figure 18-4, where network traffic is visualized at multiple levels from a single machine view to the overall network view, to improve the situational awareness of the security administrator.

---

[a] K. Lakkaraju, W. Yurcik, and A. J. Lee, "NVisionIP: Netflow Visualizations of System State for Security Situational Awareness," *Proceedings of the ACM Workshop on Visualization and Data Mining for Computer Security* (2004).

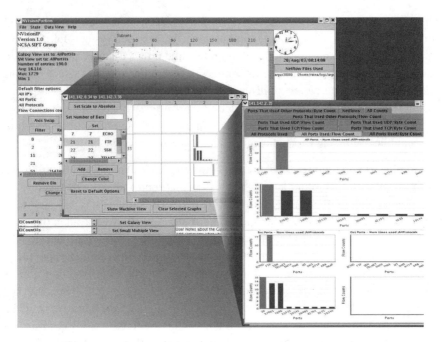

*FIGURE 18-4. NVisionIP interface (courtesy of NCSA)*

Security administration is distinct from other types of system administration, in several ways. First, while most system administration groups own some kind of computing resources (such as database administrators who own the database management software, the network team that owns the networking equipment, switches, firewall, etc.), the security administration team doesn't own the computing hardware or software for which they are responsible. This can lead to problems when other administrators don't share the same urgency in deploying fixes. Second, other administrators are mainly fighting against bugs and poorly working code; with security administrators, on the other hand, there are literally people out to get them. This problem is severe enough that one of the administrators we observed mentioned that he had asked to be left out of any public listing of security engineers, because attackers put extra effort into compromising machines and data belonging to security people.

As computer systems continue to grow in number and complexity, and as network traffic continues to increase, security work will only get harder unless better tools are developed. Based on our observations and discussion, we believe that the most important directions for tool development include:

• Standardization of event formats to permit easier integration between tools

• Tools to integrate and correlate events from multiple distributed systems, either automatically or manually via user-defined data flow

• Application of data mining and other analytics in activity classification, analysis, and noise reduction

- Automatic event stream processing

- Effective workspace, activity, and information management tools

- Improved collaboration and information-sharing tools

- Scalable, customizable, programmable visualizations

## Conclusion

Security work seems very much like war, espionage, or intense gaming. The security admins know things the attackers don't, and vice versa, and each is trying to use his knowledge to the other's disadvantage, while keeping the knowledge secret. It seems very much like watching a game of cat-and-mouse as the security admins take advantage of vulnerabilities in the attackers' tools to observe their activity, deliberately allowing machines to remain compromised in order to trace the attack. Meanwhile, the attackers keep discovering new vulnerabilities to make further attacks.

Security administrators work on the front lines defending against people who are trying to compromise the computer systems that support much of our modern society. At times, security admins might appear paranoid, but there really *are* people out to get them. In this chapter, we introduced the work practices, tools, and needs of this important group as revealed through our field observations and interviews. Security work involves research into emerging threats, situational awareness of system status, integration and processing of data from multiple sources, and, most importantly, human judgment as to whether a particular pattern of activity is legitimate. As computer systems continue to increase in number and complexity, and as network traffic continues to increase, this work will only get harder unless better tools are developed.

## Acknowledgments

We are grateful to our field study subjects, who remain nameless to preserve their anonymity. They cheerfully answered our questions and weren't bothered by our crowding their offices with extra people and video equipment, all the while continuing to perform a crucial job.

## About the Authors

 Eser Kandogan is a research staff member at IBM Almaden Research Center. He holds a Ph.D. degree from the University of Maryland, College Park, where he studied computer science with a specialization in human-computer interaction. His current interests include human interaction with complex systems, policy-based system management, ethnographic studies of system administrators, information visualization, and end-user programming.

 Eben M. Haber works on human-computer interaction at IBM Almaden Research Center. He holds a Ph.D. from the University of Wisconsin-Madison, where he worked on improving user interfaces for database systems. His interests include databases, user interfaces, and the visualization of structured information. He has worked in industry on data mining and visualization, and user interface design, and is currently studying human interaction with complex systems in the USER group at IBM Almaden.

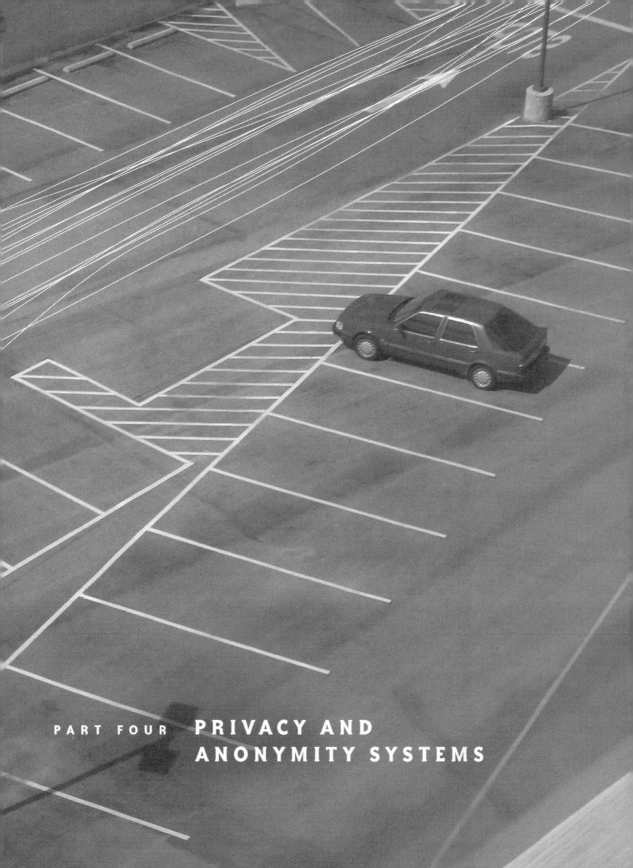

PART FOUR  **PRIVACY AND
ANONYMITY SYSTEMS**

# CHAPTER NINETEEN

# Privacy Issues and Human-Computer Interaction

MARK S. ACKERMAN AND SCOTT D. MAINWARING

**P**RIVACY CAN BE A KEY ASPECT OF THE USER EXPERIENCE WITH COMPUTERS, ONLINE SYSTEMS, AND new technologies. Knowing what to consider about users and their views of computer systems can only improve privacy mechanisms. *Human-Computer Interaction* (HCI) is the subfield of computer science that studies how people interact with—and through—computational technologies. This chapter examines what HCI, as a research area, offers to both those designing and those researching privacy mechanisms.

## Introduction

HCI is a large research field in its own right. HCI's roots were in human factors and the design and evaluation of "man-machine" interfaces for airplanes and other complex and potentially dangerous mechanical systems. The first papers in what would later be known as HCI were published in the 1970s and concerned the design of user interfaces in time-sharing systems. The field took off with the advent of personal computers and the single-user interface in the early 1980s. HCI's roots then were in cognitive-oriented, single-user interfaces—the so-called *user interface*.

HCI has since expanded to consider a variety of subareas—design methodologies, usability and usability testing, intelligent interfaces, adaptive interfaces, and so on. Of particular interest in this chapter is *Computer-Supported Cooperative Work* (CSCW), sometimes known as *groupware*. CSCW is interested in how groups of people work or interact together using computational technologies. Indeed, HCI has grown in general to consider the effects of organizational, institutional, and even societal factors on how computer systems are put together and how users interact with systems.[1] These topics have become increasingly important as the Internet has expanded the definition of "users" to potentially include billions of people in all of the world's countries and most of its cultures.

This chapter largely views HCI in its broader context. HCI is not just about user interfaces but also about the *user experience* of systems: how people perceive and understand, reason and learn about, and react and adapt to digital technologies. To borrow the terminology Sasse and Flechais use in discussing security,[2] HCI has come to deal not only with *process* (how systems are used, designed, and developed) and *product* (the systems themselves and their interfaces), but also with *panorama* (cultural and organizational contexts that support, discourage, or otherwise shape the systems they envelop). Privacy, like security, implicates all of these levels. It is, by its nature, concerned with the user and his data and also with the user and others' use of that data. Our interests, therefore, are those of HCI-writ-large.

As HCI has gone through several generations of computational technologies, it has carried a number of research themes forward. This chapter considers the various HCI themes and their research findings that may be important when designing, constructing, or evaluating privacy mechanisms. Before exploring these HCI research streams, however, we first need to articulate a working definition of privacy, and to compare and contrast privacy concerns with HCI concerns.

## Privacy and HCI

This chapter necessarily juggles two somewhat amorphous terms: HCI and privacy. HCI has already been introduced, along with its core concerns of improving ease of use and the overall user experience. *Privacy* is an even broader term. Unlike HCI, it is a term in everyday language, and so its meanings are rooted in larger cultural practices and understandings. It has technical meanings in, for example, law, ethics, and social theory, but also engenders strong, emotional connotations in common usage and daily experience. Many of these meanings are different and, at times, even contradictory.

For the purposes of this chapter, a simple but useful definition of privacy is:

> The ability of individuals to control the terms under which their personal information is acquired and used.[3]

---

1   Jonathan Grudin, "The Organizational Contexts of Development and Use," *ACM Computing Surveys* 28:1 (1996), 169–171.

2   See Chapter 2, this volume.

3   Mary J. Culnan, "Protecting Privacy Online: Is Self-Regulation Working?" *Journal of Public Policy and Marketing* 19:1 (2000), 20–26.

As such, privacy is about individuals' capabilities in a particular social situation to control what they consider to be personal data. Although fairly simple, this definition immediately raises a number of important points:

- Privacy is based on information and the effectiveness of individuals in controlling its flow, and so has a natural relationship with the concerns of HCI (as well as with the field of computer security). Indeed, as systems have increasingly involved the processing of personal information, particularly in the context of financial and governmental transactions, issues of privacy have naturally risen in prominence within the field of HCI.

- Privacy, like security, concerns risk, its perception, and its management. Privacy problems often lie in the potential future consequences of present behavior, which may be deemed risky or safe according to standards of judgment (not necessarily those of the participants involved). As such, privacy harkens back to HCI's origins in ergonomics and the safe operation of complex machinery.

- Privacy is about control, trust, and power in social situations, and so it rapidly implies ethical, political, and legal issues. It appeals to notions of individual autonomy and freedom: control of one's person, and access to one's person, in the form of personal information.[4] But this freedom is almost always constrained and may often have to be traded off in certain transactions, such as to access credit or to maintain the quality of health care.[5] These are, in general, issues for social, behavioral, and political science, but HCI does include many useful examples of interdisciplinary applied research.[6]

As this chapter will argue, privacy is individually subjective and socially situated. Indeed, privacy, as part of social interaction in general, is not a unified experience. What may be privacy for people involved in e-commerce or online banking may be a very different problem for people involved in social computing. In the following sections, we will see that people differ widely in their attitudes as well. That is, people's experience of privacy, their expectations and goals, and their problems concerning privacy may all differ when moving among areas of computation, society, and even tasks. We'll leave further discussion of the definitional problems inherent in "privacy" to other authors in this book, and use Culnan's broad definition. As we have seen, it suggests *prima facie* similarities between the concerns of HCI and of privacy at a number of different levels. It raises important issues as well, particularly regarding the irreducibility of privacy concerns to purely functional issues of efficiency and ease of use. The broader conceptions of HCI will be needed to deal with complex real-world social and ethical issues like privacy.

---

4  Irving Altman, *The Environment and Social Behavior: Privacy, Personal Space, Territory and Crowding.* (Monterey, CA: Brooks/Cole Publishing, 1975).

5  Roger Clarke, "Introduction to Dataveillance and Information Privacy, and Definition of Terms"; *http://www.anu.edu.au/people/Roger.Clarke/DV/Intro.html.*

6  For example, see Chapter 24 and Chapter 25, this volume.

# Relevant HCI Research Streams

HCI is composed of numerous research streams, as is any scientific area. Thus, we cannot hope to cover the field here. Useful surveys include the *Handbook of Human-Computer Interaction*[7] and *Readings in Human-Computer Interaction: Toward the Year 2000*,[8] especially the chapter introductions. See also the annotated bibliography of HCI resources provided by Karat, Brodie, and Karat.[9]

In any case, several research streams within HCI are of immediate interest to the examination of privacy and the design of privacy mechanisms. These include:

- Basic design considerations—designing for general usability and the evaluation of usability (usability engineering).

- How people interact with and through systems (Computer-Supported Cooperative Work, or CSCW).

- How individuals differ in their capabilities and how that affects the human-computer interface (individual differences and tailorability).

- The role of HCI in next-generation architectures (ubiquitous computing, pervasive computing).

Each is covered in the following sections.

## Usability Engineering

Over the last 20 years, considerable interest and effort have gone into improving the usability of computers. Advances in the 1980s such as mice and GUIs greatly expanded the market by removing ease-of-use barriers. Subsequent investment in and by the HCI community has yielded a wide variety of usability engineering and testing methods. It is now generally recognized that modern software and hardware cannot ignore usability. Potential users simply will not adopt or use features that are difficult to use, and organizations will not deploy hardware and software that are difficult to manage.

Addressing these usability requirements has become an acknowledged part of most development methodologies. In software engineering, it has been adopted into process models such as the prototyping, iterative, and even spiral models.[10] Generally, these recognize the need to iteratively design, develop, and test against real users in order to create usable systems. An excellent example of this process for a privacy mechanism can be seen in Cranor's implementation of Privacy Bird, which went through five iterations of development

---

7   Martin G. Helander, Thomas K. Landauer, and Prasad V. Prabhu, *Handbook of Human-Computer Interaction, 2nd Edition* (New York: Elsevier, 1997).

8   Ronald M. Baecker, William Buxton, Jonathan Grudin, and Saul Greenberg, *Readings in Human-Computer Interaction: Toward the Year 2000* (New York: Morgan Kaufmann, 1995).

9   See Chapter 4, this volume.

10  Ian Sommerville, *Software Engineering* (Reading, MA: Addison Wesley, 2001).

and evaluation.[11] Only through successive refinement can software engineers meet users' needs, capabilities, and expectations.

Privacy mechanisms are no exception. In many respects, they can be treated as any other critical platform feature, and addressed with existing usability engineering methods. Karat, Brodie, and Karat[12] provide an excellent overview of these methods and their application for security and privacy. They also point out some key differences between privacy (and security) mechanisms and kinds of functional features with which usability engineering is more typically concerned, caveats that are worth paraphrasing and reflecting upon here:

*While valued, privacy is not the users' primary task*
We would just add that calling attention to privacy and making it an explicit task at any level can be problematic. For example, Cranor discusses users' difficulties in explicitly articulating their privacy preferences.[13] The goal with privacy, then, is often not so much to measure and refine task performance as it is to refine task invisibility or lightweightness.

*Designs must encompass many different types of users*
Indeed, we devote a later section of this chapter to a discussion of techniques for dealing with individual differences.

*Privacy raises the stakes*
Badly designed features can lead not only to user rejection and increased development costs, but also to potential injury (even bodily injury, in the case of stalking via location-tracking technologies).

*Systems must respond to the legal and regulatory environment*
We note that this places additional demands for specialized expertise on the makeup of usability engineering efforts, beyond their traditional interdisciplinary competencies.

Karat, Brodie, and Karat outline the various phases of system development and the types of methods appropriate to each. Instead of repeating that here, we conclude this section by emphasizing and introducing a number of general approaches from usability engineering and user-centered design of particular use to people seeking to understand a design domain in depth. These may be of particular use for new, "disruptive" technologies that do not yet have substantial deployments in the field.

*Context*
Privacy is extremely contextual, based in the specifics of by whom, for what, where, why, and when a system is being used. Understanding people's needs and attitudes, and developing the necessary empathy to understand the world from their point of view, is

11 See Chapter 22, this volume.
12 Karat, Brodie, and Karat.
13 Cranor.

best derived by observing them "in the wild" and asking them open-ended questions. There really is no substitute for getting out into the field, and a number of more or less structured ethnographic methods have been developed. For example, contextual design[14] is a highly structured methodology for pulling out the task requirements and context—that is, going beyond the user interface and considering how users will use the privacy mechanisms in their tasks. Other approaches include discount ethnography[15] and rapid ethnography;[16] all of these seek to balance the valuable open-endedness and freedom of ethnographic investigations with practical requirements of timely return on research investments.

### Nuanced control

Control over one's personal data is often very nuanced and unconscious in everyday life. In order to understand what people are doing, it is often necessary to get them talking; observation alone is not enough because it does not provide the subjective understanding of the situation. Nor are discussions of past behavior: people are often not conscious of their actions, and the memory of what they did and why they did it can fade within minutes. For this reason, think-aloud protocols[17] were developed. In this methodology, users continuously describe their actions and reasons aloud. The researcher (or designer) may prompt the user from time to time to keep him talking, but the user provides a steady stream of reasons and subjective judgments. Over longer periods, related methodologies such as experience sampling[18] and diary keeping[19] may be useful.

### Low and high fidelity

Systems need not be fully constructed in order to evaluate their usability. Both low-fidelity and high-fidelity prototypes can be used by potential users. An often fruitful method is the Wizard of Oz study. In a Wizard of Oz study, the functionality of the system is simulated by people. For example, if the system requires the parsing of natural-language text, this can be effectively done by a person who simulates the functioning, for example, of a natural-language processing component of the potential system. In this way, designers can evaluate the adequacy of the system without constructing the system itself.

---

14 Hugh Beyer and Karen Holtzblatt, *Contextual Design: A Customer-Centered Approach to Systems Designs* (San Francisco: Morgan Kaufmann, 1997).

15 John Hughes, Val King, Tom Rodden, and Hans Andersen, "Moving Out from the Control Room: Ethnography in System Design," *Proceedings of the ACM Conference on Computer-Supported Cooperative Work (CSCW '94)* (1994), 429–439.

16 David R. Millen, "Rapid Ethnography: Time Deepening Strategies for HCI Field Research," *Proceedings of the ACM Conference on Designing Interactive Systems: Processes, Practices, Methods, and Techniques* (2000), 280–286.

17 Clayton Lewis, "Using the 'Thinking Aloud' Method in Cognitive Interface Design," IBM Research Report, RC-9265 (1982); K. Anders Ericsson and Herbert A. Simon, *Protocol Analysis: Verbal Reports as Data* (Cambridge, MA: MIT Press, 1993).

18 For example: Sunny Consolvo and Miriam Walker, "Using the Experience Sampling Method to Evaluate Ubicomp Applications," *IEEE Pervasive Computing* 2:2 (2003), 1536–1268.

19 For example: Leysia Palen and Marilyn Salzman, "Voice-mail Diary Studies for Naturalistic Data Capture Under Mobile Conditions," *Proceedings of the CSCW'2002* (2002), 87–95.

*Hybrids*

The previous approaches—delving into users' worlds, helping them to articulate and self-reflect, and getting prototypes into their hands—can be combined, elaborated on, and experimented with in almost limitless ways. Some particularly interesting hybrids include experience prototyping, bodystorming, and informance.[20] These design techniques go beyond what is traditionally meant by usability engineering, but show promise for more adequately addressing the real-world nuances of domains like privacy.

None of these usability requirement-gathering and usability evaluation techniques was constructed for privacy per se. However, because of the inherent complexity of privacy mechanisms, the large research stream about usability and user-centered design in HCI is potentially of considerable use.

The next research stream to be discussed considers how privacy mechanisms might be made more usable given the wide range of concerns and preferences that people have about their personal data.

## Computer-Supported Cooperative Work

An important stream of HCI research is Computer-Supported Cooperative Work (CSCW).[21] As already mentioned, HCI began by examining largely single-user applications and systems. Starting in the late 1980s, CSCW started as a counter-effort to consider collaborative computer use. Although this subarea of HCI began in the consideration of cooperative or collaborative work, it quickly grew to include many different forms of coordination and social organization. Much of the early work in CSCW simply ignored the issue of privacy: researchers implicitly assumed that people working jointly on a project had no reason to screen information from each other.

The interest of CSCW researchers in privacy began in the 1990s as a side effect of work on "shared spaces"—remote spaces that were electronically linked through audio and video.[22] An example of such a shared space was a video wall linking two lunchrooms in different

---

20  Marion Buchenau and Jane Fulton Suri, "Experience Prototyping," *Proceedings of the Conference on Designing Interactive Systems: Processes, Practices, Methods, and Techniques* (2000), 424–433.

21  Jonathan Grudin, "Computer-Supported Cooperative Work: History and Focus," *IEEE Computer* 27:5 (1994), 19–26; Gary M. Olson and Judith S. Olson, "Research on Computer Supported Cooperative Work," in M. Helander (ed.), *Handbook of Human Computer Interaction* (Amsterdam: Elsevier, 1997).

22  For example: Paul Dourish and Sara Bly, "Portholes: Supporting Awareness in a Distributed Work Group," *Proceedings of the ACM CHI '92 Conference on Human Factors in Computing Systems* (1992), 541–547; William Buxton, "Telepresence: Integrating Shared Task and Person Spaces," in R. M. Baecker (ed.), *Readings in Groupware and Computer-Supported Cooperative Work* (San Mateo, CA: Morgan Kaufman, 1993), 816–822; Sara A. Bly, Steve R. Harrison, and Susan Irwin, "Media Spaces: Bringing People Together in a Video, Audio, and Computing Environment," *Communications of the ACM* 36:1, (1993), 28–47.

cities. Media spaces had privacy problems that today are obvious. In one important study,[23] one of the authors found that she forgot a camera was on and began to change clothes. Other authors have reported similar events. Thus began a more systematic investigation into the issue of privacy within the context of CSCW.

Unlike HCI, which found its history in the literature of cognitive psychology, CSCW's literature came from the field of social interaction—specifically, social psychology and cognitive anthropology. Not only is this background important to understanding current CSCW research, but it also is critical in understanding privacy overall. For that reason, we next survey some of the key social theorists. (We follow this with an overview of the current CSCW literature appropriate to privacy mechanisms.) In many ways, these theorists' views have become almost assumptions within CSCW, and many CSCW studies have borne out their theories. The theorists' views most important to a discussion of privacy include the following:

- As those interested in privacy are aware, people have very nuanced views of their interactions with other people and find it problematic when those social interactions are constrained.[24] They handle this nuance with agility and contextually.[25]

- Goffman[26] noted that people present a "face" to others. Goffman, fascinated by spies and scam artists, proposed that everyone presents bits and pieces of themselves as socially appropriate to the other and, in fact, may wish to present themselves differently depending on the circumstances. A person may present himself as a loyal employee to his supervisor and a job seeker to another company. People find it very disconcerting when that capability is removed.

- Harold Garfinkel, in his examination of how people make sense of their everyday worlds, showed that people find it disconcerting when what they believe to be their everyday "normal" world is disrupted.[27] Some people may even become violently angry when they believe the rules of conduct or "normal" behavior are violated.

Privacy mechanisms, in specific, suffer from these issues. People have extremely nuanced views of other people (and groups, companies, and institutions), and want to safeguard their ability to properly present themselves to those others. At the same time, they will find it very difficult when those modes of presenting themselves change, or when the "rules" about their privacy and safeguards change.

---

23 Paul Dourish, Annette Adler, Victoria Bellotti, and Austin Henderson, "Your Place or Mine? Learning from Long-Term Use of Audio-Video Communication," *Computer Supported Cooperative Work* 5:1 (1996), 33–62.

24 Anselm L. Strauss, *Continual Permutations of Action* (New York: Aldine de Gruyter, 1993).

25 Lucy A. Suchman, *Plans and Situated Actions: The Problem of Human-Computer Communication* (New York: Cambridge University Press, 1987).

26 Erving Goffman, *The Presentation of Self in Everyday Life* (New York: Anchor-Doubleday, 1961).

27 Harold Garfinkel, *Studies in Ethnomethodology* (Englewood Cliffs, NJ: Prentice Hall, 1967).

Drawing on these theorists, CSCW research relevant to privacy can be roughly divided into three categories: media space applications, other collaborative applications with privacy concerns, and studies discussing privacy in relation to awareness.

Other applications raised similar privacy concerns. Palen[28] explored the issues with shared calendars and sharing information about users' schedules with co-workers, managers, and employees. For example, Palen noted that some workers used viewing their supervisors' open calendars to determine whether layoffs were likely, a move that might not have been in the company's interest. Other work on shared or public displays has raised concerns about automatically generated views or making information public. Finally, allowing people to view one another's temporal information, such as when people are available for communication, also raises obvious privacy concerns.[29]

These privacy problems have been analyzed in a series of papers that discuss the tradeoffs between awareness and privacy. *Awareness* is knowing what others are doing or even that they are around. First raised in media space studies[30] and other shared work investigations,[31] awareness is a critical issue in distributed, collaborative applications—one needs to know what other people are doing in the shared space. Hudson and Smith[32] went on to discuss the fundamental tradeoff between awareness and privacy. In their view, awareness requires the release of personal information; this necessitates the disruption of privacy or at least requires one's attention to controlling the release of personal data. They proposed a number of interesting technical solutions to solving the privacy-awareness tradeoff. Their video solution allowed cameras to provide awareness of a presence, but the blurred image did not allow the viewer to see details.[33] Their audio solution allowed one to hear voices in a media space, but not to make out the exact words. Neither solution required a user's attention, and yet particularly egregious problems, such as seeing too much or overhearing private conversations, were eliminated for workplace environments.

28 Leysia Palen, "Social, Individual and Technological Issues for Groupware Calendar Systems," *Proceedings of the ACM Conference on Human Factors in Computing Systems* (1999), 17–24.

29 James Bo Begole, Nicholas E. Matsakis, and John C. Tang, "Lilsys: Sensing Unavailability," *Proceedings of the ACM Conference on Computer Supported Cooperative Work* (2004), 511–514.

30 For example: Paul Dourish and Victoria Bellotti, "Awareness and Coordination in Shared Workspaces," *Proceedings of the Conference on Computer-Supported Cooperative Work (CSCW '92)* (1992), 107–114.

31 For example: Christian Heath and Paul Luff, "Collaboration and Control: Crisis Management and Multimedia Technology in London Underground Line Control Rooms," *Computer Supported Cooperative Work Journal* 1:1 (1992), 69–94.

32 Scott E. Hudson and Ian Smith, "Techniques for Addressing Fundamental Privacy and Disruption Tradeoffs in Awareness Support Systems," *Proceedings of the ACM Conference on Computer-Supported Cooperative Work (CSCW '96)* (1996), 248–257.

33 This idea was also considered in Michael Boyle, Christopher Edwards, and Saul Greenberg, "The Effects of Filtered Video on Awareness and Privacy," *Proceedings of the ACM Conference on Computer Supported Cooperative Work* (2000), 1–10.

More recently, however, Neustaedter, Greenberg, and Boyle have found that blurring is not always sufficient to protect privacy in home environments.[34]

Work on privacy continues within CSCW. Recently, Palen and Dourish[35] pointed out that privacy is a dynamic, dialectic process. Based on the work of Altman,[36] Dourish and Palen analyze the relational nature of privacy. Ackerman[37] has discussed the difficulty of privacy, and has suggested that because of the relational, nuanced, and situated complexity of privacy issues for many people, there is likely to be a gap between what we know we must do socially and what we know how to do technically. He calls this the *social-technical gap*, and sees it as a major stumbling block for building effective user-centered controls for privacy mechanisms.

## Individual Differences

Users differ widely in their privacy concerns. We know from the research literature that individuals do not view "privacy" uniformly, even in e-commerce. Types of concerns and degrees of concern segment the population:

*People have differing types of concerns*

Culnan and Armstrong[38] make the argument that people have two kinds of privacy concerns. First, they are concerned about unauthorized others accessing their personal data because of security breaches or the lack of internal controls. Second, people are concerned about the risk of secondary use; that is, the reuse of their personal data for unrelated purposes without their consent. This includes sharing with third parties who were not part of the original transaction. It also includes the aggregation of personal data to create a profile. Smith, Milberg, and Burke[39] raise two additional concerns: People have a generalized anxiety about personal data being collected, and people are also concerned about their inability to correct any errors.

*People also differ in their level of concern*

The research literature generally describes a general anxiety and its extent, but some research provides more detail. A persistent finding is that it is useful to consider U.S. consumers not as one homogenous group. Westin[40] found three separate groups: the

---

34 C. Neustaedter, S. Greenberg, and M. Boyle, "Blur Filtration Fails to Preserve Privacy for Home-Based Video Conferencing," *ACM Transactions on Computer Human Interactions (TOCHI)* (2005, in press).

35 Leysia Palen and Paul Dourish, "Unpacking 'Privacy' for a Networked World," *Proceedings of the ACM Conference on Human Factors in Computing Systems (CHI)* (2003), 129–136.

36 Altman.

37 Mark S. Ackerman, "The Intellectual Challenge of CSCW: The Gap Between Social Requirements and Technical Feasibility," *Human-Computer Interaction* 15:2–3 (2000), 179–204.

38 Mary J. Culnan and Pamela K. Armstrong, "Information Privacy Concerns, Procedural Fairness and Impersonal Trust: An Empirical Investigation," *Organization Science* 10:1 (1999), 104–115.

39 Jeff H. Smith, Sandra J. Milberg, and Sandra J. Burke, "Information Privacy: Measuring Individuals' Concerns about Organizational Practices," *MIS Quarterly* (June 1996), 167–196.

40 Alan F. Westin, *Harris-Equifax Consumer Privacy Survey 1991* (Atlanta: Equifax, Inc., 1991).

# THUNDERWIRE: A CSCW RESEARCH STUDY

Thunderwire was an experimental audio-only media space prototype developed at Interval Research. It provided a kind of "party line" shared audio connection that was continuously available to a small, fixed group of spatially distributed users. Thunderwire had an intentionally minimalist interface (to see how simple such interfaces could be while still usable): basically an on/off switch. When *on*, microphones fed local audio into the party line and lit a red "on the air" light to notify the user (and any passersby). When *off*, microphones and lights were deactivated. Users of the system comprised a video analysis and analysis tool-building team that routinely worked with audio, facilitating the addition of Thunderwire to their work practices. Their manager wanted to use the system as an awareness technology, aimed at more tightly integrating the team across locations within two buildings.

The field study lasted two months and consisted of nine users. Overall, the success of the Thunderwire experiment was mixed. But for a small core of habitual users, it became a valued and enlivening aspect of their workplace, a predominantly social medium allowing for intermittent chat among friends. These benefits came with privacy problems, chiefly the inability to tell who at any given time was present on the party line, as well as recurring problems with leaving the system on by mistake and unintentionally broadcasting phone conversations, bodily noises, and other distractions. Unintentional broadcasting was a serious issue; similar to other media space studies, participants forgot that they were part of a live, shared space. Of particular interest was how the group developed informal social norms about how the system was and was not to be used, as well as how exceptions were to be handled. In this way, the participants were able to make the system usable for themselves.

The researchers used multiple methods to collect data about the system over a two-month study period. A central server continuously logged when each user connected or disconnected. Two weeks of audio activity were recorded (with all users' knowledge and permission). An outside researcher (the first author) was contracted to study the system. He observed the users' work, and he interviewed the users before, during, and after the system deployment. He and his students also transcribed and analyzed 18 hours of the system's audio, which captured the nuances of actual system use. Having an "outsider" as principal investigator was important to ensure the confidentiality of the people's data and to encourage openness on the part of interviewees. It also brought new perspectives and disciplinary backgrounds to the research team.

For a full analysis, see Mark S. Ackerman, Debby Hindus, Scott D. Mainwaring, and Brian Starr, "Hanging on the Wire: A Field Study of an Audio-Only Media Space," *ACM Transactions on Computer-Human Interaction* 4:1 (1997), 39–66.

---

marginally concerned, the privacy fundamentalists, and the pragmatic majority. The groups differ significantly in their privacy preferences and attitudes. The marginally concerned group is mostly indifferent to privacy concerns; the privacy fundamentalists, on the other hand, are quite uncompromising about their privacy. The majority of the

U.S. population, however, are members of the pragmatic majority. The pragmatic majority are concerned about their privacy but are willing to trade personal data for some benefit (e.g., customer service).

These groupings have been consistent across studies.[41] (Spiekermann, Grosslags, and Berendt divided the pragmatics into those who were concerned with revealing their identity and those who were more concerned about making their personal profiles available.) Estimates of these groups' sizes differ, and they appear to be changing over time. Westin found population estimates shown in Table 19-1; notice that Westin 2003 is a study after 9/11. Spiekermann *et al.* noted a larger group of privacy fundamentalists and fewer marginally concerned in Germany. Note, however, that despite these groupings, consumers still want adequate measures to protect their information from inappropriate sale, accidental leakage or loss, and deliberate attack.[42] Indeed, in Ackerman, Cranor, and Reagle,[43] the concerns of pragmatists were often reduced significantly by the presence of privacy protection measures such as privacy laws or privacy policies on web sites.[44]

*TABLE 19-1. Population estimates, by privacy cluster*

|  | Privacy fundamentalists | Marginally concerned | Pragmatic majority |
|---|---|---|---|
| Westin 1995 | 25% | 20% | 55% |
| Westin 2000 | 25% | 12% | 63% |
| Westin 2003 | 37% | 11% | 52% |

Given this diversity in how users view privacy, how might one design for these differences among users' capabilities, concerns, and preferences? An old research theme in HCI is that of individual differences. Experimental and cognitive psychology, as literatures, have largely ignored differences among subjects, seeing them as part of experimental error. As well, as Egan[45] notes, "Differences among users have not been a major concern of commercial computer interface designers." However, HCI's heritage in man-machine interfaces (human factors) led HCI to appreciate how people varied. Human factors had found this critical: when constructing airplane cockpits, industrial lighting, or even office chairs, differences among individuals can be critical for safety, comfort, and usability. This concern about human factors led into user interfaces and HCI research.

41 For example: Mark S. Ackerman, Lorrie Cranor, and Joseph Reagle. "Privacy in E-Commerce: Examining User Scenarios and Privacy Preferences," *Proceedings of the ACM Conference in Electronic Commerce* (1999), 1–8; Sarah Spiekermann, Jens Grossklags, and Bettina Berendt. "E-Privacy in 2nd Generation E-Commerce: Privacy Preferences Versus Actual Behavior," *Proceedings of the ACM Conference on Electronic Commerce* (2001), 38–46.

42 Gurpreet S. Dhillon and Trevort T. Moores, "Internet Privacy: Interpreting Key Issues," *Information Resources Management Journal* 14:4 (2001), 33–37.

43 Ackerman, Cranor, and Reagle.

44 Alan Westin (2003); *http://www.harrisinteractive.com/advantages/pubs/DNC_AlanWestinConsumersPrivacyandSurveyResearch.pdf.*

45 Dennis E. Egan, "Individual Differences in Human-Computer Interaction," in M. Helander (ed.), *Handbook of Human-Computer Interaction* (New York: North-Holland, 1988), 543–568.

Egan summarizes much of the work in early HCI about individual differences. Note that this research theme is largely moribund in HCI.[46] The later volume of the *Handbook of Human-Computer Interaction*,[47] published in 1997, does not have a similar chapter. However, rekindling this research stream is likely to be of help to privacy and similar mechanisms.

The interest in Egan's chapter, as well as in most of the individual differences research, was to determine the source of efficiencies and errors in using computer systems. The goal was to find ways to help users more effectively use their task knowledge and to reduce errors. As he notes, there are huge variances among users' performance (occasionally 20:1), much more extreme than among workers performing tasks (at most, 2:1). Users have, if anything, even wider variance when considering privacy. One can see that people vary not only in their system performance, but also in their understanding of the task and its implications for privacy. All of these differences, as well as their attitudes, must be considered when constructing privacy mechanisms, and as HCI found, several standard techniques can be used.

These approaches to accommodating user differences should be of considerable interest to those constructing or researching privacy mechanisms. The approaches described by Egan are still the predominant methods in HCI research and practice for handling diversity, and they are of direct relevance to privacy mechanisms. These approaches are:

*Constructing better interfaces*

As Egan stated, "This approach is similar to standard human-interface design, except that it is shaped by a concern for the variability among users."[48] This is particularly important for systems where people are not expert users and where they will remain "permanent casual users." Redesigning interfaces and systems so as to reduce usability problems is a laudable goal. Yet, because of the complexity of privacy concerns for users, it is unlikely that a "one size fits all" approach will work adequately.[49] The concomitant possibility of constructing software that has all potential privacy functionality for a task (like the solution adopted by some word processors and office applications) may not work with privacy concerns or may be too complex for users, because the functionality is likely to cut across many tasks, systems, and applications.

*Clustering users*

This approach advocates accommodating user differences by finding a set of user clusters and then interacting with the users through those classifications. This can be done

---

46 But see Andrew Dillon and Charles Watson, "User Analysis in HCI: The Historical Lesson from Individual Differences Research," *International Journal of Human-Computer Studies* 45:6 (1996), 619–637.

47 Helander, Landauer, and Prabhu.

48 Egan, 559.

49 Mark S. Ackerman, "The Intellectual Challenge of CSCW: The Gap Between Social Requirements and Technical Feasibility," *Human-Computer Interaction* 15:2–3 (2000), 179–204.

in several different ways. Egan viewed it largely as a question of developing different interfaces. One could also have different dialog or interaction patterns with different user classes. More currently, one might treat these differing clusters of users differently. As Egan states, "Identical actions from two different users may be treated quite differently if the users have been classified as different prototypes [classes]."[50] Indeed, work on several problems shows the analytical power in examining user clusters. One set of papers examines default settings.[51] Most users not only do not program their systems, but also neither customize them nor change the default settings.[52]

Another set of research shows that different groups have different mental models or technology frames.[53] Orlikowski,[54] in her study of a collaborative work system, showed that administrative personnel, managers, frontline consultants, and information technology staff all brought differing incentives and disincentives, reward and compensation expectations, and goals. For example, frontline consultants could not bill to learn the system, whereas information technology workers wanted to know as much about the system as possible. Similarly, privacy mechanisms will be used very differently by people with differing assumptions about power and control, the efficacy of regulation and law, and the benign intent of companies. Finding suitable user clusters is important, but may be challenging, especially for members of the pragmatic majority. In some situations, however, it may be possible to teach users and consumers new technology frames. Orlikowski noted the importance of training.

These two lines of inquiry have led to discussions of creating specific default and other settings for varying user clusters. Grudin[55] suggested defaults for office applications, where different groups of people (managers, administrative assistants, and knowledge workers) use the systems very differently. For privacy, while the pragmatics are a large and highly differentiated group in their everyday, contextualized preferences, it may be quite possible to treat privacy fundamentalists and the marginally concerned as user clusters. By doing so, it may be possible to create usable privacy mechanisms for at least

50 Egan, 560.

51 Wendy E. Mackay, Thomas W. Malone, Kevin Crowston, Ramana Rao, David Rosenblitt, and Stuart K. Card, "How Do Experienced Information Lens Users Use Rules?" *Proceedings of ACM CHI '89 Conference on Human Factors in Computing Systems* (1989), 211–216; Wendy E. Mackay, "Triggers and Barriers to Customizing Software," *Proceedings of ACM CHI '91 Conference on Human Factors in Computing Systems* (1991), 153–160; Jonathan Grudin, "Managerial Use and Emerging Norms: Effects of Activity Patterns on Software Design and Deployment," *Proceedings of the Hawaii International Conference on System Sciences* 37 (2004).

52 Wendy E. Mackay, "Patterns of Sharing Customizable Software," *Proceedings of ACM CSCW '90 Conference on Computer-Supported Cooperative Work* (1990), 209–221.

53 Wanda J. Orlikowski, "Learning from Notes: Organizational Issues in Groupware Implementation," *Proceedings of the Computer Supported Cooperative Work (CSCW '92)* (1992), 362–369; Wanda J. Orlikowski, "The Duality of Technology: Rethinking the Concept of Technology in Organizations," *Organization Science* 3:3 (1992), 398–427.

54 Orlikowski, "Learning from Notes."

55 Grudin, 2004.

these groups (which may be over a majority of the population). Very recently, Olson, Grudin, and Horvitz[56] explored clustering in privacy preferences. While their work is still preliminary, it suggests that there are key classes of recipients and data. While people vary overall, these classes of recipients and data may remain relatively constant.

*Adaptive systems*

These systems prevent user errors by helping users. Carroll, in a line of work,[57] promoted "training wheels" interfaces providing reduced functionality so as to avoid errors from complex interactions with the system. Similarly, critics are interface agents that help users avoid mistakes by noting when there are problems.[58] In Fischer and Lemke,[59] the critics let the users (who were kitchen designers) know when they had made a mistake, such as placing an appliance in front of a door. Ackerman and Cranor[60] used critics to help users with their privacy on the Web. Their Privacy Critics system alerted the user when, for example, he might be violating his own privacy or when sites might be problematic.

*Automated "Mastery Learning"*

HCI has had a large number of studies on training and documentation. Egan promoted using automatic training, such as tutors, to help users gain the expertise necessary to use systems effectively. Many studies[61] have noted the use of training to facilitate changing or expanding users' mental models of the system and potential tasks. To our knowledge, no such tutoring or training system has been constructed for privacy, although one clearly would be useful.

*Tailorable systems*

A fifth approach has also arisen, following from the first two approaches. With this approach, users tailor or customize the systems to fit their needs. *Customizing* usually refers to changing the surface interfaces of a system; *tailoring* usually refers to deeper changes to the functionality of an application.[62] With this approach, the designer includes large amounts of functionality, most of which any given user will not use.

---

56 Judith S. Olson, Jonathan Grudin, and Eric Horvitz, "Toward Understanding Preferences for Sharing and Privacy," Microsoft Research Technical Report (2004), 138.

57 For example: John M. Carroll and C. Carrithers, "Training Wheels in a User Interface," *Communications of the ACM* 27:8 (1984), 800–806.

58 Gerhard Fischer, Andreas C. Lemke, Thomas Mastaglio, and Anders I. Morch, "Using Critics to Empower Users," in *Proceedings of ACM CHI '90 Conference on Human Factors in Computing Systems* (1990), 337–347.

59 Gerhard Fischer and Andreas C. Lemke, "Construction Kits and Design Environments: Steps Toward Human Problem-Domain Communication," *Human-Computer Interaction* 3:3 (1988), 179–222.

60 Mark S. Ackerman and Lorrie Cranor, "Privacy Critics: UI Components to Safeguard Users' Privacy," *Proceedings of the ACM Conference on Human Factors in Computing Systems (CHI '99)* (1999), 258–259.

61 For example: Orlikowski, "Learning from Notes."

62 Jakob Hummes and Bernard Merialdo, "Design of Extensible Component-Based Groupware," *Computer Supported Cooperative Work Journal* 9:1 (2000), 53–74.

Unlike robust interfaces, which present "one size fits all" interfaces, tailorable systems allow users to pick and choose their functionality. Information technology personnel, users with computer expertise (called gardeners in Nardi[63]), or even end users customize and tailor the systems to create new or specialized applications.

Much of this work has appeared in the context of group applications (discussed earlier), because of the need to fulfill the needs of many users simultaneously. Discussions of the organizational and social requirements can be found in Trigg and Bodker.[64] Their major findings include the necessity for having both people with task knowledge and local technical support help the tailoring process. Discussions of potential system architectures and requirements can be found in Hummes and Merialdo[65] and Dourish and Edwards.[66]

In summary, then, HCI has considerable experience dealing with individual differences. In one approach suitable to privacy mechanisms, it has been found valuable to cluster users, and then to present different interfaces or functionality to those users. Another approach is to allow users to tailor the systems to their own needs; however, this often requires that they obtain tailoring help from others. And finally, two intelligent augmentations have been found to be helpful in the HCI literature—mechanisms to help users prevent errors and mechanisms to help tutor the users about, in this case, privacy.

The idea of designing for individual differences also has a downside that is important to keep in mind: the potential for amplifying power imbalances and decreasing fairness. By classifying someone as a privacy fundamentalist, say, a system could decide that he is too much trouble and put up barriers to discourage use. Conversely, unscrupulous designers could segment users in order to seek out novices or the marginally concerned, not to offer targeted assistance, but for relatively easy exploitation. These issues are not restricted to privacy, as any system that discriminates between users opens itself to the question of whether this discrimination is unfair (or paternalistic, de-individualizing, or otherwise unwarranted). It is important to acknowledge and guard against this problem, in terms of both actual effects and perception. However, this is not to say that an "individual differences" approach is to be avoided—only that it must be used with caution.

63  Bonnie Nardi, *A Small Matter of Programming: Perspectives on End User Computing* (Cambridge, MA: MIT Press, 1993).

64  Randall H. Trigg and Susanne Bodker, "From Implementation to Design: Tailoring and the Emergence of Systematization in CSCW," *Proceedings of the ACM Conference on Computer-Supported Cooperative Work* (1994), 45–54.

65  Hummes and Merialdo.

66  Paul Dourish and W. Keith Edwards, "A Tale of Two Toolkits: Relating Infrastructure and Use in Flexible CSCW Toolkits," *Computer Supported Cooperative Work Journal* 9:1 (2000), 33–51.

## Ubiquitous Computing (Ubicomp)

There is currently considerable interest in ubiquitous and pervasive computing in HCI.[67] In these architectures, one might have hundreds or even thousands of sensors and other computational devices spread out through a room, building, or other environment. People would wear them, carry them, or even have them embedded. HCI and ubicomp are not identical areas of computer science, but there is overlap in research. In particular, HCI researchers are very interested in augmented reality applications (where the digital world augments the physical), sensor-based entertainment (such as geo-games), and user-centered interfaces to ubicomp rooms.

There are significant privacy concerns for ubiquitous computing environments. Obviously, location sensors can track individuals through an environment. Sensor aggregation could tell a large amount about what any given individual might be doing. Large amounts of seemingly personal data could be collected without the notice or consent of an environment's users.

Recently, several studies have specifically examined privacy in ubicomp environments. In an ethnographic field study, Beckwith[68] found that workers and elderly residents in a sensor-network-equipped assisted-care facility had very limited understanding of the potential privacy risks of the technology. They instead trusted that the system was benign and perceived the privacy risks to be minimal. Without understanding, informed consent is very difficult. As with work in media spaces,[69] unobtrusive interfaces that encourage users to forget that they are being recorded or tracked bring benefits in ease of use but also risks to users.

Other work considers methodologies for designing for privacy in these new environments. Langheinrich, drawing upon the European Union's privacy directive of 1995, identifies the following guiding principles for ubicomp designs:

- Notice
- Choice and consent
- Anonymity and pseudonymity
- Proximity and locality

67 For an overview, see Gregory D. Abowd and Elizabeth D. Mynatt, "Charting Past, Present, and Future Research in Ubiquitous Computing," *ACM Transactions on Computer-Human Interaction* 7:1 (2000), 29–58.

68 R. Beckwith, "Designing for Ubiquity: The Perception of Privacy," *IEEE Pervasive Computing* 2:2 (2003), 40–46.

69 For example: Mark S. Ackerman, Debby Hindus, Scott D. Mainwaring, and Brian Starr, "Hanging on the Wire: A Field Study of an Audio-Only Media Space," *ACM Transactions on Computer-Human Interaction* 4:1 (1997), 39–66. Also, Dourish *et al.*

- Adequate security

- Access and recourse[70]

This work calls attention to legal frameworks not just as requirements to be met, but also as sources of design inspiration and insight. Hong *et al.* propose a methodology for prototyping ubicomp applications involving the development of a privacy risk model (a kind of heuristic evaluation, combined with validation through user testing).[71] Lederer *et al.* also provide design guidelines for privacy.[72]

Finally, Hong and Landay examine the system issues.[73] Their Confab system provides a middleware layer for building ubicomp applications. Combining a blackboard and data-flow architecture, Confab allows users to publish and services to request data with strong privacy controls. Users can place privacy tags on all data that controls access within a Confab infospace and can provide hints about how the data is to be used outside the Confab system. In addition to customizable privacy mechanisms, Confab also includes extension mechanisms, currently about location awareness.

Ubicomp research is just beginning, and over time, we expect this field to provide considerable feedback to privacy mechanisms overall.

## Conclusion

In this chapter, we presented a range of HCI research that we believe can be of help to those designing privacy mechanisms. These included usability evaluations and requirement gathering, including the large range of HCI methods for incorporating users and users' viewpoints in the process; collaborative views of information and activity, including many systems and applications as well as a range of social analyses that promote a detailed, situated view of privacy; handling diversity and difference among users, including the HCI approaches to this problem; and new approaches to new computational environments, including studies and systems for pervasive environments.

We note in passing that HCI could profit by considering privacy more fully. The direction of research should not be one-way. Cross-cultural studies of privacy could inform the nascent interest in HCI in cross-cultural interfaces and coordination. Increased understanding of the diversity and complexity of user preferences, and potential clusterings, is

---

70 Marc Langheinrich, "Privacy by Design—Principles of Privacy-Aware Ubiquitous Systems," *Proceedings of the Ubicomp 2001* (2001), 273–291.

71 Jason I. Hong, Jennifer D. Ng, Scott Lederer, and James A. Landay, "Privacy Risk Models for Designing Privacy-Sensitive Ubiquitous Computing Systems," *Proceedings of the ACM Conference on Designing Interactive Systems* (2004), 91–100.

72 Scott Lederer, Jason I. Hong, Anind K. Dey, and James A. Landay, "Personal Privacy Through Understanding and Action: Five Pitfalls for Designers," *Personal and Ubiquitous Computing* 8:6 (2004), 440–454. See also Chapter 21, this volume.

73 Jason I. Hong and James A. Landay, "An Architecture for Privacy-Sensitive Ubiquitous Computing," *Proceedings of the 2nd International Conference on Mobile Systems, Applications, and Services* (2004), 177–189.

providing new impetus for HCI research on individual differences. As well, considering visualizations and intelligent tutoring systems for privacy, in a range of applications and tasks, could germinate new emphases in HCI. We hope that HCI work grows to consider these and other aspects of privacy needs.

Privacy in digital environments is likely to remain a critical issue for the foreseeable future. As it directly engages aspects of user control and power, it is central to the concerns of HCI. We fully expect the two areas of interest—HCI and privacy—to remain closely interlocked in interest and need.

## About the Authors

Mark S. Ackerman is an associate professor of electrical engineering and computer science and of information at the University of Michigan. He has published extensively on a number of Human-Computer Interaction topics, including Computer-Supported Cooperative Work, information access, collaborative memory systems, and privacy.

Scott D. Mainwaring is a senior researcher in the People and Practices Research Lab at Intel Research. His research interests include design ethnography; home environments; the human relationship to infrastructure; and the community, trust, and privacy implications of ubiquitous computing.

# CHAPTER TWENTY

# A User-Centric Privacy Space Framework

**BENJAMIN BRUNK**

**W**ITH THE MASS POPULARIZATION OF THE **I**NTERNET AT THE END OF THE **20**TH CENTURY, hundreds of new software tools, systems, and services specifically designed for security and privacy protection became available. Many hoped that this great effort would help fight back the widely acknowledged technological assault on privacy, especially privacy in cyberspace. But most of these tools were difficult to use and, as a result, fell short of their intended goals.

Looking at the failing of existing tools, I decided to create my own tool or suite of tools that would borrow the best features from many other privacy and security tools that were available, but mine would further include a well-designed and soundly tested user interface. Like other authors in this volume, I believed that people would be motivated to protect their privacy only if they could understand and use the privacy-protecting tools that they were given.

Although I never created that ultimate privacy tool, my analysis of the space in which privacy tools exist and operate became the basis of my dissertation. Presented here, it is a useful framework for evaluating the strengths and weaknesses of many privacy and security tools.

# Introduction

Soon after I started work on my comprehensive privacy tool, I discovered that I could not decide which features it should include. Privacy tools were a new category of software tools in 1995: many had very specific and novel features that were critical to some people but useless to others. There was no consensus on which features were important to have. Nobody even knew which of the tools that were available for download even worked!

Trolling on the Internet I found some web sites that had basic descriptions of some programs; sometimes, these sites even included ratings. But I couldn't find any comprehensive catalogs of the tools that were available.

The community of people who were actually developing these tools reflected this state of confusion. Many people were working on many products, but little communication was taking place among them. Without marketing experience, open source and independent developers had difficulty communicating why their products were actually needed. Meanwhile, those companies that had strong marketing frequently promoted their products with explanations that often devolved into impenetrable euphemisms.

I realized that I needed to perform a more thoughtful and systematic analysis. No one had yet examined privacy tools from the end user's perspective. How could this be done?

At the time my study took place, personal security solutions such as ZoneAlarm, PGP, and The Anonymizer were new and growing in popularity among Internet users. I began examining these tools specifically in terms of what privacy benefits they offered to the user. Upon examining the 134 tools, systems, and services that I thought had some relationship to privacy, I ended up with a large list of privacy features. As the work progressed, I began to see patterns emerge and could place tools and features into categories. At some point during the process, I began to refer to my collection of tools as the *privacy space*. I gave the tools, systems, and services within the privacy space the generic label of *solutions*.

Time has passed since my initial survey of privacy space solutions. Many solutions have been added to the privacy space and others have disappeared or have become insignificant. Despite the ever-changing nature of the privacy space, the framework I developed remains relevant. However, before I can discuss the Privacy Space Framework and why it is useful to us, first we must place this work into the larger context of privacy, especially online privacy.

## Privacy

Noam talks about privacy as the place where the information rights of different parties collide.[1] Everyone needs privacy, but there are no "one-size-fits-all" remedies or equations

---

1   Eli Noam, "Privacy and Self-Regulation: Markets for Electronic Privacy," in *Privacy and Self Regulation in the Information Age* (Washington, D.C.: U.S. Department of Commerce, 1997).

that can decide how privacy should be balanced against other goods. Privacy is inherently a matter of individual choices and needs, a flux that is bounded by societal factors and personal preferences. To Noam, privacy is fundamentally about the flow of personal information between parties that have different preferences for how that information should be utilized.

Technology has a strong influence on our attitudes toward privacy and on how much (or how little) privacy individuals can attain. This is because the balance that Noam describes is inherently altered by the dropping cost of mass surveillance and data retention technologies. The fact that large amounts of information can be economically collected and used increases the desire of organizations to do so.

As online communication becomes more commonplace and as more information becomes available via the Internet, it is imperative that the ability of individuals to control the dissemination of their personal information keeps pace. One common way to help individuals keep pace is to prevent or limit information exchanges through the use of policy, law, and regulation. An obvious problem with such collective solutions is that the individual's perspective and individual choice almost invariably suffer. Another problem with these solutions is that they can produce a smokescreen that results in no real progress toward the goal of enhancing privacy.

Another approach to the privacy problem is to engage individuals with an array of technological privacy solutions. These solutions allow individuals to extend their senses into the cyberrealm and become aware of the information that is flowing away from each of us.

Each of us constantly makes choices whether to communicate our identities, ideas, and preferences. McLean calls this form of privacy *access privacy*.[2] Allowing access to personal information may not be a decision that we spend much time contemplating in some cases, but it is a conscious choice.

Despite the dour outlook for privacy in America documented by numerous scholars[3, 4, 5, 6], all is not lost. As individuals, each of us has the ability to retain some control over our personal information flows. Choosing tools that allow us to better understand and enforce our preferences is of paramount importance. Informed choices come from being aware of what information is being passed. The privacy space framework helps inform such choices by giving individuals a tool for making well-considered choices when it comes to their privacy.

2   Deckle McLean, *Privacy and Its Invasion* (Westport, CT: Praeger Publishers, 1995).

3   Simson Garfinkel, *Database Nation: The Death of Privacy in the 21st Century* (Sebastopol, CA: O'Reilly Media, 2000).

4   Amitai Etzioni, *The Limits of Privacy* (New York: Basic Books, 1999).

5   B. Meeks, "The Privacy Hoax," *Communications of the ACM* 42:2 (1999).

6   Winn Schwartau, *Information Warfare: Chaos on the Electronic Superhighway* (New York: Thunder's Mouth Press, 1996).

## Exoinformation

We must expect to reveal a great deal about ourselves in everyday interactions. We continually shed information about ourselves, usually with no thought whatsoever because the process is so unavoidable. This kind of personal information "broadcast" was noted by Singleton during a workshop pertaining to online profiling.[7] Or, as Sanchez says so succinctly: "Merely by walking outdoors, we put ourselves in the public domain."[8]

*Exoinformation* is the word that I use to describe what Singleton and Sanchez are talking about. Exoinformation has become an important commodity; companies such as Double-Click, Inc. gather it up and piece it together to build mosaics that more or less reflect the preferences of individuals and society as a whole. Exoinformation is gleaned from the tidbits of information that we give off during information-seeking activities. Like pottery shards, arrowheads, or other disassociated artifacts that archaeologists use to glean knowledge of past civilizations, the string you used in a search query, the timestamp of a request, a logged event on a server, or the URL typed into a browser window are all left-behind remnants of a life. As with archaeology, each individual tidbit is insignificant. But patterns emerge when the fragments are combined. Many people believe that this ability to cross-reference exoinformation and make sense out of it will one day become a powerful tool.

Although it is tempting to define exoinformation solely in terms of the human-computer interface,[9] the term can be applied universally to all of the informational byproducts of an individual's life activities.

Westin used the term *data shadow*[10] to describe exoinformation, and Olsen used the term *data exhaust*.[11] Why do we need a new term when we have been talking about this concept for years?

Although the concept of exoinformation is not new, never before have we had a clear and descriptive term that was not itself a metaphor that needed to be explained and that opened itself up to argument. McLean[12] noted that our vocabulary on privacy is extraordinarily small. By standardizing on this word *exoinformation*, I hope that we can stop discussing the existence of this privacy leakage and start discussing what to do about it.

7   Solveig Singleton, "Comments Submitted in the FTC/NTIA Workshop on Online Profiling," Cato Institute [cited Oct. 3, 2004]; *http://www.cato.org/pubs/wtpapers/991018comments.html*.

8   Julian Sanchez, "The Privacy Cage," Liberzine.com [cited Feb. 6, 2001]; *http://www.liberzine.com/juliansanchez/010205privacy.htm*.

9   Benjamin Brunk, "Exoinformation and User Interface Design," *ASIS&T Bulletin* (Aug./Sept. 2001).

10  Alan Westin, *Privacy and Freedom* (New York: Atheneum, 1967).

11  S. Olsen, "Web Browser Offers Incognito Surfing," *CNET News.com* [cited Feb. 1, 2003].

12  *Ibid*.

# EXFORMATION

As a brief aside, let us explore the origin of the word *exoinformation* and examine some related terminology. The word *exformation* was coined by Nørretranders,[a] who argued that effective communication depends on a shared body of knowledge between the persons communicating. If someone is talking about horses, for example, what is said will be unintelligible unless the person listening has some idea what a horse is, what it is good for, and in what contexts one might be encountered. By not defining the word *horse*, Nørretranders says, the speaker has deliberately discarded a body of information.

For example, writes Nørretranders, when Victor Hugo sent a telegram to his publisher asking how his most recent book, *Les Miserables*, was selling, Hugo wrote simply: "?" His publisher replied: "!" The exchange would have little meaning to a third party not privy to the shared context that was unique to Hugo and his publisher (and, now, to us).

Nørretranders called this shared context that consists of discarded but very important information *exformation*: "Exformation is everything we do not actually say but have in our heads when or before we say anything at all. Information is the measurable, demonstrable utterance we actually come out with."

Clearly, there is no way to measure how much exformation is contained in a message based solely on its information content, as the exchange between Hugo and his publisher elegantly demonstrates.

The concepts of exoinformation and exformation are related. Exformation refers to "the stuff you leave out" and exoinformation refers to "the stuff coming out of you" (hence the *exo-* prefix). Exoinformation is generated from the same stuff as exformation—the latter being the raw data from which the former is made.

Nørretranders did a superb job of describing the process by which knowledge is created through the selective shedding of information. What Nørretranders overlooked is the phenomenon in which another entity can locate and recycle someone's discarded information, usually beyond the sensory perception of the one doing the discarding. Nørretranders assumes that discarded information is lost to the world, but that is not always the case. We are only just beginning to understand what happens to this discarded information. Because of the nature of our digital technologies, it is much harder to eliminate information for good than we perceive it to be.

---

[a] Tor Nørretranders, *The User Illusion* (New York: Viking (published by the Penguin Group), 1998).

## Security and Privacy Frameworks

Before I introduce the Privacy Space Framework, let's examine some of the other frameworks that served as a basis for this effort.

# EXAMPLES OF EXOINFORMATION

Information is constantly escaping us without our knowledge. Some of this information is private information that we would rather others not see. For example, if you create a document in Microsoft Word and someone edits it for you using the Track Changes feature, the comments and edits can remain with the document even after you select Accept Changes. A third party with access to the document can recover data that most people think was deleted. It was not until several very public incidents in which hidden information was disclosed publicly that Microsoft developed and released a special add-in to "remove hidden data."[a]

Another example involves email. Suppose that someone sends you a message with a "Reply-to:" header field that redirects any replies to a different email address. Many people have been embarrassed (and even fired) for accidentally posting a message reply to a mailing list or a group of email lists instead of to an individual. A great deal of harm can ensue because an email tool's user interface does not safeguard against such actions.

The final example involves tracking web users with "web bugs,"[b] which normally take the form of 1x1-pixel invisible images. Suppose that someone posting a message to a message board includes a link to a web bug located on her own web server. Every time someone reads her message, the web bug image is loaded and the server hosting it logs the access. Unless message board surfers make note of images linked to externally, they have no way to even know their access has been logged by a third party. Their presence on that message board, in that thread, has been logged. More comprehensive use of web bugs on a message board could allow a third party to discover a wealth of information about the browsing habits and locations of otherwise anonymous peers visiting that message board.

---

[a] Microsoft, "Office 2003/XP Add-in: Remove Hidden Data," rhdtool.exe version 1.1.
[b] See Chapter 23, this volume.

## Codes of Fair Information Practice

Since the 1970s, the guidelines for Fair Information Practice (FIP) have been used as a basis for talking about privacy and ethical data usage. The first code was developed by the U.S. Department of Health, Education, and Welfare[13] in 1973. That code lays down seven basic principles, listed in Table 20-1.[14] Variations on this code represent the most common type of privacy guidelines in use today. In 1980, for example, a code known as the OECD

---

13 HEW, Secretary's Advisory Committee on Automated Personal Data Systems, Records, Computers, and the Rights of Citizens (HEW Report), U.S. Department of Health, Education, and Welfare, 1973.

14 *Ibid.*

principles[15] was devised to help standardize information-handling practices in international trade.

TABLE 20-1. Principles of Fair Information Practice

| Principle | Description |
| --- | --- |
| Openness | The existence of record-keeping systems and databanks that contain personal data must be publicly known, along with a description of the main purpose and uses of the data. |
| Individual participation | Individuals should have a right to view all information that is collected about them; they must also be able to correct or remove data that is not timely, accurate, relevant, or complete. |
| Collection limitation | There should exist limits to the collection of personal data; data should be collected by lawful and fair means and should be collected, where appropriate, with the knowledge or consent of the subject. |
| Data quality | Personal data should be relevant to the purposes for which it is collected and used; personal data should be accurate, complete, and timely. |
| Finality | There should be limits to the use and disclosure of personal data. Data should be used only for purposes specified at the time of collection; data should not be otherwise disclosed without the consent of the data subject or other legal authority. |
| Security | Personal data should be protected by reasonable security safeguards against such risks as loss, unauthorized access, destruction, use, modification, or disclosure. |
| Accountability | Record keepers should be accountable for complying with fair information practices. |

The primary drawback of using any code of fair information practice for studying the privacy space is that none of them are particularly user centered. The codes and categories deal with contractual agreements, and not with the actual solutions that may be implemented on the user's computer.

Fair Information Practice does little to enhance our understanding of the privacy space as viewed by the user, because the features examined in my study did not involve actual agreements between a data provider and a data collector.

## The ISTPA Privacy Framework

A more recent privacy framework is the International Security, Trust & Privacy Alliance (ISTPA) Privacy Framework, version 1.1.[16] The intent of the ISTPA is to build a global alliance of businesses and technology providers. Their goal is to perform research and evaluation of privacy standards, tools, and technologies and to try to set new standards for information handling. Their framework serves as an objective guideline or template for developing solutions to corporate privacy issues (especially corporations that have an interest in actively amassing sensitive personal data for use as a commodity). The ISTPA creates a means for assessing the completeness of proposed data-handling systems. The goal is to be able to account for personal information (PI) throughout its life cycle while

15 OECD, "Guidelines on the Protection of Privacy and Transborder Flows of Personal Data" (1980).

16 ISTPA, "ISTPA Privacy Framework," International Security & Privacy Trust Alliance (2002).

provably adhering to the agreements under which it was collected, even if that information changes hands many times.

The ISTPA Privacy Framework identifies the services and capabilities listed in Table 20-2.[17]

TABLE 20-2. The ISTPA Privacy Framework

| Service/Capability | Description |
| --- | --- |
| Audit | Handles the recording and maintenance of events in any service to capture the data that is necessary to ensure compliance with the terms and policies of an agreement and any applicable regulations. |
| Certification | Manages and validates the credentials of any party or process involved in processing of a PI transaction. |
| Control | Functions as "repository gatekeeper" to ensure that access to PI that is stored by a data collection entity complies with the terms and policies of an agreement and any applicable regulations. |
| Enforcement | Handles redress when a data collection entity is not in conformance with the terms and policies of an agreement and any applicable regulations. |
| Interaction | Presents proposed agreements from a data collection entity to the data subject; receives the subject's personal information, preferences, and actions; confirms actions; manages movement of data into and out of the framework. To the extent that the data subject is represented by an agent, this service comprises the interface to the agent. |
| Negotiation | Handles arbitration of a proposal between a data collection entity and a data subject. Successful negotiation results in an agreement. Humans, agents, or any combination can handle negotiations. |
| Validation (capability) | Checks for the accuracy of PI at any point in its life cycle. |
| Agent (capability) | Allows the data subject both to access the individual's PI that is held by a data collection entity, and to correct or update it as necessary. |
| Usage (capability) | Functions as a "processing monitor" to ensure that active use of PI complies with the terms and policies of an agreement and any applicable regulations. Such uses may include transfer, derivation, aggregation, pseudo-anonymization, linking, and inference of data. |

While some of the categories shown in the table are based on the same code of FIP already discussed, the ISTPA Privacy Framework is designed for the very specific purpose of creating an auditable system so that companies and organizations can collect and manage people's personal information while adhering to whatever data-handling regulations have been imposed upon them. This privacy framework is designed to help companies fend off legal challenges by showing that they have made a good-faith attempt to uphold their obligations and agreements in an untidy global regulatory environment. Similar to the codes of FIP, the ISTPA Privacy Framework is not a user-centric approach; it is a crisp system for creating formal specifications to promote trustworthy handling of sensitive data.

17 *Ibid.*

## Schneier's Security Processes Framework

The last framework we will examine is based on a discussion in Schneier,[18] which we refer to as the Security Processes Framework.

In the early 1990s, Bruce Schneier was best known as an author and researcher in the field of cryptography. But after spending years educating people about cryptography, Schneier had an epiphany: "People are erratic, capricious, and barely comprehensible." Even the strongest cryptography was no match for a person who misused it.

Schneier proceeded to take a more human-centered approach to the problem of security and quickly realized that security is a process rather than a product. He went on to describe four security processes, summarized in Table 20-3. The security processes deal with prevention, detection, response, and recovery; they focus on "attacks" from the outside, but also deal with introspective matters. Schneier has the beginnings of a truly user-oriented approach to security, but in my opinion, he still concentrates too much on an "outside looking in" perspective.

*TABLE 20-3. Security Processes Framework*

| Security process | Description/Notes |
|---|---|
| Prevent attacks | Prevention is the obvious first step, and digital security tends to rely wholly on prevention via cryptography, firewalls, and so forth. A prevention-only strategy can work if the prevention mechanisms are perfect and cannot be circumvented. The best prevention follows these principles: secure the weakest link; use choke points; compartmentalize information; use defense in depth; fail securely; leverage unpredictability; embrace simplicity; enlist the users; assure (audit); and question anomalies. |
| Detect attacks | Detection logically follows prevention because it is fundamentally impossible to prevent all attacks. On the Internet, detection can be a lot of work. A simple form of detection involves reading, understanding, and interpreting audit logs. The goal is to locate intruders in as close to real time as possible. |
| Respond to attacks | Response goes hand in hand with detection. If there is no response, then there is no reason to bother with detection. Response involves making the problem stop as well as tracking down and locating the culprits. |
| Recover from attacks | Recovering means fixing a problem after the bad guys are gone. This can mean patching the exploited code or cutting your losses and rebuilding a system from scratch. |

## The Privacy Space Framework

The Privacy Space Framework, consisting of the five categories listed in Table 20-4, is based upon the Security Processes Framework described in the previous section. Note that four of the five categories (all but Awareness) are based on work by Schneier.[19] Borrowing from this well-conceived work serves our purposes and offers a firm starting point from which to work. However, the Privacy Space Framework attempts to classify the user experience and further understand the features of privacy solutions. While the category

18 Bruce Schneier, *Secrets & Lies* (New York: John Wiley & Sons, Inc., 2002).
19 *Ibid.*

names are based on Schneier's work, the definitions have been modified to be more focused on user behaviors relating to privacy rather than security.

TABLE 20-4. Privacy Space Framework

| Category | Description |
|---|---|
| Awareness | Anything that conveys information without requiring the user to act. Awareness features are informative and help you monitor what is going on. |
| Detection | Tools or features that scan or actively look for potential problems. Often, detection tools are always running in the background; a virus scanner is a common detection tool that looks for malware and for certain dangerous operations being performed in memory. |
| Prevention | A feature or tool that is used as a precaution. Encryption or digital signatures are preventative in nature. Secure deletion of electronic documents is a good example of a preventative feature. |
| Response | Taking action after a problem has been detected is a response. Examples of responses include canceling your credit card after it has been stolen, and blocking incoming network traffic from certain IP addresses. |
| Recovery | Features and tools that help you get back to normal. Examples of recovery include restoring to the last known good state, patching bugs that allowed intruders to gain unauthorized access, and reinstalling corrupted files. |

Now that I have introduced the Privacy Space Framework, let's move on to discuss the research that led to its creation and continued development.

# Researching the Privacy Space

I developed the Privacy Space Framework to make sense of existing "privacy solutions." This study had two distinct phases: a feature analysis phase and a validation phase.

## Feature Analysis

The first phase used grounded techniques to assess a sample of solutions in order to "make replicable and valid inferences from data to their context."[20] To do this, I developed a technique known as *feature analysis*. This technique borrows heavily from the field of *content analysis*. A central idea in content analysis is that many observed pieces of data are classified into a set of content categories.[21] Text, words, phrases, or other units are classified into categories. Entries in each category are presumed to have the same or similar meanings.

Feature analysis takes a similar approach. Instead of classifying words, feature analysis classifies software features. A software feature is a capability for completing a certain task that has been designed into a system. As such, a software feature can be named and described in words, and the content of the name and description can be analyzed using

---

20 Barney Glaser and Anselm Strauss, *The Discovery of Grounded Theory* (Chicago: Aldine Publishing Company, 1967).

21 Robert Weber, *Basic Content Analysis, 2nd Edition* (Newbury Park, CA: Sage Publications, 1990).

conventional content-analytic techniques. A *privacy feature* is a software feature that offers some kind of privacy-related functionality to the user. It is often found that solutions designed for one purpose are later adapted by someone for other purposes. For our purposes, a privacy feature need not be consciously designed, or designed for protecting privacy; it only matters that the feature in question somehow relate to privacy, even if by accident.

To compile a list of privacy features, I started with a list of 134 privacy solutions. This list was compiled by examining software download web sites, privacy-related web sites, vendors' web sites, and news articles; visiting online and offline software stores; and following up on recommendations of friends and colleagues. The major product of this effort was a raw list of 1,291 privacy features and their descriptions.

The data for phase one was collected in just over a month's time during the spring of 2002. I was able to obtain trial versions or academic licenses for most solutions and install them on my own computer for testing. There were a handful of solutions that I was unable to try myself, and for these I had to rely solely on their documentation for the analysis.

To help the reader achieve a better understanding of the utility of the Privacy Space Framework and how it can be used to classify privacy solutions, here are some examples of solutions and their features.

### Example 1: PGP Freeware

PGP Freeware[22] is a program for encrypting and decrypting files and email messages using public key cryptography. The program's name (Pretty Good Privacy) and its marketing leave no ambiguity that this product was designed to help protect personal privacy.

My analysis revealed that version 7.0.3 of PGP Freeware includes 24 features that relate to privacy. Obvious privacy-related features include generating public and private keys, encrypting data, decrypting data, digitally signing and verifying data, and wiping files using a secure algorithm. Some of the less obvious privacy features I noticed relate more to the user interface—the toolbar that allows easy access to the program's features; the lock icon in the Windows tray that provides visual information about the status of the program; the key management interface that allows the user to easily import and export public and private keys; and even controls for what to do with data left on the clipboard after the program exists. I categorized most such features as relating to prevention. PGP also has many awareness-related features (e.g., graphical depictions of key lengths) and also some detection features (e.g., the ability to verify a digital signature and thus ascertain its authenticity). My analysis found no response or recovery features in this tool, however. Overall, I categorized PGP Freeware as a prevention and awareness tool.

22 PGP Freeware v. 7.0.3, PGP Corporation (1995).

## Example 2: WebWasher

One of the first tools I evaluated was WebWasher AG's WebWasher,[23] a program that removes advertisements and blocks pop-up windows on many web sites. I was already using WebWasher at the start of the Privacy Space study.

I identified 20 privacy features provided by WebWasher. Most of these relate to its web-filtering capability, such as its ability to filter cookies, web bugs, URL prefixes (e.g., *http://search.com?url=http://realurl.com* gets changed to *http://realurl.com* in order to thwart logging and advertising systems), and so on. The user interface for most of these features involves a checkbox to simply turn the feature on or off, as well as some explanatory text about what the feature accomplishes. Predictably, I found that most of these features deal with prevention and detection. WebWasher also includes some awareness features (e.g., a splash screen to let you know when it is running, warning messages when content is being filtered, and statistical information about the program's performance).

Unlike PGP Freeware, WebWasher includes a response feature in the form of a connection cutoff button that allows the user to quickly disconnect from a web site feeding harmful content. WebWasher also includes a "black list" feature that I considered to be a response feature. Thus, WebWasher covers all five categories in some fashion. Overall, I considered WebWasher to be an awareness and prevention tool, but also noted its detection capabilities, which, in this case, only mean that in order to filter certain kinds of web content, the tool would have to look for it (e.g., detect it) first.

## Example 3: ZoneAlarm

Many would argue that a personal firewall like ZoneLabs' ZoneAlarm[24] (described in Chapter 27) is a security tool and has little to do with protecting privacy. At the face level, that is true. However, if you take into consideration the user-centered approach of my study, tie in the concept of exoinformation, and acknowledge the enormous amount of sensitive data our personal computers store for us, the role that a personal firewall tool such as ZoneAlarm plays in protecting personal privacy is quite clear.

Based on my criteria, I found 13 privacy-related features in ZoneAlarm. Several of these are awareness related, such as the network traffic meter tray icon (e.g., if you are seeing heavy traffic either coming in or leaving your computer and you aren't using the network, you should probably investigate further), and the numerous different pop-up alert messages. An excellent response feature is the Internet Lock, a means of severing all network communications without having to physically unplug a wire. Passive detection features are built into ZoneAlarm, and response is highly automated, although always at the discretion of the user. For example, when a port scan is detected, ZoneAlarm can be set to automatically block the originator of the scan and thereby prevent any further access from

23 WebWasher v. 3.0, WebWasher AG, Paderborn, Germany (1998).
24 ZoneAlarm v. 2.6, ZoneLabs, Inc., San Francisco (1999).

that miscreant. To alert the user of the event, a warning message is displayed (an awareness feature). Although I found the numerous pop-up warnings to be a bit excessive, they could be tailored by severity based on personal preference. As I became more comfortable with the program, I was able to shut off all but the most severe warning messages. I found ZoneAlarm to be a fully featured personal firewall, although the version I evaluated lacked any significant recovery features.

I was unable to fit ZoneAlarm into a single overall privacy space category; I wound up noting that it was related to awareness, detection, prevention, and response. In retrospect, I would consider it primarily a prevention tool with significant detection capabilities built in.

### Phase one results

Looking at feature counts per solution (Figure 20-1), I found that 19% of solutions contained only one discernible privacy feature. Solutions having five or fewer privacy features made up almost half (47%) of the sample. I view this result as evidence of a need for a more comprehensive privacy system that would include groups of privacy features.

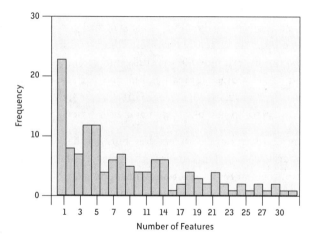

*FIGURE 20-1. Number of privacy features found in different software solutions that I studied*

Each solution was categorized using the framework; this categorization took place before the features were analyzed and categorized in an attempt to make a face-level judgment about the solution. Later, each feature was individually categorized as well and compared to the overall solution categorization. In both cases, the prevention category proved to be dominant and the other categories matched up well compared to the feature categorizations, suggesting that face-level assessments are accurate.

As indicated by Figure 20-2, very few solutions were categorized as being involved solely with recovery from intrusions. This indicates that recovery might be a likely avenue for new research and/or innovation.

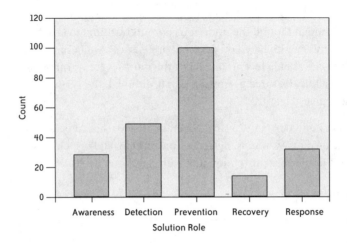

*FIGURE 20-2. Solution categorizations in different software solutions that I studied*

Another interesting trend was the heavy contribution to the privacy space made by lone entrepreneurs. Heavy emphasis was placed upon the use of basic user interface widgets (very few novel visualizations or components—just standard graphical UI fare), with the clear hope of turning a profit by targeting operating systems with the most market penetration. Many of the solutions examined in the study disappeared shortly thereafter. Some features have been adopted by larger companies and have become part of privacy software suites (e.g., Norton Internet Security 2002). I speculate that a lot of trial-and-error development has been taking place in lieu of a systematic, user-based approach.

Technological privacy solutions have had a market, but that market was smaller and less profitable than many anticipated. Today, tools such as personal firewalls are in widespread use, and spyware scanning and removal tools are just now becoming pervasive; yet it is unclear whether people understand the privacy-enhancing implications of using these tools.

## Validation

Using a sampling of the overall features list, the second phase of the study addressed the issue of validation of the Privacy Space Framework and its categories. Here, we sought to ensure that the work done was sufficiently replicable and hence that it would be useful in future privacy space projects. A stratified sampling technique was used to generate an abbreviated list of 118 unique privacy features from the raw list of 1,291 privacy features. The sampling technique created equally distributed lists of features within the five Privacy Space Framework categories. Despite the overall sample being heavily biased toward the categories of prevention and detection, we elected to use a sample unrepresentative of the actual distribution of features. The intent was to test the framework categories and the feature analysis technique, not the overall results of the first phase.

# TRADEOFFS

There are many tradeoffs to consider when designing or selecting a privacy solution.

Novice users will have no patience with privacy or security software that interferes with the tasks they are trying to complete, especially if they can see no benefit to using it. Expert users, on the other hand, do not want an interface that takes more time than is absolutely needed.

In contrast to other software applications, when privacy and security software work successfully, unexpected intrusions or other problems are averted. On the other hand, there may be no indication that the software is doing anything at all!

The dilemma here is obvious—you can't prove you don't have something. User feedback such as graphical meters, pop-up messages, and logging mechanisms give people something to look at to see that some action is going on and that their expectations are being met. Many solutions evaluated for this project were sorely lacking in these kinds of awareness-raising features, and such features are needed. At the same time, it is important not to overwhelm users—especially experienced users—with information that is too voluminous or distracting.

---

We used a modified version of the Delphi method, a consensus-building forecasting technique that uses iteration with controlled feedback where the participants remain anonymous to one another. Results of responses are summarized statistically and are fed back to the participants through the multiple rounds of the study. The Delphi method has been used for making planning decisions and setting work agendas and policy in government, business, and industry.[25] The Delphi method is also useful in soliciting opinions on subjects where there already exists a set of sampling data in order to help validate opinions.[26] It is in this second type of application that Delphi applies to the problem of validating the Privacy Space Framework.

Delphi participants were screened via email exchanges and were required to be self-reported "privacy pragmatists"[27] who routinely use or have used at least one online pri-

25 Harold A. Linstone and Murray Turoff (eds.), *The Delphi Method: Techniques and Applications* (Reading, MA: Addison Wesley, 1975).

26 Johnie Crance, *Guidelines for Using the Delphi Technique to Develop Habitat Suitability Index Curves*, National Ecology Center Division of Wildlife and Contaminant Research Fish and Wildlife Service, U.S. Dept. of the Interior (Washington, D.C.: 1987).

27 Alan Westin, *Opinion Surveys: What Consumers Have to Say About Information Privacy*, Prepared Witness Testimony for the House Committee on Energy and Commerce [cited Aug. 27, 2003]; *http://energycommerce.house.gov/107new/hearings/05082001Hearing209/Westin309print.htm*.

vacy application for a period of time. It was also required that participants be familiar with privacy issues and be using, or have used in the past, some kind of privacy software or service. Routine users of such solutions were preferred, although no formal test or survey was undertaken to ensure that criterion. It was expected that those without the appropriate background would be unable to complete the exercises, so no additional vetting process was used. Fifteen participants took part in the Delphi study.

The Delphi study consisted of an online survey of three rounds and a final exit survey. The study participants were asked to categorize each feature with one or more of the five privacy space categories (awareness, prevention, detection, response, and recovery). Each participant completed this task by assigning a value under each role category. The values ranged from 0% to 100%. If the participant felt that a feature belonged in more than one category, or wasn't sure which one(s) it belonged in, he could allocate the 100 points proportionally.

The analysis of the results involved three major comparisons:

• Author versus mean of group feature comparison (level of agreement)

• Across group differences (author versus participants, level of disagreement)

• Within group differences (level of disagreement among the participants alone)

The following summarizes the characteristics of these comparisons:

*First analysis*

In the first analysis, the Spearman correlation coefficient was employed to compare each of my answers to the corresponding mean answer from the group. The correlations revealed strong similarities between my answers and those of the group, with awareness and prevention categories showing extremely high correlations. All were statistically significant at the $p < .01$ level (two-tailed) which means that in all cases, the agreements were much more common than mere random chance.

*Second analysis*

We agreed a lot of the time, but not always. The second analysis looked at where the participants disagreed with me. To find the features that exhibited large differences between my responses and those of the group, a variable called "differences" was computed and is described as the absolute value of the observed group mean value for each feature minus my answer. I then used the standard deviation to find the outliers. For a feature to have notably high disagreement in a particular category, the difference value had to be greater than or equal to the group mean plus twice the standard deviation.

Using this technique, I generated a whole new table of values. It was soon apparent that the group agreed with me on average, but that each participant disagreed with me on certain specific features. Thus, almost all of the features were in contention, but most had only one or two participants whose differential placed them outside the threshold of two standard deviations. A good sign was that there were no discernible patterns for these disagreements. Because all Delphi participants interpreted the features differently, 100% agreement would be unlikely. As long as the analysis did not reveal 100% disagreement, we were on the right track.

*Third analysis*

The third analysis followed the same procedure as the second one except that each participant's answers were compared to those of the entire group's. The result was very similar to that of the second analysis. In each case, one or two people in the group disagreed on some features, but there was no consistency in these differences.

One conclusion we might draw from the results of these analyses is that the Delphi study did not achieve a solid consensus. In retrospect, it is possible that the design of the online surveys was to blame. It is generally acknowledged that temperamental methodologies such as Delphi are unforgiving with respect to flaws in the survey instrument.

Despite the difficulties revealed by the analysis of the second-phase data, it is clear that the participants in the Delphi study agreed with my feature categorizations a majority of the time and that this result was not a random occurrence. The within-group comparisons were also highly favorable. This part of the study involved many difficult tradeoffs. Those tradeoffs resulted in there being many uncontrolled variables at play, which, in turn, led to the results being less tidy than I had hoped. If I had the ability to repeat the validation exercise, I would increase the time commitment for each Delphi round and make the participants explain their decisions to one another in writing rather than rely on the numeric ratings alone.

## Privacy as a Process

As we progressed, it became more and more apparent that the most natural way to look at the privacy space was to view privacy as a process using the framework to model that process. In the process model, there is a "building up" of information feeding back to the user. We could say that the more categories a solution's features belong to, the more comprehensive it must be (and assume that a more comprehensive solution is better, as it gives the user more control over his privacy). Hence, the "best" solutions have features to address each stage of the process. Figure 20-3 illustrates this idea, showing examples of features from the study[28] along each stage in the privacy process.

The privacy process shown in this figure begins with general awareness of privacy needs and issues and includes feedback from each stage, with each stage adding to our knowledge and ability to make informed decisions, as follows:

- *Awareness.* Provides the basis for all privacy-protective behaviors.
- *Prevention.* Implies having awareness—we cannot try to prevent privacy invasion unless we know about the problems (e.g., why they should be addressed), as well as about techniques for prevention. Prevention is passive, but without preventative measures in place, privacy invasions are undetectable.

---

28 Features of high agreement from phase two were selected for these examples; recall that there was strong evidence to conclude that the ratings for these were highly reliable.

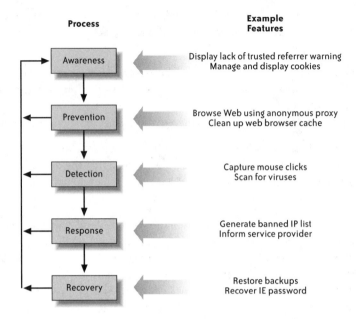

**Process** | **Example Features**

Awareness — Display lack of trusted referrer warning / Manage and display cookies

Prevention — Browse Web using anonymous proxy / Clean up web browser cache

Detection — Capture mouse clicks / Scan for viruses

Response — Generate banned IP list / Inform service provider

Recovery — Restore backups / Recover IE password

*FIGURE 20-3. The Privacy Space Framework as a process*

- *Detection.* When detection features are activated (as preventative measures), the information they relay gives us the ability to respond if a problem is found. In other words, without detection, a responsive action has no cause because no information would exist to support such an action.

- *Response.* Stops the violation from continuing.

- *Recovery.* Returns the system to an acceptable state. Because recovering before the incident is addressed would not prevent it from happening again, response must come first.

This process description may seem confusing because there is a lot of interplay between stages, and because our vocabulary to describe what is happening is somewhat limited. Still, it is important for users to understand that privacy is an ongoing process that requires continuous attention.

## Conclusion

The goal of my work was to define and analyze some privacy-related concepts that others have touched upon but that have never been systematically examined. I have defined what we mean by a privacy solution and used a grounded approach called feature analysis to examine the privacy-related features of solutions. On a grander scale, I have bounded the privacy space and suggested a model for how users can think about the privacy solutions that make up that space, as well as the features of which they themselves consist. More theoretically, this work has led to new terminology, most importantly the idea of exoinformation, which gives us a succinct way to relate the concept of information leakage when we talk about important privacy matters.

# RECOMMENDATIONS FOR DEVELOPERS OF PRIVACY SOFTWARE

Privacy is a very hard concept for most users to understand. An important role for those who develop privacy tools is to educate users about privacy.

When designing your software, think about exoinformation and how to prevent it from getting out. Many privacy tools store people's personal information in them—make sure you are not creating a honeypot for someone to exploit!

Awareness features are ubiquitous in the tools I have examined, but more could be done with them. Furnishing users with knowledge is the best defense when it comes to protecting their privacy. Help files are the minimal approach to awareness. Better awareness features can be integrated into the user interface to help users make their own decisions.

Whenever possible, privacy tools should give the user feedback that preventative features are operational. If a feature really works and problems are being averted, there is no way for users to know this unless it is pointed out to them. A simple logging mechanism might be enough to allow users to verify that a privacy tool is functioning properly.

Detection features are no good if they do not lead the user toward an adequate response!

Today's privacy solutions have few response and recovery features. Recovery is a major problem in privacy because once the information is out and has been misused, it's all over. This is what Whitten calls the "barn door" effect.[a] The incident cannot be undone. Unfortunately, even privacy solutions that have some response and recovery tools do not integrate them well with the tool as a whole.

Use the Privacy Space Framework as your guide—tools that aid users in all five steps of the privacy process offer the most comprehensive privacy solution to users.

---

[a] See Chapter 33, this volume.

Can the quest for the optimal privacy package continue? We now have some techniques and terminology to use to get us closer to that goal. Novel user interface mechanisms must evolve to help users recognize and control exoinformation. We may not achieve the fine granularity of control we desire, but at this stage, the simple ability to have on or off enforcement would be a welcome new development.

## About the Author

 Formerly a systems analyst and programmer at UNC Chapel Hill, Dr. Benjamin Brunk is now a web programmer and user interface specialist for Integrian, Inc., working on specialized digital video systems for public safety, transportation, and government applications. Dr. Brunk is also a part-time adjunct professor at the School of Information and Library Science at UNC.

# Five Pitfalls in the Design for Privacy

### SCOTT LEDERER, JASON I. HONG, ANIND K. DEY, AND JAMES A. LANDAY

**T**O PARTICIPATE IN MEANINGFUL PRIVACY PRACTICE IN THE CONTEXT OF TECHNICAL SYSTEMS, people require opportunities to understand the extent of the systems' alignment with relevant practice and to conduct discernible social action through intuitive or sensible engagement with the system. To help designers support these processes, this chapter describes five pitfalls to beware when designing interactive systems—on or off the desktop—with personal privacy implications. These are based on a review of the literature, on analyses of existing privacy-affecting systems, and on our own experiences designing a prototypical user interface for managing privacy in ubiquitous computing (ubicomp).[1]

## Introduction

One possible reason why designing privacy-sensitive systems is so difficult is that, by refusing to render its meaning plain and knowable, privacy simply lives up to its name. Instead of exposing an unambiguous public representation for all to see and comprehend, it cloaks itself behind an assortment of meanings, presenting different interpretations to

---

1   This chapter is adapted from Lederer, Hong, Dey, and Landay, "Personal Privacy Through Understanding and Action: Five Pitfalls for Designers," *Personal and Ubiquitous Computing* (Springer-Verlag, 2004).

different people. When sociologists look at privacy, they see social nuance that engineers overlook. When cryptologists consider privacy, they see technical mechanisms that everyday people ignore. When the European Union looks at privacy, it sees moral expectations that American policymakers do not. Amid this fog of heterogeneous practices, technologies, and policies that characterize the current state of privacy, designers of interactive systems face increasing market pressure and a persistent moral imperative to design systems that support users' privacy needs: systems that are *privacy-sensitive*.

> **NOTE**
>
> We will use the term *privacy-affecting* as a general description for any interactive system whose use has personal privacy implications. We will use the term *privacy-sensitive* to describe any privacy-affecting system that—by whatever criteria are contextually relevant—reasonably avoids invading or disrupting personal privacy. This chapter is intended to help designers to minimize the number of privacy-affecting systems that are not privacy-sensitive.

To meet that imperative, this chapter offers a partial set of guidelines for the design of privacy-sensitive interactive systems, on and off the desktop. We say "partial" because no design advice can ever amount to a self-contained how-to guide, especially when the domain is as sophisticated as privacy. Although systems that follow our guidelines will not necessarily support privacy, systems that *ignore* any of these guidelines without careful rationale will almost certainly not. For this reason, we present our guidelines as a set of *pitfalls* to avoid when designing privacy-affecting systems. Avoiding a pitfall does not ensure success, but falling into just one pitfall can lead to disaster.

Despite an abundance of privacy-related research and design knowledge, many systems still make it hard for people to manage their privacy. We suggest that this is largely because the designs of these systems prevent their users from both *understanding their privacy implications* and *conducting socially meaningful action* through them. We believe that designs that avoid our pitfalls will go a long way toward helping people achieve the understanding and action that personal privacy regulation requires.

Although some of these pitfalls may appear obvious, we will demonstrate in this chapter that many systems continue to fall into them. Some of the systems that have ignored them (e.g., web browsers) have been repeatedly embroiled in privacy controversies; systems that have avoided the pitfalls (e.g., instant messaging) have enjoyed considerable commercial and social success without negative connotations and regrets.

Our investigation into these pitfalls began when we fell into them ourselves in the design of a user interface prototype for managing personal privacy in ubicomp environments.[2]

---

2   Scott Lederer, Jennifer Mankoff, Anind K. Dey, and Christopher Beckmann, "Managing Personal Information Disclosure in Ubiquitous Computing Environments," Technical Report CSD-03-1257 (Berkeley, CA: UC Berkeley, 2003).

Despite the input of our formative interviews, surveys, and literature review, an evaluation indicated some fundamental missteps in our design rationale. Further analysis showed that these missteps were not exclusive to our system; we found similar problems in a number of existing commercial and research systems. Without attempting to enumerate every extant privacy design flaw, we would like to offer the design community descriptions of the most common flaws and a warning to heed them.

To help designers remember these pitfalls, we have clustered them into two categories: those that primarily affect users' *understanding* of a system's privacy implications, and those that primarily affect their ability to conduct socially meaningful *action* through the system.

## Understanding

The following pitfalls primarily affect users' understanding of a system's privacy implications:

*Obscuring potential information flow*
   Designs should not obscure the nature and extent of a system's *potential* for disclosure. Users can make informed use of a system only when they understand the scope of its privacy implications.

*Obscuring actual information flow*
   Designs should not conceal the *actual* disclosure of information through a system. Users should understand what information is being disclosed to whom.

## Action

The following pitfalls primarily affect users' ability to conduct socially meaningful action through the system:

*Emphasizing configuration over action*
   Designs should not require excessive configuration to manage privacy. They should enable users to practice privacy as a natural consequence of their normal engagement with the system.

*Lacking coarse-grained control*
   Designs should provide an obvious, top-level mechanism for halting and resuming disclosure.

*Inhibiting established practice*
   Designs should not inhibit users from transferring established social practice to new media of disclosure.

The rest of this chapter is organized as follows. First, we discuss the design and evaluation of *Faces*, our user interface prototype for managing personal privacy in ubicomp settings. The negative results of the evaluation motivated our investigation into the design missteps encoded in our five pitfalls. We then describe the five pitfalls, with illustrative examples from both our own and related work. Finally, we discuss the pitfalls' implications for the design process and we offer negative and positive case studies of systems that, respectively, fall into and avoid them.

# Faces: (Mis)Managing Ubicomp Privacy

Our investigation into the pitfalls began after we encountered them firsthand while designing Faces, a software prototype for specifying privacy preferences in ubicomp environments.

## Faces Design

Ubicomp envisions computation embedded throughout everyday environments to support arbitrary human activities,[3] but the distribution and concealment of displays and sensors can complicate interaction.[4] This can disadvantage users by leaving them unaware of or unable to influence the disclosure of personal information—such as location and identity—as they go about their activities in augmented environments. To address this, we designed Faces to do the following:

- Support the specification of disclosure preferences, such as *who* can obtain *what* information *when* (see Figure 21-1).

- Provide feedback about past disclosures in an accessible log, not unlike the financial transaction logs in Quicken and Microsoft Money (see Figure 21-2). Users would employ the feedback in the log to iteratively refine their disclosure preferences over time.

> **NOTE**
>
> Some might object to the Faces disclosure log by claiming that informing the user about a disagreeable disclosure *after the fact* is too late to be useful. Whitten and Tygar, for example, claim that a so-called "barn door property" governs privacy disclosures: "once a secret has been left accidentally unprotected, even for a short time, there is no way to be sure that it has not already been read by an attacker."[5]
>
> While this may apply to highly sensitive disclosures, a significant component of privacy maintenance is the regulation of mundane disclosures *over time* to influence an observer's historical, evolving impressions of oneself. People are remarkably capable of finessing the consequences of the occasional—and inevitable—disagreeable disclosure, and they learn to minimize repeat occurrences. The Faces disclosure log was intended to help users transfer such iterative behavior refinement to the domain of the sensed environment.

3  Mark Weiser, "The Computer for the Twenty-First Century," *Scientific American* 265:3 (1991), 94-104.

4  Victoria Bellotti, Maribeth Back, W. Keith Edwards, Rebecca E. Grinter, Austin Henderson, and Cristina Lopes, "Making Sense of Sensing Systems: Five Questions for Designers and Researchers." Conference on Human Factors in Computing Systems (CHI 2002; Minneapolis, 2002).

5  Alma Whitten and J. D. Tygar, "Why Johnny Can't Encrypt: A Usability Evaluation of PGP 5.0." 8th USENIX Security Symposium (Washington, D.C., 1999). See also Chapter 34, this volume.

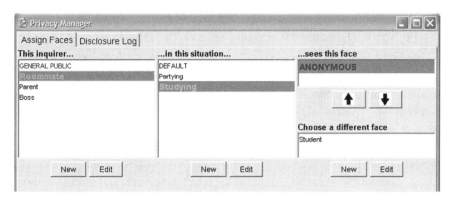

**FIGURE 21-1.** *The Faces GUI for creating and assigning faces; each face holds information precision preferences for disclosures to the associated inquirer when the user is in the associated situation; in this example, the user is choosing a face to handle inquiries from his roommate whenever he is studying*

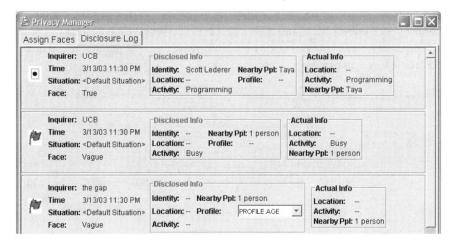

**FIGURE 21-2.** *Faces maintains a "disclosure log" that tracks the release of potentially private information; this log allows users to ascertain the characteristics of disagreeable disclosures and refine their preferences to prevent similar disclosures in the future*

Later we will show that the design of Faces involved some crucial missteps that are also present in other systems. What clued us in to the fundamental nature of these missteps is that we made them despite a substantive requirements gathering effort (details in Lederer et al.[6]). We reviewed the literature. We interviewed 12 local residents solicited from a public community web site, walking them through a series of scenarios to elicit how they might think about privacy in ubicomp. We surveyed 130 people on the Web to investigate factors that determine privacy preferences in ubicomp.[7] And we iterated through a series of low-fidelity designs. The functional upshot of our findings was that the identity of the

6 Lederer *et al.*, "Managing Personal Information Disclosure."

7 Scott Lederer, Jennifer Mankoff, and Anind K. Dey, "Who Wants to Know What When? Privacy Preference Determinants in Ubiquitous Computing." Extended Abstracts of Conference on Human Factors in Computer Systems (CHI 2003; Ft. Lauderdale, FL, 2003).

inquirer is a primary determinant of users' privacy preferences, but that the situation in which the information is disclosed is also important.

Accordingly, we designed Faces to let users assign different disclosure preferences to different *inquirers*, optionally parameterized by *situation* (a conjunction of location, activity, time, and nearby people). We employed the metaphor of *faces* to represent disclosure preferences. This is a fairly direct implementation of Goffman, who posited that a person works to present himself to an audience in such a way as to maintain a consistent impression of his role in relation to that audience—to maintain the appropriate face.[8] Prior to any affected disclosures, users employ a desktop application to specify their preferences for subsequent disclosures by creating 3-tuples of inquirers, situations, and faces, with each 3-tuple meaning "if *this* inquirer wants information about me when I am in *this* situation, show her *this* face" (Figure 21-3). Wildcards are allowed in the inquirer and situation slots to handle requests from unregistered inquirers (*General Public*) or when conditions do not meet the parameters of any registered situations (*Default Situation*). The preferences established in the desktop module are automatically synchronized with a handheld module that affords *in situ* feedback and control (Figure 21-4) and that we envisioned would communicate the user's preferences to nearby ubicomp systems in the manner of Langheinrich's Privacy Awareness System.[9]

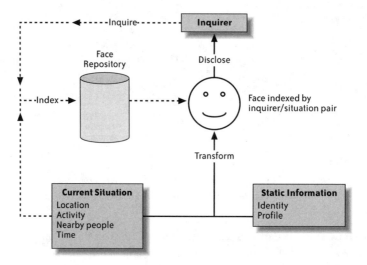

FIGURE 21-3. *Disclosure precision preferences—encapsulated in faces—are indexed on a per-inquiry basis, according to the inquirer's identity and the user's situation at the time of inquiry*

Each face alters the disclosed information by specifying the *precision* at which to disclose it. Faces supports four ordinal levels of precision—from *Undisclosed* (disclose nothing)

8  Erving Goffman, *The Presentation of Self in Everyday Life* (New York: Doubleday, 1956).

9  Marc Langheinrich, "A Privacy Awareness System for Ubiquitous Computing Environments." 4th International Conference on Ubiquitous Computing (Ubicomp 2002; Göteborg, Sweden, 2002).

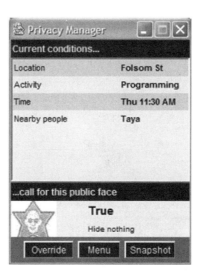

*FIGURE 21-4.* The handheld module affords in situ feedback and control; users can override active preferences and save a snapshot of current contextual variables (e.g., location, time) for subsequent use as a situation parameter; nested menus offer deeper configuration options

through *Vague* through *Approximate* to *Precise* (disclose everything). Each face lets the user apply a setting from this scale to each of four information dimensions: identity, location, activity, and nearby people (Figure 21-5). Adjusting the precision of information can desensitize it, allowing for different versions of the same information to reach different inquirers, depending on the situation.[10] For example, a woman might permit her spouse to employ a locator system to determine that she is at her physician's office (precise), but she might prefer that inquisitive friends learn only that she is downtown (vague).

Through its emphasis on inquirers, situations, and precision preferences, Faces operationalizes three of Adams and Sasse's four factors that determine the perception of privacy in richly sensed environments: recipient, context, and sensitivity.[11] We did not directly address the fourth factor—usage—because, as Faces emphasizes *a priori* preference provisioning, it is often impractical to predict how an observer will use observed information.[12]

## Formative Evaluation

A formative evaluation revealed fundamental problems with the Faces concept (details in Lederer *et al.*[13]). Flaws in the visual and surface-level interaction design of the software also contributed to negative evaluation results. However, we have been careful to focus

10  Lederer *et al.*, "Who Wants to Know What When?"

11  Anne Adams and M. Angela Sasse, "Taming the Wolf in Sheep's Clothing: Privacy in Multimedia Communications," 7th ACM International Conference on Multimedia (Orlando, FL, 1999).

12  Victoria Bellotti and Abigail Sellen, "Design for Privacy in Ubiquitous Computing Environments." 3rd European Conference on Computer Supported Cooperative Work (ECSCW 93; Milano, Italy, 1993).

13  Lederer, "Managing Personal Information Disclosure."

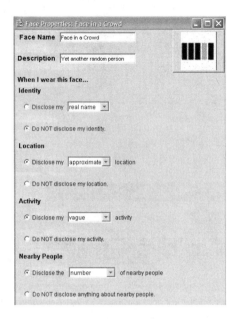

*FIGURE 21-5. Each face contains disclosure preferences for identity, location, activity, and nearby people*

our interviews with participants and our resulting analysis on problems rooted in the conceptual model behind the interaction design—problems that even optimal interaction and visual design could not sufficiently overcome.

After a thorough introduction and tutorial, five participants used the system to configure their privacy preferences regarding two inquirers and two situations of their choice. That is, they each created two inquirer entities in the Faces user interface to represent two parties whom they felt would regularly be interested in their location, activity, etc., followed by two situation entities representing situations they often find themselves in, followed by a set of faces encoding the precision preferences they felt comfortable applying to disclosures to those inquirers in those situations. At a minimum, this means they would create a single face to handle both inquirers in both situations; at a maximum, they would create four unique faces, one for each combination of the two inquirers and the two situations. We then described a series of hypothetical but realistic scenarios involving those same inquirers and situations and asked the participants to consider and state the precision levels at which they would prefer to disclose their information to those inquirers in those scenarios.

## NOTE

By *scenario* we mean a specific activity in a specific context (e.g., buying a pint of chocolate ice cream at the grocery store on Main Street at 10:00 on a Saturday night). We chose our scenarios to be specific, somewhat sensitive events that met the constraints of the more general *situations* created in the Faces user interface (e.g., shopping during the weekend).

Results showed that participants' *a priori* configured preferences often differed pointedly from their stated preferences during the scenarios. That is, when confronted with a realistic description of a specific scenario, participants' disclosure preferences differed from what they had previously thought they would be. Further, they had difficulty remembering the precision preferences they had specified inside their faces. This clouded their ability to predict the characteristics of any given disclosure: they might remember the *name* of the face that would be indexed by the characteristics of a given disclosure, but they would be hard pressed to recall exactly how that face would affect the disclosure.

Subsequent interviews with the participants corroborated these results and also brought the faces metaphor into significant question. Participants expressed discomfort with the indirection between faces and the situations in which they apply. In their minds, a situation and the face one "wears" in it are inseparable; they are, for practical purposes, the same thing.

Together these results illustrate the misstep of separating the privacy management process from the contexts in which it applies. While Faces *modeled* Goffman's theory *in* the interface, it inhibited users from *practicing* identity management *through* the interface. Users had to think explicitly about privacy in the abstract—and instruct the system to model an external representation of their privacy practices—instead of managing privacy intuitively through their actions *in situ*.[14]

Having identified these design flaws despite a reasonable design process, we reviewed other privacy-affecting systems in search of similar mistakes. The practicable outcome of this analysis is our description of a set of five pitfalls to beware when designing for personal privacy, presented in the following sections with evidence of designs both succumbing to and avoiding them. After articulating the five pitfalls, we will analyze the Faces system with respect to these pitfalls.

## Five Pitfalls to Heed When Designing for Privacy

Our pitfalls encode common problems in interaction design across several systems, constituting a preventative guide to help designers avoid mistakes that may appear obvious in retrospect but that continue to be made nonetheless. We encourage designers to carefully heed the pitfalls throughout the design cycle. Naturally, they will apply in different ways and to different degrees for each system. They should be interpreted within the context of the design task at hand.

The pitfalls fit into a history of analyses and guidelines on developing privacy-sensitive systems. They are, in part, an effort to reconcile Palen and Dourish's theoretical insights about how people practice privacy[15] with Bellotti and Sellen's guidelines for designing

---

14 Leysia Palen and Paul Dourish, "Unpacking 'Privacy' for a Networked World," Conference on Human Factors in Computing Systems (CHI 2003; Fort Lauderdale, FL, 2003).

15 *Ibid.*

feedback and control to support it.[16] In reaching for this middle ground, we have tried to honor the fair information practices—as developed by Westin[17] and more recently adapted to the ubicomp design space by Langheinrich[18]—and to encourage minimum information asymmetry between subjects and observers—as argued by Jiang, Hong, and Landay.[19]

## Concerning Understanding

Avoiding our first two pitfalls can help fortify the user's *understanding* of a system's privacy implications by illuminating the system's *potential* for information disclosure in the future and the *actual* disclosures made through it in the present and past.

### Pitfall 1: Obscuring potential information flow

To whatever degree is reasonable, systems should make clear the nature and extent of their *potential* for disclosure. Users will have difficulty appropriating a system into their everyday practices if the scope of its privacy implications is unclear. This scope includes:

- The types of information the system conveys

- The kinds of observers to which it conveys information

- The media through which information is conveyed

- The length of retention

- The potential for unintentional disclosure

- The presence of third-party observers

- The collection of meta-information like traffic analysis

Clarifying a system's potential for conveying personal information is vital to users' ability to predict the social consequences of its use.

Among the conveyable information types to elucidate are identifiable *personae* (e.g., true names, login names, email addresses, credit card numbers, Social Security numbers) and monitorable *activities* (broadly, any of the user's interpretable actions and/or the contexts in which they are performed, such as locations, purchases, clickstreams, social relations, correspondences, and audio/video records). This dichotomy of personae and activities, although imperfect and coarse, can be useful shorthand for conceptualizing a user's identity space, with personae serving as indices to dynamically intersecting subspaces and

---

16 Bellotti and Sellen.

17 Alan Westin, *Privacy and Freedom* (New York: Atheneum, 1967).

18 Marc Langheinrich, "Privacy by Design—Principles of Privacy-Aware Ubiquitous Systems," 3rd International Conference on Ubiquitous Computing (Ubicomp 03; Atlanta, 2001).

19 Xiaodong Jiang, Jason I. Hong, and James A. Landay, "Approximate Information Flows: Socially Based Modeling of Privacy in Ubiquitous Computing," 4th International Conference on Ubiquitous Computing (Ubicomp 02; Göteborg, Sweden, 2002).

activities serving as the contents of those subspaces.[20] People work to maintain consistency of character with respect to a given audience, in effect ensuring that an audience cannot access an identity subspace to which it does not already have an index. This can require considerable effort because boundaries between subspaces are fluid and overlapping. Conveying evidence of activity out of character with the apposite persona can rupture the carefully maintained boundaries between identity subspaces, collapsing one's fragmented identities and creating opportunities for social, bodily, emotional, and financial harm.[21]

Privacy-affecting systems tend to involve disclosure both between people and between a person and an organization. Designs should address the potential involvement of each, clarifying if and how primarily interpersonal disclosures (e.g., chat) involve incidental organizational disclosures (e.g., workplace chat monitoring) and, conversely, if and how primarily organizational disclosures (e.g., workplace cameras) involve secondary interpersonal disclosures (e.g., mediaspaces).

*Privacy* is a broad term whose unqualified use as a descriptor can mislead users into thinking that a system protects or erodes privacy in ways it does not. Making the scope of a system's privacy implications clear will help users understand its capabilities and limits. This, in turn, provides grounding for comprehending the *actual* flow of information through the system, addressed in pitfall 2, described in the next section.

### Evidence: Falling into the pitfall

An easy way to obscure a system's privacy scope is to present its functionality ambiguously. One example is Microsoft's Windows operating systems, whose Internet control panel offers ordinal degrees of privacy protection (from Low to High, as shown in Figure 21-6). First, the functional meaning of this scale is unclear to average users. Second, despite being a component of the operating system's control panel, this mechanism does not control general privacy for general Internet use through the operating system; its scope is limited only to a particular web browser's cookie management heuristics.

Similarly, Anonymizer.com's free anonymizing software can give the impression that all Internet activity is anonymous when the service is active, but in actuality it affects only web browsing, not email, chat, or other services. A for-pay version covers those services.

Another example is found in Beckwith's report of an eldercare facility that uses worn transponder badges to monitor the locations of residents and staff.[22] Many residents

---

20  danah boyd, "Faceted Id/Entity: Managing Representation in a Digital World," M.S. Thesis, Massachusetts Institute of Technology, 2002.

21  David J. Phillips, "Context, Identity, and Privacy in Ubiquitous Computing Environments," Workshop on Socially Informed Design of Privacy-Enhancing Solutions in Ubiquitous Computing, Ubicomp 2002 Conference (Göteborg, Sweden, 2002).

22  Richard Beckwith, "Designing for Ubiquity: The Perception of Privacy," *IEEE Pervasive* 2:2 (2003), 40–46.

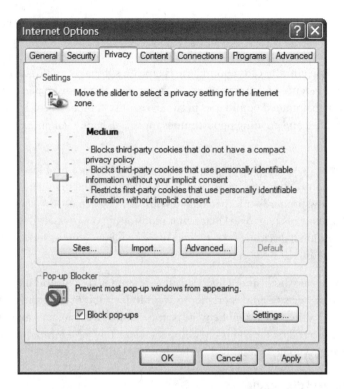

*FIGURE 21-6. The Privacy tab of Internet Explorer's Internet Options control panel offers ordinal degrees of privacy protection (from Low to High), but most users do not understand what the settings actually mean*

perceived the badge only as a call-button (which it was), but not as a persistent location tracker (which it also was). They did not understand the disclosures it was capable of facilitating.

Similarly, some hospitals use badges to track the location of nurses for efficiency and accountability purposes but neglect to clarify what kind of information the system conveys. Erroneously thinking the device was also a microphone, one concerned nurse wrote, "They've placed it in the nurses' lounge and kitchen. Somebody can click it on and listen to the conversation. You don't need a Big Brother looking over your shoulder."[23]

A recent example of a privacy-affecting system that has given ambiguous impressions of its privacy implications is Google's Gmail email system. Gmail's content-triggered advertisements have inspired public condemnation and legal action over claims of invading users' privacy.[24] Some critics may believe that Google discloses email content to advertisers—which Gmail's architecture prohibits—while some may simply protest the commercial exploitation—automated or not—of the content of personal communications. Despite

23 Putsata Reang, "Dozens of Nurses in Castro Valley Balk at Wearing Locators" *Mercury News* (Sept. 6, 2002).

24 Lisa Baertlein, "Calif. Lawmaker Moves to Block Google's Gmail," Reuters (Apr. 12, 2004).

publishing a conspicuous and concise declaration on Gmail's home page that "no email content or other personally identifiable information is ever provided to advertisers,"[25] the privacy implications of Gmail's use were unclear to many users when it launched. Equally unclear, however, is whether the confusion could have been avoided, since other factors beyond system and interaction design were in play. In particular, Google's idiosyncratic brand prominence and reputation for innovation, catalyzed by Gmail's sudden appearance, ensured an immediate—and immediately critical—market of both sophisticated and naïve users.

### Evidence: Avoiding the pitfall

Many web sites that require an email address for creating an account give clear notice on their sign-up forms that they do not share email addresses with third parties or use them for extraneous communication with the user. Clear, concise statements like these help clarify scope and are becoming more common.

Tribe.net is a social networking service that carefully makes clear that members' information will be made available only to other members within a certain number of degrees of social separation. Of course, this in no way implies that users' privacy is particularly safeguarded, but it does make explicit the basic scope of potential disclosures, helping the user understand her potential audience.

### Pitfall 2: Obscuring actual information flow

Having addressed the user's need to understand a system's potential privacy implications, we move now to instances of *actual* disclosure. To whatever degree is reasonable, designs should make clear the actual disclosure of information through the system. Users should understand *what* information is being conveyed to *whom*. The disclosure should be obvious to the user as it occurs; if this is impractical, notice should be provided within a reasonable timeframe. Feedback should sufficiently inform, but not overwhelm, the user.

By avoiding both this and the prior pitfall, designs can clarify the extent to which users' actions engage the system's range of privacy implications. This can help users understand the consequences of their use of the system thus far, and predict the consequences of future use. In the "Discussion" section, we will elaborate on how avoiding both of these pitfalls can support the user's mental model of his personal information flow.

We will not dwell on this pitfall, for it is perhaps the most obvious of the five. We suggest Bellotti and Sellen (1993) as a guide to exposing actual information disclosure.

25 Google, "About Gmail" [accessed Jan. 13, 2005]; *http://gmail.google.com/gmail/help/about.html*.

## Evidence: Falling into the pitfall

Web browser support for cookies is a persistent example of obscuring information flow.[26] Most browsers do not, by default, indicate when a site sets a cookie or what information is disclosed through its use. The prevalence of third-party cookies and web bugs (tiny web page images that facilitate tracking) exacerbates users' ignorance of who is observing their browsing activities.

Another example of concealed information flow is in the KaZaA P2P file-sharing application, which has been shown to facilitate the concealed disclosure of highly sensitive personal information to unknown parties.[27]

Another example is worn locator badges like those described in Harper *et al.*[28] and Beckwith,[29] which generally do not inform their wearers about who is locating them.

## Evidence: Avoiding the pitfall

Friedman *et al.*'s redesign of cookie management reveals *what* information is disclosed to *whom*. They extended the Mozilla web browser to provide prominent visual feedback about the real-time placement and characteristics of cookies, thereby showing users what information is being disclosed to what web sites.[30]

Some instant messaging systems employ a symmetric design that informs the user when someone wants to add that user to a contact list, allowing him to do the same. This way, he knows who is likely to see his publicized status. Further, his status is typically reflected in the user interface, indicating exactly what others can learn about him by inspecting their buddy lists.

AT&T's mMode Find People Nearby service, which lets mobile phone users locate other users of the service, informs the user when someone else is locating him. He learns *who* is obtaining *what* information.

26 Lynette I. Millett, Batya Friedman, and Edward Felten, "Cookies and Web Browser Design: Toward Realizing Informed Consent Online," Conference on Human Factors in Computing Systems (CHI 2001; Seattle, 2001). See also Chapter 24, this volume.

27 Nathaniel S. Good and Aaron Krekelberg, "Usability and Privacy: A Study of KaZaA P2P File-Sharing." Conference on Human Factors in Computing Systems (CHI 2003; Ft. Lauderdale, FL, 2003). See also Chapter 33, this volume.

28 R. H. R. Harper, M. G. Lamming, and W. H. Newman, "Locating Systems at Work: Implications for the Development of Active Badge Applications," *Interacting with Computers* 4:3 (1992), 343–363.

29 Beckwith.

30 Batya Friedman, Daniel C. Howe, and Edward W. Felten, "Informed Consent in the Mozilla Browser: Implementing Value-Sensitive Design," 35th Annual Hawaii International Conference on System Sciences (HICSS 02; Hawaii, Jan. 2002). See also Chapter 24, this volume.

## Concerning Action

Our last three pitfalls involve a system's ability to support the conduct of socially meaningful *action*. Instead of occurring through specific configurations of technical parameters within a system, everyday privacy regulation often occurs through the subtle manipulation of coarse controls across devices, applications, artifacts, and time. In other words, people manage privacy through regularly reassembled metasystems of heterogeneous media,[31] with observers discerning socially meaningful actions through the accumulation of evidence across these media. Privacy-sensitive technical systems can help users intuitively shape the nature and extent of this evidence to influence the social consequences of their behavior.

### Pitfall 3: Emphasizing configuration over action

Designs should not require excessive configuration to create and maintain privacy. They should enable users to practice privacy management as a natural consequence of their ordinary use of the system.

Palen and Dourish write:

> Setting explicit parameters and then requiring people to live by them simply does not work, and yet this is often what information technology requires.... Instead, a fine and shifting line between privacy and publicity exists, and is dependent on social context, intention, and the fine-grained coordination between action and the disclosure of that action.[32]

But because configuration has become a universal user interface design pattern, many systems fall into the configuration pitfall.

Configured privacy breaks down for at least two reasons. First, in real settings, users manage privacy semi-intuitively; they do not spell out their privacy needs in an auxiliary, focused effort.[33] Configuration imposes an awkward requirement on users, one they will often forsake in favor of default settings.[34, 35] If users are to manage their privacy at all, it needs to be done in an intuitive fashion, as a predictable outcome of their situated actions involving the system. As noted by Cranor in Chapter 22 of this volume, "most people have little experience articulating their privacy preferences."

A second reason that configured privacy breaks down is that the act of configuring preferences is too easily desituated from the contexts in which those preferences apply. Users

---

31 Matthew Chalmers and Areti Galani, "Seamful Interweaving: Heterogeneity in the Theory and Design of Interactive Systems," Designing Interactive Systems (DIS 2004; Cambridge, MA, 2004).

32 Palen and Dourish.

33 Whitten and Tygar.

34 Leysia Palen, "Social, Individual & Technological Issues for Groupware Calendar Systems," Conference on Human Factors in Computing Systems (CHI 99; Pittsburgh, PA, 1999).

35 Wendy E. Mackay, "Triggers and Barriers to Customizing Software," Conference on Human Factors in Computing Systems (CHI 91; New Orleans, 1991).

are challenged to predict their needs under hypothetical circumstances, removed from the intuitive routines and disruptive exceptions that constitute the real-time real world. If they predict wrongly during configuration, their configured preferences will differ from their *in situ* needs, creating the conditions for an invasion of privacy.

People generally do not set out to explicitly protect their privacy, an example of Whitten and Tygar's "unmotivated user" property.[36] People do not sit down at their computers to protect their privacy (or, in Whitten's case, to manage their security). Rather, they participate in some activity, with privacy regulation being an embedded component of that activity. Designs should take care not to extract the privacy regulation process from the activity within which it is normally conducted.

### Evidence: Falling into the pitfall

An abundance of systems emphasize explicit configuration of privacy, including experimental online identity managers,[37, 38] P2P file-sharing software,[39] web browsers,[40] and email encryption software.[41] In the realm of ubiquitous computing, both our Faces prototype and Bell Labs's Houdini Project[42] require significant configuration efforts prior to and after disclosures.

### Evidence: Avoiding the pitfall

Successful solutions might involve some measure of configuration but tend to embed it into the actions necessary to use the system. Web sites like Friendster.com and Tribe.net allow users to regulate information flow by modifying representations of their social networks—a process that is embedded into the very nature of these applications.

Dodgeball.com's real-time sociospatial networking service also directly integrates privacy regulation into the primary use of the system. Dodgeball members socially advertise their location by sending brief, syntactically constrained text messages from their mobile devices to Dodgeball's server, which then sends an announcement to the member's friends—and friends of friends within walking distance. Identifying one's friends to the system does require specific configuration effort, but once done, regulating location

---

36 Whitten and Tygar.

37 boyd, 2002.

38 Uwe Jendricke and Daniela Gerd tom Markotten, "Usability Meets Security—the Identity-Manager As Your Personal Security Assistant for the Internet," 16th Annual Computer Security Applications Conference (ACSAC 00; New Orleans, Dec. 2000).

39 Good and Krekelberg.

40 Millett *et al.*

41 Whitten and Tygar.

42 Richard Hull, Bharat Kumar, Daniel Lieuwen, Peter Patel-Schneider, Arnaud Sahuguet, Sriram Varadarajan, and Avinash Vyas, "Enabling Context-Aware and Privacy-Conscious User Data Sharing," IEEE International Conference on Mobile Data Management (MDM 2004; Berkeley, CA, 2004).

privacy is integrated with the very use of the system. Each use actively publicizes one's location; concealing one's location simply involves not using the system.

Georgia Tech's In/Out Board lets users reveal or conceal their presence in a workspace by badging into an entryway device.[43] Its purpose is to convey this information, but it can be intuitively used to withhold information as well, by falsely signaling in/out status with a single gesture.

Cadiz and Gupta propose a smart card that one could hand to a receptionist to grant him limited access to one's calendar to schedule an appointment; he would hand it back immediately afterward. No one would have to fumble with setting permissions. They also suggest extending scheduling systems to automatically grant meeting partners access to the user's location during the minutes leading up to a meeting, so they can infer his arrival time. The action of scheduling a meeting would imply limited approval of location disclosure.[44]

### Pitfall 4: Lacking coarse-grained control

Designs should offer an obvious, top-level mechanism for halting and resuming disclosure. Users are accustomed to turning a thing off when they want its operation to stop. Often a power button or exit button will do the trick.

Beyond binary control, a simple ordinal control may also be appropriate in some cases (e.g., audio devices' volume and mute controls). Ubicomp systems that convey location or other context could incorporate both a *precision dial* (ordinal) and a *hide button* (binary), so users can either adjust the precision at which their context is disclosed or decidedly halt disclosure.

In the general case, users can become remarkably adept at wielding coarse-grained controls to yield nuanced results.[45] Individuals can communicate significant privacy preferences by leaving an office door wide open or ajar, capping or uncapping a camera lens,[46, 47] or publicly turning off their cell phone at the start of a meeting. Coarse-grained controls are frequently easy to engage and tend to reflect their state, providing direct feedback and freeing the user from having to remember whether she set a preference properly. This

---

43  A. K. Dey, D. Salber, and G. D. Abowd, "A Conceptual Framework and a Toolkit for Supporting the Rapid Prototyping of Context-Aware Application," *Human-Computer Interaction* 16:2–4 (2001), 97–166.

44  J. J. Cadiz and Anoop Gupta, "Privacy Interfaces for Collaboration," Technical Report Msr-Tr-2001-82 (Redmond, WA: Microsoft Corporation, 2001).

45  Chalmers and Galani.

46  Bellotti and Sellen.

47  Gavin Jancke, Gina Danielle Venolia, Jonathan Grudin, J. J. Cadiz, and Anoop Gupta, "Linking Public Spaces: Technical and Social Issues," Conference on Human Factors in Computing Systems (CHI 01; Seattle, 2001).

helps users accommodate the controls and even co-opt them in ways the designer may not have intended.

While some fine-grained controls may be unavoidable, the flexibility they are intended to provide is often lost to their neglect (see Pitfall 3), which is then compensated for by the nuanced manipulation of coarse-grained controls across devices, applications, artifacts, and time.

### Evidence: Falling into the pitfall

E-commerce web sites typically maintain users' shopping histories.[48] While this informs useful services like personalization and collaborative filtering, there are times when a shopper does not want the item at hand to be included in his actionable history; he effectively wants to shop anonymously during the current session (beyond the private transaction record in the merchant's database). For example, the shopper may not want his personalized shopping environment—which others can see over his shoulder—to reflect this private purchase. In our experiences, we have encountered no web sites that provide a simple mechanism for excluding the current purchase from our profiles.

Similarly, some web browsers still bury their privacy controls under two or three layers of configuration panels.[49] While excessive configuration may itself be a problem (see Pitfall 3), the issue here is that there is typically no top-level control for switching between one's normal cookie policy and a "block all cookies" policy. Third-party applications that elevate cookie control widgets have begun to appear (e.g., GuideScope.com).

Further, wearable locator badges like those described in Harper *et al.*[50] and Beckwith[51] do not have power buttons. One could remove the badge and leave it somewhere else, but simply turning it off would at times be more practical or preferable.

### Evidence: Avoiding the pitfall

Systems that expose simple, obvious ways of halting and resuming disclosure include easily coverable cameras,[52] mobile phone power buttons, instant messaging systems with invisible modes, the In/Out Board,[53] and our Faces prototype.

48 Lorrie Faith Cranor, "'I Didn't Buy it for Myself': Privacy and Ecommerce Personalization," *Proceedings of the 2003 ACM Workshop on Privacy in the Electronic Society* (Washington, D.C., Oct. 30, 2003).

49 Millett *et al.*

50 Harper, Lamming, and Newman.

51 Beckwith.

52 Bellotti and Sellen.

53 Dey, Salber, and Abowd.

## Pitfall 5: Inhibiting established practice

Designers should beware inhibiting existing social practice. People manage privacy through a range of established, often nuanced, practices. For simplicity's sake, we might divide such practices into those that are already established and those that will evolve as new media of disclosure emerge. While early designs might lack elegant support for emergent practices—because, obviously, substantive practice cannot evolve around a system until after deployment—designs can at least take care to *avoid inhibiting established practice*.

This is effectively a call to employ *privacy design patterns*. Designers of privacy-affecting systems can identify and assess the existing disclosure practices into which their systems will be introduced. By supporting—and possibly enhancing—the roles, expectations, and practices already at play in these situations, designs can accommodate users' natural efforts to transfer existing skills to new media.

Certain metapractices are also worth noting. In particular, we emphasize the broad applicability of *plausible deniability* (whereby the potential observer cannot determine whether a lack of disclosure was intentional)[54, 55] and disclosing *ambiguous information* (e.g., pseudonyms, imprecise location). These common, broadly applicable techniques allow people to finesse disclosure through technical systems to achieve nuanced social ends. Systems that rigidly belie metapractices like plausible deniability and ambiguous disclosure may encounter significant resistance during deployment.[56]

Technical systems are notoriously awkward at supporting social nuance.[57] Interestingly, however, systems that survive long enough in the field often contribute to the emergence of new practices even if they suffer from socially awkward design in the first place (e.g., see Green *et al.*[58] and boyd[59]). In other words, emergent nuance *happens*. But being intrinsically difficult to predict, seed, and design for, it generally does not happen as optimally as we might like it to. Designers will continue to struggle to support emergent practices, but by identifying successful privacy design patterns, they can at least help users transfer *established* skills to new technologies and domains.

54 B. A. Nardi, S. Whittaker, and E. Bradner, "Interaction and Outeraction: Instant Messaging in Action," Conference on Computer Supported Cooperative Work (CSCW 00; New York, 2000).

55 A. Woodruff and P. M. Aoki, "How Push-to-Talk Makes Talk Less Pushy," International Conference on Supporting Group Work (GROUP 03; Sanibel Island, FL, Nov. 2003).

56 Lucy Suchman, "Do Categories Have Politics? The Language/Action Perspective Reconsidered," in *Human Values and the Design of Computer Technology*, Batya Friedman (ed.), 91–106 (Stanford, CA: Center for the Study of Language and Information, 1997).

57 Mark S. Ackerman, "The Intellectual Challenge of CSCW: The Gap Between Social Requirements and Technical Feasibility," *Human-Computer Interaction* 15, no. 2–3 (2000): 181–203.

58 Nicola Green, Hazel Lachoee, and Nina Wakeford, "Rethinking Queer Communications: Mobile Phones and Beyond." Sexualities, Medias and Technologies Conference (University of Surrey, Guildford, UK, June 21–22, 2001).

59 danah boyd, "Friendster and Publicly Articulated Social Networks." Conference on Human Factors in Computing Systems (Vienna, Austria, 2004).

## Evidence: Falling into the pitfall

Some researchers envision context-aware mobile phones that disclose the user's activity to the caller to help explain why his call was not answered.[60] But this prohibits users from exploiting plausible deniability. There can be value in keeping the caller ignorant of the reason for not answering.

Location-tracking systems like those described in Harper *et al.*[61] and Beckwith[62] constrain the user's ability to incorporate ambiguity into location disclosures. Users can convey only their concise location or—when permitted—nothing at all.

Returning to the privacy controversy surrounding Google's email system, one possible reason for people's discomfort with Gmail's content-triggered advertising is its inconsistency with the long-established expectation that the content of one's mail is for the eyes of the sender and the recipient only. With respect to this pitfall, the fact that Gmail discloses no private information to advertisers, third parties, or Google employees is not the issue. The issue is the plain expectation that mail service providers (electronic or physical) will interpret a correspondence's metadata (electronic headers or physical envelopes) but never its contents. Many people would express discomfort if the U.S. Postal Service employed robots to open people's mail, scan the contents, reseal the envelopes, and send content-related junk mail to the recipient. Even if no private information ever left each robot, people would react to the violation of an established social expectation, namely the inviolability—under normal conditions—of decidedly private communications.

## Evidence: Avoiding the pitfall

Mobile phones, push-to-talk phones,[63] and instant messaging systems[64] let users exploit plausible deniability by not responding to hails and not having to explain why.

Although privacy on the Web is a common concern, a basic function of HTML allows users to practice ambiguous disclosure: forms that let users enter false data facilitate anonymous account creation and service provision.

Tribe.net supports another established practice. It allows users to cooperatively partition their social networks into *tribes*, thereby letting both preexisting and new groups represent themselves online, situated within the greater networks to which they are connected. In contrast, Friendster.com users each have a single set of friends that cannot be functionally partitioned.

---

60 D. Siewiorek, A. Smailagic, J. Furukawa, A. Krause, N. Moraveji, K. Reiger, J. Shaffer, and F. Wong, "Sensay: A Context-Aware Mobile Phone." IEEE International Symposium on Wearable Computers (White Plains, NY, 2003).

61 Harper *et al.*

62 Beckwith.

63 Woodruff and Aoki.

64 Nardi, Whittaker, and Bradner.

# Discussion

Having described the five pitfalls and provided evidence of systems that fall into and avoid them, we now examine some of the deeper implications they have for design. We begin by elaborating on the influence of our first two pitfalls on the user's mental model of his information trajectories. This leads to the introduction of a new conceptual tool to help the design process. Then we present an analytical argument for why designs that avoid our five pitfalls can support the human processes of understanding and action necessary for personal privacy maintenance. Using our Faces prototype as a case study, we then show how falling into these pitfalls can undermine an otherwise ordinary design process. Finally we discuss some successful systems that have largely avoided the pitfalls.

## Mental Models of Information Flow

As we said earlier, avoiding our first two pitfalls—obscuring potential and actual information flow—can clarify the extent to which users' actions engage the system's range of privacy implications. Users can understand the consequences of their use of the system thus far, and they can predict the consequences of future use.

Illuminating disclosure contributes constructively to the user's mental model of the portrayal of her identity and behavior in the context of the system. If she has a reasonable understanding of what observers can learn about her (Pitfall 1) and of what they already know about her (Pitfall 2), she can maintain and exploit this mental model to influence the portrayal of her identity and associated activities over time.

In the context of interactive systems, the personal information a user conveys is often tightly integrated with her interaction with the system. For example, by simply browsing the Web, a user generates a rich clickstream that can be used by observers in ways that directly impact her life. When interaction and disclosure are integrated in such a way, an informed user's mental model of the system's operation and her mental model of her disclosures are interdependent.

This suggests an extension to Norman's canonical elucidation of the role of mental models in the design process. According to Norman, the designer's goal is to design the system image (i.e., those aspects of the implementation with which the user interacts) such that the user's mental model of the system's operation coincides with the designer's mental model of the same.[65]

When we take into account the coupling of interaction and disclosure, we see that the designer's goal has expanded. She now strives to design the system image such that the user's mental models of the system's operation *and* of the portrayal of his identity and behavior through it are both accurate. As with Norman's original notion, ideally the designer's and the user's models of the system's operation will coincide. But the designer generally cannot have a model of the user's personal information; that depends on the

---

65 Donald A. Norman, *The Design of Everyday Things* (New York: Basic Books, 1988).

user and the context of use. Indeed, here the designer's task is not to harmonize the user's model of his information flow with her own (she likely has none), but to harmonize the user's information model with the *observer's* (Figure 21-7). In other words, she wants to design the system image to accurately convey a model not only of *how* other parties can observe the user's behavior through the system, but also *what* they can and do observe.

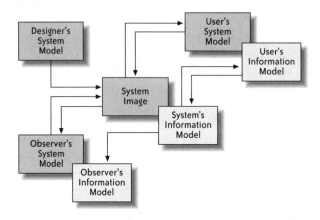

FIGURE 21-7. *Building on Norman's elucidation of the role of mental models in the design process, designers can aim to harmonize the user's and the observer's understanding of the user's personal information disclosures*

### Opportunities for Understanding and Action

We have argued that people maintain personal privacy by understanding the privacy implications of their sociotechnical contexts and influencing them through socially meaningful action. When a technical system is embedded into a social process, the primary means its designers have to engender understanding and action are its feedback and control mechanisms. We encourage designers of privacy-affecting systems to think of feedback and control mechanisms as *opportunities* for understanding and action. They are the designer's opportunity to empower those processes, and they are the user's opportunity to practice them.

This orientation can help designers reach across what Ackerman calls the *sociotechnical gap*—the difference between systems' technical capabilities and their social requirements[66]—just enough to empower informed social action. The challenge is to find that intermediate point where carefully designed technical feedback and control translates into social understanding and action. Reaching too far can overwhelm the user. Not reaching far enough can disempower him.

We believe that avoiding the pitfalls can help designers reach that intermediate point. Carefully designed feedback about potential and actual information flow can help users understand the representation and conveyance of their behavior through the system. Curtailing configuration, providing coarse-grained control, and supporting established practices can help people make productive, intuitive use of a privacy-affecting system. Designs

66 Ackerman.

that heed these suggestions make their consequences known and do not require great effort to use, helping people incorporate them meaningfully into their everyday privacy practices.

## Negative Case Study: Faces

We return now to Faces—our prototypical ubicomp privacy UI—as a case study in how to fall into the following pitfalls.

*Obscuring potential information flow*

In trying to be a UI for managing privacy across any ubicomp system, Faces abstracted away the true capabilities of any underlying system. Users could not gauge its potential information flow because it aimed to address *all* information flow. Its scope was impractically broad and effectively incomprehensible.

*Obscuring actual information flow*

Faces conveyed actual information flow through the disclosure log. Each record was accessible after the relevant disclosure. While this design intends to illuminate information flow, it is unclear whether postponing notice is optimal. Embedding notice directly into the real-time experience of disclosure might foster a stronger understanding of information flow.

*Emphasizing configuration over action*

Faces required a considerable amount of configuration. Once configuration was done, and assuming it was done correctly, the system was designed to require little *ad hoc* configuration. The user would simply go about his business. But the sheer amount and desituated nature of configuration severely limited the system's chances of operating in alignment with the user's *in situ* preferences, positioning Faces squarely in this pitfall.

*Lacking coarse-grained control*

Faces avoided this pitfall by including an override function that afforded quick transitions to alternate faces.

*Inhibiting established practice*

While Faces modeled the nuance of Goffman's identity management theory, it appeared to hinder its actual practice by requiring the user to maintain virtual representations of his fragmented identities *in addition to* manifesting them naturally through intuitive, socially meaningful behavior.

Our evaluation of Faces revealed a complex, abstract configuration requirement that belies the intuitive practice of privacy in real settings. Faces also aimed to singularly address privacy needs across an arbitrary range of ubicomp systems and information types, a task whose futility becomes apparent upon recognizing that privacy management extends across systems, involving fluid, heterogeneous assemblies of technologies, practices, and information types.

## Positive Case Study: Instant Messaging and Mobile Telephony

Interestingly, two systems that largely avoid our pitfalls—mobile phones and instant messaging (IM)—are primarily *communication* media. That is, disclosure is their central function. We will briefly assess these services against the pitfalls, focusing on their primary functions—textual and vocal communication—and on some of their secondary features that support these functions. We will not address orthogonal, controversial features like the location-tracking capabilities of some mobile phones and the capture of IM sessions, which would have to be addressed by a more robust assessment of the privacy implications of these technologies.

IM and mobile telephony each make clear the potential and actual flow of disclosed information, making for a robust, shared mental model of information flow through these cooperative interactive systems. *Potential flow* is scoped by features like Caller ID (telephony), Buddy Lists (IM), and feedback about the user's own online presence (IM). *Actual flow* is largely self-evident in the contents of the communications. Each technology requires minimal *configuration* for maintaining privacy (although secondary features often require excessive configuration), largely due to *coarse-grained controls* for halting and resuming information flow—for example, invisible mode (IM), application exit (IM), power button (telephony), and ringer volume (telephony). Finally, each supports *existing practices* of plausible deniability—people can choose to ignore incoming messages and calls without having to explain why—and ambiguous disclosure; the linguistic nature of each medium allows for arbitrary customization of disclosed information.[67, 68]

Indeed, communication media might serve as a model for designing other privacy-affecting systems not conventionally categorized as communication technologies. Disclosure *is* communication, whether it results from the use of a symmetric linguistic medium (e.g., telephony) or an asymmetric event-based medium (e.g., e-commerce, context-aware systems). Systems that affect privacy but are not positioned as communication media do nonetheless communicate personal information to observers. Exposing and addressing these disclosure media as communication media might liberate designs to leverage users' intuitive privacy maintenance skills.

## Conclusion

In this chapter, we described five common pitfalls to which designs of privacy-affecting systems often succumb. These pitfalls include obscuring potential information flow, obscuring actual information flow, emphasizing configuration over action, lacking coarse-grained control, and inhibiting established practice. We provided several examples of systems that fall into or manage to avoid these pitfalls, including Faces, our user interface prototype for managing ubicomp privacy.

We further identified a number of conceptual tools to help designers. These tools include privacy design patterns; the metaphor of personae and activities as, respectively, indices to

---

67 Nardi, Whittaker, and Bradner.

68 Woodruff and Aoki.

and contents of subspaces of a user's identity space; and an extension of Norman's elucidation of the role of mental models in the design process, in which the designer also works to align the user's mental model of his information flow with his observers'.

In closing, we encourage designers of privacy-affecting systems to employ our guidelines to help them design opportunities for users to understand the extent of a system's privacy implications and to influence those implications through socially meaningfully action.

## Acknowledgments

This work was funded by Grant No. IIS-0205644 of the United States National Science Foundation and by a United States Department of Defense NDSEG fellowship. We are grateful for the assistance and insights of Jennifer Mankoff, Chris Beckmann, danah boyd, John Canny, Karen Teng, Jeff Huang, Xiaodong Jiang, the anonymous reviewers of earlier drafts of this work, and the participants of the studies mentioned herein.

## About the Authors

Scott Lederer is a Ph.D. student in Human-Computer Interaction in the Computer Science Division at the University of California, Berkeley. His research aims to empower people to make sense of and appropriate the deeply augmented world.

*http://scott.lederer.name/*

Jason I. Hong is an assistant professor in the Human-Computer Interaction Institute (HCII) at Carnegie Mellon University. His research is centered on ubiquitous computing, focusing on privacy, end-user programming, interaction techniques, and deployment issues.

*http://www.cs.cmu.edu/~jasonh/*

Anind K. Dey is an assistant professor in the Human-Computer Interaction Institute (HCII) at Carnegie Mellon University. He joined the HCII after spending three years as a senior researcher at Intel Research Berkeley and as an adjunct assistant professor in electrical engineering and computer science at the University of California, Berkeley. Dr. Dey's research focuses on the intersection of ubiquitous computing and human-computer interaction.

*http://www.cs.cmu.edu/~anind/*

James A. Landay is an associate professor in computer science and engineering at the University of Washington, specializing in human-computer interaction. His research interests include automated usability evaluation, demonstrational interfaces, ubiquitous computing, user interface design tools, and web design. He is also the laboratory director of Intel Research Seattle, a university-affiliated research lab that is exploring the new usage models, applications, and technology for ubiquitous computing.

*http://www.cs.washington.edu/homes/landay/*

# CHAPTER TWENTY-TWO

# Privacy Policies and Privacy Preferences

**LORRIE FAITH CRANOR**

**M**ost Privacy Enhancing Technologies (PETs) research and development has focused on just one category of Benjamin Brunk's Privacy Space Framework:[1] *prevention*. In Brunk's 2002 review of available privacy technology solutions, prevention tools dominated. In the PETs research literature, we see numerous papers on cryptographic protocols, anonymous communication systems, and private information retrieval techniques, all of which are designed to prevent information from being disclosed. However, prevention tools tend to be blunt instruments that offer their users only the ability to turn protections on or off. They usually do not facilitate fine-grained control over the flow of personal information.

The concept of individual control over personal information is central to most conceptions of privacy. To facilitate user control over their information requires tools that can be tuned to allow or block information exchange at a fine-grained level based on a variety of factors. Such tools might be categorized as *awareness* tools, as they can convey privacy-related information to users to help them inform their decision making. However, we would ultimately like these tools not only to inform users, but also to take actions on their behalf. Thus, these tools might also be categorized as *detection* tools, because they can analyze privacy-related information and detect situations where preventive steps should be taken.

---

1   See Chapter 20, this volume.

New tools are being developed that straddle these three categories, offering the ability to inform users about privacy-related issues, detect conflicts with user-specified privacy preferences, and take appropriate preventive actions. In this chapter, I focus on tools that make use of computer-readable privacy policies to allow users to control the use of their personal information on the World Wide Web.

## Introduction

Alan Westin defines privacy as "the claim of individuals, groups, or institutions to determine for themselves when, how, and to what extent information about them is communicated to others." He goes on to explain that "each individual is continually engaged in a personal adjustment process in which he balances the desire for privacy with the desire for disclosure and communication of himself to others, in light of the environmental conditions and social norms set by the society in which he lives."[2] Westin's definition envisions an individual actively involved in a decision-making process. It assumes a certain level of individual awareness of the consequences of both disclosing and not disclosing personal information, and the ability to effectively control whether information is disclosed. In practice, individuals are often unable to make such informed decisions or to take the necessary actions to control information disclosure because they lack knowledge about how their personal information may be used and how they can exercise control.

Privacy policies have emerged as mechanisms for communicating about information collection and use. On the World Wide Web, privacy policies have been widely adopted. These policies are encouraged by consumer and industry groups, and in some jurisdictions are even required by law. The purpose of these policies is to inform web site visitors about how sites will use their personal information and what choices are available to them. Thus, individuals should be able to gather the information they need to take advantage of privacy-related options at the sites they visit and to choose sites based on their privacy policies. Unfortunately, while many privacy policies are posted, in practice few are read.[3] Studies have shown that consumers find privacy policies time consuming to read and difficult to understand,[4] and readability experts have found that privacy policies typically require college-level reading skills to comprehend.[5] In addition, privacy policy formats are not standardized, making comparisons between policies difficult. Consumers who do read these policies are also frustrated by the fact that they may change unexpectedly.

2   Alan F. Westin, *Privacy and Freedom* (New York: Antheum, 1967), 7.

3   Privacy Leadership Initiative, Privacy Notices Research Final Results (conducted by Harris Interactive, Dec. 2001); *http://www.ftc.gov/bcp/workshops/glb/supporting/harris%20results.pdf*.

4   Joseph Turow, "Americans & Online Privacy: The System Is Broken," a report from the Annenberg Public Policy Center of the University of Pennsylvania (June 2003); *http://www.asc.upenn.edu/usr/jturow/internet-privacy-report/36-page-turow-version-9.pdf*.

5   Carlos Jensen and Colin Potts, "Privacy Policies As Decision-Making Tools: An Evaluation of Online Privacy Notices," *Proceedings of the 2004 Conference on Human Factors in Computing Systems* (Vienna, Austria, 2004). See also Will Rodger, "Privacy Isn't Public Knowledge: Online Policies Spread Confusion with Legal Jargon," *USA Today* (May 1, 2003), 3D.

When personal information is collected electronically, the potential exists to automate the process of informing individuals about how that information will be used and to give them tools to automate their ability to exercise controls. We can imagine a world in which all web sites and electronic forms are accompanied by privacy policies,[6] and all RFID readers,[7] video surveillance cameras,[8] and other automated personal data collectors broadcast privacy policies that can be understood and acted upon by personal electronic agents. In order to realize this vision, we need standards for encoding and transferring privacy policies and electronic agents that have the ability to understand their users' privacy needs.[9]

In the next section, I discuss the Platform for Privacy Preferences (P3P), which provides a standard mechanism for encoding and transferring web site privacy policies. In the two sections that follow, I describe the design and evaluation of a P3P user agent called Privacy Bird that can read and interpret P3P-encoded privacy policies and compare them with an individual's privacy preferences. Finally, I return to the vision introduced here and discuss ways that P3P might evolve to bring us closer to that vision.

## The Platform for Privacy Preferences (P3P)

In April 2002, the World Wide Web Consortium (W3C) published the Platform for Privacy Preferences 1.0 (P3P 1.0) Specification, which defines a standard way of encoding web site privacy policies in an XML format, as well as mechanisms for locating and transporting these policies.[10] P3P was designed so that web sites can adopt it easily without the need to change their web server software. Two years after P3P 1.0 was published, 1 in 3 of the top 100 web sites and 1 in 4 of the top 500 web sites had adopted it.[11]

6   Lorrie Faith Cranor, "P3P: Making Privacy Policies More Useful," *IEEE Security and Privacy* (Nov./ Dec. 2003), 50–55.

7   Christian Floerkemeier, Roland Schneider, and Marc Langheinrich, "Scanning with a Purpose: Supporting the Fair Information Practice Principles in RFID Protocols," *Proceedings of the 2nd International Symposium on Ubiquitous Computing Systems* (Tokyo, Nov. 8–9, 2004); *http://www.vs.inf.ethz. ch/publ/papers/floerkem2004-rfidprivacy.pdf.*

8   Marc Langheinrich, "Privacy Awareness System for Ubiquitous Computing Environments," *Proceedings of the 4th International Conference on Ubiquitous Computing* (UbiComp2002; September 2002); *http://www.vs.inf.ethz.ch/publ/papers/privacy-awareness.pdf.*

9   While technology can be used to build this world, to fully realize this vision will likely require laws or other incentives for adoption of standard privacy policies, provisions for enforcement, and the availability of a meaningful "market" in which individuals who are unhappy with the privacy policies of one service can find an alternative service that better suits their needs. A discussion of legal and market issues is beyond the scope of this chapter.

10  Lorrie Cranor, Marc Langheinrich, Massimo Marchiori, Martin Presler-Marshall, and Joseph Reagle, "The Platform for Privacy Preferences 1.0 (P3P 1.0) Specification," W3C Recommendation (Apr. 16, 2002); *http://www.w3.org/TR/P3P/.*

11  Ernst & Young, P3P Dashboard Report (May 2004); *http://www.ey.com/global/download.nsf/US/P3P_ Dashboard_-_May_2004/$file/E&YP3PDashboardMay2004.pdf.*

## How P3P Works

A privacy policy encoded according to the P3P 1.0 Specification is referred to as a *P3P policy*. P3P policies include eight major components. Each component is represented as an XML element. Some of these XML elements also have subelements, and some of them are described by XML attributes. For example, the use of collected data is represented by the "purpose" element. The specification defines 11 purpose subelements, each representing a data use. In addition, each of these purpose subelements has a "required" attribute that indicates whether the data may be used for this purpose all the time, on an opt-in basis, or on an opt-out basis.

Figure 22-1 gives an overview of the major P3P policy components. The purpose, data, recipients, retention, and consequence elements are bundled together into a structure called a P3P *statement*. A P3P policy contains one or more statements. Sites use the statement structure to indicate types of data that are treated in similar ways. For example, a site might have one statement to describe the information it stores in logfiles, and one statement to describe the information it collects from individuals who make purchases at the site. A P3P policy for a site with a relatively simple privacy policy is shown in Figure 22-2. This policy includes only one statement.

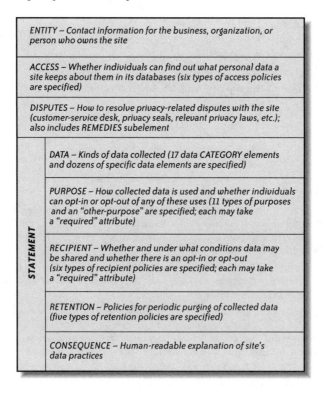

*FIGURE 22-1. The major components of a P3P policy*

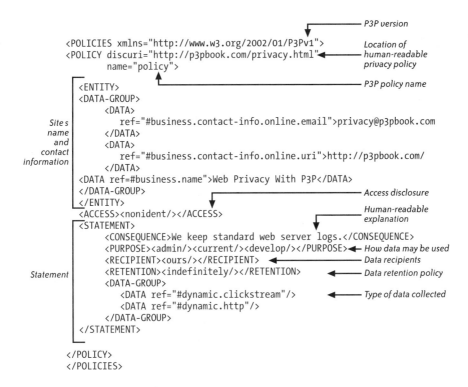

```
                                                          ──── P3P version
      <POLICIES xmlns="http://www.w3.org/2002/01/P3Pv1">
      <POLICY discuri="http://p3pbook.com/privacy.html" ◄────── Location of
             name="policy">                                     human-readable
                                                                privacy policy
          <ENTITY>                                      ──── P3P policy name
          <DATA-GROUP>
              <DATA>
                  ref="#business.contact-info.online.email">privacy@p3pbook.com
              </DATA>
              <DATA>
                  ref="#business.contact-info.online.uri">http://p3pbook.com/
              </DATA>
          <DATA ref=#business.name">Web Privacy With P3P</DATA>
          </DATA-GROUP>
          </ENTITY>                                     ──── Access disclosure
          <ACCESS><nonident/></ACCESS>                       Human-readable
          <STATEMENT>                                         explanation
              <CONSEQUENCE>We keep standard web server logs.</CONSEQUENCE>
              <PURPOSE><admin/><current/><develop/></PURPOSE> ◄── How data may be used
              <RECIPIENT><ours/></RECIPIENT>  ◄────────────── Data recipients
              <RETENTION><indefinitely/></RETENTION>  ◄────── Data retention policy
              <DATA-GROUP>
                  <DATA ref="#dynamic.clickstream"/>  ◄────── Type of data collected
                  <DATA ref="#dynamic.http"/>
              </DATA-GROUP>
          </STATEMENT>

      </POLICY>
      </POLICIES>
```

*F I G U R E 22-2. Example P3P policy*

The P3P policy syntax is extensible, allowing for the addition of new required or optional policy components without necessitating a new version of the P3P Specification.

The P3P 1.0 Specification also includes syntax for a P3P *compact policy*, an abbreviated version of an XML P3P policy that describes a web site's data practices with respect to cookies. Compact policies consist of combinations of three-letter tokens, many of which can be modified by a compact version of the required attribute. Fifty-two such tokens are specified. P3P compact policies are optional for P3P-enabled web sites; they are used by some P3P user agents to facilitate rapid cookie-blocking decisions without the need to fetch a complete P3P policy and load it into an XML parser. Web sites that have compact policies must also have full P3P policies. However, web sites with full policies are not required to have compact policies. Indeed, sites that don't have cookies have no need for compact policies at all. Because the P3P policy in Figure 22-2 does not mention cookies, there is no corresponding compact policy. A web site that uses cookies to tailor site content each time a user returns to that site (unless the user opts out) might have a compact policy that looks something like this:

```
CP="NON DSP ADM DEV PSDo OUR PRE NAV UNI STA"
```

These 10 P3P compact policy tokens have the following meanings:

*NON*
   We do not give you access to our information about you.

*DSP*

Our full P3P policy includes ways to resolve privacy-related disputes with us.

*ADM*

We may use your information to perform web site and system administration.

*DEV*

We may use your information for research and development, but without connecting any information to you.

*PSDo*

We may use your information to make decisions that directly affect you without identifying you—for example, to display content or ads based on links you clicked on previously—unless you opt-out.

*OUR*

We may share your information with companies that help us fulfill your requests (for example, shipping a product to you), but these companies must not use your information for any other purpose.

*PRE*

We may collect information about your tastes or interests.

*NAV*

We may collect information about which pages you visited on this web site and how long you stayed at each page.

*UNI*

We may collect web site login IDs and other identifiers (excluding government IDs and financial account numbers).

*STA*

We may use cookies and mechanisms that perform similar functions.

A P3P *policy reference file* is an XML-encoded file that is used to indicate the parts of a web site to which a P3P policy applies. Policy reference files specify the location of one or more P3P policies and a URL or set of URLs to which each applies. Most web sites place their policy reference files at a standard well-known location: */w3c/p3p.xml*. Thus, P3P user agents can make an HTTP GET request for this file in order to learn the location of the P3P files on a web site. After parsing this file, P3P user agents can make additional GET requests to obtain P3P policy files. As P3P policies generally apply to many (or all) URLs on a site, it is not necessary for user agents to fetch these files every time a user requests a new page on a site. By default, P3P files have a lifetime of 24 hours, meaning that if a user returns to a site within one day, no new P3P files need to be fetched. Optionally, P3P policies may be embedded in policy reference files to simplify site administration and reduce the number of round trips necessary to retrieve P3P files from a site.

While the vast majority of web sites use the well-known location,[12] P3P 1.0 also supports two additional mechanisms for locating policy reference files. Webmasters can place policy reference files at arbitrary locations on their sites and reference them through links embedded in HTML content or in special P3P HTTP headers. P3P HTTP headers are also used to transport P3P compact policies. P3P 1.1 is expected to introduce mechanisms for binding P3P policies to arbitrary XML elements so as to facilitate locating P3P policies for XForms and web services applications.

A separate W3C specification called A P3P Preference Exchange Language (APPEL) provides syntax for encoding user preferences about privacy.[13] APPEL is a rule-based language encoded in XML. P3P user agents can compare APPEL-encoded preferences with a P3P policy to determine whether a site's policy matches a user's preferences; however, P3P user agents are not required to use APPEL. Unlike the P3P 1.0 Specification, APPEL is not an official W3C Recommendation and is considered somewhat experimental. Nonetheless, it is used in several P3P software implementations.

## P3P User Agents

Most Windows computer users are probably already using P3P user agents without realizing it. That is because the Microsoft Internet Explorer 6 and Netscape Navigator 7 web browsers include basic P3P functionality. When I speak to an audience about privacy, I often ask for a show of hands to see how many people use these browsers and how many of them are aware of the P3P features. While most audience members typically use these browsers, very few are aware of the P3P features. Thus, it appears that the vast majority of these people are using P3P features at their default settings without customizing them to reflect their personal privacy preferences.

IE6 checks the HTTP headers sent with cookies for P3P compact policies automatically. Under IE6's default setting, cookies without compact policies may be blocked if they are set by a "third-party" web site—that is, if they are associated with an advertisement or other content embedded in a web page that is served from a different domain from the page in which it is embedded. Other cookies may be blocked or restricted depending on the substance of a compact policy and the user's cookie settings. As shown in Figure 22-3, a small icon featuring a picture of an eye with a do-not-enter sign appears in the lower-right corner of the browser window when a cookie is blocked or restricted. While users may not notice this icon and may be unaware of this P3P feature, web sites that set third-party cookies are becoming increasingly aware of it. When blocked cookies start interfering with the functionality of their web site, many webmasters quickly add P3P policies and compact policies to their sites.[14]

---

12 Simon Byers, Lorrie Cranor, and David Kormann, "Automated Analysis of P3P-Enabled Web Sites," *Proceedings of the Fifth International Conference on Electronic Commerce (ICEC 2003)* (Pittsburgh, PA, Oct. 1–3, 2003); *http://lorrie.cranor.org/pubs/icec03.html.*

13 Lorrie Cranor, Marc Langheinrich, and Massimo Marchiori, "A P3P Preference Exchange Language 1.0 (APPEL1.0)," W3C Working Draft (April 15, 2002); *http://www.w3.org/TR/P3P-preferences/.*

14 Lorrie Cranor, "Help! IE6 is Blocking My Cookies," O'Reilly Network (Oct. 2002); *http://www. oreillynet.com/pub/a/javascript/2002/10/04/p3p.html.*

*FIGURE 22-3. IE6 icon indicating cookie is blocked or restricted*

IE6 also offers a "privacy report" feature that users can select from the browser's View menu. Selecting this feature causes the browser to check for a site's full P3P policy. If the browser is able to fetch the policy, it parses the XML and displays a human-readable representation of the policy, as shown in Figure 22-4.

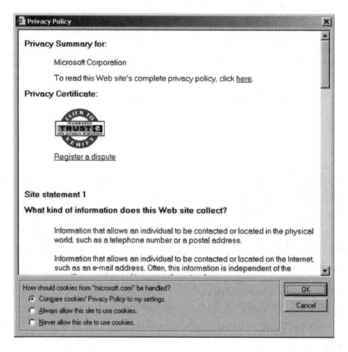

*FIGURE 22-4. First screen of the IE6 privacy report for Microsoft.com*

Navigator 7 has P3P features similar to those in IE6. It employs a slightly different cookie interface and default settings. Netscape can also generate a human-readable version of a site's P3P policy, as shown in Figure 22-5. The Netscape version of a P3P policy is shorter and uses sentence fragments and bulleted lists where IE6 uses complete sentences and paragraphs.

I led the development of AT&T Privacy Bird, an IE5/6 add-on available as a free download from *http://privacybird.com/*. Once installed, a bird icon appears on the right side of the IE6 title bar, as shown in Figure 22-6. Privacy Bird checks for P3P policies at every site a user visits and compares them with the privacy preference settings the user has configured through a menu accessed by clicking on the bird. At sites that match a user's privacy preferences, the bird icon turns green; at sites that do not match, the icon turns red; and at sites that are not P3P enabled, the icon turns yellow. Symbols in the bird's song "bubble"

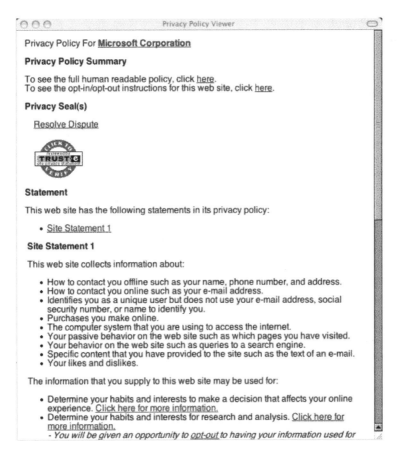

*FIGURE 22-5. First screen of the Netscape Navigator 7 privacy report for Microsoft.com*

also help distinguish these three icons. In addition, users can optionally configure Privacy Bird to play distinctive sounds corresponding to the appearance of each icon.

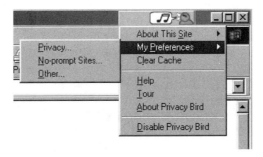

*FIGURE 22-6. The Privacy Bird "green bird" icon and My Preferences menu*

Privacy Bird can also generate and display a human-readable version of a site's P3P policy. Similar to the Netscape version, this version also uses short phrases and bulleted lists.

Privacy Bird offers more configuration options than IE6 and Netscape 7, and it allows users to import APPEL preference files. However, Privacy Bird (version beta 1.2) does not have cookie-blocking capabilities.[15]

## Privacy Bird Design

I began designing a P3P user agent in parallel with the development of the P3P specification. Over a four-year period, during which time many changes were made to the P3P specification, I worked on four prototype P3P user agents.[16] Experience with these prototypes informed the eventual design of Privacy Bird. The first public Privacy Bird beta was released in February 2002. A second beta was released a year later, following a user study.[17] In 2004, AT&T made the Privacy Bird source code publicly available. My goals in developing Privacy Bird and the earlier prototypes were to provide feedback into the P3P specification development process based on implementation experience, and to demonstrate the capabilities of P3P. I hope that other P3P user agent developers will be able to learn from Privacy Bird.

Privacy Bird is implemented as a browser helper object, which loads whenever IE starts up.[18] Users download Privacy Bird as a 1.4 MB self-extracting file that includes an installation wizard. A P3P user agent built into a web browser would likely perform better and be able to more easily integrate with cookie managers and other browser functionality.[19] Much of the Privacy Bird design could be incorporated into a browser implementation.

Designers of P3P user agents face two major design challenges: designing an interface for capturing user privacy preferences, and designing an interface for communicating with users about web site privacy policies. These challenges and our approaches to addressing them are discussed in the sections that follow.

### Capturing User Privacy Preferences

Unless you are a privacy researcher, it is unlikely that you have ever had a discussion with someone about his privacy preferences. If you are interested in building privacy tools, especially tools that help individuals control the collection and use of their personal information, I recommend that you spend some time talking to people about their privacy preferences and the type of control they would like to have.

---

15  We originally planned to implement cookie blocking in Privacy Bird, but discovered that it is fairly difficult to get this to work in a browser helper object. Martin discusses this problem in the context of Bugnosis. See Chapter 23, this volume.

16  See Chapter 14 of Lorrie Faith Cranor, *Web Privacy with P3P* (Sebastopol, CA: O'Reilly Media, 2002), 236–265.

17  Praveen Guduru and Manjula Arjula were the primary developers of the Privacy Bird betas at AT&T Labs.

18  D. Esposito, "Browser Helper Objects: The Browser the Way You Want It," MSDN Library (Jan. 1999); *http://msdn.microsoft.com/library/default.asp?url=/library/en-us/dnwebgen/html/bho.asp.*

19  We faced many of the same challenges as the Bugnosis team did, because of the fact that both projects were implemented as browser helper objects. See Chapter 23, this volume.

While working on P3P and Privacy Bird, I spoke with many people about their privacy preferences. In this process, I learned a few important lessons:

*Most people have little experience articulating their privacy preferences*
Most people have never been asked to do this before.

*Privacy preferences are often complex and nuanced*
Initially, most people with whom I have discussed privacy preferences tell me that their privacy preferences are pretty simple—for example, "I don't want companies to give my information to anyone else." But as our conversations continue, people usually start to articulate a variety of exceptions to their initial simple rules. "If I order something from them, then they can provide my information to fulfill the order and ship a package to me. And if I tell them about my hobby, then it would be OK if they send me catalogs related to that hobby or let me know about clubs I might be interested in." Some people, eager for a good deal, go further: "I should have the right to control my information, but junk mail doesn't really bother me so much. So if they are willing to give me something for free, I don't mind throwing away their junk mail. But if they are profiting from my information, I should get something too." And when the discussion turns to the sharing of location or presence information with other individuals, privacy preferences tend to get very complex.

*Most people are unfamiliar with much of the terminology used by privacy experts*
Privacy policies, privacy laws, and privacy principles tend to be full of privacy jargon.

*Most people do not understand the privacy-related consequences of their behavior*
People tend to assume that if they have nothing to hide, there probably isn't any risk associated with sharing their personal information. Often, they are unaware of the potential for information from multiple sources to be combined, perhaps years after the information was initially collected. It is hard for them to imagine how information might be used against them, both accurately and inaccurately.

For these reasons, it is very difficult for most people to articulate anything close to a set of privacy-related rules that might be applied by an automated agent. It is no wonder that Westin describes privacy control as a process in which individuals are "continually engaged."[20] To develop software that can serve as the user's proxy in this continuous decision-making process is indeed a challenge.

To make matters worse, privacy policies are also complex and nuanced. Some natural-language privacy policies are almost incomprehensible to anyone without a law degree, and even those who have law degrees may find internal inconsistencies in some policies. P3P improves the situation somewhat by forcing P3P adopters to articulate their privacy policies in multiple-choice format. Most P3P elements have a fixed set of choices, and P3P adopters have to decide which choices apply. However, if we look at the combinations of data category, purpose, recipient, and retention, there are more than 5,000 possibilities. If

20 Westin.

we also factor in the access element, whether opt-in or opt-out is provided, specific data elements collected, or any of the other elements or subelements available in a P3P policy, the number of combinations explodes. When we include free text fields, the number of combinations is infinite. We could simply ask P3P user agent users to tell us their preferences for each field individually. However, often their preferences are dependent on multiple fields. "I don't mind if they share my preferences about food or sports or things like that, but I don't want them to share information like my address or phone number, especially if it might result in more unsolicited marketing." Clearly there are too many combinations to ask users to articulate a preference about each one.

I attempted to design a Privacy Bird configuration interface that would allow users to specify all of their preferences on a single screen. As shown in Figure 22-7, the Privacy Bird configuration screen allows users to select from 12 conditions under which they might wish to receive privacy warnings. These conditions were selected after reviewing privacy survey results (primarily of American Internet users, as we were designing a user agent with this group in mind) to determine the aspects of privacy policies that would likely be of most interest to users.[21] The three areas that appeared repeatedly as most important were the type of data collected, how data would be used, and whether data would be shared (represented by the P3P data, purpose, and recipient elements). Among data uses, telemarketing calls and marketing lists seemed to cause the greatest concern. Among data types, financial data and medical data appeared to be most sensitive. In addition, individuals did not like having their data used to build profiles of their interests or activities. We focused our configuration interface on these areas of concern.

Focus group participants that discussed our early P3P user agent prototypes expressed two seemingly contradictory preferences: they wanted the interface to be extremely simple, but they also were reluctant to have their choices reduced to several pre-configured settings such as high, medium, and low. In an attempt to satisfy the preferences expressed by the focus group, we included radio buttons that allow a user to select from High, Medium, Low, and Custom settings. When a user selects one of the three prepackaged settings, the boxes next to the corresponding warning conditions are checked automatically. (In Figure 22-7, for example, the Medium setting has been selected and the six boxes corresponding to that setting are checked.) This provides immediate feedback about what each of the settings does. In addition, it makes it easy for users to make modifications to a prepackaged setting.

It is likely that the choice of what aspects of P3P policies should be highlighted in the user interface will need to be revisited over time and as specialized P3P user agents are developed. For example, although detailed location data such as global positioning system (GPS) data is very sensitive, we did not include a setting that dealt with location data in

21 Mark S. Ackerman, Lorrie Faith Cranor, and Joseph Reagle, "Privacy in E-Commerce: Examining User Scenarios and Privacy Preferences," *Proceedings of EC '99* (Denver, CO: ACM Press, Nov. 1999), 1–8.

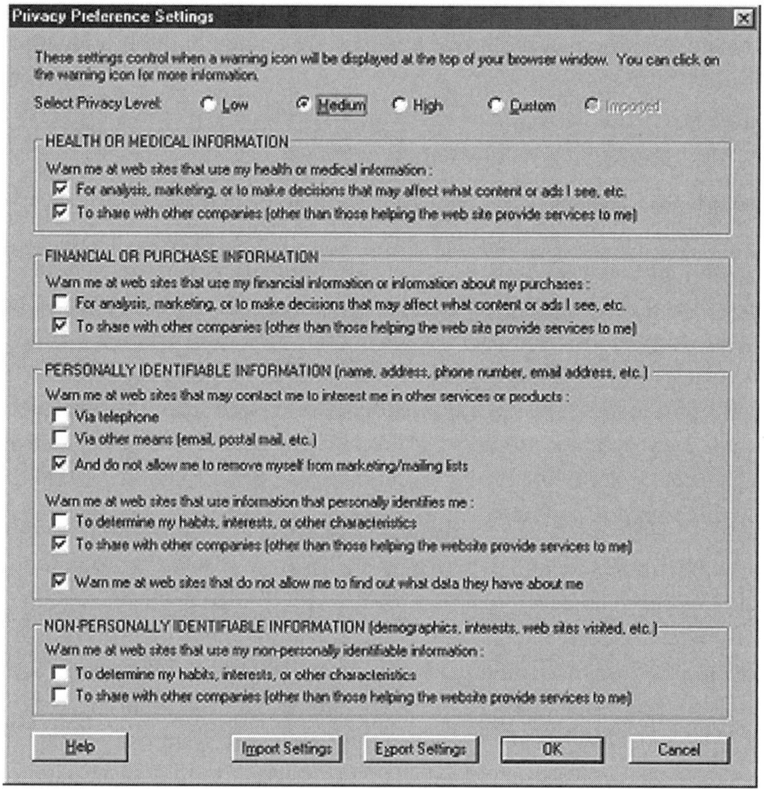

*FIGURE 22-7.* Privacy Bird Privacy Preference configuration

this interface because Privacy Bird is designed for use on personal computers rather than mobile devices, and thus we do not anticipate that Privacy Bird users will be visiting many web sites that track a user's location. However, as users increasingly use wireless networks to access the Internet from laptop computers, applications that track user location may become more common. Certainly, a P3P user agent for wireless handheld devices should highlight a web site's use of GPS data.

Many of the distinctions made in the P3P vocabulary are unlikely to be important to most users—although it is quite likely that the distinctions users find most important will change over time and perhaps even vary across regions of the world. We bundled vocabulary elements together that users may think about in similar ways in order to reduce the apparent complexity of the P3P vocabulary. For example, the P3P "recipients" element offers web sites six choices for describing their data-sharing practices. We bundled these choices into two groups—*sharing* and *nonsharing*—and described the sharing practice as sharing data "with other companies (other than those helping the web site provide services to me)." Sites that disclose data only to their agents and to delivery companies are considered to be nonsharing, while those that disclose data to any other recipients are considered to be sharing. Thus, P3P vocabulary distinctions between sites that share data with companies having similar privacy policies, companies having different privacy policies, and companies with unknown privacy policies are hidden in the Privacy Bird preference specification interface.

The fact that the Privacy Bird configuration interface reduces a potentially infinite space of choices to 12 is clearly a limitation. With further testing, we might become more confident that the 12 choices we selected are indeed the best ones, or that a few changes might improve them. We might decide that a few additional choices are needed to better capture the kinds of preferences Privacy Bird users have. But ultimately, as more web sites become P3P enabled, and as P3P user agent functionality becomes better integrated into web browsers and other tools, I suspect that users will find themselves wanting to add dozens of rules to handle special cases not adequately captured by the 12 choices provided. Users may not mind very much if Privacy Bird provides unnecessary warnings, because these warnings can be easily ignored. However, if Privacy Bird were taking automated actions, such as blocking cookies or filling out forms, users would likely be more demanding, and require more nuanced privacy rules.

As I discussed earlier, users are unlikely to have the interest or ability to articulate a complete set of privacy rules. Indeed, a tool that required users to go through a lengthy configuration process would fall directly into one of the pitfalls described by Lederer *et al.*[22] Instead, I envision P3P user agents with a configuration interface similar to Privacy Bird's that is used as a starting point. Then, as users visit sites and discover that their agent is giving them advice that doesn't completely match their preferences, they can ask their agent to create new rules on the fly. Ideally their agent will also be able to observe patterns in the user's behavior and suggest new rules that would be appropriate. A good agent would also be able to provide educational information to users that would help them understand the privacy implications of the rules they select. An agent that is able to learn and adapt over time will be especially important if P3P user agents are used in the context of a privacy policy framework that goes beyond web sites, similar to the framework described in the "Introduction" section of this chapter.

## Communicating with Users About Web Site Privacy Policies

One important function of a P3P user agent is to present users with information about web site privacy policies so that they can make informed decisions about their interactions with those sites. Implementing this function might not be particularly challenging if standard, easy-to-understand privacy notices were in widespread use. Imagine, for example, that we were developing a nutrition user agent in the form of a handheld device that people could take to the grocery store and point at items they were considering purchasing. The agent would display nutrition information, customized for each individual's needs. Because people have already become familiar with legally mandated nutrition labels, it might make sense to use the standard nutrition label format as a starting point. I could

---

22 See Chapter 21, this volume.

then augment this label to take advantage of the fact that it is being displayed on an electronic device rather than a static paper label. For example, I might design a label in which the serving size was adjusted to the amount each individual was likely to actually eat. Individuals who were counting calories, or carbs, or avoiding dairy products, or whatever, could have the display customized to highlight the fields most relevant to their diet. Clicking on a field could bring up additional information such as definitions, health tips, or comparisons with other products.

There has been discussion among privacy advocates, regulators, and industry representatives about the need for a standard privacy notice format, similar to a nutrition label. This is sometimes referred to as a *short notice* or a *layered notice* because it is envisioned as a summary of, rather than a replacement for, a full privacy policy. Industry groups tend to advocate formats that offer a lot of flexibility and allow companies to use their own language to fill in a number of prescribed privacy-related fields.[23] On the other hand, consumer advocates tend to prefer much more restrictive formats with standard language and even checkboxes to indicate which practices apply.[24] In the meantime, a standard privacy notice format has yet to emerge.

We developed our own privacy notice format for use as the Privacy Bird "Policy Summary," as shown in Figure 22-8. The Policy Summary begins with a Privacy Policy Check, which indicates the cause of the mismatch at sites that do not match a user's privacy preferences. For example, a site's policy might match a user's preferences except for the fact that the site engages in telemarketing. If the site provides a way for users to opt out of receiving telemarketing solicitations, the policy summary includes a hyperlink that takes users to the opt-out instructions. Below the Privacy Policy Check is a summary derived from the site's P3P policy. It includes a bulleted summary of each statement in the policy, as well as information from the P3P access, disputes, and entity elements, including images of any privacy seals referenced. Rather than use the full definitions of each element from the P3P specification, we developed abbreviated descriptions using plain language. We append the words "unless you opt-out" to those purposes for which an opt-out is available, and provide a hyperlink to the site's instructions for opting out. We append the words "only if you request this" to purposes that occur only if a user opts in. Future versions of Privacy Bird will use the standardized plain-language descriptions developed for P3P 1.1.

---

23  See, for example, comments submitted by the Center for Information Policy Leadership at Hunton & Williams (CIPL) in response to the request for public comments in the Advance Notice of Proposed Rulemaking on Alternative Forms of Privacy Notices under the Gramm-Leach-Bliley Act (March 29, 2004); *http://www.hunton.com/info_policy/pdfs/CIPL_Notices_ANPR_Comments_3.04.pdf*.

24  See, for example, comments submitted by Privacy Rights Clearinghouse, Consumers Union of U.S., Inc., Consumer Action, Identity Theft Resource Center, World Privacy Forum, and Privacy Activism in response to Federal Agencies' Joint Request for Comment: Alternative Forms of Privacy Notices (March 26, 2004); *http://www.privacyrights.org/ar/ftc-noticeANPR.htm#AttachA*.

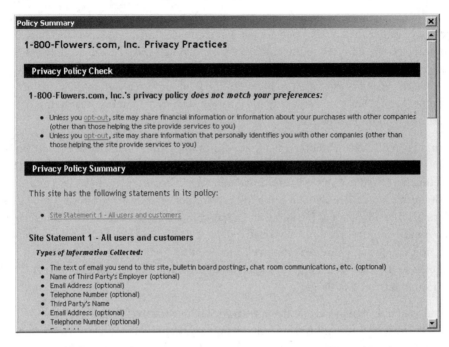

*FIGURE 22-8*. A Privacy Bird beta 1.1 Policy Summary for a site that does not match the user's preferences

As discussed earlier, P3P policies include one or more statements that describe how a set of data may be used by a web site. Many P3P policies include just two or three statements—for example, a statement describing clickstream data sent automatically by the web browser, and a statement describing information users type into web forms. However, some policies include 6 to 10, or even more statements. At sites with a small number of statements, it is easy for a user to quickly scan each one to look for objectionable data practices. However, at sites that have a large number of statements, such a scan can be laborious. In Privacy Bird beta 1.2, we tried to address this concern by adding the ability to expand and collapse elements of the Policy Summary display. When the Policy Summary opened, users could view a list of statements with short descriptions of each one (generated from the human-readable "consequence" fields in the P3P policy), as shown on the left side of Figure 22-9. Users who want more details about a statement can expand it, as shown on the right side of Figure 22-9.

We found some confusion among users about how to access the expand/collapse feature (as a result of the fact that it was not obvious that the + and - were clickable), but once they figured it out, users seemed to find the feature helpful. Nonetheless, it does not seem to completely address a problem that many users would like to solve: to see at a glance whether and how a web site will share their personal information or contact them for marketing purposes. In the future, I would like to experiment with displaying a summary of this information gathered from across all of the statements in a policy. For example, a

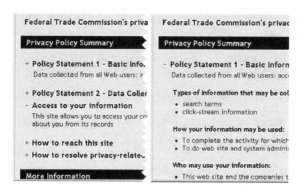

FIGURE 22-9. The Privacy Bird beta 1.2 expand/collapse interface

summary statement might say, "This site will not share your personal information, *except with delivery companies*. This site will send you marketing email *only if you specifically request it*." The italicized phrases could be hyperlinked to the statements where these particular practices are explained.

## Privacy Icons

Privacy Bird uses icons to provide immediate feedback about whether a site's policy matches a user's preferences. Thus, if a user sees that a policy matches her preferences, in many cases she would not need to look any further. Developing an appropriate icon set and determining where to locate the icon on the screen was a challenge. Other privacy tools have frequently used symbols involving eyes, window shades, and keyholes. Informal feedback and feedback from our focus groups suggested that while these symbols may convey a sense that the tool has something to do with privacy, individuals typically have little idea about exactly what these symbols mean. Furthermore, when designing Privacy Bird, we wanted to select symbols that would convey the messages "your preferences are matched" and "your preferences are not matched" rather than "your privacy is protected" and "your privacy is not protected." Thus, we focused on finding symbols that would suggest an agent providing advice. In one prototype, we used a thumbs-up and thumbs-down symbol color-coded with traffic light colors. Our usability test results indicated that this symbol effectively conveyed our intended meaning. However, it appeared that users were relying on the colors more than the symbols, and that they were having difficulties distinguishing the symbol shapes when they appeared as small icons on the computer screen. We later learned that the thumbs-up gesture is interpreted as a rude gesture in some cultures.[25]

When other aspects of our interface design required us to change the shape of the icon from a square to a horizontal rectangle, we revisited the symbol question and came up with the following bird symbols (retaining the traffic light colors), also shown in Figure 22-10.

---

25 See *http://www.msc.navy.mil/msccent/taboos.htm*.

- A happy green bird indicates a site that matches a user's preferences.

- The same green bird with an extra red exclamation point indicates a site that matches a user's preferences but contains embedded content that does not match or does not have a P3P policy.

- A confused yellow bird indicates a site that does not have a P3P policy.

- An angry red bird indicates a site that does not match a user's preferences.

- A sleeping gray bird indicates that the tool is turned off.

The bubbles are designed to be distinguishable by colorblind users and users who do not have color displays. Sounds associated with the red, green, and yellow birds serve to reinforce the visual icons (users can choose whether they want to hear these "earcons"). When a user hovers a mouse over the bird icon, a text message explains the meaning of the icon as well.

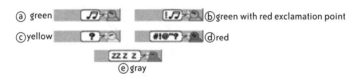

FIGURE 22-10. Privacy Bird icons: (a) Site matches user's preferences; (b) site matches user's preferences but contains embedded content that does not match or does not have a P3P policy; (c) site is not P3P enabled; (d) site does not match user's preferences; (e) Privacy Bird is disabled

Our choice of traffic light colors seems to resonate well with users. However, it does send one message that has the potential to be misleading. Web sites that don't have P3P policies are given yellow birds, and sites with policies that don't match a user's preferences are given red birds. This suggests that the sites with policies that are known to conflict with a user's preferences are worse than those with unknown policies. Whether sites that are not P3P enabled should be considered better or worse than those that are P3P enabled but have unacceptable policies is a debatable question. By assigning sites with unknown policies a yellow bird, we convey the message that users should be cautious when visiting these sites, but that they aren't as bad as sites that have red birds. Arguably, to promote P3P adoption, it would be better to assign these sites a symbol that users would interpret as worse than the symbol assigned to sites that do not match their preferences. However, users might find this approach discouraging while the majority of sites they visit are not P3P enabled.

We decided to locate the bird icons in the top-right corner of the browser's title bar for several reasons. First, this enables us to have a separate icon for every browser window a user has open and to have those icons remain visible. Attaching the icon to another part of the browser window (for example, in the button area) would cause it to disappear when browser windows are opened as pop-up windows. Placing the icon on a separate toolbar

## WHY A BIRD?

We selected a bird to personify the agent because of some of the images it brings to mind, such as "a little bird told me" and a canary in a coal mine serving as an early warning of hazardous gases. More recently, sentinel chickens have served as an early warning of the West Nile virus, and it has been pointed out to us that in the Biblical story of Noah's Ark, a bird was dispatched to determine whether the flood was over. Because the bird symbol does not suggest anything related to privacy, users do not know what it means out of context, and often must read the Privacy Bird tutorial or spend some time using the software before the meaning of the bird symbols is completely clear. In one of our studies, when we asked subjects to associate a meaning with the Privacy Bird icons before they read the tutorial, several subjects suggested a literal meaning of the icons—for example, the singing bird might indicate a site that plays music, and the swearing bird might indicate that a site uses foul language. Despite this confusion, subjects did seem to understand intuitively the idea of the bird as a trusted agent. Because Privacy Bird users have to proactively download and install this software, we felt that it was more important that the symbol convey the tool's role as an agent without misleading users into believing that their privacy would be protected for them, rather than conveying that this was a privacy tool. If Privacy Bird were built directly into a browser or other software, it would be more important to communicate to users that this symbol was part of a privacy-related feature.

We have received some suggestions for minor changes to the bird artwork to make the bird symbols more easily recognizable on a computer screen. While we have received occasional feedback that the bird is not a serious enough symbol to be used when discussing important privacy concerns, as well as some concerns about slang uses of the term "bird," most of the feedback we have received about our choice of symbols has been positive. In addition, anecdotal evidence suggests that some users are attracted to Privacy Bird because they want to have a "cute" bird in their browser window, and only after downloading the software do they learn about its privacy-related features.

---

would result in a single icon that applies only to the browser window currently in focus.[26] Placing the icon at the bottom of the browser window would result in an icon situated in an area of the screen where most users rarely look.[27] However, this is where the Internet Explorer 6 privacy icon—a do-not-enter sign superimposed on an eye—appears to indicate that cookies have been blocked or restricted.

26 In our beta 1.2 release, in response to user requests, we did end up introducing an option that allows users to move the bird off the title bar and place it wherever they want on the screen, but this option has the same drawback as the toolbar option.

27 J. McCarthy, M. A. Sasse, and J. Riegelsberger, "Could I Have the Menu Please? An Eye Tracking Study of Design Conventions," *Proceedings of HCI 2003* (Bath, UK, Sept. 8–12, 2003).

Some of the most passionate feedback we received about Privacy Bird concerned the sounds that users can configure to accompany the appearance of the bird symbols. While many users found the sounds to be a useful reinforcement for the visual symbols, and some found them to be generally enjoyable, some users complained that they found the sounds extremely annoying. One user complained, "Damned crow caw really grates on you after a while," and another wrote, "I was driven almost to a state of collapse; I used to jump when I heard the same bird call in my yard...." In response to user requests, we introduced an option that effectively results in the sounds being played only once a day at each site a user visits.

## Privacy Bird Evaluation

We performed two studies to evaluate the usefulness and usability of Privacy Bird, investigating how it is used in a controlled laboratory setting as well as how it is used in practice. We conducted a laboratory study that allowed us to make detailed firsthand observations of how first-time users interacted with the Privacy Bird software and to compare Privacy Bird with another P3P user agent. In addition, we were able to observe users performing the same tasks with and without the benefit of a P3P user agent and thus evaluate the effectiveness of the user agent. We also conducted a user survey to gather information about how Privacy Bird is used in practice. This survey provided us with self-reported data from individuals who had been using the software for several months in their own homes or offices.

### User Survey

We received informal feedback on our first beta release of Privacy Bird from demo audiences and from some of the approximately 30,000 users who downloaded it. Email from our users focused on requests for new features and ports to other platforms, and stability and compatibility problems. In order to get additional feedback and gain a better understanding of how people were actually using Privacy Bird, we conducted a survey of Privacy Bird users in August 2002.[28] We sent email invitations to complete a 35-question online survey to 2,000 of the email addresses provided by individuals who had downloaded Privacy Bird during the first six months of our beta trial and had given their permission to be contacted for user studies. We received 309 completed surveys.

We asked respondents to evaluate how easy or difficult it was to use several aspects of Privacy Bird. Because our results indicated that users had the most difficulty in understanding the Policy Summary, we focused most of our attention on that aspect of Privacy Bird for the beta 1.2 release.

28 Lorrie Faith Cranor, Manjula Arjula, and Praveen Guduru, "Use of a P3P User Agent by Early Adopters," *Proceeding of the ACM Workshop on Privacy in the Electronic Society* (ACM Press, 2002), 1–10.

A frequent criticism respondents had of Privacy Bird was that a yellow bird appeared at most web sites (because most web sites are not yet P3P enabled[29]). The survey indicated that respondents would find Privacy Bird considerably more useful if most web sites were P3P enabled, and if Privacy Bird were capable of blocking cookies at web sites where the red bird was displayed.

We asked users whether they had learned anything about web site privacy policies as they used Privacy Bird that caused them to change their online behavior. A total of 88% indicated that their use of Privacy Bird had resulted in some change in behavior: about 37% of respondents reported that they fill out fewer forms online; 37% reported taking advantage of opt-out opportunities; 29% reported that they stopped visiting some web sites; and 18% reported comparing privacy policies at similar sites and trying to frequent the sites with the better privacy policies. While the fact that these are responses from self-selected survey respondents is probably a factor, these results do suggest that P3P has the potential to influence user behavior.

As a result of this study, we made several changes to the Privacy Bird interface before releasing the beta 1.2 version.

## Laboratory Study

We conducted a laboratory study involving 12 Microsoft Internet Explorer users who had never used Privacy Bird or the P3P features in IE6.[30] Subjects were given a brief tutorial on Privacy Bird beta 1.2 and the IE6 P3P features and were then asked to use these tools to answer several questions about a web site's privacy policy. As a control, they were also asked to read an English-language privacy policy at a different web site and answer the same questions. Subjects filled out pre-test and post-test questionnaires and discussed their experience with a moderator.

Subjects were asked to respond to questions and follow instructions provided by a web-based interface on a personal computer running Windows NT and IE6. This interface allowed us to record the subjects' responses and to collect information automatically about how long it took the subjects to perform each task.

Each subject was asked to perform a set of tasks using Privacy Bird and IE6, and by reading a site's English-language privacy policy. Subjects were randomly assigned an order in which to complete these three sets of tasks. The tasks involved visiting a specified well-known commercial web site and answering four questions frequently asked about web site privacy policies. The four questions required subjects to determine:

- Whether the site might send a visitor unsolicited email

- Whether the site might share a visitor's email address with another company that might send the visitor unsolicited email

---

29 In August 2002, Ernst & Young reported that 24% of the top 100 domains and 16% of the top 500 domains visited by U.S. Internet users had been P3P enabled (see *http://www.ey.com/global/download. nsf/US/P3P_Dashboard_-__August_2002/$file/P3PDashboardAugust2002.pdf*).

30 Lorrie Faith Cranor, Praveen Guduru, and Manjula Arjula, "User Interfaces for Privacy Agents," *ACM Transactions on Computer Human Interactions (TOCHI)* (2006, in press).

- Whether the site uses cookies
- What steps a visitor could take to exercise opt-out or unsubscribe options

Post-test questionnaires asked subjects to rate several aspects of the ease of use of each user agent and the likelihood that they would use it in the future or recommend it to a friend.

Subjects found using either P3P user agent preferable to reading web site privacy policies; however, they preferred Privacy Bird to IE6. Many subjects remarked that they liked the structured nature of the Privacy Bird policy summary and found the bulleted items easy to read and understand. They liked the fact that Privacy Bird presents information in a consistent format. They also remarked that although the IE6 policy summary uses a standard format, they found it to be far too verbose, which made it difficult to quickly scroll through it to find particular information. In fact, we observed that some subjects attempted to use the browser's search feature to find information in both the English-language privacy policies and in the IE6 policy summary. When searching English-language privacy policies, they usually had to try several terms until they figured out what terminology a particular web site was using to describe a given data practice, and sometimes this strategy proved ultimately unsuccessful. They were unable to search the IE6 policy summary as no search tool is provided. Furthermore, the IE6 policy summary does not include important information needed to answer some of the questions we posed to our subjects.

Our results suggest that individuals who are looking for a specific piece of information in a privacy policy will likely find that information faster using Privacy Bird than using IE6 or reading the policy. The Privacy Bird policy summary could be further improved so that it highlights information that users are most likely to seek and provides a summary of this information across all the statements in a P3P policy. The policy summary might also be customized based on the privacy preferences specified by each user. Observations of users making privacy-related decisions while browsing the Internet in their own home or work environments would help inform policy summary refinements.

## Beyond the Browser

Privacy Bird, in its current form, is useful mostly as a tool to raise user awareness about web site privacy practices. By integrating it with a cookie manager—as Microsoft and Netscape have done with their P3P user agents—we could help facilitate more meaningful automated cookie management. If enough sites adopt P3P, and P3P user agents become widely used, the increased transparency about web site privacy practices may lead to the adoption of more privacy-friendly policies—as a result of either market forces or new regulations.[31] However, the real potential for use of an automated privacy policy framework may lie in applications that go beyond the web browser.

---

31 Lorrie Cranor and Rigo Wenning, "Why P3P Is a Good Tool for Consumers and Companies," Gigalaw.com (April 2002); *http://www.gigalaw.com/articles/2002/cranor-2002-04.html*.

# ADVICE FOR PRIVACY SOFTWARE DEVELOPERS

- *Avoid the use of privacy jargon.* Privacy terms used by experts are unfamiliar to most users. However, all of the P3P user agents we examined used jargon such as *access, profiling, third-party cookie,* and *implicit consent.*

- *Provide persistent privacy-related indicators.* The Privacy Bird icon serves as an indicator of web site privacy practices that users could always find in their browser window. Users reported that they liked having the ability to get high-level privacy-related information at a glance.

- *Provide meaningful summaries of privacy-related information in standardized formats.* Privacy-related information is complicated and can be time consuming and difficult for users to read. Users appreciate short summaries, as long as these summaries do not hide critical information. Standardized formats allow them to find the information of most interest quickly. For P3P user agents, summaries should highlight data sharing and marketing practices, as well as opt-out information. Summary information may combine information about multiple aspects of privacy or reduce the granularity of information if this will help users understand the information being conveyed to them or allow them to more easily make configuration decisions.

- *Provide mechanisms for accessing detailed information,* Users have differing privacy information needs. While most have narrow interests in privacy policy information, some want to see more detailed information. This information should be readily available to users who want it. It is especially important that information be available to explain why privacy warnings were raised or protective actions such as blocking a cookie were taken.

- *Make configuration fast and easy.* Users don't want to spend a lot of time configuring privacy tools, but they will be upset if the tools do not do what they are expecting them to do, or if they interfere with their normal activities. Reasonable defaults should be provided along with a number of easily accessible alternative options.

- *Allow users to fine-tune their configuration.* Users have nuanced privacy preferences, which they may want to articulate more explicitly over time. Tools should allow users to fine-tune their configurations as needed.

- *Convey meaningful information to users about the agent's capabilities and current state.* Most users do not have a good understanding of privacy issues or of privacy software, and thus may have misconceptions about what the software actually does. It is important that users do not assume that their privacy software is providing protection that it is not capable of providing. Likewise, software that has capabilities that can be turned on or off should clearly indicate its state to users.

- *Provide educational opportunities to users over time as they use the tool.* While users may be reluctant to read a lot of material up front, there seems to be an interest in learning more about privacy over time through use of a privacy user agent.

Today it is quite difficult for individuals to take privacy into consideration while comparison shopping. Web sites exist that compare similar products based on user reviews. Other sites compare price and shipping charges across vendors that offer the same product. But consumers who wish to purchase a product from the site that has the best privacy practices must tediously compare lengthy human-readable privacy policies across many sites. If all of the sites under consideration were P3P enabled, a consumer could visit these sites with a P3P user agent and determine which ones best meet their privacy preferences. However, the comparison process would be eased by a tool that could perform the comparison directly. I can imagine the addition of a privacy comparison feature to any of the price comparison services currently available. To facilitate privacy comparisons more generally, it would be useful to have such a feature built into a general-purpose search engine.

Simon Byers, David Kormann, Patrick McDaniel, and I have developed a prototype P3P-enabled search engine using the Google API.[32] Our prototype returns a Google-style search result page with Privacy Bird icons annotating each result to indicate whether it matches the privacy preference level configured by the user. We have demonstrated the feasibility of such a service and have experimented with ways to reduce the associated performance overhead. Further work is needed on the best approach to configuring preferences and displaying results. For example, we would like to investigate how to reorder search results so that sites with better privacy policies appear toward the top while ensuring that top search results are good matches to users' queries.

To realize the vision I introduced at the beginning of this chapter in which computer-readable privacy policies were associated with all automated data collection, tools are needed that can detect the presence of data collection devices, read their privacy policies, and take appropriate actions. In some cases, these tools might be able to signal back to the data collection device that the user does not want his data collected, and the device might respond by turning off data collection until the user is no longer in proximity. Devices might also be able to take steps to anonymize data upon request—for example, substitute an image of an "anonymous face" on a video recording.[33] When data collection cannot be suppressed, privacy tools might alert their users and suggest routes that will avoid these devices.

Besides helping users avoid data collection, privacy tools may also facilitate controlled sharing of data. For example, in ubiquitous computing environments, users may wish to advertise their location or presence to friends or co-workers, or to devices that might perform useful services, while preventing other people and devices from gaining access to this information. In this case, privacy rules might take into account not only privacy policies, but also information about the user's relationship with other individuals and the types of

---

32 Simon Byers, Lorrie Cranor, Dave Kormann, and Patrick McDaniel, "Searching for Privacy: Design and Implementation of a P3P-Enabled Search Engine," *Proceedings of the 2004 Workshop on Privacy Enhancing Technologies* (PET 2004; Toronto, May 26–28, 2004).

33 E. Newton, L. Sweeney, and B. Malin, "Preserving Privacy by De-Identifying Facial Images," *IEEE Transactions on Knowledge and Data Engineering* 17:2 (2005), 232–243.

services offered by devices. Semantic knowledge captured using semantic web tools could facilitate the creation of and reasoning about such rules.[34]

There is clearly a lot of work to be done before it will be prudent to entrust to an automated agent the many nuanced privacy-related decisions we make on a daily basis.[35] Work on the problems of capturing privacy preferences and displaying privacy-related information is bringing us closer to this vision.

## About the Author

 Lorrie Faith Cranor is an associate research professor in the School of Computer Science and Department of Engineering & Public Policy at Carnegie Mellon University, where she directs the CMU Usable Privacy and Security Laboratory (CUPS). She came to CMU in December 2003 after seven years at AT&T Labs-Research. Dr. Cranor's research has focused on a variety of areas where technology and policy issues interact, including online privacy, electronic voting, and spam.

*http://lorrie.cranor.org/*

34 F. Gandon and N. Sadeh, "Semantic Web Technologies to Reconcile Privacy and Context Awareness," *Web Semantics Journal* 1:3, 2004.

35 See Chapter 5, this volume.

# CHAPTER TWENTY-THREE

# Privacy Analysis for the Casual User with Bugnosis

**DAVID MARTIN**

**B**UGNOSIS[1] **IS A PRIVACY ANALYSIS TOOL FOR THE TYPICAL END USER.** Like Privacy Bird (described in the previous chapter), Bugnosis is a benevolent snoop: it taps into your web browser so that it can deduce the privacy characteristics of the web sites you visit. It uses some of the same Internet Explorer facilities as Privacy Bird, and presents results with a similar balance of approachability and charm as opposed to technical detail. But these two IE add-ons are concerned with different parts of the web privacy question. Privacy Bird uses the Platform for Privacy Preferences (P3P) to decide whether a web site's privacy *policy* is consistent with the user's desires, and Bugnosis identifies a particular type of web site privacy *practice*—one that says a lot about the nature of the Web—namely, the use of web bugs to gather information about web users.[2]

## Introduction

Briefly, *web bugs* are invisible elements on a web page used to record the fact that the page was visited, and sometimes to communicate additional information about the user or

---

1   Bugnosis is available from *http://www.bugnosis.org/*.
2   We're talking about bugs as in "This room is bugged, so be careful what you say."

computer doing the viewing. It can be pretty hard to say what the purpose of a particular web bug is without looking at the ultimate processing of the data that it helps gather, and Bugnosis doesn't even try. Rather, Bugnosis just helps to drive home this simple fact: the Web isn't just a glimmering, clickable newspaper. *The Web watches you read.*

Now, people who work on the production side of the Web already know this, and might even find it to be blazingly obvious. But for the majority of web users who aren't in the business of running web servers, this truth—when remembered at all—remains abstract. With Bugnosis installed, users see and hear the previously hidden bugs, and can look at the information that they transmit in order to form a concrete mental image of the process. So while Bugnosis performs privacy analysis, it ultimately contributes to *awareness* of how users are watched on the Web: a necessary prerequisite to any interest in exerting control over their own personally identifiable information.

In this chapter, we'll explain exactly what Bugnosis detects and how it communicates with the user, and along the way, we'll present some lessons we learned by constructing this Internet Explorer monitoring tool.

## The Audience for Bugnosis

We wanted to make Bugnosis as widely available as possible. Our strategy for this was to make it appealing to mainstream technology journalists and policy makers—the bellwethers of personal and desktop computing. We did assume that these users knew at least vaguely that web surveillance was an issue, but otherwise we were faced with a wide spectrum of technical ability, so we assumed a generally low level of technical sophistication. Bugnosis really needed to do just one thing, and it needed to do it well. It needed to install cleanly, require little configuration, and tell its story simply. And finally, when the user got tired of it, it needed to go away quietly.

## Cookies, Web Bugs, and User Tracking

Bugnosis defines a reasonable notion of web surveillance and alerts users when it sees it so that users can just trust the Bugnosis analysis rather than always trying to remember and imagine what's going on behind the scenes. Now, what does it really mean to say "the Web watches you read"? It's not really that complicated, but it's very easy to get bogged down in details.

When a web browser fetches a web page with an HTTP transaction, the remote web server has an opportunity to log the event. In the event log, the server generally gets only these pieces of information:

- IP address of the web browser
- URL of the web page that referred the browser to the requested page (if any)
- Current time
- User agent string, usually indicating the type of browser and type of operating system

- Cookie value that the same web server previously sent to that web browser

- Type of document desired in response to the query

- (Human) language and character coding desired in the response

Web servers are configured to record this type of information *by default*. For example, a recent distribution of the popular Apache web server automatically records the first four items in the preceding list.[3] You should just assume that each web site you visit creates a record of the web pages that it delivers to you.

Conspicuously missing from the preceding list are the user's real name, email address, national identity number, political affiliations, passwords, embarrassing habits, and so on—that is, the extremely sensitive personal information that an underinformed user might imagine flowing over the wire. The actual information transmitted isn't all that immediately alarming, and there is a case to be made for all of it to be there.

Now, how can a web site use this information to identify a user and not just the IP address of the user's computer? Certainly some users have stable and unique IP addresses—for these folks, it could make sense to associate the user's IP address with the actual user. But a large number of us end up with dynamically assigned addresses or shared addresses because of our network provider's policies, a nearby firewall, or a network address translator.

Instead of using the incoming IP address to recognize the computer's current network address, it's far more reliable to use the cookie facility to recognize the web browser itself, and associate *that* with the user.[4] In the next section, we'll see how it works.

### Tracing Alice Through the Web

Suppose that Alice has just bought a new computer and starts visiting web sites. The web server's algorithm for establishing and recognizing users can be extremely simple:

```
if the web transaction arrived with a cookie then
    # that cookie value is this user's ID string
else
    # it's a new user
    cookie := get_currently_unused_user_ID( )
    return cookie to user's web browser as its new persistent cookie value
endif
deliver requested page
```

Having never visited the site before (at least through this browser), Alice will get a new ID. When she returns to the site through the same browser, she'll be recognized by that automatically transmitted ID. The ID string can be used by the server as a key into a database

---

3   Apache version 2.0.46 built in Nov. 2004 and packaged for RedHat Enterprise Linux; *httpd-2.0.46-40.ent.i386.rpm*.

4   David Kristol and Lou Montulli, "RFC 2965: HTTP State Management Mechanism" (Oct. 2000); *http://www.ietf.org/rfc/rfc2965.txt*.

of other information they maintain about her—for instance, any information she types into the site, such as an email address, password, or postal code.

Altogether, this cookie facility only allows a server to remember something it already knows about the user behind a particular web browser: there is no way for an evil web server to use a cookie to snatch files from a user's computer, for instance. And there are plenty of good applications for cookies. Probably the most prominent application—the one envisioned by Lou Montulli, who invented cookies while working at Netscape—was to make it possible to implement web shopping carts:

> It began in the summer of 1994 when I was working on the first version of Netscape Navigator. We had a meeting with a group of customers and some internal application builders who were trying to do a shopping application. They kept running into a consistent problem of not being able to easily store what the user was looking to shop for—basically a shopping cart problem. Because HTTP [hypertext transfer protocol] is a connectionless protocol, each time you ask for a different page it closes and reestablishes a connection. It is very difficult to know when the same user is asking for the next page so that you could associate that user with the previous session and also to know that this was a consistent shopping experience. So, we wanted to come up with a mechanism that would allow a session identifier and also to be able to store shopping cart information and other preferences for the user. The cookie is a very simple mechanism that allows the server to store information with the client and have that return each time the client returns to the site.[5]

### Visiting multiple sites

If Alice visits multiple web sites, then each of the web servers will independently create a new ID for Alice, as pictured in Figure 23-1.

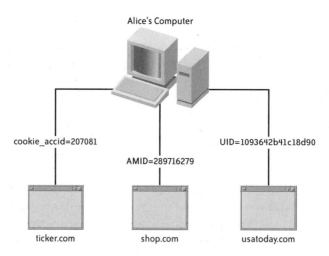

Alice's Computer

cookie_accid=207081

AMID=289716279

UID=1093642b41c18d90

ticker.com          shop.com          usatoday.com

*FIGURE 23-1. Sample cookies actually assigned by various web sites; in effect, each site has a different name for Alice*

---

5   Lou Montulli, interview by the Privacy Foundation (April 16, 2001); *http://web.archive.org/web/20010815233421/http://www.privacyfoundation.org/resources/montulli.asp.*

Because each web server knows Alice by a different ID, it's difficult to combine all of their records into one giant dossier of activity, even if all the servers wanted to do so. After all, if I've gathered a lot of information about Marion Morrison, and you know everything about the movie star John Wayne, would we even suspect that we could combine our information and so get a better picture of the man? We'd first have to learn that John Wayne was Morrison's stage name. Without that knowledge, we would have to treat them as two different people. This is where *third-party cookies* become important.

### Unique identification with referrers and third-party cookies

*Whenever* a browser fetches web content over HTTP, it automatically sends the appropriate cookie to the destination server, even when it is getting content that wasn't explicitly requested by the user.[6] This means that when Alice loads *http://www.nytimes.com/*, her browser sends her *nytimes.com* cookie.[7] That page is delivered to her browser. Now, assuming that the page includes an instruction to fetch an image from *http://m3.doubleclick.net/*, her browser will go grab it automatically. But along with the request to *m3.doubleclick.net*, her browser will also transmit her *doubleclick.net* cookie along with the URL of the page whose content this transaction is part of:

```
Host: m3.doubleclick.net
Cookie: id=80000021e26e40b
Referrer: http://www.nytimes.com/
```

This excerpt shows that the third-party site *m3.doubleclick.net* receives enough information to recognize Alice by her *doubleclick.net* ID even though she's really just trying to visit *nytimes.com*, a different site altogether. Unexpectedly, a third-party image provider is actually in a better position to observe Alice's browsing than the web sites she's intentionally visiting. This is because when Alice's browser contacts the third party to obtain images, it helpfully sends them her third-party cookie ID along with the Referer line. And more to the point, *every site* that embeds content from *doubleclick.net*—not just *nytimes.com*—will transmit the same *doubleclick.net* ID. So *doubleclick.net* can tell that all of these transactions refer to the same person, whereas each individual site like *nytimes.com* could only gather data about her and file it under its own peculiar pseudonym. In other words, the third party can use a consistent name for the user, no matter what site the user is visiting.

Of course, this technique allows the third party to track Alice's clickstream (the sequence of pages she visits) only on those pages that actually mention the third party. If the desired

6  Browsers do send cookies by default, but every popular browser allows this behavior to be reconfigured. The choice is made available to users precisely so that they can decide whether the functionality benefits of cookies are more important to them than the privacy threats.

7  The *http://www.nytimes.com/* web site does use third-party images from *doubleclick.net* as described in this section. Many, many sites have similar relationships with third-party image providers. See *http://www.nytimes.com/ref/membercenter/help/privacy.html* and *http://www.doubleclick.com/about_doubleclick/privacy/* for information about these sites' use of cookies.

web page doesn't include *any* content from a third-party site, then the user's web browser has no reason to send any information at all to the third party.

So, the ideal web clickstream tracker would be a third-party image provider that many different web sites use to provide their images. Two types of businesses come to mind:

- *Internet advertising firms.* A web site sells screen space to an advertiser, and the advertiser actually provides the images from its own server, potentially recording the user's web browsing in the process.

- *Content distribution networks (CDNs).* A CDN provides images, videos, or other server-intensive content and guarantees high reliability, usually by replicating the content and pushing it as close to end users as possible.

## Using Web Bugs to Enable Clickstream Tracking

The automatic transmission of third-party cookies with third-party images makes centralized clickstream tracking possible. *But that doesn't mean that clickstream tracking is actually taking place.* Sites contract with content delivery networks to make their sites load quickly and reliably, not necessarily to perform clickstream tracking. And third-party advertisers do provide a valuable service: they provide actual information to users and send actual customers to their clients. None of this requires them to generate or analyze user clickstream logs.

For example, the DoubleClick company states in its privacy policy that it does not attempt to learn the "real-world identity" behind its cookies, and that in its role as an advertisement delivery agent, it won't use the collected information for its own business purposes. Presumably, this would include combining a user's clickstream on various unrelated client sites into one giant clickstream dossier. DoubleClick does use its cookies to remember which ads it has already shown a user, so it doesn't repeat the same one too often—an excellent use, really. So yes, DoubleClick uses cookies, but with apparently good reason.

But what if a web site doesn't care about actually displaying anything and just wants a third party to record the clickstream event? The site can still use the same cookie-laden image delivery scheme—except that it doesn't need the image to be large or at all interesting. The standard way to do this is with a single-pixel GIF, with that pixel set to the "transparent" color. Here's an example pulled from a page at the *New York Times* web site:

```
<IMG height=1 src="http://ad.doubleclick.net/ad/N2097.nytimes.comSD6440/
B1318936.3;sz=1x1" width=1 border=0>
```

A $1 \times 1$-pixel image is fairly invisible on the screen, but when it's the same color as the background, there's really no hope of seeing it. Obviously, the purpose of this image isn't really to display the invisible dot on the screen. The purpose is to inform the remote server that the user loaded the web page.[8] Otherwise, why bother with the extra work? This is a

---

8   Remember that when this basically invisible image is fetched, the Doubleclick.net server will also be told the URL of the page that the user is trying to view (the "referrer" web page).

*web bug*. The *New York Times* (which placed the bug on its page) and DoubleClick (which delivered the actual invisible image) are cooperatively logging the event that the user viewed this page.

### The web bug: a definition

In Bugnosis, a web bug is an image embedded on a web page that:

- Is a third party to the main web page (it has the *domain* property)
- Has an associated persistent third-party cookie (the *tpcookie* property)
- Is too small to be seen (the *tiny* property)

This isn't quite enough: web designers often put tiny images on pages in order to force the page layout engine to invoke its image alignment rules and achieve a desired presentation effect. We've tried to exclude such images from consideration by observing that they often appear multiple times on a page with the same name each time. So, in addition to the aforementioned descriptions, a web bug also:

- Has a URL that appears only once on this web page (the *once* test)

And, finally, Bugnosis keeps a small list of regular expressions for URLs that are known to be web bugs or known not to be web bugs (the *recognized* property): membership in one of these lists overrides all of the other tests.[9] Together, these properties identify images that generate a loggable event at the third-party site without delivering interesting visual material.

### What about second-party transactions?

We don't really need to see web bugs in order to conclude that users are being watched by the second parties (the web sites that the users intend to visit). As explained previously, web sites tend to log clickstreams by default. But this ability is fundamental to the client-server architecture of the Web. There is no easy way to programmatically determine whether a web site is *interested* in the tracking, or whether it actually does record it. When we see web bugs, we see evidence that a site has established a business relationship for the purpose of tracking its users' clickstreams. Although this could be explained by a business that does not have access to its own web server logfiles or that lacks the technical wherewithal to analyze them, usually it is because the organization wants more detail about its users than is possible from analyzing the logs alone.

---

9   For example, URLs that match the regular expression ^http://216\.239\.(3[2-9]|[45][0-9]|6[0-3])\
    .[[:digit:]]{1,3}/ are never identified as web bugs. A Google spokesperson explained that they
    use these URLs in order to measure network delays, and that they use IP addresses rather than
    names ending in *.google.com* in order to eliminate delays having to do with the use of the Domain
    Name System (DNS).

## Bugnosis: Theory of Operation

Bugnosis sniffs for web bugs according to the preceding definition. It watches a user browse the Web, and whenever it sees a web bug, it alerts the user. Bugnosis has absolutely no way of knowing what the third party does with the data it collects, but it can legitimately conclude that wherever there are web bugs, there is logging (or there used to be).

Without focusing on web bugs, an observer would simply see a blur of third-party transactions and cookies go by—but that type of traffic flows normally and automatically, so it's not a reliable indicator of anything other than the *possibility* of logging. This is the primary insight behind Bugnosis: instead of trying to explain how clickstream tracking works in principle, and that it *might* be used to track your movements on the Web, Bugnosis just looks for indisputable evidence that the Web is watching you, and makes that visible. Web bugs are about the simplest such evidence we could imagine.

> **NOTE**
>
> The last several pages described how user tracking can happen with cookies. Bugnosis takes a far simpler approach. By merely detecting web bugs—evidence of interest in information about users—Bugnosis avoids having to explain cookie tracking to its users.

### One-sided errors

By concentrating on web bugs, we're overlooking many other practical ways for web sites to watch people surfing the Web. For example, suppose that a web designer decided to use Cascading Style Sheets (CSS) stored on third-party servers to trigger a cookie transmission. Because CSS elements aren't images, Bugnosis won't consider them to be web bugs, even though they can be used to record exactly the same type of information as web bugs. This is a *negative error*—Bugnosis fails to identify the surveillance element. And again, it doesn't even attempt to account for ordinary server logs at second-party web sites (the ones the users intend to visit). We designed Bugnosis to be conservative in its analysis, so negative errors are OK. We would much rather have Bugnosis underestimate the amount of intentional surveillance on the Web than have it make *positive errors*—those in which it mistakenly indicates that an innocent web element is there for surveillance.

### Detecting but not blocking web bugs

When Bugnosis detects a web bug, it simply alerts the user: it does *not* try to interfere with the associated data flow. We really wanted Bugnosis to be a sensory booster: more like an extra pair of eyes on the back of the head than a can of Mace in the purse. Besides, given the large number of negative errors Bugnosis is bound to make, "protecting" the user by blocking a few web bugs is not likely to make much of a difference in the long run.

### Presenting the Analysis

Installing Bugnosis adds its functionality to Internet Explorer: there is no separate program to run. It makes itself minimally visible as a toolbar, as shown in Figure 23-2. From left to right, we see a drop-down menu button for configuration and help; a bug button (  ), a vacant four-bar "severity meter," and text summarizing the page.

FIGURE 23-2. *Bugnosis toolbar summarizing analysis of the Froogle page, containing two images and no web bugs*

Clicking on the bug button toggles the visibility of Bugnosis's detailed analysis window. In Figure 23-3, the button is visibly depressed and the analysis is shown. Bugnosis creates its analysis as a separate HTML document consisting primarily of a table showing the analyzed web page's "interesting" elements, one per row. In this case, Bugnosis found two images. The first image was $276 \times 110$ pixels—definitely not a web bug. A reduced version of the image is also shown in the analysis window. The second image on the page is unusual: it is the result of the HTML construct `<IMG height=1 alt="" width=1>` which, curiously, doesn't specify a URL for the image. This image is apparently used for alignment purposes. IE considers it an incompletely downloaded $0 \times 0$ image, and Bugnosis considers it harmless, because it doesn't refer to a third-party site.

Normally, Bugnosis wouldn't even mention these two unremarkable images, so as to avoid overwhelming the user with irrelevant detail. But in this case, we enabled the Bugnosis "List unsuspicious images" option.

## Alerting the User

Normally, the user will browse with the analysis window closed, as in Figure 23-2. Bugnosis quietly continues to update its toolbar status line. But when it discovers a web bug on a viewed page (such as in Figure 23-4), Bugnosis:

- Sounds an alarm: "uh-oh!" in a cute child's voice
- Automatically displays the analysis window
- Makes the web bugs visible
- Adds red color to the severity meter in its toolbar status line

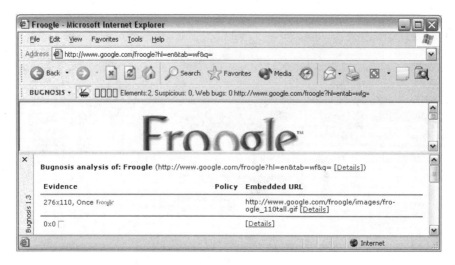

FIGURE 23-3. *With the bug image depressed, the Bugnosis details window takes over some browser screen space*

No user acknowledgment or other action is required. These are the default alerts at installation, but each of these alert methods can be configured: the sound can be changed or disabled; the automatic analysis display can be disabled; and the web bug visibility can be disabled. The toolbar can also be hidden through IE's standard View → Toolbars menu.

Figure 23-4 shows IE's appearance when a web bug has been found at the *freedownloadscenter.com* site. The severity meter on the Bugnosis toolbar is lit up with yellows and reds. The analysis window has been forced to appear, and it shows the offending image along with the names of the tests that support its conclusion. It also shows cookie information (VISID=...) in the lefthand column and the embedded image URL in the righthand column. This URL is interesting because it reveals that the *freedownloadscenter.com* site has grabbed the URL of its own referrer and put that into the URL of the web bug. The site is basically saying, "Someone is visiting me who came directly from *www.bugnosis.org*" (where there is indeed a link to the site shown). Amusingly, the third-party site is within the *spylog.com* domain. Now that's refreshingly transparent.

Two other images with dimensions of 88×31 are highlighted in yellow below the web bug. They are yellow because they're merely "suspicious"—because they're actually visible, they're not web bugs, even though they're able to convey just as much information as web bugs. Bugnosis presents an analysis of such images as well, but it will never alert the user without seeing an actual web bug. Note also that the web bug and the last image both contact the same third-party host, and both include an "rn=*[apparently random number]*" field in their embedded URL. This is probably done in order to ensure that the image transfer isn't served by a cache somewhere between the user's browser and the third-party server. A manual inspection of this page's HTML shows that all of these images were constructed by a JavaScript program that ran after the main page loaded.

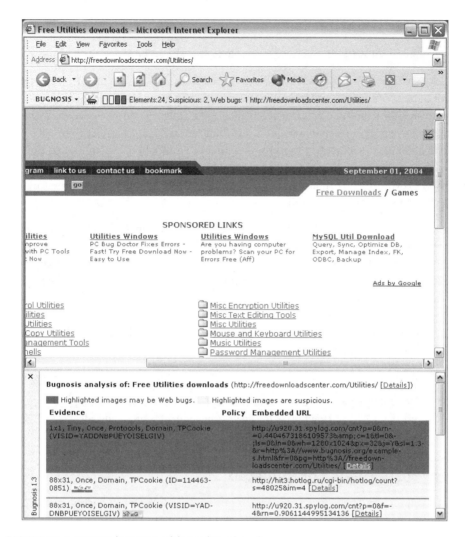

FIGURE 23-4. Bugnosis discovers a web bug and sounds an alarm

Finally, we can actually see the web bug cartoon image in the upper righthand part of the screen. When Bugnosis detected the web bug on this page, it put this image in its place. This cartoon image is an animated GIF and gallops mildly, in order to improve its own visibility. This makes the analysis seem even more real: not only is there a web bug on the page, but *there it is*, right there on the screen. Hovering the pointer over this image also shows some of the web bug's analysis.

A lot of information is available here, but you have to drill down to see it. An ordinary user will simply hear the alarm, see a bunch of coded jargon appear, remember that he is being watched, and move on.

# The Graphic Identity

If you're building software that you want people to use, then find yourself an artist.

In 2000, when we initially released Bugnosis, concerns about web privacy were getting a lot of press attention, web bugs were just starting to become recognized as a part of the cookie equation, and P3P was not yet available. Although its simplicity certainly had some appeal, Bugnosis attracted far more users than we anticipated—more than 100,000 download attempts in its first five months. The Privacy Foundation, which funded the development of Bugnosis, had experience with public relations. An integral part of the publicity effort was the incorporation of an attractive graphic identity, both at the Bugnosis web site and in the software itself.

According to a study performed by the Stanford Persuasive Technology Lab, consumers asked to assess a web site's credibility cited the "design look" of the site more often than any other factor (such as information structure or accuracy) in reaching their conclusions. [10] This study did investigate web sites, not software. However, some of the consumer comments can easily be considered relevant to software as well—valuing a "positive, professional look" over "put together in 5 minutes" and "cheesy graphics." And in any case, Bugnosis is distributed from a web site, which certainly gives users an impression of the credibility of the organization that produced it.

> NOTE
>
> Designing an appealing look takes very different skills from designing privacy software. Don't make the mistake of adding features and gadgets at the expense of visual coherence.

# Making It Simple Is Complicated

Internet Explorer's extensibility, particularly its Browser Helper Object facility, made Bugnosis's unobtrusive user interface possible. But things didn't always snap together as easily as we would have liked. In the following sections, we'll look at some of the details of the architecture that required special attention.

## Using Browser Helper Objects and the Document Object Model

The design decision with the largest impact was where to put the analysis engine. Fairly obviously, it had to run on the end user's computer (rather than on a remote server) in order to maintain acceptable speeds. We also considered the idea of running an HTTP proxy on the user's computer, which would be able to intercept the browser's HTTP

---

10 B. J. Fogg, Cathy Soohoo, David Danielson, Leslie Marable, Julianne Stanford, and Ellen R. Tauber, "How Do People Evaluate a Web Site's Credibility? Results from a Large Study," Consumer Web Watch (Oct. 29, 2002); *http://www.consumerwebwatch.org/*.

requests involved in rendering its web pages. But there were many problems with the proxy approach:

*Some users already rely on a proxy for web access*
> To support these users, we would have to install our proxy in front of theirs, and then their old proxy would appear to vanish from their Internet Options configuration dialog. How confusing!

*The web browser visually indicates the multiple steps in fetching a page*
> These include resolving the DNS name, contacting the remote host, fetching the page, etc. But when a proxy is installed, it has to perform those tasks itself, and there's no standard way for a proxy to send updates directly to the browser's status line. Less visual feedback overall makes the combination of browser and proxy seem sluggish.

*The proxy would have to parse HTML in order to apply the relevant web bug tests*
> For example, the *once* test (which excludes images with URLs that are repeated on a page) requires counting how many times the image appears on the page, not just counting how many times it is fetched from the network. These two measures are not identical because of browser caching. Similarly, an image's visible size is determined both by its native size (from the image file itself) *and* by any HTML width and height attributes used in the <IMG> element that fetches the image.

*Proxies cannot intercept HTTPS (encrypted) connections to perform any kind of page analysis*
> This is the case because proxies don't have the decryption keys. But web bugs are easily deployed on HTTPS pages, and we wanted Bugnosis to be able to detect them. In fact, this would present a valuable lesson about security on the Web: seeing the little lock icon doesn't mean that you're safe from all forms of surveillance.

*Some web bugs are created by client-side scripts, usually JavaScript programs*
> In fact, we've seen web bugs generated by JavaScript code that sense the user's operating system type, screen resolution, window size, and JavaScript version, and that encode that information in a web bug. We'd like Bugnosis to detect these dynamically created web bugs as well. But no one could actually write a proxy that would reliably detect a JavaScript program's intent to create a web bug.

*The Bugnosis web page analysis needs to be visible somewhere*
> If it is provided by a proxy, it would either have to be displayed in a separate window or mixed into the HTML content of the analyzed page. Keeping a separate window open just because Bugnosis is installed is clunkier than we'd like, and the alternative of adding extra HTML content to an arbitrary external page without disturbing its layout is very tricky.

So, instead of the proxy approach, we built the analysis directly into the Internet Explorer (IE) web browser using its Browser Helper Object (BHO) hooks.[11] Naturally, this restricted our audience to IE users. But it gave us direct access to the browser's view of the world,

11 Scott Roberts, *Programming Internet Explorer 5 (Microsoft Programming Series)* (Microsoft Press, 1999). See also the Microsoft Developer Network at *http://msdn.microsoft.com/*.

including its toolbars, status line, and sidebars. Most importantly, it provided read/write access to the Document Object Model (DOM) representation of the page.[12] This conferred a number of advantages:

- In order to find the images on the page, we don't have to parse any HTML at all: we just walk through the DOM data structures, looking for elements that are images.

- To find out an image's size, we query its width and height properties: this tells us precisely how the image is rendered, taking into account both the image's native size and its scaling by HTML's width and height attributes.

- Internet Explorer handles the loading of pages, and our code just sees the results. So, we can analyze encrypted web pages just as easily as unencrypted ones.

- By hooking into DOM events, our code can notice when images are created as a result of client-side scripting and analyze them as well.

## The Event Model

Bugnosis is an event-driven BHO. When IE starts up, it creates our Component Object Model (COM) object called IEMonitor, which then identifies itself as an event sink for the containing WebBrowser object. IE subsequently calls IEMonitor::Invoke( ) with appropriate parameters when it receives reportable events, such as UI manipulation and element download progress. The events of particular interest to us are:

BeforeNavigate2

> This event indicates that the browser is loading a new web page, and a parameter gives the new page's URL. Later, we'll compare the embedded element URLs against this URL so that we can identify those that are third party.

DownloadBegin *and* DownloadEnd

> When IE downloads an embedded element, it brackets the download with this pair of events. Unfortunately, the events don't carry parameters indicating *which* element is being downloaded. These events are really just an indication that something is happening. However, individual elements can be inspected for completeness by querying their ReadyState property, and you can gain access to all DOM elements on the page by walking through the web browser's Document property.

DocumentComplete

> Once all of the elements on a page have been downloaded (or had their downloads aborted) and the page is fully rendered, IE fires this event along with a parameter indicating which window (such as the main window, or a frame in a frameset, or a pop-up) is complete. This is our main indication to analyze the page for web bugs and to trigger an alert, if any are found.

---

12 World Wide Web Consortium, "Document Object Model (DOM) Level 2 Core Specification" (Nov. 2000); *http://www.w3.org/DOM/*.

## Provisional analysis

Of course, web pages don't load instantly—there can be a significant delay between the `BeforeNavigate2` and `DocumentComplete` events. Bugnosis analyzes the document provisionally during this period so that it can update its toolbar status line as the embedded elements arrive. This makes the tool appear alive and responsive, and ensures that the status line always refers to the current page somehow, not to a page that it visited previously. (Bugnosis also puts the main page URL in its status line in order to avoid confusion about exactly what it's analyzing; see Figure 23-4). During the downloading period, it never alerts the user about a web bug, but it may begin to mark elements as suspicious.

These provisional analyses are triggered by the arrival of `ProgressChange` events, which IE fires when it updates its visual meter indicating how much of the page has been loaded. The accompanying parameter is merely the percentage of the line that has been drawn on the screen so far; it is not a certain indicator of anything, but it arrives regularly and roughly in sync with page-loading activity, so it's a reasonable signal to rescan. `DownloadComplete` events also cause a provisional scan.

## Rescanning, refreshing, and Old Paint

Things change during the post-`DocumentComplete` period: Bugnosis remains alert so that it can see more web bugs arrive. This can happen if a client-side script loads an image after the main page has been fully delivered. If so, and the image is not served from the browser's cache, then the new image will trigger `DownloadComplete` and `ProgressChange` events, and so we will rescan the document and react to the addition.

At the same time, we don't want Bugnosis to keep chirping "uh-oh!" whenever a web bug is found somewhere on the page. The goal is to alert the user once when the first web bug on a page is found, and perhaps again later if a new web bug appears—but more than that would be really annoying!

What if the user clicks the Refresh button to reload the page? This puts us in kind of a spot. Because the URL of the page doesn't change, no `BeginNavigate2` event is posted: in fact, no event is delivered indicating that the page is being reloaded at all. All we can count on is some `DownloadBegin`, `DownloadComplete`, and `ProgressChange` activity: this is indistinguishable from client-side scripts loading data. But we'll probably recognize all of the images being loaded because they were loaded on this page already, so nothing will seem new, and so no alarm will sound—even if the user specifically pressed Reload in order to have Bugnosis rescan the page! Our compromise is that Bugnosis rescans the entire document whenever a triggering event arrives without considering whether the images are new or old, but it imposes a limit of one "uh-oh!" every three seconds.

Finally, complications arise when Bugnosis makes web bugs visible:

- The standard galloping bug ( 🐛 we affectionately call him "Old Paint") is delivered as a GIF that is embedded inside the Bugnosis executable. After a web bug has been identified, it's a simple matter to change its image's `src` property to point to this URL, and IE changes the image. However, this also triggers the image-downloading events, which causes the document image to be rescanned. What was once a tiny image obtained from a third-party site with an accompanying cookie is now an $18 \times 18$ image served out of the local filesystem, which Bugnosis wouldn't find suspicious at all.

- To further complicate matters, changing an image's `src` property sometimes disturbs its `ReadyState` property. Bugnosis uses this property to determine whether a page is not ready for a full web bug scan. But we had observed that in IE 6, whenever a web bug is made visible by changing its `src`, its `ReadyState` never again becomes "fully ready."

To address these issues, before making any web bug visible, Bugnosis adds properties to the image object that record its previous dimensions and URL. When rescanning the document later on, Bugnosis recognizes them and reports these original characteristics rather than its updated ones, and excludes the image from further testing.

Unfortunately, on HTTPS (encrypted) web pages, changing an embedded `https://` URL to a `file://` URL in order to make the web bug visible displays a warning dialog; IE complains that this encrypted web page contains unencrypted content. We couldn't find an acceptable workaround, so in this case, Bugnosis simply leaves the original invisible image in place. Sorry, Old Paint!

### The Analysis Pane and Toolbar

The analysis pane in the lower part of the main IE window (Figure 23-1) is not intrinsically attached to the browser helper object; it's another type of IE extension called a *comm bar*. Comm bars (as well as *explorer bars*, which are oriented vertically instead of horizontally) serve only to take control of part of the IE window. Once claimed, IE provides some decoration for the pane including space for the pane's title ("Bugnosis 1.3" rotated 90°), a "close" button, and the horizontal line separating IE's main window from the comm bar. The user can move the separator with the pointer and in this way change the relative size of the two windows.

### The discovery dance

The toolbar is yet another type of IE extension, similarly claiming screen space and window decoration (namely, the ability to move the toolbar around). IE invokes these three types of extensions—the browser helper object for sinking events, the toolbar, and the comm bar—at startup time, by individually calling their `IObjectWithSite::SetSite(IWebBrowser2*)` functions with the surrounding web browser as a parameter. IE knows to do so because entries in the system registry indicate that these objects are installed. And, naturally, the three objects need to communicate with each other at runtime. However, IE *doesn't* call these objects' `SetSite` functions in a predictable order. Bugnosis therefore uses a data structure shared by all three of the objects (which luckily run in the same process) as a rendezvous point so that the objects can discover each other.

### Making the Analysis Pane feel natural

As mentioned earlier, IE doesn't manage the space it gives to the analysis pane (comm bar). Bugnosis populates this blank space with a newly created *web browser control*—a self-contained web-rendering engine provided by IE itself that provides only an HTML rendering space, and no toolbars of any kind. Bugnosis causes its analysis to appear in this pane by obtaining the web browser control's <body> element and writing onto its innerHTML property. By providing this text output as HTML, Bugnosis matches the look-and-feel of the web browser, and also simplifies the problem of saving or printing Bugnosis output.

Because the main IE window doesn't know that it contains an embedded IE window (only Bugnosis knows that), a little more work is required to make the embedded window feel natural. Specifically, when the user moves the mouse pointer over a link, we want the URL of the link to appear in the main browser window status bar. Although the web browser control does generate an event indicating that *some* status bar should be updated during a mouse-over, this event is not connected to the user's main web browser, because the main web browser doesn't even know that the embedded control is there. Bugnosis connects the dots by intercepting status bar update events emitted by the control and transforming them into explicit changes to the status bar text in the main web browser.

Right-clicking the pointer within the analysis pane brings up a little menu (see Figure 23-5), allowing a user to export the analysis in various forms. This is essentially the same menu available through the drop-down menu on the Bugnosis toolbar, aside from some extra options available here (such as Copy text). The export options cause the analysis to be regenerated in a form that removes some of the embedded JavaScript and other constructs that would not work properly if viewed outside of a web browser control managed directly by Bugnosis.

*FIGURE 23-5. Context menu in the analysis pane*

### Analyzing pop-up windows

Pop-up windows were another challenge. Where and how can we present analysis results for these windows—windows that normally don't contain any toolbar at all? We considered taking screen space from pop-ups, just as we do for the main browser window, but decided against it. Whereas ordinary web pages don't have control over the dimensions of their window, pop-ups are often made to be just large enough to hold their content. Taking away screen space from pop-ups would usually mean rendering their content poorly. Instead, Bugnosis keeps a record of all of the analyses it has made, and allows the user to bring up an old analysis with the Pages Analyzed submenu in Figure 23-5. Therefore, the user can get the analysis by controlling the Bugnosis analysis that *is* visible. This also allows users to retrieve a page's analysis if the page has changed quickly—for example, by an automatic redirect.

Pop-up windows also caused us a fair number of coding headaches because of an apparent bug in IE 6. We observed that pop-up windows sometimes just don't generate a `DocumentComplete` event, which we need as our trigger to begin real (nonprovisional) scans of the document. To compensate for this, Bugnosis treats newly created windows very suspiciously: if no `DocumentComplete` arrives in a new window but other (less reliable) indicators of completeness are present, then Bugnosis performs its full scan anyway. We observed similar problems during "file download" operations (fetches of content that are not rendered natively by IE); sometimes, these generate `DocumentComplete` events carrying a parameter that doesn't appear to refer to *any* previously encountered window.

In spite of Bugnosis's attempt to compensate for these irregularities, it still occasionally waits for a signal that never arrives and thus stops analyzing documents properly. Sometimes it seems that IE is itself confused: for example, we have seen the IE status line continuing to display "Opening page [URL]…" (and we can observe that Bugnosis is also still awaiting a completion signal), yet the animated icon indicating "document loading" in the upper-righthand corner of IE has stopped swirling and the page appears to be fully present. Bugs like these are hard to isolate and hard to fix; we are merely grateful that Bugnosis's own errors tend to under-alarm rather than over-alarm users.

### Installation and Uninstallation

Installation and uninstallation are extremely important because they form the first and last impression of a piece of software. On this account, the first release of Bugnosis failed miserably. Here's what went wrong.

Because Bugnosis is packaged as a COM object inside a dynamic link library (DLL), it was possible to use IE's ActiveX delivery capability for installation. This technique is very straightforward: an `<object>` tag on a web page specifies a URL for the object. If it's not already present on the user's computer, IE fetches it. This appealed to us—we envisioned a potential user being able to read about Bugnosis at our web site, and then being able to install it with just a click or two. IE would post a security warning dialog showing information from the software publisher's certificate (the Privacy Foundation, in our case) and ask the user's permission before proceeding. To uninstall, users would select the Uninstall option from the Bugnosis menu, which would delete the Bugnosis entries from the registry and effectively decouple Bugnosis from IE for the future.

## Installation/uninstallation problems

In theory, and in closed test environments, our approach to installation and uninstallation worked reasonably well. But there were many disadvantages:

* Although this method was consistent with IE under IE's *default* security settings, some users ran IE with ActiveX downloads disabled—perhaps they were privacy fundamentalists, or just extra careful. It was a little embarrassing to tell them that they had to temporarily lower their security settings in order to install Bugnosis.

* Immediately after an installation attempt, Bugnosis would display a web page that detected whether it worked, and would give appropriate advice to the user. The sensing mechanism turned out to be unreliable for unknown reasons. Sometimes Bugnosis would activate quickly, and other times it would require an IE restart. When a restart was required, our web page gave the wrong advice—this was, of course, confusing and frustrating to users.

* On a few systems, Bugnosis simply would not install, in spite of apparently correct settings. We never learned why.

* Probably the worst scenario happened when the Bugnosis browser helper object installed successfully, but the comm bar didn't. This left the user with a browser in which Bugnosis was working—and occasionally saying "uh-oh!"—but with no visible controls. Even the Uninstall menu option was hidden! To get it to shut up, users had to hunt down and remove the *.DLL* file, or scrape out a registry entry or two, or run *regsvr32.exe* manually, or perform some other equivalently complicated maneuver. The simplest-sounding of these—removing the *.DLL* file—may have actually been the hardest, because the file was automatically stored by IE in a hidden directory (which was named differently on various Windows platforms).

* We thought it was nice that IE would pick a directory in which to store the *.DLL* file all by itself. And because Bugnosis is not very large (less than 1 MB), we thought it wasn't critical to remove it during uninstallation. Some users, however, aren't comfortable with merely disconnecting Bugnosis from IE—they really want to delete it when they uninstall. So, these users also had to navigate to the hidden directory to remove it.

We soon realized this was becoming a disaster and put together a traditional installation mechanism: a self-extracting *.EXE* holding a wizard-driven installation dialog. This had the advantage of familiarity, which we should have valued more highly up front. To uninstall Bugnosis, the user is now directed to the Add/Remove Programs dialog in the control panel.

## Windows XP Service Pack 2

Microsoft's Service Pack 2 for Windows XP now restricts ActiveX installations even further, so it's good we got away from that installation model when we did. In SP2, IE also provides an "add-in manager" to give the user finer control over the currently installed browser extensions. On the whole, this is great, but it now also gives the user the ability to *individually* disable the Bugnosis toolbar or the Bugnosis browser helper object. This results in runtime configurations that previously weren't easily accessible. The next version of Bugnosis ought to ensure that all of the newly available configurations result in sensible behavior.

## Looking Ahead

Bugnosis was a bigger success than we planned for, but it remains a very simple tool. It still needs improvement in two main areas: email web bugs and P3P. Future improvements are likely to take it further afield. But first, let's enumerate its current deficiencies.

### Exposing Email Tracking

Bugnosis looks only for surveillance built into web pages. However, because HTML is widely supported by email user agents, the same techniques for tracking users on the Web can be used against email users. This is a far more serious situation. Email addresses correspond to individuals, not to computers or network devices, so they are more personal than IP addresses. When a user views a bugged email, the watcher gets a server hit for the embedded images and can generate a log entry recording which *particular* email recipient read the message. And if the user forwards it to someone else, the watcher gets *another* hit when the other user reads it, and so on.

> **NOTE**
>
> As an example, we recently received a party invitation via the Evite company, which describes itself as "the social planning site."[13] The email contained a web bug (part of the URL was named "mailDetect") that appeared to be associated uniquely with the invitation that was sent. Evite couldn't have known beforehand that this invitation would be forwarded to a mailing list of a few hundred people (as it was), but they certainly were equipped to figure that out after the fact, when their server logs showed the email being viewed on many different IP addresses. Some of those recipients who had previously registered at Evite would have been recognized merely upon reading the invitation, if their mail agents (or web mail readers) were configured to send along their Evite cookies. Evite's privacy policy makes it clear that they're interested in such information.

We don't know of any systematic studies of sender-based email surveillance. Email user agents increasingly defer fetching images and sending cookies precisely in order to prevent this form of user tracking, but that doesn't mean that the watchers are giving up. In the past year, we've seen email tracking being used by several large pharmaceutical companies, various nonprofit organizations, spammers (of course), and, ironically, even a web consumer advocacy group (in a newsletter that included an article about spyware

---

13 See *http://www.evite.com/* and their privacy policy at *http://www.evite.com/pages/custservice/privacy.jsp*.

defenses!). We hope to make a version of Bugnosis that is able to detect email tracking, but it's harder to build and deploy as effectively, mostly because of the large number of different email readers in common use.

### Platform for Privacy Preferences Project

Bugnosis is presently unaware of P3P policies (which are described along with Privacy Bird in Chapter 22). But it should take them into consideration, because a site that commits to privacy disclosure in this way is arguably not trying to hide, even if it does use invisible images to generate log entries. Yet Bugnosis still has a role to play even in a world where every site publishes a P3P policy, because it can measure whether a web site's *practices* are consistent with its policy, at least regarding the narrow question of clickstream logging. A site that claims not to collect clickstream information yet does use web bugs is sending very mixed messages.

### Further Privacy Awareness Tools and Research

Users often send emails to the Bugnosis support address asking privacy and security questions that aren't directly related to Bugnosis. In the language of Chapter 5, Bugnosis possesses a level of *learned trust*: many people have installed it; they've become slightly more enlightened; they didn't get burned in the process; and so they see it as an authoritative resource for privacy questions. How can this trust be leveraged to improve the user community's awareness of Internet privacy? Bugnosis could incorporate social processes techniques such as those highlighted in Chapter 25, to allow privacy mavens to bring their enthusiasm and expertise to the community without becoming C++ developers. Bugnosis would be a natural launching pad for detecting spyware. Speaking of spyware, Bugnosis could also be used to *gather* information about how users interact with privacy mechanisms for privacy research purposes—with appropriate anonymizing of gathered data, and user opt-in, of course.

> **NOTE**
> If you are interested in building upon the Bugnosis code base, please do! Bugnosis and its source code are available from *http://www.bugnosis.org/*.

## Acknowledgments

Adil Alsaid did most of the original Bugnosis implementation work as a graduate student at the University of Denver. Many others contributed to various design decisions, including Stephen Keating, Andy Cervantes, and Richard M. Smith. John Boak designed the graphic theme and elements, along with the initial web site. Thanks to the editors and reviewers for valuable feedback on this chapter.

## About the Author

David Martin (*dm@cs.uml.edu*) is an assistant professor in the Department of Computer Science at the University of Massachusetts (Lowell, MA). He became interested in Internet privacy as a graduate student at Boston University. As a faculty member at the University of Denver, he collaborated with the Privacy Foundation, a consumer privacy awareness and advocacy group. He is currently co-chair of the program committee of the Privacy Enhancing Technologies Workshop, which meets annually to bring privacy researchers together to discuss their ideas and projects.

*http://www.cs.uml.edu/~dm/*

# CHAPTER TWENTY-FOUR

# Informed Consent by Design

### BATYA FRIEDMAN, PEYINA LIN, AND JESSICA K. MILLER

**C**ONSUMER PRIVACY ATTITUDES HAVE SHIFTED SIGNIFICANTLY OVER THE PAST DECADE, from being a concern of a minority in the 1980s, to being a concern of the majority. As of 2001, more than three-quarters of Americans (77%) were "very concerned" about potential misuse of their personal information.[1] Consumers not only want to be informed about how their personal information will be used, but also want the opportunity to choose: 88% of Internet users would like "opt-in" privacy policies that require Internet companies to ask consumers for permission to share their personal information with others "always" (based on a four-tier scale from "never" to "always"). In addition, if consumers could choose not to have their personal information collected, 56% would "always" opt out, and 34% would "sometimes" opt out.[2]

While informed consent may not eliminate all privacy concerns for all groups, it can help to gain users' trust by accurately articulating business practices for personal information and by allowing users autonomous choice.

---

1  Alan Westin, "Opinion Surveys: What Consumers Have to Say About Information Privacy" (2001) [cited Dec. 9, 2004]; *http://energycommerce.house.gov/107/hearings/05082001Hearing209/Westin309.htm.*

2  The McGraw-Hill Companies Inc., "Business Week/Harris Poll: A Growing Threat" (2000) [cited Dec. 9, 2004]; *http://www.businessweek.com/2000/00_12/b3673010.htm.*

How, then, might the information systems community design for informed consent? We take up that challenge here. Toward answering this question, we ground our work in the interactional theory and tripartite methodology of Value Sensitive Design.[3, 4, 5] Our approach integrates conceptual, technical, and empirical investigations. We consider the impact of information systems on both direct and indirect stakeholders.

## Introduction

Changes in consumer attitudes are occurring against the backdrop of two major trends: (1) the evolution of the concept of privacy; and (2) the erosion of historical protections for privacy.

The conception of privacy and, correspondingly, that of informed consent, has evolved through changes in political, legal, economic, social, and technological spheres. In earlier times, privacy (and the security it afforded) existed primarily in relation to physical property. Consequently, protections were given against trespasses of physical property and against battery to a person's body. Liberty meant "freedom from actual restraint."[6] In the late 1800s, advances in photographic technology made it possible to take pictures surreptitiously. Thus, the implicit consent given when "sitting" for a portrait became an inadequate safeguard against the improper capturing of one's portrait for circulation and profit. In reaction to these changes, in a landmark 1890 *Harvard Law Review* article, "The Right to Privacy,"[7] Samuel Warren and Louis Brandeis urged the courts to recognize an individual's "right to be let alone," to be free from unwarranted intrusions into personal affairs. While Warren and Brandeis were referring primarily to publishable records (e.g., photography and popular media articles), inherent to their plea was the change in meaning of "the right to life," from merely protecting physical property to "the right to enjoy life" spiritually, emotionally, and intellectually. Important for purposes here, the article established a clear relationship between the "right to privacy" and informed consent: that "the right to privacy ceases upon the publication of the facts by the individual, or upon his consent." In addition, having the ability to consent—to prevent or allow publication—afforded peace of mind, relief, and freedom from fear of injury.[8]

3   Batya Friedman (ed.), *Human Values and the Design of Computer Technology* (Cambridge: CSLI Publications Center for the Study of Language and Information, 1997).

4   Batya Friedman, "Value Sensitive Design," in William Sims Bainbridge (ed.), *Berkshire Encyclopedia of Human-Computer Interaction* (Great Barrington, MA: Berkshire Publishing Group, 2004), 769–777.

5   Batya Friedman, Peter Kahn, and Alan Borning, "Value Sensitive Design and Information Systems," in D. Galleta and Ping Zhang (eds.), *Human-Computer Interaction in Management Information Systems* (Armonk, NY: M.E. Sharpe, in press).

6   Samuel D. Warren and Louis D. Brandeis, "The Right to Privacy," *Harvard Law Review* IV:5 (1890).

7   *Ibid.*

8   *Ibid.*

Paralleling this evolution in conceptions of privacy, protections for privacy have eroded, in large part brought about by technological advances. For example, in earlier times, the mere format in which personal information was collected (paper) afforded reasonable privacy protection. Inconvenient access to information, limited reproduction capabilities, and the inability to easily link, sort, and process information acted as "natural" shields protecting personal data. Nowadays, networking and digitization have stripped the public of that "natural shielding," and continuously beg for the reconceptualization of privacy and its protection. How is this relevant for today's businesses and for technology design?

Accounting for privacy in technology design does not merely address a moral concern, it safeguards the design host company from financial risks and public relations backlashes. For example, the built-in unique processor-identifier of Intel's Pentium III processor, also known as the Processor Serial Number (PSN) technology, was introduced to help corporations manage inventories.[9] Even though the PSN is a number attached to a processor, not a person, and even though Intel took precautionary actions by creating a control utility that allowed users to turn off the identifier, the introduction of security at the potential expense of privacy generated consumer distrust. Intel was faced with consumer boycotts and legal action attacks from privacy advocacy groups. According to a 1999 report on CNET news, "The serial number has sparked a definite negative emotional core with segments of the population."[10] Other technologies, such as commonplace workstations that contain microphones without hardware on/off switches[11] and the more exotic Active Badge Location system of the Palo Alto Research Center (PARC),[12] are examples of designs that similarly compromised privacy for the sake of other functionalities and that were met with resistance from some groups.

In this chapter, we first present a conceptual model of informed consent for information systems. Next we present three cases in which the conceptual model has been applied: cookie handling in web browsers; secure connections for web-based interactions; and Google's Gmail web-based email service. Each case discussed here involves a widely deployed technology in use at the time our investigations were conducted; each invokes privacy or security concerns for the public at large; and each highlights a unique set of challenges and design possibilities for informed consent. In reporting on these cases, our goal is not only to articulate how these three specific systems might be improved, but also more generally to illustrate how the model can be used proactively to design information systems that support the user experience of informed consent. Finally, we propose design principles and business practices to enhance privacy and security through informed consent.

9   Intel Corporation, "Intel Pentium III Processor" (2003) [cited Dec. 10, 2004]; *http://support.intel.com*.

10  Stephanie Miles, "How Serious Is Pentium III's Privacy Risk?" (1999) [cited Dec. 1, 2004]; *http://news.com.com/How+serious+is+Pentium+IIIs+privacy+risk/2100-1040_3-222905.html*.

11  John C. Tang, "Eliminating a Hardware Switch: Weighing Economics and Values in a Design Decision," in Batya Friedman (ed.), *Human Values and the Design of Computer Technology* (Cambridge: CSLI Publications Center for the Study of Language and Information, 1997), 259–269.

12  Roy Want, Andy Hopper, Veronica Falcao, and Jon Gibbons, "The Active Badge Location System," *ACM Transactions on Information Systems* 10 (1992), 91–102.

# VALUE SENSITIVE DESIGN

Value Sensitive Design[a] emerged in the 1990s as an approach to the design of information and computer systems that accounts for human values in a principled and comprehensive manner throughout the design process. While emphasizing the moral perspective (e.g., privacy, security, trust, human dignity, physical and psychological well-being, informed consent, intellectual property), Value Sensitive Design also accounts for usability (e.g., ease of use), conventions (e.g., standardization of technical protocols), and personal predilections (e.g., color preferences within a graphical interface).

Key features of Value Sensitive Design involve its interactional perspective, tripartite methodology, and emphasis on direct and indirect stakeholders:

*Interactional theory*

Value Sensitive Design is an interactional theory: values are viewed neither as inscribed into technology nor as simply transmitted by social forces. Rather, people and social systems affect technological development, and new technologies shape (but do not rigidly determine) individual behavior and social systems.

*Tripartite methodology: conceptual, empirical, and technical*

Value Sensitive Design systematically integrates and iterates on three types of investigations. *Conceptual investigations* comprise philosophically informed analyses of the central constructs and issues under investigation. For example: what values have standing? How should we engage in tradeoffs among competing values (e.g., access versus privacy, or security versus trust)? *Empirical investigations* focus on the human response to the technical artifact and on the larger social context in which the technology is situated. The entire range of quantitative and qualitative social science research methods may be applicable (e.g., observations, interviews, surveys, focus groups, measurements of user behavior and human physiology, contextual inquiry, and interaction logs). *Technical investigations* focus on the design and performance of the technology itself, involving both retrospective analyses of existing technologies and the design of new technical mechanisms and systems. The conceptual, empirical, and technical investigations are employed iteratively such that the results of one type are integrated with those of the others, which, in turn, influence yet additional investigations of the earlier types.

*Direct and indirect stakeholders*

*Direct stakeholders* are parties who interact directly with the computer system or its output. *Indirect stakeholders* are all other parties who are otherwise affected by the use of the system. For example, online court record systems impact not only the direct stakeholders, such as lawyers, judges, and journalists who access the court records, but also an especially important group of indirect stakeholders: the people documented in the court records.

---

[a] Adapted from Batya Friedman, "Value Sensitive Design" in William Sims Bainbridge (ed.), *Berkshire Encyclopedia of Human-Computer Interaction* (Great Barrington, MA: Berkshire Publishing Group, 2004), 769–777.

# A Model of Informed Consent for Information Systems

The model of informed consent for information systems we present here was first developed in 2000 by Friedman, Felten, and Millett[13] in the context of online interactions.[14] This model is based on six components:

- Disclosure

- Comprehension

- Voluntariness

- Competence

- Agreement

- Minimal distraction

The word *informed* encompasses the first two components: disclosure and comprehension. The word *consent* encompasses the following three components: voluntariness, competence, and agreement. In addition, the activities of being informed and giving consent should happen with minimal distraction, without diverting users from their primary task or overwhelming them with intolerable nuisance.

## Disclosure

Disclosure refers to providing accurate information about the benefits and harms that might reasonably be expected from the action under consideration. What is disclosed should address the important values, needs, and interests of the individual, explicitly state the purpose or reason for undertaking the action, and avoid unnecessary technical detail. The information should also disabuse the individual of any commonly held false beliefs. Moreover, if the action involves collecting information about an individual, then the following should also be made explicit:

- What information will be collected?

- Who will have access to the information?

- How long will the information be archived?

- What will the information be used for?

- How will the identity of the individual be protected?

## Comprehension

Comprehension refers to the individual's accurate interpretation of *what* is being disclosed. This component raises the question: how do we know when something has been adequately comprehended? While there is no easy answer here, at least two methods seem

---

13 Batya Friedman, Edward Felten, and Lynette I. Millett, "Informed Consent Online: A Conceptual Model and Design Principles," *CSE Technical Report* (Seattle: University of Washington, 2000).

14 See also Ruth R. Faden and Tom L. Beauchamp, *A History and Theory of Informed Consent* (New York: Oxford University Press, 1986).

viable: (1) being able to restate in different words what has been disclosed, and (2) being able to apply what has been disclosed to a set of hypothetical events. Take, for example, a web-based recommendation system, such as an e-commerce site recommending products based on the customer's prior purchases or on purchases of other customers with similar profiles. Based on information disclosed to the customer—about what data is being collected and how it will be used—can the customer answer reasonable questions about the data's use, such as:

- Will information about the customer's last three purchases be included in the recommendation system?

- Will some other user of the recommendation system be able to determine what the customer has purchased in the past?

- Will information about the customer's past purchases be a part of the recommendation system two years from now?

In face-to-face interactions, two-way dialog, facial expressions, and other physical cues help ensure the adequate interpretation of any information disclosed. Technologically mediated interactions, however, lack many of the cues and opportunities to ascertain and ensure comprehension. Typical web-based interactions present the disclosure of information in a web page or dialog box, and users are expected to agree to or decline participation by clicking on a button. Rarely are email or chat facilities provided during the process of disclosure. As more and more interactions move online or become mediated by technology, ensuring comprehension becomes more challenging. Nevertheless, comprehension is a crucial component of informing, and it should not be dismissed.

## Voluntariness

A voluntary action is one in which an individual could reasonably resist participation should she wish to. Voluntariness, then, refers to ensuring that the action is not coerced or overly manipulated.

*Coercion* is an extreme form of influence that controls by compulsion, threat, or prevention. A canonical example of coercion occurs as follows: Person A holds a gun to Person B's head and says, "Fly me to Havana or I'll shoot." Often, coercion can occur without notice when there is only one reasonable way for individuals to receive certain needed services or information (or, if other ways do exist, they are too costly in terms of finance, time, expertise, or other costs to be viable options.) This form of coercion is a serious concern for online interactions and other technology mediated interactions. As more and more critical services move online in their entirety, such as applying for medical insurance or to universities for higher education, individuals who want to obtain these services or information will have to engage in web interactions. Given the lack of substantive choice among web sites and web browsers, users can be, in effect, coerced into web-based interactions that compel them to give up personal information or engage in other activities.

*Manipulation* of certain forms can also undermine voluntariness. Manipulation can roughly be defined as "any intentional and successful influence by a person by noncoercively altering the actual choices available to the person or by nonpersuasively altering the person's perceptions of those choices."[15] The key here is that manipulation alters the individuals' choices or perception of choices by some means other than reason. This sort of manipulation can be achieved in at least three ways:

- *Manipulation of options.* The first way entails manipulation of the options presented to the individual such that the presentation encourages certain choices or behaviors. For example, consider an e-business that asks the user for more information than is necessary to complete a purchase but does not indicate to the user that completing some fields is optional.

- *Manipulation of information.* The second way entails manipulation of information. This manipulation uses information intentionally to overwhelm the individual or to provoke or take advantage of an individual's fear or anxiety. For example, some web sites have packaged information into multiple cookies—information that could have been packaged more concisely—so that the user who elects to accept cookies on a case-by-case basis would be bombarded with numerous requests to set cookies from a single site. As a result, the user may turn on the "agree to all cookies" option to avoid the overwhelming requests for information, or fail to notice an undesirable cookie.

- *Psychological manipulation.* The third way is psychological. This form of manipulation includes any intentional act that influences a person by causing changes in the individual's mental processes by any means other than reason. Flattery, guilt induction, and subliminal suggestions are a few relevant influences. Recent work by Reeves and Nass and their colleagues[16, 17] indicates that individuals are vulnerable to psychological manipulation in online interactions, particularly with respect to psychological manipulations from the technology's interface. For example, in their research, Reeves and Nass have shown that users respond to flattery from a computer, judge computers that criticize rather than praise others to provide more accurate information, and apply gender stereotypes to the technology simply on the basis of subtle gender cues, to name but a few of their results. Web sites that use psychological manipulation—for instance, to flatter the user into divulging information or into attributing greater accuracy to online recommendations—may violate the criterion of voluntariness.

15 *Ibid.,* 354.

16 B. Reeves and C. Nass, *The Media Equation: How People Treat Computers, Television, and New Media Like Real People and Places* (New York: Cambridge University Press, 1996).

17 C. I. Nass, Y. Moon, J. Morkes, E. Kim, and B. J. Fogg, "Computers Are Social Actors: A Review of Current Research," in Batya Friedman (ed.), *Human Values and the Design of Computer Technology* (New York: Cambridge University Press, 1997), 137–162.

## Competence

Competence refers to possessing the mental, emotional, and physical capabilities needed to give informed consent. For example, a person with Alzheimer's may lack the mental capability to make her own medical decisions. Or, in the online environment, a 15-year-old may have the technical competence, but lack the mental and emotional capability to make reasoned judgments about when to provide personal information to e-businesses and in online chat rooms.

For example, at roughly the same time as the Year 2000 Census was being conducted in the United States, the Barbi web site presented Barbi as a census taker who asked web site visitors—mostly young girls under the age of 12—to help Barbi with her census work by completing a form that requested personal information. Troublesome from the perspective of informed consent, these young girls often lacked the mental and emotional competence necessary to judge the appropriateness of the information they volunteered to the web site.

Designers of web sites and other technologies targeted to children and adolescents will need to be especially cognizant of the component of competence. For example, the United States Children's Online Privacy Protection Act (COPPA) requires written parental consent when web sites collect information from children aged 12 and under. Another model is that used by many Institutional Review Boards; it suggests obtaining informed consent from both the adolescent and the adolescent's guardian for adolescents between the ages of 13 and 17 (inclusive). However, the case of adolescents is not straightforward: a tension exists between ensuring that adolescents can adequately assess the impacts of the type of information being collected from them and maintaining adolescents' privacy (as this is typically the time in a person's life that privacy vis a vis one's parents begins to become an important value). This tension should be considered when determining whether it is necessary to obtain consent from the adolescent's guardian as well as from the adolescent.

## Agreement

Agreement refers to a reasonably clear opportunity to accept or decline to participate. Aspects to consider include:

- Are opportunities to accept or decline visible, readily accessible, and ongoing?

- Is agreement by the participant ongoing?

In traditional human subjects research, the component of agreement is ongoing. Participants may withdraw their agreement to participate at any time and for any reason (participants do not need to provide a reason for discontinuing participation). While the arena of research differs in important ways from interactions with information systems, and while considerable complexity exists concerning how to apply the guidelines from one to the other, still the aspect of ongoing agreement may have relevance for information systems. For example, in the case of recommendation systems, users could be provided with the opportunity to withdraw or prevent further use of their data from the recommendation system at any time. Many of today's recommendation systems lack such an ability.

A related issue for ongoing agreement arises in the context of discussion groups and online chat rooms where dialog that may often feel like "ethereal" online conversation is archived and, in reality, is more permanent and accessible than most other forms of communication. In these online forums, participants in the flurry of heated conversation may forget that they have agreed to have their online conversation recorded and archived and, if given the opportunity, might even suspend that agreement. Mechanisms that periodically remind participants that online dialog may be archived (and perhaps allow participants to remove dialog from the archive) could help preserve informed consent in these interactions.

Not all forms of agreement need to be explicit. As a society, we have a good deal of experience with implicit consent where, by virtue of entering into a situation, the individual has, in effect, agreed to the activities that are broadly known to occur in that context. For example, when a player steps out onto the football field in football garb and enters the game, the individual has implicitly agreed to participate in the normal activities of the game—namely, to being bumped, bashed, and smashed by other players who have entered into identical agreements. Implicit consent holds in this case because the other components have also been met: disclosure and comprehension (via reasonable expectation), competence (if we assume that the individual is of a reasonable age and of sound mind and body), and voluntariness (if we assume that the individual was not coerced or manipulated to dress in football garb and to go out onto the field). For implicit consent to hold for information systems, similar criteria need to be met.

## Minimal Distraction

This criterion for informed consent arose from empirical investigations in which users, overwhelmed by the activities of "being informed" and "giving consent," became numbed to the informed consent process and disengaged from the process in its entirety. Specifically, minimal distraction refers to meeting the preceding criteria of disclosure, comprehension, competence, voluntariness, and agreement without "unduly diverting the individual from the task at hand."[18] This criterion is challenging to implement, because "the very process of informing and obtaining consent necessarily diverts users from their primary task,"[19] yet it is crucial if informed consent is to be realized in practice.

With a model of informed consent for information systems in hand, we turn now to examine how this model can be used to analyze, assess, and improve the design of existing information systems.

18  Batya Friedman, Daniel C. Howe, and Edward Felten, "Informed Consent in the Mozilla Browser: Implementing Value-Sensitive Design." Thirty-Fifth Hawaii International Conference on System Sciences (Hawaii, 2002).

19  *Ibid.*

# Possibilities and Limitations for Informed Consent: Redesigning Cookie Handling in a Web Browser

In this section, we demonstrate that the proposed model of informed consent can be used to:

- Assess how effectively a particular system design supports informed consent

- Guide successive design

- Identify how the underlying technology may constrain the range of possible solutions to support users' informed consent

Specifically, we examine the role the web browser plays in obtaining informed consent for cookies.

## What Are Cookies and How Are They Used?

A cookie is a text file stored on the user's machine that can be used to maintain information about the user, such as an identifier or a log of the user's navigation on the web site. One accepted way companies use cookies is to customize their web site to the user (e.g., Amazon uses cookies to remember what users like to buy and what users put in their shopping baskets). However, cookies can also be abused by surreptitiously collecting information about the user.

When a user wants to retrieve a particular web page from the Internet, the user opens a web browser and enters the web page's address. The browser sends the request for the web page to the appropriate web server. The web server then retrieves the requested web page and sends it back to the user's browser where it is displayed. This process involves a couple of additional steps if the web server wants to set a cookie. When sending the requested web page back to the browser, the server sends the browser a request to store the cookie. Depending on how it has been programmed, and on any cookie-related preferences that have been set, the browser may or may not store the cookie as requested. If the browser stores the cookie on the user's computer, the browser will volunteer the cookie each time the user revisits that web page and possibly any other web pages in that domain, depending on the scope of the cookie.

## Web Browser as Gatekeeper to Informed Consent

In the previous description, the browser acts as a gatekeeper by determining which web server requests to fulfill. In addition, with respect to informed consent, the web browser plays at least two other critical gatekeeping roles:

- The web browser controls whether the user is notified about a server request and, to a large extent, controls the content of that notification. Thus, the components of disclosure and comprehension largely reside in the web browser.

- The web browser controls whether the user has an opportunity to agree to or decline the web server's request (e.g., prompting for user input each time a server requests to place a cookie as opposed to the browser handling the request without user input). Thus, the component of agreement also resides in the browser.

Admittedly, a proactive web site could supplement the functionality provided by the web browser by explicitly addressing disclosure and agreement (e.g., privacy policies). However, relying on all web sites to do this individually would result in ad hoc methods and require users to become familiar with each web site's policies and practices.

## Web Browser Development and Progress for Informed Consent: 1995–1999

With a conceptualization for informed consent online in hand, Millett, Friedman, and Felten[20] conducted a retrospective analysis of how cookie handling in Netscape Navigator and Internet Explorer evolved with respect to informed consent over a five-year period, beginning in 1995. Specifically, they used the criteria of disclosure, comprehension, voluntariness, competence, and agreement to evaluate how well each browser in each stage of its development supported the users' experience of informed consent for the use of cookies. (At this early stage in their work, the criterion of minimal distraction had not yet been identified.)

Through this analysis, they found that cookie technology had improved over time regarding informed consent. For example, there had been increased visibility of cookies, options for accepting or declining cookies, and access to information about cookie content. However, as of 1999, some startling problems remained:

- While browsers disclosed to users some information about cookies, the right kind of information—that is, information about the potential harms and benefits from setting a particular cookie—was still not disclosed.

- In Internet Explorer, if a user wanted to decline all third-party cookies, the burden fell on the user to do so one cookie at a time.

- Users' out-of-the-box cookie experience (i.e., the default setting) was no different in 1999 from what it had been in 1995: to accept all cookies. That is, the novice user installed a browser that accepted all cookies and disclosed nothing about that activity to the user.

- Neither Internet Explorer nor Netscape Navigator alerted a user when a cookie was sent back to a site, as opposed to when a cookie was stored.

## Redesigning the Browser

After completing the retrospective analysis, Friedman, Howe, and Felten[21] considered how to redesign the browser to better support informed consent. First, they identified four overarching design goals:

- Enhance users' understanding of specific cookie events

- Enhance users' global understanding of the common uses of cookie technology, including what a cookie is and its potential benefits and risks

---

20 Lynette I. Millett, Batya Friedman, and Edward Felten, "Cookies and Web Browser Design: Toward Realizing Informed Consent Online," CHI (Seattle, WA, March 2001).

21 Friedman, Howe, and Felten.

- Enhance users' ability to manage cookies

- Achieve these goals while minimizing distraction for the user

By iterating through three design prototypes, each followed by small-scale usability studies (see the earlier sidebar, "Value Sensitive Design"), Friedman et al. redesigned the Cookie Manager tool of the Mozilla browser (the open source version of Netscape Navigator).[22]

In consideration of the design goals and design strategies, Friedman et al.[23] implemented a *peripheral awareness* mechanism by implementing a small application they named the "Cookie Watcher" docked in Mozilla's existing sidebar. In their final design (see Figure 24-1), users were notified in real time not only about the occurrence of cookie events, but also about the domain and type of cookie being set. Visual cues such as background color and font style were used to represent domain and duration information, respectively, as follows: third-party cookies were displayed in red; cookies from the same domain were displayed in green; italicized fonts were used for session cookies; and bold fonts were used for cookies with durations of more than a year.

Two just-in-time interventions were implemented:

- Users can click on any installed cookie (once displayed in the sidebar) to bring up a cookie manager tool. With that tool, the user can learn more information about the specific cookie, delete the cookie, and ban that site from resetting cookies.

- At the bottom of the sidebar, users can click on a "Learn About Cookies" button to prompt a Cookie-Information Dialog Box with information about the potential benefits and harms of cookies, and label information on what the colors and font sizes represent.

Participants of the usability studies commented favorably on the just-in-time management tools. Their comments suggested that the Cookie Watcher helped to enhance understanding about cookies as well as eased cookie management. Evidence showed that direct access to information on individual cookies supported the design goals.

## Technical Limitations to Redesigning for Informed Consent

Although the Mozilla prototypes made good progress toward achieving the design goals, there remained changes that Friedman et al. were unable to make as a result of the underlying technology. For example, many users would like to know not only when a web site wants to set a cookie, but also when a web site wants to *use* a cookie. However, because the web browser automatically volunteers cookies whenever the user revisits the domain, it is currently not possible to provide users with that information.

In order to fully disclose when and why a particular cookie is being set and then used—and its potential harms and benefits—changes would need to be made to the network

---

22 Mozilla version 0.8 was used in the prototype designs.
23 Friedman, Howe, and Felten.

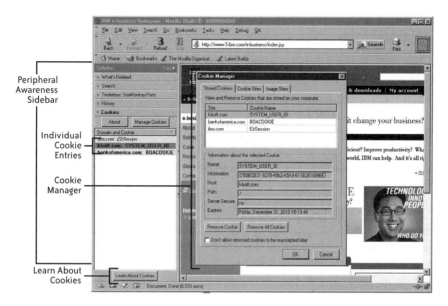

*FIGURE 24-1.* Taking advantage of Mozilla's sidebar structure, a new peripheral awareness sidebar (the Cookie Watcher) was developed to dynamically notify users whenever a cookie is set (as shown above); in addition, two just-in-time mechanisms were implemented and supported in the Cookie Watcher: (1) by clicking on a cookie, the user can bring up a cookie manager tool (as shown above); (2) by clicking on the Learn About Cookies button, the user can bring up a dialog box with information about the potential harms and benefits of cookies, and about what the colors and font styles in the Cookie Watcher represent (not shown)

protocol that, in turn, would necessitate changes to the web browser and the remote web site, as follows:

- The underlying network protocol (in this case, HTTP) would need to support the description of the harms and benefits of the cookie as well as provide a means for the web site to request to *use* (not just set) a cookie.

- The browser then would need to be programmed to display these harms and benefits in a clear and accessible way both when the cookie is being set and when the cookie is requested.

- Finally, the web site would need to provide accurate information by filling in the appropriate HTTP fields.

While each entity has a critical role to play, the network protocol constrains possibilities for the other two.

## Reflections

This section has highlighted how the model of informed consent can be used to evaluate and design information systems. We note that some of the design ideas presented here, such as the use of peripheral awareness mechanisms, can now be seen in the current version of both Mozilla (version 1.73) and Internet Explorer (version 6). For example, both browsers now use a peripheral awareness mechanism in the form of a small "eye" icon displayed in the bottom righthand corner of the browser window to indicate when a web site attempts to set a cookie that is restricted or blocked by the users' privacy preferences. Thus, the design methods presented in this section have pragmatic value.

We have also explicated the interaction between the underlying technical infrastructure (in this case, the HTTP protocol) and what solutions can be designed and implemented to support users' informed consent. Along these lines, the Platform for Privacy Preferences (P3P) (discussed in Chapter 22 in this volume) represents one recent effort that works around the protocol limitations to provide a mechanism that evaluates web site privacy practices against user-specified privacy preferences.

Finally, we point to the interaction between technical implementation and business practice: even if there were no technical limitations on redesigning the web browser for informed consent, in order for the web browser to provide complete disclosure to the user, web sites would need to provide an accurate and clear description of what information their cookies collect and how the collected information will be used. In this and other ways, business practice must work in consort with technical implementations.

## Informing Through Interaction Design: What Users Understand About Secure Connections Through Their Web Browsing

The process of informing the user can happen as the user interacts with the system instead of through simple, explicit text disclosure. That is, in addition to the user's existing knowledge about how the system functions, the visual cues during interaction and the text displayed on the interface (web pages, browser, etc.) may lead the user to develop an idea or mental model of how the system functions. An issue of concern arises when there is a mismatch between the disclosed text and the interaction cues—in particular, when the latter heavily influences the user's perception of how the system works. As a result, in a best-case scenario, the user could end up confused but not jeopardize any personal data; in a worst-case scenario, the user could construct inaccurate mental models about the security of the system and make poor decisions on what actions to take or not to take to protect personal information.

With the design strategy of informing through interaction in mind, in this section we describe a study by Friedman, Hurley, Howe, Felten, and Nissenbaum[24] on how users across diverse communities conceptualize web security.

### Participants

Seventy-two individuals, 24 each from a rural community in Maine, a suburban professional community in New Jersey, and a high-technology community in California, partici-

---

24 Batya Friedman, David Hurley, Daniel C. Howe, Edward Felten, and Helen Nissenbaum, "Users' Conceptions of Web Security: A Comparative Study," in *Extended Abstracts of CHI* (2002), 746–747.

pated in an extensive (two-hour) semistructured interview concerning users' conceptions, views, and values about web security. Equal numbers of men and women participated from each community. We report here on one section of the interview that focused on users' mental models of web security. Both verbal and nonverbal techniques were used to assess users' understandings.

## Users' Conceptions of Secure Connections

Participants were asked to define and portray secure connections in various ways, as we describe in the following subsections.

### Definition of a secure connection

Participants were first asked to define a secure connection. Participants' definitions of a secure connection encompassed one of the following concepts:

- *Transit.* Protecting the confidentiality of information while it moves between machines on the Web

- *Encryption.* The specific mechanism of encoding and decoding information

- *Remote site.* Protecting information once it has arrived at its destination on the Web

High-technology participants (83%) provided correct definitions of a secure connection more frequently than rural participants (52%) ($p < .05$) did. Statistically, there was no difference in responses between the high-technology (83%) and suburban (68%) participants.

### Recognition of a connection as secure or not secure

Next, participants were shown four screenshots of a browser connecting to a web site and were asked to recognize a secure connection. For each screenshot, participants were asked to state whether the web connection was secure or not secure, as well as to provide the rationale for their evaluation.

Table 24-1 shows the types of evidence participants used to evaluate a connection. As shown, participants depended primarily upon six types of evidence.

1. HTTPS protocol—for example, "usually, it says http for nonsecure or standard and https for secure, the s meaning secure".

2. Icon—for example, "[the site is secure] just because the key is there".

3. Point in transaction—for example, "it looks like one of the main pages on the site and usually main pages are nonsecured connections".

4. Type of information—for example, "that at least has the indication of a secure connection; I mean, it's obviously asking for a Social Security number and a password".

5. Type of web site—for example, "I can't imagine a bank would be online and not have security measures in there".

6. General distrust—for example, "I'm wary of the computer itself…I basically don't think any of the sites are secure".

*TABLE 24-1. Percentage of types of evidence participants used to evaluate a connection as secure or not secure*

| Type of evidence[a] | Correct evaluation | | Incorrect evaluation | |
|---|---|---|---|---|
| | Not secure | Secure | Not secure | Secure |
| 1. HTTPS protocol | 16 | 20 | 0 | 9 |
| 2. Icon (lock or key) | 45 | 53 | 45 | 18 |
| 3. Point in transaction | 11 | 2 | 0 | 9 |
| 4. Type of information | 2 | 18 | 27 | 27 |
| 5. Type of web site | 2 | 0 | 27 | 0 |
| 6. General distrust | 5 | 0 | 0 | 18 |
| 7. Blue line | 3 | 4 | 0 | 0 |
| 8. Amount/presence of Information | 1 | 0 | 0 | 0 |
| 9. Accessibility of site | 2 | 0 | 0 | 9 |
| 10. Text from web site | 6 | 0 | 0 | 9 |
| 11. Alerts on screen | 2 | 2 | 0 | 0 |
| 12. Security conventions | 1 | 0 | 0 | 0 |
| 13. Transaction completed | 1 | 2 | 0 | 0 |
| 14. Unspecified | 3 | 0 | 0 | 0 |
| 15. Uncodeable | 2 | 0 | 0 | 0 |

[a] Some participants provided multiple types of evidence. All types of evidence were coded for each participant.

Secure connections were recognized by roughly half the participants evenly across the three communities. In contrast, nonsecure connections were correctly recognized more frequently by high-technology participants (92%) than by either rural (59%) or suburban (50%) participants ($p < .05$).

**Visual portrayal of a secure connection**

Finally, to elicit participants' models about web security, participants were asked to revise a drawing of the Web that they had made earlier in the interview to reflect a secure connection. Participants sketched primarily five different representations:

• Screenshot (12%), a symbol on the screen such as the key icon

• Direct connection (12%), a direct line between the user's computer and the target web site

- Secure boundary (14%), a barrier, such as a firewall, that surrounds or protects the user's computer, a server, or the target web site

- Encryption (40%), scrambling the information while it is in transit, including both message encoding and decoding in more sophisticated drawings

- No difference (11%), drawings that remained unchanged from the participant's initial drawing

Participants' drawings were then analyzed for their representation of a secure connection as something that applies to information while it is in transit from one machine to another (a correct understanding) (see Figure 24-2), or as something that applies to a specific "place" on the Web (an incorrect understanding) (see Figure 24-3).

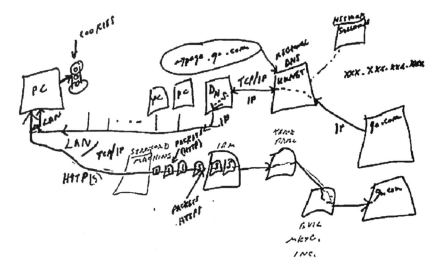

FIGURE 24-2. Participant drawing showing security as transit; the drawing shows a secure connection in terms of encryption while the information is in "transit"; the darker solid lines represent the secure connection

High-technology participants (74%) provided transit (i.e., correct) representations more frequently than did either rural (33%) or suburban (46%) participants (p < .05).

## Reflections

Based on empirically derived typologies, results (Table 24-1) suggest that many users across diverse communities inaccurately evaluated a connection as secure when it was not, and vice versa. In addition, users who correctly recognized connections as secure or not secure sometimes did so for incorrect reasons. Furthermore, the high-technology participants did not always have more accurate or sophisticated conceptions of web security than did their rural and suburban counterparts.

Through this study, we highlighted two main points: that informing can happen through interaction, and that users develop mental models that shape their understanding about the system and about its security.

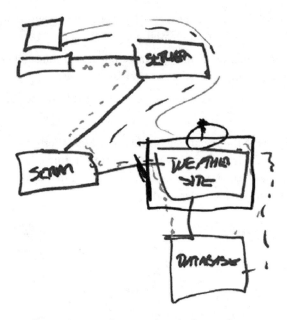

FIGURE 24-3. *Participant drawing showing security as a place; the drawing shows a secure connection in terms of a secure boundary around a specific "place" on the Web; the darker solid lines represent the secure connection*

We also mentioned that poor, inadequate, or misguided mental models about security may lead to poor privacy behavior—believing personal information is adequately protected when it is not, or not taking the appropriate actions to protect personal information. These negative consequences could be reduced through web browser design that helps users construct more accurate understandings of a secure connection. Such design work can profit from this study's typologies. For example, the most frequently used icons to represent the security status of a connection—the key or padlock—convey the idea of a "place" that can be made secure. Such a conception runs counter to the more accurate meaning of a secure connection (referring to the security of the information in transit). More generally, well-designed interactions—conceptualized to match the underlying security model and validated empirically with users—can lead users to construct reasonable models for system security. In so doing, the interaction design can go a good distance toward tacitly informing users of potential privacy and security risks.

## The Scope of Informed Consent: Questions Motivated by Gmail

In the first two cases, we provided "proof-of-concept" projects for ways in which the information systems community can design for informed consent. In our third case—Google's Gmail web mail (web-based email) system—we examine the scope of informed consent—namely, are there issues concerning privacy and security that informed consent cannot reasonably address? And, if so, how do these issues affect informed consent?

## What Is Gmail?

Gmail (*http://www.gmail.com*) is Google's web mail system, currently in beta testing. Similar to other free email services, such as those provided by Yahoo! Mail or Hotmail, Gmail provides three key additional features:

- A larger amount of storage space for one's email than is typically provided (as of December 2004, 1 GB of storage as compared to Yahoo! Mail's 250 MB or Hotmail's 250 MB)

- The ability to use Google search technology to search one's email messages

- Grouping an email and the replies to it as a conversation

As with most free web mail services, Gmail subscribers see advertising alongside their email. However, unlike other free web mail providers, Gmail determines which advertisements to display based on the *content* of the subscriber's email message. For example, if a Gmail subscriber receives an email message from a friend asking to borrow the subscriber's bicycle, the subscriber would likely see advertisements related to online bicycle vendors alongside the email message (see Figure 24-4).

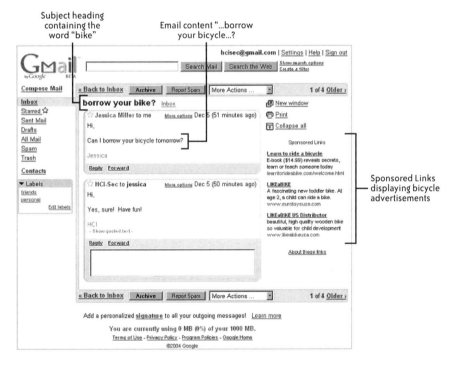

*F I G U R E   2 4 - 4 .* Viewing an email message in Gmail; advertisements targeted to the content of the body of the message—in this case, bicycles—appear to the right of the email message, under the label Sponsored Links

## How Gmail Advertisements Work

Let's look briefly at both the Gmail business model and its technology:

- *The business model.* In a nutshell, Google charges advertisers only when a user clicks on an advertisement. When advertisers submit their advertisements to Google, they negotiate a "rate-per-user-click" and designate keywords they believe to be most relevant to their advertisement.[25]

- *The technology.* The following automated process occurs dynamically each time a Gmail subscriber clicks on an email entry. The Gmail system retrieves the message and scans the text (attachments are not scanned) for keywords (provided earlier by advertisers) in the body of the email message.[26] Based on the results of scanning the message, as well as on how well the advertisement keywords match the email content, the amount advertisers pay per user-click, and the prior click-through rate (i.e., the number of clicks divided by the number of times the advertisement has been displayed), Google computers select and determine the order in which to display advertisements. The selected advertisement is displayed near the subscriber's message; no link is established between the advertisement and the email message. The only information Google relinquishes to its advertisers is the number of times their advertisement was chosen for display and the click-through rate. No personal information about subscribers or the content of email messages is released to advertisers.

## Gmail and the Six Components of Informed Consent

In the context of this business model and technical implementation, how well does Gmail meet the criteria for informed consent? To make this assessment, we analyzed Gmail's Terms of Use,[27] Program Policy,[28] and Privacy Policy[29] in relation to Gmail's functionality as described above. Between these documents, Gmail's registration interface, and the user interface, Google addresses each of the different components of informed consent in a reasonably thorough manner.

### Disclosure

As of December 2004, the Gmail privacy policy explicitly states:

*What information will be collected about subscribers and their activities*
For example, "personal information including your first and last name, a user name...and a password," "log information...browser type you used, your Internet

---

25  Google, *Google Adwords* (2004) [cited Dec. 2004]; *https://adwords.google.com/select/*.

26  According to Ana R. Yang (product marketing manager, Gmail), personal email (Dec. 4, 2004).

27  Google, *Gmail Terms of Use* (2004) [cited Dec. 2, 2004]; *http://gmail.google.com/gmail/help/terms_of_use.html*.

28  Google, *Gmail Program Policies* (2004) [cited Dec. 1, 2004]; *http://gmail.google.com/gmail/help/program_policies.html*.

29  Google, *Gmail Privacy Policy* (2004) [cited Nov. 15, 2004]; *http://gmail.google.com/gmail/help/privacy.html*.

Protocol address, and the date and time of day...the unique ID provided by our cookie and the URL of the last site you visited."

*Who will have access to the information*

For example, "No human reads your email...without your consent," "Google will never sell, rent or share your personal information...with any third parties for marketing purposes without your express permission."

*What the information will be used for*

For example, subscribers' accounts will be used "internally to deliver the best possible service to you, such as improving the Gmail user interface, preventing fraud within our advertising system, and better targeting related information."

*How the identity of the individual will be protected*

For example, employees who have access to user information are monitored and educated to protect the user's privacy.[30]

Overall, Google discloses an impressive amount of the right type of information to enable informed consent. We note one anomaly: Google provides only vague details about how long information is kept.

## Comprehension

The Privacy Policy uses fairly clear, jargon-free English; this goes a good distance toward helping ensure comprehension. To further support comprehension, Google could provide an opportunity for dialog and clarification about Gmail policies and practices by publishing a way to contact the appropriate Google personnel (e.g., email address, phone number, or online chat).

## Voluntariness

Gmail subscribers' consent can be considered voluntary for two reasons:

- Gmail's Terms of Use and Privacy Policy contain reasonably neutral language that does not attempt to coerce or manipulate users to use Gmail.

- Other free web mail services are available, albeit with substantially less storage space and perhaps not as high-quality search technology, that do not scan users' email for the purpose of displaying content-targeted advertisements.

## Competence

Competence is difficult to assess in online interactions, and how to do so remains an open problem for the information systems community. Within the bounds of current knowledge and practice, Gmail's Terms of Use addresses the competence of minors by stating:

---

30 *Ibid.*

"Due to the Children's Online Privacy Protection Act of 1998 (which is available at *http:// www.ftc.gov/ogc/coppa1.htm*), you must be at least thirteen (13) years of age to use this Service."[31]

## Agreement

Google requires explicit consent with Gmail's Terms of Use before the user receives a Gmail account. In practice, the user must click a large button at the end of the registration process signaling agreement to the Terms of Use. However, the Terms of Use does not provide information about whether subscribers can withdraw from the agreement and, if so, whether it is possible to delete their Gmail accounts. Indeed, it is possible to do both, but subscribers must be able to navigate through several different layers of menus to do so.

## Minimal distraction

Setting aside users' tendency not to read agreement policies during online registration processes, we address the criterion of minimal distraction under the confinements of online interactions. Links to Gmail's Terms of Use and Privacy Policy are always at the bottom of a user's email, thus making it easy for the user to see what he has agreed to while not being distracted from the task at hand: reading and sending email.

## Two Questions Related to Informed Consent

Despite Google's reasonable handling of informed consent, privacy advocates have made claims that scanning personal email to place content-targeted advertisements is still a privacy invasion. Their claims revolve around two primary questions:[32]

- Does using machines to read personal email constitute a privacy violation?
- Should the consent of indirect stakeholders (i.e., email senders) also be obtained?

We turn now to discuss these two questions and their relation to informed consent.

## The question of machines reading personal content

This question is not so much one of informed consent as it is one of privacy. Namely, what do we mean by privacy and, in turn, who or what can violate a person's privacy? Consider the following two definitions of privacy:

- *Parent's definition.* W. A. Parent defines privacy as the "condition of not having undocumented personal information about oneself known by others."[33] This definition

---

31 Google, *Gmail Terms of Use.*

32 Chris Jay Hoofnagle, Beth Givens, and Pam Dixon, *Violation of California Civil Code § 631 by Google Gmail Service*, Electronic Privacy Information Center (EPIC, 2004) [cited Nov. 15, 2004]; *http:// www.epic.org/privacy/gmail/agltr5.3.04.html.*

33 W. A. Parent, "Recent Work on the Conception of Privacy," *American Philosophical Journal Quarterly* 20 (1983), 341.

requires an "other" who can "know" something. Putting aside artificial intelligence claims for machine agency, this definition implies that the information must be imparted to another human. Google assumes such a definition when making the claim that Gmail's content-targeted advertising does not violate privacy because no *human being* ever reads subscribers' email.

- *Bloustein's definition.* In contrast, consider an alternative definition by Edward Bloustein: privacy preserves one's inviolate personality, independence, and dignity.[34] For Bloustein, a privacy violation concerns the act of intrusion upon the self, independent of the state of mind (or knowledge) of the intruder. Privacy advocates troubled by Google's practices likely share Bloustein's view of privacy when they claim that by extracting meaning from a subscriber's email message—whether with a machine reader or a human reader—Google is violating privacy. Moreover, some privacy advocates are more concerned about machine than human readers because of computer efficiency, memory capacity, and power.

### The question of indirect stakeholders

Many privacy advocates also assert that content-targeted advertisements should not be allowed without the consent of *all* parties involved in an email exchange. While Gmail does obtain the consent of the subscriber, it does not obtain the consent of the email sender. Yet personal content from an email sender is scanned to generate content-targeted advertisements to the email receiver.

Google argues that Gmail's practices are not a violation of the sender's privacy "since no one other than the recipient is allowed to read their email messages, and no one but the recipient sees targeted ads and related information."[35] A further argument against obtaining sender consent could be made by adopting the United States' model of ownership for physical mail. As soon as physical mail is delivered to receivers, it is considered to be the receivers' property; at that point, receivers may do whatever they please with the mail. Thus, the question becomes, "Is the model of ownership for physical mail an adequate or desirable model for ownership of email?"

### Reflections

In this case, we have argued that privacy advocates' claims against Gmail are not claims about informed consent per se, but rather, claims that concern differing views of privacy and ownership. Google has done a reasonable job obtaining informed consent under its notions of privacy and property, but it is possible that these notions are inappropriate for email and need to be reconsidered. Overall, the case of Gmail illustrates that at times,

34 Edward J. Bloustein, "Privacy As an Aspect of Human Dignity," in Ferdinand David Schoeman (ed.), *Philosophical Dimensions of Privacy: An Anthology* (Cambridge University Press, 1964), 156–202.

35 Google, *More on Gmail and Privacy* (2005) [cited July 30, 2005]; *http://mail.google.com/mail/help/more. html*; <*https://iexchange.ischool.washington.edu/exchweb/bin/redir.asp?URL=http://mail.google.com/mail/help/more.html*>.

considerations beyond the scope of informed consent (e.g., privacy, ownership) need to be understood in order to ascertain when informed consent is relevant.

## Design Principles for Informed Consent for Information Systems

In our view, design refers not only to the design process and resulting technology, but also to policy and business practice. Given this broad context for design, and based on the model of informed consent for information systems and the three cases, we now distill 10 design principles:

1. Decide what technical capabilities are exempt from informed consent.

   Obtaining users' informed consent comes with a high cost to users. Information must first be disclosed and comprehended by users, who must then have an opportunity to agree or decline. And while all of this is being done, the user has been diverted from the task at hand—the thing that the user really wanted to do. Let us refer to these costs for obtaining the user's informed consent as "the nuisance factor." If all interactions with information systems required explicit informed consent, the nuisance factor would be unmanageable. Users would simply crumble under the burden.

   Fortunately, a fair number of interactions with information systems may be considered exempt from the need to obtain users' informed consent. But how are designers to determine which interactions are exempt? While there are no hard and fast rules, the Belmont Report[36] on human subjects research offers some useful guidelines. According to the report, an individual's participation is considered exempt from the need to obtain informed consent when the following three conditions are met:

   - Participation can in no way put the individual in physical, legal, psychological, or social jeopardy. To this list of harms, for interactions with information systems we also include that participation does not place the individual's privacy, data, or hardware in jeopardy.

   - The purpose and sponsorship of the activity is known (or clearly stated to the individual).

   - No coercion is involved.

   Designers can invoke these three criteria to scrutinize information system–based interactions for exemption from informed consent. Granted, it may be difficult to make these judgments in advance; however, defensible assessments should be made, and if the initial assessments are in error, then remedies should be implemented.

---

36 The National Commission for the Protection of Human Subjects of Biomedical and Behavioral Research, "The Belmont Report: Ethical Principles and Guidelines for the Protection of Human Subjects of Research" (1978).

2. Invoke the sanction of implicit consent with care.

On the surface, implicit consent seems a reasonable umbrella to cover most online interactions. After all, users do not interact online—as in the canonical example—with a gun held to their heads. However, unless users have comparable (with respect to costs such as time, effort, knowledge, and expense) alternative access to comparable services, products, information, and so forth, then information system use may not be regarded as wholly noncoercive. Given the rapidity and widespread movement with which access to goods and services has moved online and the corresponding movement to discontinue or minimize traditional means of access, the viability of alternative comparable access to goods and services is at times slim and getting slimmer. In this climate, we advocate presuming that implicit consent is not a viable option, and only in special circumstances and after careful consideration invoking the sanction of implicit consent.

Further challenges for implicit consent arise from the criterion of disclosure. The disclosure issue can be understood as follows: although the user may be told what mechanisms are enabled, the user may not be aware of the full implications of those mechanisms. For example, while many users were aware of and enabled cookies, few users understood the implications of cookies for individual privacy (until an extensive public discussion took place).

3. Understand the scope of informed consent and how informed consent interacts with other values.

Informed consent concerns the important but limited activities of "informing" those affected by using, or the use of, an information system and obtaining their "consent" for that participation. Thus, informed consent closely interacts, but is not synonymous, with other values such as privacy, trust, and security. Nonetheless, how those other values are defined (e.g., can a machine invade a person's privacy?) has implications for what activities may require consent—for example, obtaining user consent for machine reading of personal content in an email message.

4. Consider both direct and indirect stakeholders.

Designers and usability engineers too often focus only on those users who interact directly with the information system without considering the system's impact on others, whom we refer to as indirect stakeholders. At times, it may be important to obtain informed consent from indirect as well as direct stakeholders (see the earlier sidebar, "Value Sensitive Design").

5. Put users in control of the "nuisance factor."

Different users place differing degrees of importance on different types of harm. Correspondingly, how much of a nuisance factor a user is willing to tolerate to obtain informed consent will depend on the particular user. Rather than mandating a single mechanism for obtaining informed consent for all users in all situations, designers need to provide users with a range of mechanisms and levels of control so that users are positioned to manage the nuisance factor in accordance with their concerns.

Successful designs will likely contain a reasonable balance among overarching controls (e.g., "never accept cookies" or "always accept cookies"), micromanaged controls (e.g., "ask about each cookie"), and intermediate controls that mix well-chosen overarching controls with micromanaged subsets (e.g., "decline all third-party cookies and ask me about all other cookies").

6. **Defaults matter.**

   It is well established that most users do not change preference settings. Thus, default settings should err on the side of preserving informed consent. Notably, for many years, the default setting for cookies on current browsers was "accept all cookies," which neither informs nor obtains consent from users. Default settings will also need to take into account the nuisance factor to obtain users' informed consent (see Design Principle 5).

7. **Avoid technical jargon.**

   Follow the well-established interface principle to avoid technical jargon in favor of clear language that directly addresses the user's values, needs, and interests.

8. **Inform through the interaction model.**

   In addition to using words to explicitly inform users, take advantage of the mental models that users construct through their interaction with a system to reinforce reasonably accurate conceptions of how information is secured and flows through the system. Avoid interaction models that may lead to misleading or ambiguous user conceptions of information flow (e.g., in web browsers, the use of locks that suggest a secure "place" to indicate a secure connection for information while it is in "transit" over the Internet).

9. **Field test to help ensure adequate comprehension and opportunities for agreement.**

   Because information systems will likely rely on automated means to realize informed consent, designers face significant challenges in ensuring adequate disclosure, comprehension, and opportunities for agreement. Thoughtful interface design will need to be coupled with equally thoughtful field tests to validate and refine the initial designs. Moreover, because informed consent carries a moral imperative, the components of disclosure, comprehension, and agreement need to work reasonably well for all users. Thus, it becomes a requirement (and not simply better practice) to include a reasonable range of both representative and atypical users in the field tests.

10. **Design proactively for informed consent.**

    More frequently than not, information systems are conceived of and implemented without consideration of informed consent. Once introduced, practices evolve around these new interactions, and these, too, develop without consideration of informed consent. When issues of informed consent at last come to the fore, designers face a nearly insurmountable task: to retrofit the information system capability and interaction. The solution, in part, is to design proactively for informed consent.

# Acknowledgments

This work was funded, in part, by NSF Award IIS-0325035.

# About the Authors

Batya Friedman is a professor in the Information School and an adjunct professor in the Department of Computer Science and Engineering at the University of Washington, where she co-directs the Value Sensitive Design Research Laboratory. Dr. Friedman's research interests include human-computer interaction, especially human values in technology and design methodology. Her recent work has focused on informed consent, privacy, trust, and human dignity engaging such technologies as web browsers, urban simulation, robotics, open source, and location-enhanced computing.

*http://www.ischool.washington.edu/vsd/*

Peyina Lin is a Ph.D. student in the Information School at the University of Washington, where she works in the Value Sensitive Design Research Laboratory. Ms. Lin holds an M.Sc. in information management (Syracuse University) and an M.A. in telecommunication digital media arts (Michigan State University). Her research investigates the impact of information technologies on community, sense of place, and value tradeoffs, such as privacy-security, and privacy-social awareness.

*http://students.washington.edu/pl3/*

Jessica K. Miller is a Ph.D. student in the Department of Computer Science and Engineering at the University of Washington, where she works with Batya Friedman and Alan Borning in the Value Sensitive Design Research Laboratory. Ms. Miller is principally interested in human-computer interaction, and specifically how user-centered design methodologies can be used to develop technologies that impact social relationships such as the Internet, wearable computing devices, and pervasive computing.

*http://www.cs.washington.edu/jessica/*

# CHAPTER TWENTY-FIVE

# Social Approaches to End-User Privacy Management

JEREMY GOECKS AND ELIZABETH D. MYNATT

**T**HOUSANDS OF YEARS AGO, THE EARLIEST HUMANS LIVED TOGETHER IN TRIBES. They hunted in bands to maximize their effectiveness, shared stories in the evening to entertain themselves, and migrated together to preserve and enhance the knowledge that a tribe had acquired over the years. Today, Internet and communication technologies make it possible for colleagues to collaborate over large distances, for extended families to share experiences via digital photos, and for multinational businesses to easily aggregate and utilize organizational knowledge.

These two snapshots of human society, taken at its dawn and at its present state, reveal the innate social nature of people and how they leverage this nature to beneficial ends. People work, learn, and play together. Every day, each individual engages in numerous social activities and processes with close friends and family, acquaintances, and strangers alike. Because social activities are woven into everyday life, people have substantial experience and expertise in employing social processes to meet various needs, from hearing about local news to learning new skills to acquiring advice for decision making. It makes sense, then, that users can benefit by leveraging social processes when they are managing their digital privacy.

In this chapter, we discuss how a software system can employ social processes to help end users manage their privacy. End users are users who are not computer experts. They have a general understanding of computers but are unlikely to be familiar with most facets of privacy. We first describe a concrete, end-user privacy management problem— the managing of web browser cookies—and introduce Acumen, a software system that leverages social processes to help users manage cookies. We then step back and describe how a system can use social processes to support common activities that end users perform while managing their privacy. Next, we discuss challenges that arise in privacy management systems that utilize social processes. Finally, we outline a general approach for building such systems.

## A Concrete Privacy Problem

To ground the discussion in this chapter, we introduce a concrete privacy problem and a potential solution to the problem; we will refer back to both this problem and its solution throughout the chapter. The privacy problem that we examine is that of web cookies, and our solution is Acumen, a system that we have developed. Acumen uses social processes to help users manage their cookies.

*Browser cookies* are a general mechanism used by web sites to maintain state across multiple web page requests from a single user.[1] While cookies can store arbitrary data, in practice, web sites frequently use cookies as persistent identifiers for users. Using cookies, then, a web site can identify all web page requests that a user makes to the site.

One concern that many Internet users have is the collection of personal data by entities such as corporations and government agencies; these users want the ability to control when, how, and what information they share with such entities. Browser cookies are particularly troublesome in this respect because web sites can use cookies to collect and aggregate information about users. In fact, many web sites can and do use cookies to monitor users' browsing activities and then link this data to personally identifiable information volunteered by users (e.g., name, email address), thereby creating personally identifiable profiles of users.[2] (Another tool used by such web sites is web bugs, discussed by David Martin in Chapter 23.)

Cookies are nearly ubiquitous among the most popular web sites.[3] As such, managing cookies on an individual or per-request basis is often confusing, tedious, and overly invasive for many users. Existing solutions for managing cookies, such as Platform for Privacy Preferences (P3P) user agents,[4] Privoxy,[5] and web browsers' tools, are insufficient at

---

1  RFC 2965: HTTP State Management Mechanism; *http://www.rfc-archive.org/getrfc.php?rfc=2965*.

2  Federal Trade Commission, "Privacy Online: Fair Information Practices in the Electronic Marketplace: A Federal Trade Commission Report to Congress, May 2000"; *http://www.ftc.gov/reports/privacy2000/privacy2000.pdf*.

3  *Ibid*.

4  Lorrie Faith Cranor, *Web Privacy with P3P* (Sebastopol, CA: O'Reilly Media, 2002). See also Chapter 22, this volume.

5  Privoxy software, *http://www.privoxy.org*.

times. These tools are often not well understood by users, offer little awareness of ongoing cookie activity, and provide inflexible settings that do not adapt to changes in users' needs and attitudes.[6, 7] Cookies, then, remain an outstanding privacy problem, and there is a need for tools that enable users to better manage their cookies.

# Acumen: A Solution Using Social Processes

The Acumen system (see Figure 25-1) captures and makes visible people's cookie management actions. By making this information visible, Acumen enables users to employ social processes to maintain awareness of, learn about, and make decisions about their browser cookies. Acumen enables a group of users to manage their cookies via indirect collaboration through their actions; each individual user benefits by leveraging the group's collective knowledge and experiences.

Acumen is a fully functional system—the first system to make the actions of users within a community visible so that other members of that community can employ social processes when managing their privacy. Nevertheless, Acumen is a prototype, not a production system. Acumen is principally an exploratory system—both in design and in implementation—rather than a model of how to build a privacy management system that leverages social processes. We encourage other designers to draw from Acumen's features according to their users' privacy management needs.

## Acumen Overview

Acumen enables users to manage cookies at the web site level, allowing or blocking each web site's cookies. Acumen allows all cookies by default; this default reflects the fact that most Internet users do not actively manage their cookies and thus do not block cookies. Acumen is an independent cookie management system and, as a consequence of architectural constraints, cannot interact with web browsers' cookie management tools. Thus, Acumen does not know which cookies are blocked by a web browser, and, conversely, cookies blocked by Acumen are never seen by the browser.

Acumen captures and makes the following data visible in aggregate:

* The number of community members who have "visited" a web site (i.e., requested a file from the site)

* The number of community members who allow the site's cookies

* The number of community members who block the site's cookies

---

6   Lynette Millett, Batya Friedman, and Edward Felten, "Cookies and Web Browser Design: Toward Realizing Informed Consent Online," *Proceedings of the 2001 Conference on Human Factors in Computing Systems* (2001), 46–52.

7   Batya Friedman, David Howe, and Edward Felten, "Informed Consent in the Mozilla Browser: Implementing Value-Sensitive Design," *Proceedings of the 35th Hawaii International Conference on Systems and Science* (2002), 247; CD-ROM for full paper. See also Chapter 24, this volume.

The "community" here is, of course, the community of Acumen users itself. This data is easy to collect because the collection imposes no additional burdens: users simply manage their cookies through the Acumen interface; Acumen records their actions and the resulting data, and aggregates the data for the benefit of the entire community, allowing users to see how others are managing their cookies.

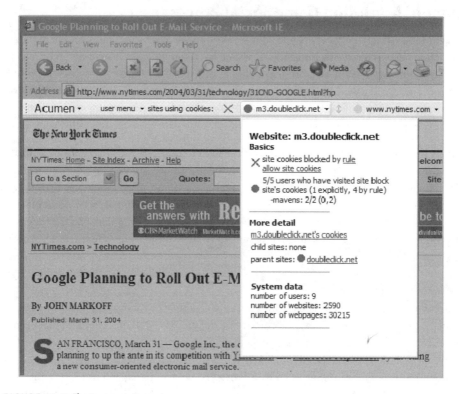

FIGURE 25-1. The Acumen system

The data that Acumen provides can be utilized for many purposes: maintaining awareness of cookies, learning about cookies, and offering advice when deciding whether to allow or block a web site's cookies.

Manually managing all cookies is tedious for users, and hence Acumen enables users to automatically manage cookies by employing simple rules that leverage Acumen's community-generated data. Users can create rules of the form:

> If X% of users have [blocked/allowed] cookies from a web site, then automatically [block/allow] the site's cookies.

Users choose a rule's threshold percentage when they create the rule. The percentage of users that block (or allow) a site's cookies includes both users that block cookies explicitly and those that block cookies by rule. Thus, when one user's rule blocks a site's cookies, it can cause another user's rule with a higher threshold to block the site's cookies as well, and so on. This chain of rule applications acts like a social epidemic,[8] and it can propagate the blocking of a site's cookies quite quickly among users. We discuss the benefits and drawbacks of supporting such social epidemics later in this chapter.

Acumen makes data visible from all users and also from a select subset of users called *mavens*.[9] Mavens are, roughly, the users who are most active in explicitly blocking and allowing cookies. Users can specifically leverage mavens' data in Acumen's automation rules. We discuss mavens in more detail later as well.

## The Acumen User Interface

Acumen's user interface is integrated into web browsers so that it can provide ongoing, just-in-time support for cookie management. Acumen provides Internet Explorer users with a toolbar interface and Netscape/Mozilla/Firefox users with a Sidebar Tab interface; a Sidebar Tab[10] is a small (typically about 150–200 pixels wide), full-length, vertical window to the left of the main browsing window. Both interfaces present the same data, and we use the toolbar (shown in Figure 25-2) as the exemplar for this discussion.

Acumen's toolbar uses a just-in-time approach to provide cookie information. The toolbar lists the web sites that are using cookies on the page that the user is currently visiting. Next to each web site using cookies are two icons. The icon to the far left of the site name denotes whether the user allows or blocks the site's cookies; a *green* double arrow indicates that they are allowed, and a *red* X indicates that they are blocked.

The circle icon to the immediate left of the web site's name denotes Acumen's community data for the site. Recall that this data is the number of Acumen users who have blocked/allowed a web site's cookies. The icon itself has two regions: an inner region and an outer region. The inner region's color denotes cookie management data for mavens; the outer region denotes data for all users (see Figure 25-2).

Regions are colored using a stoplight motif. (The Privacy Bird uses a similar motif; see Chapter 22.) *Green* indicates that a great majority of users (90% or more) allow the site's cookies; *yellow* indicates that most users (75% to 90%) allow the site's cookies; and *red* indicates that only some users (less than 75%) allow the site's cookies. These thresholds are biased so that Acumen's user data icon will change color even if only a small number of users or mavens have blocked a site's cookies; we discuss these thresholds in more detail shortly.

Clicking on a web site's name in the toolbar opens the site's menu (Figure 25-3). The menu's top section elaborates on the icons next to the site in the toolbar. If cookies are blocked, the menu indicates why; a link is provided to block/allow the site's cookies. User

8   Malcolm Gladwell, *The Tipping Point: How Little Things Can Make a Big Difference* (New York: Back Bay Books, 2000).

9   *Ibid.*

10  Mozilla Sidebar Tabs; *http://www.mozilla.org/catalog/web-developer/sidebar/*.

data is presented numerically, and the number of users who block the site's cookies explicitly and by rule are indicated.

FIGURE 25-2. *The outer circle is green, indicating that the majority of users accept cookies from this site; the inner circle is red, indicating that mavens do not allow cookies*

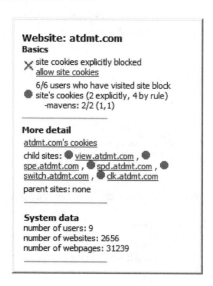

FIGURE 25-3. *The web site menu offers detailed information about a web site*

The menu's middle section provides a link to view the cookies that a site uses (Figure 25-4) and provides links to menus for child and parent sites. An icon next to each child and parent site denotes the site's user data. These links enable users to explore Acumen's data via relationships between parent and child sites. For example, the menu for the site *view.atdmt.com* enables a user to easily navigate to the menu for its parent, *atdmt.com*, and block all cookies from this site. Blocking cookies from a parent site blocks cookies from all its child sites as well.

The menu's lower section provides system information; the number of users, number of web sites, and number of documents in Acumen's database are displayed. This information is intended to serve as an incentive for users to utilize Acumen; users are more likely to use Acumen if they know that others are using the system and that there is data in the system.

The toolbar also provides a user menu. The menu links to Acumen's rule interface (Figure 25-5) and indicates whether the user is currently a maven.

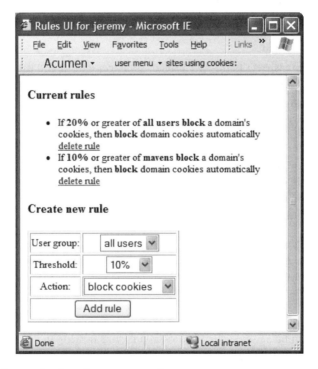

**More detail**

image.weather.com's cookies

| 11 Cookie(s) | | Close popup |
|---|---|---|
| **Name** | **Value** | **Expires** |
| ads | ba.020604_1_... | ? |
| ctCounter | yes | ? |
| footprint | 1%7Cdriving | ? |
| fq4 | unicast | ? |
| LocID | 30329 | ? |
| oob | dewy.020904_... | ? |
| pCounter | 1 | ? |
| rCounter | yes | ? |

*FIGURE 25-4. Details about the cookies that a web site is using; each cookie's name, value, and expiration date are shown; because of architectural constraints, Acumen cannot always identify the expiration date for a cookie*

*FIGURE 25-5. User interface for cookie management rules*

# Supporting Privacy Management Activities with Social Processes

End-user privacy management is rarely a simple task. Instead, there are often multiple and ongoing activities that users must perform in order to manage their privacy. The most common activities for end users performing privacy management are the following; these activities frequently proceed in the order in which they are listed.

- *Awareness and motivation.* An end user must achieve some level of awareness—or the system must provide awareness—of a potential privacy risk. Such awareness is necessary because it motivates the user to engage the risk.

- *Learning and education.* The user must learn about the privacy risk and its accompanying management activity.

- *Decision making.* Based on the user's awareness of and knowledge about the risk, he must make decisions about how to manage the risk.

In other domains, users maintain awareness, learn, and make decisions better when using social processes than they do individually.[11, 12] It makes sense that users can also benefit from employing social processes to perform these activities in the context of privacy management. In the following sections, we discuss these activities in detail, how social processes can facilitate them, and how Acumen supports them.

## Awareness and Motivation

Motivation is a critical aspect of end-user privacy management. If end users do not perceive a privacy risk, they will not use privacy management tools. Hence, a privacy management system frequently needs to raise awareness for the risk in order to motivate users to manage it.

Often, users must maintain ongoing awareness of a privacy risk. However, ongoing awareness can be overwhelming and distracting to users. Privacy management is rarely a primary activity for end users; rather, it is a secondary activity that is integrated into and performed alongside principal tasks.[13] For example, the primary activity for Internet users is browsing the Internet; managing cookies is a secondary activity, if that.

Because privacy management is a secondary activity at best, awareness of privacy risks and requisite management should be limited so as not to distract the user. Ideally, a privacy management system should filter information and alert users only to potentially important or new concerns and threats.

Raising end users' awareness of a privacy risk—and thereby raising users' motivation to manage the risk—can be accomplished via social means. Knowing that others recognize a risk and are managing it can serve to motivate a user to do the same; at the least, most users will take more notice of a risk if they observe that others are concerned about the risk. While there are users who will disregard the activities of others, most users will find others' activities to be useful information.

11  Alan J. Fridland, Daniel Reisberg, and Henry Gleitman, *Psychology* (New York: W.W. Norton & Company, 2003).

12  Ilan Yaniv, "Receiving Other People's Advice: Influence and Benefit," *Journal of Organizational Behavior and Human Decision Processes* 93:1, 1–13.

13  Victoria Bellotti and Abigail Sellen, "Design for Privacy in Ubiquitous Computing Environments," *Proceedings of 1993 European Conference on Computer-Supported Cooperative Work* (1993), 77–92.

## Awareness and motivation in Acumen

Acumen offers minimal and context-driven awareness. Acumen's toolbar is integrated into the web browser and displays information about only the web sites that are using cookies on the current web page. Thus, the toolbar provides relevant but limited information that a user can easily glance at and understand.

Acumen's icons make it clear that others are managing their cookies and also serve to alert users to potentially problematic cookies. Recall that there are two colored icons next to each site using cookies on the page: an arrowhead or X that indicates whether cookies are allowed/blocked, and the circle icon that denotes the site's user management data.

Just a quick glance by a user often provides valuable information about the cookies on the page. Problematic cookies stand out immediately because their site's user data icon is colored *yellow* or *red*, indicating that others have blocked the site's cookies. In addition, a user can glance at the two icons next to a web site name and determine whether her decision to allow/block the site's cookies matches others' decisions. A user's decision matches that of others if the icons are the same color; if not, the icons have different colors (see Figure 25-2). It is worthwhile to note that color perception and comparison are preattentive processes that are very fast and require little cognitive effort.[14]

Recall that Acumen uses nonlinear, biased thresholds for the color categories:

- Green indicates that 90% or more of all visitors allow a web site's cookies.
- Yellow indicates that 75% to 90% of visitors block a site's cookies.
- Red indicates that less than 75% of visitors allow a site's cookies.

Thus, a yellow or a red icon, both indicating caution, will appear next to some web sites even though a majority of users have not blocked the site's cookies.

We chose these thresholds to reflect the often sensitive and conservative nature of privacy management. Even if only a few users block a site's cookies, this information is reflected in an icon's color and is thus communicated to the user. Because few users ever change default settings, these biased thresholds accentuate any deviation in the community's data from Acumen's default of allowing cookies.

## Learning and Education

Many users have only passing familiarity with privacy management. They are often unfamiliar with privacy risks, the terminology used in describing privacy issues, and the methods that they can use to manage their privacy. For example, many users have concerns about Internet privacy but do not link those concerns to the issue of cookies. Users often do not understand how a cookie acting as a "persistent identifier" can be used to intrude

---

14 Chris G. Healey, K. S. Booth, and James T. Enns, "Harnessing Preattentive Processes for Multivariate Data Visualization," *Proceedings of 1993 Graphics Interface* (1993), 107–117.

upon their privacy, nor do they understand the difference between "first-party" and "third-party" cookies—terminology that is common in the cookie management systems built into Internet Explorer and other web browsers.

Because end users have a limited understanding of privacy, one important role of a privacy management system is to educate. Two of the more effective forms of social learning are modeling[15] and legitimate peripheral participation:[16]

- *Modeling.* In modeling, a novice learns by observing other people perform a task and models his behavior after what he has observed. Modeling is a simple process, but it is difficult for the novice to learn why others chose the behaviors that they did; a novice must infer why another person behaved in a particular way, and such inferences may be incomplete or incorrect.

- *Legitimate peripheral participation (LPP).* This is a more complex form of social learning. In LPP, a novice participates in a larger process that is administered by a group of experts. Initially, the novice has small, "peripheral" responsibilities in the process; however, as the novice becomes more experienced, he is given more important, "central" tasks. In LPP, novices learn through a combination of observation, experimentation, and direct interactions with experts. LPP is a longer process than modeling, but it offers novices the opportunity to learn why experts chose the behaviors that they did and also how to handle exceptional and unusual circumstances.

### Learning and education in Acumen

Acumen supports modeling; users can view the cookie management activities of other people in order to learn which cookies others are blocking. This information can help them begin to infer why others made the choices that they made. For example, a user may observe that others are more apt to block cookies from third-party web sites (e.g., advertising sites) than they are to block first-party cookies. The user may then choose to follow up on this information and learn more about why other people may have blocked third-party cookies; alternatively, the user may simply choose to block third-party cookies because others have.

Acumen currently provides little support for LPP. However, Acumen does support experimentation by novices; users can choose to toggle between blocking and allowing a web site's cookies to observe how the web page they are viewing changes. Only the user's final cookie setting is recorded; thus, a user's experimentation is private and occurs on the periphery of the group's cookie management processes.

It is difficult for a software system to facilitate LPP because doing so requires significant effort and commitment from both experts and novices. We are, however, experimenting

---

15 Albert Bandura, *Social Learning Theory* (Englewood Cliffs, NJ: Prentice Hall, 1977).

16 Jean Lave and Etienne Wenger, *Situated Learning: Legitimate Peripheral Participation* (Cambridge: Cambridge University Press, 1991).

with techniques to mitigate the required efforts of Acumen users. For instance, we are investigating methods to quickly and easily elicit why experts chose to block a cookie and methods to aggregate experts' data so that novices can more easily learn from it.

## Decision Making

Maintaining awareness of a privacy risk and learning about that risk lays the foundation for making decisions about, or managing, the risk. Decision making is likely the activity in which users can benefit most by leveraging social processes. The social process that supports decision making is called social navigation.

*Social navigation* is the process of observing other users' activities, inferring information from these observations, and using this information to make an informed decision.[17] Social navigation is quite common in everyday life; a very simple instance of social navigation occurs when an individual observes a crowd outside an unfamiliar restaurant. When the individual sees the crowd, she may infer that many people enjoy the food at the restaurant and that the restaurant generally serves good food. Hence, she is more likely to dine at the restaurant than she otherwise would be because the crowd provides information about how much other people like the restaurant. The crowd's behavior, then, is a simple form of data or advice that she can use to make a decision.

Social navigation is an especially promising approach for privacy management. A software system that supports social navigation offers a technological complement to end-user privacy management processes. Users' privacy management settings evolve to reflect changes in how their information is collected or used or changes in norms surrounding the use of their information.[18] Social navigation systems evolve as well because users' activities shape the system, and thus the system evolves as users' activities change.

Privacy management is frequently a collaborative process; conventions regarding privacy management develop among groups of people, and an individual's management decisions are made in the context of these conventions.[19] Social navigation systems support a similar process. Conventions are made visible through user data aggregation, and an individual's decisions are made in the context of, and often directly using, this data. Finally, as discussed earlier, privacy management is often a complementary activity that is situated in a principal activity; similarly, social navigation systems are situated in principal activities and support decision making in them.

Social navigation can take on many forms. One important facet of a social navigation system is the type of data that it collects and uses; this data can be either implicit or explicit.

17 Andreas Dieberger, Paul Dourish, Kristina Hook, Paul Resnick, and Alan Wexelblat, "Social Navigation: Techniques for Building More Usable Systems," *Interactions* 7:6 (2000), 36–45.

18 Leysia Palen and Paul Dourish, "Unpacking 'Privacy' for a Networked World," *Proceedings of 2003 Conference on Human Factors in Computing Systems* (2003), 129–136.

19 Victoria Bellotti, "What You Don't Know Can Hurt You: Privacy in Collaborative Computing," *Proceedings of the 1996 HCI Conference on People and Computers* (1996), 241–261.

*Implicit data* is generated by users as a by-product of their activities; *explicit data* must be intentionally generated by users. A system that collects implicit data can do so at a very low cost to users. However, implicit data requires users to infer why people behaved in a particular way or made a particular decision. A system collecting explicit data imposes a substantial burden on users by requiring them to expend effort to contribute data to the system, but explicit data is potentially more useful than implicit data because it requires users to make fewer inferences and judgments.

### Decision making and herd behavior

Social navigation is an intuitive and straightforward process, and supporting social navigation in Acumen is simple. In order to minimize the efforts of users, Acumen collects only implicit data from users; future versions of Acumen may collect explicit data using low-cost methods. Acumen's data, when made available to an individual user, provides information about how others are managing their cookies, and this data can be employed by the user as a form of advice when deciding whether to block or allow a web site's cookies.

There is, however, a particular challenge in using social navigation: herd behavior. Some users may choose to blindly follow the decisions of other users rather than make their own decisions; if enough users blindly follow the majority decision, a herd mentality arises and other people's data becomes detrimental because users simply choose the increasingly majority opinion.[20]

Acumen tries to mitigate herd behavior by identifying and using mavens. A *maven* is a domain expert, someone who has both a deep understanding of a domain and also an intrinsic desire to learn as much as they can about the domain; mavens have been identified in many areas.[21] Internet privacy mavens almost certainly exist as well; for example, people that read and contribute to the Electronic Privacy Information Center (EPIC) web site (*http://www.epic.org*) and those that use free cookie management software such as Privoxy are likely to be privacy mavens.

Acumen leverages mavens' expertise by anonymously identifying and finally providing the data of mavens as a group separately to the large Acumen community. To identify mavens, Acumen computes a "maven rating" for each user; a user's rating is the sum of the square roots of a user's actions across all the web sites that he visited:

$$R_m = \sum_{websites} \sqrt{num\_user\_actions_n}$$

Each time a user explicitly blocks or allows a site's cookies, Acumen increments the user's action count for that site. This function has two interesting features:

---

20 Abhijit V. Banerjee, "A Simple Model of Herd Behavior," *Quarterly Journal of Economics* 107:3 (1992), 797–818.

21 Gladwell.

- Taking the square root of the number of actions decreases the influence that each additional action has on a user's maven rating; for example, the first four actions a user performs on a site will increase his rating by 2.0, but the subsequent four actions that he takes on the site will increase his rating by only 0.82.

- Taking the square root of actions performed for each site rather than the square root of actions performed across all sites, the function balances breadth and depth of user actions, although breadth is slightly favored.

The function, then, identifies mavens as users with considerable breadth and depth of cookie management actions. However, later user actions count less than earlier actions; this is advantageous for two reasons:

- It is well established that people often learn more in early experiences as compared to later experiences;[22] the function reflects this feature of learning as inexperienced users' ratings increase more quickly with additional actions than do experienced users' ratings.

- The function makes it progressively more difficult for users to increase their rating and become mavens artificially.

It is not clear what percentage of users should be labeled as mavens; we are not aware of any estimates about how many mavens are present in a typical domain. Acumen labels the users with ratings in the top 20% as mavens. Labeling a relatively large number of users as mavens increases the likelihood that Acumen's user data for a site will include a maven's data.

It is too early to say how well the function described here identifies mavens and how effective mavens are at mitigating herd behavior; we are actively exploring these questions.

## Deployment, Adoption, and Evaluation

So far, we have discussed how end-user privacy management systems can employ social processes to help users more effectively manage their privacy. In this section, we address how to deploy, foster adoption of, and evaluate such systems.

### Deployment and Adoption

Successfully deploying and fostering adoption of a privacy management system that employs social processes is difficult. Such systems are *groupware*: software systems that support groups of people rather than individuals or whole organizations. A groupware deployment is deemed successful when enough individuals adopt the system so as to sustain its use. Several known obstacles prevent successful deployment and adoption of

22 Fridland, Reisberg, and Gleitman.

groupware.[23] For privacy management systems that are also groupware, perhaps the two most significant obstacles are obtaining critical mass and mitigating the disparity between work and benefit for users.

A groupware system must obtain a sizable number of users—a critical mass—if it is to succeed. Without a critical mass of users, the system often cannot provide enough benefits to those that use the system, and eventually use of the system stops. Critical mass differs among various groupware systems. Moreover, for some groupware, it is never advantageous for any single user to use it, and thus adoption must be considered from a group perspective rather than an individual perspective.

A groupware system will fail if it requires that some or all users expend significant effort contributing to the system but obtain little benefit from it. It is important for a groupware system to balance the work required and the benefits received for all users; this is especially true for knowledgeable users who, given sufficient motivations or benefits, contribute more to the system than others.

### Deployment and adoption in Acumen

Acumen's critical mass is highly correlated with the degree of coverage that its data can obtain. Acumen is most effective when it can provide data about many of the potential decisions a user may face; in other words, Acumen is most effective when it can provide user cookie management data for many different web sites. In a deployment of Acumen, we found that Acumen achieves significant coverage over the most popular web sites with as few as nine users. We discuss Acumen's coverage in more detail in this section.

In general, the critical mass for a privacy management system that employs social processes will be the number of users necessary to obtain sufficient coverage such that users find the system useful. Sufficient coverage is difficult to predict or offer guidelines for because it is dependent on the privacy management domain and on the system's users.

Acumen attempts to avoid disparities in users' efforts and benefits by using implicit data and by automatically extracting mavens' data. While it is appealing to encourage cookie management experts to contribute explicit knowledge to Acumen about how and why they are blocking particular cookies, this would increase the amount of effort that experts would have to expend without any additional benefits to them. Ultimately, experts would be less likely to participate in Acumen under these circumstances.

### User Needs Evaluation

Evaluating a privacy management system that employs social processes can be difficult. Often, multiple sets of criteria are important when performing an evaluation.

One critical set of criteria concerns how well the system meets user needs and supports user practices. Assuming that user-centered design practices (see Chapter 2) are followed,

---

23 Jonathan Grudin, "Groupware and Social Dynamics: Eight Challenges for Developers," *Communications of the ACM* 37:1 (1994), 92–105.

users' privacy management needs should be clear; these needs will often fall into one or more of the three general user activities discussed earlier. The goal of evaluating a privacy management system that employs social processes, then, is to determine whether the processes supported by the system help users address their privacy management needs effectively.

Standard evaluation instruments (see Chapter 3) can be used to perform such an evaluation, but some caveats must be recognized and accounted for. The main caveat is that it is very difficult to evaluate groupware in a laboratory setting because group culture and dynamics will play a role in how the system is used. Evaluation, then, often benefits from an authentic deployment of the system to its intended users for an extended period of time. Ideally, the system should not be evaluated until users have adopted it and developed norms surrounding its use.

### User needs evaluation in Acumen

We deployed Acumen to nine users for six weeks in order to perform a preliminary evaluation of the system. Users employed Acumen on a voluntary basis. We asked users to employ Acumen in the context of their normal browsing activities; we did not ask them to be more proactive in managing cookies than they otherwise would be, although the presence of Acumen's toolbar likely encouraged them to manage cookies more than they would have otherwise.

After the deployment, we obtained evaluation data using informal interviews with users, logging data, and data from Acumen's database. We used informal interviews to qualitatively assess whether and how well Acumen raised users' awareness of cookies, what effect Acumen's data had on users' decisions to block or allow cookies, and how useful mavens' data was to users. We used logging data and data from Acumen's database to obtain some objective metrics regarding system usage, such as how often users explicitly blocked cookies as compared to using rules to block cookies.

Our findings from this deployment are promising. Acumen does raise users' awareness of cookie management and helps users manage their cookies in an informed way. Because privacy is highly subjective, it is difficult to assess whether users allowed "good" cookies and blocked "bad" cookies, but our data indicates a degree of consensus among users for some cookies.

For example, advertisers' cookies (e.g., *atdmt.com* and *hitbox.com*) were often blocked by a significant number of users; web sites that use cookies to provide personalized services (e.g., *yahoo.com* and *amazon.com*) were often allowed. There were, however, some sites for which users disagreed about whether to block or allow cookies (e.g., *msn.com* and *google.com*); often such sites were well known and trusted but offered users little or no tangible benefits for the use of cookies. We speculate that users consider two factors when deciding whether to allow or block a site's cookies: first, trust in the site; and second, the benefit/cost ratio associated with the site's use of cookies. We report our complete findings from this deployment elsewhere.[24]

## Technological Evaluation

Systems that support social processes by making users' activities visible to each other have some rather unique technological requirements. Hence, it is often useful to evaluate such systems from a technological standpoint.

We previously discussed the relationship between achieving critical mass and data coverage in a privacy management system that utilizes social processes. Data coverage is both a social and a technological issue; coverage reflects not only which activities users perform, but also the ability of the system to capture and record data.

A purely technological issue for a privacy management system is its response time. Privacy management systems are most effective when they respond quickly to user input. Real-time interaction enables users to experiment with privacy management; as discussed earlier, experimentation is valuable for learning. Achieving real-time interaction, however, can be difficult to do in systems that are driven by large numbers of users and by the data that they generate. Replicating system components and databases and using cached but perhaps slightly inaccurate data may be acceptable if the system appears to respond in real time to users. (In order to respond in real time using cached data, a system would update the cached data based on a user's action and show the updated, cached data to the user.)

### Technological evaluation in Acumen

Data coverage appears to be a challenging issue for Acumen. For the purposes of this discussion, we assume that Acumen provides data coverage for a web site if two or more users have visited the site. Thus, any user who visits the site can observe how at least one other person manages the site's cookies.

There are millions of web sites, and Acumen will not contain data for every site—or likely even most sites. However, Acumen's data is tied to users' browsing activities; users will manage only cookies that they encounter while browsing. Hence, Acumen's data coverage mirrors the coverage obtained by users' browsing activities. Traffic among web sites on the Internet has been shown to obey a *power law distribution*.[25] A basic power law distribution for web traffic says that the $n$th most popular web site receives about $1/n$ as much traffic as the most popular web site. It follows that traffic to the most popular sites is a very, very large proportion of total traffic.

---

24 Jeremy Goecks and Elizabeth D. Mynatt, "Supporting Privacy Management via Community Experience and Expertise," *Proceedings of the Second Communities and Technologies Conference* (Milano 2005).

25 Bernardo Huberman, *The Laws of the Web: Patterns in the Ecology of Information* (Cambridge, MA: MIT Press, 2001).

Acumen, then, should contain data for the most popular web sites and be significantly less likely to have data for less popular sites. Data obtained from our deployment of Acumen confirmed this hypothesis:

- Among the most popular 20% of web sites, nearly half are covered by Acumen's data.

- Among the most popular 40% of web sites, about two in five are covered.

- Among the most popular 60% of web sites, one-third are covered.

Power law distributions are quite common in human activity, and they can mitigate issues of data coverage in other systems that employ social data.

Acumen achieves real-time interaction with users by utilizing a modular, replication-based architecture that distributes user interaction and data processing across many components (see the sidebar, "Acumen Architecture"). Acumen utilizes multiple instances of the components that users interact with to ensure that the system responds in real time. Each component has a very short-term cache that decreases response time as well; data is cached for 1–3 seconds.

## Gaming and Anti-gaming

*Gaming* is the process by which an entity manipulates a system to serve her personal interests while harming other users. A system that uses social processes is susceptible to gaming by an entity, whether the entity is a single user, a group of users, or an organization that is acting through users. Using basic economics[26] as an analysis lens, we can infer the conditions under which gaming will occur; these conditions are:

- There is an entity with an incentive to game the system.

- The benefit that the entity obtains from gaming the system is greater than the cost incurred by the entity to game the system.

Consider a hypothetical instance of gaming in Acumen: a group of employees working for a company decide to block cookies from a competitor's web site, hoping that other users will follow suit, either manually or using rules. Many web sites are dependent upon cookies in order for their site to perform well and provide a good user experience; hence, for users who block its cookies, the competitor's site may offer only a limited user experience. Consequently, these users may be less likely to use the competitor's site and more likely to use the web site of the employees' company. Thus, the employees have gamed the system; they have successfully modified the system to obtain an outcome that is desirable for them but not for the larger community.

It is difficult to make a system that utilizes social processes completely immune to gaming, but there are techniques that can make gaming more difficult. A general rule of thumb is

---

26 Campbell R. McConnell and Stanley L. Brue, *Economics, 15th Edition* (New York: McGraw-Hill, 2001).

# ACUMEN ARCHITECTURE

Four component types comprise the Acumen system: (1) remote web proxies; (2) a central database; (3) Acumen's toolbar; and (4) web services that act as data intermediaries between the database and the toolbar. The components, shown in Figure 25-6, communicate securely using Secure Sockets Layer (SSL) channels.

All users' web traffic goes through one of Acumen's web proxies. A proxy performs two actions: it records the web sites that a user has visited and the cookies used by those sites; and it blocks cookies from web page requests and responses if a user has explicitly or by rule blocked the site's cookies.

Acumen's database acts as a central repository for all data used by the system. For each web site that a user has visited, the database maintains a user web site history; the history contains the cookies that the site uses for the user, whether a user blocks or allows the site's cookies, and, if cookies are blocked, how so.

Acumen's web service acts as the intermediary between its database and its toolbar. When a user visits a web page, the toolbar obtains data about the page from the service; the data is in the form of an XML file. The service also handles user actions (e.g., blocking a cookie, changing a rule) and updates the database accordingly.

Acumen's web proxies and web services are the performance bottlenecks in the architecture. In order to make these components as responsive as possible, Acumen supports dynamic replication and deployment of the components and uses caches in both components.

Acumen attempts to mitigate privacy concerns by ensuring that user data is anonymous at both the user interface level and the system level. Acumen's interface enables users to view only aggregated data; users are never able to view another individual's data. Acumen does not record any identifying information about its users beyond a persistent identifier, and it records a user's browsing activities only if she is logged into the system. Finally, Acumen provides a simple interface for users to see what data the system has collected about them; this interface enables a user to exclude some or all of her data from Acumen's community data.

Acumen's architecture ensures that the system's complexity is hidden from users. To use Acumen, a user needs only to install Acumen's toolbar, set her browser to use Acumen's proxy, and create a pseudonym for persistent identification by Acumen.

that it should be difficult (and sometimes forbidden) for a single user or a small group of users to significantly alter the system. Instead, users should be able to produce only incremental changes, and there should be a cost for performing such changes. The cost should be sufficient to discourage manipulative behavior.

Ultimately, more research is needed about gaming and anti-gaming techniques in social systems, especially those used to support privacy management. Exploring how people game a social system is difficult, however, because an environment that encourages gaming must be fostered; often a system must be in sustained use over a significant period of time in order for an instance of gaming to arise.

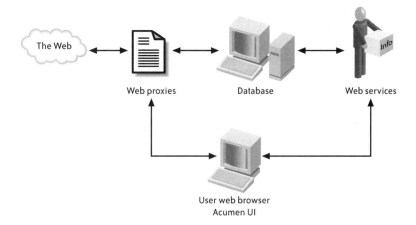

*FIGURE 25-6. Acumen architecture*

### Anti-gaming Techniques in Acumen

Acumen's anti-gaming techniques are quite rudimentary. Recall that Acumen's maven formula uses a square root function and a summation function to make it difficult for users to become mavens artificially.

We are currently exploring other methods to prevent gaming in Acumen. Acumen could decrease a user's maven rating over time; such decay would increase the effort it takes for users to remain mavens. A related problem is that of a user signing up for multiple accounts and using these accounts to exert more than his fair share of influence in the system. To address this problem, we are experimenting with an activity threshold such that data from users with less than a certain amount of activity (e.g., less than a certain number of sites visited) would not be included in the data shown by Acumen's interface.

## Generalizing Our Approach

So far, we have focused on addressing the privacy management challenges that web site cookies pose. There are, however, numerous other domains where users would benefit from using social processes to manage their privacy. In this section, we generalize our approach and describe its necessary components; in the process of this generalization, we discuss how social processes could be used to address another privacy problem: adware and spyware.

Advertiser-supported software, or *adware*, is software that displays advertisements while running; revenue from the advertisements goes to the software's developers. Because the ads displayed by adware may use cookies, adware poses the same privacy risks as traditional cookies do. In fact, often adware is simply a web browser add-on that displays unwanted pop-up windows.

*Spyware* is software that gathers and transmits information about a user to an external party unbeknownst to, and without the consent of, the software's user; often, the external party is a marketing company. Of course, spyware presents privacy risks to users, as it is designed to invade users' privacy.

Adware and spyware are overlapping categories of software. Adware can be spyware; spyware need not be adware; and often spyware is bundled and installed with other software. Many users object to adware and spyware because such software violates their privacy, and hence adware and spyware often go to great lengths to hide how and when they collect information about users. The privacy management problem that users face, then, is distinguishing adware and spyware from other software on their computer and on the Internet, and deciding whether to install or uninstall a piece of software.

Existing tools that detect and remove adware and spyware, such as AdAware[27] and Spyware Eliminator,[28] are often effective but are also limited in some respects. These tools are not always able to recognize and remove the most current adware and spyware. In addition, using an adware/spyware removal program requires that the user trust the program's categorizations of adware and spyware. However, research has shown that people respond to and make more use of personal, concrete information than they do abstract information.[29] A privacy management system that employs social processes can be used to address these weaknesses. Such a system is likely to be more dynamic than other adware/spyware removal tools; the system would also leverage concrete information.

## Four Key Questions for a Privacy Management System

Four key questions must be addressed when building a privacy management system that uses social processes. The answers to these questions will significantly influence both the system's architecture and how useful users find the system. These questions are:

1. *What data will the system collect?* The collected data must be useful to users when they are managing their privacy. Moreover, it is important to be mindful of the tradeoffs between collecting implicit data and collecting explicit data.

2. *Where and how will the data be stored?* Data can be stored on a user's computer or it can reside in a central database; it is easier to aggregate data that is stored in a database, but there are security concerns when using a single, remote data store.

27 Lavasoft AdAware software; *http://www.lavasoftusa.com/software/adaware/*.

28 Alaria Spyware Eliminator software; *http://www.aluriasoftware.com/homeproducts/spyware/*.

29 Eugene Borigda and Richard E. Nisbett, "The differential impact of abstract and concrete information on decisions," *Journal of Applied Social Psychology* 7:3, 258–271.

3. *When will the system display its data?* Ideally, the system will display the data only when the user is managing his privacy, although attaining this ideal is rarely possible.

4. *How will the system display its data?* Data can be displayed in raw form, reflecting the data exactly as it was captured; it can also be transformed or visualized in order to abstract details away and make the data easier to understand.

## Sketching a System Design

Using these four questions, we can sketch the design for a system that will help end users identify adware and spyware and determine whether to install or uninstall a piece of software.

Data that may be useful to users for this management activity is likely best conceptualized as focused around a piece of software. For a particular piece of software, then, useful implicit data might be (a) how many people have installed and currently use the software? (b) how many people have installed and then uninstalled the software? Other information, such as how long, on average, users have had the software installed, may be useful as well. Explicit information that would be useful includes (a) why did people uninstall the software and (b) why did some people consider installing the software but choose not to?

Note that the implicit data is a surrogate for the information that we want—namely, whether users want a piece of software on their computer. While there are many reasons that a user would uninstall software from their computer, adware and spyware, over time, are likely to have a higher uninstall rate than other software. It is also important not to underestimate people's social intelligence.

People are often able to make informed judgments on the basis of ambiguous, implicit information; people also often use such information as a starting point, using the information to indicate which software might be of concern and then using other sources of information to determine whether to install/uninstall it. Thus, explicit information, while useful, is not always needed for users to employ social processes.

It is important not to overlook the technological and social challenges of obtaining this information. In order to collect this information, it is necessary to write and install code on users' computers that listens for when a user installs or uninstalls software; moreover, the code must be able to transmit this information to the data store. Implementing these behaviors may be difficult.

Obtaining explicit data is largely dependent on users' motivation. We can infer that some users, upset about the ads displayed by an adware program or alarmed by the data a spyware program is collecting, will want to share their experiences. Many users, however, will not take the time to provide explicit data to the system. Consequently, the system must be useful even in the absence of explicit data.

A central database is the most straightforward solution for storing user data. While there are security concerns about storing data in one location, this is a popular and robust method for housing data. An alternative to a central database is distributed hash tables[30] (DHT), which facilitate storage of data across multiple servers; DHTs ensure that a single security breach cannot compromise all the system's data.

Regardless of where the data is actually stored, it may be useful to enable users to employ conceptually different databases. For example, there might be a database for a particular organization and another one for the general population; we assume that the data in the organization's database would better reflect the organization's views than the data in the general database. An individual in the organization could choose which database to use and may want to compare data in the databases.

There are obvious instances during which the system should display its data. When a user is installing or uninstalling a piece of software, the system should display its data about the software. However, the system should also make its data available to users when they are browsing the Internet and considering whether to install a piece of *shareware* (software that is free to try, but further use must be paid for) or *freeware* (free software). In these instances, it makes sense to develop a web-based, searching interface to the system, such as a toolbar or other browser add-on, that makes it simple for users to find the system's data about a piece of software.

We recommend following the well-known information visualization principle "overview, zoom/filter, detail on demand"[31] when creating an interface to display the system's data. The interface should use simple, iconic representations to provide an overview of the data; using colors and shapes is an effective mechanism for summarizing the data. A red-yellow-green color motif may be a good way to indicate whether the majority of users have installed or uninstalled a piece of software. The iconic representation should be interactive, enabling users to zoom in and obtain more details about the software, such as how many users have the software installed versus the number who have uninstalled it. Filtering may be useful to support as well; for example, a user may want to see data from only the last month rather than all data.

## Conclusion

Leveraging social processes to help end users manage their privacy is a promising approach. End users engage in awareness, learning, and decision-making activities in order to effectively manage their privacy, and social processes offer users intuitive, robust

---

30 Antony Rowstron and Peter Druschel, "Storage Management and Caching in PAST, a Large-Scale, Persistent Peer-to-Peer Storage Utility," *Proceedings of 2001 Conference on Operating Systems Principles* (2001), 188–201.

31 Christopher Ahlberg and Ben Shneiderman, "Visual Information Seeking: Tight Coupling of Dynamic Query Filters with Starfield Displays," *Proceedings of 1994 Conference on Human Factors in Computing Systems* (1994), 313–317.

methods to support these activities. This chapter has discussed the principal features of end-user privacy management systems that employ social processes.

## About the Authors

 Jeremy Goecks is a Ph.D. student in the College of Computing at the Georgia Institute of Technology. He is a member of the Everyday Computing Lab and is affiliated with the GVU Center. His research interests center on collaborative computing, supporting large-group activities and social decision processes, and privacy. He received his B.S. in computer science from the University of Wisconsin-Madison.

*http://www.cc.gatech.edu/~jeremy*

 Elizabeth D. Mynatt is an associate professor and Sloan Fellow in the College of Computing at the Georgia Institute of Technology. She is also the associate director of Georgia Tech's GVU Center. Her research program, Everyday Computing, examines the human-computer interface implications of having computation continually present in many aspects of everyday life.

*http://www.cc.gatech.edu/gvu/people/faculty/mynatt.html*

# CHAPTER TWENTY-SIX

# Anonymity Loves Company: Usability and the Network Effect

**ROGER DINGLEDINE AND NICK MATHEWSON**

**O**THER CHAPTERS IN THIS BOOK HAVE TALKED ABOUT HOW USABILITY IMPACTS SECURITY. One class of security software is anonymizing networks—overlay networks on the Internet that provide privacy by letting users transact (for example, fetch a web page or send an email) without revealing their communication partners.

In this chapter, we'll focus on the network effects of usability on privacy and security: usability is a factor as before, but the size of the user base also becomes a factor. As we will see, in anonymizing networks, even if you were smart enough and had enough time to use every system perfectly, you would nevertheless be right to choose your system based in part on its usability for *other* users.

## Usability for Others Impacts Your Security

While security software is the product of developers, the security it provides is a collaboration between developers and users. It's not enough to make software that *can* be used securely; software that is hard to use often suffers in its security as a result. For example, suppose there are two popular mail encryption programs: HeavyCrypto, which is more secure (when used correctly), and LightCrypto, which is easier to use. Suppose you can use either one, or both. Which should you choose?

You might decide to use HeavyCrypto because it protects your secrets better. But if you do, it's likelier that when your friends send you confidential email, they'll make a mistake and encrypt it badly or not at all. With LightCrypto, you can at least be more certain that all your friends' correspondence with you will get some protection.

What if you use *both* programs? If your tech-savvy friends use HeavyCrypto and your less sophisticated friends use LightCrypto, then everybody will get as much protection as they can. But can all your friends really judge how able they are? If not, then by supporting a less usable option, you've made it more likely that your nonsavvy friends will shoot themselves in the foot.

The crucial insight here is that for email encryption, security is a collaboration between multiple people: both the sender and the receiver of a secret email must work together to protect its confidentiality. Thus, in order to protect your own security, you need to make sure that the system you use is usable not only by yourself, but also by the other participants.

This observation doesn't mean that it's always better to choose usability over security, of course; if a system doesn't address your threat model, no amount of usability can make it secure. But conversely, if the people who need to use a system can't or won't use it correctly, its ideal security properties are irrelevant.

Hard-to-use programs and protocols can hurt security in many ways:

- *Insecure modes of operation.* Programs with insecure modes of operation are bound to be used unknowingly in those modes.

- *Optional security.* Optional security, once disabled, is often never re-enabled. For example, many users who ordinarily disable browser cookies for privacy reasons wind up re-enabling them so that they can access sites that require cookies, and later leaving cookies enabled for all sites.

- *Badly labeled off switches.* Such switches for security are prone to accidental selection and vulnerable to social attackers who trick users into disabling their security. As an example, consider the page-long warning your browser provides when you go to a web site with an expired or otherwise suspicious SSL certificate.

- *Inconvenient security.* Inconvenient security is often abandoned in the name of day-to-day efficiency. People often write down difficult passwords to keep from forgetting them, and share passwords in order to work together.

- *False sense of security.* Systems that provide a false sense of security prevent users from taking real measures to protect themselves. Breakable encryption on zip archives, for example, can fool users into thinking that they don't need to encrypt email containing zip archives.

- *Bad mental models.* Systems that provide bad mental models for their security can trick users into believing that they are safer than they really are. For example, many users interpret the "lock" icon in their web browsers to mean that "You can safely enter personal information," whereas its actual meaning is closer to "Nobody can read your information on its way to the named web site."[1]

## Usability Is Even More Important for Privacy

Usability affects security in systems that aim to protect data confidentiality. But when the goal is privacy, usability can become even more important. A large category of *anonymizing networks*, such as Tor, JAP, Mixminion, and Mixmaster, aim to hide not only what is being said, but also who is communicating with whom, which users are using which web sites, and so on. These systems have a broad range of users, including ordinary citizens who want to avoid being profiled for targeted advertisements, corporations that don't want to reveal information to their competitors, and law enforcement and government intelligence agencies that need to do operations on the Internet without being noticed.

Anonymizing networks work by hiding users among users. An eavesdropper might be able to tell that Alice, Bob, and Carol are all using the network, but should not be able to tell which of them is talking to Dave. This property is summarized in the notion of an *anonymity set*—the total set of people who, as far as the attacker can tell, might include the one engaging in some activity of interest. The larger the set, the more anonymous the participants.[2] When more users join the network, existing users become more secure, even if the new users never talk to the existing ones![3] Thus, "anonymity loves company."[4]

In a data confidentiality system like PGP, Alice and Bob can decide by themselves that they want to get security. As long as they both use the software properly, no third party can intercept the traffic and break their encryption. However, Alice and Bob can't get anonymity by themselves: they need to participate in an infrastructure that coordinates users to provide cover for each other.

---

1   Or more accurately, "Nobody can read your information on its way to someone who was able to convince one of the dozens to hundreds of CAs configured in your browser that they are the named web site, or who was able to compromise the named web site later on—unless your computer has been compromised already."

2   Assuming that all participants are equally plausible, of course. If the attacker suspects Alice, Bob, and Carol equally, Alice is more anonymous than if the attacker is 98% suspicious of Alice and 1% suspicious of Bob and Carol, even though the anonymity sets are the same size. Because of this imprecision, recent research is moving beyond simple anonymity sets to more sophisticated measures based on the attacker's confidence.

3   Alessandro Acquisti, Roger Dingledine, and Paul Syverson, "On the Economics of Anonymity," in Rebecca N. Wright (ed.), *Financial Cryptography* (Springer-Verlag, LNCS 2742, Jan. 2003); Adam Back, Ulf Möller, and Anton Stiglic, "Traffic Analysis Attacks and Trade-offs in Anonymity Providing Systems," in Ira S. Moskowitz (ed.), *Information Hiding* (IH 2001), (Springer-Verlag, LNCS 2137, Apr. 2001).

4   This catch phrase was first made popular in our context by Michael Reiter and Aviel Rubin, "Crowds: Anonymity for Web Transactions," *ACM Transactions on Information and System Security* 1:1 (June 1998).

No organization can build this infrastructure for its own sole use. If a single corporation or government agency were to build a private network to protect its operations, any connections entering or leaving that network would be obviously linkable to the controlling organization. The members and operations of that agency would be easier, not harder, to distinguish.

Thus, to provide anonymity to any of its users, the network must accept traffic from external users, so the various user groups can blend together.

In practice, existing commercial anonymity solutions (like Anonymizer.com) are based on a set of single-hop proxies. In these systems, each user connects to a single proxy, which then relays the user's traffic. Single proxies provide comparatively weak security, because a compromised proxy can trivially observe all of its users' actions, and an eavesdropper needs to watch only a single proxy to perform timing correlation attacks against all its users' traffic. Worse, all users need to trust the proxy company to have good security itself as well as to not reveal user activities.

The solution is *distributed trust*: an infrastructure made up of many independently controlled proxies that work together to make sure that no transaction's privacy relies on any single proxy. With distributed-trust anonymizing networks like the ones discussed in this chapter, users build tunnels or *circuits* through a series of servers. They encrypt their traffic in multiple layers of encryption, and each server removes a single layer of encryption. No single server knows the entire path from the user to the user's chosen destination. Therefore, an attacker can't break the user's anonymity by compromising or eavesdropping on any one server.

Despite their increased security, distributed-trust anonymizing networks have their disadvantages. Because traffic needs to be relayed through multiple servers, performance is often (but not always) worse. Also, the software to implement a distributed-trust anonymizing network is significantly more difficult to design and implement.

Beyond these issues of the architecture and ownership of the network, however, there is another catch. For users to keep the same anonymity set, they need to act like each other. If Alice's client acts completely unlike Bob's client, or if Alice's messages leave the system acting completely unlike Bob's, the attacker can use this information. In the worst case, Alice's messages stand out entering and leaving the network, and the attacker can treat Alice and those like her as if they were on a separate network of their own. But even if Alice's messages are recognizable only as they leave the network, an attacker can use this information to break exiting messages into "messages from User1," "messages from User2," and so on, and can now get away with linking messages to their senders as groups, instead of trying to guess from individual messages. Some of this *partitioning* is inevitable: if Alice speaks Arabic and Bob speaks Bulgarian, we can't force them both to learn English in order to mask each other.

What does this imply for usability? More so than with encryption systems, users of anonymizing networks may need to choose their systems based on how usable others will find them, in order to get the protection of a larger anonymity set.

## Case Study: Usability Means Users, Users Mean Security

Let's consider an example. Practical anonymizing networks fall into two broad classes: high latency and low latency.

- *High-latency networks.* Networks like Mixminion and Mixmaster can resist strong attackers who can watch the whole network and control a large part of the network infrastructure. To prevent this "global attacker" from linking senders to recipients by correlating when messages enter and leave the system, high-latency networks introduce large delays into message delivery times, and are thus suitable only for applications like email and bulk data delivery—most users aren't willing to wait half an hour for their web pages to load.

- *Low-latency networks.* Networks like Tor, on the other hand, are fast enough for web browsing, secure shell, and other interactive applications, but have a weaker threat model. An attacker who watches or controls both ends of a communication can trivially correlate message timing and link the communicating parties.

Clearly, users who need to resist strong attackers must choose high-latency networks or nothing at all, and users who need to anonymize interactive applications must choose low-latency networks or nothing at all. But what should flexible users choose? Against an unknown threat model, with a noninteractive application (such as email), is it more secure to choose security or usability?

Security, we might decide, is more important than usability. If the attacker turns out to be strong, then we'll prefer the high-latency network, and if the attacker is weak, then the extra protection doesn't hurt.

But because many users might find the high-latency network inconvenient, suppose that it gets few actual users—so few, in fact, that its maximum anonymity set is too small for our needs. In this case, we need to pick the low-latency system, because the high-latency system, although it always protects us, never protects us enough; whereas the low-latency system can give us enough protection against at least *some* attackers.

This decision is especially messy because even the developers who implement these anonymizing networks can't recommend which approach is safer, since they can't predict how many users each network will get, and they can't predict the capabilities of the attackers we might see in the wild. Worse, the anonymity research field is still young, and doesn't have many convincing techniques for measuring and comparing the protection we get from various situations. So even if the developers or users could somehow divine what level of anonymity they require and what their expected attacker can do, the researchers still don't know what parameter values to recommend.

## Case Study: Against Options

Too often, designers faced with a security decision bow out, and instead leave the choice as an option: protocol designers leave implementors to decide, and implementors leave the choice for their users. This approach can be bad for security systems, and is nearly always bad for privacy systems. With security:

- Extra options often delegate security decisions to those least able to understand what they imply. If the protocol designer can't decide whether the AES encryption algorithm is better than the Twofish encryption algorithm, how is the end user supposed to pick?

- Options make code harder to audit by increasing the volume of code, by increasing the number of possible configurations *exponentially*, and by guaranteeing that nondefault configurations will receive little testing in the field. If AES is always the default, even with several independent implementations of your protocol, how long will it take to notice if the Twofish implementation is wrong?

Most users stay with default configurations as long as they work, and reconfigure their software only as necessary to make it usable. For example, suppose the developers of a web browser can't decide whether to support a given extension with unknown security implications, so they leave it as a user-adjustable option, thinking that users can enable or disable the extension based on their security needs. In reality, however, if the extension is enabled by default, nearly all users will leave it on whether it's secure or not; and if the extension is disabled by default, users will tend to enable it based on their perceived demand for the extension rather than on their security needs. Thus, only the most savvy and security-conscious users—the ones who know more about web security than the developers themselves—will actually wind up understanding the security implications of their decision.

The real issue here is that designers often end up with a situation where they need to choose between "insecure" and "inconvenient" as the default configuration—meaning that they've already made a mistake in designing their application.

Of course, when end users *do* know more about their individual security requirements than application designers do, adding options is beneficial, especially when users describe their own situation (home or enterprise; shared versus single-user host) instead of trying to specify what the program should do about their situation.

In privacy applications, superfluous options are even worse. When there are many different possible configurations, eavesdroppers and insiders can often tell users apart by which settings they choose. For example, the Type I or "Cypherpunk" anonymous email network uses the OpenPGP encrypted message format, which supports many symmetric and asymmetric ciphers. Because different users prefer different ciphers, and because different versions of encryption programs implementing OpenPGP (such as PGP and GnuPG) use different cipher suites, users with uncommon preferences and versions stand out from the rest, and get little privacy at all.

Similarly, the Type I network allows users to pad their messages to a fixed size so that an eavesdropper can't correlate the sizes of messages passing through the network—but it forces the user to decide what size of padding to use! Unless a user can guess which padding size will happen to be most popular, the option provides attackers with another way to tell users apart.

Even when users' needs genuinely vary, adding options does not necessarily serve their privacy. In anonymizing networks, for example, because the default option usually prevails for casual users, this option actually provides more security for security-conscious users—*even when it would not otherwise be their best choice*! For example, when an anonymizing network allows user-selected message latency (like the Type I network does), most users tend to use whichever setting is the default, so long as it works. Of the fraction of users who change the default at all, most will not, in fact, understand the security implications; those few who do will need to decide whether the increased traffic-analysis resistance that comes with more variable latency is worth the decreased anonymity that comes from splitting away from the bulk of the user base.

## Case Study: Mixminion and MIME

We've argued that providing too many observable options can hurt privacy, but we've also argued that focusing too hard on privacy over usability can hurt privacy itself. What happens when these principles conflict?

We encountered such a situation when designing how the Mixminion anonymous email network[5] should handle MIME-encoded data. MIME (Multipurpose Internet Mail Extensions) is the way a mail client tells the receiving mail client about attachments, which character set was used, and so on. As a standard, MIME is so permissive and flexible that different email programs are almost always distinguishable by which subsets of the format, and which types of encodings, they choose to generate. Trying to "normalize" MIME by converting all mail to a standard works only up to a point: it's trivial to convert all encodings to *quoted-printable*, for example, or to impose a standard order for *multipart/alternative* parts, but demanding a uniform list of formats for *multipart/alternative* messages, normalizing HTML, stripping identifying information from Microsoft Office documents, or imposing a single character encoding on each language would likely be an impossible task.

Other possible solutions to this problem could include limiting users to a single email client or simply banning email formats other than plain 7-bit ASCII. But these procrustean approaches would limit usability and turn users away from the Mixminion network. Because fewer users means less anonymity, we must ask whether users would be better off in a larger network where their messages are more likely to be distinguishable based on the email client, or in a smaller network where everyone's email formats look the same.

---

5 George Danezis, Roger Dingledine, and Nick Mathewson, "Mixminion: Design of a Type III Anonymous Remailer Protocol," *2003 IEEE Symposium on Security and Privacy*, IEEE CS (May 2003), 2–15.

Some distinguishability is inevitable anyway, because users differ in their interests, languages, and writing styles: if Alice writes about astronomy in Amharic, her messages are unlikely to be mistaken for Bob's, who writes about botany in Basque. Also, any attempt to restrict formats is likely to backfire. If we limited Mixminion to 7-bit ASCII, users wouldn't stop sending each other images, PDF files, and messages in Chinese. Instead, they would follow the same evolutionary path that led to MIME in the first place, and encode their messages in a variety of distinguishable formats, with each client software implementation having its own *ad hoc* favorites. So, imposing uniformity in this case would not only drive away users, it would probably fail in the long run, and lead to fragmentation at least as dangerous as that we were trying to avoid.

With Mixminion, we also had to consider threat models. To take advantage of format distinguishability, an attacker needs to observe messages leaving the network, and either exploit prior knowledge of suspected senders ("Alice is the only user who owns a 1995 copy of Eudora"), or feed message format information into traffic analysis approaches ("Because half of the messages to Alice are written in English, I'll assume they mostly come from different senders than the ones in Amharic"). Neither attack is certain or easy for all attackers; even if we can't defeat them in the worst possible case (where the attacker knows, for example, that only one copy of LeetMailPro was ever sold), we can provide vulnerable users with protection against weaker attackers.

In the end, we compromised: we perform as much normalization as we can, and warn the user about document types such as Microsoft Word that are likely to reveal identifying information, but we do not forbid any particular format or client software. This way, users are informed about how to blend with the largest possible anonymity set, but users who prefer to use distinguishable formats rather than nothing at all still receive and contribute protection against certain attackers.

### Case Study: Tor Installation, Marketing, and GUI

Usability and marketing have also proved important in the development of Tor, a low-latency anonymizing network for TCP traffic. The technical challenges Tor has solved, and the ones it still needs to address, are described in its design paper,[6] but at this point, many of the most crucial challenges are in adoption and usability.

While Tor was in its earliest stages, its user base was a small number of fairly sophisticated privacy enthusiasts with experience running Unix services, who wanted to experiment with the network (or so they say; by design, we don't track our users). As the project gained more attention from venues including security conferences and articles on Slashdot.org and Wired News, we added more users with less technical expertise. These users can now provide a broader base of anonymity for high-needs users, but only when they receive good support themselves.

---

6   Roger Dingledine, Nick Mathewson, and Paul Syverson, "Tor: The Second-Generation Onion Router," *Proceedings of the 13th USENIX Security Symposium* (August 2004).

For example, it has proven difficult to educate less sophisticated users about DNS issues. Anonymizing TCP streams (as Tor does) does no good if applications reveal where they are about to connect by first performing a nonanonymized hostname lookup. To stay anonymous, users had to do one of the following:

- Configure their applications to pass hostnames to Tor directly by using SOCKS4a or the hostname-based variant of SOCKS5

- Manually resolve hostnames with Tor and pass the resulting IPs to their applications

- Direct their applications to application-specific proxies that handle each protocol's needs independently

None of these is easy for an unsophisticated user, and when users misconfigure their systems, they not only compromise their own privacy, but also provide no cover for the users who *are* configured correctly: if Bob leaks a DNS request whenever he is about to connect to a web site, an observer can tell that anybody connecting to Alice's web site anonymously must not be Bob. Thus, experienced users have an interest in making sure that inexperienced users can use the system correctly. Having Tor be hard to configure is a weakness for everybody.

We've tried a few solutions that have not worked as well as we had hoped. Improving documentation helped only the users who read it. We changed Tor to warn users who provided an IP address rather than a hostname, but this warning usually resulted in several email exchanges to explain DNS to the casual user, who typically had no idea how to solve his problem.

At the time of this writing, the most important solutions for these users have been to:

- Improve Tor's documentation for how to configure various applications to use Tor

- Change the warning messages to refer users to a description of the solution ("You are insecure; see this web page") rather than a description of the problem ("Your application is sending IPs instead of hostnames, which may leak information; consider using SOCKS4a instead")

- Bundle Tor with the support tools that it needs, instead of relying on users to find and configure them on their own

### Case Study: JAP and its Anonym-o-meter

The Java Anon Proxy (JAP) is a low-latency anonymizing network for web browsing developed and deployed by the Technical University of Dresden in Germany.[7] Unlike Tor, which uses a *free-route* topology where each user can choose where to enter the network

---

7   Oliver Berthold, Hannes Federrath, and Stefan Köpsell, "Web MIXes: A System for Anonymous and Unobservable Internet Access," in Hannes Federrath (ed.), *Designing Privacy Enhancing Technologies: Workshop on Design Issues in Anonymity and Unobservability* (Springer-Verlag, LNCS 2009, July 2000).

and where to exit, JAP has fixed-route *cascades* that aggregate user traffic into a single entry point and a single exit point. The JAP client includes a GUI, shown in Figure 26-1.

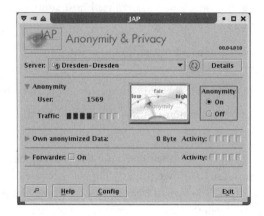

FIGURE 26-1. *JAP client GUI*

Notice the "anonymity meter," which gives the user an impression of the level of protection for his current traffic.

How do we decide the value that the anonym-o-meter should report? In JAP's case, it's based on the number of other users traveling through the cascade at the same time. But alas, because JAP aims for quick transmission of bytes from one end of the cascade to the other, it falls prey to the same end-to-end timing correlation attacks as we described earlier. That is, an attacker who can watch both ends of the cascade won't actually be distracted by the other users.[8] The JAP team has plans to implement full-scale padding from every user (sending and receiving packets all the time, even when they have nothing to send), but—for usability reasons—they haven't gone forward with these plans.

As the system is now, anonymity sets don't provide a real measure of security for JAP, since any attacker who can watch both ends of the cascade wins, and the number of users on the network is no obstacle to this attack. However, we think the anonym-o-meter is a great way to present security information to the user, and we hope to see a variant of it deployed one day for a high-latency system like Mixminion, where the amount of current traffic in the system is more directly related to the protection it offers.

## Bootstrapping, Confidence, and Reputability

Another area where human factors are critical in privacy is in bootstrapping new systems. Because new systems start out with few users, they initially provide only small anonymity sets. This starting state creates a dilemma: a new system with improved privacy properties will attract users only once they believe it is popular and therefore has high anonymity

---

8   George Danezis, "The Traffic Analysis of Continuous-Time Mixes," in David Martin and Andrei Serjantov (eds.), *Privacy Enhancing Technologies (PET 2004)* (May 2004).

sets; but a system cannot be popular without attracting users. New systems need users for privacy, but need privacy for users.

Low-needs users can break the deadlock. The earliest stages of an anonymizing network's lifetime tend to involve users who need only to resist weak attackers who can't know which users are using the network and thus can't learn the contents of the small anonymity set. This solution reverses the early-adopter trends of many security systems: instead of first attracting the most security-conscious users, privacy applications must begin by first attracting low-needs users and hobbyists.

But this analysis relies on users' accurate perceptions of present and future anonymity set size. As in market economics, expectations themselves can bring about trends: a privacy system that people believe to be secure and popular will gain users, thus becoming (all things being equal) more secure and popular. Thus, security depends not only on usability, but also on *perceived usability by others*, and hence on the quality of the provider's marketing and public relations. Perversely, over-hyped systems (if they are not too broken) may be a better choice than modestly promoted ones, if the hype attracts more users.

Yet another factor in the safety of a given network is its reputability: the perception of its social value based on its current users. If I'm the only user of a system, it might be socially accepted, but I'm not getting any anonymity. Add a thousand Communists, and I'm anonymous, but everyone thinks I'm a Commie. Add a thousand random citizens (cancer survivors, privacy enthusiasts, and so on) and now I'm hard to profile.

The more cancer survivors on Tor, the better for the human rights activists. The more script kiddies, the worse for the normal users. Thus, reputability is an anonymity issue for two reasons. First, it impacts the sustainability of the network: a network that's always about to be shut down has difficulty attracting and keeping users, so its anonymity set suffers. Second, a disreputable network attracts the attention of powerful attackers who may not mind revealing the identities of all the users to uncover the few bad ones.

While people therefore have an incentive for the network to be used for "more reputable" activities than their own, there are still tradeoffs involved when it comes to anonymity. To follow the previous example, a network used entirely by cancer survivors might welcome some Communists onto the network, although of course they'd prefer a wider variety of users.

The impact of public perception on security is especially important during the bootstrapping phase of the network, in which the first few widely publicized uses of the network can dictate the types of users it attracts next.

## Technical Challenges to Guessing the Number of Users in a Network

In addition to the social problems we've described that make it difficult for a typical user to guess which anonymizing network will be most popular, there are some technical challenges as well. These stem from the fact that anonymizing networks are good at hiding what's going on—even from their users. For example, one of the toughest attacks to solve is that an attacker might sign up many users to artificially inflate the apparent size of the network. Not only does this *Sybil attack* increase the odds that the attacker will be able to successfully compromise a given user transaction,[9] but it might also trick users into thinking that a given network is safer than it actually is.

And finally, as we saw when discussing JAP, the feasibility of end-to-end attacks makes it hard to guess how much a given other user is contributing to your anonymity. Even if he's not actively trying to trick you, he can still fail to provide cover for you—because his behavior is sufficiently different from yours (he's active during the day, and you're active at night), because his transactions are different (he talks about physics, you talk about AIDS), or because network design parameters (such as low delay for messages) mean the attacker is able to track transactions more easily.

## Conclusion

Users' safety relies on their behaving like other users. But how can they predict other users' behavior? If they need to behave in a way that's different from the rest of the users, how do they compute the tradeoffs and risks?

There are several lessons we might take away from researching anonymity and usability. On the one hand, we might remark that anonymity is already tricky from a technical standpoint, and if we're required to get usability right as well before anybody can be safe, it will be hard indeed to come up with a good design. If lack of anonymity means lack of users, then we're stuck in a depressing loop. On the other hand, the loop has an optimistic side too. Good anonymity can mean more users: if we can make good headway on usability, then as long as the technical designs are adequate, we'll end up with enough users to make everything work out.

In any case, declining to design a good solution means leaving most users to a less secure network or no anonymizing network at all. Cancer survivors and abuse victims would continue communications and research over the Internet, risking social or employment problems; and human rights workers in oppressive countries would continue publishing their stories.

---

9   John Douceur, "The Sybil Attack," *Proceedings of the 1st International Peer to Peer Systems Workshop (IPTPS)* (March 2002).

The temptation to focus on designing a perfectly usable system before building it can be self-defeating, because obstacles to usability are often unforeseen. We believe that the anonymity community needs to focus on continuing experimental deployment.

## About the Authors

Roger Dingledine is a security and privacy researcher. While at MIT, he developed Free Haven, one of the early peer-to-peer systems that emphasized resource management while retaining anonymity for its users. He consults for government, industry, and NGOs to design and develop systems for anonymity and traffic analysis resistance. Roger is the project leader for Tor, the second-generation onion routing network, and one of the principal designers for Mixminion, the latest anonymous remailer design. Past work includes anonymous publishing and communication systems, traffic analysis resistance, censorship resistance, attack resistance for decentralized networks, and reputation.

Nick Mathewson is a researcher in security, privacy, and anonymity. He has been a core designer and developer on Tor since 2003, and is currently sponsored by the EFF to improve and expand the Tor software and network. He is also one of the main designers and the main developer on Type III (a.k.a. Mixminion), the protocol that will replace the one currently used by the Mixmaster anonymous remailer. He lives in Cambridge, Massachusetts.

PART FIVE **COMMERCIALIZING USABILITY: THE VENDOR PERSPECTIVE**

# CHAPTER TWENTY-SEVEN

# ZoneAlarm: Creating Usable Security Products for Consumers

**JORDY BERSON**

**W**HEN ZONEALARM 2.0 DEBUTED IN JANUARY 2000, it was downloaded more than 1 million times in the first 10 weeks. We had tapped into a sorely needed space—an easy-to-use personal firewall—and the 20 or so Zone Labs employees suddenly found themselves strapped to a rocket and struggling to hold on. By 2005, the company had grown to more than 180 employees. The ZoneAlarm product family now has more than 30 million users, making it the most widely used software firewall in the world. We believe our products have been so successful because they are both highly secure and easy to use.

We make our products secure by employing multiple layers of security, so when a threat gets past one layer, another is there to stop it. We use a signature-independent foundation, so we're as good at catching unknown threats as we are at catching known threats. And we don't cut corners: we must pass every test thrown at us, or have lightning-fast resolution if we fail. And security at Zone Labs adheres to a simple rule—block everything that's not specifically allowed by the user. In such a user-centric model, ease of use is critical.

We make our products easy to use by knowing who our target users are; tailoring our products to their needs—not ours; and making the user a key part of the security process.

At Zone Labs, we haven't always executed our ease-of-use principle perfectly. But we've done it consistently enough to spread protection from advanced to more novice users and to be the industry leader. We've also proven that a user-centric security model can be a secure model. In this chapter, I describe some of our most important practical principles and provide examples of how we create our software.

## About ZoneAlarm

ZoneAlarm is a firewall that blocks all incoming traffic unless the user has specifically allowed it. It does this using "stealthing" technology that hides the protected computer from probing hackers on the Internet. The firewall also monitors all programs trying to make outbound connections from the computer, preventing any program from connecting to the Internet or acting as a server without the user's permission. The user is assisted in this decision-making with the Automatic Program AlertAdvisor.

The product interaction consists of a graphic user interface (GUI), alerts, and a system tray icon. Most interaction is done through the alerts, so users rarely interact with the GUI (shown in Figure 27-1).

The ZoneAlarm product family is designed for consumer use and for single or networked PCs. Stressing "set and forget" security, these products go about their job as silently as possible. There are several versions of ZoneAlarm, from a basic free version to a suite containing email worm prevention, privacy control, antivirus, antispam, antiphishing/fraud, instant messaging encryption and protection, and a few other security and convenience features. All ZoneAlarm products are built around the same core: our award-winning stateful inspection firewall.

## Design Principles

This section describes the basic principles underlying the design of ZoneAlarm:

- Know your audience
- Think like your audience
- Eliminate clutter
- Eliminate complexity
- Create just enough feedback
- Be a customer advocate when usability and competitive pressure collide

### Know Your Audience

Our company held a weekly lunch meeting series in which we could hear an architect explain a bit of the technology within our firewall. The first meeting was packed with people anxious to learn, and about half of us were from marketing. As the words began to spill out of the architect's mouth, those of us in marketing quickly realized that the lecture

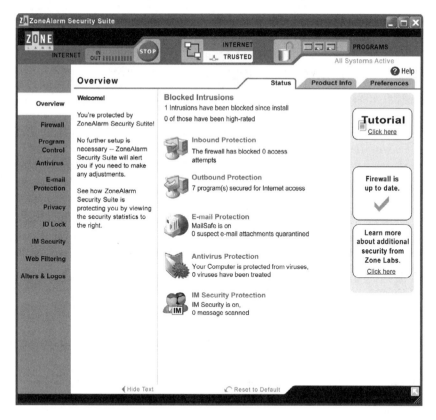

FIGURE 27-1. *Interacting with this ZoneAlarm Security Suite GUI is seldom necessary, as most user interaction occurs through the alerts*

may as well have been in Latin. What the architect had to say may have been brilliant, but it failed for the very simple reason that it didn't reach the audience.

Now imagine getting this wrong on your interface design, considering the thousands of hours it takes to design, build, test, and market a product. If you're not speaking your audience's language, all that work is wasted. But even a minor mismatch with your audience means that your product will be less successful than it could be, that it could lose its edge on the competition. and that the very customers you are trying to protect may make wrong decisions that will leave them exposed. That's why you must know your audience intimately. Skip this step, and you leave opportunity on the table. Even if your product doesn't fail outright, it won't be as good as it could have been.

A mistake I made early in my career was thinking that knowing the audience was simply inherent in my job title. I, the product manager with the arts and humanities major and a background in writing, should naturally know better than the nerdy engineers what my audience wants. Of course, I was wrong. To know the audience, I needed to get out of the office and talk to them. Without this information, your guess is no better than anybody else's. If you're the key decision-maker for your product's design, this concept is powerful

## MINIMIZING USER EFFORT SAFELY

Striving to provide the strongest security that's also easy to use may seem impossible at times. For example, antivirus, standard intrusion detection, and other signature-based solutions are very easy to use but offer little protection against emerging and as-yet-unknown viruses and malware. But combating old as well as brand-new threats often involves an aware user who can react to real-time attacks and understand the difference between a real threat and something benign. You know, that user we spoke about who doesn't want to spend any of her time using your software? As pointed out in Chapter 2, "Security is dependable only if it is actually used as intended." While there is no single way to solve this conundrum, here are a few tips that help us to get closer to achieving good security:

- Create interaction points only when you absolutely must. If you interrupt users with pop-ups that have noncritical or less meaningful information, then the user is less likely to pay attention to critical information.

- If you cannot answer a question yourself, or you have a tough time explaining the question to others, your users probably cannot answer the question either. Come up with a different question to ask that may get to the same answer.

- Set up multiple layers of security so that even if a threat gets past one layer, another will stop it. This way, user errors don't have to be catastrophic.

- Create automation if you can do so securely. There may be technical solutions that can lessen or eliminate the need for user interaction. But keep in mind the raison d'être for your product and do not sacrifice security in the process.

- Explore alternative interfaces, such as wizards. Often, a carefully designed wizard can take what would be a tough decision and break it down into easier and more intuitive questions. But stay away from wizards that are too long. And if a wizard contains questions that are as tough to answer as the original question the wizard was intended to replace, then the wizard is not worth doing.

- When you're analyzing the effectiveness of your product's security, always include the customer in your analysis. If it is likely that the customer will make an error and reduce security, either redesign the experience to minimize the risk or, in extreme cases, consider revamping the technology or leaving it as an advanced option rather than a default setting.

- Remember that a false sense of security is worse than no security at all. It is better to leave out a portion of functionality if it's highly prone to failure, than to include it.

and indispensable. Know your audience, and you'll not only be able to create much more successful design, but also earn the respect and credibility of your team so that you're empowered to make good decisions. But even if you're not personally talking to users, make sure that someone on your team is.

This does not have to be a huge endeavor, by the way. If you dedicate even a four-hour, uninterrupted time slot each week to call people on the phone, send out surveys, talk to people at trade shows, visit people's homes, or even hang out at Best Buy and talk to people there, that's probably more than your competitors are doing. Of course, the more time you spend in this area, the better you will know your audience.

## Think Like Your Audience

So, you know your audience. That's a terrific start, and you're already well on your way to creating usable security. Now begins the difficult step of applying what you've learned about your audience and, in a way, *becoming* them. This means overcoming noise—anything that takes away your focus on the customer. For an interface designer, noise could be sticking entirely to classroom theory and ignoring the realities of the customer or the market. An architect or developer may try to create such an efficient, elegant architecture that the customer needs cannot be accommodated. Marketing may focus too much on revenue opportunities and forget that the best way to gain and keep customers is to focus on the needs and desires of the customers. If you are the lead decision-maker on a design, it's your job to filter all of this noise for the sake of the customer. You must truly step out of your noise-filled head and into the heads of your audience to make a design successful.

One of the best ways to do this is to present your design to others throughout the design process. This forces your mind to shift perspectives and see the product through others' eyes. It's always amazing to me when, after working hundreds of hours on a design, we present it to others at a review meeting. Predictably, problems leap from the screen within a minute of the presentation as if we've put no thought at all into the design. This should be expected. There is a reason why every professional writer has an editor: once you produce something, you can no longer truly step out of your own head and see it for what it is. It's the same with software design: it takes someone else to help you find errors and tailor your product to the intended audience.

Another great way to step out of your own head is to identify a representative person or two from your target audience and design for them. When I began considering our antivirus software design, many of the guiding principles I used came from observing my roommate, Julie, one night after work. There she sat at her desk, anxious because she had heard about a virus outbreak and wondering if her computer was safe. It took her wading through multiple panels of her antivirus product before she got the information she wanted—and discovered that her antivirus software had been out of date for months.

What an advantage I had having witnessed her experience. Stepping into her head, I knew what questions to ask of our own design: can she glance at the antivirus area and know instantly and without a doubt that she's protected? Will she clearly know when her antivirus software is out of date or expired? Isn't it better for her if we put the most common controls and displays into a single panel, and we relegate all the advanced settings she'll probably never use to an Options dialog? The end result of considering this user and the other members of our target audience in these decisions was a very clear, easy-to-use interface that customers and reviewers have praised.

## Eliminate Clutter

William Zinsser, author of *On Writing Well*,[1] calls clutter "the disease of American writing." "We are a society," he says, "strangling in unnecessary words, circular constructions, pompous frills and meaningless jargon." In writing, any words that do not help to get the main idea across only weaken it. As with so many writing principles, this is also true of software design. And while designing software is difficult in itself, designing a security product—something that so few people understand to begin with—presents an even bigger challenge. Simply put, our job is to make the complex underpinnings of a security product into tasks and metaphors that our customers can understand. We are the intermediary. So it's critical that we strive for purity in our design so that every word, button, and pixel that's present in that design is used to explain an idea or a task and that any clutter is removed.

## Eliminate Complexity

Whereas clutter occurs at the detail level of our designs, complexity can permeate our designs at a higher and more profound level, which can end up not only confusing a user, but also slowing time to market and introducing stability problems.

If you can barely explain your design to somebody else, then the design is too complex. From an R&D perspective, if functionality takes unusually long to write, if the code is so tricky that it creates bugs, or if the functionality permutations would take QA too long to test, that is also a reason to simplify.

A good example of this point comes from a startup wizard we were creating for a new product version (see the upcoming sidebar). The first step of the wizard had three possible branches. Moreover, each wizard permutation would turn product functionality on or off, but only if no conflicting software was found on the user's computer. This complexity bothered everyone on the team, but we proceeded heads-down toward our deadline anyway. Eventually we decided to try to do something to improve the wizard. It didn't take too long to come up with a fantastic solution: we realized that this segment of the wizard wasn't doing a bit of good for the customer, and it certainly wasn't making our job easy. When we moved the necessary functionality to a new location, it was simple and understandable.

So, when a portion of your design seems overly complex or problematic, ask yourself: is it essential? Does it make things better or worse? Can it be done in another way, at a different time, or somewhere else? One of the keys to avoiding complexity is to give priority to the most common and likely use cases. So often, someone on the design team will ask, "What if the user wants to (*insert extremely unlikely action*)?" While it's important to ferret out those rare-use cases and ensure that they don't end in catastrophic failure, you've also got to be able to say you're not going to sacrifice the common use cases to design for a case that may never happen.

---

1   William Zinsser, *On Writing Well* (New York: Harper & Row, 2001).

# A WIZARD MAKEOVER

ZoneAlarm Pro includes a network detection wizard that automatically pops up whenever the software detects a new network. The goal of the wizard is to help the user select the security level appropriate for the resources needed on the network. The existing wizard, shown in Figure 27-2, wasn't achieving that goal as well as we'd hoped and was difficult for novice users. Adding to the design challenge, we were outside of a regular development cycle. Changing any functionality or introducing any stability risk to the code base was forbidden; our opportunity lay only in aesthetic and textual changes. So we set out to achieve the goal of the wizard as directly and powerfully as possible, keeping and promoting those items that supported that goal and cutting all else. Each time we changed our design, we would get outside opinions from anyone who was available to make sure we were in our users' mind. Getting this outside perspective was critical to the design's success. Much like editing a document, we found clutter to remove with every pass. Our improved wizard is shown in Figure 27-3.

Here is the analysis and what was changed:

- The original wizard involved four steps: announce the new network; assign a security level; name the network (optional); and announce completion. Had the wizard been a one-time occurrence, four screens might have been OK. But traveling users would get this wizard with each new location they traveled to. This was a major point of clutter. Because only one of the four screens directly supported the goal for the wizard, we cut the others and saw instant improvement.

- The pop-up was too wordy and technical. For something that comes up multiple times, possibly at inopportune times, the text had to be a quick read with direct information. The text itself had clutter that we edited and tested out with multiple reviews.

- The formatting was wrong. Paragraphs of text overburdened the display and made it difficult to extract at-a-glance information. The text that we created was put into short bullet points. In addition, we were very careful to keep the number of different elements in the pop-up to a minimum so that it appeared simple.

- The wizard was tailored to the wrong audience. The text-heavy pop-up was intimidating, as were some of the technical terms. We substituted icons for text to immediately decrease the intimidation factor and create more whitespace. The page focus was now on simple icons and text bullets, perfect for our primary audience. The more technical information for the secondary audience remained, but with less focus.

- The optional and noncritical task of naming the network was placed at the bottom of the pop-up, purposely in second place to the main goal.

*—continued—*

As with nearly all designs I've encountered, our improved design wasn't the only way to succeed. And deeper technical work could have made the wizard even easier to use. But the quick design proved successful at helping users choose the right security level. It also reduced support calls and was noticed favorably by the press and our distributors—definitely a lot of gain for a small amount of coding.

This example shows the many ways that clutter can be present in software design. It also shows how important it is to have a design goal and to identify the main and secondary audiences. Finally, it shows that multiple user reviews with the target audience are the key to making a design successful.

*FIGURE 27-2. The four-step wizard was ungainly and difficult for less experienced users*

### Create Just Enough Feedback

Among the bad assumptions a security product designer can make is that people actually want to spend any time at all interacting with their security. This point is made throughout this book, but it is so important that I'd be remiss not to mention it here as well. Don't ask users to do anything unless it absolutely cannot be done safely without them. If you keep this in mind, you'll greatly reduce the likelihood that your users will make errors that defeat their security.

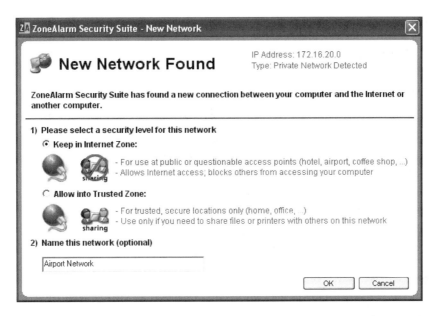

FIGURE 27-3. *The single-step wizard keeps the critical items and removes the clutter for a much easier and more effective user experience*

Keep in mind that users may not always agree with this principle. We have survey results where users of varying skill levels say they want to be involved in every decision made. But our usability studies consistently contradict this. So, what do users want? They want to be kept in the know about their security, to be reassured that they're being protected. But in general, they want this knowledge in unintrusive ways.

So, while I talk about removing interface clutter, showing pop-ups and wizards only when absolutely necessary, and keeping the security product behind the scenes as much as possible, there are some elements of the product you should expose to the user.

When we redesigned the ZoneAlarm product family, we built in some reassuring interaction points. On the main panel, two subtle lines at the top of the page report how many intrusions have been blocked since installation, and how many of those are high risk. These two little lines are cited in many of the fan-mail letters we receive, and are often mentioned by customers at trade shows. Our system tray icon is another subtle place for feedback that indicates whenever traffic moves from client to Internet. And if the product ever fails to load, the icon becomes an attention-grabbing X.

There are times for more pronounced feedback as well. Our subscription expiration screen, for example, pops up and demands attention when the subscription is about to or already has expired. We wanted this alert to stick out because out-of-date software is one of the major factors in security attacks. Another example of pronounced feedback occurs when we find a virus. Although the virus is treated automatically, we still let users know what has happened so that they know we're actively protecting them.

Our customers consistently tell us they like the reassurance we give them because they know that the software is working and that they are protected. When we provide this reassurance, we are also demonstrating the value of our products, generating loyalty, and building brand. Providing feedback is also very important as a security enhancement to alert users to a lapse in security.

## Be a Customer Advocate When Usability and Competitive Pressure Collide

While sound usability principles are probably understood by most designers in the security software industry, they are obviously not always followed. Competitive pressure and tight internal schedules are often the reason. Although ideally everyone on your team *should* be the user/customer advocate, you (or whoever is in the lead position) *must* be. Otherwise, things that have nothing to do with designing for the audience, such as engineering restrictions, timelines, budget, and politics, will edge out the needs of the audience. Phrases like "that's the way we've always done it," or "we cannot do that" can weigh too heavily at the expense of the goals at hand to the extent that you are left asking, "what's the point?" While this type of noise is very real and must be dealt with, you must make sure you don't penalize the user by letting such things get in your way. And while there are realities that may sometimes end up making the user second, you must keep your allegiances as much as possible to the user.

Balancing customer needs with competitive pressure requires compromise on all sides, including yours. Sometimes implementing your proposed changes could affect the stability of the project or take developers away from other critical work. So you must think like a superhero. A mission may seem impossible, but you need to make it happen. Start by making sure that you know the exact goal of the intended design. Then decide if you can make headway on that goal by doing part of the work. Often, developers can help you eliminate the most risky, time-eating portions of the design that perhaps can be put off until the next release. It is very rarely an "all or nothing" decision that cannot be somewhat improved through other means.

The wizard makeover discussed in the earlier sidebar was done after the VP of development told me that I couldn't do it. So I made a deal with him: if I could come up with changes within a week that would not affect client stability or push out the ship date, he would let the improvements be checked into the product code. As long as QA found no problems, we could leave the improvements in; otherwise, they would be pulled. I worked very closely with a seasoned developer who was supportive of my goals. I came up with a design that the developer had confidence in, quickly validated it with a UI designer and some 10-minute usability testing around the office, and by deadline time, the code was checked in. After holding my breath for a day to see if bugs would show up, we were in the clear and the VP was true to his word. In fact, he later congratulated me for pushing the changes because they offered such a vast improvement.

## CREATING THE PROGRAM ADVISOR

We had a difficult problem. One of the most protective layers of our firewall had become too difficult to use for a large part of our audience. This layer, program control, asks users to decide when a program should or should not have Internet access and server rights. When we first released program control, our audience of more technical users was up to the task of making these decisions. But as our product spread to less technical users, we found ourselves breaking our own principles by asking users questions they couldn't answer. Some of our competitors appeared to be providing a solution to this problem, but their methods of doing so could be so easily defeated that they rendered the feature worthless. Although we knew this, our customers did not. So we had enormous pressure to "catch up" to competitors—in a secure way—and to repair this failing security layer for our users.

Our company founder was well aware of the problem and created what at first seemed to be a complex system. This system is now in use on most of our products and has been among the single biggest usability improvements in our history. For the user, the solution is simple: we answer the pop-up so that the user doesn't have to. The underpinnings are complex, however, and require the Zone Labs security team to maintain a list of thousands of programs and their matching checksums along with a security policy for each program. Each client calls to the program policy server when it tries to access the Internet, and the server provides an instant policy to the client. This policy can be manually reviewed by the user or automatically accepted, according to user preference. Each policy can be changed by Zone Labs at any time.

In some ways, this system breaks with some of the fundamentals I described earlier—namely, complexity. For users, however, the system couldn't be simpler. On average, users see 90% fewer alerts than they did before, a critical security improvement. With this system, we also know that programs are getting configured correctly, so our users' security is vastly improved over what was already an excellent system. The bottom line is that we realized that to maintain security, we had to make these critical decisions for the user.

# Efficient Production for a Fast Market

Creating good usability for a single feature can take months of research, testing, and iterative design. But in demanding market conditions, we're often forced to create designs in much less time. This can weaken design and can even end up costing more time and expense if design flaws are discovered after code has already been written. In such a fast-paced environment, here are a few tips for making the most of your time:

*Get as much design time as possible from management*
> Remind them that cutting time from the beginning of the design process often means doubling or tripling time and expense later in the cycle when unforeseen design problems occur.

*Form teams early*

A process that works well for us involves getting key people from engineering, marketing, and QA together to serve as consultants to the designers throughout the design process. It's remarkable how many problems can be eliminated early so that when development begins to code, there are virtually no issues. This also means that the spec will be better understood and that you will more likely get the end product that you want. Documentation and support should also be involved early so that they can learn the design gradually as it's developed, instead of having it dumped on them when it's done.

*Make sure that engineering is involved early*

This relates to the previous point, but it is worth stressing on its own. Engineers can help guide design decisions that are easier and faster to develop and that have little or no effect on market requirements. Inclusion is much better for ensuring that your requirements will be understood and developed correctly—many errors occur when design is done in isolation and then dumped on development in a long, tedious document. Finally, including developers in the design creation process makes them take ownership and share in the excitement of the product, which in turn leads to a better product.

*Spend concentrated effort with the whole team when you can*

Especially at the beginning of the project, getting the core team members to focus on the design together for a half day often eliminates a lot of emailing and guessing and is more efficient than bothering people for five minutes at a time throughout the day and week.

*Test*

Even if formal usability testing has been cut, you can still find fast and creative ways to test. Some of the most valuable feedback I've gotten is through co-workers who are not directly involved with my project. One of our designers brings in his friends and family to watch them use the software. It's amazing how many problems we can find and eliminate in just a couple of hours a week, saving on support costs and delivering a much better product to our customers.

*Don't write until the design is done*

We focus mostly on pictures, iterating them as we perfect the design. Only when the pictures are generally approved by decision-makers in the company do we start to write down the interaction details. Words are tedious and time consuming to change. Pictures are much less so.

*Use as few words as possible while still getting the facts across*

We know that our customers don't like to read anything, and I've found that people inside the company aren't much different. The spec that design, QA, and documentation will work from should be as small as you can make it, with as few words and repetition as possible. As with the previous point, people are much more inclined to look at pictures than to read, so use more pictures than words.

*Use prototyping if possible*

It is amazing what you can miss in a design that's written on paper and what you can catch when you can actually interact with the product. A prototype is an invaluable way to find flaws before heavy-duty coding and documentation begins.

*Involve executives and higher-up decision-makers as you go.*

This lets them feel that they are a part of the process, helps them understand the design, and is a good way to ensure that your design won't be changed late in the game by an executive who has been left out.

## Conclusion

Design for the ZoneAlarm product line can be best summed up by two things: identify and study the target audience, and apply that knowledge to the design. Following these principles doesn't guarantee great design, but without them, design fails. There is no question that designing usable security is difficult, and no company I've seen, including Zone Labs, does it flawlessly. By reading this book, you are benefiting from the research and experience of all of us and will be well prepared to join us in this ongoing battle to protect computer users of every kind from Internet-borne threats.

## About the Author

Jordy Berson is a senior product manager at Zone Labs and has guided the design of the ZoneAlarm product line since 2000. His focus at Zone Labs is on creating software that "his mom could use" to combat Internet threats. He is a graduate of Colorado State University in technical journalism with a mechanical engineering concentration.

# CHAPTER TWENTY-EIGHT

# Firefox and the Worry-Free Web

**BLAKE ROSS**

**A**S THE PRIMARY BARRIER BETWEEN MILLIONS OF UNSUSPECTING WEB USERS AND THE CON ARTISTS who want their credit card numbers, Firefox developers are acutely aware of the challenges in securing the Web. And so, it seems, are our users. More than 15 million people downloaded Firefox 1.0 in its first two months—a gold rush driven by Firefox's speed and reliability, no doubt, but also driven by the barrage of media warnings against online identity theft, data loss, and continuing security problems with Microsoft's Internet Explorer (IE).

## Usability and Security: Bridging the Gap

The Mozilla Foundation has undergone a profound transformation during its short lifetime. It began as a loose organization responsible for shepherding the open source community to help develop Netscape 6. In those formative years, the foundation was a technology provider, working primarily with technology vendors like ActiveState and IBM. Although the foundation's work was significant, its developers were always at least two degrees away from the customers who would eventually use its products.

Enter Firefox, the organization's first-ever product designed for and marketed directly to end users without any middlemen. The factors and circumstances that motivated such a tremendous shift in direction make for an interesting business case study, but aren't really of interest here. What is relevant is the attitude shift that the change necessitated.

As a technology provider, the Mozilla Foundation didn't need to concern itself with designing and focus testing usable interfaces. That was, by and large, the burden of the vendor using its technology. Instead, Mozilla's job was nearly the opposite: to provide an interface that exposed all of its capabilities, allowing vendors to pick and choose with ease.

As a maker of consumer products, the organization had to realize one key insight: whereas vendors wanted to use the *technology*, users want to use the *Web*. They care about Firefox's features and capabilities only to the extent that the technology helps them maximize their productivity while online. Designing for this audience required a fundamental paradigm shift. The end result is a browser that can do most of the things the old Netscape and Mozilla browsers could do, but with a simpler interface sporting a tiny fraction of the older programs' options and windows.

Firefox has a simple design philosophy: those features that are not perceived to significantly improve the online experience of the collective web population are hidden, and those that do improve the experience—such as pop-up blocking and tabbed browsing—are pushed to the forefront. In a world of programs that seem to get more complex with each iteration, Firefox's approach and clean interface have won plaudits from the media and users alike.

So, how do our security obligations fit into this picture? Quite easily, actually. We are committed to designing products that help people use the Web easily, and we don't compromise this vision to help them use it securely. Our decisions about security, and when to expose an interface to the user that manages security, hinge on three basic assumptions:

• Users want to believe that their products are keeping them secure.

• Users do not want to be responsible for, nor concern themselves with, their own security.

• We know more about security than our users do.

Perhaps this betrays a kind of brazen confidence on our part, but that's the point: users want their software to protect them, because they don't know—and don't want to know—about the details of security.

Our chief competitor, Microsoft, has publicly expressed doubt that a marriage of usability and security can last. Upon releasing Windows XP Service Pack 2 (SP2), an Internet Explorer program manager wrote this comment in the IE team's public blog: "We are absolute [sic] dead serious about security now. It's permeated everything we do, and we're willing to impinge on the user experience if needed."[1]

---

1  Tony Chor, "IE in Windows XP SP2," Internet Explorer Team Blog; *http://blogs.msdn.com/ie/archive/2004/08/10/212008.aspx#212128*.

Indeed, many aspects of the revamped IE interface in SP2 illustrate the compromises that were made. Things that once took a single click to accomplish now take three or four; whereas users previously endured one warning, they must now endure two. Realistically, however, what we're seeing in SP2 is probably more Microsoft's overreaction to public criticism than it is the inability to realize an experience that is both secure and usable. For years, Microsoft took the heat for allowing spyware installation with a single click of the mouse; SP2 is a natural reaction toward the other extreme.

We believe that it's possible to straddle the line and deliver products that are silently secure while outwardly usable. This chapter will walk through the methodology we employ and the assumptions (listed earlier) that power it.

# The Five Golden Rules

It's too easy for developers to throw up their hands and say, "Users are the weakest link." In fact, the blame frequently lies with developers for not understanding how users interact with technology and designing interfaces that facilitate mistakes. When designing interfaces that need to both serve users and protect them, a few questions come up again and again: when should the program turn to the user for input? When it does, how should the program solicit that input? This section will offer answers to these questions as we have fine-tuned them during our work on Firefox.

### Identifying "The User"

There are undoubtedly people who will take offense at some of the statements made in the following sections. It's important to realize that "the user," as discussed here, is meant to represent the intended majority of our Firefox audience—the dentists, lawyers, teachers, stay-at-home dads, and other members of society who aren't in the computer profession and don't know anything about security beyond what they read in the news. Although Firefox is becoming increasingly popular in enterprises, this chapter does not apply to corporate customers, who usually have more interest in their own security and frequently have trained IT departments who have security as an explicit responsibility. Firefox offers different solutions for corporations—without harming the Firefox consumer users—often by simply putting advanced options behind a technical wall that's impenetrable by most home users.

### 1. Enforce the Officer/Citizen Model

Society has constructed a variety of organizations to regulate and protect itself. The police maintain order and enforce the law. Insurance companies protect against unpredictable disasters. Lawyers defend personal rights and freedoms. People want to delegate their security to experts who specialize in the field and are able to guarantee it.

It's easy to forget that the same is true of their online security. The old Mozilla software is a chronicle of indecision within the walls of Netscape. Every option, confirmation window, and question to the user marks another case where two internal camps couldn't agree on the most secure way to proceed and instead deferred to the user's decision. This approach, of course, is absurd. Consider arriving home to an unsolicited package on your doorstop. You call the bomb squad, and after some analysis, the lead officer comes to brief you: "An X-ray of the package was perfectly normal, and the organization that sent it seems to be reputable, but a chemical swab of the exterior yielded some concerning figures. Gee, I dunno. Your call."

The example seems over the top until you consider the questions the average user encounters every day on the Internet. Figure 28-1 illustrates a particularly mystifying one that IE users can encounter while attempting to navigate to certain sites, many of which are in fact trustworthy. The "View Certificate" button opens a window containing what amounts to Greek to a majority of web users; in our real-world analogy, it's the equivalent of the officer providing you with the raw data output of the chemical swab.

*FIGURE 28-1. Internet Explorer 6.0 users can encounter this baffling dialog in day-to-day surfing*

Before coding up such confirmation windows, software developers—the group most notorious for encouraging them as a suitable compromise—should ask *themselves* a question: if I can't figure it out, how are users supposed to? What additional qualifications do users possess that will help them arrive at a better conclusion? What evidence is there to suggest that most users even know what a certificate is in the digital sense?

In developing Firefox, we challenge ourselves daily to do something that has proven difficult in the software industry: *make decisions.* We want users to know that they can go about their business on the Internet with security in the back of their minds, because it's on the front of our minds. The intent is not to be covert, or to pretend that security isn't a concern; we do want our users to know that we're making decisions on their behalf. But we want them to have confidence in our ability to make such judgments (hence our slogan, "the browser you can trust").

So, how do you discern the bombs from the fruitcakes when there's not enough information to make the call? You need to err on the side of caution, but *only if the circumstances justify it*. That means that if 99.9% of sites matching the profile outlined in Figure 28-1 are reputable sites that forgot to dot the i's in their certificates, you owe it to your users to just navigate to the site—especially because usability studies indicate that almost all of them will click "Yes" without reading the question.[2] On the other hand, if there's a strong likelihood that users are in danger, you owe it to them to take protective actions on their behalf—especially, again, because they're likely to make the wrong choice ("Yes") if you ask them. In other words, if you're doing things right, you should be making the decision users would make anyway when it's probably the right one, and correcting them in the cases where they're likely making the wrong one. You've achieved status quo or better, and you're down one annoying confirmation window.

Skeptics will point out that mistakes will be made and we will have broken our contract with the user, but that's only partly true. Our promise to users is that they can trust us to do the due diligence on their behalf, and they understand that we are more likely to choose "Yes" or "No" correctly than they are. We purport to be the browser they can trust, not the browser without security problems. While we believe—and evidence suggests—that our products are more secure than our competitors' out of the box, trust is a more nuanced reward that must be won on many fronts.

The media is chiding Microsoft not because IE has so many exploits, but because IE has so many exploits *as a result of prioritizing other things above security* (as its manager conceded[3]), because vulnerabilities are often public for weeks before being patched, and because Microsoft is denying some security features to users who won't upgrade to Windows XP. The Microsoft attacks are motivated by a perception that the company isn't doing everything it could be to protect users, in the same way that a doctor will come under fire for malpractice if his perceived negligence injures his patient. Because we design Firefox with security in mind, proactively seek out vulnerabilities by paying experts who discover them, and generally provide 24-hour turnaround to patch them when they arise, our users do not feel cheated when exploits are discovered, and continue to trust us to make decisions on their behalf.

## 2. Don't Overwhelm the User

Put a usability guru in a room with a developer who wants to add a dialog box, and sparks will fly. What's the big deal about asking the user for a decision, anyway?

There's nothing inherently wrong with turning to the user for input, but our own usability studies corroborate the widely held belief that doing so too often is detrimental—both

---

2   Mary Ellen Zurko, Charlie Kaufman, Katherine Spanbauer, and Chuck Bassett, "Did You Ever Have to Make Up Your Mind? What Notes Users Do When Faced with a Security Decision," *18th Annual Computer Security Applications Conference* (2002).

3   Chor.

to users and to developers. As discussed earlier, Firefox is built entirely on the principle that people want to use the Web, and not the web browser. Dialogs and confirmation windows—especially when they pose questions as inane as the one pictured in Figure 28-1—interrupt the user's thoughts and delay the payoff (the loading of the web site). Even before the user has a chance to begin reading the question, he is already frustrated and predisposed to dismiss it in the quickest way possible. This is not the state of mind you want your users to be in when making a security decision with potentially devastating consequences.

So, dialog abuse can harm users, but how does it harm us as developers? When users are inundated with questions that are cryptic or of little interest, they begin to lose faith in our commitment to pester them only when absolutely necessary, and they no longer find it incumbent upon themselves to read future questions—even when they have not seen them before. Consequently, we as developers lose another tool in our toolbox of ways to warn users. A particularly apt example from modern society is found in the U.S. Department of Homeland Security's color-based threat level. The government bumps the national threat level up and down so frequently that studies indicate many citizens have stopped reacting to the changes. The tool no longer acts to mobilize public awareness, and thus the government must resort to even more pervasive means to grab their attention. This only frustrates and interrupts them even more, and a vicious cycle ensues.

With Firefox, we seek to break this cycle by distinguishing the problem from its symptoms. The problem is that users do not want to be bothered unless they perceive it to be necessary; that they grow jaded of the interruptions and begin to ignore them is just a symptom, and should not be perceived as an invitation to interrupt them more forcefully. Instead of introducing dialogs that animate, change color, use bold text, or otherwise try to one-up the traditional dialog and capture the user's attention, we acknowledge our users' preference to surf the Web without a shadow, and try to make decisions on their behalf in line with the officer/citizen model described earlier. There is growing evidence that the software industry is moving in this direction. For example, antivirus programs that once (ridiculously) notified the user of a virus and asked whether to delete it now simply delete the virus and notify the user of the action taken.

Of course, it would be disingenuous to suggest this as the be-all and end-all solution to the great dialog problem. There are circumstances that mandate user input and can't be avoided. In Firefox, for example, a user who encounters a web site that is trying to install software (such as extensions) *must* decide whether to permit the installation. To enforce an indiscriminate ban on software installation would be to marginalize one of Firefox's greatest advantages and destroy an ecosystem that has subsisted since the project's inception. On the other hand, allowing all software installation would put our users at great risk.

The dialog problem isn't binary, though. Just because we can't avoid asking the user a question doesn't mean a dialog is the only venue to pose the question. Wherever possible, we try to replace dialogs with UI widgets that are less jarring to the user experience while still maintaining the better features of a dialog from a usability perspective: easy to notice and difficult to ignore. In the case of software installation, for example, we replaced the dialog asking users whether to install the software with a transient toolbar of sorts (Figure 28-2). The toolbar appears automatically upon installation attempt, and it is distracting only to the extent that the page shifts slightly to allocate space for it. This has proven to be a good compromise both from a pure usability perspective and in the context of security. As far as usability is concerned, our users report that the toolbar is appreciably less intrusive than a dialog appearing when the page loads, and say they like being able to install the software at their leisure instead of being forced to decide immediately. This explains the security win as well. Because the interface respects the user's workflow in not demanding a decision, users are not inclined to dismiss it instinctively.

> To protect your computer, Firefox prevented this site (extensionroom.mozdev.org) from installing software on your computer.    Edit Options...

FIGURE 28-2. *Firefox 1.0 displays this nonintrusive toolbar when an unknown site tries to install software*

Spyware is a major problem for computer users today: a 2004 study conducted by the ISP Earthlink found that the average computer user has 28 spyware programs installed on his computer.[4] We believe this is because most versions of Internet Explorer require the user to allow or reject software installation immediately upon visiting a site, prompting the user to just hit OK in frustration. Our interface is there if they want to install the software, and if not, they can just leave it be. As of Windows XP Service Pack 2, Internet Explorer uses a similar toolbar—but again, this benefits only Windows XP users. Our challenge in the future will be to resist the temptation to use this toolbar for other, less important purposes, because it would then incur the same user apathy as the dialog.

Dialogs still have their place in end-user software, and indeed Firefox has plenty. While usability studies tend to agree on the scenarios outlined thus far, there is evidence that users are more receptive to dialogs that directly result from their own deliberate actions. In other words, most users probably wouldn't perceive a dialog that appears on page load to be a consequence of their choosing to navigate to that page. But a dialog that appears upon clicking a button is more reasonable and more likely to be read if it seems to exist to help the user achieve his goal.

Although they often don't realize it, many developers add security controls and dialogs because they want the user to know the steps they've taken to keep the user safe. There is, after all, something disheartening about spending all day implementing an unbreakable encryption scheme only to end up with a product that is, as far as most users are concerned, exactly the same as yesterday's. There's just one problem with developers wanting to show off their accomplishments: most users simply don't care.

---

4   Earthlink, Inc., "Inaugural Report Charts 28 Spies per Computer" [cited Jan. 2005]; *http://www. earthlink.net/spyaudit/press/.*

Still, there's something to the idea that users want occasional reassurance of their safety. The key is to provide it in a way that doesn't annoy them. People want to see the uniformed security at the airport checkpoints, but they don't want to be singled out for a strip search. You can count on your marketing department to play up security for you, but it's still important to have some feedback built into the product itself. Just make sure you don't overload users with details they don't care about, and make sure the information doesn't interrupt their actually *using* the product.

### 3. Earn Your Users' Trust

Perhaps the most compelling impetus to use dialogs in a product is liability. Dialogs force the user to decide so that the company doesn't have to, a sleight of hand that the in-house lawyers appreciate later when it turns out that the user's decision was wrong.

The problem is that while your users may know next to nothing about security or computers, they know plenty about corporate dishonesty. They are aware of and disgusted by the fine print, immune to the psychology of "$39.99," and wary of privacy policies the size of novels. They are intuitively aware of when a company is furthering its own goals at their expense, and the moment they suspect this of you and your product, you have ceded their loyalty to your competitor.

Google is a perfect (if overused) case study of a company that ostensibly has valued its user trust above all else. Google has decided that cultivating its brand image over time will eventually yield greater revenues than instant-revenue schemes, and the result is a front page that's as pristine and free of advertising as the day the service was launched. With its stated policy of "don't be evil" and its congenial public image, it seems easy for people to forget that, at the end of the day, Google is a multibillion-dollar business.

So, how does this apply to security? In conversations with our users, we've learned two things. The first is that most users simply don't understand complicated security questions, as already discussed. But the second is that some mentally categorize such questions in the same way they do the fine print on advertising—as intentionally obfuscated warnings that companies can point to later and say "Look, we warned you!" if it becomes necessary. People recognize the deceptiveness of fine print, and whether they perceive a company as a group of human beings or a faceless monolith relies in part on whether the company recognizes it, too.

Without delving too much into human psychology, our basic premise in designing Firefox is that most users really don't want to be responsible for their own security, an idea that again invokes the officer/citizen model discussed earlier. The thought of having to fend for yourself in a Web that has been deemed "harmful" and "corrupt" by the press is daunting and overwhelming. Our users expect us, as Internet security experts, to make decisions that keep them safe, instead of passing the buck to them and washing our hands if they mess up.

This probably sounds a bit pie-in-the-sky to lawyers: sure, products would be nice and usable if we could just leave the user alone forever, but what happens when we make the wrong security decision on their behalf? Given the heat Microsoft is taking for its security problems in IE, this is very much a concern of ours with Firefox, and we certainly haven't excised all security dialogs. But one thing we've learned is that if users come to perceive your company as a group of human beings, as discussed earlier, then they are much more willing to tolerate your mistakes. The key is handling such mistakes properly, as discussed in the following section.

## 4. Put Out Fires Quickly and Responsibly

The release of Firefox sparked a mass exodus of Microsoft Internet Explorer users, driving IE's market share below 90% for the first time in years.

We believe that the exodus from IE was driven as much by disillusionment with *Microsoft* as with the heavily publicized security exploits in the company's browser. The security problems are largely viewed as a symptom of a more dire problem: Microsoft just doesn't seem concerned about its users. Whereas Google has built a reputation for intimately caring about customers, Microsoft has created an image of apathy by leaving security exploits unpatched for weeks after they have been announced, and by telling users of its older operating systems that they need to upgrade. Users can accept security exploits if it's clear that you work diligently to prevent them and then work diligently to respond to them when they do arise. Likewise, provided that the police work hard to deter criminals, the public isn't outraged when a crime does occur—unless the police completely botch the investigation afterward.

Many companies seem to forget that announcing a security problem is only half the battle: what the company does next matters just as much. When a security bug is found in Firefox, there's no time for a sigh and a postmortem. The public eye is upon us, watching us closely to see how we respond. The Mozilla security team generally strives for a 24-hour turnaround on security patches, a policy that has been lauded by users and the media alike. It's important to recognize that at this point, the principles of usability extend beyond your product to your web site. Can users find your security update easily? Does it seem like you are being publicly accountable, or are you trying to brush it under the rug, burying it in a remote section of your web site? Remember: the user is expecting corporate tricks.

Admittedly, security response is an area where Firefox lagged behind for much of its history. Security information used to be difficult to find on the Mozilla web site, and only recently did we introduce a built-in update system that automatically notifies Firefox users of security patches and installs them. The usability of such a system is critical: if it's too aggressive in trying to persuade users to get patches (as critics of Windows XP's system have complained), users will ignore it for the same reasons they ignore persistent security dialogs. On the other hand, if it's too passive, users won't get the critical updates.

And if you've read this far, this should just be a reminder: users really don't care that you're patching exploit #25F104A in the handling of XML remote procedural calls. Give them the option to view details about the update, but don't overwhelm them with information in the initial screen. They just want to be safe.

## 5. Teach Your Users Simple Tricks

Many of the reasons given thus far to explain why products offer security dialogs and other controls have been rather cynical: because they are easy to code, because they are the path of least resistance between two warring camps, and because they reduce a company's liability. To be fair, many good-intentioned developers add dialogs or other interface text for a more noble purpose: to educate users and make them better citizens in your product's community (in Firefox's case, the Web). Alas, most people are more interested in using a product to get stuff done than to learn security trivia.

Distinguished companies like eBay and CitiBank learned this lesson the hard way in their fight against phishers. Many scam artists direct users to a fraudulent web site that appears to be legitimate because the artist is using a sophisticated technique to mask the web address. For years, the corporate victims of such attacks tried to educate their users about the intricacies of the Internet URL scheme so that they could discern the masked addresses from the real ones. This was largely a failure, and recently companies have resorted to developing and deploying software that automatically recognizes phishing sites for users, a strategy that is proving more effective. eBay, for example, rolled out its Web Caller ID toolbar and enjoyed a resulting decline in successful phishing attacks.

So, what went wrong? Users, it seems, are willing to learn only as much as they need to know to get the job done using the product—and nothing more. They are willing to learn that the odd convention of wrapping "CNN" in "www." and ".com" gets them to the CNN web site, but they don't know or care what magic makes that happen. And despite the best efforts of many different organizations to popularize the term "URL," most of our users still have no idea what that acronym means. Accordingly, we don't use it anywhere in our interface. While it would certainly make our lives easier if our users were well versed in Internet technologies, it's not their job to know such trivia, nor is it our job to lecture them about it.

The fact that most of our users are baffled by the Web's navigation presents a number of challenging usability and security concerns. For example, the "s" in "https" indicates that the given site uses SSL to encrypt its transmissions, but many users don't know that and won't ever learn it. How do we let them know when they are at a secure site without burdening them with such detail or disturbing them with a dialog? Other browsers have historically solved this problem by displaying a small lock icon in the status bar on secure pages. That solution is on the right track, but it has two problems: many users don't notice it, and those that do don't make the connection between the icon and the page. In Firefox, our solution is to remove all doubt and make it as dead simple as possible: we turn the entire address bar a bright shade of yellow at secure sites. It's impossible to miss; the connection with the page is clear because it highlights the page address; and it's obvious what it means because it's punctuated by a large lock.

Such simplicity is crucial in trying to make something as complex and varied as security a usable aspect of your product. Whenever you feel compelled to educate users about your support for 128-bit encryption or TLS 1.0, ask yourself: will users be able to use the product without this knowledge? If the answer is yes, odds are that they won't bother reading what you have to say.

That sounds blasé, but it's a very frustrating problem. There are many severe security problems in Firefox that we could fix easily if we could educate our users about certain concepts. For example, a serious problem we're currently battling is spoofing on the user interface level: sites spawn a new browser window that replicates the entire browser interface, with a fake address bar that displays a legitimate web address like "http://www.ebay.com/". The window loads a spoofed eBay page in a frame, so for all intents and purposes, it looks exactly as if the user were at the real eBay site. This is all possible due to a common browser feature that allows sites to hide the standard browser UI from windows they open (which is useful for web applications that want to provide their own interface). Our original solution was to disallow sites from hiding the address bar so that even if they replicated the entire interface with a fake address bar, our real address bar (with the real address) would show as well. But although this was foolproof deterrence, it proved completely useless, because users perceived the duplicate address bar as a Firefox glitch and still believed they were at the correct site. In response, one Mozilla developer came up with another foolproof idea that was brilliant: on each launch of Firefox, paint the Firefox interface with a nonintrusive, randomly generated pattern. Because sites wouldn't be able to replicate this pattern, users would know when they were viewing spoofed UI. Again, though this approach would make any developer drool with delight, this is just not a concept that most of our users would grasp, and so it fails to be a viable solution. In a sense, our security battles are not just against malicious hackers, but against our own users. Both have proven stubborn foes.

## Conclusion

Our decisions in Firefox—security and otherwise—are guided entirely by one core, humbling belief shared by all members of the team: software is just a means to an end. Don't overwhelm your users with talk of ciphers and encryption and other jabberwocky. Empathize with them, and force yourself to make the tough decisions so that they don't have to. Be human, not corporate, and respond to security fire drills with tenacity and alacrity. Do all of these things, and usability will follow.

## About the Author

Blake Ross is an undergraduate student at Stanford University. After working at Netscape for several years, he helped create Firefox (then called Phoenix) in fall 2002. He is also working with Dan Boneh and others in the Stanford cryptography group to develop new tools to protect people against phishing attacks.

*http://www.blakeross.com/*

# CHAPTER TWENTY-NINE

# Users and Trust: A Microsoft Case Study

**CHRIS NODDER**

**B**ACK IN THE GOOD OLD DAYS, if you lived in a small town, you wouldn't think twice about leaving your house unlocked while you ran errands, about letting kids play in the streets, or about sharing details of your family's life with other people in the town.

However, as the small town grew, and more new people started to arrive, you might have started to hear about unusual things happening: property disappearing, park benches getting vandalized, strange behavior from the new neighbors.

Over time, you'd learn that maybe it was safer to lock your door, to ask your kids where they would be going, not to lend out your lawnmower. Normally, you would learn this through newspaper articles or stories that friends told you. Sometimes, if you were unlucky, you'd learn through personal experience of having something bad happen to you—something that would never have happened in the good old days.

The Internet has paralleled this move from small town to larger city life. With the advent of the first HTML browsers, the Internet became the World Wide Web, and many new neighbors moved in to what had previously been a relatively trusting small town. The new neighbors brought with them confidence tricks, unwanted mail, viruses, and lots of candy that it really wasn't safe to take.

The major difference between real-life small towns and the Internet is the compressed time scale of the Internet's growth. That growth rate, along with the relative anonymity afforded by the Internet and the extreme ease of creating a presence on the Web, has meant that many regular users of the Internet have not had enough time to build or adjust their perceptions of trust to deal well with the online environment.

Instead, the responsibility for helping users decide whom to trust online has fallen to the infrastructure providers: manufacturers of browsers and email programs, antivirus applications, and spyware scanners.

In the early days of the World Wide Web, fewer people were attempting to exploit the gaps in technological or social trust online. As the technologies matured and the user base grew, such exploits became more lucrative.

To counter this rise in the number of exploits, the infrastructure providers have incorporated technologies and user interface elements aimed at shaping users' behaviors, teaching them whom they can trust, and, where necessary, giving them the cues they need to make trust decisions. However, the code that infrastructure providers produce is much better at dealing with problems that have a logical right and wrong outcome (virus/no virus) than problems that have shades of emotional response, such as social engineering attacks.

Obviously, Microsoft is one of those technology providers. This chapter describes how research into users' trust mechanisms led to changes in user interface design philosophy for Internet Explorer and several other products at Microsoft. The changes represent a first step in respecting the emotional aspect of trust decisions, and in giving users the information they need to make good trust decisions within Microsoft applications.

## Users and Trust

As part of continual usability research, usability engineers at Microsoft had observed hundreds of users answering questions posed by the computer (consent dialogs) in Internet Explorer, Windows Client and Server, Microsoft applications, and other companies' products. It was clear that users often weren't following the recommendations that the products made. The question was: why not?

Having seen this behavior over multiple usability sessions, we ran some specific studies to gain more insight. We conducted in-depth interviews about trust with 7 participants, and lab-based research with 14 more. We then used the results of this work to develop user interface prototypes that incorporated design elements suggested by the initial research, and observed a further 50 participants working with various iterations of the designs in different trust scenarios. Later, we had the chance to verify the concepts and designs with participants who were helping us evaluate the interface for Windows XP Service Pack 2 both in multiple lab sessions and through feedback and instrumentation from a very large user panel.

We found that it was not just that users didn't understand the questions being posed by the computer, although that was definitely part of it. It was also that the computer was not their only source of trust information. It turns out that users aggregate many "clues" about trustworthiness and then trade those off against how much they want the item in question. Interestingly, computers weren't presenting all of the clues that they could have to help users, and some of the clues they were presenting were so obscure that they just confused users.

---

## WHAT IS USER RESEARCH AT MICROSOFT?

A User Researcher's role is, specifically, to bring data to the table about how people interact with PCs, what they want to do but can't do, and what's coming around the corner technologically that they'll need to do but don't even have a clue about. Then, the researcher works closely with designers, user assistance creators, and the feature program managers to ensure that we build the right features to meet user scenarios, that those features work the way users expect, and that all the other myriad design considerations are taken into account.

User Research at Microsoft draws on multiple data sources to build a picture of user behavior and user needs. Along with traditional lab-based studies of everything from paper prototypes to finished code, we also conduct site visits to watch users in their own environments, perform in-depth interviews on specific topics, and administer large-scale international surveys. In addition, we rely on community feedback and our panel of instrumented users. This user panel is composed of regular people who have opted to run special software that provides us with data on their computer settings and their behavior. Interpolating from all of these areas as well as market research and published academic studies helps us to understand what drives users.

Lab work (usability "testing") is actually quite a small part of what User Researchers do. While we're in the lab, though, along with measuring users' success on tasks, we also measure things like desirability, learnability, and comprehension. Having the controlled environment of the usability lab allows us to isolate specific issues more easily. We iterate the design and test again with more users until we get the user experience to a point where participants can be successful and satisfied with the task.

The data serves other purposes too. Knowing what proportion of users are likely to perform a certain task—say, one that keeps them more secure—is very useful in meetings where other team members are inclined to make wild guesses based on their own experiences. The realities can be very sobering. Being able to show how that proportion grows after injection of some user-centered design into the task is a major encouragement for teams to think and design in a user-centered way.

---

## Users' Reactions to Trust Questions

Trust questions appear at many points in computer interfaces. Typically, they are shown as dialogs when the computer requires input or consent from the user before proceeding—for example, before downloading a file or before performing an action that could lead to data loss.

These trust question dialogs are often designed to serve a useful dual purpose of both informing users and requesting input. During usability research at Microsoft, we found that these dialogs regularly failed on both counts from users' perspectives. Some observations we made about the information and questions in trust dialogs were:

*Often, the question being presented is a dilemma rather than a decision*
> In such cases, the user feels that he has no way of choosing between the options being presented. Without suitable assistance, the user will be forced into making a choice that may or may not be the right one for him. Superstitious behavior builds up this way.

*Computers can't help interpret emotional clues because they behave in a purely logical way*
> This means that computer software has to defer decisions to users even if the outcomes of those decisions look logically "bad."

*Users don't want to deal with the trust issues presented to them*
> The larger the scope of the decision, and the less context that is given, the more likely they are not to consent to the action being presented to them.

*Users don't want to reveal personal data*
> The closer the question being asked is to revealing personal data, the less likely users will be to comply.

So, users do not respond to dialogs the way we might anticipate. This is because they are often forced to make a decision that is at odds with their understanding of the situation, and the information being provided is both incomplete and only partially intelligible to them.

## Users' Behavior in Trust Situations

The research I performed also showed that users have some interesting things going on in their heads during their interactions with trust situations on their computers:

*What users say they'll do and what they actually do often differ*
> For example, while users may claim to run virus-checking software, and be careful to whom they give personal data, in reality they are more lax than they describe.

*Users don't necessarily want to think about the consequences of their behavior*
> They may "forget" that they've changed a setting or allowed a certain application to access their data, and thus be confused when they suffer consequences such as a broken user experience or unexpected email.

*Users make one-off decisions about trust*
Trying to get them to make a global decision to "always do X" will upset them and potentially lead to their declining that global decision where, in fact, they would want to accept in some specific instances.

*Users conceive of security and privacy issues differently than developers do*
Users don't have the background understanding of issues, are surrounded by myths and hoaxes, and have a different relationship with "junk" mail than application developers do.

*Users have many superstitions about how viruses are propagated*
They confuse hacking and viruses. They also interchange terms for software bugs and viruses. They often fall prey to virus hoaxes in an attempt to protect themselves, while simultaneously engaging in risky behavior likely to lead to virus transmission.

Users do not tend to consider events requiring trust decisions in the same way that technologists do. This is because their focus is not on the technology, but *on the outcome of the trust event and its impact on their lives.*

## Security Versus Convenience

The worst dilemma for users, and the one that is also the hardest to resolve through user experience design, is that from a user perspective, increases in security are most frequently accompanied by a reduction in convenience. Likewise, when users try to accomplish a task in a convenient way, they often encounter security warnings.

For instance, choosing to set the browser security level to High in Internet Explorer or other browser products will turn off many of the features of the product that can be used to exploit users. However, this same action can degrade the browsing experience to a point where most users will be dissatisfied, as they will no longer have access to the plug-in components and scripting functions that they have come to expect on a web site. It is this dilemma that user experience designers must seek to resolve for users, presenting them instead with understandable options that allow them to perform their tasks with a minimum of inconvenience.

## Making Decisions Versus Supporting Decisions

It is important to note that the emphasis here is not on allowing the computer to make trust decisions, but on how a computer can assist users with their trust decisions. Of course, there are some instances where the computer can make that decision—for instance, when it detects the presence of a known virus in something the user plans to download. Here, the decision is easy—protect the user from the virus. Computers can be programmed to make this kind of decision. Most of the time, however, the decision is less clear cut, and so it still rests with the user. The challenge is to achieve the correct balance between exhausting the user with multiple questions and automating the process to the point where the computer runs the risk of making erroneous decisions.

Having observed that users have a tendency to simply dismiss any dialog that gets in their way, the tendency among interface designers is often to try to remove the dialog. If the dialog can be completely removed (if the computer can make the decision), that's great. If, however, the dialog still needs to exist, our studies have shown that users make a much more secure, appropriate, reasoned decision if the dialog is presented in the context of their task.

Placing the decision in an initial options screen or hiding it in a settings dialog removed in space and time from the point where users carry out their task requires them to think in a logical rather than an emotional way about a class of task rather than about a specific instance.

As noted earlier, users found it easier to make a specific decision rather than a generic decision. It was much easier for them to agree to trust a specific person at a specific time for a specific transaction than to agree to trust a whole category of people every time a transaction occurred.

Users could easily make a decision without too much interruption to their task if the dialog presented the facts they needed in a way they could understand. We classified this as *presenting a decision, not a dilemma.*

For common or repetitive tasks, obviously the fewer interruptions a user experiences, the better. In these situations, it makes sense to give the user an option to always apply his current decision to the situation. If you can scope the situation suitably, the user will be happy to have that decision applied consistently.

For less common tasks, it's not necessarily the number of screens between a user and his goal that determines the quality of the interaction. Instead, a major factor is whether all of those screens are perceived by the user to be flowing toward his end goal.

After eliciting from users some of the clues they use, and understanding the philosophies that they bring to their trust interactions, we worked out which clues can be provided by a computer, and then worked out how and when to present them in the trust process such that they aided in the decision. The tone of the interaction was dictated to a large degree by a wish to stay within users' comfort zones while simultaneously educating them.

## Consent Dialogs

The name of this much maligned interface element suggests something that isn't always apparent in the design—dialog boxes are supposed to be a conversation ("dialog") between the computer and the user. The consent dialog has a specific conversation topic: "Do you want this thing to happen?" Frequently, consent dialogs ask trust questions. If the question is well phrased, users should have little difficulty making a decision, completing the dialog, and continuing on their way. However, well-phrased dialogs seem to be difficult to design.

After observing many users working with dialogs in the lab, I would suggest the hierarchy of decision points shown in Figure 29-1 that users follow in order to continue with what they perceive as their real task—the one that the dialog box interrupted.

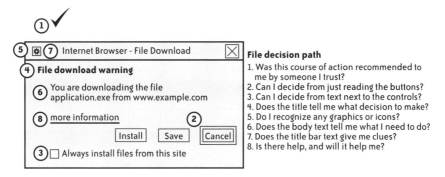

FIGURE 29-1. Decision points users make in evaluating a (hypothetical) consent dialog

Note that before users even start to evaluate the information provided in the dialog, they have already engaged their emotional feelings about the situation (1, in the figure). If these feelings are strong and positive (a friend or someone the user trusts recommended the application, for instance), then his desire to continue down this path may overrule his usual caution. In this situation, the user has made an emotional decision that is unlikely to be changed by any logical information or warning on the screen.

Users also gravitate toward the buttons and other controls (checkboxes, radio buttons) on the screen—they realize that these are the elements that will propel them toward their desired outcome, so they start by reading the text on and next to controls (2 and 3, in the figure) to see if these provide enough clues to let them continue. The wording of the buttons, and even which one is highlighted by default, are clues that users can employ in their trust decisions.

If they are unsuccessful after reading the button labels, users typically proceed to read the text on the screen. The primary statement is read first, normally because it is first on the main page area and in a larger or bold font (4, in the figure).

Dialogs with graphical elements also assist users with the trust decision—have they seen that graphic before? Is it from a company they trust? Obviously, if the only graphics are system elements such as the icon of the program that launched the dialog box, then users may gain a false sense of security (5, in the figure).

Now users are really scraping around for clues and cues to help with their trust decision. Body text in the dialog box, the title bar, and potentially help links from the dialog box are all read with increasing levels of irritation and desperation, if at all (6, 7, and 8, in the figure).

## Consent Dialog Redesign

There is very little that a computer can do to counter an emotional decision by the user. Unfortunately, this is the place where social engineering attacks (e.g., so-called "phishing" attacks) happen—before the computer interface has a chance to influence the decision.

However, there are user interface design elements that can assist users with making trust decisions if they choose to make use of the information presented by the consent dialog. Figure 29-2 shows these elements laid out in a figurative consent dialog. For an example of how these elements are used in a real consent dialog, see Figure 29-8.

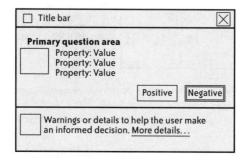

FIGURE 29-2. Figurative elements of a more informative (hypothetical) consent dialog

Considering that users tend to gravitate to the buttons on the dialog, the default button (which will be clicked if the user simply presses Enter) should always follow the path recommended by the computer. This may not necessarily be the most secure path ultimately, but instead may be the best tradeoff of security and convenience.

The button labels should also be verbose enough to allow users to make an informed decision. For instance, consider the difference in meaning between the button pair Install and Cancel and the button pair Install Anyway and Cancel. In the second instance, the button label itself contains a caution that something may require further investigation before installation. Of course, in conjunction with the button labels, the dialog text needs to make it clear what the issue is that requires investigation, and suggest a path of resolution.

The dialog should contain a summary statement or focused question placed in the primary area of the dialog box. This statement or question should provide users with an understanding of the decision they are being asked to make (what they are "consenting" to).

If further text is required, it should follow the summary statement, but what appears from testing to be more useful to users at this point is evidence that they can use to evaluate their response to the question being asked. In an ideal world, this information would probably contain recommendations from trusted sources; in reality, with today's software and certification mechanisms, the best that can be done is often to provide what information the application knows about the situation to the user in the form of clues he can use to help him arrive at a decision (the Property: Value pairs in Figure 29-2). Typically, this means items such as the filename, publisher, and download location of a file, the name of an application or user who is requesting something, or other such short strings. The computer can often also assign some degree of confidence to these clues by letting the user know whether the statement is corroborated by a certificate. Although users often have totally erroneous concepts of what certification entails or guarantees, this can be abstracted to an extent within the dialog.

For users who still do not have sufficient information to make a decision, there is space to provide additional assistance text and even a link to a help article. Note that this information is placed in a separate area at the bottom of the dialog that does not interfere with the primary dialog controls. User testing has shown that people who are seeking out this information will still find it in this location, whereas if it is placed above the action buttons, it interferes with the task for users who do not require the additional, often generic, text. This information is accompanied by an icon that rates the severity of the decision outcome—informational, warning, or danger/stop.

## Windows XP Service Pack 2—A Case Study

In August of 2003, senior executives at Microsoft made it clear that continuing with a reactive patching approach to fixing security exploits was insufficient. Instead, users needed a system that was able to deal with whole classes of exploits and to prevent infection. The technologies required to achieve this required a major rewrite of several components of the operating system, and also required us to make changes to the default behaviors in Windows.

While this last point may not sound like a big deal, this would be the first time in the history of Windows that a service pack release made significant changes to the user experience of the product. By working with the program managers for Service Pack 2, we presented evidence from user studies, surveys, instrumentation reports, and site visits to the Windows executives demonstrating that the release would not be successful without several large-scale changes to the user experience.

This data had been collected primarily from research into Passport, Hailstorm, XP Service Pack 1, and early work on Windows Codename "Longhorn"—the next version of Windows. It was fortuitous that it could be applied so directly to the problems that were addressed by XP Service Pack 2. We also worked to ensure that many of the changes could be controlled through group policy in order to satisfy corporate customers.

Some of the major attack points in Windows are found in the Internet-related features—Internet Explorer (IE), Outlook Express (OE), and the Application Execution Service (which prompts users to save or run downloaded or attached files). Various other system components, such as the Windows Firewall and Automatic Updates, are designed to help protect users but require user interaction in order to work correctly.

The user experience focus for SP2 was on making security and privacy "just work," and where that was not possible, making the security and privacy issues understandable to users so that they can make informed decisions.

To that end, we took several components of Windows and gave them a design overhaul. The following sections show before and after images with some commentary on the reasons for the changes. Most frequently, the reasons are based on the consent dialog redesign described earlier.

## ActiveX Dialogs

It was very clear from user testing that the ActiveX dialog box in Windows XP and XP Service Pack 1 (XP SP1) (see Figure 29-3) was not very successful at giving users the information they needed in order to make an informed consent decision.

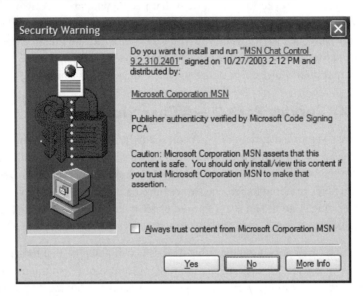

*FIGURE 29-3. Original ActiveX consent dialog*

Instead of just applying the consent dialog redesign to this interface, we considered ways of also increasing user satisfaction. This dialog box typically appears while a page is loading—often before any content has appeared on the first page of a site that a user visits. As such, it is both a frustration because it gets in the way of the user's primary task, and a dilemma because the user cannot judge the value of agreeing to the dialog box (if she even understands what it is asking).

Taking a design element from Outlook Express, where additional information about email format options and blocked content is displayed in a "bar" in the message title area, we developed an in-context but discreet notification called the Information Bar, which animates down from the Internet Explorer Toolbar.

The Information Bar (shown in Figure 29-4) provides the most condensed information possible to inform users in context that the web site they are on is requesting that they consent to a specific action. They can continue to browse the Web without responding to the Information Bar, or they can interact with the bar to enable downloads of files or ActiveX controls, or to enable blocked pop-ups.

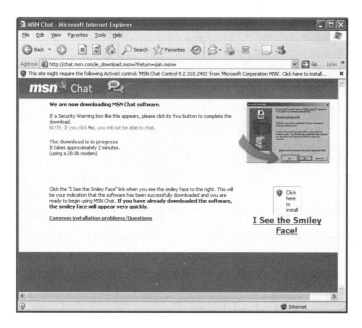

FIGURE 29-4. The Information Bar in Windows XP Service Pack 2

For ActiveX controls, clicking the Information Bar produces the redesigned consent dialog shown in Figure 29-5.

FIGURE 29-5. The updated Active X consent dialog; even if they read nothing else, users will see their options from the button labels

The consent dialog from XP SP1 had contained a checkbox option to "Always trust" the given publisher, and thus not be pestered by these consent dialogs in the future. Once ActiveX controls got co-opted for unsavory uses, we observed users wanting a checkbox for "Never trust" more frequently than for "Always trust." After trying several iterations of these designs, we ended up with the "More options" button, shown in its expanded state in Figure 29-6.

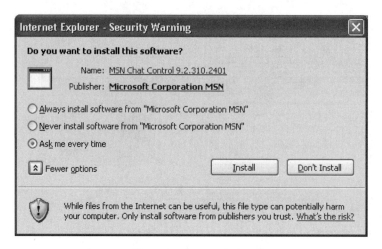

FIGURE 29-6. Expanded version of the redesigned ActiveX dialog; the options include a "never install" choice often requested by users

Note that the redesigned ActiveX consent dialog has several changes:

- *Button defaults.* Buttons have a secure default: clicking Enter chooses the Don't Install option.

- *Button labels.* Button labels change from OK and Cancel to Install and Don't Install. Users can now see the implication of clicking the button (something will be installed) without reading any other text on the dialog.

- *Primary text.* Primary text on the screen is a simple question. In the previous design, it wasn't even clear to most users that there was any question at all in the text.

- *Evidence.* "Evidence" that the computer knows to be true (via certificates) is presented to the user. Clicking on the items allows experienced users to see certificate details and the originating site. This helps prevent users from being fooled into clicking on a consent dialog that appears to be from the site they are on but that was actually produced by a pop-under advertisement (trust by association).

- *Assistance text.* Assistance text is shown in a separate area at the bottom of the screen, with a link to further assistance. This is useful if this is the first time a user has seen this dialog or if the user sees such dialogs infrequently. However, the text is out of the way if the user knows what he is doing.

## File Download Dialogs

File download dialogs are mainly triggered by user actions in Internet Explorer. However, sometimes the user can be tricked into downloading software through a variety of code or social engineering manipulations. While XP SP2 removed several of the code exploits, it was still important to ensure that users knew what they were getting themselves into with file downloads, considering that the consequences could be catastrophic if the file were actually a virus.

The file download dialog in Windows XP and XP SP1 (shown in Figure 29-7) was a relatively innocuous dialog that took an informative approach but did not really help the user.

FIGURE 29-7. Original file download dialog; users have to read the entire dialog in order to see the question

Note the relatively useless text "You are downloading the file:", which takes precedence over the real question in the dialog—"Would you like to open the file or save it to your computer?" This question is also misleading. In the case of a Word document download, you truly are "opening" the file. However, in the case of an executable program file, from a user perspective you are not so much opening the file as running it.

Note also how the More Info button has as much precedence on the dialog as the much more important decision buttons.

Applying some of the trust concepts described earlier, we arrive at the dialog shown in Figure 29-8.

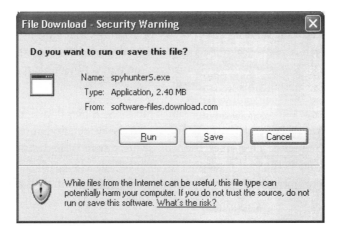

FIGURE 29-8. Redesigned file download dialog; the question is immediately apparent, and the additional information that users need for a trust decision is readily available

Note the purposeful similarities with the ActiveX control redesign:

*Button defaults*

Buttons have a secure default; clicking Enter chooses the Cancel option.

*Button labels*

Button labels are more accurate descriptions of the accompanying actions. In the previous version, users were invited to "open" an executable file in the same way that they might "open" a text file. Changing the terminology for executable files is one extra clue to users about the nature of the downloaded file.

*Primary text*

Primary text on the screen is a simple question. Also, making the question into the primary text reduced its length, as there was no need to refer back to the previous statement in the dialog.

*Evidence*

"Evidence" that the computer can ascertain is presented to the user. The user can see the originating site, check that the filename matches his expectations, and also check that the size of the file seems appropriate for the type of application he expected.

*Assistance text*

Assistance text is shown in a separate area at the bottom of the screen, with a link to further assistance. This link replaces the large and distracting More Info button.

Another problem with file downloads in previous Windows versions was that once the file was saved to the computer, it lost any identifying marks. Thus, a user could choose to download a file from the Internet, mindful of the risks, but then later open it on his machine without realizing its potentially dangerous history.

The Application Execution Service (AES) is a part of Windows that most users never have to think about. Its job is to check that files are pretty much what they say they are, and then run them. In XP SP2, this little workhorse got some new functionality, and the issue then became how to message this functionality to users.

The basic premise was that with the changes made in XP SP2, files that were downloaded from the Internet would be tagged as such, and would always retain that reduced level of "trustedness" until a user decided otherwise. This reduced trust carried with it a requirement that users explicitly consent to running the application. As such, the interface for the new Application Execution Service functionality became the consent dialog shown in Figure 29-9.

Again, this dialog has purposeful similarities with the File Download control redesign:

- *Button defaults.* Buttons have a secure default; clicking Enter chooses the Cancel option.

- *Primary text.* Primary text on the screen is a simple question. While it may seem to be an overly obvious question (after all, the user just double-clicked on an icon), often executable files masquerade as documents for just this reason. In these situations, the AES recognizes the subterfuge and presents the consent dialog, thus alerting the user to the true nature of the file.

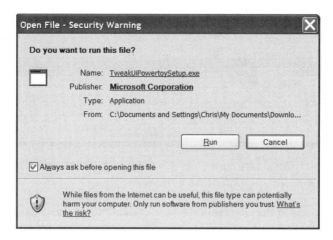

*FIGURE 29-9. The Application Execution Service consent dialog; this dialog takes over from the file download dialog if users choose to save rather than run a downloaded file*

- *Evidence.* "Evidence" that the computer can ascertain is presented to the user. The user can see the software publisher and check that the filename matches his expectations.

- *Checkbox.* There is a "don't show me this again" checkbox on the dialog, but it is purposefully phrased as a positive statement.

- *Assistance text.* Assistance text is shown in a separate link at the bottom of the screen, with a link to further assistance. This dialog is new, and most users will see it infrequently, so the assistance text is available but not in the way of the primary decision.

## Pop-Up Blocking

Pop-up blocking was new to Windows XP Service Pack 2. Pop-ups are windows that are generated by a web page to show additional content. A legitimate use for pop-ups may be to provide a glossary term, assistance, or a product photo when users click a link on a web page. This would allow the user to stay on the same page, but gain additional information that was not deemed important enough to have screen real estate devoted to it.

Unfortunately, the legitimate uses of pop-ups are outweighed many times by the more frustrating or downright dangerous uses. Typically, pop-up technology has been used to display advertisements to users in separate windows, to open (or "spawn") additional windows when the user navigates away from a site in order to trap them on the site, or to cover parts of a dialog box so that it appears to users that they have fewer choices—for example, to hide a part of the ActiveX consent dialog (Figure 29-3) so that only the Yes button appears rather than the No and "More info" buttons.

The issue is that there are times when the pop-up may be seen as legitimate by users, so it is important that users be aware when pop-ups have been blocked, and also have the opportunity to view the pop-up if they think that it is one they invoked. The Information Bar, discussed already in the "ActiveX Dialogs" section, provides a useful mechanism both for notifying users that a pop-up has been blocked and for giving them access to that pop-up should they choose to see it, as shown in Figure 29-10.

*FIGURE 29-10. Information Bar showing a blocked pop-up; the bar animates down from the top of the page area, accompanied by a sound similar to tapping on a glass monitor screen*

This notification occurs in the context of the user's task, but in a way that does not prevent him from continuing with his current task. In user testing, this implementation provided the best tradeoff between the ability for users to ignore unwanted pop-ups and to act on ones they wanted to see. It builds on and reinforces the use of the Information Bar for ActiveX control consent. Judging from users' positive remarks during testing and after release, this feature seems to have struck the right balance between security and convenience.

## The Ideal

The redesigned consent dialogs presented in this chapter all follow the consent dialog redesign format that we based on user research into trust issues. During the process of creating this format, we came across infrastructure and technical constraints that prevented us from taking the design as far as we would have liked in the timeframe we had.

Certificate Authorities such as VeriSign allow Internet browsers to have a level of confidence that statements made by software publishers are true. However, only a few pieces of information are currently certified, such as publisher name and issuer name. With changes in the Certificate Authority model, it should be possible to also have certified graphics (for the icon area in the dialog redesign earlier), certified membership of communities such as TRUSTe, and even a certified audit of the software with accompanying statements about privacy, security, and reliability. Having a certified audit would bring the concept of certification much closer to users' ideals than today's reality.

Users typically see recommendations from a friend as trustable. This is true even when it is a tenuous recommendation (the friend sends a link to a site that wants to download something). Users also often have trusted friends whom they will ask whether something is safe to download. It is not difficult to imagine mechanisms that allow this type of interaction to occur from within the consent dialog using synchronous communication channels such as Instant Messaging.

Taking this one stage further, consider expert or community ratings. It is highly likely that many other people will already have downloaded a specific piece of software or will have consented to a certain action. Their comments on this software form a trust rating. Certain users may subscribe to a particular guru's ratings; others may subscribe to Slashdot, CNET, or even Good Housekeeping's ratings. These ratings could appear as part of the consent dialog process to assist users with their decision. An early version of this process has already been implemented in SpyNet, the part of the (post-XP SP2) Windows antispyware application that analyzes user recommendations in order to make determinations as to what is and is not spyware.

## Conclusion

Throughout this chapter, I have focused on design solutions for the user behavior that I have observed with multiple participants in usability studies of many products. I have shown examples of those design concepts being turned into practical dialogs within Internet Explorer. The following recommendations can—and should—be applied to any trust interaction on computers:

*Let users make trust decisions in context*
> Decisions made at the time the issue arises contain the scope users need, which would be missing in a disjointed experience such as a setup dialog. Users who are forced to make isolated decisions are often overly cautious, which can later hurt their experience with the application and lead to suboptimal user experiences.

*Make the most trusted option the default selection*
> Users are not well placed to make trust decisions. They seldom have all the details. As long as they trust your application, they will frequently select the defaults.

*Present users with choices, not dilemmas*
> Ensure that the user is able to understand the consequences of choosing a certain option, and that wherever possible there is a trusted way for him to complete his task.

*Always respect the user's decision*
> Once you have alerted the user to the consequences, the rest is up to him. Your application cannot know the emotional context of a trust decision, only the potential worst-case logical outcome. Users often place more weight on the emotional context.

This last point deserves further emphasis, as it is the cornerstone of a successful trust user experience design. Usable and useful trusted software has to accommodate the emotional and social aspects of users' experience. It must allow them instant gratification, help them to fill in the rest of the picture, and gracefully submit when a user chooses a different path for reasons the computer will never understand.

## About the Author

Chris Nodder is a user experience specialist with Nielsen Norman Group. Before joining NN/g, Chris worked as a senior user researcher at Microsoft Corporation. During his seven years at Microsoft, Chris worked on products as diverse as videoconferencing, programming tools for web developers, home networking, online communities, and delivering Internet content over cell phones. In 2004, he was responsible for the user experience for XP Service Pack 2, a major upgrade to Windows XP. He has created personas, reality TV episodes, and even whole rooms ("usertoriums") as ways of getting developers to walk in their customers' shoes.

# CHAPTER THIRTY

# IBM Lotus Notes/Domino: Embedding Security in Collaborative Applications

**MARY ELLEN ZURKO**

**T**HERE ARE A MULTITUDE OF APPROACHES TO MAKING SECURITY USABLE AND USEFUL. Some approaches concentrate on the usability of the security information, mechanisms, and displays themselves. Some approaches concentrate on making as much security as possible disappear into the context of more task-directed functions, from the point of view of as many (types of) users as possible. Under the best circumstances, security and usability, along with performance, are considered and integrated in initial architectural and design discussions. As products evolve and mature, new challenges in these areas arise, and the solutions need to work well with existing, deployed code and data. The breadth of risks, threats, and features often generates a range of solutions that are more or less integrated, depending on context, process, and history.

## Usable Secure Collaboration

Collaborative applications offer a particularly rich environment to explore approaches to usable security, as can be seen in several of the vendor chapters in this book. Because they are user-to-user applications, collaborative applications have high profiles and aggressive usability goals. Collaborating on potentially sensitive topics requires both open sharing and tight control, depending on the users, the tasks, and the information being manipulated. Both administrators and end users are involved directly and indirectly in using collaborative application security features. In fact, end users sometimes act as administrators for groupings of collaborative objects, increasing the power and complexity of the functions they are expected to take on.

This chapter discusses several specific security features that have been embedded in the collaborative application infrastructure of IBM® Lotus® Notes® and IBM Lotus Domino® (see the sidebar). The goal of embedding security in this collaborative platform is to make it a seamless and integral part of tasks that are meaningful to users. The features we discuss illustrate both successes and current shortcomings to both this approach and our execution of it. The features covered here include public key infrastructure (PKI), security-specific information displays, and security controls on active content.

The Lotus Domino public key infrastructure is perhaps the most widely deployed PKI in the world, with more than 114 million licenses. It is embedded in the Notes end user and administrative architectures; many features cannot be used without it. It is used for authentication of the Notes client to the Domino server, signing and encrypting mail messages, and administrative accountability and trust. In the next section, we discuss how many confusing key management and related concepts are completely hidden from users through the use of application-specific features and enterprise-use norms. Users do need both the Notes rich client and their own keyfile to take advantage of many of these features, although recent architectural updates are making mail encryption and signing available from the Domino browser user interface.

There are two major areas of security-related information for end users: security information about themselves and security information about an application database. User security information was brought together in a single security panel in a recent release of Notes. The Access Control dialog displays the control information for a database that holds a single instance of a Notes application. Later in this chapter, we discuss the usability process for, and features of, these dialogs, and the benefits we are seeing from them.

Protections on active content were introduced into version 4.5 of Notes. We were able to observe both the usability of the controls and how easily they can be used to ensure secure behavior on the part of users in a study of a 500-person organization. The study showed that when you tell people to click a button to get a more secure configuration, most will do so. The same study showed that when the same user population is asked if they would like to subvert that security to proceed with their current task, most will do so. Later, we discuss the implications of pushing security-relevant decisions down to the user.

## Embedding and Simplifying Public Key Security

The Lotus Domino PKI is not a free-standing product: it is integral to the Lotus Notes end-user and administrative experience. Every new user of the Notes desktop client is given, by his administrator, a public/private key pair in a keyfile called his *ID file*.[1] The user types in his password to decrypt and make use of the ID file. The Lotus Notes client uses a private key to authenticate to the Domino server, providing two-factor authentication (the

---

1  Notes 6 provides a feature that allows the user to generate his own public/private keypair.

# IBM LOTUS NOTES AND DOMINO

The IBM Lotus Notes and Domino architecture supports a suite of products that provide a client/server infrastructure for collaboration applications, as well as specific support for electronic messaging and calendaring and scheduling. Lotus Notes is a rich desktop client to the Domino server. It communicates with the Domino server through a proprietary, public key cryptographic protocol called Notes Remote Procedure Call (NRPC). Notes client security features are generally accessed through the user security panel (Figure 30-1). A user's password (Figure 30-2) decrypts the file that contains her public/private keys.

The Lotus Domino server provides the foundation for custom collaboration applications, messaging, and web applications. Full enterprise deployment of this server can take advantage of administrative features such as clustering, partitioning, and automatic failover, for performance and scalability. A separate rich client, the Administrative client, provides the server administration features in a user interface experience tuned to the administrator's tasks and skills..

Each Domino application is associated with a design template that is instantiated in a Domino database. Access control lists are set and managed at the database level (see Figures 30-3 and 30-4). Domino Designer is application development software that provides the features that make up a Domino application, including forms, views, pages, framesets, integrated instant messaging, XML, Java, JavaScript, and LotusScript. These Domino applications can be accessed via either Notes or a web browser. Multiple instances of the same application are supported via multiple disjoint databases associated with that application design. This allows a site to use the same team room design for different groups and topics, for example. The Notes client supports full-featured offline functionality with Domino applications through local copies of the Domino application databases. Both Notes and Domino run on a variety of hardware platforms and operating systems. A full overview of Notes/Domino security features as of version 5 is available.[a] A timeline of all Notes/Domino security features from the first release in 1989 through the 2001 releases also lists some of the security features that were put into version 6.[b] From the scope of the features, the reader can see that in this chapter we touch on the usability aspects of only a few of them. Resource and schedule constraints generally concentrate explicit usability attention on the highest priority or most widely used security features of each release.

---

[a] Susan Bryant and Christie Williams (with Katherine Spanbauer), "Overview of Notes/Domino Security," Iris Today Archives [cited Oct. 2004]; *http://www-10.lotus.com/ldd/today.nsf/lookup/security_overview.*
[b] Katherine Spanbauer, "Milestones in Notes/Domion Security," Iris Today Archives [cited Nov. 2004]; *http://www-10.lotus.com/ldd/today.nsf/Lookup/security_milestones.*

password the user knows, and the private key the user has stored in his keyfile).[2] By and large, the user is unaware of this use of public key cryptography. He knows only that he needs access to a copy of his ID file to use Notes.

## Signing and Decrypting Email

The same private key used in authentication can be used to sign and decrypt mail. A single email is explicitly signed or encrypted via a checkbox in the set of optionally manipulated delivery options of a mail message. Those features can also be enabled by default for all mail messages in user preference information.

Checking signatures on email from people in your organization is quite seamless. Notes has a native, proprietary format for signing and encrypting, because the feature was originally developed before S/MIME and X.509 certificate standards had the widespread use they have today. Notes supports those standards now as well, but the usability and integration of the earlier formats is superior, because it exploits other native features of Notes/Domino, such as the organization and syntax of enterprise names and usernames in the directory.

Notes Certificate Authorities are arranged in a naming hierarchy that parallels the enterprise organization naming hierarchy. Each user receives in his ID file a public key certificate for his private key and the certificate of every authority in his hierarchy. Any signature from another user who shares a common hierarchical authority with the recipient is automatically checked when the message is read. The name of the signer, the time of the signature, and the name of the shared authority is displayed in a message bar at the bottom of the window. For example, the Notes name of Mary Ellen Zurko/Westford/IBM will have certificates for that name, /Westford/IBM, and /IBM in its ID file. That username can automatically validate signatures from anyone under the /IBM authority. Hierarchical names constrain the format of names, but simplify the explicitly available trust relationships. Within an enterprise, users never have to be asked confusing questions about trust and authorities. Hierarchical names also provide excellent security properties, limiting the amount of damage a misbehaving or compromised Certificate Authority can do.[3]

## Encrypting Email

Encrypting mail messages is more challenging, even within the circumscribed limits of an enterprise, because it requires access to information not always available locally on the client (trustworthy public key information for the recipient). When the user is on the network, and sending email to a colleague with a record in the directory configured as his

---

2   The keyfile is stored on each user's local computer, making it inaccessible to attackers who have not penetrated the local computer. However, the keyfile is protected by the password and may potentially be compromised without a user's knowledge. In addition, copies of the keyfile may be stored elsewhere. Thus, Lotus Domino may be considered to have one and one-half factor authentication.

3   Virgil D. Gligor, Shyh-Wei Luan, and Joseph N. Pato, "On Inter-Realm Authentication in Large Distributed Systems," *IEEE Computer Society Symposium on Research in Security and Privacy* (1992), 2–17.

directory server, encryption is as easy as signing. The directory server automatically finds the recipient's name and public key information. However, an enterprise may have many Domino directories; all need to be configured to be available to the sender's directory server. Sending encrypted mail offline has another set of issues that are addressed in the product, but can require preconfiguration or other extra interactions with the user.

While excellent integration within an enterprise or organization hides many confusing key management concepts, using encryption or signature checking across those boundaries exposes them, leading to many of the known difficulties with PKI. Users receiving signed email from beyond their enterprise hierarchy are asked if they trust the root authority of the sender, with a display of that authority's fingerprint (a sequence of letters and numbers encapsulating the public key). In theory, the user is supposed to verify the fingerprint's association with a trustworthy entity associated with the presumed organization of that authority. In practice, users are more likely to be confused or simply click OK to start trusting that certificate. Encrypting for a recipient in another organization is even more complex, involving acquiring the certificate from the potential recipient and placing it into a personal directory. Lotus Notes provides features that allow the user to do that so that he does not have to rely on administrative intervention. However, explicit use of such features takes some sophistication on the part of the user.

From the point of view of promoting both the active use and the understanding of security concepts, signing and encrypting are perhaps too embedded in Notes, as their integration has made them invisible in the most common use cases. Many Internet browser users feel a sense of security when they see the padlock icon indicating that the Secure Sockets Layer (SSL) is in use. The same users are unaware that an electronic pay stub delivered by Notes is encrypted and signed.

Although users might get an enhanced feeling of trust if they see a similar icon on signed or encrypted mail messages, display of this information needs to be traded off with the many other informative messages and icons displayed in Notes email (including message priority, whether an attachment is included, and whether the message is a calendar invitation). How to balance ease of use and simplicity with user awareness and trust is an ongoing design issue.

One of the major places where the public key infrastructure still intrudes is the need for the ID file to be present for Notes authentication, decryption, and signing. This has posed a challenge for kiosk use, where a desktop with the Notes client might be used by many employees of a single enterprise. It is an even bigger issue for browser-based access to Domino applications, including mail. The emphasis on local information that makes signing, signature checking, and decrypting both easy and extremely secure in the rich Notes client makes the same operations a challenge, and potentially less secure, in a browser-based environment.

Lotus Domino can operate in a browser environment using special server-side processes for signing and encrypting email. To use these processes, however, the user must be willing to place his ID files on the server, allow the files to be decrypted, and allow the processes to access the user's private keys.

The Lotus Notes PKI has provided excellent security and usability for six versions and 15 years. The benefits have been most noticeable in an enterprise setting that can take advantage of both the proprietary features and the organization's structure. This has enabled many simplifications not available to fully flexible, free-standing PKIs.

## Designing Security Displays

Information about security attributes can, in theory, occur almost anywhere in a user interface. This placement makes good sense from a task perspective. For example, users can find all their email configuration options in one place, from delegating access to their mail to changing the text placed automatically at the bottom of each mail message. Sometimes, though, users are looking for a security feature and are not sure what task or context it might be associated with. Or they are trying to get a better sense of the overall security picture of the application to form a useful mental model. This latter task is more likely to arise for evaluators, reviewers, and administrators, people who provide guidance to larger populations, than for individual end users.

In this section, we discuss the usability of two displays that provide useful centralized security information in Lotus Notes.

### User Security Panel

User-related security information was brought together in a single security panel in Notes 6, as shown in Figure 30-1. The motivation behind consolidating that information in one place is to make it easier to find. For example, information in only one of the resulting tabs, the Mail Security tab, was gathered from five different places in the previous product version. Consolidation can also make it easier to understand, and can help users learn about security features that they might not have noticed otherwise. The Lotus Notes User Security panel was explicitly designed with an eye toward making difficult security concepts easier to understand and use. In addition, access to security-sensitive information is protected with a password prompt (to ensure that it is not viewed or manipulated by anyone other than the user). Interleaving sensitive security and other types of information meant that a user had to type his password unnecessarily in some circumstances. Therefore, localizing that information made the usability of other paths better. An informative and entertaining article also accompanied the change,[4] using humor to highlight the

---

4   Jane Marcus and Cara Haagenson, "Bonding with User Security in Notes 6,"
    Lotus Software [cited Oct. 2004]; *http://www-10.lotus.com/ldd/today.nsf/0/*
    *232e604b847d2cad88256ab90074e298?OpenDocument.*

potential utility of the security information. Informal feedback from users and customers to both the panel and the article has been enthusiastic.

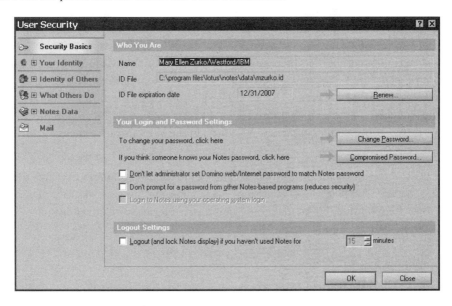

FIGURE 30-1. User Security panel

The initial design of the User Security panel was performed by a security engineer. This allowed someone knowledgeable about the content of the panel to provide initial organization and explanations. The dialogs were designed to explain topics and information directly to the user. Each was structured to highlight basic information or useful task-specific security procedures.

After the initial panel design by a security engineer, design walkthroughs were held with a usability expert. These walkthroughs found and corrected many visual design problems that impeded usability. They applied color and whitespace to make data items and the relationships between them more understandable. Visual design discussions included whether tabular information should be organized by concept (such as infrastructure and specific applications) or by the likelihood of being used. A mixed model of a single first tab for the most-used items, followed by a conceptual grouping for all of the other tabs, was adopted.

The walkthroughs also clarified basic security concepts useful to many users, because they were understood by the usability expert who could offer specific informed suggestions for improvement around them. Making terminology more understandable generated some robust discussions. Security features targeted at technology, not user artifacts, are often the most difficult to explain. For example, Lotus Domino supports several protocols, and therefore several methods of authentication. Notes authentication, as described earlier, uses a password to unlock a private key; subsequently, public key cryptography authenticates the Notes user to the Domino server. Browser access to the Domino server uses web-standard, password-based mechanisms with password checking against a hashed version stored in the directory. These two passwords can easily be unsynchronized, leaving the user with two different Domino passwords: one for Notes RPC and one for other protocols. Usability experts found the term *Internet password*, used by Notes developers to refer to one of the passwords, to be precise but not informative to users. They recommended *web password*, which they believed would be meaningful to the user, and descriptive. Administrative developers pointed out that the password is used for all supported Internet protocols: HTTP, IMAP, POP, and LDAP, making *web password* imprecise and therefore inaccurate. The resolution of the debate was to choose different terminology for the different types of users: the end user and the administrator. *Domino web/Internet password* is used in the Notes client for the end user, and *Internet password* is used in the administrative client for the administrator.

This small example shows the difficulty in balancing the needs of different user constituencies against the need for product consistency. The choice in this case was to tune terminology to each user group, but to make sure that the two terms were linked in some obvious fashion.

### Displaying public key certificates

Even with detailed explanations from security experts, usability experts found it difficult to understand the more advanced security concepts. This made it difficult to apply usability knowledge to the domain. Display of public key certificates and tasks that use them continues to be a challenge when their use cannot be hidden.

One open design question on the "Your Certificates:" display in the Your Identity tab was just how much information about a certificate users need to see, and under what circumstances they would need to see it. Most users do not even know they have certificates (and that is a good thing). The decision was made to include help text directly on the dialog displaying all the certificates of a certain type (such as Notes, Internet, certification authority, and so on), explaining the type and what it is used for. This design approach is similar to some of the safe staging work in Lime.[5] The display of any specific certificate also contains most basic information that each type has in common: who it is issued to and by, when it was issued and when it expires, its type, and its identifier. All other information about a certificate in the general display panel was deemed intended for security experts only, and hidden behind an Advanced button.

In another example, in the context of configuring an Internet certificate for use, the Internet-style mail security options were hidden under a button to simplify the dialog. The motivating use cases for viewing this information would be error paths, not common tasks. We had little information about what information was most commonly needed in error cases.

---

5   Alma Whitten, "Making Security Usable." Ph.D. dissertation, Carnegie Melon University, 2004, CMU-CS-04-135. See also Chapter 34, this volume.

One error case that is well thought through in the Notes security user interface is mistyping a password. Notes has a feature that attempts to help you catch password mistypes before you hit Return. The Notes password prompt dialog (shown in Figure 30-2) displays a changing picture of a keyring and keys on the lefthand side. Starting with the fifth character typed, the picture changes to one of a set of keyring pictures, determined by a hash of the current string of characters that have been typed. Mistyping a password will show an unexpected sequence of keyrings (and most likely a different final one). If the user does mistype his password and clicks OK, he is reminded of the most common error case—that passwords are case sensitive.

FIGURE 30-2. Password dialog

### Limitations and results

The scope of the User Security panel design was to overlay a user interface on existing features. Bringing diverse security information together can highlight issues and opportunities in the existing security model, providing just the first step for enhanced usability of security. For example, the User Security panel displays all types of names that can be used to refer to the user. Some names are used for security (access control lists), and some names are used for sending email (either within a Domino domain or through the Internet). Further work could make the naming model more consistent, allowing either type of name in both functions, at least within the context of the Notes client and a Domino administrative domain.

Some useful manual security procedures were implemented as actions in the User Security panel dialogs. Because the scope of the task was only the user interface, in some situations, the procedures still require multiple steps for the user to execute. One example is the Compromised Password button in the Security Basics panel tab (see Figure 30-1). The procedure to recover from password compromise is usefully encapsulated in a single dialog. However, it requires four steps:

1. Change the password that protects the private key.

2. Ask your administrator to turn on extra password checks so that even someone with your private key and your old password cannot access your server data (a feature that takes the place of certificate revocation lists in our proprietary PKI).

3. Get a new signing key.

4. Update all the copies of your keyfile if you have them in multiple places.

The two automated steps are interleaved with procedures not currently automated in Notes: contacting your system administrator, and manually copying files to unspecified hosts. The former would be automatable if the system had some configured notion of how to contact the right system administrator on behalf of the user.

While security remains an area that requires deep domain expertise to understand, and while application of many usability techniques requires a full understanding of the domain applied to, deep cross-domain expertise in both areas will be needed to make progress using standard usability techniques, such as expert reviews and consultation. This exercise did find real value in the application of those techniques to the more commonly used security information displays.

### Database Access Control Information

The other area that displays useful security information is the database Access Control List (ACL) dialog, shown in Figure 30-3. Each instance of a Notes application is associated with a specific database. The Access Control List dialog displays the overall control information for a database.[6]

Domino database ACLs are quite simple, compared to the hierarchical access control features found elsewhere in the literature and in filesystem and directory products. The general approach here and elsewhere was to provide something basic, secure, and usable. There is a single list of users and groups who have access to the database. Attributes on those entries include access levels and their permissions. Seven access levels are defined, from No Access to Manager. Each of these levels has both implicit and explicit abilities or permissions. There are nine explicit permissions, represented as checkboxes. Some permissions are required to be enabled or disabled at a particular level, and others are optional. The default values for a new entry for both access level and permissions is taken from the entry selected when the new entry is added. One theme in customer requests in this area is the ability to create custom access levels. The concept of a level is quite useful in general, but each customer has his own notion of how fine-grained permissions should be allocated across his organizational roles.

There is no notion of the ability to deny a permission. Instead, the ACL evaluation algorithm proceeds from the most specific user entry found to the least specific matching entry (Anonymous), granting the permissions found at the first level of specificity where the user has a match. Thus, a user in a group with a powerful permission (level) can be denied that level by adding his name with a more restricted permission level to achieve deny-like semantics. This straightforward approach to both ACL evaluation and the ability to deny permissions has worked well in the majority of Notes applications.

---

6 Rob Slapikoff and Russ Lipton, "The ABC's of Using the ACL," Iris Today Archives [cited Oct. 2004]; *http://www-10.lotus.com/ldd/today.nsf/8a6d147cf55a7fd385256658007aacf1/ be08e4acfc72cd72852565d9004cb61c?OpenDocument*.

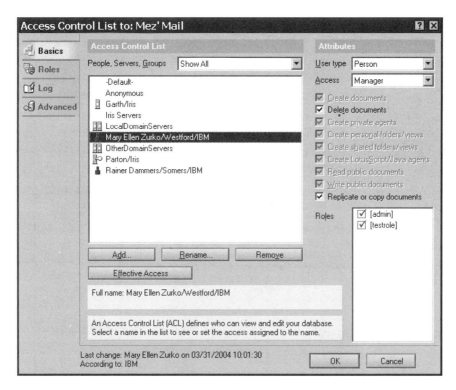

FIGURE 30-3. Access Control List main tab

The large-grained, general database ACL is a useful and understandable starting point, but some applications need to grant and manage more fine-grained access. Over time, several mechanisms were added to provide more detailed control.

Other ACL display tabs cover role definition and the logging of changes to the ACL, shown in Figure 30-4. Notes roles are groups defined and managed locally in a specific database ACL (not in the directory where enterprise-wide groups are defined). They are used by Notes applications to provide application-specific custom semantics on application operations. For example, the Domino database application defines roles for UserCreator and GroupModifier. The Reader List on a document overrides the database ACL to specify a much more limited set of readers for sensitive documents. The Authors List on a document specifies which users who have Author access to the database also have the ability to modify a specific document as its author.

### Adding power and complexity

In Notes 6, we added the Extended ACL (xACL) feature that allows sites to partition and delegate the access control administration of their Domino directory to allow for regional administrators and to enable hosting. We layered this support on the LDAP ACL standards

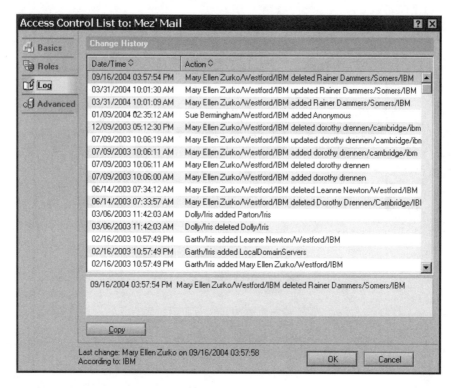

FIGURE 30-4. Notes ACL log

work that was proceeding in the IETF.[7] This access control model is a substantial increase in complexity over what we had provided before. It allows access control to be set at any point in the hierarchy of documents, on any type of document, on a field type within a document type, and on a per-document basis. This flexibility went beyond the targeted use case requests from customers, but was attractive because it could cover future use cases, and was anticipated as a standards-compliant approach.

The very fine-grained and flexible model seemed that it might be an invitation to usability-related security problems. When an early version of the Extended ACL user interface was available, four experienced Notes administrators participated in a classic, lab-based usability test on the feature. They were given a scenario with 13 tasks to complete. A usability specialist constructed and ran the test, and worked with developers on the feedback and lessons learned from the testing. The tasks ranged from using xACLs to restrict a specific user to reading, but not changing, a particular field, through defining limited administrative delegation access to another user.

Generally, the test subjects were in favor of having the advanced features and controls. The usability tests found a number of user interface problems that were easily fixed with

7   E. Stokes, B. Blakley, R. Byrne, R. Huber, and D. Rinkevich, "Access Control Model for LDAPv3," [cited Oct. 2004]; *http://www.ietf.org/proceedings/01aug/I-D/draft-ietf-ldapext-acl-model-08.txt.*

more straightforward or consistent terminology or with a simple rearrangement of dialog features. The most challenging scenario for the test users was to give a specified group only read and create access to a particular type of document (the Person form), but not to give them delete or modify permission access to that same type. Only one of the four test subjects was able to complete that task successfully.

One of the most substantial security-specific findings from this and other tasks in the scenario was that three out of the four test subjects could not figure out how permissions interacted between the extended ACL and the familiar database ACL. The Effective Access button was added to help with that confusion. It is available at the database level, and at any specific items protected by extended ACLs. It returns what access any specified user has to that data and, if groups are involved, shows the user's groups that were used to calculate that access.

Our experience with the usability methods applied to both security information displays is that they can find and correct a number of basic usability problems early in the design cycle. They did not address fundamentally complex models such as xACLs. The separation between the creation of the security model in a standards organization and the evaluation of the usability of the use cases of that model makes providing usable standards-based security particularly challenging. In neither of our usability evaluation contexts were deeper methods such as contextual interview and design applied to the more complex underlying security models. That approach has yielded good results in the research context,[8] when coupled with user interface models that tame and simplify the complexity of the models.

## User Control of Active Content Security

Developers, administrators, and users are all involved in making (or avoiding) security decisions. Developers determine many of the decisions available to (or imposed on) administrators and users, and administrators do the same for their users. Users have the most context for making those decisions, but have the least time (and often the least experience) for thinking about security impacts and risks. Conversely, any security-related decision not made available to the user or administrator is one less way they can protect themselves.

All of these considerations inform the design of security features. In addition, security features should be policy neutral. They should ensure that the system is securable, but not impose a particular security policy on it. However, any security-related decisions that are made available to users need to have a default behavior chosen for them. Users may find it difficult to evaluate why the default might not be right for them.

8   Mary Ellen Zurko, Rich Simon, and Tom Sanfilippo, "A User-Centered, Modular Authorization Service Built on an RBAC Foundation," *IEEE Symposium on Security and Privacy* (1999), 57–71.

Choice of the default will determine how open or secure the feature is. Defaults can have a large impact on both the usability and the security of a system. Open defaults have traditionally allowed security and usability concerns to remain unaddressed, because the security features were not part of the initial user experience of the system. They have also allowed users to deploy systems in an unsecured state, increasing the chance of successful attacks.

When protections on active content were introduced into version 4.5 of Notes, the default shipping policy was open. Any active content, whether signed or unsigned, would be executed. This was in part to ease the transition; active content shipped before that version had no policy controls at all, and no signatures. Administrators could change that default for users before they installed, and could specify whether users had the ability to change their own Execution Control List (ECL) policy. Subsequent administrative updates could be enabled by supported application template programming extensions that provided an ECL update via some other frequently accessed Notes application (such as email) or with a specific button that the user had to click (which could be shared via email). In practice, as with many administrative security features, the shipped defaults were widely deployed. As organizations gained experience with the feature, they came to understand that security would be enhanced with tighter policy.

## Deployment Study

When we changed to a secure default ECL policy in R5.02e, we were able to observe both the usability of the active content controls and how easily they can be used to ensure secure behavior on the part of users. We studied a 500-person organization securing their ECL defaults (we call them SoftwareHouse).[9] After the administrative ECL was secured at SoftwareHouse, a prestigious security guru sent email to everyone in the company. The email included a button for a user to click to tighten his ECLs from the new administrative defaults, as well as an extensive explanation of those new secure defaults. It also provided an example of an unsigned Execution Security Alert (which notifies users that unsigned active content is trying to run on their system), explaining the potential danger it could represent, and giving instructions about how users who received such alerts should handle them safely and to whom they should report these alerts.

Three months later, we performed a test. We used active content in a survey email to obtain data on the state of ECLs in SoftwareHouse. Users received mail from another colleague at SoftwareHouse, also from the security team. This mail message included unsigned active content, which users had been warned about in the previous email. The active content sent mail back to the person who sent the mail (Jane Doe). If a user opened this second mail and had unsecured ECL settings, the response email was sent on behalf of the recipient to Jane Doe with no user interaction. If the user opened this second mail

---

9   Mary Ellen Zurko, Charlie Kaufman, Katherine Spanbauer, and Chuck Bassett, "Did You Ever Have to Make Up Your Mind? What Notes Users Do When Faced with a Security Decision," *18th Annual Computer Security Applications Conference* (2002), 371–381.

message and had secured policy settings that disallowed unsigned active content, they saw two unsigned ECL alerts mapping to the two operations necessary to send the response email. Choosing to allow unsigned active content to run is not the default on those dialogs. However, if they overrode the default and allowed the active content to run, a response mail was also sent to Jane Doe. The response mail message had a timer indicating the amount of elapsed time between the two operations, to differentiate between the unsecured policy and the overridden secure policy cases. We also attempted to gather self-reported statistics on who did not allow the unsigned active content to run. The text of the mail message explained the survey and encouraged people who didn't allow the unsigned code to execute to send the contact person mail telling him so, for data-gathering purposes. We called that list of people the *Gold Star list* to further encourage self-reporting.

We found that 62% of the people on the email list (334) responded within two days of the survey. In addition, 68% of the respondents (227) had secured their defaults to not allow unsigned code to run on their behalf, and 31% of the respondents (102) had open ECL defaults. This number demonstrates that many users in this fairly computer-savvy population would, in fact, take an explicit action to secure themselves when asked to do so by someone they know and trust who explains the request.

We also found that 71% of the responses (237), or 44% of the entire recipient list, allowed the unsigned active content to run, either because their defaults were open or because they explicitly allowed it when the alert dialogs came up. This number clearly shows that if users must make explicit and informed choices that are likely to stop the flow of their work (instead of continue it) in order to maintain their security, many will not. This finding is related to recent trends showing how hopeless it is to tell users to practice good mail attachment hygiene to stop viruses.

### Solutions and Challenges

Better administrative tools can take the burden of setting secure defaults off of the user. Domino 6 included policy management features that allowed administrators to push down updates to the ECL policy to users, without needing to ask the users to take an extra step (like clicking a button) or tying it to use of a particular Notes application. This tool allows administrators to achieve 100% compliance with the portions of the policy set by the administrator, under the constraints they choose. Administrators working in a very structured organization in which code signers are preauthorized can set their policy to override the user's policy whenever the administrative policy is changed, and disallow users from changing their local personal versions of the policy.

Unfortunately, many organizations don't work in a structure where all trustworthy active content creators are preauthorized. In fact, such a target is at odds with the desire to simplify the creation and reuse of simple active content (such as RSVP buttons). Some of the other usability features deployed in Domino can help with that model. ECL policy updates can be pushed down to the user on a daily basis, and can merge with, rather than override, user-specific settings. In combination with allowing users to change their own policy, this can be used to ensure that the most egregiously unsafe settings, such as the permissions allowed to unsigned active content, are done away with.

## Conclusion

This chapter discussed just some of the many security and usability challenges faced by the full-featured collaborative application infrastructure provided by IBM Lotus Notes and Domino. Up-front design that simplified the security functions and integrated them tightly into collaboration tasks has provided the best usability benefits. Coping with the addition of new features and flexible standards has proved to be a continuing challenge for tight integration and usability of the security features. Usability testing or expert review yields clear benefits on the basics, but hasn't scaled to cover big concept additions or changes in our environment. It also does not address many issues around integrating security information display into user tasks, perhaps because more information is available than should be put into the default view of an application task. Data on how users actually use and respond to security features is an excellent motivator for further enhancements. We continue to work to move the necessity for security decisions off end users and administrators, and still provide them with a secure and usable product.

## About the Author

Mary Ellen Zurko leads security architecture and strategy for Lotus Software at IBM. She defined the field of User-Centered Security in 1996. She is on the steering committee for the New Security Paradigms Workshop and the International World Wide Web Conference series. She has worked in security since 1986, at The Open Group Research Institute and Digital Equipment Corporation, as well as at IBM.

# CHAPTER THIRTY-ONE

# Achieving Usable Security in Groove Virtual Office

GEORGE MOROMISATO, PAUL BOYD, AND NIMISHA ASTHAGIRI

**W**HEN WE DESIGNED **GROOVE VIRTUAL OFFICE,** we struggled to balance security and usability. Ray Ozzie, whose vision we were executing, set out the following core principles early in the design phase:

- Users should not be required to be administrators. Users care about getting their work done. They are not interested in setting up accounts, configuring network topologies, or distributing security keys. Groove Virtual Office should "just work."

- The highest possible level of security should be built into the system from day one.

Ozzie's experience creating Lotus Notes convinced him that users care about security and privacy and that a robust security infrastructure would be necessary in the globally connected Internet. Unfortunately, these two core principles conflict. High-security systems are often not usable; and often, in the quest to be usable, security is traded off. How we reconciled these two conflicting principles and how we developed a user-friendly security model for Groove Virtual Office are the subjects of this chapter.

## About Groove Virtual Office

Groove Virtual Office (GVO) is a peer-to-peer-based solution that allows distributed groups to share information inside and outside an organization. Many enterprises today need to share information with clients or remote workers outside of the corporate network. Thus, GVO encrypts data over the wire automatically. But that is not enough. Laptops can be stolen or otherwise compromised even if the data on them is not being transmitted. Thus, GVO also encrypts data stored locally.

In the years after September 11, the U.S. Military and the U.S. Department of Homeland Security became interested in GVO as a way of sharing sensitive information across organizational boundaries. The rapid way in which GVO can be deployed, and the high security of the system, have satisfied many of the government's requirements.

Information shared within GVO takes a number of different forms—images in the Pictures tool, files in the Files tool, events in the Calendar tool, reports in the Forms tool, minutes in the Meetings tool, and so on. In all, GVO supports more than 50 different tools, each appropriate to the nature of the data being shared. New tools can be created by customers and then "plugged in" to GVO's existing framework.

In Iraq, for example, Coalition Forces and more than 30 humanitarian organizations used a custom Rapid Assessment tool in GVO to distribute aid to the people of Iraq. The Rapid Assessment form (shown in Figure 31-1) allowed a field team to evaluate the aid needs of individual communities and automatically transmitted the information to distribution sites. In the wrong hands, the data shared by these groups could have been disastrous, potentially tipping off insurgents about the location of military forces. Connections to the network were dubious at best. In one case, the only connection to be found came from a completely insecure Internet café. Rarely is the need for information security in a hostile environment stronger.

## Groove Virtual Office Design

In the following sections, we look at the key design issues for Groove Virtual Office.

### The Weakest Link

In *Secrets and Lies*, Bruce Schneier concludes that correct cryptographic algorithms are necessary but not sufficient for creating secure systems.[1] Indeed, in complex systems, the cryptographic algorithms are the last place that anyone attacks. Why exploit a weakness in the random number generator when users will launch any email attachment that promises them a visual thrill? Why set up an elaborate man-in-the-middle attack when users are likely to write their passwords down on sticky notes? A system is only as secure as its weakest link, and in many systems, the weakest link is often the user.

Of course, security professionals have been aware of the limitations of the user ever since Troy accepted a free horse. There are two common user interface techniques for strengthening the user link:

---

1   Bruce Schneier, *Secrets and Lies* (Indianapolis: Wiley Publishing, Inc., 2000).

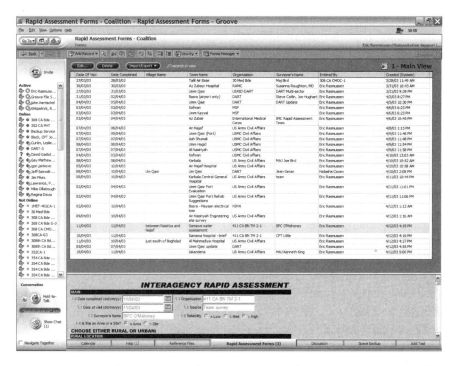

FIGURE 31-1. *Groove Workspace was used in the Iraq War to assess the humanitarian assistance needs of people affected by the fighting; Groove was chosen for its ability to work in austere networking infrastructures*

- Prevent the user from doing the wrong thing—for example, enforce strong password policies

- Teach the user how to do the right thing—for example, teach people how to choose a strong password

Both techniques have their place, but unfortunately, both also have limitations. Jakob Nielsen writes that as passwords become stronger (and thus more difficult to remember), users tend to write their passwords down on sticky notes.[2] Thus, Nielsen argues, enforcing strong passwords *weakens* security as a direct consequence of being less usable. We would argue, however, that the effect on security is subtler. If strong passwords are enforced, remote attacks (i.e., attacks over the Internet) become harder but insider attacks become easier (because passwords will be on sticky notes).

Teaching the user to do the right thing also has tradeoffs. For most users, computers are tools used to get their job done. Most users are not motivated to learn about security procedures. When we first designed Groove, we decided to encourage people to use strong passwords by prompting for a *passphrase* in our login and account creation screens. We felt that this would be a subtle reminder that people could and should use a phrase rather

2   Jakob Nielsen, "Alert Box" (Nov. 26, 2000); *http://www.useit.com/alertbox/20001126.html.*

than a word for their login credentials. Unfortunately, this minor deviation from user expectation ended up causing more confusion than it was worth. In usability testing, we found that users struggled in the account creation screens. Several users were confused by the word *passphrase* and were not sure what to enter. Moreover, this unfamiliar term reinforced the perception that Groove Virtual Office was nonstandard and thus more complicated than software people were used to. This would lead users to choose to send sensitive information via email rather than Groove. Because email is often sent in the clear, this left the user worse off from a security perspective. However, the performance of workers is rarely measured by the security measures they take. For this reason, they are likely to choose the medium that allows them to accomplish their task (sending a file) quickly and comfortably. Thus, given a choice between an easy solution that is insecure and a difficult solution that is secure, the user is likely to choose the former. Groove Virtual Office had to be a solution that is both easy to use and secure.

## Do the Right Thing

From experiences like these, we concluded that we needed a flexible security model. This was all the more important given the different security needs of our diverse target audience—ranging from office workers who mainly use email and Microsoft Word, to military and intelligence personnel. Each user group requires different levels of security but also has different tolerance levels for security inconveniences. The security model of Groove Virtual Office accommodates all of these groups. Depending on the needs and abilities of the user, and the properties of the networking environment, Groove applies one or both of the two user interface (UI) techniques (i.e., enforcing and teaching) to maximize the security of the system.

The main user groups for Groove are:

- *Office workers.* Most office workers want to think about their work, not their infrastructure. They tend to avoid products that force them to learn new concepts, and they want security to be as invisible as possible. For these users, Groove relies on a centralized server to enforce security policies and to serve as a certification authority. As we describe later in this chapter, a central server allows Groove to provide secure communications without any user intervention or effort.

- *Road warriors.* Another type of user that Groove Virtual Office needs to satisfy is the road warrior. People who travel in their business may have to deal with multiple central servers (their company's server and their client's server, for example). They may even have to make do without one at all. Groove uses various UI techniques (such as colors and prompts) to help the user understand how to work securely. For example, Groove can warn users if they are communicating with someone who has not been certified by their own central server.

- *Military and intelligence users.* Finally, Groove needs to support users in the military and intelligence community. Groove's architecture works particularly well in austere networking environments such as ad hoc field networks with only occasional Internet connectivity. These users need a high level of security but cannot rely on a centralized server to enforce policies or manage identities and access control. Moreover, these users often communicate with people across organizational and, sometimes, warfront boundaries. Groove allows these users to communicate securely, even without a central server, by teaching them to authenticate each other directly. Direct authentication (described later in this chapter) guarantees secure communications over insecure infrastructure without requiring a trusted third party.

We knew that forcing the office worker to use the intelligence users' level of security would lead to user frustration and, eventually, abandonment of our product. The challenge, then, was to find a way to serve all of these user types with all of their various environments and expectations. This led us to our primary guiding principle: a flexible approach to security that keeps the users and their environments in mind will, in the end, be significantly stronger than one that merely mandates security upon the user.

Secure communications in Iraq are a good example. Naturally, the U.S. military has secure, closed networks such as SIPRNET that were designed for the transmission of highly sensitive data. Nevertheless, because the mission in Iraq involves reconstruction projects as well as military operations, soldiers often need to communicate with humanitarian organizations, private contractors, and local Iraqi civilians. Most of these people do not have access to SIPRNET. Instead, some battalions in Iraq now use Groove to communicate both with their rear command and with humanitarian and civilian organizations. Because Groove does not mandate a central certification authority, it can be deployed without an administrator. In addition, because Groove can send encrypted communications over insecure networks, it allows Iraqi civilians to communicate with the U.S. military securely.

The security architecture of Groove Virtual Office takes advantage of the environment that it finds itself in to maximize the security for the user, given the constraints of the system. In other words, Groove scales the security offered to the user based on the desires and abilities of the user and the existing infrastructure. This approach allowed us to satisfy Ozzie's core principles.

## Is That You, Alice?

An example of this flexible approach is the design of the identity and authentication system in Groove Virtual Office. All communications and collaboration systems need to convey the identity of users to each other, and questions inevitably arise:

- Is that really a message from Alice?

- How do I know that the Alice Smith in the directory is really the Alice Smith that I know (and not an impostor)?

- How do I know that Alice Smith is the Alice Smith that works in my company and not a similarly named Alice Smith who works for a competitor?

There are well-known algorithms for securely answering all these questions. Most systems use public-private key cryptography to prove that the owner of a given public key composed a message. Next, most systems use a centralized certification authority to vouch that the owner of a given public key is named, for example, "Alice Smith." Finally, most systems have a centralized, hierarchical directory that disambiguates among different people with the same name.

Groove, unfortunately, cannot always rely on a central server for certifying and disambiguating identities. Relying on a central server makes sense in many cases, but Groove Virtual Office must be able to function without one. For example, negotiators in the talks between the Sri Lankan government and Tamil Tiger rebels used Groove Virtual Office. Neither side wanted the other to run a certifying server. Even cross-certification was unacceptable because of intense political sensitivities.[3] Groove's flexible approach pays off in this situation because it supports direct authentication. With direct authentication, two parties who want to communicate securely can authenticate each other without having to trust a third party or even each other. In the case of the Sri Lanka peace talks, this allowed the two sides to communicate in a neutral space that no one controlled. In the corporate world, direct authentication allows you to securely communicate with an external party without having to wait for your IT department to issue a certificate.

## Colorful Security

Groove uses public key cryptography to provide message-level security, without requiring user intervention, special knowledge, or centralized administration. For example, when Bob receives a message from Alice, Groove displays the message as originating from a person named "Alice." The message is encrypted with Bob's public key, so no one but Bob can read it. The message is also signed with Alice's private key, so only the person possessing that private key could have written it.

A problem remains. Although the underlying Groove cryptographic layer protects the message cryptographically, it cannot guarantee that the message was written by the Alice that Bob expects. The Groove user interface must help Bob to determine whether Alice is an impostor. When Bob sees that he has a message from Alice, the name "Alice" will be displayed in a color that represents the authentication level for Alice. The authentication color answers the question: "Which Alice is this?" If Bob and Alice are both employees of the same company, their management server will vouch for the identity of Alice and Bob.[4] In that case, Alice's name will display in *teal* on Bob's screen (and vice versa).

---

3   "To Engender and Sustain a Holistic and Integrated Peacebuilding Process in Sri Lanka"; *http://www.info-share.org/*.

4   Cryptographically speaking, Alice's Groove identity certificate is signed with the management server's Certificate Authority (CA) private key. Because Bob knows the server's CA public key (it's his server too) he can trust that Alice's identity is valid, at least as far as the management server is concerned.

But what if Bob and Alice don't work for the same company? The companies can choose to cross-certify each other's employees. The Groove UI automatically helps Bob recognize Alice by displaying Alice's name in *blue*, a color designated for certified contacts outside the company. We chose to explicitly distinguish between certified contacts within the company and those outside the company so that users can easily detect company affiliations of a contact list before exchanging company-confidential information.

In some cases, however, the additional administrative overhead of cross-certification is not desired. This is where more user training is required. The most secure way is for Bob to use an out-of-band method (such as a phone conversation) to verify that the public key that he sees for Alice is what Alice knows her public key to be. To make this easier, the Groove user interface displays a *fingerprint*[5] for each person displayed in the UI. Once verified, Bob can directly authenticate Alice. Thereafter, all messages and communications from Alice will show Alice's name in *green*. This method of authentication is similar to PGP's web of trust model.

Groove will also warn the user if there is already a different user with the name Alice. That is, if two people with different public keys both claim to be Alice, both Alices are shown in *red* and Bob is asked to disambiguate the two. The Groove UI shows the user the various contexts in which the two Alices have communicated with Bob. For example, the user interface might indicate that the first Alice is in a marketing *workspace* with Bob and the second Alice is in a family photo-sharing workspace. Bob can use this information to disambiguate the two Alices, and then alias[6] one or both of the Alices so that he can keep them straight in the Groove user interface. This technique protects Bob from spoofing attacks after he has communicated with the real Alice. Any subsequent people claiming to be Alice will appear in *red* in the UI, and Bob can determine whether the second Alice is an impostor. Figure 31-2 shows the Resolve Name Conflict screen.

The technique of displaying authentication and certification information with a name is what makes it possible for Groove to support different user groups. Office workers in an enterprise environment do not have to worry about security because a management server authenticates their contacts. An office worker will generally see all names as *teal* (certified) without taking additional steps. Road warriors, on the other hand, can use the colors to distinguish between people inside their own company (who show as *teal*), people who are trusted but are outside their company (who show as *blue*), and people who are unauthenticated (who show as *black*). In addition, all users can benefit from notifications about duplicate names (which show as *red*). Finally, users in the intelligence community can be trained to use direct authentication without any server infrastructure (out-of-band exchange of fingerprints) to authenticate users (who show as *green*). These color codes are shown in Figure 31-3.

---

5   The fingerprint is a cryptographic hash of the public key and thus is easier to compare manually.

6   An *alias* is a user-local name given to a contact; Groove does not share your aliases with others.

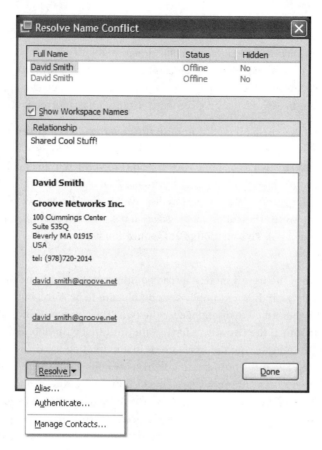

*FIGURE 31-2. The Resolve Name Conflict dialog box allows the user to disambiguate two people with the same name but different public keys; being able to handle different people with the same name is crucial for software that requires no central naming authority; this is also the first line of defense against spoofing attacks*

Are *five* distinct authentication and certification colors too many? Will they overwhelm users and add unneeded complexity? Will users find them distracting or useful? Will users understand the significance of these colors? These are questions we asked when testing and adapting the usability of our "flexible" UI security model. What we have found is that the system works well because it evolves with the user's environment and use of GVO. For example, office workers see and need to learn only three of the five colors that are pertinent to their role:

- *Teal* (for certified users within their company)

- *Black* (warning for uncertified users)

- *Red* (high warning for name conflict and possible attack)

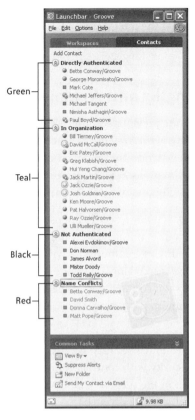

Green —

Teal —

Black —

Red —

*FIGURE 31-3. Groove keeps track of how each person is authenticated; some people (shown in green) are directly authenticated, which means that the user has validated the digital fingerprint of the person's contact; other people (shown in teal) are certified by the organization's certificate authority; those not authenticated are shown in black, and those with name conflicts are shown in red*

Two additional colors are displayed only for more advanced users:

• Road warriors in multiple environments (*blue* for certified users outside of their company)

• Intelligence analysts in austere circumstances (*green* for direct authentication)

Because color coding may, at first, appear new and foreign to users, we employ standard UI techniques such as tooltips and context-sensitive help to teach users these (as of yet) nonstandard features. Of course, as we receive more user feedback, we will adapt our model to satisfy our diverse user community. For example, we may provide end-user and administrative tools to customize the colors according to their local environment and preferences.

Most importantly, all three of these user communities can interact with each other using their own local policies and without compromising security. For example, an intelligence analyst does not have to trust an office worker's administrator to communicate with the office worker. Because the intelligence analyst can directly authenticate the office worker, the security of the authentication is in the control of the intelligence analyst and can be as secure as he wishes. In contrast, if the intelligence analyst had to rely on an administrator's certification, the administrator would be another (possibly vulnerable) link in the security chain.

## Administrators' Strengths and Weaknesses

The user interface described in the previous sections is an example of teaching and guiding the user to maintain the security of the system. As much as possible, Groove exposes security information (such as authentication colors) in a simple way that the user can understand. Nevertheless, there are situations in which more controlled mechanisms are needed. Groove also uses the technique of enforcing behaviors when appropriate.

A corporation can set up a management server to impose certain policies on its employees. For example, a corporation that does not need to communicate across enterprise boundaries might restrict Groove's ability to communicate with nonemployees. In that case, the Groove UI might *warn* Bob if he is receiving a message from someone who cannot be directly authenticated or who is not certified (i.e., someone who could be an impostor). In some cases, it might even be important to *prevent* such unauthenticated and uncertified communications.

As discussed, Groove provides as much security as possible without an administrator and provides increasing levels of security with centralized management. But administrators can themselves be a weak point in the security chain. Many users forget their passwords. Most systems provide a way for an administrator to recover or reset a user's password. When we originally designed a centralized password reset system, we relied on administrators to properly authenticate users before resetting their passwords. The process required administrators to verify out-of-band a temporary digital fingerprint generated for the user. The new password, therefore, did not need to be communicated in the clear since it was strongly encrypted in the user's temporary keys. In theory, this was a secure protocol because the out-of-band channel need only be an authenticated channel, rather than a confidential one.

Unfortunately, administrators are users too, and they are not familiar with this level of security. As a result, many Groove domain administrators skipped the important signature verification step and significantly weakened the overall system. Ideas for forcing the administrator to verify the fingerprint (e.g., by preventing progress until the fingerprint was manually typed in) were proposed, but were later rejected by customers. We learned that most administrators strongly favor using systems whose interfaces are similar to those of other popular applications, even if it means less security. In addition, a system that eliminates administrator intervention would, in practice, be more secure and deployable. Later designs of centralized password reset take these human elements into account and provide a relatively secure system that does not require administrator intervention and uses more common technologies (e.g., email, questions and answers, hints).

# Security and Usability

Like all systems, Groove makes tradeoffs between security and usability to achieve the user's goals. And like all security software engineers, we know that the user is often the weakest link in the system. But instead of only preventing the user from performing insecure actions or forcing the user to learn proper security protocols, we chose to flexibly adapt our security around the strengths and weaknesses of users and the environment in which they work.

---

## CORE PRINCIPLES

1. Design for the strengths and weaknesses of the user. A flexible approach to security is significantly stronger than one that imposes security on the user.
2. Do not force users to be administrators.
3. Remember that administrators are users too.
4. Build in the highest possible security from day one—it will be harder to add it later.
5. Design the user interface so that it is similar to those of existing popular systems. User confusion leads to security compromises.
6. Ensure that security features meant for one user group do not negatively impact the usability for another group.

---

When we started the design of Groove Virtual Office, the twin goals of high security and high usability seemed mutually exclusive. Security and usability are disciplines that are half art and half science. There are no algorithms to ensure the security of a system, any more than there are algorithms that guarantee usability. But in both disciplines, the first principle is the same: design for the strengths and weaknesses of the user. Once we adopted this view into our design process, reconciling the two disciplines was easier.

## About the Authors

George Moromisato is chief product designer at Groove Networks, Inc. He has had the great fortune to participate in the design and development of Ray Ozzie's software for the last 14 years.

Paul Boyd manages the Design Team at Groove Networks and is responsible for the user interface design and usability of Groove Virtual Office.

Nimisha Asthagiri has managed the Security Team at Groove Networks and has led the design and implementation of all aspects of security in Groove Virtual Office.

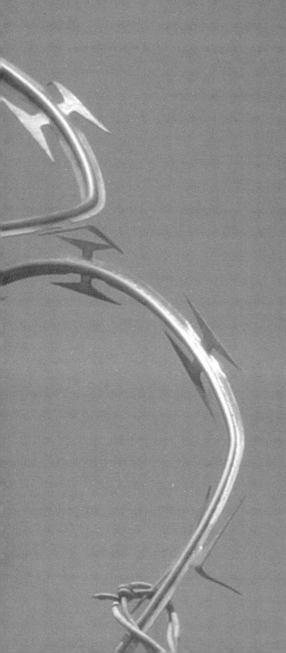

# CHAPTER THIRTY-TWO

# Users Are Not the Enemy

## *Why Users Compromise Security Mechanisms and How to Take Remedial Measures*

**ANNE ADAMS AND M. ANGELA SASSE**

**C**ONFIDENTIALITY IS AN IMPORTANT ASPECT OF COMPUTER SECURITY. It depends on authentication mechanisms, such as passwords, to safeguard access to information. Traditionally, authentication procedures are divided into two stages:[1, 2]

- *Identification* (user ID), to identify the user

- *Authentication*, to verify that the user is the legitimate owner of the ID

It is the latter stage that requires a secret password. To date, research on password security has focused on designing technical mechanisms to protect access to systems; the usability of these mechanisms has rarely been investigated. Hitchings[3] and Davis and Price[4] argue

---

1   A. Adams and M. A. Sasse, "Users Are Not the Enemy," *Communications of the ACM* 42:12 (Dec. 1999). © 1999 Association for Computing Machinery, Inc. Reprinted by permission.

2   D. B. Parker, "Restating the Foundation of Information Security," in G. C. Gable and W. J. Caelli (eds.), *IT Security: The Need for International Co-operation* (Holland: Elsevier Science Publishers, 1992).

3   J. Hitchings, "Deficiencies of the Traditional Approach to Information Security and the Requirements for a New Methodology," *Computers and Security* 14 (1995), 377–383.

4   D. Davis and W. Price, *Security for Computer Networks* (Chichester, U.K.: Wiley, 1987).

that this narrow perspective has produced security mechanisms that are, in practice, less effective than they are generally assumed to be. Because security mechanisms are designed, implemented, applied, and breached by people, human factors should be considered in their design. It seems that, currently, hackers pay more attention to the human link in the security chain than security designers do, for example, by using social engineering techniques to obtain passwords.

The key element in password security is the crackability of a password combination. Davies and Ganesan[5] argue that an adversary's ability to crack passwords is greater than usually believed. System-generated passwords are essentially the optimal security approach; however, user-generated passwords are potentially more memorable and thus are less likely to be disclosed (because users do not have to write them down). The U.S. Federal Information Processing Standards[6] (FIPS) suggest several criteria for assuring different levels of password security. *Password composition,* for example, relates the size of a character set from which a password has been chosen to its level of security. An alphanumeric password is therefore more secure than one composed of letters alone. Short *password lifetime*—changing passwords frequently—is suggested as reducing the risk associated with undetected compromised passwords. Finally, *password ownership,* in particular individual ownership, is recommended to:

- Increase individual accountability
- Reduce illicit usage
- Allow for an establishment of system usage audit trails
- Reduce frequent password changes due to group membership fluctuations

There is evidence that many password users do not comply with these suggested rules. DeAlvare[7] found that once a password is chosen, a user is unlikely to change it until it has been shown to be compromised. Users were also found to construct passwords that contained as few characters as possible.[8] These observations cannot be disputed, but the conclusion that this behavior occurs because users are inherently careless—and therefore insecure—needs to be challenged.

## The Study

A web-based questionnaire was used to obtain initial quantitative and qualitative data on user behaviors and perceptions relating to password systems. The questionnaire focused

5  C. Davis and R. Ganesan, "BApasswd: A New Proactive Password Checker," *Proceedings of the National Computer Security Conference '93* (1993), 1–15.

6  FIPS 112, *Password Usage,* Federal Information Processing Standards Publication (May 30, 1985).

7  A. M. DeAlvare, "A Framework for Password Selection," *Proceedings of Unix Security Workshop II* (Portland, Aug. 29–30, 1998).

8  A. M. DeAlvare, "How Crackers Crack Passwords or What Passwords to Avoid," *Proceedings of Unix Security Workshop II* (Portland, 1990).

mainly on password-related user behaviors (password construction, frequency of use, password recall, and work practices) and in particular, memorability issues. A total of 139 responses were received, approximately half from employees of Organization A (a technology company), and the other half from users in organizations throughout the world. There was a wide range of frequency and duration of password use among respondents. The questionnaire was followed by 30 semistructured in-depth interviews with a variety of users in Organization A and Organization B (a company in the construction sector). Interview questions covered password generation and recall along with systems and organizational issues raised by respondents in the questionnaire. The interview format allowed participants to introduce new issues to the discussion that they regarded as related to password usage. Results from the open-ended sections of the questionnaire were brought together with results from the in-depth interviews to give a wide sample for analysis.

The analysis, using a social science–based method called *Grounded Theory*,[9] provided a framework of issues affecting user behavior, with a step-by-step account of password usage problems and possible intervention points. Four major factors influencing effective password usage were identified within the framework:

- Multiple passwords
- Password content
- Perceived compatibility with work practices
- Users' perceptions of organizational security and information sensitivity

Because the findings from the study are too numerous to discuss in detail here, key points of interest from each factor are presented.

Many users have to remember multiple passwords, that is, use different passwords for different applications and/or change passwords frequently because of password expiration mechanisms. Having a large number of passwords reduces their memorability and increases insecure work practices, such as writing passwords down—50% of questionnaire respondents wrote their passwords down in one form or another.[10] One employee emphasized this relationship when he said "...because I was forced into changing it every month I had to write it down." Poor password design (for example, using "password" as the password) was also found to be related to multiple passwords. "Constantly changing passwords" were blamed by another employee for producing "...very simple choices that are easy to guess, or break, within seconds of using 'Cracker'.[11] Hence, there is no security." It is interesting to note here that users, again, perceive their behavior to be caused by a mechanism designed to increase security. At the same time, users often devise their own procedures to increase

---

9  A. Strauss and J. Corbin, *Basics of Qualitative Research: Grounded Theory Procedures and Techniques* (Newbury Park, CA: Sage, 1990).

10 The response was the same for all users who answered these questions—the other 50% of users left these questions blank.

11 A password dictionary checker.

password memorability and security. Some users devise their own methods for creating memorable multiple passwords through related passwords (linking their passwords via some common element)—50% of questionnaire respondents employed this method. Many users try to comply with security rules by varying elements in these linked passwords (name1, name2, name3, and so forth). However, instead of improving memorability and security, this method actually decreases password memorability because of within-list interference,[12] causing users to write down passwords, and this, of course, compromises password security levels.

Users' knowledge of what constitutes secure password content (the character content of the password) was inadequate. Without feedback from security experts, users created their own rules on password design that were often anything but secure. Dictionary words and names are the most vulnerable forms of passwords, but many users do not understand how password cracking works. Members of the security department in Organization A were appalled to discover that one of their employees suggested: "I would have thought that if you picked something like your wife's maiden name or something, then the chances of a complete stranger guessing *********, in my case, were pretty remote."

At the same time, restrictions introduced to create more secure password content may produce less memorable passwords, leading to increased password disclosure (because users write passwords down). Many users circumvent such restrictions to produce passwords they find easy to remember. However, the resulting passwords tend to be less secure in terms of content. Even worse, having to circumvent security procedures lowers users' regard for the overall security arrangements in the organization, which, in turn, increases password disclosure.

Another new finding of this study is the importance of compatibility between work practices and password procedures. Organization A employed individually owned passwords for group working that users perceived as incompatible with their working procedures (they advocated shared passwords for themselves). Users in Organization B experienced this incompatibility in reverse: they emphatically rejected the departmental policy of group passwords for individual personal information (such as email).

One reason why Organization A insisted on individual passwords was to establish the users' perception of accountability through audit trails of system usage. We found, however, that most users had not considered the possibility that their actions might be tracked. It is telling that the only user who made the connection cheerfully revealed that he avoided being tracked by using other users' passwords for certain transactions so that "...if there's any problem, they get it in the neck, not you."

The study clearly showed that users are not sufficiently informed about security issues. This causes them to construct their own model of possible security threats and the impor-

---

12 C. D. Wickens, *Engineering Psychology and Human Performance, 2nd Edition* (New York: Harper Collins, 1992).

tance of security, and these are often wildly inaccurate. Users tend to be guided by what they actually see—or don't. As one manager stated: "I don't think that hacking is a problem—I've had no visibility of hacking that may go on. None at all." Another employee observed that "...security problems are more by word of mouth...." This lack of awareness was corroborated by results from the web questionnaire. A complex interaction between users' perceptions of organizational security and information sensitivity was identified. Users identified certain systems as worthy of secure password practices, and others were perceived as "not important enough." Without any feedback from the organization, users rated confidential information about individuals (personnel files, email) as sensitive; but commercially sensitive information (such as customer databases and financial data) was often seen as less sensitive. Some users stated that they appreciated printed document classifications (for example, *Confidential, Not for Circulation*), indicating their need for information sensitivity guidance and rules for levels of protection in online documentation.

Two main problems in password usage were identified:

- System factors, which users perceive they are forced to circumvent
- External factors, which are perceived as incompatible with working procedures

Both of these problems result from a lack of communication between security departments and users: users do not understand security issues, and security departments lack an understanding of users' perceptions, tasks, and needs. The result is that security departments typecast users as "inherently insecure": at best, they are a security risk that needs to be controlled and managed; at worst, they are the enemy within. Users, on the other hand, perceive many security mechanisms as laborious and unnecessary—an overhead that gets in the way of their real work.

## Users Lack Security Knowledge

Parker[13] points out that a major doctrine in password security, adopted from the military, is the *need-to-know* principle. The assumption is that the more that is known about a security mechanism, the easier it is to attack; restricting access to this knowledge therefore increases security. Users are often told as little as possible because security departments see them as "inherently insecure." One clear finding from this study is that inadequate knowledge of password procedures, content, and cracking lies at the root of users' "insecure" behaviors.

Both Organizations A and B had replaced system-generated passwords with user-generated ones, thus shifting the responsibility for creating secure passwords to the users. However, known rules for creating secure passwords were rarely communicated to users. Users were asked to complete a skilled design job without adequate training or online feedback.

13 D. B. Parker, "Restating the Foundation of Information Security," in G. C. Gable and W. J. Caelli (eds.), *IT Security: The Need for International Co-operation* (Holland: Elsevier Science Publishers, 1992).

This problem was compounded by the security departments' implicit need-to-know policy on the sensitivity of particular information, potential security breaches, and risks. Users perceived threats to the organization to be low because of their own judgments of the information's lack of importance or visible threats. This misunderstanding led to the general misconception that password cracking is done on a "personal" basis. They perceived the risk to be low because their role in the system was not important. Organization A decided to provide online support and feedback to users in the process of password design; a cracker program was installed, with constructive advice provided on secure password design for all users whose passwords were cracked. Online information on threats to password security ("Monthly security report and update") is also being considered.

Finally, we found that users do not understand the authentication process, confusing the user identification (ID) and password sections. Many users assumed that IDs were another form of password to be secured and recalled in the same manner. This increased users' perception of the mental workload associated with passwords, which then reduced their motivation to comply with the suggested behavior. The IDs, within the organizations investigated, could have caused this misconception by having no standardized format for different applications and often being nonwords without meaning. In response to this finding, Organization A decided to introduce a single sign-on for users with a high number of passwords and is considering the use of smart cards as an identification mechanism. User authentication using physical attributes (biometrics) does not require ID recall, and thus offers a mechanism with reduced mental overhead. The main drawback of these methods is the cost of both installation and monitoring. Organizations also have to consider whether the level and consequences of "false positive" alarms are acceptable to their business. Finally, there is a question of how to combine the specialized equipment required for such methods with remote access to systems, which is an increasing requirement in an age of nomadic professionals.

## Security Needs User-Centered Design

Insufficient communication with users produces a lack of a user-centered design in security mechanisms. Many of these mechanisms create overheads for users, or require unworkable user behavior. It is therefore hardly surprising to find that many users try to circumvent such mechanisms.

Requiring users to have a large number of passwords (for multiple applications and change regimes) was found to create serious usability problems. Although change regimes are employed to reduce the impact of an undetected security breach, our findings suggest that they reduce the overall password security in an organization. Users required to change their passwords frequently produce less secure password content (because they have to be more memorable) and disclose their passwords more frequently. Many of the users felt forced into these circumventing procedures, which subsequently decreased their own security motivation. Ultimately, this produces a spiraling decline in users' password behavior ("I cannot remember my password, I have to write it down, everyone knows it's on a Post-it in my drawer, so I might as well stick it on the screen and tell everyone who wants to know"). Organization A was understandably worried to discover such attitudes, as social engineers rely on password disclosure and low security awareness and motivation to breach security mechanisms. The cost associated with resetting passwords in Organization A was one of the visible consequences, prompting the study that is the basis for this article. Recognizing the impact that cognitive overheads introduced by some password mechanisms have on users' security motivation, the security and human factors groups in Organization A have joined forces to develop a user-centered approach to the design of password and other security mechanisms. Such approaches will also have to take into account that the number of passwords required outside the workplace is growing constantly, thus increasing the cognitive load of users.

## Motivating Users

A technical bias toward security mechanisms has produced a simplistic approach to user authentication: restricting access to data by identification and authentication of a user. This simplistic approach may work well in military environments, but it limits usable solutions to the security problems of modern organizations seeking to encourage work practices such as teamwork and shared responsibility. Such organizations require support for trust and information sharing. The authoritarian approach has also led to security departments' reluctance to communicate with users with regard to work practices. It has been suggested by the U.S. Federal Information Processing Standards[14] that individual ownership of passwords increases accountability and decreases illicit usage of passwords, because of the possibility of audit trailing—a by-product of authentication. However, both of these assumptions rely on users' perceptions, which, as previously mentioned, do not always comply with those of the security departments. FIPS[15] also suggests that shared passwords for groups are insecure. This study has identified that—when users perceive they are using shared passwords for work carried out in a team—this may increase their perceptions of group responsibility and accountability. If a password mechanism is incompatible with users' work practices, they perceive the security mechanism as "not sensible" and circumvent it (for example, by disclosing their password to other group members). This can lead to a perception that *all* password mechanisms are "pointless," circumventing all of them and decreasing overall security. This does not mean that individual passwords should not be used in organizations with team-based working; it is worth considering protecting access to shared information with a shared password while leaving individual passwords for individual activities. The increased mental load of an additional shared password may cause fewer problems than the spiraling decline in security behavior caused by "incompatible" mechanisms.

It is important to challenge the view that users are never motivated to behave in a secure manner. Our results show that the majority of users were security conscious, as long as

14 FIPS 112.
15 *Ibid.*

they perceive the need for these behaviors (for example, because of obvious external threats or the perceived sensitivity of the information protected). These findings are supported by research within Organization B, where both physical and computer security levels were low and security threats were evident to users. In this situation, users demonstrated exemplary behavior with their own passwords. We argue that the need-to-know principle should be jettisoned. The main argument of its proponents is that by informing users about the rationale behind security mechanisms, along with real and potential threats to security, they may be lowering security by increasing the possibility of information leaks. This attitude has led to a two-fold problem:

- Users' lack of security awareness
- Security departments' lack of knowledge about users, producing security mechanisms and systems that are not usable

These two factors lower users' motivation to produce secure work practices. This in turn reinforces security departments' belief that users are "inherently insecure" and leads to the introduction of stricter mechanisms, which require more effort from users. This vicious circle needs to be broken. Communication between security departments and users is therefore often restricted to "ticking off" users caught circumventing the rules. This approach does not fit with modern distributed and networked organizations, which depend on communication and collaboration. Users have to be treated as partners in the endeavor to secure an organization's systems, not as the enemy within. System security is one of the last areas in IT in which user-centered design and user training are not regarded as essential—this has to change.

## Users and Password Behavior

Insecure work practices and low security motivation have been identified by research on information security as major problems that must be addressed.[16,17,18,19] The research presented here does, however, clearly identify the cause of these user-related problems; in the sidebar "Recommendations," we summarize methods for addressing these problems. There is an implicit assumption that users are not inherently motivated to adopt secure behavior, but that such behavior can be achieved through drills and threats of punishment in case of noncompliance. Knowledge from psychology and human-computer interaction indicates that users' behavior is likely to be more complex than a simple conditioned response. This study demonstrates that users forced to comply with password mechanisms incompatible with work practices may produce responses that circumvent the whole procedure. Insecure work practices and low security motivation among users can be caused

16 DeAlvare, *Crackers*.

17 Davis.

18 W. Ford, *Computer Communications Security: Principles, Standard Protocols and Techniques* (Englewood Cliffs, NJ: Prentice Hall, 1994).

19 S. Gordon, *Social Engineering: Techniques and Prevention* (Computer Security, 1995).

# RECOMMENDATIONS

The results from the studies reported have led to the formulation of the recommendations summarized here. The construction of secure passwords can be supported through the recommendations under "Password Content" and "Multiple Passwords." Recommended ways of ensuring that users comply with security mechanisms are described under "Users' Perceptions of Security" and "Work Practices."

## Password Content

- Provide instruction and training on how to construct usable and secure passwords. Users must be shown, proactively, how to construct memorable passwords that do not circumvent security mechanisms.

- Provide constructive online feedback during the password construction process, incorporating explanation if/when a password is rejected as insecure. This should also help to refresh users' knowledge of password design procedures.

## Multiple Passwords

- Asking users to remember multiple passwords decreases memorability and increases cognitive overheads associated with the password mechanism.

- If multiple passwords cannot be avoided, four or five is the maximum for unrelated, regularly used passwords that users can be expected to cope with. The number is lower if passwords are used infrequently.

- Related passwords are a frequently used technique employed by users who have to remember multiple passwords, but within-list interference creates another, even worse, memory problem. Where users have to work with a large number of different systems, single sign-on and physical security mechanisms such as smart cards should be considered to alleviate memory problems.

## Users' Perceptions of Security

- System security needs to be visible and seen to be taken seriously by the organization. Providing feedback during the password construction process not only assists users in the construction of secure passwords, but also is an example of security in action and increases users' awareness of system security and its importance.

- Inform users about existing and potential threats to the organization's systems and sensitivity of information contained in them. Awareness of threats and potential loss to the organization is the raison d'être for security mechanisms; without it, users are likely to perceive security mechanisms as tedious motions they have to go through. The role of passwords in the fight against perceived threats should be made explicit.

*—continued—*

- Users' awareness of the importance of security and threats to it needs to be maintained over time. This requires a balancing act. While we advise against "punishing" users who circumvent security mechanisms, such behavior needs to be detected and challenged in a constructive manner: if security is compromised and no action is taken, users tend to assume that "it doesn't matter anyway." At the same time, an environment giving the impression that its security mechanisms are invincible is likely to foster careless behavior among users, because the level of perceived threats to security is low.

- Provide users with guidance as to which systems and information are sensitive, and why. The current tendency is for security departments to treat all information as equally sensitive, with as little explanation as possible. Without such indicators and guidance, users tend to make arbitrary judgments based on their own—usually patchy—knowledge and experience. Explain how security levels relate to different levels of information sensitivity.

### Work Practices

- Password mechanisms need to be compatible with organizational and work procedures. Shared work and responsibility require users to perceive that they are using shared passwords, whereas information or work specific to individual users should be protected by individual passwords.

---

by security mechanisms and policies that take no account of users' work practices, organizational strategies, and usability. These factors are pivotal in the design and implementation of most computer systems today. Designers of security mechanisms must realize that they are the key to successful security systems. Unless security departments understand how the mechanisms they design are used in practice, there will remain the danger that mechanisms that look secure on paper will fail in practice.

## About the Authors

Dr. Anne Adams is a research fellow at the UCL Interaction Centre, a visiting senior lecturer at Middlesex University, and an external examiner at Bath University. Dr. Adams' research interests vary from security to digital libraries, HCI, and social issues. Research projects have been based in clinical, industrial, and academic settings. She has been both an invited and a keynote speaker for academic, industrial, and health organizations around the world (e.g., Royal Society of Medicine, Google).

*a.adams@ciderpress.demon.co.uk*

M. Angela Sasse is the professor of human-centred technology in the Department of Computer Science at University College London. After obtaining an M.Sc. in occupational psychology (from the University of Sheffield) and a Ph. D. in computer science (from the University of Birmingham), she joined UCL in 1990 to teach and research on design and evaluation of emerging technologies. Since 1997, her research has focused on user-centered approaches to security, privacy, and trust.

*A.Sasse@cs.ucl.ac.uk*

# CHAPTER THIRTY-THREE

# Usability and Privacy:
# A Study of KaZaA P2P File Sharing

**NATHANIEL S. GOOD AND AARON KREKELBERG**

**P**2P FILE SHARING SYSTEMS SUCH AS GNUTELLA, FREENET, AND KAZAA, while primarily intended for sharing multimedia files, frequently allow other types of information to be shared. This raises serious concerns about the extent to which users may unknowingly be sharing private or personal information.[1]

IIn this chapter, we report on a cognitive walkthrough and a laboratory user study of the KaZaA file sharing user interface. The majority of the users in our study were unable to tell what files they were sharing, and sometimes incorrectly assumed that they were not sharing any files when, in fact, they were sharing *all* files on their hard drive. An analysis of the KaZaA network suggested that a large number of users appeared to be unwittingly sharing personal and private files, and that some users were indeed taking advantage of this and downloading files containing ostensibly private information.

---

[1]  N. S. Good and A. Krekelberg, "Privacy and Trust, Usability and Privacy: A Study of Kazaa P2P File-Sharing," *Proceedings of the Conference on Human Factors in Computing Systems* (CHI '03', April 2003). © 2003 Association for Computing Machinery, Inc. Reprinted by permission.

# Introduction

The excitement about P2P systems has been encouraged by recent innovations that foster easier sharing of files, such as downloading simultaneously from multiple sources, and the sharing of many different file types, as well as improvements to the usability of these clients. Of the current P2P systems, KaZaA is by far the most popular and widely used, with more than 120 million downloads worldwide and an average of 3 million users online at any given time. The user interface (UI) for finding files is straightforward: the user types a query into a textbox and, from the results, selects a matching filename to download. If sharing is enabled, the files that the user downloads are then shared automatically with other users on the network. The success of a P2P file sharing network depends on people sharing files with one another, so this feature helps promote file sharing by recycling files in the network.

While facilitating file sharing and searching, the systems do a poor job of preventing users from accidentally sharing personal files. Users attracted to the simplicity of downloading files provided by the P2P network can inadvertently allow access to their private data files, such as email, tax reports, work-related spreadsheets, and private documents. This is especially problematic in a single-machine, multiple-user situation typical of families sharing a single computer. In such a setting, a parent could have a secure VPN connection to a corporation for downloading and working on important confidential files, only to have them inadvertently shared by a teenage son or daughter, without either party's knowledge. This is not simply a theoretical problem but describes a scenario that is possible in the current reality. Our research suggests that people are unintentionally sharing what appear to be personal or confidential files via KaZaA. Queries for files such as Inbox for Outlook Express (*.dbx* files), data for financial applications, and *.pst* files (Microsoft Outlook mail folders) returned numerous results.

In order to understand how this can take place, we examined KaZaA's UI and use from a variety of perspectives to determine if usability issues could account for such fatal errors. KaZaA is interesting from a usability perspective because it is widely used by millions of users with varying degrees of computer experience, has crossed over from a select group of expert users to a more general population, and has challenging UI issues that it must address to preserve users' privacy while facilitating file sharing. We feel that lessons learned from KaZaA are applicable to designers working with other P2P systems, as well as with other kinds of continually connected systems where users manage access control and share information (e.g., KM applications, expert finding, etc.). From a more general perspective, we hope that our study provides a concrete example of the challenges in designing UIs that both encourage participation and protect privacy, and guidelines for building these kinds of systems.

Recent literature examined usability guidelines for user interfaces for security applications. Whitten and Tygar[2] looked into usability problems that affected users sending secure messages via PGP,[3] and how inadequate design caused users to make fatal mistakes, such as sending unencrypted messages that they felt were encrypted, or sending people their private keys. Yee[4] has expanded on this work, and provides a list of guidelines and case studies for usability of security applications. His work builds on that of Saltzer and Schroeder,[5] which focused on understanding the design requirements for developing secure systems.

While KaZaA is not a security application like PGP or personal firewall software, it nonetheless has privacy implications for its users. It must help them ensure that data is not accidentally shared with others. We used an approach inspired by the success of Whitten and Tygar in identifying the flaws within PGP 5.0. We performed a cognitive walkthrough and a user study to analyze the interface of KaZaA and determine usability issues that could cause users to share files unintentionally with the KaZaA network. The results detailed in the following sections show that usability issues alone could account for unintentional file sharing. Indeed, we were able to determine from our user studies that it was possible for users to share all files on their hard drive and not even know it.

### Abuses on KaZaA Today

We looked at other P2P networks, such as Gnutella, for similar problems. We found that over a 24-hour period, we were able to find files such as *inbox.dbx* on these networks as well, yet in fewer numbers than KaZaA. We attribute this to the much smaller user base of Gnutella. Because Gnutella is an open protocol, unlike KaZaA, there are many different client programs that use it, each with a different interface. Focusing on the KaZaA interface gave us the benefit of a large user base and a consistent UI, from which we hoped we could generalize a solution for all kinds of P2P clients.

We were curious to see how widespread the problem of unintended file sharing is on the current KaZaA network, and whether users are currently taking advantage of others' mistakes to download private files from them. In order to do this, we scripted searches to run every 1.5 minutes for a 12-hour period. KaZaA operates on a closed protocol, so it is not possible to determine the full extent of people sharing personal files, as one cannot tell exactly how much of the network is being searched with every query.

2   A. Whitten and J. D. Tygar, "Why Johnny Can't Encrypt" *Proceedings of the 8th USENIX Security Symposium* (Aug. 1999). See also Chapter 34, this volume.

3   PGP: Pretty Good Privacy, *http://www.pgp.com*.

4   K. P. Yee, "User Interaction Design for Secure Systems," ICSIS, Singapore (2002).

5   J. H. Saltzer and M. D. Schroeder, "The Protection of Information in Computer Systems" in *Proceedings of the IEEE* 63:9 (Sept. 1975), 1278–1308; *http://web.mit.edu/Saltzer/www/publications/protection/*.

## Unintended File Sharing Among KaZaA Users

In our searches of the KaZaA network, we purposely limited ourselves to queries only, and did not download any user files to verify their contents. The targets of the searches were files that end in *.dbx*, with particular emphasis on *inbox.dbx*. DBX files are Microsoft Outlook Express email files. This is a good indicator that users are unintentionally sharing files, for several reasons. First, DBX files are commonly found on Windows machines because they are packaged with Internet Explorer and Windows. Second, they contain private email correspondence that most users would not likely intend to share. Finally, we had discovered that users who have their inbox shared typically had other files shared that contained what appeared to be private information.

The results of 443 searches in 12 hours showed that unintentional file sharing is quite prevalent on the KaZaA network. We found that 61% of all searches performed in this test returned one or more hits for *inbox.dbx*. By the end of the 12-hour period, 156 distinct users with shared inboxes were found.

To further demonstrate that this indicates unintentional file sharing, we examined 20 distinct cases of shares on the *inbox.dbx* file by manually using the "find more from same user" feature. We found that 19 of the 20 users shared the other email files found in the default Microsoft Outlook Express installation (Sent Items, Deleted Items, Outbox, etc.). In addition, nine users had exposed their web browser's cache and cookies, five had exposed word processing documents, two had what appeared to be data from financial software, and one user had files that belong in the system folder for Windows.

## Users Downloading Others' Private Files

After we determined that users were indeed sharing private files, we were interested in whether other users on the KaZaA network were taking advantage of this fact and downloading files from others. We ran a dummy client populated with dummy files (such as *Credit Cards.xls, Inbox.dbx, Outlook.pst*, and other types of files that were intended to appear to be private) over a 24-hour period.

From our dummy server, we received a total of four downloads from two unique users of an *Inbox.dbx* file (Figure 33-1).

*FIGURE 33-1. Inbox.dbx files being downloaded from our dummy client by other KaZaA users*

We also received four downloads from four unique users for an Excel spreadsheet named *Credit Cards.xls* (Figure 33-2).

| Credit Cards | Credit Cards.xls | Completed |
| Credit Cards | Credit Cards.xls | Completed |
| Credit Cards | Credit Cards.xls | Completed |

*FIGURE 33-2. Credit Card.xls files KaZaA users downloaded from our dummy client*

## Usability Guidelines

By looking at the KaZaA network, we surmised that abuses are occurring, and their frequency demonstrates that they are not isolated events.

Based on a list of security guidelines provided by Whitten and Tygar,[6] we created a modified list of usability guidelines adapted for peer-to-peer file sharing applications that take into account the unique demands of continuously connected systems that distribute personal files.

---

### USABILITY GUIDELINES FOR P2P FILE SHARING

*Definition*: Peer-to-peer file sharing software is safe and usable if users:

- Are clearly made aware of what files are being offered for others to download
- Are able to determine how to share and stop sharing files successfully
- Do not make dangerous errors that can lead to unintentionally sharing private files
- Are comfortable with what is being shared with others and confident that the system is handling this correctly

---

We then conducted a cognitive walkthrough and user study, paying close attention to whether the interface was able to meet these guidelines and, if not, why users were confused.

## Results of the Cognitive Walkthrough

Recent versions of the KaZaA application have made some progress in addressing access control issues. Default installation of KaZaA for users using a recent version of KaZaA 1.7.1 is relatively safe: it creates a shared file folder, assigns this as the default download file, and indexes these folders for the *My KaZaA* library. Various versions of KaZaA had various settings, and had different default configurations. The latest version of KaZaA 1.7.2 (the most

6   Whitten and Tygar.

recent at this time) and other previous versions of KaZaA offered to search for files to share with users during the initial setup. In the latest version at the time of this writing and in some previous versions, file sharing is enabled. While a default setup where file sharing is disabled, as in version 1.7.1, is relatively safe, user modifications of various settings are not. By adding or changing directories to be shared, there are potential interface issues that can create misunderstandings about what files the system is sharing with other users, regardless of the version of KaZaA that the user is using. There are a number of reasons why a user would change default settings. Three common scenarios are driven by users' desire to save the files being downloaded to a different location, to share more files with other users, or to add files to their shared files folder. In the following sections, we will walk through each of these scenarios and the various ways that KaZaA allows these to be accomplished. We will look at the various safeguards that KaZaA employs to prevent users from sharing private files, or files that they do not want others to see, and describe where they seem likely to fail.

### Changing the Download File Directory

In KaZaA, as in most P2P applications, the default shared directory provides the dual purpose of specifying the files that the user decides to share with the network, and the place where these files will be stored. The default shared directory is (confusingly) alternatively referred to as *My Media, My Shared Folder, My KaZaA,* and the *folder for downloaded files* in KaZaA.

*My Shared Folder* refers both to a folder created on the machine by KaZaA and abstractly to all folders that the user shares. For simplicity, we will refer to *My Shared Folder* as the actual folder that KaZaA creates by default to share files, and all files allocated for sharing as the *shared files*. The *My Media* and *My KaZaA* folders list all the shared files, yet organize them according to media type, such as music, video, documents, etc. For purposes of simplicity, we will refer only to *My Media*. The *folder for downloaded files* refers to the folder where download files will be stored, but also to the root folder of all shared files. Although each folder is used in a different context, they are essentially different names for the same thing: a list of files that KaZaA can share with others.

While the *My KaZaA* and *My Media* folders are accessible through clearly visible buttons, specifying shared files and the *folder for downloaded files* are managed through the Options menu, in the Tools tab (Figure 33-3). Additionally, the Options → Tools tab contains a checkbox for users to determine whether they would like to share files with the KaZaA community. Users may type in the name of the directory they would like to download files to, or alternately browse their filesystem and select the folder they would like to use to store downloaded files (Figure 33-4).

If the user has decided to share files with others, then all files in this directory, as well as the directories below it, are recursively shared and added to *My Media* files. The wording of the download folder is confusing. The word *folder* is singular, implying one folder, and

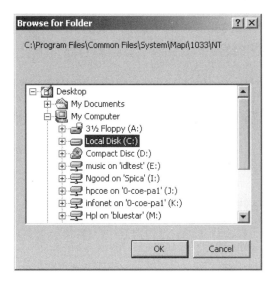

FIGURE 33-3. The Traffic tab in the Options menu; here is where users specify the download and My Shared directory as well as toggle sharing of all files

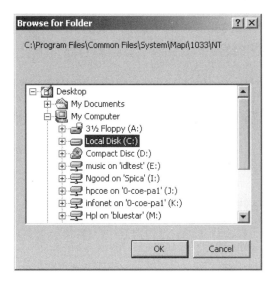

FIGURE 33-4. Browsing and selecting interface for the shared download folder; note that the interface says browse for folder, and does not mention that subfolders will be recursively searched for files

does not hint that all folders below it will be recursively shared with others. More misleadingly, the name *download folder* implies that it will be used to store files that are downloaded and has nothing to do with sharing. It does not mention that this folder (and the folders and files underneath) will also be shared with others, if sharing is enabled.

Another factor leading to user error is that hierarchical filesystems can be very difficult for some users to navigate and conceptualize. Vicente and Williges[7] demonstrated that users with low spatial ability have trouble navigating hierarchical filesystems compared to those with high spatial ability. Novice users are "notoriously bad" at navigating hierarchical file structures and prefer breadth (as opposed to depth) in browsing and searching for files or information. The tradeoffs between depth and breadth in hierarchical structures have been well studied by the psychological and human-computer interaction communities.[8, 9, 10, 11] Most reach the conclusion that breadth is better than depth. "Shortcuts" on the Windows desktop are frequently created to allow users one-click access to file folders buried in hierarchies. However, by automatically recursing through directories for files, KaZaA presumes, at the same time, that all users have a detailed knowledge of their filesystem and its contents. At the very least, users should be given a choice whether to recursively add files when asked to share a folder.

## Sharing Files

Two interfaces that KaZaA provides for sharing files are located in the Tools menu, under Find Shared Files for version 1.7 and above. Selecting this menu item brings up a dialog box with several choices (Figure 33-5).

One choice is to have KaZaA automatically discover files for the user by clicking the Search Wizard button. The other is for the user to browse his machine and determine which directories to share, which is accessible by selecting the Folder List tab, or clicking the Folder List button. The Find function uses a wizard interface to walk users through selecting drives to search, and select which folders to share after the process has been completed. After searching, KaZaA returns a list of folders that it recommends that the user share with other KaZaA users (Figure 33-6). In the latest version of KaZaA, it recommends folders containing documents (such as the default Windows *My Documents* folder), image files, and multimedia files, such as music and video. On a side note, it does not indicate whether any of these directories it has found are already being shared using other means. A message (that could easily be ignored) above the listbox tells users the steps that they will need to perform in order to stop sharing files in the folders that they select.

One problem with the Search Wizard interface (Figure 33-6) is that it does not describe what criteria it uses to find folders to share. For example, it does not say what files in the

---

7 K. J. Vicente and R. C. Williges, "Accommodating Individual Differences in Searching a Hierarchical File System," *International Journal of Man-Machine Studies* (1988), 29.

8 J. I. Kiger, "The Depth/Breadth Tradeoff in the Design of Menu-Driven Interfaces," *International Journal of Man-Machine Studies* 20 (1984), 201–213.

9 K. Larson and M. Czerwinski, "Web Page Design: Implications of Memory, Structure and Scent for Information Retrieval," *Conference Proceedings on Human Factors in Computing Systems*, 25–32.

10 G. A. Milier, "The Magical Number Seven Plus or Minus Two: Some Limits on Our Capacity for Processing Information," *Psychological Review* 63 (1956), 81–97.

11 D. P. Miller, "The Depth/Breadth Tradeoff in Hierarchical Computer Menus," *Proceedings of the Human Factors Society* (1981), 296-300.

F I G U R E 3 3 - 5 . Selection interface to find or select shared folders

*My Documents* folder will be shared, or describe the particular attributes of the *My Documents* folder that caused it to be recommended for sharing. The interface relies on the user's knowledge of what is capable of being shared by a file sharing program and what the program is looking for. It presumes that users have perfect knowledge of what kinds of files (and subdirectories with further files) are contained in those folders and that these contents will be shared recursively.

The "tip" portion is the only part of the interface that warns users that they risk sharing files that they would rather not. It is unclear whether users read this message and, if so, remember the instructions and places they need to go in order to stop sharing such files. It also mentions that users must remove the files one by one if they choose not to share them. Overall, while the search interface affords sharing more files, it makes browsing, searching, and stopping the sharing of specific files within shared folders difficult and tedious.

The other function, which we will call the Folder Select function, has a UI that allows the user to browse the current filesystem and select a folder or folders to share (Figure 33-7). Folders are shared by selecting a checkbox, and are restricted from sharing by deselecting

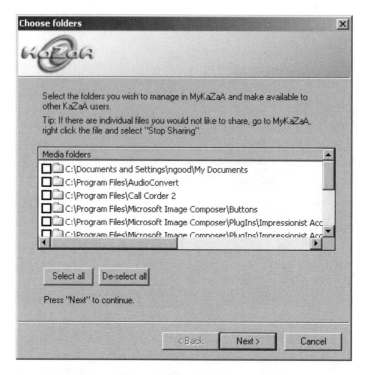

**FIGURE 33-6.** *Search interface*

the checkbox. When a user selects a directory, the directories below it are selected automatically for the user (Figure 33-8). When they deselect a directory, the directories below are also deselected.

If a user selects a drive (such as the C drive), a message pops up (Figure 33-9) warning the user that this action will share all files with all KaZaA users for this drive. This warning will not appear again if any user on a given machine decides to check "Do not show this again," and future users sharing the same machine will not be able to see this warning.

We noticed that if file sharing was enabled (through the UI in Figure 33-3) and the user had changed the download directory to something else, this change was not reflected in the Folder Select window (Figure 33-7). For example, if a user changes his download directory to *C:\* and sharing is enabled, he is sharing his whole hard drive. All of these files are indexed by *My Media*, but there is no indication in the checkbox, like the one in Figure 33-9, in the Folder Select function (Figure 33-7). We found this to be a critical flaw that the participants in the study discussed shortly found to be misleading. In effect, it allowed users to share anything through the download folder, and not be aware of it through the Folder Select function. In the user studies discussed shortly, this error had serious repercussions for user expectations of shared folders and files.

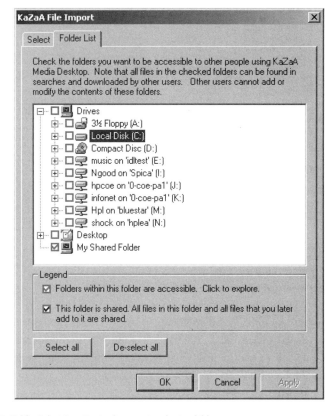

*FIGURE 33-7.* Folder Select Function to share or stop sharing folders

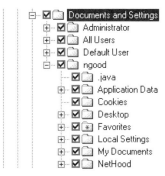

*FIGURE 33-8.* Expanded view of folders selected by selecting Documents and Settings

## Adding Files to the My Media Folder

KaZaA, like most file sharing programs, comes with a built-in media player that allows playback of a variety of audio and video formats. Playback of these formats is done through the My KaZaA tab, which organizes files based on their content into file folders, similar to the interface provided by Microsoft Internet Explorer. To add files to the *My*

*FIGURE 33-9. Warning to not share the entire folder from the Folder Select Function*

*Media* folder, they must be shared or included in the download directory as described earlier or through another button that "imports" files into *My Media*, using similar techniques to those described earlier.

Files imported into the *My Media* folder can be turned on and off individually via a context menu, accessible by right-clicking the file with the mouse, or with an icon above the file folders. The context menu is activated only for individual files, and does not work at the top folders or root folders of the directory structure. For example, if a user wanted to disable sharing of applications in the software folder, the only choice he has is to disable sharing entirely, or stop sharing each individual file. Also, there is no indication of exactly what folders are being shared on the user's hard drive. In the usability study described shortly, the *My Media* folder was a source of general confusion. The participants' opinions about its purpose and contents varied greatly.

## Uploading Files

During the walkthrough, we examined the Transfer File interface that allows users to determine what is currently being uploaded to and downloaded from the KaZaA network. It consisted of two scrollable lists. Files being transferred to others are appended to the bottom of the file transfer list, and this list is cleared every time KaZaA is restarted, erasing any past transactions. Users therefore have to be very attentive to what is being transferred in KaZaA, in order to be aware of any unwanted file shares.

## Summary of Usability Guidelines

Here we summarize the results of the cognitive walkthrough in relation to how well KaZaA satisfies each of the earlier proposed guidelines:

1. *FAILED*: Users should be made clearly aware of what files are being offered for others to download.

   From the cognitive walkthrough, we see that bugs, assumptions of users' knowledge in searching and selecting files, and unclear labeling clearly make it difficult for users to determine what is offered for others to download. Nowhere in the interface were we able to determine which types of files can be shared.

2. *FAILED*: Users should be able to determine how to successfully share and stop sharing files.

The cognitive walkthrough revealed many ways to share files, but demonstrated that there are few ways to stop sharing files. The ways that do exist are complicated and difficult to find. Again, unclear labeling is confusing and misleading, complicating the problem.

3. *FAILED*: Users should not be able to make dangerous errors that can lead to unintentionally sharing private files.

Files and folders shared through the *download* folder are not indicated as such in other parts of the interface. This is a serious flaw that could easily allow users to make fatal mistakes.

4. *FAILED*: Users should be sufficiently comfortable with what is being shared with others and confident that the system is handling this correctly.

In the cognitive walkthrough, it was difficult to determine which types of files could be shared, when KaZaA was sharing them, and with whom. Without constantly monitoring KaZaA, it is difficult to tell what the system is doing with the files and with whom they are sharing them.

## A Two-Part User Study

We attempted to devise a test to determine how easy it is for users to misconfigure their system. After several trials, we discovered that our attempts to devise a realistic scenario involving sharing and specifying file locations became contrived and only confused our test participants. Nor could we simulate the length of time over which settings are most likely changed and then forgotten during real use. In addition, we could not speculate on all of the various reasons users would want to change their default settings, although we knew from our data that they were indeed modifying the settings and were not aware of it.

From anecdotal evidence, we know that KaZaA users often work in shared computer settings, so it is quite possible for one user to change all the settings and another to know nothing about it. We were able to contact and interview four online users who had accidentally shared their inboxes and to talk to them about their configurations. These users indicated that they had either changed the settings to make files easier to find (1 of 4) or that they shared a computer with other people who may have changed the settings without their knowledge (3 of 4). For this reason, and given the difficulties with any other realistic trial described earlier, we decided to make a very simple test to simulate this scenario. We would share all files on the hard drive (as if we were a user sharing the same machine) and see how easy it was for participants to determine what, if anything, was being shared.

Our study consisted of 12 participants: 10 of these had used file sharing applications (such as Morpheus, Gnutella, KaZaA, and Napster) before, and two had not. All the users spent more than 10 hours a week on their computers.

## Parts of the Study

The two parts of the study are described in the following sections.

### KaZaA sharing comprehension questions

We were interested in the participants' conceptions of the types of files that peer-to-peer file sharing applications can share, as well as whether they were able to perform the specified task. We asked the participants to indicate what types of files could be shared over peer-to-peer networks.

### Current sharing settings discovery task

The participants were initially presented with the KaZaA interface, which had been pre-configured in the following manner:

- File sharing was enabled (thus *My Shared Folder* was being shared).
- The *download* directory was set to C:\, effectively sharing all files on the hard drive as well.
- KaZaA indexed all of C:\, and displayed the file information into the *My Media* folder.

In order to prevent others from downloading our files, we set up KaZaA behind a firewall and blocked incoming requests to download files. This prevented others from actually accessing our files, but still allowed KaZaA to index all the files and provide them for sharing.

Participants were given a short tutorial on file sharing and the concept of a shared folder. They were then asked to discover which files were currently being shared, if any, on a KaZaA media desktop running KaZaA version 1.7.1. All participants were given the same setup and were told to take as much time as they needed. They were allowed to use only the KaZaA interface, and at the end of their search were asked to provide a clear answer of whether they thought files were being shared, and if so, which folders they were in.

If participants correctly determined that files were being shared, we asked them to stop sharing them, and share only *My Shared Folder*.

## Results

The following sections summarize the results of the two parts of the study.

### KaZaA sharing comprehension questions

Only 2 of the 12 participants indicated correctly that all files could be shared. One more participant indicated correctly that it was also possible to share office documents, source code files, and email folders. The nine remaining participants believed that only multimedia files such as music, video, and pictures could be shared. After completing the task, some participants were very surprised to learn that all files could be shared with others, and some couldn't understand why. One participant exclaimed, "You mean it shares *all* files?" and expressed concern about why it would be able to share anything other than multimedia files. These results from our study bolster those from our cognitive walkthrough to demonstrate that KaZaA is in clear violation of the first guideline listed under "Usability Guidelines": participants should be made clearly aware of what files are being offered for others to download.

## Current sharing settings discovery task

Only 2 of the 12 participants were able to determine correctly which files and folders were currently being shared. Of those 2, both were able to turn off sharing completely using the Stop Sharing feature (Figure 33-3), but were not able to determine how to stop sharing a single given folder. Of the remaining participants:

- 5 of 12 determined incorrectly that *My Shared Folder* was the only folder being shared, based on the information they saw from the Folder Select feature (Figure 33-7), which, as we found in our cognitive walkthrough, does not update itself based on current sharing status.

- 2 of 12 used the Find Files interface to search for folders they were sharing. When everything showed up unchecked (Figure 33-6), the participants concluded incorrectly that nothing was being shared.

- 2 of 12 browsed Help and used it to determine incorrectly that the only folder they could share was *My Shared Folder*.

- 1 of 12 was unable to determine what folder was being shared after going through every menu item in the application and the Help. The participant said that the files in *My Shared Folder* were probably being shared but admitted that he couldn't determine what, if anything, was in that folder.

Many participants found the initial interface difficult to navigate. Several participants traversed the web interface to look for help in determining what KaZaA shared, and how. In the Help section, some participants tried to use the Search function, assuming incorrectly that it searched Help and not the KaZaA network. Of the participants who were able to make it to the menus in the toolbar at the top of the application, only one was able to make the connection between the *download* folder (Figure 33-4) and *My Shared Folder* described in the help and shown on the Folder Select feature (Figure 33-7). Participants had difficulty finding the main menus in the top toolbar, and had difficulty understanding the labeling on the menu items, which made it hard for them to traverse the menu hierarchies to determine where they could control file sharing. One participant later described the experience as a "buckshot approach" to find out what was where. The participant mentioned that "he had no clue" where to look for shared folders, and resorted to looking through every menu item for something that made sense.

There was considerable confusion about *My Media*. Less than half of the participants thought that items in *My Media* were being shared with others, the rest either thought it held an archive of all media on the machine for personal use, or assumed it contained some shared and some unshared items. Only three participants could determine which items were shared and which were not by looking at the file icons, but all were unsure of which folders in *My Media* contained shared items and which contained items not being shared without browsing each individual folder.

### Suggested Design Improvements

Based on what we found in the surveys, participant studies, and cognitive walkthrough, we have several suggestions that may help improve the current interface:

- Prohibit or curtail sharing of files that are not multimedia files. For example, nonmultimedia files could be shared using a more safety conscious, or advanced participant interface. As most participants in our study were unaware of the fact that they could share files other than multimedia, this would realign users' expectations with the current reality. We feel that the current interface is weighted too heavily in favor of sharing files. Our usability studies suggest that improvements can be made to create a balance between sharing files easily (to encourage KaZaA uptake by making sure there is a wealth of content available) and protecting and preserving users' privacy.

- Provide better "feedforward" about the consequences of recursion in sharing of folders and subfolders.

- Provide a more rigorous interface that explicitly supports users' efforts to make exceptions to recursively shared folders, or otherwise warns users that they have not checked subfolders in a folder that is being selected for sharing.

## Conclusion

While the interface provided by KaZaA affords simple sharing and file download features, we find that its sharing interface is problematic. The design presupposes sophisticated user understanding of file sharing, and fails all four of the usability guidelines that we developed based on Whitten and Tygar's work.

By being provided with several different locations and interfaces to manage file sharing and not integrating them, users are not made aware of which files are being offered for others to download and are not able to determine how to successfully share and stop sharing files. Ambiguity and erroneous assumptions about recursion and which types of files can be shared allow users to make dangerous errors, such as sharing an entire hard drive. Finally, the confusing multiple purposes of the *My Media* interface cause confusion about what is actually being shared. Given the potential violation of user privacy and the current abuses that we noted earlier, it should be a top priority for file sharing applications to look into usability for security applications, and to design their applications accordingly.

We believe that measures to protect privacy need not reduce the amount of content that attracts users to such shared networks. Rather, they will simply avoid the unintentional sharing of a large amount of personal and confidential content that is unlikely to appeal to bona fide users anyway.

## Acknowledgments

Thanks to Mary Czerwinski, Paul Dourish, Marti Hearst, and the IDL group at HP Labs for helping with early drafts of this document. Special thanks to Victoria Bellotti and Marti Hearst for help with the final draft, and to the University of Minnesota Office of Information Management for allowing us to use their computers to run our study.

## About the Authors

Nathaniel Good is a Ph.D. student at the University of California's School of Information Management and Systems and the Samuelson Clinic at Boalt Law School, concentrating on human computer interaction and privacy. A fundamental goal of his research is making networked systems and devices usable and respectful of people's privacy. His work on privacy includes studies of RFID, spyware, and P2P networks. He has testified on his work with P2P systems and privacy before the U.S. House of Representatives, Senate, and FTC. This study was done while he was an intern at IDL in Hewlett-Packard Labs, Palo Alto California.

*http://www.sims.berkeley.edu/~ngood*

Aaron Krekelberg has been developing software for over 13 years. As a consultant, he developed information solutions for companies such as Medtronic, Mayo Clinic, and Boston Scientific. As an owner and primary software engineer of Borealis Communications, LLC, he developed vertical market solutions for wireless, mobile platforms. As a researcher, he has been involved in studying P2P network protocols and information content. He has testified before the House Committee on Government Reform and the Senate judiciary in regard to usability and privacy issues with P2P systems. He is currently a consultant for Allianz Life.

*aaron.krekelberg@gmail.com*

# CHAPTER THIRTY-FOUR

# Why Johnny Can't Encrypt
## *A Usability Evaluation of PGP 5.0*

**ALMA WHITTEN AND J. D. TYGAR**

**U**SER ERRORS CAUSE OR CONTRIBUTE TO MOST COMPUTER SECURITY FAILURES, yet user interfaces for security still tend to be clumsy, confusing, or near nonexistent. Is this simply because of a failure to apply standard user interface design techniques to security? We argue that, on the contrary, effective security requires a different usability standard, and that it will not be achieved through the user interface design techniques appropriate to other types of consumer software.[1]

To test this hypothesis, we performed a case study of a security program that does have a good user interface by general standards: PGP 5.0. Our case study used a cognitive walk-through analysis together with a laboratory user test to evaluate whether PGP 5.0 can be used successfully by cryptography novices to achieve effective electronic mail security. The analysis found a number of user interface design flaws that may contribute to security failures, and the user test demonstrated that when our test participants were given 90 minutes in which to sign and encrypt a message using PGP 5.0, the majority of them were unable to do so successfully.

---

1   This paper was originally published in the *Proceedings of the 8th USENIX Security Symposium* (Washington, D.C., Aug. 23–36, 1999), 169–184.

We conclude that PGP 5.0 is not usable enough to provide effective security for most computer users, despite its attractive graphical user interface, supporting our hypothesis that user interface design for effective security remains an open problem. We close with a brief description of our continuing work on the development and application of user interface design principles and techniques for security.

## Introduction

Security mechanisms are effective only when used correctly. Strong cryptography, provably correct protocols, and bug-free code will not provide security if the people who use the software forget to click on the Encrypt button when they need privacy, give up on a communication protocol because they are too confused about which cryptographic keys they need to use, or accidentally configure their access control mechanisms to make their private data world readable. Problems such as these are already quite serious: at least one researcher, Matt Bishop,[2] has claimed that configuration errors are the probable cause of more than 90% of all computer security failures. Because average citizens are now increasingly encouraged to make use of networked computers for private transactions, the need to make security manageable for even untrained users has become critical.[3, 4]

This is inescapably a user interface design problem. Legal remedies, increased automation, and user training provide only limited solutions. Individual users may not have the resources to pursue an attacker legally, and may not even realize that an attack took place. Automation may work for securing a communications channel, but not for setting an access control policy when a user wants to share some files and not others. Employees can be required to attend training sessions, but home computer users cannot.

Why, then, is there such a lack of good user interface design for security? Are existing general user interface design principles adequate for security? To answer these questions, we must first understand what kind of usability security requires in order to be effective. In this chapter, we offer a specific definition of usability for security, and identify several significant properties of security as a problem domain for user interface design. The design priorities required to achieve usable security, and the challenges posed by the properties we discuss, are significantly different from those of general consumer software.We therefore suspect that making security usable will require the development of domain-specific user interface design principles and techniques.

To investigate further, we looked to existing software to find a program that was representative of the best current user interface design for security, an exemplar of general user interface design as applied to security software. By performing a detailed case study of the

---

2  Matt Bishop, *UNIX Security: Threats and Solutions*, presentation to SHARE 86.0 (March 1996).

3  "The End of Privacy," *The Economist* (May 1, 1999), 21–23.

4  Stephen Kent, "Security," *More Than Screen Deep: Toward Every-Citizen Interfaces to the Nation's Information Infrastructure* (Washington, D.C.: National Academy Press, 1997).

usability of such a program, focusing on the impact of usability issues on the effectiveness of the security the program provides, we were able to get valuable results on several fronts. First, our case study serves as a test of our hypothesis that user interface design standards appropriate for general consumer software are not sufficient for security. Second, good usability evaluation for security is itself something of an open problem, and our case study discusses and demonstrates the evaluation techniques that we found to be most appropriate. Third, our case study provides real data on which to base our priorities and insights for research into better user interface design solutions, both for the specific program in question and for the domain of security in general.

We chose PGP 5.0[5, 6, 7] as the best candidate subject for our case study. Its user interface appears to be reasonably well designed by general consumer software standards, and its marketing literature[8] indicates that effort was put into the design, stating that the "significantly improved graphical user interface makes complex mathematical cryptography accessible for novice computer users." Furthermore, because public key management is an important component of many security systems being proposed and developed today, the problem of how to make the functionality in PGP usable enough to be effective is widely relevant.

We began by deriving a specific usability standard for PGP from our general usability standard for security. In evaluating PGP 5.0's usability against that standard, we chose to employ two separate evaluation methods: a direct analysis technique called cognitive walkthrough,[9] and a laboratory user test.[10] The two methods have complementary strengths and weaknesses. User testing produces more objective results, but is necessarily limited in scope; direct analysis can consider a wider range of possibilities and factors, but is inherently subjective. The sum of the two methods produces a more exhaustive evaluation than either could alone.

5   At the time of this writing, PGP 6.0 has recently been released. Some points raised in our case study may not apply to this newer version; however, this does not significantly diminish the value of PGP 5.0 as a subject for usability analysis. Also, our evaluation was performed using the Apple Macintosh version, but the user interface issues we address are not specific to a particular operating system and are equally applicable to Unix and Windows security software. [Note added in July 2005: Since the original 1999 publication of our paper, PGP has been substantionally modified. The current version of PGP shipping is PGP Desktop 9.0.]

6   Simson Garfinkel, *PGP: Pretty Good Privacy* (Sebastopol, CA: O'Reilly Media, 1995).

7   Pretty Good Privacy, Inc., *User's Guide for PGP for Personal Privacy*, Version 5.0 for the Mac OS. Packaged with software, 1997.

8   Jeffrey Rubin, *Handbook of Usability Testing: How to Plan, Design, and Conduct Effective Tests* (New York: John Wiley & Sons, Inc., 1994).

9   Cathleen Wharton, John Rieman, Clayton Lewis, and Peter Polson, "The Cognitive Walkthrough Method: A Practioner's Guide," *Usability Inspection Methods* (New York: John Wiley & Sons, Inc., 1994).

10  Rubin.

We present a point-by-point discussion of the results of our direct analysis, followed by a brief description of our user test's purpose, design, and participants, and then a compact discussion of the user test results. A more detailed presentation of this material, including user test transcript summaries, may be found in Whitten and Tygar.[11]

Based on the results of our evaluation, we conclude that PGP 5.0's user interface does not come even reasonably close to achieving our usability standard—it does not make public key encryption of electronic mail manageable for average computer users. This, along with much of the detail from our evaluation results, supports our hypothesis that security-specific user interface design principles and techniques are needed. In our continuing work, we are using our usability standard for security, the observations made in our direct analysis, and the detailed findings from our user test as a basis from which to develop and apply appropriate design principles and techniques.

# Understanding the Problem

Before describing the user test, we provide a specific definition of usability for security, identify the key properties of security as a problem domain for user interface design, and define a usability standard for PGP.

## Defining Usability for Security

Usability necessarily has different meanings in different contexts. For some, efficiency may be a priority; for others, learnability; for still others, flexibility. In a security context, our priorities must be whatever is needed in order for the security to be used effectively. We capture that set of priorities in the following definition:

*Definition*: Security software is usable if the people who are expected to use it:

- Are reliably made aware of the security tasks they need to perform
- Are able to figure out how to successfully perform those tasks
- Don't make dangerous errors
- Are sufficiently comfortable with the interface to continue using it

## Problematic Properties of Security

Security has some inherent properties that make it a difficult problem domain for user interface design. Design strategies for creating usable security will need to take these properties explicitly into account, and generalized user interface design does not do so. We describe five such properties here; it is possible that there are others that we have not yet identified.

11 Alma Whitten and J. D. Tygar, *Usability of Security: A Case Study*, Carnegie Mellon University School of Computer Science Technical Report CMU-CS-98-155 (Dec. 1998).

1. The unmotivated user property

Security is usually a secondary goal. People do not generally sit down at their computers wanting to manage their security; rather, they want to send email, browse web pages, or download software, and they want security in place to protect them while they do those things. It is easy for people to put off learning about security, or to optimistically assume that their security is working, while they focus on their primary goals. Designers of user interfaces for security should not assume that users will be motivated to read manuals or go looking for security controls that are designed to be unobtrusive. Furthermore, if security is too difficult or annoying, users may give up on it altogether.

2. The abstraction property

Computer security management often involves security policies, which are systems of abstract rules for deciding whether to grant access to resources. The creation and management of such rules is an activity that programmers take for granted, but that may be alien and unintuitive to many members of the wider user population. User interface design for security will need to take this into account.

3. The lack of feedback property

The need to prevent dangerous errors makes it imperative to provide good feedback to the user, but providing good feedback for security management is a difficult problem. The state of a security configuration is usually complex, and attempts to summarize it are not adequate. Furthermore, the correct security configuration is the one that does what the user "really wants," and because only the user knows what that is, it is hard for security software to perform much useful error checking.

4. The barn door property

The proverb about the futility of locking the barn door after the horse is gone is descriptive of an important property of computer security: once a secret has been left accidentally unprotected, even for a short time, there is no way to be sure that it has not already been read by an attacker. Because of this, user interface design for security needs to place a very high priority on making sure users understand their security well enough to keep from making potentially high-cost mistakes.

5. The weakest link property

It is well known that the security of a networked computer is only as strong as its weakest component. If a cracker can exploit a single error, the game is up. This means that users need to be guided to attend to all aspects of their security, not left to proceed through random exploration as they might with a word processor or a spreadsheet.

## A Usability Standard for PGP

People who use email to communicate over the Internet need security software that allows them to do so with privacy and authentication. The documentation and marketing literature for PGP presents it as a tool intended for that use by this large, diverse group of people, the majority of whom are not computer professionals. Referring back to our general definition of usability for security, we derived the following question on which to focus our evaluation:

> If an average user of email feels the need for privacy and authentication, and acquires PGP with that purpose in mind, will PGP's current design allow that person to realize what needs to be done, figure out how to do it, and avoid dangerous errors, without becoming so frustrated that he decides to give up on using PGP after all?

Stating the question in more detail, we want to know whether that person will, at minimum:

- Understand that privacy is achieved by encryption, and figure out how to encrypt email and how to decrypt email received from other people

- Understand that authentication is achieved through digital signatures, and figure out how to sign email and how to verify signatures on email from other people

- Understand that in order to sign email and allow other people to send him encrypted email, a key pair must be generated, and figure out how to do so

- Understand that in order to allow other people to verify his signature and to send him encrypted email, he must publish his public key, and figure out some way to do so

- Understand that in order to verify signatures on email from other people and send encrypted email to other people, he must acquire those people's public keys, and figure out some way to do so

- Manage to avoid such dangerous errors as accidentally failing to encrypt, trusting the wrong public keys, failing to back up his private keys, and forgetting his passphrases

- Be able to succeed at all of this within a few hours of reasonably motivated effort

This is a minimal list of items that are essential for correct use of PGP. It does not include such important tasks as having other people sign the public key, signing other people's public keys, revoking the public key and publicizing the revocation, or evaluating the authenticity of a public key based on accompanying signatures and making use of PGP's built-in mechanisms for such evaluation.

## Evaluation Methods

We chose to evaluate PGP's usability through two methods: an informal cognitive walkthrough[12] in which we reviewed PGP's user interface directly and noted aspects of its design that failed to meet the usability standard described in the preceding section, and a user test[13] performed in a laboratory with test participants selected to be reasonably representative of the general population of email users. The strengths and weaknesses inherent

12 Wharton.
13 Rubin.

in each of the two methods made them useful in quite different ways, and it was more realistic for us to view them as complementary evaluation strategies[14] than to attempt to use the laboratory test to directly verify the points raised by the cognitive walkthrough.

*Cognitive walkthrough* is a usability evaluation technique modeled after the software engineering practice of code walkthroughs. To perform a cognitive walkthrough, the evaluators step through the use of the software as if they were novice users, attempting to mentally simulate what they think the novices' understanding of the software would be at each point, and looking for probable errors and areas of confusion. As an evaluation tool, cognitive walkthrough tends to focus on the learnability of the user interface (as opposed to, say, the efficiency), and as such it is an appropriate tool for evaluating the usability of security.

Although our analysis is most accurately described as a cognitive walkthough, it also incorporated aspects of another technique, *heuristic evaluation*.[15] In this technique, the user interface is evaluated against a specific list of high-priority usability principles; our list of principles is comprised by our definition of usability for security (in the section "Defining Usability for Security") and its restatement specifically for PGP (in the section "A Usability Standard for PGP"). Heuristic evaluation is ideally performed by people who are "double experts," highly familiar both with the application domain and with usability techniques and requirements (including an understanding of the skills, mindset, and background of the people who are expected to use the software). Our evaluation draws on our experience as security researchers and on additional background in training and tutoring novice computer users, as well as in theater, anthropology, and psychology.

Some of the same properties that make the design of usable security a difficult and specialized problem also make testing the usability of security a challenging task. To conduct a user test, we must ask the participants to use the software to perform some task that will include the use of the security. If, however, we prompt them to perform a security task directly, when in real life they might have had no awareness of that task, then we have failed to test whether the software is designed well enough to give them that awareness when they need it. Furthermore, to test whether they are able to figure out how to use the security when they want it, we must make sure that the test scenario gives them some secret that they consider worth protecting, comparable to the value we expect them to place on their own secrets in the real world. Designing tests that take these requirements adequately into account is something that must be done carefully, and with the exception of some work on testing the effectiveness of warning labels,[16] we have found little existing material on user testing that addresses similar concerns.

14  B. E. John, and M. M. Mashyna, "Evaluating a Multimedia Authoring Tool with Cognitive Walkthrough and Think-Aloud User Studies," *Journal of the American Society of Information Science* 48:9, 1997.

15  Jakob Nielsen, "Heuristic Evaluation," *Usability Inspection Methods* (New York: John Wiley & Sons, Inc., 1994).

16  M. S. Wogalter and S. L. Young, "Enhancing Warning Compliance Through Alternative Product Label Designs," *Applied Ergonomics* 25 (1994), 3–57.

# Cognitive Walkthrough

Because this chapter is intended for a security audience and is subject to space limitations, we present the results of our cognitive walkthrough in summary form, focusing on the points that are most relevant to security risks.

### Visual Metaphors

The metaphor of *keys* is built into cryptologic terminology, and PGP's user interface relies heavily on graphical depictions of keys and locks. The PGPtools display, shown in Figure 34-1, offers four buttons to the user, representing four operations: Encrypt, Sign, Encrypt & Sign, and Decrypt/Verify, plus a fifth button for invoking the PGPkeys application. The graphical labels on these buttons indicate the encryption operation with an icon of a sealed envelope that has a metal loop on top to make it look like a closed padlock and, for the decryption operation, an icon of an open envelope with a key inserted at the bottom. Even for a novice user, these appear to be straightforward visual metaphors that help make the use of keys to encrypt and decrypt an intuitive concept.

FIGURE 34-1. PGPtools display

Still more helpful, however, would be an extension of the metaphor to distinguish between public keys for encryption and private keys for decryption; normal locks use the same key to lock and unlock, and the key metaphor will lead people to expect the same for encryption and decryption if it is not visually clarified in some way. Faulty intuition in this case may lead them to assume that they can always decrypt anything they have encrypted, an assumption that may have upsetting consequences. Different icons for public and private keys, perhaps drawn to indicate that they fit together like puzzle pieces, might be an improvement.

*Signatures* are another metaphor built into cryptologic terminology, but the icon of the blue quill pen that is used to indicate signing is problematic. People who are not familiar with cryptography probably know that quills are used for signing, and will recognize that the picture indicates the signature operation, but what they also need to understand is that they are using their private keys to generate signatures. The quill pen icon, which has nothing keylike about it, will not help them understand this and may even lead them to think that, along with the key objects that they use to encrypt, they also have quill pen objects that they use to sign. Quill pen icons encountered elsewhere in the program may be taken to be those objects, rather than the signatures that they are actually intended to represent. A better icon design might keep the quill pen to represent signing, but modify it to show a private key as the nib of the pen, and use some entirely different icon for signatures, perhaps something that looks more like a bit of inked handwriting and incorporates a keyhole shape.

Signature verification is not represented visually, which is a shame because it would be easy for people to overlook it altogether. The single button for Decrypt/Verify, labeled with an icon that only evokes decryption, could easily lead people to think that "verify" just means "verify that the decryption occurred correctly." Perhaps an icon that showed a private key unlocking the envelope and a public key unlocking the signature inside could suggest a much more accurate model to the user, while still remaining simple enough to serve as a button label.

### Different Key Types

Originally, PGP used the popular RSA algorithm for encryption and signing. PGP 5.0 uses the Diffie-Hellman/DSS algorithms. The RSA and Diffie-Hellman/DSS algorithms use correspondingly different types of keys. The makers of PGP would prefer to see all the users of their software switch to use of Diffie-Hellman/DSS, but have designed PGP 5.0 to be backward compatible and to handle existing RSA keys when necessary. The lack of forward compatibility, however, can be a problem: if a file is encrypted for several recipients, some of whom have RSA keys and some of whom have Diffie-Hellman/DSS keys, the recipients who have RSA keys will not be able to decrypt it unless they have upgraded to PGP 5.0; similarly, those recipients will not be able to verify signatures created with Diffie-Hellman/DSS without a software upgrade.

PGP 5.0 alerts its users to this compatibility issue in two ways. First, it uses different icons to depict the different key types: a blue key with an old-fashioned shape for RSA keys, and a brass key with a more modern shape for Diffie-Hellman/DSS keys, as shown in Figure 34-2. Second, when users attempt to encrypt documents using mixed key types, a warning message is displayed to tell them that recipients who have earlier versions of PGP may not be able to decrypt these documents.

| Name | Validity | Trust | Creation | Size |
|---|---|---|---|---|
| Alma Whitten <alma@cs.cmu.edu> | | | 9/24/98 | 1024/2048 |
| Alma Whitten <alma@cs.cmu.edu> | | | | |
| Alma Whitten <alma@cs.cmu.edu> | | | 9/24/98 | |
| Bill Blanke <wjb@pgp.com> | | | 5/14/97 | 1024/4096 |
| Brett A. Thomas <bat@pgp.com> | | | 5/19/97 | 1024/2048 |
| Jason Bobier <jason@pgp.com> | | | 6/4/97 | 1024/2059 |
| Jeff Harrell <jeff@pgp.com> | | | 5/20/97 | 1024/2048 |
| Jeffrey I. Schiller <jis@mit.edu> | | | 8/27/94 | 1024 |
| jude shabry <jude@pgp.com> | | | 6/9/97 | 1024/2048 |
| Lloyd L. Chambers <lloyd@pgp.com> | | | 5/20/97 | 1024/4096 |
| Mark B. Elrod <elrod@pgp.com> | | | 6/4/97 | 1024/2048 |
| Mark H. Weaver <mhw@pgp.com> | | | 6/10/97 | 1024/2048 |

*FIGURE 34-2. PGPkeys display*

Unfortunately, information about the meaning of the blue and brass key icons is difficult to find, requiring users either to go looking through the 132-page manual, or to figure it out based on the presence of other key type data. Furthermore, other than the warning message encountered during encryption, explanation of why the different key types are significant (in particular, the risk of forward compatibility problems) is given only in the manual. Double-clicking on a key pops up a Key Properties window, which would be a good place to provide a short message about the meaning of the blue or brass key icon and the significance of the corresponding key type.

It is most important for the user to pay attention to the key types when choosing a key for message encryption, because that is when mixed key types can cause compatibility problems. However, PGP's dialog box (see Figure 34-3) presents the user with the metaphor of choosing people (recipients) to receive the message, rather than keys with which to encrypt the message. This is not a good design choice, not only because the human head icons obscure the key type information, but also because people may have multiple keys, and it is counterintuitive for the dialog to display multiple versions of a person rather than the multiple keys that person owns.

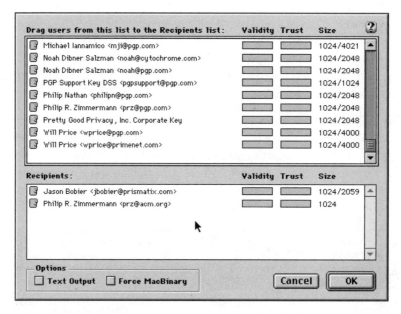

FIGURE 34-3. PGP dialog box

## Key Server

Key servers are publicly accessible (via the Internet) databases in which anyone can publish a public key joined to a name. PGP is set to access a key server at MIT by default, but others are available, most of which are kept up-to-date as mirrors of each other. PGP offers three key server operations to the user under the Keys pull-down menu shown in Figure 34-4: Get Selected Key, Send Selected Key, and Find New Keys. The first two of those simply connect to the key server and perform the operation. The third asks the user to type in a name or email address to search for, connects to the key server and performs the search, and then tells the user how many keys were returned as a result, asking whether to add them to the user's key ring.

*FIGURE 34-4. Keys pull-down menu*

The first problem we find with this presentation of the key server is that users may not realize that it exists, because there is no representation of it in the top level of the PGPkeys display. Putting the key server operations under a Key Server pull-down menu would be a better design choice, especially as it is worthwhile to encourage the user to make a mental distinction between operations that access remote machines and those that are purely local. We also think that it should be made clearer that a remote machine is being accessed, and that the identity of the remote machine should be displayed. Often the "connecting—receiving data—closing connection" series of status messages that PGP displayed flashed by almost too quickly to be read.

At present, PGPkeys keeps no records of key server accesses. There is nothing to show whether a key has been sent to a key server, or when a key was fetched or last updated, and from which key server the key was fetched or updated. This is information that might be useful to the user for key management and for verifying that key server operations were completed successfully. Adding this record keeping to the information displayed in the Key Properties window would improve PGP.

*Key revocation*, in which a certificate is published to announce that a previously published public key should no longer be considered valid, generally implies the use of the key server to publicize the revocation. PGP's key revocation operation does not send the resulting revocation certificate to the key server, which is probably as it should be, but there is a risk that some users will assume that it does do so, and fail to take that action themselves. A warning that the created revocation certificate has not yet been publicized would be appropriate.

## Key Management Policy

PGP maintains two ratings for each public key in a PGP key ring. These ratings may be assigned by the user or derived automatically. The first of these ratings is *validity*, which is meant to indicate how sure the user is that the key is safe to encrypt with (i.e., that it does belong to the person whose name it is labeled with). A key may be labeled as completely valid, marginally valid, or invalid. Keys that the user generates are always completely valid. The second of these ratings is *trust*, which indicates how much faith the user has in the key (and, implicitly, the owner of the key) as a certifier of other keys. Similarly, a key may be labeled as completely trusted, marginally trusted, or untrusted, and the user's own keys are always completely trusted.

What users may not realize, unless they read the manual very carefully, is that there is a policy built into PGP that automatically sets the validity rating of a key based on whether it has been signed by a certain number of sufficiently trusted keys. This is dangerous. There is nothing to prevent users from innocently assigning their own interpretations to those ratings and setting them accordingly (especially because "validity" and "trust" have different colloquial meanings), and it is certainly possible that some people might make mental use of the validity rating while disregarding and perhaps incautiously modifying the trust ratings. PGP's ability to automatically derive validity ratings can be useful, but the fact that PGP is doing so needs to be made obvious to the user.

## Irreversible Actions

Some user errors are reversible, even if they require some time and effort to reconstruct the desired state. The ones we list here, however, are not, and potentially have unpleasant consequences for the user, who might lose valuable data:

*Accidentally deleting the private key*

A public key, if deleted, can usually be obtained again from a key server or from its owner. A private key, if deleted and not backed up somewhere, is gone for good, and anything encrypted with its corresponding public key will never be able to be decrypted, nor will the user ever be able to make a revocation certificate for that public key. PGP responds to any attempt to delete a key with the question "Do you really want to delete these items?" This is fine for a public key, but attempts to delete a private key should be met with a warning about the possible consequences.

*Accidentally publicizing a key*

Information can only be added to a key server, not removed. A user who is experimenting with PGP may end up generating a number of key pairs that are permanently added to the key server, without realizing that these are permanent entries. It is true that the effect of this can be partially addressed by revoking the keys later (or waiting for them to expire), but this is not a satisfactory solution. First, even if a key is revoked or expired, it remains on the key server. Second, the notions of revocation and expiration are relatively sophisticated concepts: concepts that are likely to be unfamiliar to a novice user. For example, as discussed earlier, the user may accidentally lose the ability to generate a revocation certificate for a key. This is particularly likely for a user who was experimenting with PGP and generating a variety of test keys that he intends to delete. One way to address this problem would be to warn the user when he sends a key to a server that the information being sent will be a permanent addition.

*Accidentally revoking a key*

Once the user revokes a public key, the only way to undo the revocation is to restore the key ring from a backup copy. PGP's warning message for the revocation operation asks "Are you sure you want to revoke this key? Once distributed, others will be unable to encrypt data to this key." This message doesn't warn the user that, even if no distribution has taken place, a previous backup of the key ring will be needed if the user wants to undo the revocation. Also, it may contribute to the misconception that revoking the key automatically distributes the revocation.

*Forgetting the passphrase*

PGP suggests that the user make a backup revocation certificate so that if the passphrase is lost, at least the user can still use that certificate to revoke the public key. We agree that this is a useful thing to do, but we also believe that only expert users of PGP will understand what this means and how to go about doing so. Under PGP's current design, this requires the user to create a backup of the key ring, revoke the public key, create another backup of the key ring that has the revoked key, and then restore the key ring from the original backup.

*Failing to back up the key rings*

We see two problems with the way the mechanism for backing up the key rings is presented. First, the user is not reminded to back up the key rings until he exits PGPkeys; it would be better to remind him as soon as keys are generated, so as not to risk losing them to a system crash. Second, although the reminder message tells the user that it is important to back up the keys to some medium other than the main hard drive, the dialog box for backing up presents the main PGP folder as a default backup location. Because most users will just click the OK button and accept the default, this is not a good design.

## Consistency

When PGP is in the process of encrypting or signing a file, it presents the user with a status message that says it is currently "encoding." It would be better to say "encrypting" or "signing" because seeing terms that explicitly match the operations being performed helps to create a clear mental model for the user, and introducing a third term may confuse the user into thinking there is a third operation taking place. We recognize that the use of the term "encoding" here may simply be a programming error and not a design choice per se, but we think this is something that should be caught by usability-oriented product testing.

## Too Much Information

In previous implementations of PGP, the supporting functions for key management (creating key rings, collecting other people's keys, constructing a *web of trust*) tended to overshadow PGP's simpler primary functions, signing and encryption. PGP 5.0 separates these functions into two applications: PGPkeys for key management, and PGPtools for signing and encryption. This cleans up what was previously a rather jumbled collection of primary and supporting functions, and gives the user a nice simple interface to the primary functions. We believe, however, that the PGPkeys application still presents the user with far too much information to make sense of, and that it needs to do a better job of distinguishing between basic, intermediate, and advanced levels of key management activity so as not to overwhelm its users.

Currently, the PGPkeys display (see Figure 34-2) always shows the following information for each key on the user's key ring: owner's name, validity, trust level, creation date, and size. The key type is also indicated by the choice of icon, and the user can toggle the display of the signatures on each key. This is a lot of information, and there is nothing to help the user figure out which parts of the display are the most important to pay attention to. We think that this will cause users to fail to recognize data that is immediately relevant, such as the key type; that it will increase the chances that they will assign wrong interpretations to some of the data, such as trust and validity; and that it will add to making users feel overwhelmed and uncertain that they are managing their security successfully.

We believe that, realistically, the vast majority of PGP's users will be moving from sending all of their email in plain text to using simple encryption when they email something sensitive, and that they will be inclined to trust all the keys they acquire, because they are looking for protection against eavesdroppers and not against the sort of attack that would try to trick them into using false keys A better design of PGPkeys would have an initial display configuration that concentrated on giving the user the correct model of the relationship between public and private keys, the significance of key types, and a clear understanding of the functions for acquiring and distributing keys. Removing the validity, trust level, creation date, and size from the display would free up screen area for this, and would help the user focus on understanding the basic model well. Some security experts may find the downplaying of this information alarming, but the goal here is to enable users who are inexperienced with cryptography to understand and begin to use the basics, and to prevent confusion or frustration that might lead them to use PGP incorrectly or not at all.

A smaller set of more experienced users will probably care more about the trustworthiness of their keys; perhaps these users do have reason to believe that the contents of their email are valuable enough to be the target of a more sophisticated, planned attack, or perhaps they really do need to authenticate a digital signature as coming from a known real-world entity. These users will need the information given by the signatures on each key. They may find the validity and trust labels useful for recording their assessments of those signatures, or they may prefer to glance at the actual signatures each time. It would be worthwhile to allow users to add the validity and trust labels to the display if they want to, and to provide easily accessible help for users who are transitioning to this more sophisticated level of use. But this would make sense only if the automatic derivation of validity by PGP's built-in policy were turned off for these users, for the reasons discussed in the section "Key Management Policy."

Key size is really only relevant to those who actually fear a cryptographic attack, and could certainly be left as information for the Key Properties dialog, as could the creation date. Users who are sophisticated enough to make intelligent use of that information are certainly sophisticated enough to go looking for it.

# User Test

This section describes the purpose, design, and results of the user test.

## Purpose

Our user test was designed to evaluate whether PGP 5.0 meets the specific usability standard described in the section "A Usability Standard for PGP." We gave our participants a test scenario that was both plausible and appropriately motivating, and then avoided interfering with their attempts to carry out the security tasks that we gave them.

## Description

This section outlines the characteristics of the test design and participants.

### Test design

Our test scenario was that the participant had volunteered to help with a political campaign and had been given the job of campaign coordinator (the party affiliation and campaign issues were left to the participant's imagination, so as not to offend anyone). The participant's task was to send out campaign plan updates to the other members of the campaign team by email, using PGP for privacy and authentication. Because volunteering for a political campaign presumably implies a personal investment in the campaign's success, we hoped that the participants would be appropriately motivated to protect the secrecy of their messages.

Because PGP does not handle email itself, it was necessary to provide the participants with an email handling program to use. We chose to give them Eudora, as that would allow us to also evaluate the success of the Eudora plug-in that is included with PGP. Because we were not interested in testing the usability of Eudora (aside from the PGP plug-in), we gave the participants a brief Eudora tutorial before starting the test, and intervened with assistance during the test if a participant got stuck on something that had nothing to do with PGP.

After briefing the participants on the test scenario and tutoring them on the use of Eudora, we gave them an initial task description, which provided them with a secret message (a proposed itinerary for the candidate), the names and email addresses of the campaign manager and four other campaign team members, and a request to please send the secret message to the five team members in a signed and encrypted email. In order to complete this task, a participant had to generate a key pair, get the team members' public keys, make their own public key available to the team members, type the (short) secret message into an email, sign the email using their private key, encrypt the email using the five team members' public keys, and send the result. In addition, we designed the test so that one of the team members had an RSA key while the others all had Diffie-Hellman/DSS keys; thus, if a participant encrypted one copy of the message for all five team members (which was the expected interpretation of the task), they would encounter the mixed key types warning message. Participants were told that after accomplishing that initial task, they should wait to receive email from the campaign team members and follow any instructions they gave.

Each of the five campaign team members was represented by a dummy email account and a key pair: these were accessible to the test monitor through a networked laptop. The campaign manager's private key was used to sign each of the team members' public keys, including her own, and all five of the signed public keys were placed on the default key server at MIT so that they could be retrieved by participant requests.

Under certain circumstances, the test monitor posed as a member of the campaign team and sent email to the participant from the appropriate dummy account. These circumstances were:

1. The participant sent email to that team member asking a question about how to do something. In that case, the test monitor sent the minimally informative reply consistent with the test scenario (i.e., the minimal answer that wouldn't make that team member seem hostile or ignorant beyond the bounds of plausibility).[17]

2. The participant sent the secret in a plain-text email. The test monitor then sent email posing as the campaign manager, telling the participant what happened, stressing the importance of using encryption to protect the secrets, and asking the participant to try sending an encrypted test email before going any further. If the participant succeeded in doing so, the test monitor (posing as the campaign manager) then sent an updated secret to the participant in encrypted email and the test proceeded as from the beginning.

3. The participant sent email encrypted with the wrong key. The test monitor then sent email posing as one of the team members who had received the email, telling the participant that the team member was unable to decrypt the email and asking whether the participant had used that team member's key to encrypt.

4. The participant sent email to a team member asking for that team member's key. The test monitor then posed as that team member and sent the requested key in email.

5. The participant succeeded in carrying out the initial task. They were then sent a signed, encrypted email from the test monitor, posing as the campaign manager, with a change for the secret message, in order to test whether they could decrypt and read it successfully. If at that point, they had not done so on their own, they received email prompting to remember to back up their key rings and to make a backup revocation certificate, to see if they were able to perform those tasks. If they had not sent a

---

17 This aspect of the test may trouble the reader in that different test participants were able to extract different amounts of information by asking questions in email, thus leading to test results that are not as standardized as we might like. However, this is in some sense realistic; PGP is being tested here as a utility for secure communication, and people who use it for that purpose will be likely to ask each other for help with the software as part of that communication. We point out also that the purpose of our test is to locate extreme usability problems, not to compare the performance of one set of participants against another, and that while inaccurately improved performance by a few participants might cause us to fail to identify some usability problems, it certainly would not lead us to identify a problem where none exists.

separately encrypted version of the message to the team member with the RSA key, they also received email from the test monitor posing as that team member and complaining that he couldn't decrypt the email message.

6. The participant sent email telling the team member with the RSA key that he should generate a new key or should upgrade his copy of PGP. In that case, the test monitor continued sending email as that team member, saying that he couldn't or didn't want to do those things and asking the participant to please try to find a way to encrypt a copy that he could decrypt.

Each test session lasted for 90 minutes, from the point at which the participant was given the initial task description to the point when the test monitor stopped the session. Manuals for both PGP and Eudora were provided, along with a formatted floppy disk, and participants were told to use them as much as they liked.

## Participants

The user test was run with 12 different participants, all of whom were experienced users of email, and none of whom could describe the difference between public and private key cryptography prior to the test sessions. The participants all had attended at least some college, and some had graduate degrees. Their ages ranged from 20 to 49, and their professions were diversely distributed, including graphic artists, programmers, a medical student, administrators, and a writer More detailed information about participant selection and demographics is available in Whitten and Tygar.[18]

## Results

We summarize the most significant results we observed from the test sessions, again focusing on the usability standard for PGP that we gave in the section "A Usability Standard for PGP." Detailed transcripts of the test sessions are available in Whitten and Tygar.[19]

### Avoiding dangerous errors

Three of the twelve test participants (P4, P9, and P11) accidentally emailed the secret to the team members without encryption. Two of the three (P9 and P11) realized immediately that they had done so, but P4 appeared to believe that the security was supposed to be transparent to him and that the encryption had taken place. In all three cases, the error occurred while the participants were trying to figure out the system by exploring.

One participant (P12) forgot her passphrase during the course of the test session and had to generate a new key pair. Participants tended to choose passphrases that could have been standard passwords, 8 to 10 characters long and without spaces.

18 Whitten and Tygar.
19 Whitten and Tygar.

### Figuring out how to encrypt with any key

One of the twelve participants (P4) was unable to figure out how to encrypt at all. He kept attempting to find a way to "turn on" encryption, and at one point believed that he had done so by modifying the settings in the Preferences dialog in PGPkeys. Another of the 12 (P2) took more than 30 minutes[20] to figure out how to encrypt, and the method he finally found required a reconfiguration of PGP (to make it display the PGPMenu inside Eudora). Another (P3) spent 25 minutes sending repeated test messages to the team members to see if she had succeeded in encrypting them (without success), and finally succeeded only after being prompted to use the PGP Plug-In buttons.

### Figuring out the correct key to encrypt with

Among the 11 participants who figured out how to encrypt, failure to understand the public key model was widespread. Seven participants (P1, P2, P7, P8, P9, P10, and P11) used only their own public keys to encrypt email to the team members. Of those seven, only P8 and P10 eventually succeeded in sending correctly encrypted email to the team members before the end of the 90-minute test session (P9 figured out that she needed to use the campaign manager's public key, but then sent email to the entire team encrypted only with that key), and they did so only after they had received fairly explicit email prompting from the test monitor posing as the team members. P1, P7, and P11 appeared to develop an understanding that they needed the team members' public keys (for P1 and P11, this was also after they had received prompting email), but still did not succeed at correctly encrypting email. P2 never appeared to understand what was wrong, even after twice receiving feedback that the team members could not decrypt his email.

Another of the 11 (P5) so completely misunderstood the model that he generated key pairs for each team member rather than for himself, and then attempted to send the secret in an email encrypted with the five public keys he had generated. Even after receiving feedback that the team members were unable to decrypt his email, he did not manage to recover from this error.

### Decrypting an email message

Five participants (P6, P8, P9, P10, and P12) received encrypted email from a team member (after successfully sending encrypted email and publicizing their public keys). P10 tried for 25 minutes but was unable to figure out how to decrypt the email. P9 mistook the encrypted message block for a key, and emailed the team member who sent it to ask if that was the case; after the test monitor sent a reply from the team member saying that no key had been sent and that the block was just the message, she was then able to decrypt it

---

20 This is measured as time the participant spent working on the specific task of encrypting a message, and does not include time spent working on getting keys, generating keys, or otherwise exploring PGP and Eudora.

successfully. P6 had some initial difficulty viewing the results after decryption, but recovered successfully within 10 minutes. P8 and P12 were able to decrypt without any problems.

**Publishing the public key**

Ten of the twelve participants were able to successfully make their public keys available to the team members; the other two (P4 and P5) had so much difficulty with earlier tasks that they never addressed key distribution. Of those ten, five (P1, P2, P3, P6, and P7) sent their keys to the key server, three (P8, P9, and P10) emailed their keys to the team members, and P11 and P12 did both P3, P9, and P10 publicized their keys only after being prompted to do so by email from the test monitor posing as the campaign manager.

The primary difficulty that participants appeared to experience when attempting to publish their keys involved the iconic representation of their key pairs in PGPkeys. P1, P11, and P12 all expressed confusion about which icons represented their public keys and which their private keys, and were disturbed by the fact that they could only select the key pair icon as an indivisible unit; they feared that if they then sent their selection to the key server, they would be accidentally publishing their private keys. Also, P7 tried and failed to email her public key to the team members; she was confused by the directive to "paste her key into the desired area" of the message, thinking that it referred to some area specifically demarcated for that purpose that she was unable to find.

**Getting other people's public keys**

Eight of the twelve participants (P1, P3, P6, P8, P9, P10, P11, and P12) successfully got the team members' public keys; all of the eight used the key server to do so. Five of the eight (P3, P8, P9, P10, and P11) received some degree of email prompting before they did so. Of the four who did not succeed, P2 and P4 never seemed aware that they needed to get the team members' keys; P5 was so confused about the model that he generated keys for the team members instead; and P7 spent 15 minutes trying to figure out how to get the keys but ultimately failed.

P7 gave up on using the key server after one failed attempt in which she tried to retrieve the campaign manager's public key but got nothing back (perhaps because she mistyped the name). P1 spent 25 minutes trying and failing to import a key from an email message; he copied the key to the clipboard but then kept trying to decrypt it rather than import it. P12 also had difficulty trying to import a key from an email message: the key was one she already had in her key ring, and when her copy-and-paste of the key failed to have any effect on the PGPkeys display, she assumed that her attempt had failed and kept trying. Eventually, she became so confused that she began trying to decrypt the key instead.

### Handling the mixed key types problem

Four participants (P6, P8, P10, and P12) eventually managed to send correctly encrypted email to the team members (P3 sent a correctly encrypted email to the campaign manager, but not to the whole team). P6 sent an individually encrypted message to each team member to begin with, so the mixed key types problem did not arise for him. The other three received a reply email from the test monitor posing as the team member with an RSA key, complaining that he was unable to decrypt their email.

P8 successfully employed the solution of sending that team member an email encrypted only with his own key. P10 explained the cause of the problem correctly in an email to that team member, but didn't manage to offer a solution. P12 half understood, initially believing that the problem was due to the fact that her own key pair was Diffie-Hellman/DSS, and attempting to generate herself an RSA key pair as a solution. When she found herself unable to do that, she then decided that maybe the problem was just that she had a corrupt copy of that team member's public key, and began trying in various ways to get a good copy of it. She was still trying to do so at the end of the test session.

### Signing an email message

All of the participants who were able to send an encrypted email message were also able to sign the message (although in the case of P5, he signed using key pairs that he had generated for other people). It was unclear whether they assigned much significance to doing so, beyond the fact that it had been requested as part of the task description.

### Verifying a signature on an email message

Again, all of the participants who were able to decrypt an email message were by default also verifying the signature on the message, because the only decryption operation available to them includes verification. Whether they were aware that they were doing so, or paid any attention to the verification result message, is not something we were able to determine from this test.

### Creating a backup revocation certificate

We would have liked to know whether the participants were aware of the good reasons to make a backup revocation certificate and were able to figure out how to do so successfully. Regrettably, this was very difficult to test for. We settled for direct prompting to make a backup revocation certificate, for participants who managed to successfully send encrypted email and decrypt a reply (P6, P8, and P12).

In response to this prompting, P6 generated a test key pair and then revoked it, without sending either the key pair or its revocation to the key server. He appeared to think that he had completed the task successfully. P8 backed up her key rings, revoked her key, then sent email to the campaign manager saying she didn't know what to do next. P12 ignored the prompt, focusing on another task.

### Deciding whether to trust keys from the key server

Of the eight participants who got the team members' public keys, only three (P1, P6, and P11) expressed some concern over whether they should trust the keys. P1's worry was expressed in the last five minutes of his test session, so he never got beyond that point. P6 noted aloud that the team members' keys were all signed by the campaign manager's key, and took that as evidence that they could be trusted. P11 expressed great distress over not knowing whether she should trust the keys, and got no further in the remaining 10 minutes of her test session. None of the three made use of the validity and trust labeling provided by PGPkeys.

## Conclusion

This section summarizes the conclusions of our case study.

### Failure of Standard Interface Design

The results seen in our case study support our hypothesis that the standard model of user interface design, represented here by PGP 5.0, is not sufficient to make computer security usable for people who are not already knowledgeable in that area. Our 12 test participants were generally educated and experienced at using email, yet only one-third of them were able to use PGP 5.0 to correctly sign and encrypt an email message when given 90 minutes in which to do so. Furthermore, one-quarter of them accidentally exposed the secret they were meant to protect in the process, by sending it in email they thought they had encrypted but had not.

In the earlier section "Defining Usability for Security," we defined usability for security in terms of four necessary qualities, which translate directly to design priorities. PGP 5.0's user interface fails to enable effective security where it is not designed in accordance with those priorities: test participants did not understand the public key model well enough to know that they must get public keys for people to whom they wish to send secure email; many who knew that they needed to get a key or to encrypt still had substantial difficulties in figuring out how to do so; some erroneously sent secrets in plain text, thinking that they had encrypted; and many expressed frustration and unhappiness with the experience of trying to use PGP 5.0, to the point where it is unlikely that they would have continued to use it in the real world.

All this failure is despite the fact that PGP 5.0 is attractive, with basic operations neatly represented by buttons with labels and icons, and pull-down menus for the rest, and despite the fact that it is simple to use for those who already understand the basic models of public key cryptography and digital signature-based trust. Designing security that is usable enough to be effective for those who don't already understand it must thus require something more.

## Usability Evaluation for Security

Because usable security requires user interface design priorities that are not the same as those of general consumer software, it likewise requires usability evaluation methods that are appropriate to testing whether those priorities have been sufficiently achieved. Standard usability evaluation methods, simplistically applied, may treat security functions as if they were primary rather than secondary goals for the user, leading to faulty conclusions. A body of public work on usability evaluation in a security context would be extremely valuable, and will almost certainly have to come from research sources, as software developers are not eager to make public the usability flaws they find in their own products.

In our own work, which has focused on personal computer users who have little initial understanding of security, we have assigned a high value to learnability, and thus have found cognitive walkthrough to be a natural evaluation technique. Other techniques may be more appropriate for corporate or military users, but are likely to need similar adaptation to the priorities appropriate for security. In designing appropriate user tests, it may be valuable to look to other fields in which there is an established liability for consumer safety; such fields are more likely to have a body of research on how best to establish whether product designs successfully promote safe modes of use.

## Toward Better Design Strategies

The detailed findings in our case study suggest several design strategies for more usable security, which we are pursuing in our ongoing work. To begin with, it is clear that there is a need to communicate an accurate conceptual model of the security to the user as quickly as possible. The smaller and simpler that conceptual model is, the more plausible it will be that we can succeed in doing so. We thus are investigating pragmatic ways of paring down security functionality to that which is truly necessary and appropriate to the needs of a given demographic, without sacrificing the integrity of the security offered to the user.

After a minimal yet valid conceptual model of the security has been established, it must be communicated to the user, more quickly and effectively than has been necessary for conceptual models of other types of software. We are investigating several strategies for accomplishing this, including the possibility of carefully crafting interface metaphors to match security functionality at a more demanding level of accuracy.

In addition, we are looking to current research in educational software for ideas on how best to guide users through learning to manage their security. We do not believe that home users can be made to cooperate with extensive tutorials, but we are investigating gentler methods for providing users with the right guidance at the right time, including how best to make use of warning messages, wizards, and other interactive tools.

# Related Work

We have found very little published research to date on the problem of usability for security. Of what does exist, the most prominent example is the Adage project,[21, 22] which is described as a system designed to handle authorization policies for distributed applications and groups. Usability was a major design goal in Adage, but it is intended for use by professional system administrators who already possess a high level of expertise, and as such it does not address the problems posed in making security effectively usable by a more general population. Work has also been done on the related issue of usability for safety-critical systems,[23] like those that control aircraft or manufacturing plants, but we may hope that unlike the users of personal computer security, users of those systems will be carefully selected and trained.

Ross Anderson discusses the effects of user noncompliance on security,[24] and Don Davis analyzes the unrealistic expectations that public key–based security systems often place on users.[25] Beyond that, we know of only one paper on usability testing of a database authentication routine,[26] and some brief discussion of the security and privacy issues inherent in computer-supported collaborative work.[27] John Howard's thesis[28] provides interesting analyses of the security incidents reported to CERT[29] between 1989 and 1995, but focuses more on the types of attacks than on the causes of the vulnerabilities that those attacks exploited, and represents only incidents experienced by entities sophisticated enough to report them to CERT.

# Acknowledgments

We thank Robert Kraut for helpful advice on the design of our user test. This work was supported in part by the National Science Foundation and the United States Postal Service.

The contents of this publication are solely the responsibility of the authors.

21 The Open Group Research Institute, *Adage System Overview*; published on the Web in July 1998.

22 Mary Ellen Zurko and Richard T. Simon, *User-Centered Security*, New Security Paradigms Workshop (1996).

23 Nancy G. Leveson, *Safeware: System Safety and Computers* (Reading, MA: Addison Wesley, 1995).

24 Ross Anderson, "Why Cryptosystems Fail," *Communications of the ACM* 37:11, 1994.

25 Don Davis, "Compliance Defects in Public-Key Cryptography," *Proceedings of the 6th USENIX Security Symposium* (1996).

26 Clare-Marie Karat, "Iterative Usability Testing of a Security Application," *Proceedings of the Human Factors Society 33rd Annual Meeting* (1989).

27 HongHai Shen and Prasun Dewan, "Access Control for Collaborative Environments," *Proceedings of CSCW '92*.

28 John D. Howard, *An Analysis of Security Incidents on the Internet 1989-1995*, Ph.D. Thesis, Carnegie Mellon University (1997).

29 CERT is the Computer Emergency Response Team formed by the Defense Advanced Research Projects Agency, located at Carnegie Mellon University.

## About the Authors

 Alma Whitten now works for Google.

 Doug Tygar is Professor of Computer Science at UC Berkeley, where he holds joint appointments in the Electrical Engineering and Computer Science (EECS) Department and the School of Information Management and Systems (SIMS). He is also Adjunct Professor of Computer Science at Carnegie Mellon University. Dr. Tygar works broadly on problems in computer security and privacy and is one of the creators of the NSF Science and Technology Center TRUST: Team for Research on Ubiquitous Security Technologies. Dr. Tygar served as chair of the Department of Defense's Information Science and Technology Study Group on Security with Privacy. He has written three books and numerous papers. He received his doctorate from Harvard University and his bachelor's degree from UC Berkeley.

*http://www.tygar.net*

# INDEX

## Symbols

@ (at sign) in URLs, 290

## Numbers

802.1x, 324
    EAP-TLS mode, 323

## A

A P3P Preference Exchange Language
    (APPEL), 453
ability, trustworthiness and, 88
abundance, authentication security, 120
access control, on World Wide Web, 328
accessibility of authentication
    mechanisms, 106, 115–117
    disabled users, 117
        biometric authentication, 191
    environmental considerations, 124
    hardware/software requirements, 116
    online banking example, 126
Ackerman, Mark S., 399
active storage, 223
ActiveX dialogs, Windows XP, 598
Acumen, 525–528
    anti-gaming techniques, 541
    architecture, 540
    deploying, 536
    technological evaluation, 538
    users
        awareness/motivation of, 531
        educating, 532
        needs, evaluating, 537
Adage project, 691
Adams, Anne, 649
adaptive systems, interface design, 395
AdAware, 542
add-on software, sanitization techniques, 308–
    310
admonition, security by, 259
adware, 542
AEGIS (Appropriate and Effective Guidance
    for Information Security), 23
agreement, informed consent model, 502

alerts (see attacks)
Ambient Intelligence (AmI), 98
ambiguous disclosure, 440
AmI (Ambient Intelligence), 98
Anderson, Ross, 142
anonymity (see anonymizing networks)
anonymity sets, 549
The Anonymizer, 402
anonymizing networks, 547, 550–558
    case studies of, 551–553
anti-gaming, gaming and, 539
antiphishing tools, 269
Anti-Phishing Working Group (APWG), 276
AntiVirus (Symantec), 360
AOL (America Online), message system
    defense against phishing attacks, 291
APPEL (P3P Preference Exchange
    Language), 453
Apple Macintosh (see Macintosh)
applicability, challenge question systems, 147
applications
    collaborative, embedding security in, 607–
        622
    developing (see applications, developing)
    distributed/collaborative, user
        awareness, 389
    for keystroke biometrics, 204
    malware and, 337
applications, developing
    design, 23
    design/development phases, 52–56
    postrelease phase, 56
    privacy policy management tool, usability
        case study, 65–73
        policy authoring, evaluating, 71–73
        privacy needs, identifying, 66
        prototypes, designing/evaluating, 68–71
        users, interviewing, 67
    privacy software developers, advice
        for, 419, 469
    Problem Severity Classification Matrix, 54
    requirements phase, 50–52
    secure software architecture, 354
    security application, usability case
        study, 57–65

# C

CapDesk research project, 272
capture, biometric authentication, 190
Cascading Style Sheets (CSS), 480
case studies
  anonymizing networks, 551–553
    Mixminion, 553
  Casca, work group applications, iPKIs
    and, 326–328
  Chameleon interface development, 345–
    351
  Faces software prototype, 443
  JAP, 555
  KaZaA user study, 663–666
  network intrusion alert, 366
  Network-in-a-Box, 322–326
  PGP v5.0, 683–689
  PKI deployment for wireless
    networks, 331
  privacy policy management tool, 65–73
  privacy, designing for, 444
  security administration, 364–375
  security application, usability of, 57–65
  sensitive information on discarded
    drives, 298–305
  SpoofGuard, 290
  Tor, 554
  Web, usable access control for, 328
  Windows XP Service Pack 2, 597–603
CDNs (content distribution networks), 478
cell phones
  context-aware, 440
  disclosure function, 438, 444
  disposable, 41
  exploiting plausible deniability, 440
CERT (Computer Emergency Readiness
  Team), 361
certificate authorities, iPKIs and, 330–332
challenge questions systems, 18
  criteria for building/evaluating, 145–147
  designing, 149–155
challenge-response systems (see challenge
  questions systems)
Chameleon, 335–355
  email attachments, security and, 337
  interface, 340–344
    development, 345–351
    X Windows implementation, 351–355
  low-fidelity prototyping, 341
  network access, 339
  roles, 337–340
  simplicity of interface, 345
  usability/security, 338

chat rooms, security administrators,
  communications among, 360
chattr command (Linux), 311
Children Online Privacy Protection Act
  (COPPA), 502
cipher utility (Windows), 310
classification, biometric authentication, 201
clickstreams, 478
  tracking, web bugs enabling, 478–479
code samples, as vulnerability detection
  tool, 361, 370
coercion, 500
Coffetti, Paolo, 242
cognitive walkthrough, usability
  technique, 675
  KaZaA user study, results of, 655–662
  PGP v5.0, 676–682
cognometric authentication (see graphical
  authentication)
collection limitation, privacy criterion for
  challenge questions system, 145
communications
  Chameleon, 337, 354
  secure interaction design, 255
  security administrators, coordinating efforts
    of, 360, 373
community, sense of, trust design, 96
Compatible Time Sharing System (CTSS), 315
competence, informed consent model, 502
comprehension, informed consent model, 499
Computer Emergency Readiness Team
  (CERT), 361
Computer-Supported Cooperative Work (see
  CSCW)
Confab system, 398
confidentiality, 639
  authentication security, 121
configuration, 9
  detecting changes in, 360
  gesture-based approach to, 325
  iPKIs and, 331
  KaZaA user study, 663–666
  options, Privacy Bird, 456
  privacy system design, emphasizing user
    action, 435–437
consent dialogs, trust issues and, 594–597
content distribution networks (CDNs), 478
contextual design, 385
controlled answers/questions, challenge
  questions, 148
convenience, authentication accessibility, 116
cookies, 474–483, 504, 524
  adware and, 542
  blocking, 456
  development of, 476

## R

random passwords, 110
    authentication time, 117
    centrally assigned, 141
    meaningfulness of, 118
    memorability of, 138
    predictability of, 120
Rapid Assessment tool, Groove Virtual
    Office, 624
recall
    knowledge-based authentication keys, 106
    uncued/cued, 108
recognition, 108
    authentication mechanism based on, 112
        inclusivity, 117
    picture effect, graphical passwords
        and, 159
    retrieval strategy for graphical
        passwords, 118
recovery, step in privacy process, 418
Reiter, Michael, 174
Renaud, Karen, 128
repeatability, challenge questions system, 147
reputation systems, trust design element, 96
requirements phase, product
    development, 50–52
research-based attacks, 122
response, step in privacy process, 418
retina verification, biometrics
    authentication, 184
retrieval strategies, memorability and, 117
return on investment (ROI) analysis, case
    study of security application, 64
rings, multiple, security model for Internet, 43
risks, 81
    managing, decision-making process
        and, 533–535
    risk and threat analysis, 28
ROI (return on investment) analysis, case
    study of security application, 64
rootkits, 370
    hunting, 360
Ross, Blake, 587

## S

Salvaneschi, Paolo, 242
sanitization, 294
    cryptographic approach to, 308
    standards, U.S. Department of Defense, 306
    usability and, 308–317
SANS (SysAdmin, Audit, Network,
    Security), 361
Sasse, M. Angela, 30, 649
Save As command, overwriting files, 313

Schneier's Security Processes Framework, 409
search tools, file access security, 265
Secure Empty Trash command (Macintosh),
    replacing with Shred Trash command, 316
secure interaction design, 248–273
    authority management, 250
    browsers, 508–512
    conflict between security/usability, 248
    design guidelines, 250–259
        authorization, 251–255
        communications, 255
    design strategies, 259–272
    implementations of, 272
    iterative design, 249
    privacy, designing for, 429–443
Secure Sockets Layer (SSL), 321
SecureID, 113
security
    by admonition, 259
    authentication and, 119–123
        environmental considerations, 125
        online banking example, 127
    breaches in business sector, 14
    challenge questions systems and, 146
    collaborative applications, embedding
        in, 607–622
    as collaborative effort, 547
    complexity and, 1
    contextual design, 385
    cookies, managing, 266–268
    credentials, using challenge questions to
        recover, 144
    culture, 13, 15, 27, 28
        ethnographic studies, 359
    by designation, 259
        file access, securing, 265
    on desktops, 335, 335–355
    graphical passwords, evaluating, 163–170
    image problem, 28
    mechanisms (see security mechanisms)
    memorability and, tradeoff in password
        selection, 130
    policies (see security policies)
    problematic properties of, 672
    retrofitting usable, inability to, 329
    supporting task, 22
    systems (see security systems)
    usability and (see security and usability,
        balancing)
    user knowledge, 643
    web (see web security)
    (see also Chameleon; security
        administration)
security administration, 357–375
    attack analysis, 369–371
    case studies, 364–375

usability (*continued*)
    portable devices, 226–229
    in postrelease phase of product
        development, 56
    privacy and, 549–556
        P2P systems, 651–666
    in privacy policy management tool, case
        study, 65–73
        policy authoring, evaluating, 71–73
        privacy needs, identifying, 66
        prototype, designing/evaluating, 68–71
        users, interviewing, 67
    remote data collection/system
        evaluation, 56
    in requirements phase of product
        development, 50–52
    in security application, case study, 57–65
        interface, testing, 59–64
        ROI analysis, 64
        work context, field study of, 58
    smart cards, 229–240
    in software/hardware life cycle, 48–57
    systemic approach to, 222
    tests (see testing)
    unique aspects of, in privacy/security
        domain, 48–50
    user error and, 316
    value-sensitive design, 498
    (see also sanitization; security and
        usability, balancing)
    (see also security and usability, balancing)
usable biometrics, 175–196
    (see also biometric authentication)
USB tokens, 113, 225
    recommendations, 240
    usability study of, 229–240
        aim/scope of, 229
        context/roles definition, 229–231
        measurement apparatus, 232
        results/interpretation, 235–240
        user selection, 231
use limitation, privacy criterion for challenge
    questions system, 146
USENET newsgroups, patch distribution, 8
user experiences, eBay user profiles, 96
user group meetings, survey/questionnaire
    data collection/analysis, 57
users
    in academic environments, 363
    actions of
        phishing attack defense, 289
    alerting, Bugnosis, 481–483
    anonymity sets, 549
    attackers and, exploiting differences, 33
    authentication centered on (see
        authentication, user-centered)

    awareness of, 648
    distributed/collaborative
        applications, 389
    information disclosure, 448
    privacy-protective behaviors, 417
    web security, Bugnosis, 474
behavior in sociotechnical systems, 16–21,
    92
    policing, consequences of, 27
    security culture, building, 28
    (see also biometric authentication; trust)
beliefs/attitudes, 27, 92
biometric authentication (see biometric
    authentication)
browsers, hidden information, 294
children/adolescents, 502
clustering, interface design approach, 393
compliance of, 140
consent indications, 252
decision-making process, 533–535
demands on, 16–19
    reducing, 36, 566
disabled (see accessibility of authentication
    mechanisms)
in e-commerce transactions, assessing
    risks, 83
educating, 15
    privacy management, 531
    Shred Trash command, 316
    (see also password selection, existing
        advice on)
efforts of, minimizing, 566
expectations, security operations, 248
experiences, 382
    biometric authentication and, 189
    on eBay, 78
    (see also HCI; CSCW)
feedback in postrelease, 56
gesture-based configuration, 325
groups of, behaviors (see CSCW)
hard drives, directly addressable data, 299
    (see also sanitization)
identifying
    keystroke digraphs, 201
    (see also identification; keystroke
        biometrics)
information about
    collecting/analyzing with online
        tools, 56
    concerns about publicizing, 423
    downloading files, 654
    user fine-grained control, 447
    (see also identification, biometric
        authentication)
informing through interaction design, web
    browsers, 508–512

Web Caller-ID antiphishing tool, 269
web cookies (see cookies)
web forums, user feedback, 56
web logs, 474
    clickstreams, 478
web mail system, Google Gmail, 513
web security
    ambiguous disclosure forms, 440
    communications about, P3P user agent
        design, 456, 460–463
    keystroke biometrics, 202
    Mozilla Firefox, 577–587
    MyDoom virus, scanning logs for, 366
    password selection, restricting, 38
    scanning logs, 374
    user awareness, Bugnosis and, 474
    user understanding of, 79, 508–512
    (see also P3P)
web servers
    as certificate authorities, 328
    secure communications between, 321
web sites
    Barbi, violating informed consent
        principles, 502
    clickstreams, logging, 478
    credibility assessments, 84
    fake password prompts, 255
    forged, 269, 276, 281
        (see also phishing attacks)
    low-fi prototyping, 341
    mirror, 79
    online banking example, 126
    P3P policies, human-readable version, 455
    password selection, existing advice on, 131
    pop-ups, Bugnosis design, 489
    privacy policies (see P3P; privacy policies/
        preferences; web security)
    trusted designs, 84, 91, 484
        examples, 97
        influence of time, 86
    underground, attackers using, 370
Whitten, Alma, 692
Wilkerson, Matt, 220
WindowBox project, Chameleon and, 336
Windows 2000
    cipher utility, 310
Windows systems
    cipher utility, 310
    drag-and-drop installation, adopting, 264

email access, securing, 265
file access, securing, 264–265
file extensions, hidden, 258
hotkeys, designating reserved, 255
overwriting data and, 315
P3P user agents on, 453
software installation/removal, 253
viruses/worms, 43
Windows XP
    ActiveX dialogs, 598
    cipher utility, 310
    Service Pack 2, 7
        Bugnosis architecture and, 491
        case study of, 597–603
        pop-up blocking, 603
wireless networks
    PKI and, 323, 331
    war driving, 4
Wizard of Oz study, 386
work group applications, securing with
    iPKIs, 326–328
World Wide Web Consortium (W3C), P3P
    specifications, 449, 453
worms, 43
Wu, Min, 292

# X

X Windows implementation of
    Chameleon, 351–355
XML (extensible markup language), P3P
    and, 450

# Y

Yan, Jeff, 142

# Z

Zone Labs, 563
    (see also ZoneAlarm)
ZoneAlarm, 402, 563–572
    design principles, 564–572
    firewall in, 564
    program advisor in, 573
    security by admonition, 260
ZoneAlarm Pro, network detection
    wizard, 569
Zurko, Mary Ellen, 622

# ABOUT THE EDITORS

LORRIE FAITH CRANOR is an Associate Research Professor in the School of Computer Science and in the Engineering and Public Policy Department at Carnegie Mellon University. She is director of the CMU Usable Privacy and Security Laboratory (CUPS). She came to CMU in December 2003 after seven years at AT&T Labs-Research. Cranor's research has focused on a variety of areas where technology and policy issues interact, including online privacy, electronic voting, and spam. She is chair of the Platform for Privacy Preferences Project (P3P) Specification Working Group at the World Wide Web Consortium and author of the book *Web Privacy with P3P* (O'Reilly, 2002). She served as general chair of the 2005 Symposium On Usable Privacy and Security (SOUPS). In 2003, she was named one of the top 100 innovators 35 or younger by *Technology Review* magazine. Cranor spends most of her free time with her husband, Chuck, and her children, Shane and Maya, but sometimes she finds time to play the tenor saxophone or design and create award-winning quilts.

SIMSON GARFINKEL is a postdoctoral fellow at the Center for Research on Computers and Society at Harvard University's department of Electrical Engineering and Computer Science. He came to Harvard after completing his Ph.D. in Computer Security at MIT's Computer Science and Artificial Intelligence Laboratory, where he studied computer security, usability, and forensics. Garfinkel is also the founder of Sandstorm Enterprises, Inc., a supplier of computer security auditing tools. Garfinkel writes a monthly column on computer security for *CSO Magazine*, for which he has received the 2004 and 2005 Neal Business Journalism award. This is Garfinkel's 14th book; he doesn't have any free time.

# COLOPHON

OUR LOOK IS THE RESULT of reader comments, our own experimentation, and feedback from distribution channels. Distinctive covers complement our distinctive approach to technical topics, breathing personality and life into potentially dry subjects.

Mary Brady was the production editor and Audrey Doyle was the copyeditor for *Security and Usability*. Sada Preisch proofread the book. Adam Witwer and Claire Cloutier provided quality control. Lydia Onofrei and Marlowe Shaeffer provided production assistance. Nancy Crumpton wrote the index.

MendeDesign designed and created the cover artwork and the part page artwork of this book. Karen Montgomery produced the cover layout with Adobe InDesign CS using the Akzidenz Grotesk and Orator fonts.

Marcia Friedman designed the interior layout. Melanie Wang and Phyllis McKee designed the template. This book was converted by Keith Fahlgren to FrameMaker 5.5.6 with a format conversion tool created by Erik Ray, Jason McIntosh, Neil Walls, and Mike Sierra that uses Perl and XML technologies. The text font is Adobe's Meridien; the heading font is ITC Bailey; and the code font is LucasFont's TheSans Mono Condensed. The illustrations that appear in the book were produced by Robert Romano, Jessamyn Read, and Lesley Borash using Macromedia FreeHand MX and Adobe Photoshop CS.

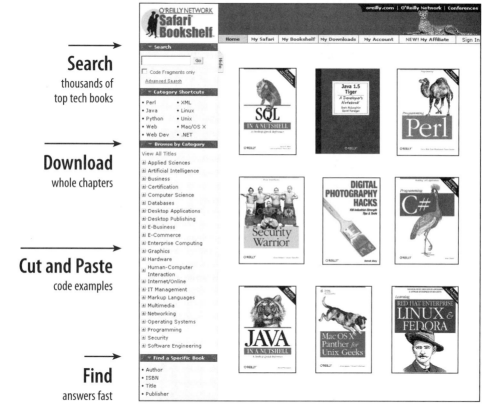

# Related Titles from O'Reilly

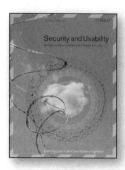

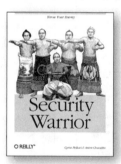

## Security

802.11 Security

Apache Security

Building Internet Firewalls, *2nd Edition*

Building Secure Servers with Linux

Hardening Cisco Routers

Kerberos: The Definitive Guide

Linux Security Cookbook

Managing Security with Snort and IDS Tools

Mastering FreeBSD OpenBSD Security

Network Security Assessment

Network Security Hacks

Network Security with OpenSSL

Network Security Tools

Practical Unix and Internet Security, *3rd Edition*

Programming .NET Security

RADIUS

Secure Coding: Principles and Practices

Secure Programming Cookbook with C and C++

Security Warrior

Security and Usability

SSH, The Secure Shell: The Definitive Guide, *2nd Edition*

Snort Cookbook

SpamAssassin

Web Security, Privacy and Commerce, *2nd Edition*

# O'REILLY®

Our books are available at most retail and online bookstores.

To order direct: 1-800-998-9938 • *order@oreilly.com* • *www.oreilly.com*

Online editions of most O'Reilly titles are available by subscription at *safari.oreilly.com*

# Keep in touch with O'Reilly

## Download examples from our books

To find example files from a book, go to: *www.oreilly.com/catalog* select the book, and follow the "Examples" link.

## Register your O'Reilly books

Register your book at *register.oreilly.com* Why register your books? Once you've registered your O'Reilly books you can:

- Win O'Reilly books, T-shirts or discount coupons in our monthly drawing.
- Get special offers available only to registered O'Reilly customers.
- Get catalogs announcing new books (US and UK only).
- Get email notification of new editions of the O'Reilly books you own.

## Join our email lists

Sign up to get topic-specific email announcements of new books and conferences, special offers, and O'Reilly Network technology newsletters at:

*elists.oreilly.com*

It's easy to customize your free elists subscription so you'll get exactly the O'Reilly news you want.

## Get the latest news, tips, and tools

*www.oreilly.com*

- "Top 100 Sites on the Web"—PC Magazine
- CIO Magazine's Web Business 50 Awards

Our web site contains a library of comprehensive product information (including book excerpts and tables of contents), downloadable software, background articles, interviews with technology leaders, links to relevant sites, book cover art, and more.

## Work for O'Reilly

Check out our web site for current employment opportunities:

*jobs.oreilly.com*

## Contact us

O'Reilly Media, Inc.
1005 Gravenstein Hwy North
Sebastopol, CA 95472 USA
Tel: 707-827-7000 or 800-998-9938
　　 (6am to 5pm PST)
Fax: 707-829-0104

## Contact us by email

For answers to problems regarding your order or our products: **order@oreilly.com**

To request a copy of our latest catalog: **catalog@oreilly.com**

For book content technical questions or corrections: **booktech@oreilly.com**

For educational, library, government, and corporate sales: **corporate@oreilly.com**

To submit new book proposals to our editors and product managers: **proposals@oreilly.com**

For information about our international distributors or translation queries: **international@oreilly.com**

For information about academic use of O'Reilly books: **adoption@oreilly.com** or visit: *academic.oreilly.com*

For a list of our distributors outside of North America check out: *international.oreilly.com/distributors.html*

## Order a book online

*www.oreilly.com/order_new*

---

Our books are available at most retail and online bookstores.
To order direct: 1-800-998-9938 • *order@oreilly.com* • *www.oreilly.com*
Online editions of most O'Reilly titles are available by subscription at *safari.oreilly.com*